Dictionary of the Modern Politics of Southeast Asia

The past two decades since the end of the Cold War have been years of remarkable change and transformation for Southeast Asia. Long seen as an arena for superpower rivalry, Southeast Asia is increasingly coming into its own by locating itself at the forefront of regional integration initiatives that involve not only the Association of Southeast Asian Nations, but major external powers such as the United States, China, India, Japan and Australia as well. At the same time, the past two decades have seen the revival of old animosities as well as the emergence of new security challenges confronting the region. Old animosities include unresolved territorial disputes, while new challenges range from regional and global financial crises to terrorism and pandemics. Significant changes within the eleven Southeast Asian countries covered in this book have also transpired that have affected not only the complexion of domestic politics, but have impacted regional diplomacy as well, such as the creation of the eleventh 'Southeast Asian' country – Timor-Leste.

Extensively updated and revised in light of these changes and developments, this fourth edition of the *Dictionary of the Modern Politics of Southeast Asia* contains profiles of each Southeast Asian country. Following this, it provides more than 450 alphabetically arranged individual entries giving detailed accounts and analyses on major episodes and treaties, political parties and institutions, civil society movements, and regional and international organizations. Biographies of significant political leaders and personalities, both past and present, are also provided. Entries are comprehensively cross-referenced, and an index by country directs readers to all entries concerning a particular country. The *Dictionary* also includes an extensive bibliography that serves as a guide to further reading.

It is an essential reference tool for all scholars and students of Asian politics and international affairs, and a vital resource for journalists, diplomats, policy-makers and others with an interest in the region.

Joseph Chinyong Liow is Dean and Professor of Comparative and International Politics at the Rajaratnam School of International Studies, Nanyang Technological University, Singapore. Joseph concurrently holds the inaugural Lee Kuan Yew Chair in Southeast Asian Studies at the Brookings Institution, Washington DC, USA. He is the author of *The Politics of Indonesia–Malaysia Relations* (2005) and co-editor of *The Routledge Handbook of Asian Security Studies* (2010, with Sumit Ganguly and Andrew Schobell) and *Order and Security in Southeast Asia: Essays in Memory of Michael Leifer* (2005, with Ralf Emmers), all published by Routledge.

Dictionary of the Modern Politics of Southeast Asia

Fourth Edition

Joseph Chinyong Liow

LONDON AND NEW YORK

First published in 1995
by Routledge

Third edition published 2001
by Routledge

Fourth edition published 2015
by Routledge
2 Park Square, Milton Park, Abingdon, Oxon OX14 4RN

and by Routledge
711 Third Avenue, New York, NY 10017

Routledge is an imprint of the Taylor & Francis Group, an informa business

British Library Cataloguing in Publication Data
A catalogue record for this book is available from the British Library

Library of Congress Cataloging-in-Publication Data
Liow, Joseph Chinyong, 1972- author.
Dictionary of the modern politics of Southeast Asia/Joseph Chinyong Liow. — Fourth edition.
pages cm
Previous edition published as: Dictionary of the modern politics of South-East Asia/Michael Leifer.
Includes bibliographical references and index.
1. Southeast Asia—Politics and government—1945- —Dictionaries.
I. Leifer, Michael. Dictionary of the modern politics of South-East Asia.
II. Title.
DS526.7.L56 2014
959.05'4--dc23
2014011545

ISBN: 978-0-415-62531-9 (hbk)
ISBN: 978-0-415-62532-6 (pbk)
ISBN: 978-1-315-75384-3 (ebk)

Typeset in Palatino and Optima
by Florence Production Ltd, Stoodleigh, Devon, UK

Printed and bound by CPI Group (UK) Ltd, Croydon, CR0 4YY

Contents

Introduction 1

Brunei, Sultanate of 3
Cambodia, Kingdom of 6
Indonesia, Republic of 10
Laos, People's Democratic Republic of 16
Malaysia, Federation of 19
Myanmar (Burma) 25
Philippines, Republic of 31
Singapore, Republic of 38
Thailand, Kingdom of 43
Timor-Leste, Democratic Republic of 51
Vietnam, Socialist Republic of 54

Abangan (Indonesia) 59
Abdul Rahman, Tunku (Malaya/Malaysia) 59
Abdul Rahman Yakub, Tun (Malaysia) 60
Abdullah, Zaini (Indonesia) 60
Abhisit Vejjajiva (Thailand) 60
ABIM (Malaysia) 62
ABRI (Indonesia) 62
Abu Sayyaf Group (ASG) (Philippines) 64
Aceh Independence Movement (Indonesia) 65
ADMM (ASEAN Defence Ministers' Meeting) (Brunei/Cambodia/Indonesia/Laos/Malaysia/Myanmar/Philippines/Singapore/Thailand/Vietnam) 66
ADMM-Plus (Brunei/Cambodia/Indonesia/Laos/Malaysia/Myanmar/Philippines/Singapore/Thailand/Vietnam) *see* ADMM 67
AFTA (Association of Southeast Asian Nations Free Trade Area) 1993– (Brunei/Cambodia/Indonesia/Laos/Malaysia/Myanmar/Philippines/Singapore/Thailand/Vietnam) 67
Ahmadiyah (Indonesia) 68
Aljunied Group Representation Constituency (Singapore) 70
Alkatiri, Mari (Timor-Leste) 70
Alliance Party (Malaya/Malaysia) 71
Al-Ma'unah (Malaysia) 71
Ambalat (Indonesia/Malaysia) 72
Anand Panyarachun (Thailand) 73
Ananda Mahidol, King (Thailand) 73
Angkatan Belia Islam Malaysia (Malaysia) *see* ABIM
Angkatan Perpaduan Ummah (Malaysia) 74
Anglo-Malayan/Malaysian Defence Agreement 1957–71 (Malaya/Malaysia/Singapore) 74
Anti-Fascist People's Freedom League (AFPFL) (Burma/Myanmar) 75
Anupong Paochinda, General (Thailand) 75
Anwar Ibrahim (Malaysia) 75
APEC (Asia-Pacific Economic Cooperation) 1989– (Brunei/Indonesia/Malaysia/Philippines/Singapore/Thailand/Vietnam) 77
Aquino, Benigno (Philippines) 78
Aquino III, Benigno Simeon Cojuangco (Philippines) 79
Aquino, Corazón (Philippines) 80
Archipelago Declaration 1957 (Indonesia) 81
Article 11 Coalition (Malaysia) 81
ASA (Association of Southeast Asia) 1961–7 (Malaya/Malaysia/Philippines/Thailand) 82
ASEAN (Association of Southeast Asian Nations) 1967– (Brunei/Cambodia/Indonesia/Laos/Malaysia/Myanmar/Philippines/Singapore/Thailand/Vietnam) 82
ASEAN Charter (Charter of the Association of Southeast Asian Nations) (Brunei/Cambodia/Indonesia/Laos/Malaysia/Myanmar/Philippines/Singapore/Thailand/Vietnam) 85
ASEAN Community (Brunei/Cambodia/Indonesia/Laos/Malaysia/Myanmar/Philippines/Singapore/Thailand/Vietnam) 86

ASEAN Regional Forum (ARF) 1994– (Brunei/Cambodia/Indonesia/Laos/Malaysia/Myanmar/Philippines/Singapore/Thailand/Timor-Leste/Vietnam) 87
Asia–Europe Meeting (ASEM) 1996– (Brunei/Cambodia/Indonesia/Laos/Malaysia/Myanmar/Philippines/Singapore/Thailand/Vietnam) 88
Asian–African Conference, Bandung 1955 (Indonesia) 89
Asian Financial Crisis 1997–8 (Indonesia/Malaysia/Thailand) 90
August Revolution 1945 (Vietnam) 91
Aung San (Burma/Myanmar) 92
Aung San Suu Kyi (Myanmar) 92
Azahari, A. M. (Brunei) 94

Ba'asyir, Abu Bakar (Indonesia) 95
Badawi, Tun Abdullah Ahmad (Malaysia) 95
Bali Summit (ASEAN) 1976 (Indonesia/Malaysia/Philippines/Singapore/Thailand) 97
Bali Summit (ASEAN) 2003 (Brunei/Cambodia/Indonesia/Laos/Malaysia/Myanmar/Philippines/Singapore/Thailand/Vietnam) 97
Bali Summit (ASEAN) 2011 (Brunei/Cambodia/Indonesia/Laos/Malaysia/Myanmar/Philippines/Singapore/Thailand/Vietnam) 97
Baling Talks 1955 (Malaya/Malaysia) 98
Bandar Seri Begawan Summit (ASEAN) April 2013 (Brunei/Cambodia/Indonesia/Laos/Malaysia/Myanmar/Philippines/Singapore/Thailand/Vietnam) 99
Bandar Seri Begawan Summit (ASEAN) October 2013 (Brunei/Cambodia/Indonesia/Laos/Malaysia/Myanmar/Philippines/Singapore/Thailand/Vietnam) 99
Bandung Conference 1955 (Indonesia) *see* Asian–African Conference, Bandung 1955
Bangkok Declaration (ASEAN) 1967 (Indonesia/Malaysia/Philippines/Singapore/Thailand) 99
Bangkok Summit (ASEAN) 1995 (Brunei/Cambodia/Indonesia/Laos/Malaysia/Myanmar/Philippines/Singapore/Thailand/Vietnam) 99
Banharn Silpa-archa (Thailand) 100
Bank Bumiputera Crisis (Malaysia) 100
Bao Dai, Emperor (Vietnam) 101
Barisan Alternatif (BA) (Malaysia) 101
Barisan Nasional (BN) (Malaysia) 102
Barisan Revolusi Nasional (Thailand) 103
Barisan Revolusi Nasional-Coordinate (Thailand) *see Barisan Revolusi Nasional*
Barisan Sosialis (Singapore) 103
Bersih (Malaysia) 104
Bhumibol Adulyadej, King (Thailand) 105
Boat People (Vietnam) 107
Boediono (Indonesia) 108
Bolkiah, Sultan Hassanal (Brunei) 108
Bouasone Bouphavanh (Laos) 109
Brevié Line (Cambodia/Vietnam) 109
Brunei Revolt 1962 (Brunei) 110
Buddhism (Cambodia/Laos/Myanmar/Thailand/Vietnam) 110
Bumiputra (Malaysia) 111
Burma Socialist Programme Party (BPSPP) (Burma/Myanmar) 111
Buy British Last Policy (Malaysia) 112

Cam Ranh Bay (Vietnam) 114
Cambodia National Rescue Party (Cambodia) 114
Cambodian People's Party (CPP) (Cambodia) 115
Cebu Summit (ASEAN) 2006 (Brunei/Cambodia/Indonesia/Laos/Malaysia/Myanmar/Philippines/Singapore/Thailand/Vietnam) 116
Cham (Cambodia/Vietnam) 116
Chamlong Srimuang, General (Thailand) 116
Chart Pattana Party (Thailand) 118
Chart Thai Party (Thailand) 118
Chatichai Choonhavan, General (Thailand) 119
Chavalit Yongchaiyuth, General (Thailand) 120
Chea Sim (Cambodia) 121
Chiam See Tong (Singapore) 121

Chiang Mai Initiative (Brunei/Cambodia/Indonesia/Laos/Malaysia/Myanmar/Philippines/Singapore/Thailand/Vietnam) 122
Chin (Myanmar) 122
Chin Peng (Malaya/Malaysia) 122
Chinese Communities in Southeast Asia 123
Choummaly Sayasone (Laos) 125
Chuan Leekpai (Thailand) 125
Clark Air Base (Philippines) 126
Cobbold Commission 1962 (Malaya/Malaysia) 126
Cobra Gold Military Exercises (Thailand/Singapore/Indonesia/Malaysia/Philippines) 127
Communism in Southeast Asia 127
Comprehensive Agreement on the Bangsamoro (CAB) 2014 (Philippines) 130
Confrontation (Indonesia/Malaysia) 131
Constitution 2008 (Myanmar) 132
Constitutional Crises (Malaysia) 132
Constructive Engagement (Myanmar/Thailand) 133
Contemplacion, Flor: Hanging 1995 (Philippines/Singapore) 134
Corregidor Affair 1968 (Philippines/Malaysia) 135

Daim Zainuddin, Tun (Malaysia) 136
Dakwah (Malaysia) 136
Darul Islam (Indonesia) 137
Declaration of ASEAN Concord 1976 (Indonesia/Malaysia/Philippines/Singapore/Thailand) 137
Declaration of ASEAN Concord II 2003 (Brunei/Cambodia/Indonesia/Malaysia/Myanmar/Laos/Philippines/Singapore/Thailand/Vietnam) 137
Declaration of ASEAN Concord III 2011 (Brunei/Cambodia/Indonesia/Malaysia/Myanmar/Laos/Philippines/Singapore/Thailand/Vietnam) 138
Declaration on the Conduct of Parties in the South China Sea (ASEAN) 2002 (Brunei/Cambodia/Indonesia/Laos/Malaysia/Myanmar/Philippines/Singapore/Thailand/Vietnam) 138
Declaration on the South China Sea (ASEAN) 1992 (Brunei/Cambodia/Indonesia/Laos/Malaysia/Myanmar/Philippines/Singapore/Thailand/Vietnam) 139
Democracy Uprising 1988 (Myanmar) 140
Democrat Party (Thailand) 141
Democratic Action Party (DAP) (Malaysia) 142
Democratic Kampuchea (Cambodia) 143
Democratic Kampuchea, Coalition Government of (CGDK) 1982–90 (Cambodia) 144
Democratic Soldiers (Thailand) 145
Demokrasi Terpimpin (Indonesia) *see* Guided Democracy
Diem, Ngo Dinh (Vietnam) 145
Dien Bien Phu, Battle of, 1954 (Vietnam) 146
Do Muoi (Vietnam) 146
Doi Moi (Vietnam) 147
Domino Theory (Cambodia/Laos/Vietnam) 147
Dong, Pham Van (Vietnam) *see* Pham Van Dong
Duan, Le (Vietnam) *see* Le Duan
Dung, Nguyen Tan (Vietnam) 148
Dwi Fungsi (Indonesia) 148

East Asia Summit 2005– (Brunei/Cambodia/Indonesia/Laos/Malaysia/Myanmar/Philippines/Singapore/Thailand/Vietnam) 150
EDSA (Epifanio de los Santos Avenue) (Philippines) 151
EDSA II (Philippines) 151
Elections 1990 (Myanmar) 151
Elections 2010 (Myanmar) 152
Elysée Agreement 1949 (Vietnam) 152
Emergency 1948–60 (Malaya/Malaysia) 153
Enrile, Juan Ponce (Philippines) 153
Estrada, Joseph (Philippines) 154
Exchange of Letters 2009 (Brunei/Malaysia) 155

Five Power Defence Arrangements (FPDA) 1971– (Malaysia/Singapore) 157
Framework Agreement on the Bangsamoro 2012 (Philippines) 157
Free Papua Movement (Indonesia) 158
Fretilin (Timor-Leste) 159
Friendship Bridge (Laos/Thailand) 160

Front Pembela Islam (Indonesia) 160
Fuad, Tun Muhammad (Donald Stephens) (Malaysia) 161
FUNCINPEC (Cambodia) 162

Geneva Agreements on Indochina 1954 (Cambodia/Laos/Vietnam) 164
Geneva Agreements on Laos 1962 (Laos) 165
Gerakan Rakyat Malaysia (Malaysia) 166
Gerindra (Indonesia) 166
Gestapu (Indonesia) 167
Ghazalie Shafie, Tun Mohamad (Malaysia) 167
Giap, General Vo Nguyen (Vietnam) 168
Goh Chok Tong (Singapore) 169
Goh Keng Swee (Singapore) 170
Golkar (Indonesia) 170
Guided Democracy (Indonesia) 171
Gulf of Tonkin Incident 1964 (Vietnam) *see* Tonkin Gulf Incident 1964
Gusmão, José 'Xanana' (Timor-Leste) 171

Habibie, B. J. (Indonesia/Timor-Leste) 173
Hadi Awang, Abdul (Malaysia) 174
Hambali (Riduan Isamuddin) (Indonesia) 174
Hanoi Summit (ASEAN) 1998 (Brunei/Cambodia/Indonesia/Laos/ Malaysia/Myanmar/Philippines/ Singapore/Thailand/Vietnam) 175
Hanoi Summit (ASEAN) April 2010 (Brunei/Cambodia/Indonesia/Laos/ Malaysia/Myanmar/Philippines/ Singapore/Thailand/Vietnam) 175
Hanoi Summit (ASEAN) October 2010 (Brunei/Cambodia/Indonesia/Laos/ Malaysia/Myanmar/Philippines/ Singapore/Thailand/Vietnam) 176
Harris Mohamad Salleh, Datuk (Malaysia) 176
Hatta, Mohammad (Indonesia) 177
Haz, Hamzah (Indonesia) 177
Heng Samrin (Cambodia) 178
Hertogh, Maria: Riots 1950 (Singapore) 178
Herzog Affair 1986 (Malaysia/Singapore) 178
Hindraf (Hindu Rights Action Force) (Malaysia) 179
Hizbut Tahrir Indonesia (Indonesia) 180
Hmong (Laos) 181
Ho Chi Minh (Vietnam) 181
Ho Chi Minh Trail (Vietnam) 182
Horsburgh Lighthouse (Malaysia/ Singapore) 182
Hua Hin Summit (ASEAN) February 2009 (Brunei/Cambodia/Indonesia/Laos/ Malaysia/Myanmar/Philippines/ Singapore/Thailand/Vietnam) 183
Hua Hin Summit (ASEAN) October 2009 (Brunei/Cambodia/Indonesia/Laos/ Malaysia/Myanmar/Philippines/ Singapore/Thailand/Vietnam) 183
Hukbalahap Movement (Philippines) 184
Hun Sen (Cambodia) 184
Hussein Onn, Tun (Malaysia) 185

Ieng Sary (Cambodia) 187
Indochina Wars (Cambodia/Laos/ Vietnam) 188
Insurgencies, Myanmar (Myanmar) 190
Insurgency, Southern Provinces (Thailand) 193
International Conference on Cambodia, New York 1981 (Cambodia) 194
International Conference on Cambodia, Paris 1989 (Cambodia) 195
International Conference on Cambodia, Paris 1991 (Cambodia) 195
Irian Jaya (Indonesia) 196
Iskandar Development Region (Malaysia/ Singapore) 198
Islam (Brunei/Cambodia/Indonesia/ Malaysia/Myanmar/Philippines/ Singapore/Thailand) 198

Jakarta Conference on Cambodia 1970 (Cambodia/Indonesia) 204
Jakarta Summit (ASEAN) 2011(Brunei/ Cambodia/Indonesia/Laos/ Malaysia/Myanmar/Philippines/ Singapore/Thailand/Vietnam) 204
Jatuporn Prompan (Thailand) 205
Jemaah Islamiyah (Indonesia/Malaysia/ Philippines/Singapore) 205
Jeyaretnam, J. B. (Singapore) 206
Johor, Strait of (Malaysia/Singapore) 207

Kachin (Myanmar) 208
Kalla, Yusuf (Indonesia) 208
Kampuchea, People's Republic of (PRK) (Cambodia) 209

Kampuchean People's Revolutionary Party (KPRP) (Cambodia) 209
Karen (Myanmar) 210
Kaysone Phomvihan (Laos) 211
Khamtay Siphandon (Laos) 212
Khieu Samphan (Cambodia) 213
Khin Nyunt, General (Myanmar) 214
Khmer People's National Liberation Front (KPNLF) (Cambodia) 215
Khmer Republic (Cambodia) 215
Khmer Rouge (Cambodia) 215
Khmer Rouge Trials (Cambodia) 217
Kiet, Vo Van (Vietnam) *see* Vo Van Kiet
Konfrontasi (Indonesia/Malaysia) *see* Confrontation
Kriangsak Chomanan, General (Thailand) 218
Kuala Lumpur Declaration 1971 (Indonesia/Malaysia/Philippines/ Singapore/Thailand) 219
Kuala Lumpur Summit (ASEAN) 1977 (Indonesia/Malaysia/Philippines/ Singapore/Thailand) 219
Kuala Lumpur Summit (ASEAN) 2005 (Brunei/Cambodia/Indonesia/Laos/ Malaysia/Myanmar/Philippines/ Singapore/Thailand/Vietnam) 220
Kukrit Pramoj (Thailand) 220
Kumpulan Militan Malaysia (Malaysia) 221
Kumpulan Mujahidin Malaysia (Malaysia) *see Kumpulan Militan Malaysia*
Kwam Wang Mai (Thailand) *see* New Aspiration Party

Laban ng Demokratikong Pilipino (LDP) (Philippines) 222
Lahad Datu Crisis 2013 (Malaysia/ Philippines) 223
Lakas–CMD (Philippines) 223
Lakas–NUCD (Philippines) *see Lakas*–CMD
Lanzin (Burma/Myanmar) *see* Burma Socialist Programme Party
Lao Dong (Vietnam) 224
Lao Patriotic Front (Laos) *see Neo Lao Hak Sat*
Lao People's Revolutionary Party (Laos) 224
Laskar Jihad (Indonesia) 225
Le Duan (Vietnam) 225
Le Duc Anh, General (Vietnam) 226
Le Duc Tho (Vietnam) 226
Le Kha Phieu, General (Vietnam) 227
Lee Hsien Loong (Singapore) 227
Lee Kuan Yew (Singapore) 228
Legislative Council (Brunei) 230
Liberal Party (Philippines) *see Partido Liberal ng Pilipinas*
Lim Guan Eng (Malaysia) 231
Lim Kit Siang (Malaysia) 231
Lim Yew Hock (Malaysia/Singapore) 232
Limbang Claim (Brunei/Malaysia) 232
Lina Joy Issue (Malaysia) 233
Linh, Nguyen Van (Vietnam) 233
Loi Tack (Malaya/Malaysia) 234
Lon Nol (Cambodia) *see* Nol, Lon
Low Thia Khiang (Singapore) 234
Luong, Tran Duc (Vietnam) 235

Macapagal, Diosdado (Philippines) 236
Macapagal-Arroyo, Gloria (Philippines) 236
Madiun Revolt 1948 (Indonesia) 237
Magsaysay, Ramón (Philippines) 237
Maguindanao Massacre 2009 (Philippines) 238
Maha Vajiralongkorn, Prince (Thailand) 238
Mahathir Mohamad, Tun (Malaysia) 239
Majelis Mujahidin Indonesia (Indonesia) 241
Majelis Ulama Indonesia (Indonesia) 241
Malacca Strait (Indonesia/Malaysia/ Singapore) 242
Malacca Strait Patrol (Indonesia/Malaysia/ Singapore/Thailand) 243
Malayan Union Proposal 1946 (Malaya/ Malaysia) 243
Malaysian Chinese Association (Malaya/ Malaysia) 244
Malaysian Indian Congress (MIC) (Malaya/Malaysia) 245
Malik, Adam (Indonesia) 245
Maluku Violence 1999–2002 (Indonesia) 246
Manila Hostage Crisis 2010 (Philippines) 247
Manila Pact 1954 (Cambodia/Laos/ Philippines/Thailand/Vietnam) 247
Manila Summit (ASEAN) 1987 (Brunei/ Indonesia/Malaysia/Philippines/ Singapore/Thailand) 248
Maphilindo (Indonesia/Malaysia/ Philippines) 249
Marcos, Ferdinand (Philippines) 249
Marcos, Imelda (Philippines) 250
Marshall, David (Singapore) 251
Mas Selamat Kastari (Singapore) 252
Masyumi (Indonesia) 252

May 13 Racial Riots 1969 (Malaysia) 253
Megawati Sukarnoputri (Indonesia) 254
Mekong River Project (Cambodia/Laos/Myanmar/Thailand/Vietnam) 255
Melayu Islam Beraja (Brunei) 256
Memali Incident 1985 (Malaysia) 256
Misuari, Nur (Philippines) 257
Mok, Ta (Cambodia) *see* Ta Mok
Moro Islamic Liberation Front (Philippines) 258
Moro National Liberation Front (Philippines) 259
Muhammadiyah (Indonesia) 261
Muhyiddin Yassin, Tan Sri (Malaysia) 262
Muoi, Do (Vietnam) *see* Do Muoi
Murdani, General L. B. (Indonesia) 262
Murtopo, General Ali (Indonesia) 263
Musa Hitam, Tun (Malaysia) 263
Muslim Unity Front (Malaysia) *see* *Angkatan Perpaduan Ummah*
Mustapha bin Datuk Harun, Tun (Malaysia) 264

Nacionalista Party (Philippines) 265
Nahdlatul Ulama (Indonesia) 265
Najib Tun Razak, Datuk Seri Mohamad (Malaysia) 266
Nasakom (Indonesia) 267
Nasution, General Abdul Haris (Indonesia) 267
Natalegawa, Raden Mohammad Marty Muliana (Indonesia) 268
National Congress for Timorese Reconstruction (Timor-Leste) 268
National Democratic Front (Philippines) 269
National League for Democracy (Myanmar) 270
National Liberation Front of South Vietnam (Vietnam) 271
National Mandate Party (Indonesia) *see* *Partai Amanat Nasional*
National Unity Party (Myanmar) 272
Natuna Islands (Indonesia) 272
Naypyidaw (Myanmar) 273
Ne Win, General (Myanmar) 273
Neo Lao Hak Sat (Laos) 274
New Aspiration Party (Thailand) 274
New Economic Mechanism (Laos) 275
New Economic Model (Malaysia) 275
New Economic Policy (Malaysia) 276
New Order (Indonesia) 276
New People's Army (Philippines) 277
Ngo Dinh Diem (Vietnam) *see* Diem, Ngo Dinh
Nguyen Ai Quoc (Vietnam) *see* Ho Chi Minh
Nguyen Co Thach (Vietnam) *see* Thach, Nguyen Co
Nguyen Manh Cam (Vietnam) 278
Nguyen Minh Triet (Vietnam) 278
Nguyen Phu Trong (Vietnam) 278
Nguyen Tan Dung (Vietnam) 279
Nguyen Tat Thanh (Vietnam) *see* Ho Chi Minh
Nguyen Van Linh (Vietnam) *see* Linh, Nguyen Van
Nguyen Van Thieu (Vietnam) *see* Thieu, Nguyen Van
Nik Abdul Aziz Nik Mat (Malaysia) 279
Nixon Doctrine 1969 (Vietnam) 280
Nol, Lon (Cambodia) 280
Nong Duc Manh (Vietnam) 281
Norodom Ranariddh (Cambodia) *see* Ranariddh, Prince Norodom
Norodom Sihanouk (Cambodia) *see* Sihanouk, King Norodom
Nouhak Phoumsavan (Laos) 281
Nu, U (Burma/Myanmar) 282

One Malaysia (1Malaysia) (Malaysia) 283
Ong Boon Hua (Malaya/Malaysia) *see* Chin Peng
Ong Teng Cheong (Singapore) 283
Organisasi Papua Merdeka (OPM) (Indonesia) *see* Free Papua Movement

Pakatan Rakyat (Malaysia) 285
Pancasila (Indonesia) 286
Panglong Agreement (Burma/Myanmar) 286
Papua Freedom Movement (Indonesia) *see* Free Papua Movement
Paris Peace Agreements 1973 (Vietnam) 287
Partai Amanat Nasional (Indonesia) 288
Partai Bulan Bintang (Indonesia) 289
Partai Demokrasi Indonesia (Indonesia) *see* *Partai Demokrasi Indonesia–Perjuangan*
Partai Demokrasi Indonesia–Perjuangan (Indonesia) 289
Partai Demokrat (Indonesia) 290
Partai Keadilan Sejahtera (Indonesia) 291

Partai Kebangkitan Bangsa (Indonesia) 292
Partai Persatuan Pembangunan (Indonesia) 292
Partai Rakyat Brunei (Brunei) *see* People's Party
Parti Bangsa Dayak Sarawak (Malaysia) 293
Parti Bersatu Sabah (Malaysia) *see* Sabah United Party
Parti Islam Se-Malaysia (Malaysia) 294
Parti Keadilan Rakyat (Malaysia) 295
Parti Pesaka Bumiputera Bersatu (Malaysia) 296
Partido Liberal ng Pilipinas (Philippines) 296
Patani United Liberation Organization (Thailand) 297
Pathet Lao (Laos) 298
Paukphaw Relationship (Burma/Myanmar) 298
Pedra Branca (Malaysia/Singapore) *see* Horsburgh Lighthouse
Pembela (Malaysia) 299
Pemerintah Revolusioner Republik Indonesia (PRRI) (Indonesia) *see* Revolutionary Government of the Republic of Indonesia 1958–61
People Power (Philippines) 299
People's Action Party (Singapore) 299
People's Alliance for Democracy (Thailand) 300
People's Constitution 1997 (Thailand) 301
People's Consultative Assembly (Indonesia) 302
People's Party (Brunei) 302
People's Power Party (Thailand) 303
Perak Legislature Takeover 2009 (Malaysia) 303
Permesta (Indonesia) 304
Peta (Indonesia) 304
Pham Van Dong (Vietnam) 304
Phan Van Khai (Vietnam) 305
Pheu Thai Party (Thailand) 305
Phibul Songkram, Field Marshal (Thailand) 306
Phieu, General Le Kha (Vietnam) *see* Le Kha Phieu, General
Philippines–US Security Treaty 1951 (Philippines) 306
Philippines' Claim to Sabah (Malaysia/Philippines) 307
Phnom Penh Summit (ASEAN) 2002 (Brunei/Cambodia/Indonesia/Laos/Malaysia/Myanmar/Philippines/Singapore/Thailand/Vietnam) 307
Phnom Penh Summit (ASEAN) April 2012 (Brunei/Cambodia/Indonesia/Laos/Malaysia/Myanmar/Philippines/Singapore/Thailand/Vietnam) 309
Phnom Penh Summit (ASEAN) November 2012 (Brunei/Cambodia/Indonesia/Laos/Malaysia/Myanmar/Philippines/Singapore/Thailand/Vietnam) 309
Pol Pot (Cambodia) 310
Port Klang Free Zone Controversy (Malaysia) 311
Prabowo Subianto (Indonesia) 312
Praphas Charusathien, Field Marshal (Thailand) 312
Prayuth Chan-ocha, General (Thailand) 313
Preah Vihear Temple Dispute (Cambodia/Thailand) 313
Prem Tinsulanonda, General (Thailand) 314
Pribumi (Indonesia) 315
Pridi Phanomyong (Thailand) 315
Provisional Revolutionary Government of the Republic of South Vietnam (PRG) 1969–76 (Vietnam) 316
Pulau Batu Puteh (Malaysia/Singapore) *see* Horsburgh Lighthouse

Rajaratnam, Sinnathamby (Singapore) 317
Ramos, Fidel (Philippines) 317
Ramos-Horta, José (Timor-Leste) 318
Ranariddh, Prince Norodom (Cambodia) 319
Razak, Tun Abdul (Malaysia) 320
Razaleigh Hamzah, Tengku (Malaysia) 320
Reform the Armed Forces Movement (RAM) (Philippines) 321
Regional Comprehensive Economic Partnership (Brunei/Cambodia/Indonesia/Laos/Malaysia/Myanmar/Philippines/Singapore/Thailand/Vietnam) 321
Reproductive Health Bills (Philippines) 322
Revolutionary Government of the Republic of Indonesia 1958–61 (Indonesia) 322
Rizal, José (Philippines) 323
Roadmap to Democracy (Myanmar) 323
Rohingya (Myanmar) 323
Roxas, Manuel A. (Philippines) 324
Ruak, Taur Matan (Timor-Leste) 325
Rukunegara 1970 (Malaysia) 325

Sabah United Party (Malaysia) 327
Saffron Revolution 2007 (Myanmar) 327
Saloth Sar (Cambodia) *see* Pol Pot
Sam Rainsy (Cambodia) 328
Sam Rainsy Party (Cambodia) 329
Samak Sundaravej (Thailand) 329
Samphan, Khieu (Cambodia) *see* Khieu Samphan
Samrin, Heng (Cambodia) *see* Heng Samrin
San Yu, General (Myanmar) 330
Sangkum Reastre Niyum (Cambodia) 330
Sann, Son (Cambodia) *see* Son Sann
Sanoh Thienthong (Thailand) 331
Santri (Indonesia) 331
Sarawak National Party (Malaysia) 331
Sarawak United People's Party (Malaysia) 332
Sarit Thanarat, Field Marshal (Thailand) 332
Sary, Ieng (Cambodia) *see* Ieng Sary
Scarborough Shoal Dispute (Philippines) 333
SEATO (Southeast Asia Treaty Organization) 1955–77 (Philippines/Thailand) 334
Semangat '46 (Malaysia) 334
Sen, Hun (Cambodia) *see* Hun Sen
Seni Pramoj (Thailand) 334
Shan (Myanmar) 335
Shwe Mann (Myanmar) 335
Sihamoni, King Norodom (Cambodia) 336
Sihanouk, King Norodom (Cambodia) 336
Sin, Cardinal Jaime (Philippines) 338
Singapore Strait (Indonesia/Malaysia/Singapore) 339
Singapore Summit (ASEAN) 1992 (Brunei/Indonesia/Malaysia/Philippines/Singapore/Thailand) 340
Singapore Summit (ASEAN) 2007 (Brunei/Cambodia/Indonesia/Laos/Malaysia/Myanmar/Philippines/Singapore/Thailand/Vietnam) 340
Sipadan–Ligitan (Indonesia/Malaysia) 341
Sisón, José María (Philippines) 341
Sjahrir, Sutan (Indonesia) 342
Somchai Wongsawat (Thailand) 342
Son Sann (Cambodia) 343
Son Sen (Cambodia) 344
Sondhi Limthongkul (Thailand) 344
Sonthi Boonyaratglin, General (Thailand) 345
Souphanouvong, Prince (Laos) 346
South China Sea (Brunei/Indonesia/Malaysia/Philippines/Vietnam) 346
Southeast Asia Command 1943–6 348
Souvanna Phouma, Prince (Laos) 348
State Law and Order Restoration Council (Myanmar) 349
State Owned Enterprise Reform (Vietnam) 350
State Peace and Development Council (Myanmar) 350
Subandrio (Indonesia) 352
Subic Bay Naval Base (Philippines) 352
Suchinda Kraprayoon, General (Thailand) 353
Suharto (Indonesia) 354
Sukarno (Indonesia) 355
Sukarnoputri, Megawati (Indonesia) *see* Megawati Sukarnoputri
Supersemar (Indonesia) 357
Supreme National Council (Cambodia) 357
Surabaya, Battle of, 1945 (Indonesia) 358
Surayud Chulanont, General (Thailand) 358
Surin Pitsuwan (Thailand) 359

Ta Mok (Cambodia) 361
Taib Mahmud, Datuk Patinggi Abdul (Malaysia) 361
Tanjung Priok Riot 1984 (Indonesia) 362
Tarbiyah (Indonesia) 362
Terrorism in Southeast Asia (Indonesia/Malaysia/Philippines/Singapore) 363
Tet Offensive 1968 (Vietnam) 364
Thach, Nguyen Co (Vietnam) 365
Thai–Lao Border War 1987–8 (Laos/Thailand) 365
Thai Rak Thai Party (Thailand) 366
Thaksin Shinawatra (Thailand) 367
Thammasat University Massacre 1976 (Thailand) 368
Than Shwe, Senior General (Myanmar) 369
Thanat Khoman (Thailand) 370
Thanin Kraivichian (Thailand) 370
Thanom Kittikachorn, Field Marshal (Thailand) 370
Thein Sein (Myanmar) 371
Thieu, Nguyen Van (Vietnam) 372
Thongloun Sisoulith (Laos) 372
Thongsing Thammavong (Laos) 372
Timor Gap Cooperation Treaty (Indonesia/Timor-Leste) 373
Timor-Leste Crisis 2006 (Timor-Leste) 374

Timor Sea Treaty 2002 (Timor-Leste) *see* Timor Gap Cooperation Treaty
Tonkin Gulf Dispute (Vietnam) 375
Tonkin Gulf Incident 1964 (Vietnam) 375
Tran Duc Luong (Vietnam) *see* Luong, Tran Duc
Trans-Pacific Partnership (Brunei/Malaysia/Singapore/Vietnam) 375
Treaty of Amity and Cooperation (ASEAN) 1976 (Brunei/Cambodia/Indonesia/Laos/Malaysia/Myanmar/Philippines/Singapore/Thailand/Timor-Leste/Vietnam) 376
Treaty of Friendship and Cooperation 1977 (Laos/Vietnam) 377
Treaty of Friendship and Cooperation 1978 (Vietnam) 377
Treaty of Peace, Friendship, and Cooperation 1979 (Cambodia/Vietnam) 377
Tripoli Agreement 1976 (Philippines) 378
Truong Chinh (Vietnam) 378
Truong Tan Sang (Vietnam) 379
Tsunami 2004 (Indonesia/Malaysia/Thailand) 379
Tudung Controversy 2002 (Singapore) 380
Tuol Sleng (Cambodia) 381

UMNO (United Malays National Organization) (Malaya/Malaysia) 382
Union Solidarity and Development Association (Myanmar) *see* Union Solidarity and Development Party
Union Solidarity and Development Party (Myanmar) 384
United Front for Democracy Against Dictatorship (Thailand) 384
United Nations: Cambodia 1991–3 (Cambodia) 385
United Nations: East Timor 1999–2002 (Indonesia/Timor-Leste) 387
United Nations: Irian Jaya 1962–9 (Indonesia) 388
United Nations: Northern Borneo 1963 (Indonesia/Malaysia/Philippines) 389
United Sabah National Organization (USNO) (Malaysia) 389
UNTAC (United Nations Transitional Authority in Cambodia) (Cambodia) 390

Ver, General Fabian (Philippines) 391
Vientiane Action Plan (ASEAN) 2004 (Brunei/Cambodia/Indonesia/Laos/Malaysia/Myanmar/Philippines/Singapore/Thailand/Vietnam) 391
Vientiane Agreement on the Restoration of Peace and Reconciliation in Laos 1973 (Laos) 392
Vientiane Summit (ASEAN) 2004 (Brunei/Cambodia/Indonesia/Laos/Malaysia/Myanmar/Philippines/Singapore/Thailand/Vietnam) 392
Viet Cong (Vietnam) 393
Viet Minh (Vietnam) 393
Vietnam–US Strategic Partnership (Vietnam) 393
Vietnam War (Cambodia/Laos/Vietnam) 394
Vietnamization (Vietnam) 397
Vo Nguyen Giap, General (Vietnam) *see* Giap, General Vo Nguyen
Vo Van Kiet (Vietnam) 397

Wahid, Abdurrahman (Indonesia) 399
Widodo, Joko (Indonesia) 400
Workers' Party (Singapore) 400

Xayaburi Dam (Cambodia/Laos/Thailand/Vietnam) 402

Yang di-Pertuan Agong (Malaysia) 403
Yeo, George Yong-Boon (Singapore) 403
Yingluck Shinawatra (Thailand) 404
Young Turks (Thailand) 405
Yudhoyono, Susilo Bambang (Indonesia) 405
Yusuf, Irwandy (Indonesia) 406

ZOPFAN (Zone of Peace, Freedom and Neutrality) 1971 (Indonesia/Malaysia/Philippines/Singapore/Thailand) 408

Postscript 409
Further Reading 411
Index by Country 418

Introduction

There is a common Malay idiom: '*Gajah sama gajah bergadu, kancil mati di tengah-tengah*' (trans: 'When elephants fight, the mouse deer gets trampled between'). For scholars of international politics, this idiom will resonate. It suggests the precarious circumstances small states find themselves in when caught between major powers inclined towards rivalry. In many respects, this scenario describes much of the international politics of Southeast Asia since the colonial era. Over the course of history, Southeast Asia has found itself an arena for great power politics. This has taken the form of the carving up of the region by various European (and North American, in the case of the Philippines) powers, Japanese hegemony and occupation during World War Two couched as the 'liberation' of Asia under the banner of 'Asia for the Asiatics', Cold War rivalry between the United States, the Soviet Union and the People's Republic of China which found bloody expression in the Vietnam conflict, and, with the end of the Cold War, the rise of China and the United States' reassessment of its engagement with the region. At the same time, through these various epochs of great power rivalry, regional states have demonstrated a remarkable deftness and dexterity, not unlike the mouse deer in Malay folklore, in how they have navigated the rough waters of intervention and proxy warfare during the Cold War, in the process cultivating a sense of regional identity and purpose which has ensured that regional interests have not been overwhelmed.

Following Timor-Leste's independence in 2002, Southeast Asia now comprises eleven states. As a geographic region, Southeast Asia is situated to the east of the Indian subcontinent, to the south of the People's Republic of China and to the north of Australia. The region is divided geographically (between mainland and island zones), culturally (between Buddhist and Islamic civilizations), and politically (along a spectrum ranging from democracies such as Indonesia and the Philippines, to Communist states such as Laos and Vietnam, to the absolute monarchy of Brunei). Since the almost-overnight change in Indonesia from an authoritarian state under President Suharto to a multi-party democracy in the late-1990s, Southeast Asia has experienced growing pressures towards political liberalization. Such pressures have led to the gradual erosion of the standing of hitherto strong ruling regimes in Cambodia, Malaysia, Singapore and Vietnam. Arguably the most recent dramatic change in domestic politics is the political transformation currently underway in Myanmar, which in 2010 witnessed the inauguration of its first nominally civilian government in half a century.

Since 1967, the identity of Southeast Asia has been registered through the institution of the Association of Southeast Asian Nations, best known by its acronym, ASEAN. From its relatively inauspicious beginnings with five regional states, ASEAN has developed into a regional institution of consequence, as demonstrated in its central role in regional affairs from the resolution of the third Indochina conflict to the provision of a diplomatic platform for US–China bilateral engagement in the aftermath of the Cold War. Economic adversity in the form of the Asian Financial Crisis in the late 1990s further prompted the deepening of regional economic integration both within ASEAN and between ASEAN and its dialogue partners, resulting in the creation of regional trade and monetary institutions such as the ASEAN Economic Community, the Regional Comprehensive Economic Partnership (RCEP) and the Chiang Mai Initiative.

Yet notwithstanding ASEAN's efforts at integration, it is still plagued by a host of tensions and challenges of both bilateral and multilateral nature. On the bilateral front, the resurgence of hostilities between Cambodia and Thailand over a border dispute centred at the historic Preah Vihear Temple in 2008 served as a sobering reminder that despite progress in regional community and identity building, obstacles in the form of mutual mistrust remain. Competing claims over the South China Sea, which lies geographically at the heart of Southeast Asia, are another potentially destabilizing flashpoint, all the more so given China's unyielding claim to almost the entire area.

Since 1995, the *Dictionary of the Modern Politics of Southeast Asia* has attempted to map, capture and illuminate the contours of domestic and international politics in the region. When the first edition was published that year, authored by the late Michael Leifer, its main preoccupation was to identify and analyse the key players and institutions that emerged, and events that transpired, as the region came of age during the era of the Cold War. Subsequently two revised editions, published in 1996 and 2001, added to the wealth of information as events unfolded. This fourth edition builds on the legacy of Michael Leifer's monumental effort, taking the story of Southeast Asia into the twenty-first century.

The politics of the region have undergone considerable change since the last edition of this *Dictionary* was published. In October 2002, Indonesian terrorists conducted heinous suicide operations on the resort island of Bali, catapulting terrorism and political violence onto the region's political and security agenda overnight. Over the last decade, periodic terrorist attacks in Indonesia along with resurgent ethnoreligious belligerence in Thailand, the Philippines and Indonesia contrived to keep them there. At the same time, the evolution of regional institutionalism, carefully tracked in the previous three editions, progressed rapidly, resulting in the proliferation of a multitude of regional initiatives over the last decade. Underlying this has been ASEAN's concern for its continued relevance in light of the rise of China and India, and the possible centrifugal forces this might generate. Driven by this concern, ASEAN set about reconceptualizing regionalism. What resulted from this exercise was a decidedly more proactive form of regional integration which, among other things, witnessed the landmark signing of the ASEAN Charter, creation of the East Asia Summit and ASEAN Defence Ministers' Meeting, and the conceptualization of the ASEAN Community. During this period, the world also witnessed the historic independence of Timor-Leste in 2002 after a United Nations referendum in 1999 ended twenty-four years of Indonesian occupation. In recognition of this monumental change, Timor-Leste is introduced in this edition as a country in its own right (in the previous three editions it took the form of the entry 'East Timor' under the list of Indonesian entries).

Given the events that have transpired since the turn of the century, it should be no surprise that this fourth edition contains significant revisions. Aside from a new entry for Timor-Leste as the eleventh Southeast Asian state, this book contains more than 155 new and 171 revised entries, including revised and updated surveys of the original ten states of Southeast Asia. In addition, readers will also see that several entries have been retained for their historical significance and continued salience in the broader context of the region's unfolding political history. A project of this nature obviously encounters the proverbial 'shifting goalposts' conundrum as it seeks to be as up-to-date and relevant as possible. To that end, this fourth edition takes the discussion up to the end of May 2014, after Indonesia's parliamentary election which took place on 9 April and the military coup in Thailand on 22 May.

I wish to acknowledge the help I received from the following in the preparation of this revised manuscript: Royce Chan, Rajni Gamage, Theophilus Kwek, Brian McCartan, Afif Pasuni, Mohamed Redzuan and Hanisah Sani.

I would also like to express my deepest gratitude to Barry Desker, outgoing Dean of the S. Rajaratnam School of International Studies, for his unstinting support of this and many other projects in my career.

Joseph Chinyong Liow
Singapore
May 2014

Brunei, Sultanate of

The Sultanate of Brunei or *Brunei Darussalam* (Abode of Peace), which is located along the northern coast of Borneo, is the sole ruling monarchy in Southeast Asia. Its head of state and government, Sultan **Hassanal Bolkiah**, has been on the throne since October 1967. In August 1998, he installed his eldest son, Al-Muhtadee Billah, as crown prince. In the fifteenth and sixteenth centuries, Brunei exercised suzerainty over much of Borneo (giving its name to the island) and into the south of the Philippines archipelago. Its territorial extent was whittled down considerably over the centuries, while its separate identity was only preserved through British colonial intervention, albeit with further loss of territory. Brunei became a protected state in 1888 and only acquired internal self-government in 1959, with internal security powers transferred in 1971 when Britain gave up an automatic defence guarantee for a consultative defence arrangement. It became fully sovereign in January 1984 when Britain transferred its residual responsibility for foreign affairs. Brunei then comprised two territorial enclaves of some 5,765 square kilometres accessible from one another only by water and surrounded on the landward side by the Malaysian state of Sarawak. Its population is estimated at around 300,000, of whom some 230,000 are Malay-Muslim who dominate the political and bureaucratic life of the sultanate. Ethnic Chinese, most of whom lack citizenship, number around 50,000. Non-Malay indigenous people add up to about 10,000, while the balance is made up of expatriates, including skilled professionals from the West and construction and factory workers from other parts of Southeast Asia. The official religion is Islam, while the state is represented as a Malay Islamic Monarchy (***Melayu Islam Beraja***) in the interest of sustaining political conservatism. The sultan, by combining religious and royal roles, seeks to contain radical Islam, which is viewed as a threat to the established political order. In recent times however, Islam has come to assume a more prominent place in this traditional Malay kingdom. This trend was underscored in October 2013 when the government announced its intention to extend the authority of its *shari'a* court beyond its traditional confines of family law to the national penal code, a move that came to fruition in February 2014 when an Islamic penal code was implemented formally.

Modern Brunei is bound up with the discovery and exploitation of oil and natural gas. Onshore production of oil began in 1929 with the active involvement of the Shell Company, which in time became the joint venture Brunei Shell in which the government of the sultanate owns a fifty per cent share. Offshore oil production began in 1963 and corresponding natural gas production in 1973, with the involvement of Mitsubishi and with the subsequent engagement of Elf Petroleum. A consortium comprising Fletcher Challenge Energy of New Zealand, Unocol Borneo Utara and the government of Brunei is involved in the biggest offshore drilling programme for a decade. Six operational offshore oil and gas fields account for virtually the whole of the sultanate's great wealth, either directly, or indirectly through overseas investments funded from oil and gas revenues. National reserves have never been disclosed, nor has the great personal wealth of the sultan and other members of the royal family. At one time, national reserves were estimated at over US$100 billion but are believed to have been run down dramatically as a result of the collapse, with losses estimated at US$15 billion, of the country's largest private company, Amedeo Development Corporation, headed by the Sultan's youngest brother, Prince Jefri. In March 2000, he was the subject of a civil law suit brought by the Brunei government for misappropriating funds from the Brunei Investment Agency (BIA), which he also used to head. The government sought to recover B$25.8 billion but the matter was settled out of court in May 2000 with an agreement that all assets acquired with funds derived from the BIA and under the control of Prince Jefri and his family be returned to the agency.

Brunei's economic tribulations came to a head during the peak of economic crisis within Southeast Asia, compounded in its case by the relatively low world oil price. By the turn of the century that price had recovered significantly to Brunei's advantage. In the past, the huge resources at the disposal of the state, which gave it (at US$25,000) one of the highest average per capita incomes in the world, enabled the introduction of a unique system of social welfare. Free education and health care as well as guaranteed pensions and housing have been provided on a generous basis but have been under review because of changing economic circumstances. Economic planning has concentrated on developing alternative forms of employment to the energy industry and government service in the interest of political stability but with very limited success. In July 2000, radical economic reforms were announced in an attempt to broaden the revenue base before the depletion of oil and gas reserves which were expected to run out in twenty-five years. In the last decade, Brunei has vigorously pushed an economic diversification policy and shifted its economic gravity away from the oil and gas industries. Launched in July 2009, the success of Brunei Halal has had a positive spill-over effect by providing business opportunities for local small and medium sized enterprises while also expanding the size of the regional market by establishing a presence in Singapore, Malaysia and Indonesia.

The government of Brunei is literally a family business with the sultan as prime minister as well as holding the portfolios of finance and defence. One brother, Prince Mohamed Bolkiah, has been foreign minister since January 1984, while Prince Jefri was finance minister until his dismissal in 1998. Speculation remains rife about the rivalry between the three brothers. During British protection, the current sultan's father, the late Sir Omar Ali Saifuddin, was persuaded to introduce a measure of democracy. Elections in September 1962 gave a majority of elective seats to the radical **People's Party** (*Partai Rakyat*) with links to the Indonesia of President **Sukarno**. In December 1962, after the sultan had refused to convene the Legislative Council, the People's Party led by **A. M. Azahari**, launched a revolt, which was put down through British military intervention from Singapore. Brunei has been ruled by decree ever since without any reversion to electoral politics and with all political parties effectively proscribed. Moreover, in order to hold off British pressure for democratization, Sultan Sir Omar Ali Saifuddin abdicated in favour of his son, Hassanal Bolkiah, in October 1967 shortly before he was due to graduate from the British Military Academy at Sandhurst. Sir Omar remained a powerful and decisive influence behind the throne until his death in 1986. Following his father's death, Sultan Hassanal Bolkiah sought to throw off the playboy image depicted in western media and to demonstrate a seriousness of political purpose in the absence of political change. Despite the neo-conservatism associated with the sultan, expressed in a ban on the public consumption of alcohol in January 1991, social delinquency has grown among a young unemployed sector. The vulnerability of monarchical rule is well understood in royal circles, especially to a military coup arising from social discontent. For that reason, the armed forces, on whom some ten per cent of the national budget is spent, are well paid and provided for in modern equipment. The officer corps is also monitored and personal interests balanced in a way that ensures loyalty. Since the revolt was crushed in 1962, a battalion of British Gurkha Rifles had been deployed in the sultanate on rotation from their brigade headquarters (which until mid–1997 was located in Hong Kong) under a secret exchange of letters, ostensibly in a training role. In addition, the sultanate recruits a further battalion of retired Gurkhas directly from Nepal. These forces serve as a deterrent against any challenge by rebellious elements.

In September 1984, shortly after independence, Sultan Hassanal Bolkiah addressed the General Assembly of the United Nations maintaining: 'We wish to be left alone and free from foreign intervention'. Brunei had been reluctant to assume full independence from Britain because of an acute sense of vulnerability arising from experience of hostile relations with both Indonesia and Malaysia. At one stage, Brunei had contemplated joining the Federation of Malaysia on its inception in 1963 but decided against political union. The **Brunei Revolt** had served as Indonesia's pretext for its campaign of **Confrontation**, while, during the mid-1970s, Malaysia had sought to destabilize the sultanate in part to consolidate its control in northern Borneo. It was only in the late 1970s that the evident cohesion of **ASEAN** (Association of Southeast Asian Nations), to which Indonesia and Malaysia were strongly committed, encouraged Brunei to assume full independence and place its security in membership of ASEAN; which was openly pledged to uphold the sanctity of national sovereignty. Even then, independence was accomplished through a treaty of friendship with Britain in 1979 which contained a unique five-year grace period before the transfer of full sovereign status in January 1984. On independence, Brunei joined the Commonwealth and the Organization of the Islamic Conference as well as the United Nations and ASEAN. It also participated in **APEC** from its advent in 1989 and hosted the APEC Economic Leaders' Meeting in November 2000, as well as the **ASEAN Regional Forum** (ARF) and the **Asia–Europe Meeting** (ASEM) from their respective inceptions in 1993 and 1996. Diplomatic relations have been gradually expanded beyond Britain, the United States ASEAN and other major powers to the Islamic world and the People's Republic of China. In 2005, Brunei joined the Trans–Pacific Strategic Economic Partnership Agreement (TPSEP), which was initiated by Chile, New Zealand and Singapore. TPSEP would eventually expand to become the **Trans–Pacific Partnership** (TPP) in 2011. The TPP was considered a more comprehensive and higher-standard free trade agreement concerning trade in goods, services and intellectual property as well as investment. Tensions existed with Malaysia over its **Limbang Claim**: the district of Limbang was incorporated into Sarawak in 1890 after Britain's protectorate had been established. In 2009, Brunei and Malaysia signed a package of arrangements to solve the territorial dispute. Brunei agreed to give up territorial ownership over Sarawak and Limbang, in exchange for oil exploration and development rights in Borneo's offshore waters.

In addition, there are differences with Malaysia over maritime jurisdiction in Brunei Bay and also with China and Vietnam over jurisdiction within that part of the sea space within the Spratly Islands which falls within Brunei's continental shelf. Among its neighbours, Brunei has enjoyed a special relationship with Singapore with which a common vulnerability over size and location has been shared. Singapore bases an infantry battalion in the Temburong enclave, while military exercises are conducted with Australian forces. Relations have improved significantly with Indonesia, which has assumed a protective regional role, while an underlying coolness remains in the relationship with Malaysia. A residual relationship has been maintained with Britain, which still plays an important role in training and servicing the Royal Brunei Armed Forces. An agreement to deploy the Gurkhas beyond 1998 was concluded between the sultan and Britain's prime minister in London in December 1994, when they also signed a memorandum on defence sales. In addition, limited military links have been established with the United States. In December 2002, the sultan of Brunei paid a visit to Washington. Following the impasse at the ASEAN Foreign Ministers Meeting in Phnom Penh the previous year which resulted in the absence of a joint communiqué, in April 2013 Brunei, which had taken over chairmanship of the organization, adroitly steered the association away from further controversy and managed to secure collective re-commitment to the **Declaration on the Conduct of Parties in the South China Sea** (DOC).

see also: APEC; ASEAN; ASEAN Regional Forum (ARF); Asia–Europe Meeting (ASEM); Azahari, A. M.; Bolkiah, Sultan Hassanal; Brunei Revolt 1962; Confrontation; Declaration on the Conduct of Parties in the South China Sea (ASEAN) 2002; Islam; Limbang Claim; *Melayu Islam Beraja*; People's Party.

Cambodia, Kingdom of

Cambodia is situated in the central-south of the Indochina peninsula adjoining Thailand, Vietnam and Laos. It is 181,000 square kilometres in size and has a population of around 14.8 million who mostly adhere to Theravada Buddhism. Formerly a great Hindu empire, its culture still plays an important role in the country. The ethnic breakdown of the population shows an overwhelming majority of Khmers, with a minority yet sizeable representation of Vietnamese and Chinese ethnic groups. Due to its geographical location, Cambodia has historically been periodically drawn into conflicts involving warring polities of Vietnam and Thailand. This lasted until 1863, when King Norodom sought protection from France, and Cambodia became a French protectorate.

Under its colonial rule, France restored Cambodia's historical monuments from the Angkor period which helped generate a sense of ethnic and cultural pride among the people. The French retained the institution of the monarchy and ruled Cambodia through the royal family. In 1941 they returned the title of king to the senior branch of the royal family in favour of **Norodom Sihanouk**, then in his late teens. It was assumed that he would be a pliant instrument of colonial rule, then subject to the authority of the government in Vichy. This was a gross miscalculation which failed to take account of his innate ability to exploit the aura of monarchy among a predominantly peasant population which regarded him as semi-divine. Cambodian politics after the end of the Pacific War were marked by factional struggles representing royalist, republican and revolutionary interests. This development may be traced to the modest opening of the political system by the French on the restoration of their rule following the interregnum of Japanese occupation. King Norodom Sihanouk exploited the aura of monarchy and French failure to restore colonial authority to outmanoeuvre his republican and revolutionary opponents. Through political theatre, he was able to claim the credit for France conceding independence in November 1953. Once independence had acquired international recognition through the **Geneva Agreements on Indochina** in July 1954, Norodom Sihanouk abdicated the throne in favour of his father Norodom Suramarit, reverting to the title of prince so as to enjoy full political freedom. King Suramarit ruled Cambodia as a populist but ruthless leader in part through the vehicle of ***Sangkum Reastre Niyum*** (Popular Socialist Community), a mass movement subject to his manipulation. Prince Sihanouk became head of state after the death of his father in April 1960.

Prince Sihanouk's commitment to neutrality in foreign policy had served to keep Cambodia out of the Vietnam War until Communist use of his country's territory provided a pretext for his republican opponents to oust him when he was visiting the Soviet Union in March 1970. Cambodia then experienced five years of civil war, becoming the **Khmer Republic** under the leadership of Marshal **Lon Nol**. Prince Sihanouk went into exile in Beijing where he established a united front in opposition to the new regime in Phnom Penh. He was joined in this front by a revolutionary faction led by a close-knit group of Cambodian intellectuals, the **Khmer Rouge**. The overthrow of Prince Sihanouk propelled Vietnam's Communists to invade Cambodia to destroy Lon Nol's army and extracted the administration of the eastern part of the country from the government of Phnom Penh, which served to assist the Khmer Rouge to become a formidable military force. Aided by association with Prince Sihanouk, the Khmer Rouge fought their way to power by mid-April 1975 just two weeks before the fall of Saigon. The Khmer Rouge under the leadership of the notorious **Pol Pot** subjected the people of Cambodia to a terrible ordeal in the name of revolutionary idealism between April 1975 and the end of 1978. They sought the total transformation of Cambodian society by murdering its political and religious elite and by driving the inhabitants of the towns into the countryside, where they were engaged in a primitive and punishing agriculture. The unstable and precarious new state of **Democratic Kampuchea** generated a great deal of internal strife marked by paranoia and treachery, and eventually it fell to an invasion by the Vietnamese on 25 December 1978, who then established the **People's Republic of Kampuchea** in January 1979. Prince Sihanouk, who had returned to Cambodia to experience house arrest, was able to leave the country on a Chinese aircraft and to go on from Beijing to the United Nations in New York to condemn both his jailors and the Vietnamese occupiers.

While the Vietnamese invasion revealed the full extent of the horrors perpetrated by the Khmer Rouge, the new government in Phnom Penh failed to receive full international recognition. As a regional organization with an immediate interest in stability in Indochina, **ASEAN** (Association of Southeast Asian Nations) stood at the forefront of international condemnation of Vietnam's invasion of Cambodia and lobbied extensively for Vietnamese withdrawal at various international forums. Vietnam eventually withdrew in September 1989 following the collapse of the Soviet Union and its own economic failure, abandoning the government in Phnom Penh and leaving behind a fractious society ridden by civil war. After protracted diplomacy, an **International Conference on Cambodia** in Paris concluded an accord in October 1991 whereby the United Nations would assume responsibility for implementing a peace plan tied to general elections in 1993. The **Supreme National Council** was established under Prince Sihanouk's chairmanship as a formal repository of sovereignty which would delegate powers to **UNTAC** (United Nations Transitional Authority in Cambodia) with a supervisory role in administration and responsibilities for peacekeeping and conducting elections. However, the Khmer Rouge refused to cooperate with UNTAC, charging them with failure to verify the withdrawal of Vietnamese forces, and called for the replacement of the Phnom Penh administration by the **Supreme National Council**. They were prepared to participate in elections only if they would serve to advance their prospect of resuming power. Contending factions with force at their disposal were bent on abusing the rules of the electoral game in their own interests.

By early 1993, the Paris Agreement appeared to be in serious jeopardy. The Khmer Rouge had called for a boycott of the elections, which they disrupted through acts of violence. Nonetheless, UNTAC went ahead with the elections as scheduled during 23–28 May, which were conducted surprisingly without serious disruption, despite intimidation of opponents by the **Cambodian People's Party** (CPP). Some 4.6 million voters had been registered, of whom nearly ninety per cent cast their ballots in a poll which the United Nations Security Council judged to have been free and fair. **FUNCINPEC** (National United Front for an Independent, Neutral, Peaceful and Cooperative Cambodia) led by Prince **Norodom Ranariddh** won a narrow plurality with fifty-eight seats in the Constituent Assembly of 120 members. The incumbent government's Cambodian People's Party (CPP) secured fifty-one, while the Buddhist Liberal Democratic Party obtained ten seats. The CPP contested the outcome, threatening territorial secession in eastern provinces; UNTAC stood firm but conceded a provisional coalition government, while the Constituent Assembly set about drafting a new constitution. That constitution, which reinstated the monarchy, was promulgated by Norodom Sihanouk on 24 September 1993. He was then enthroned nearly four decades after he had abdicated the throne. Prince Ranariddh and the former prime minister, **Hun Sen**, became first and second prime ministers respectively in a fragile coalition sustained by a common fear of the Khmer Rouge and of a loss of external assistance. Control of the armed forces and the police remained with the CPP, whose dominant position in the rural administration had not been challenged, despite the greater electoral success of FUNCINPEC.

The last UN peacekeepers left the country towards the end of 1993 amidst simmering tensions within and between the component parties of the ruling coalition as well as charges of endemic corruption. Ironically, the Khmer Rouge were unable to benefit from the degeneration of Cambodian politics after the advent of the coalition government and were eventually outlawed by the National Assembly in July 1994. Human rights abuses and draconian press laws, on top of the murder and intimidation of journalists marred Cambodia's precarious coalition government. Similarly, members of the coalition government who did not follow the script were harshly dealt with. Finance minister **Sam Rainsy** was dismissed in October 1994 for his persistence against corruption. Rainsy continued his campaign out of office and was stripped of his membership of FUNCINPEC before being expelled from the National Assembly in June 1995 without debate or vote. Foreign minister Prince Norodom Sirivudh, was imprisoned on a trumped-up charge of attempted assassination after being removed from office. By 1997, the working relationship between Norodom Ranariddh and Hun Sen had broken down with both sides competing to solicit defections from the Khmer Rouge. One such defection which dealt a major blow to the Khmer Rouge was that of Ieng Sary, one-time deputy prime minister of Democratic Kampuchea and Pol Pot's brother-in-law who had been sentenced to death *in absentia* in September 1996. However, he was subsequently granted a royal pardon, a move which elicited criticism from the UN Commission of Human Rights (UNHCR) and paved the way for the formation of the Khmer Rouge Tribunal (KRT) (*see* **Khmer Rouge Trials**) to try senior leaders of the Khmer Rouge for grave human rights violations including genocide between April 1975 and January 1979. Conservative estimates put the number of deaths during the Khmer Rouge regime at 1.7 million, almost twenty-five per cent of the population at the time.

In July 1997, while Norodom Ranariddh was out of the country, Hun Sen seized power through a violent coup in Phnom Penh to effectively end the coalition government. Cambodia's bid to join ASEAN towards the end of July 1997 was shelved due to the coup, which had caused embarrassment to ASEAN whose governments decided to postpone Cambodia's entry. Cambodia was only admitted into ASEAN in April 1999 following fresh elections and the formation of a new government in Cambodia. The elections in July 1998, which were supervised by international monitors, were predictably won by the CPP after which Hun Sen assumed the exclusive office of prime minister with Norodom Ranariddh relegated to chair the National Assembly. An ageing and ailing Norodom Sihanouk played a role in brokering an agreement whereby a new coalition government was formed in November 1998, but without any effective sharing of power, which had become concentrated in the hands of Hun Sen. It was clear by this time that the dawn of a new era had arrived, effectively obliterating the remnants of Khmer Rouge influence. Pol Pot died in April 1998 in a remote jungle base, apparently of a heart attack. The final surrender of Khmer Rouge forces took place in December 1998 ending any prospect of a return to a murderous rule, whose legacy casts a continuing shadow over Cambodia. Even so, the KRT, monitored closely by the UN, continued the process of formulating the tribunal despite it being fraught with difficulties (*see* Khmer Rouge Trials). The KRT successfully completed its first case in February 2012, giving a life sentence to Duch, who had been in charge of running a notorious prison and was held responsible for some 15,000 deaths. It is now looking into its second case of four senior Khmer Rouge leaders – 'Brother Number Two' Nuon Chea, former head of state **Khieu Samphan**, **Ieng Sary** and his wife Ieng Thirith, a former social action minister. All four have been accused of genocide, crimes against humanity and war crimes during the 1970s.

In 2003, Cambodia held its third parliamentary elections since the signing of the 1991 Paris Peace Accords. Even with claims of a corrupt electoral process in favour of the incumbent party, the CPP did not manage to secure the two-thirds majority vote required to re-elect a prime minister and form a new government. The elections also saw support for FUNCINPEC dwindle while support for the **Sam Rainsy Party**, a liberal party whose vocal and persistent opposition to the ruling government had gained steady momentum, increased. A new government was finally installed in July 2004 following a coalition between CPP and FUNCINPEC. Following the impasse of the 2003 parliamentary elections, Hun Sen sought to amend the constitution and do away with the two-thirds requirement in favour of a simple majority. This constitutional amendment was put in place in 2006. Meanwhile, the ailing King of Cambodia, Norodom Sihanouk, finally relinquished his position in 2004 making him one of the longest serving political figures in history. The mercurial Sihanouk spent his final years in China and passed away in Beijing in October 2012. The 2008 parliamentary elections saw twelve parties contending, with the CPP winning a clear mandate with ninety out of 123 seats in parliament. On the other hand, support for FUNCINPEC continued to dwindle as they managed to retain only one seat in parliament, while the Sam Rainsy Party saw growing support and came in second to the CPP with twenty-six. The story at the 2013 election however, was markedly different. Spurred on by growing urban disenchantment, high unemployment, persistent land conflicts, the return of opposition figure Sam Rainsy from self-imposed exile (even though he was eventually barred from contesting) and the formation of a new coalition in the form of the **Cambodia National Rescue Party** (CNRP), opposition forces tapped into wellsprings of discontent and combined as the CNRP to limit the CPP to sixty-eight seats on the way to winning fifty-five seats themselves. This considerable reduction in support, which amounted to the loss of a two-thirds parliamentary majority, was unprecedented given how the CPP had gained in every election since competitive elections were reintroduced in 1993. In the event, the CNRP refused to accept the result, alleging widespread electoral fraud, and subsequently boycotted parliament and called for fresh elections. In December 2013, anti-government protests erupted as tens of thousands took to the streets in a clear demonstration of widespread discontent with the personalized rule of Hun Sen. The government retaliated with a crackdown on protestors, and in April 2014 Cambodian courts convicted thirteen people, purportedly from an opposition organization known as the Khmer National Liberation Front, of treason and plotting to overthrow the government and sentenced them to up to nine years' imprisonment.

After October 1993, despite persistent tensions with immediate neighbours Thailand and Vietnam, Cambodia sought regional integration through engagement with ASEAN. It signed the Association's **Treaty of Amity and Cooperation** in 1995, and was expected to join ASEAN towards the end of July 1997 together with Myanmar and Laos at a meeting of foreign ministers commemorating the thirtieth anniversary of its formation. Membership was attained only in April 1999 after fresh elections and a new government in Cambodia. Cambodia's chairmanship of ASEAN in 2012 was marked by controversy over brewing tensions in the **South China Sea** involving China and the Philippines. At the July 2012 ministerial meeting in Phnom Penh, differences between Cambodia on the one hand and the Philippines and Vietnam on the other over the issue of a reference to the **Scarborough Shoal** dispute resulted in the inability of ASEAN to agree on a joint communiqué for the first time in the organization's history. The imbroglio drew attention to China's influence in Southeast Asia, in particular over regional states which are heavily reliant on Chinese economic support.

see also: ASEAN; Cambodian National Rescue Party; Cambodian People's Party; Democratic Kampuchea; FUNCINPEC; Geneva Agreements on Indochina; Ieng Sary; International Conference on Cambodia; Khieu Samphan; Khmer Republic; Khmer Rouge; Khmer Rouge Trials; Hun Sen; Nol, Lon; Pol Pot; Ranariddh, Prince Norodom; Sam Rainsy; Sam Rainsy Party; *Sangkum Reastre Niyum*; Scarborough Shoal Dispute; Sihanouk, King Norodom; South China Sea; Supreme National Council; Treaty of Amity and Cooperation; UNTAC.

Indonesia, Republic of

The Republic of Indonesia is the largest and most populous country in Southeast Asia. It comprises a distended archipelago of some 18,000 islands that extend from south of the Indian sub-continent to north of Australia; the most sizeable and important of these are Sumatra, Java (on which is located the capital Jakarta), the major portion of Kalimantan (Borneo), Sulawesi (Celebes) and West Papua Province (known as West Irian Jaya until 2007). They comprise a land area of almost two million square kilometres. Its population of around 260 million is the fourth largest after China, India and the United States. Some ninety per cent of its citizens profess an adherence to Islam and constitute statistically the largest Muslim community in the world. The degree of religious observance varies, however, and orthodox Islamic practice is diluted and combined regionally with underlying Hindu–Buddhist and animist traditions. Islam has been denied a prerogative place in political life through a state philosophy, ***Pancasila***, which was enunciated before independence by the country's first president, **Sukarno**. *Pancasila* enjoins all Indonesians to believe in a single deity but permits them to worship any god of their choice. This philosophy was introduced initially in the interests of religious and cultural tolerance but was then exploited to serve the cause of political demobilization during the authoritarian rule of the country's second president, and former general, **Suharto**. An Islamic revival encouraged from the late 1980s for political advantage found expression in sectarian conflict between Muslims and the country's Christian minority from the late 1990s attendant on an acute economic adversity, which paved the way for the resignation of President Suharto in May 1998. A transitional rule under his constitutional successor, Vice-President **B. J. Habibie**, enabled a return to democratic practice, which was followed by the election in October 1999 of **Abdurrahman Wahid** as Indonesia's fourth president. Although Indonesia is a unitary republic, a law came into effect in January 2001 that gave provincial administrations greater autonomy in education, health, land rights and transport policies as well as investment approvals. Further changes were introduced to the political system in August 2002, when the **People's Consultative Assembly** of Indonesia (*Majelis Permusyawaratan Rakyat Republik Indonesia*, MPR) approved an amendment that required all legislators to be elected to office. Henceforth, the MPR could no longer elect the country's president and vice-president. Instead, they would be directly elected with a significant majority of more than half of the popular vote and at least twenty per cent of the vote in half the provinces otherwise there would be a second round of elections. This amendment eventually saw **Susilo Bambang Yudhoyono** of ***Partai Demokrat*** (Democrat Party, PD) become the sixth president of Indonesia and the first to be directly elected through elections in 2004. Another significant change was the establishment of the House of Regional Representatives (*Dewan Perwakilan Daerah*, DPD), which held its first elections in 2004, replacing the 200 unelected members of the MPR who represented various provinces, districts and municipalities across the country.

Indonesia is a unitary republic without historical antecedent within its contemporary territorial bounds, which were established by a waxing Dutch colonial rule from the end of the sixteenth century. Independence was proclaimed by Sukarno and Vice-President **Mohammad Hatta** on 17 August 1945 shortly after the end of a cruel Japanese occupation from March 1942. Full international status was attained only on 27 December 1949 after a bitter national revolutionary struggle against the returning colonial Dutch, who refused to transfer the western half of the island of New Guinea. In October 1965 an abortive coup (*see* ***Gestapu***) attributed to the Communist Party of Indonesia paved the way to a fundamental change in Indonesia's political system and priorities. The circumstances of the coup discredited Sukarno and enabled the armed forces led by Major General Suharto with Muslim support to take violent measures against the Communists and their alleged supporters. On 11 March 1966 Sukarno was obliged to transfer executive authority to Suharto, promoted to lieutenant general, who became acting president in the following year. Confirmed as president in March 1968, Suharto held office continuously with military support for over three decades. He secured re-election for a seventh successive term in March 1998 but was obliged to give up office within two months against a background of social and political unrest, known in the Indonesian political lexicon as *era reformasi*, generated by economic collapse. For the most part, however, his authoritarian rule had provided a stable background for notable economic development, which rested initially on the exploitation of natural resources, especially oil and natural gas. Foreign direct investment enabled that process of development to extend to manufacturing for export, generating high levels of growth. However, with accelerated development came a culture of corruption, to the advantage, in particular, of Suharto's close family and business circle. The attendant structural weaknesses in the economy were exposed with the onset of devastating economic crises from the late 1990s. Nevertheless, Suharto's clout went beyond his years in office. Hutomo Putra Mandal, better known as Tommy Suharto, the youngest son of the former president was jailed for fifteen years for the assassination of a Supreme Court judge who had convicted him of graft. However, he was released from jail on 30 October 2006, serving just five years. The Indonesian government's persistent attempts to charge Suharto with graft were never successful and the charges were formally dropped with his demise on 27 January 2008.

Under President Suharto's proclaimed **New Order**, political participation was strictly controlled, while the media were subject to draconian controls. Parliamentary elections were resumed in 1971 but political parties were compelled to merge into two groupings entitled to canvass popular support only every five years. The government revived an association of functional groups, ***Golkar***, to serve as its electoral vehicle. *Golkar* secured approximately two-thirds of the votes cast in parliamentary elections between 1971 and 1997 but lost support dramatically after the political downfall of Suharto. Members of parliament and political nominees, including representatives of the armed forces, made up the constitutionally supreme MPR, which re-elected Suharto to a seventh consecutive five-year term of office in March 1998. Suharto had previously assumed the title of 'father of development' in a demonstration of his claim to legitimacy. By that juncture, however, Indonesia was deep in economic crisis. Suharto appeared determined to soldier on to the end of his term and had secured the appointment of B. J. Habibie as vice-president on the assumption that he would be a politically unwelcome successor. In the event, a reluctance to meet the economic priorities of the International Monetary Fund served to accelerate the process of economic crisis, which gave rise to serious social and political unrest in Jakarta, in particular, including anti-Chinese violence. The catalyst in generating political change was a student-led activism, which was met by force from the security services killing four students at Trisakti University in Jakarta. It was in this turbulent context that Suharto found himself unable to reconstitute his cabinet and without the support of the armed forces' leadership he decided to resign on 21 May 1998. The end of his personalized quasi-monarchical rule left a political vacuum distinguished by the absence of viable national economic and legal institutions. He was succeeded by Vice-President Habibie who restored the practice of democracy but attempted to use it to secure a fresh term of office. In January of 1999, President Habibie, in an unprecedented move, suggested the possibility of a referendum on independence for East Timor. This triggered a chain of events that culminated in international intervention and eventually, East Timorese independence on 20 May 2002. In the post-Suharto dispensation, there was a proliferation of political parties. Forty-eight of them contested parliamentary elections in June 1999. The most successful was the ***Partai Demokrasi Indonesia–Perjuangan*** (Democratic Party of Indonesia–Struggle,

PDI–P), which secured 154 of 462 elective seats. It was led by **Megawati Sukarnoputri**, the daughter of the republic's first president. The PDI (Democratic Party of Indonesia) was one of three legal parties during Suharto's rule but PDI–P was its prevailing faction. A much diminished and divided *Golkar* came second with 120 seats. In third place with fifty-eight seats, in alliance with smaller parties, was the Islamic ***Partai Persatuan Pembangunan*** (United Development Party, PPP), another legal party from the Suharto era. Fifth with fifty-one seats was the ***Partai Kebangkitan Bangsa*** (National Awakening Party, PKB), which was new in form but represented the interests of the moderate Islamic ***Nahdlatul Ulama*** and its leader Abdurrahman Wahid, which had once been a constituent part of the PPP. The ostensibly constitutionalist but modernist-Islamic ***Partai Amanat Nasional*** (National Mandate Party, PAN) which also contested in the 2009 presidential elections, came last among the more successful participants with thirty-five seats. With the exception of the Islamic ***Partai Bulan Bintang*** (Crescent Star Party, PBB) with fourteen seats, thirteen other parties secured six seats or less each. Amongst these thirteen parties that failed to have an impact on the elections was the *Partai Keadilan* (Justice Party, PK) which reconstituted itself as the ***Partai Keadilan Sejahtera*** (Prosperous Justice Party, PKS). The PKS eventually became a major player in Indonesian politics when it gained significant electoral ground in the 2004 elections as the best-organized of Indonesia's Islamist parties. The parliamentary elections placed Megawati as front-runner for president. However, she did not command a working majority either in the Parliament or in the MPR. Moreover, an Islamic-based coalition led by Amien Rais of PAN coalesced against her. In the event, Abdurrahman Wahid was elected president on 20 October 1999 defeating Megawati by 373 votes to 313. She was then elected vice-president on the following day in an act of political reconciliation, while Amien Rais became speaker of the MPR.

President Wahid adopted a populist leadership style, marred by a willingness to tolerate acts of intimidation by members of the youth wing of his party against his political detractors. An immediate major challenge for his presidency was the management of sectarian conflict between Muslims and Christians on the Moluccan Island chain, with around 4,000 fatalities, as well as on Sulawesi and the island of Lombok. The **Maluku Violence** that saw a declaration of civil emergency in Ambon city in July 2000 was further exacerbated by the arrival of external militant forces such as ***Laskar Jihad***, which turned the conflict into a full-fledged religious war. Religio-political violence was also engulfing Poso in central Sulawesi. The Wahid administration was unable to contain the violence and allowed it to simmer for almost two years. The violence was contained in 2002 only when *Laskar Jihad* was persuaded by its military patrons to unilaterally disband itself immediately after the Bali bombings in October. The early promise of President Wahid's tenure gave way after six months to disillusionment at home and abroad as a result of his erratic style of leadership, which neglected economic priorities, particularly banking reforms and corporate restructuring. The rupiah continued to deteriorate and inflation was at ten per cent. In August 2000, he sought to reassert his authority through reconstituting his cabinet at the cost of alienating the majority parties in Parliament as well as his vice-president. However, he failed to impose any effective control over the armed forces beyond the removal of General Wiranto, former armed forces commander and minister of defence. President Wahid also faced immense pressure from the international community because of the deteriorating security situation in East Timor and the ensuing sectarian conflicts.

President Wahid's popularity was steadily declining as he failed to address the dire economic situation of the country and the escalation of socio-political and religious conflicts. Therefore on the basis of incompetence along with accusations of corruption, President Wahid was impeached on 23 July 2001. Megawati replaced Abdurrahman Wahid as the fifth president of Indonesia. Megawati was able to bring about a measure of political stability but her government was dogged by issues of corruption, slow economic growth, separatist conflicts and escalation of terrorist activity in the country.

Indonesia witnessed the deadliest terrorist attack on home soil on 12 October 2002 at the popular tourist resort island of Bali, which killed nearly 200 people. The island was again targeted in October 2005 by terrorists. On 9 November 2008, Imam Samudra, Amrozi Nurhasyim and Huda Abdul Haq, members of the ***Jemaah Islamiyah*** (JI) network, were executed for their role in the 2002 Bali bombings. Western targets continued to come under terrorist attack. Car bombs exploded on 5 August 2003 at the Marriott Hotel in Jakarta, and outside the Australian Embassy on 9 September 2004. The Marriott Hotel in Jakarta was again bombed in a July 2009 twin attack that also included the bombing of the Ritz Carlton Hotel. Indonesian counterterrorism operations, epitomized by the effective *Densus 88*, have managed to control the scourge of terrorism through operations that have led to the arrest and killing of several key terrorist leaders. At the same time, terrorist organizations have managed to survive through a combination of legal incapacities, displayed in the judiciary's inability to outlaw JI, and metamorphosis, as factions of JI have over the years managed to transform themselves and relocate to other areas of Indonesia. Much maligned for the passivity of her government, Megawati lost the presidency to Susilo Bambang Yudhoyono after the 2004 election, and her PDI–P remained in opposition.

Although Indonesia showed signs of stabilizing both politically and economically by the time Susilo Bambang Yudhoyono's first term in office drew to a close, residual challenges remained in the form of Islamist vigilantism which found expression in organizations such as ***Front Pembela Islam*** (Islamic Defenders Front, FPI), ***Majelis Mujahidin Indonesia*** (Indonesian Mujahidin Council, MMI) and the Islamic Community Forum (*Forum Umat Islam*, FUI). These vigilante movements were well entrenched in Indonesian society through their association with international Islamist organizations which had local networks, and they became the self-proclaimed voice of disenchanted Muslims in Indonesia. It was pressure from such groups that forced a 2008 decree banning the ***Ahmadiyah*** which was viewed as heretical and deviant by these fundamentalist movements. The decree in many respects made it easier for these movements to resort to violence when closing down a number of *Ahmadiyah* mosques and disrupting their gatherings. The Christian community was also not spared periodic violence against them. The moral postulations of these movements were further justified by the state with the passing of the equally controversial anti-pornography bill in October 2008 which was aimed at pleasing certain segments of the Islamist parties and their supporters. While President Yudhoyono's first term was generally viewed as a success, assessments of his second term have been considerably more ambivalent. Yudhoyono has been criticized for his inability to take firm decisions on critical issues, most notably on the matter of costly fuel subsidies that were popular but a huge drain on the country's finances, his faltering campaign against corruption, which became starkly evident with a series of high-profile corruption cases involving members of his own ***Partai Demokrat*** (Democrat Party), and his inability to rein in coalition members.

Indonesia's parliamentary elections of 9 April 2014 saw the PDI–P emerge with the most votes. Even then, its nineteen per cent fell short of the twenty-five per cent required for a party to nominate a presidential candidate of its own. In the event, the party now anchors a coalition that includes the PKB, which put in a strong performance to regain some of its previous lustre by securing nine per cent of the vote, and two smaller parties, the National Democratic Party and Hanudra. The coalition has nominated popular Jakarta governor **Joko Widodo**, or 'Jokowi', as their candidate for the July 2014 presidential election. His vice-presidential candidate is **Yusuf Kalla**, the former vice-president and *Golkar* party chairman, known to be a competent organizer and administrator. A second coalition emerged, comprising ***Gerindra***, *Golkar*, PAN, PKS and PBB. *Gerindra*'s controversial strongman **Prabowo Subianto**, a former military general and confidante of Suharto, and PAN leader Hatta Rajasa declared their candidacies as president and vice-president on 20 May. The July presidential race has been cast as a contest between a humble Jakarta governor whose popularity has been built on his broad appeal and willingness to engage with the grassroots, and a former Suharto-era general known for fiery rhetoric and promises of firm leadership, but who also carries the baggage of alleged past involvement in human rights abuses while serving in the military.

A separatist challenge in Aceh in northern Sumatra was mitigated with a ceasefire signed in May 2000. In the wake of continued violence however, martial law was imposed in Aceh in May 2003, putting the brakes on back-channel talks that had at the time begun to take place between the Indonesian government and *Gerakan Aceh Merdeka* (**Aceh Independence Movement**, GAM). At the end of 2004, Aceh was hit by a major calamity when a tsunami caused the death of more than 150,000 Acehnese, with tens of thousands more missing, and the wholesale destruction of coastal villages and towns in Aceh (*see* **Tsunami 2004**). The humanitarian crisis that followed focused the attention of the world on Aceh and compelled both parties to set aside differences in order to cooperate in disaster relief operations. The disaster also created a new set of conditions for negotiations, which after a stuttering reboot culminated in the signing of a memorandum of understanding on 15 August 2005 in Helsinki, which allowed for special autonomy status, amnesty for GAM separatists and the withdrawal of government troops from the region. In return, GAM undertook to abandon its goal of independence and to disarm. In the following year, a pro-GAM independent candidate and former separatist leader, **Irwandy Yusuf**, was elected governor of Aceh. **Zaini Abdullah**, co-founder of GAM who was directly involved in the negotiations leading up to Helsinki, succeeded Irwandy Yusuf in 2012.

Indonesia returned to the United Nations in September 1966 and reinstated a declaratory policy of non-alignment, while forging close economic and political links with the United States and Japan as well as suspending diplomatic ties with China. General Suharto presided over the end of the **Confrontation** with Malaysia and played a decisive role in cementing regional reconciliation through promoting the formation of **ASEAN** (Association of Southeast Asian Nations) in August 1967. Within Indonesia, ASEAN was conceived as a vehicle for managing regional order to the exclusion of the major powers. Indonesia's central place within ASEAN was registered in June 1976 when its secretariat was located in Jakarta. Another cornerstone of Indonesian foreign policy has been a strategic perspective that centres on an **Archipelago Declaration** proclaimed in December 1957. That declaration asserted the same right of jurisdiction over waters surrounding and intersecting the islands of Indonesia as over its land space. Indonesia's archipelagic status, with prerogative rights, was recognized in the Convention concluded at the Third United Nations Conference on the Law of the Sea in 1982, which came into force in 1994. After Vietnam's invasion of Cambodia in December 1978, Indonesia's foreign ministers played leading roles in the diplomacy of the Cambodian conflict. Foreign Minister Ali Alatas served as co-chair of the international conference in Paris in October 1991 which resolved the conflict, although it was the permanent members of the United Nations Security Council that were instrumental in fashioning the final settlement. In August 1990, after the end of the Cold War, Indonesia restored diplomatic relations with China, which removed an impediment to a long-sought goal of assuming the chair of the Non-Aligned Movement, whose summit was held in Jakarta in September 1992. Indonesia also hosted an **APEC** summit in Bogor in November 1994. Despite recurrent tensions with the United States over human rights, Indonesia has maintained an informal strategic relationship and has permitted US naval vessels access to the port of Surabaya for repair and supply, although the United States did impose an arms ban on Indonesia between 1999 and 2006 in response to human rights violations by the Indonesian military in East Timor and Irian Jaya.

The post-Cold War relationship with the United States was augmented indirectly in December 1995 through an unprecedented security agreement with Australia that then fell victim to acrimony over East Timor in September 1999, when Indonesia's condition of economic adversity and international pressure obliged President Habibie to tolerate the intervention of a United Nations-sanctioned international force led by Australia to restore order and to transfer responsibility for the territory to the world body in October that year. The deepening of security cooperation with the United States and Australia in the past decade has no doubt been driven foremost by concerns over terrorism and the perceived need to strengthen Indonesia's counterterrorism capabilities. This was particularly so in the early 2000s, when it was not yet clear that Indonesia's security forces could handle the emergent terrorist threat in the form of JI, as well as the various sectarian crises that were spawning across the archipelago. As Indonesia recovered from the turbulence of the immediate post-Suharto era, it shifted its foreign policy orientation towards more proactive leadership within ASEAN. Seizing upon its hosting of the **Ninth ASEAN Summit in Bali** in 2003, Indonesia rolled out the Declaration of ASEAN Concord II which provided a blueprint for the establishment of an **ASEAN Community** by 2020. Symbolically, this declaration was made twenty-seven years after the first ASEAN Summit was held, also in Bali, and when the foundational ASEAN documents – ASEAN Concord and the **Treaty of Amity and Cooperation** – were signed. Under President Yudhoyono, Indonesia pursued a foreign policy that extended beyond its traditional focus on ASEAN. Indonesia was a non-permanent UN Security Council member in 2008–9. By virtue of its size and potential, Indonesia was invited to join the G-20 forum in 2009, the only ASEAN country in the organization. Yudhoyono has also promoted Indonesia's democratic experience internationally through the Bali Democracy Forum. Indeed Indonesia's confidence was demonstrated at a regional level when Indonesia took over the chairmanship of ASEAN in 2011, two years before its turn. At the same time, it has also offered to play a mediation role in a number of conflicts ranging from the Israel–Palestinian conflict, to the **South China Sea** territorial claims, to the internal conflict raging in Thailand's southern border provinces.

see also: Ahmadiyah; APEC; Archipelago Declaration; ASEAN; ASEAN Community; Confrontation; *Front Pembela Islam*; Aceh Independence Movement; *Gerindra*; *Golkar*; Habibie, B. J.; Hatta, Mohammad; Yusuf, Irwandy; *Jemaah Islamiyah*; Kalla, Yusuf; *Laskar Jihad*; *Majelis Mujahideen Indonesia*; Maluku Violence; Megawati Sukarnoputri; *Nahdlatul Ulama*; New Order; Bali Summit (ASEAN) 2003; *Pancasila*; *Partai Amanat Nasional*; *Partai Bulan Bintang*; *Partai Demokrasi Indonesia–Perjuangan*; *Partai Demokrat*; *Partai Keadilan Sejahtera*; *Partai Kebangkitan Bangsa*; *Partai Persatuan Pembangunan*; People's Consultative Assembly; Prabowo Subianto; Suharto; Sukarno; South China Sea; Treaty of Amity and Cooperation; Tsunami 2004; Wahid, Abdurrahman; Widodo, Joko; Yudhoyono, Susilo Bambang; Zaini Abdullah.

Laos, People's Democratic Republic of

The People's Democratic Republic of Laos was established on 2 December 1975 in succession to the Kingdom of Laos. The political change was effected by the ruling **Lao People's Revolutionary Party** (LPRP), which had been created in the 1950s as a virtual branch of the Communist Party of Vietnam. The party had assumed power progressively during 1975 as a direct consequence of Communist victories in Cambodia and Vietnam in April that year. It has ruled Laos continuously with close reference to the changing priorities of its senior fraternal partner in Hanoi. While maintaining this relationship, China has had an increasing influence on the party's decisions.

Laos is an elongated landlocked state of around 240,000 square kilometres situated in the mainland of Southeast Asia. The country is bounded to the north by the People's Republic of China, to the east by Vietnam, to the south by Cambodia, to the west by Thailand and minimally to the northeast by Myanmar. Its topography is very mixed with a great contrast between the fertile valley of the River Mekong to the west and the forested mountainous uplands in the east. A population of some six million is distinguished by an ethnic diversity, in particular between the lowland Lao with linguistic and cultural affiliations to Thailand, and the upland hill tribes who have kinship links across the eastern border in the upland area of Vietnam. The contemporary configuration of the state owes much to colonial intervention in the late nineteenth century, with a French protectorate established initially over the kingdom of Luang Prabang in 1893. The imposition and expansion of French colonial dominion prevented the absorption of the several local principalities by the expanding Thai and Vietnamese states. An occupied France was obliged to give up territory west of the Mekong to Thailand in May 1941. Japan inspired the independence of Laos in April 1945 but the protectorate was reinstated at the end of August 1945 after Japan's surrender to the Allied powers.

The restoration of French rule and the establishment of the kingdom of Laos was resisted by a nationalist revolutionary movement which received direction and military support from a patron movement in Vietnam. From the end of the Pacific War, the country was caught up in a wider struggle for Indochina whose prime locus was in Vietnam (*see* **Indochina Wars**). Civil conflict within the Lao elite over ideology and external patronage attracted intervention from the United States and Thailand as well as from China, the Soviet Union and Vietnam and was contained only temporarily by the settlement reached in the **Geneva Agreements on Indochina** in July 1954 which confirmed national independence. After a revival of conflict, a further settlement exclusively for Laos was reached in the **Geneva Agreements on Laos** in July 1962 and the country was ostensibly neutralized under a coalition government comprised of warring political factions. Neutralization failed and the country continued to be a hostage to the fortunes of competing sides in the **Vietnam War**. On 21 February 1973, just weeks after the **Paris Peace Agreements** for Vietnam, hostilities in Laos were ended by the **Vientiane Agreement on the Restoration of Peace and Reconciliation in Laos**. Another coalition government was established in which the balance of advantage shifted inexorably to the Communist side until their complete seizure of power in December 1975, when King Savang Vatthana abdicated.

Laos began its socialist era with a commitment to the same doctrinal priorities that inspired the ruling party in Hanoi. Indeed, Laos has moved in both domestic and international policy in parallel with its eastern neighbour, which has served as mentor and patron for over three decades. In July 1977 a **Treaty of Friendship and Cooperation** between Laos and Vietnam affirmed a special relationship in a context of deteriorating Sino-Vietnamese relations which overcame any Laotian desire at the time for greater political autonomy. Laos shared

Vietnam's experience of miscalculating the pitfalls of an accelerated collectivization of agriculture and nationalization of industry and commerce, and suffered economic distress as a consequence. That distress was aggravated after the onset of the Cambodian conflict in which Laos sided with Vietnam to its cost. Parallel with Vietnam, Laos was obliged from the start of the 1980s to sacrifice ideology and to embark tentatively on market-based economic reforms while striving to maintain single-party rule. Those reforms were pursued vigorously from the mid-1980s concurrently with the ending of the Cold War and Vietnam's loss of Soviet patronage, which had the attendant effect of weakening but not dissolving the special relationship enshrined by treaty. Laos made corresponding adjustments in foreign policy by improving fractured ties with China and Thailand which have become important economic partners. In July 1992 in Manila, Laos acceded to ASEAN's (Association of Southeast Asian Nations) **Treaty of Amity and Cooperation** thereby securing observer status at annual meetings of ASEAN's foreign ministers. In July 1993 in Singapore, Phoune Sipaseuth, foreign minister of Laos, took part in the inaugural dinner meeting of the **ASEAN Regional Forum**. Laos became a member of ASEAN in July 1997. However, in October 1999, a meeting in Vientiane of the heads of government of Cambodia, Laos and Vietnam indicated a reversion to a political alignment in opposition to ASEAN that had been forged during the height of the Cambodian conflict. In recent years, Vietnam's influence over Laos has waned somewhat as China's influence has grown. At the same time foreign institutions, especially development banks, as well as international non-governmental organizations and investment corporations have had increasing influence in the country. Laos applied to join the World Trade Organization (WTO) in 1998 and became a member of the WTO in February 2013. In 2004 Laos successfully hosted the ASEAN summit in Vientiane.

Laos has long ceased to be a battleground in Indochina but has been troubled by a limited revival of insurgency on the part of the **Hmong** minority who were recruited by the American CIA to fight on the anti-Communist side in a spill-over from the Vietnam War. By 2010 the insurgency was confined to remnants and the remaining Hmong refugees in Thailand had been returned to Laos. Laos continues to be governed by an administration drawn from the LPRP, which is the sole legal political organization and in which the military exercise a leading role. Following the death of founding leader, **Kaysone Phomvihan**, General **Khamtay Siphandon** took over as head of the party in November 1992. In March 2006 he was succeeded by General **Choummaly Sayasone** as head of the party and later as president in June 2006. General Sisavath Keobounpanh, who took over as prime minister from Khamtay in 1998 was succeeded by Boungnang Vorachith in 2001. In 2006, Boungnang became vice-president and was replaced by **Bouasone Bouphavanh** who remained prime minister until December 2010 when he was suddenly replaced by **Thongsing Thammavong**. The ease with which political succession has repeatedly been accomplished indicates an underlying party control. Only one out of ninety-nine members of the National Assembly elected in December 1997 was not from the ruling party. By the 2006 elections, the assembly had expanded to 115 members, of which two were non-members of the LPRP. In the 2011 elections, the assembly was expanded again to 132 seats, all but four of which were won by LPRP members. Despite that control, Laos is a weak state for which subsistence agriculture remains the primary economic activity. Annual average per capita income is around US$2,700. Laos was badly hit by the economic crisis that afflicted Southeast Asia at the end of the 1990s, primarily as a result of Thailand's acute difficulties leading to collapse of its currency, the *kip*. In August 1999, Laos' finance minister and the governor of its central bank were dismissed on grounds of mismanaging the country's fiscal and banking policy in terms that suggested an involvement in corruption. Laos' economic conditions have improved since the turn of the century driven by its tourism industry, including gambling, and exports of textiles, minerals and hydropower. Agricultural production is also up, stimulated by foreign investment, largely from China, Vietnam and Thailand. China has shown the greatest increase in investment and its economic influence is expanding. Still, the country is heavily dependent on economic investment for foreign exchange. Laos faces major problems in creating an adequate infrastructure to overcome physical and human resources barriers to development. China has invested heavily in improving the infrastructure, especially in the northern portion of the country. Although slow to have an impact, the **Friendship Bridge** linking Vientiane with Thailand, together with several newer bridges across the Mekong, has increased trade, especially through an improved road network linking Laos with China, Thailand and Vietnam. As Laos becomes increasingly connected with the region it is becoming a crossroads for trade in mainland Southeast Asia. While the government has opened up the economy, it has been reluctant to enact reforms geared towards making it more transparent and accountable. There are also growing concerns about the widening gap between rich and poor, and between rural and urban areas. There is also growing concern about the influx of Chinese migrants as a result of their expanding economic influence.

Laos' ruling party, like that in Vietnam, remains cautious in opening up the country to foreign influences that might pose a threat to its conservative political system. Still, it has shown signs in recent years of increasing transparency and accountability. Though exchanges with China have increased in importance, the Laotian leadership have been careful to make sure their growing relationship with Beijing does not undermine their traditional close political and military relationship with Vietnam.

see also: ASEAN; ASEAN Regional Forum; Bouasone Bouphavanh; Choummaly Sayasone; Friendship Bridge; Geneva Agreements on Indochina; Geneva Agreements on Laos; Hmong; Indochina Wars; Kaysone Phomvihan; Khamtay Siphandon; Lao People's Revolutionary Party; Paris Peace Agreements; Thongsing Thammavong; Treaty of Amity and Cooperation; Treaty of Friendship and Cooperation; Vientiane Agreement on the Restoration of Peace and Reconciliation in Laos; Vietnam War.

Malaysia, Federation of

The Federation of Malaysia was established on 16 September 1963 from former British colonial possessions in Southeast Asia around the core of the Federation of Malaya. It contains a population of almost thirty million within a land area of around 330,000 square kilometres. Comprising the Malay Peninsula and much of northern Borneo, Malaysia shares common land and maritime boundaries with Thailand, Brunei and Indonesia, and maritime boundaries with Singapore, the Philippines and Vietnam, some of which are contested. The federal enterprise was designed primarily to protect the political dominance of the indigenous Muslim community of the Malay Peninsula from the economically based challenge of ethnic Chinese of migrant origin. It was intended also to facilitate a smooth process of decolonization.

Malay-Muslim political dominance in the federation is symbolized in a constitutional monarchy whose incumbent is drawn, on a rotating five-year basis, from the sultans or rulers of the states of the Malay Peninsula (*see* ***Yang di-Pertuan Agong***). It has more practical expression in the commanding role of **UMNO** (United Malays National Organization), and the distribution of parliamentary seats and cabinet posts. As that political dominance became more entrenched under the leadership of Prime Minister **Mahathir Mohamad** since 1981, intra-Malay contention has become more evident. Successful economic development with diversification into export-led growth in manufactures in addition to plantation agriculture and extractive industry, including oil and natural gas, has provided a strong material base for political stability in a plural society. Such stability has been enforced also by authoritarian government which has curbed the role of independent institutions in providing those political checks and balances associated with parliamentary democracy. That authoritarianism became more pronounced in the wake of the economic crisis at the end of the 1990s during which Mahathir met a political challenge by removing his deputy, **Anwar Ibrahim**. Malay reaction to his arrest, trial and imprisonment on charges of corruption and sexual misconduct provided an opportunity for ***Parti Islam Se-Malaysia*** (PAS), the main Malay opposition party, to make considerable gains at UMNO's expense in elections in November 1999, although UMNO managed to retain its two-thirds parliamentary majority. Anwar's continued incarceration however, catalysed a nationwide movement for political reform which culminated in the incumbent ***Barisan Nasional*** (National Front, BN) coalition losing its two-thirds majority for the first time in elections in 2008. The momentum of the reform movement catapulted opposition parties, which coalesced into the ***Pakatan Rakyat*** (People's Alliance, PR) to further gains in the elections of 2013. By then, Anwar had been released and had taken on the role of *de facto* leader of the opposition.

Malaysia superseded the Federation of Malaya, which had been independent since 31 August 1957. The ambit of the government of Malaya, based in Kuala Lumpur, was extended to the self-governing island of Singapore and two British colonial possessions in northern Borneo – Sarawak and Sabah – located several hundred miles away across the **South China Sea**. The British-protected sultanate of Brunei, also in northern Borneo, had contemplated membership but in the event did not join. Singapore's membership was short-lived. The island constituent was expelled from the Federation on 9 August 1965.

Malaysia was established in a climate of controversy because of objections, from President **Sukarno**'s Indonesia in particular, to the extension of Kuala Lumpur's political domain across the South China Sea to a common border in Borneo. That dispute was resolved after Sukarno's downfall in 1966 and Indonesia and Malaysia became founder members of **ASEAN** (Association of Southeast Asian Nations) in 1967. The initiative for extending Malaya into Malaysia came from the prime minister, **Tunku Abdul Rahman**, who viewed the federal undertaking as a way of securing the dominant political position of the Malay community represented by UMNO which he led. That initiative, first made public in May 1961, had been inspired by apprehension at the prospect of the self-governing island of Singapore, joined to the Malay Peninsula by a causeway, becoming fully independent. Its predominantly Chinese population and the growing influence of the Communist Party of Malaya made Singapore a potential source of political infection. The Malayan government's wish to neutralize Singapore through political encapsulation was tempered by a fear of the consequences of the demographic change for the Malay community. It was to avoid such an outcome that the two Borneo states were included in Malaysia on the facile assumption that their non-Chinese indigenous people, akin to Malays, would help to maintain the right kind of racial and political balance.

The peninsular Malaya model of politics – based on intercommunal coalition government led by its Muslim component – was extended to northern Borneo, although there remains a strong indigenous political spirit which has prevented peninsular political parties from gaining a foothold especially in Sarawak. Concomitantly, attempts to sustain this **Alliance Party** model in a very different racial context provoked recurrent federal–state tensions which have persisted. When Singapore's ruling **People's Action Party** (PAP) entered peninsular Malaysia elections in 1964 to challenge the Chinese partner of UMNO in the federal coalition cabinet, it laid the ground for expulsion from Malaysia in August 1965. The challenge was construed as masking an ulterior intent to displace UMNO from its leading political role. The sequel took the form of intercommunal violence (the **May 13 Racial Riots**) in Kuala Lumpur in 1969 in the wake of general elections. UMNO had lost support from its communal constituency, while non-Malay opposition parties publicly trumpeted their success at the expense of UMNO's non-Malay coalition partners. A state of emergency was imposed and government placed in the hands of a National Operations Council. When it was lifted, the rules of politics had been revised in the Malay interest. To that end, a **New Economic Policy** was introduced to ensure that a constitutionally founded dominance would be underpinned by corporate economic ownership. Prime Minister Tunku Abdul Rahman, associated with appeasing Chinese interests, was obliged to resign. He was succeeded in September 1970 by his deputy, **Tun Abdul Razak**, who was identified with Malay rural development. From that juncture, Malay political dominance has never been challenged. That said, non-Malay voting support for the wider ruling intercommunal BN, which replaced the Alliance, has diminished even as intra-Malay contention has intensified.

A critical factor in modifying the pattern of politics in Malaysia has been the resurgence of **Islam** as a result of international and local causes. The experiment of incorporating the Malay opposition PAS into the ruling coalition from the early 1970s failed by the end of the decade. More successful was the cooption of non-Malay parties, including those from the northern Borneo states. When Mahathir became Malaysia's fourth prime minister in July 1981, he decided to reinforce UMNO's Islamic identity in order to overcome its political vulnerability because of its close cooperation with non-Malay parties. That policy was expressed more in form than in substance. It proved effective, however, for example, through his cooption of Anwar Ibrahim, a one-time radical Islamic youth leader, who rose rapidly through ministerial ranks to become deputy prime minister by the end of 1993. At the same time, the opposition PAS also began to take on an even more Islamic complexion with their introduction of clerical rule. Acrimony and mutual distrust between UMNO and PAS, which at one level epitomized intra-Malay contention, resulted in a dangerous game of religious brinkmanship as each sought to embellish their own Islamic credentials while undermining the other.

Mahathir found himself troubled far more by challenges based on personal ambition from among his cabinet colleagues than from racial tension or Islamic resurgence. Major internal discord was signalled from February 1986, when the deputy prime minister, Musa Hitam, resigned from the government complaining of Mahathir's managerial style. In April 1987 **Tengku Razaleigh Hamzah**, minister for trade and industry, who had been demoted from finance, launched an abortive challenge to Mahathir for the presidency of UMNO at the party's triennial elections. He did so in tandem with Musa Hitam, who failed to retain the office of deputy president. The contest exposed deep factional divisions within UMNO. Those divisions became institutionalized after a challenge in the courts to the credentials of a number of UMNO branches led to the party being declared an unlawful society. After a confrontation between Mahathir and senior members of the judiciary, during which its head was removed from office, UMNO was reconstituted as a new party with the power to screen applications for admission. In May 1988 Tengku Razaleigh registered ***Semangat '46*** as a new party. Its meaning (Spirit of 1946) was intended to convey direct lineal descent from UMNO, which had been established in that year. The sustained challenge to Mahathir was then mitigated by Musa Hitam's announcement in January 1989 that he was rejoining UMNO; this was possibly prompted by the heart attack suffered by the prime minister, whose health was restored through bypass surgery.

Any doubts about Mahathir's mastery of Malaysian politics were laid to rest in October 1990 when he led UMNO to a third successive electoral victory since assuming office. *Semangat '46* had entered into an electoral pact with PAS within a Muslim Unity Front which gave them an overwhelming victory only in the legislature in Tengku Razaleigh's home state of Kelantan, where his nephew was sultan. The ruling coalition was also unable to displace ***Parti Bersatu Sabah*** (PBS), which had defected from the ruling federal coalition only days before the election but eventually returned to the ruling stable in 2002. Nonetheless, UMNO secured more than the two-thirds parliamentary majority required to amend the federal constitution at will. Mahathir's political dominance was further asserted when an impetuous act by the sultan of Johor provided the opportunity in 1993 to have the legal immunity of the Malay rulers removed by constitutional amendment and to diminish their political influence. Mahathir's position has been underpinned by the good health of Malaysia's economy as well as by a skilful employment of attendant patronage. Jockeying for political succession, however, became evident in the run-up to UMNO's general elections in November 1993 at which Anwar Ibrahim displaced the deputy prime minister, Ghafar Baba, from the office of deputy president in a generational change reflected also in the team which he carried into the three posts of vice-president. Prime Minister Mahathir was returned unopposed as president of the dominant party but its activists had indicated their choice of the next prime minister. Mahathir showed no inclination to step aside.

Malaysia was afflicted by the regional economic crisis, which came to a head during 1998. In the wake of the downfall of President **Suharto** in May 1998, Mahathir judged that his deputy prime minister and finance minister, Anwar Ibrahim, was making a bid to replace him. Anwar was dismissed from both offices on 2 September 1998 and expelled from UMNO on the following day. He was arrested later in the month and charged with corruption (abuse of power) and sexual misconduct. On his first appearance in court, Anwar's neck and arms were badly bruised and he had a black eye. He was found guilty on four charges of corruption in April 1999 and of a further count of sodomy in August 2000. One reaction to Anwar's arrest, trial and imprisonment was public disorder in Kuala Lumpur put down with a heavy hand by security forces. Another was the emergence of a new political entity promoted by Anwar's wife Wan Azizah Ismail, ***Parti Keadilan Nasional***, which would later morph into, ***Parti Keadilan Rakyat*** (People's Justice Party, PKR). The first of a stream of political sequels to the Anwar affair was the outcome of elections in November 1999 in which the BN was returned to federal office with a reduced majority of 148 seats in a legislature expanded to 193. UMNO suffered a major reverse, however, to the advantage of PAS, which increased its federal representation to twenty-seven seats from seven. PAS had entered into an electoral pact with other Malay opposition parties, including PKR (that at the time was still *Parti Keadilan Nasional*), which won five seats, and the non-Malay **Democratic Action Party** (DAP) within a ***Barisan Alternatif*** (Alternative Front). PAS also displaced UMNO as the government in the state of Terengganu, while holding onto government in Kelantan, and provided the leader of the federal parliamentary opposition for the first time. Mahathir replaced Anwar with **Abdullah Ahmad Badawi** as deputy prime minister in January 1999. He was confirmed, without contest, as deputy president of UMNO in May 2000. In 2002, Mahathir dramatically announced his intention to step down during an UMNO general assembly. The announcement evidently caught the party leadership by surprise, and upon their appeal Mahathir decided to delay his retirement by a year. In October 2003 after twenty-two years at the helm, Mahathir handed over the reins of power to Badawi.

Badawi's tenure began with a resounding mandate at the 2004 election, when the BN won a landslide 198 out of 219 parliamentary seats as Malaysians welcomed a new era of more consultative government compared to the strong-arm leadership of Mahathir. Nevertheless, Badawi's promises of a more responsive government never quite materialized. Inter-ethnic relations were strained by increasingly assertive Malay-Muslim activism. In addition, Badawi's attempts to curtail futile megaprojects inherited from the Mahathir years were met with visceral recrimination by his predecessor, who remained vocal on the sidelines after his retirement and eventually started a media campaign to criticize Badawi's leadership. Meanwhile, civil society movements were mobilizing against the inertia of the Badawi administration, whose performance by then was a far cry from the hope he inspired when he first took over. Massive movements like **Hindraf** and ***Bersih*** demonstrated the extent of popular frustration. Released in 2004 when his 1999 conviction was overturned, Anwar galvanized a hitherto disparate reform movement as opposition to the BN swelled, especially among non-Malays. He anchored a pact between opposition parties DAP, PAS and PKR, which later became institutionalized as the PR, and which resulted in a massive swing of support away from the ruling coalition at the 2008 elections. It proved at that time to be the BN's worst ever performance, as it lost not only its two-thirds parliamentary majority, but also the state governments of Kelantan, Kedah, Penang, Selangor and Perak, although Perak would return to the BN fold a year later following a controversial takeover of the state legislature after defections from the PR. Prior to that, Anwar attempted to engineer his own takeover, in this instance of the federal government, by declaring that thirty-one parliamentarians were prepared to defect from the BN on the occasion of 'Malaysia Day' on 16 September 2008 to join the opposition, thus enabling them to form the government. Though Anwar's gambit failed, it was widely believed that he had managed to secure enough potential defectors, and the plan was only thwarted when the government recruited some of them for a government-sponsored 'study trip' to Taiwan in September. Still smarting from the debacle at the 2008 polls, which provided a *casus belli* for added pressure from Mahathir, Badawi was forced to resign in April 2009. This paved the way for the appointment of **Najib Tun Razak**, son of the second prime minister of Malaysia, Tun Abduk Razak, to ascend to high office.

Clearly cognizant of the challenge before him, Najib Razak positioned himself as a technocrat and reformer. In order to win back some of the non-Malay vote lost in 2008, he bravely asserted that blanket affirmative action was no longer viable. He also introduced an ambitious Economic Transformation Programme geared towards achieving high-income nation status for Malaysia. Nevertheless, without his own election mandate, Najib's reform initiatives met with stiff resistance from within both the party and the bureaucracy. Malay right-wing segments of UMNO, and their civil society allies, continued to espouse inflammatory racial rhetoric with impunity, which generated and played on existential fears especially of rural Malays. At the same time, corruption and mismanagement of state resources continued to plague the government. A particularly visible scandal was uncovered that saw a sitting minister's family use funds allocated to the National Feedlot Corporation for the purchase of livestock to purchase private properties in Singapore instead. The growth of alternative and social media amplified discontent, resulting in a further swing of support away from the BN at the 2013 elections, when the incumbent managed to secure only 133 parliamentary seats. More significant was the fact that the BN secured only forty-seven per cent of the popular vote to the fifty-one per cent won by the PR, and lost the vast majority of the ethnic Chinese vote. The election itself was plagued by allegations of massive fraud and irregularities, and the result was disputed by Anwar Ibrahim and the PR which staged a series of post-election rallies. Since the election, the BN has struggled to regain support from the ethnic Chinese community. Prime Minister Najib also came under heavy domestic and international criticism for his government's poor handling of the mysterious disappearance of Malaysian Airlines flight MH370 in March 2014.

Malaysia's foreign policy has for the most part reflected domestic political change. Its first prime minister, Tunku Abdul Rahman, was an Anglophile who valued the Commonwealth connection and who was obliged to draw on British and Commonwealth support to cope with the threat posed by Indonesia's **Confrontation**. Reconciliation with Indonesia and membership of **ASEAN** (Association of Southeast Asian Nations) encouraged an extension of international links, especially membership of the Non-Aligned Movement, under the leadership of Tun Abdul Razak. He was identified with a proposal to neutralize Southeast Asia and took the initiative in 1974 in establishing diplomatic relations with the People's Republic of China in order to gain support from his large number of ethnic Chinese constituents. Following Razak's premature death in 1976, **Hussein Onn** succeeded but without imposing any distinctive stamp on foreign policy. He did, however, curtail an adventurist tendency expressed in particular in an attempt to destabilize Brunei.

Foreign policy did not change in great substance when Mahathir became prime minister in 1981 after Hussein Onn had retired because of ill health. ASEAN remained at the centre of regional calculations but Malaysia became more self-assertive under his leadership. He acquired a reputation as a sharp-tongued spokesman in support of Third World causes and early in his tenure directed his anger at Britain, which was subject to economic discrimination (*see* **Buy British Last Policy**) in retaliation for insensitivity to Malaysia's interests. Membership of the Commonwealth was reconsidered, while international Islamic links were strengthened. Initiatives were taken to promote international cooperation in control of drug trafficking and over Antarctica and South–South relationships. A change of political heart over the utility of the Commonwealth resulted in Malaysia playing host to the meeting of its heads of government in October 1989. In 1994 Mahathir returned to attack the former colonial power over British press allegations of his financial impropriety. He was also vocal over the alleged hypocrisy of the west through its failure to safeguard human rights in Bosnia. Mahathir's personal role in foreign policy gave rise to some tensions in regional relations. For example, he interpreted Singapore's willingness to receive the president of Israel in November 1986 as an insult because of his own identification with the Palestinian cause. Relations with Indonesia were uneasy partly because of an unwillingness to respect President Suharto's seniority. Such unease was reinforced in the early 1990s, after Mahathir had unilaterally put forward a proposal for the establishment of an East Asian Economic Caucus to cope with a global trend towards trade blocs. That proposal generated tensions with the United States and Australia. Tensions with the United States were generated also during 1998 when Mahathir claimed that an international Jewish conspiracy was behind Malaysia's economic tribulations. Malaysia took a strong stand on incorporating Myanmar and the states of Indochina within ASEAN and aligned with Vietnam against other regional partners in supporting Cambodia's early membership, despite the violent coup in Phnom Penh in July 1997. Malaysia has also been prominent within ASEAN in promoting close relations with China. An agreement to boost defence cooperation and to use peaceful means to resolve tensions over disputed maritime jurisdiction in the **South China Sea** was concluded in Beijing in June 1999. That agreement gave rise to suspicions that Malaysia had come to terms with China at the expense of ASEAN partners. Tellingly, in June and August 1999, Malaysia occupied two unoccupied features in the Spratly Islands, which provoked a strong protest from the Philippines but only a mild rebuke from China. The key to Mahathir's ability to receive a hearing internationally for his outspoken views was the underlying success of Malaysia's economy. The economic crisis of the late 1990s had the effect of diminishing his credibility in preaching to the West.

While testy during the Mahathir years, relations with Singapore improved significantly following Abdullah Badawi's appointment as prime minister. This upturn found expression in the creation the **Iskandar Development Region** in the southern Malaysian state of Johor bordering Singapore. Ties advanced further under Najib Razak, with both governments agreeing to build a high-speed railway between Singapore and Kuala Lumpur to deepen integration. During Badawi's tenure Malaysia chaired the Organization of the Islamic Conference in 2003, the Non-Aligned Movement from 2003 to 2006, and ASEAN in 2005 when the **East Asia Summit** was inaugurated. Malaysia's foreign policy focus on Islamic countries has gradually deepened since the Mahathir administration. Malaysia was at the forefront of regional opposition to the American invasion of Iraq, which it criticized as a manifestation of the neo-conservative Washington government's assault on the Islamic faith. Malaysia's resolute support for the Palestinian cause was marked by Prime Minister Najib's landmark visit to Gaza in January 2013, when he signed an agreement with the Hamas government to help rebuild the prime minister's office which was destroyed by Israeli forces in November the previous year.

see also: Abdul Rahman, Tunku; Alliance Party; Anwar Ibrahim; APEC; ASEAN; Badawi, Tun Abdullah Ahmad; *Barisan Alternatif*; *Barisan Nasional*; *Bersih*; Buy British Last Policy; Confrontation; Democratic Action Party; East Asia Summit; Hindraf; Hussein Onn, Tun; Iskandar Development Region; Islam; Mahathir Mohamad, Tun; May 13 Racial Riots 1969; Musa Hitam, Tun; Najib Tun Razak, Datuk Seri Mohamad; New Economic Policy; *Pakatan Rakyat*; *Parti Bersatu Sabah*; *Parti Islam Se-Malaysia*; *Parti Keadilan Nasional*; People's Action Party; Razak, Tun Abdul; Razaleigh Hamzah, Tengku; *Semangat '46*; South China Sea; Suharto; Sukarno; UMNO; *Yang di-Pertuan Agong*.

Myanmar (Burma)

Myanmar (Burma) is the second largest country in Southeast Asia with an area of 676,000 square kilometres. It is situated to the east of India and Bangladesh, to the southwest of the People's Republic of China and to the west of Laos and Thailand. Its coastline extends from Bangladesh to Thailand and fronts the Bay of Bengal. The country has an estimated population of over fifty-five million, the vast majority of whom are devotees of Theravada Buddhism. A host of ethnic minorities, long disaffected from the central government, inhabit the border areas of the state. Myanmar's primarily agricultural economy has barely advanced beyond its condition under colonialism. Indeed, for almost fifty years, it regressed economically in the charge of a military junta for whom power became an end in itself, reflected in defence expenditure consuming a third of the annual budget. In reconstituted form since 1988, that junta attempted to open the county to foreign investment and trade, in particular from the early 1990s but with only superficial success. The initial momentum of foreign investment was reversed, partly as a consequence of external sanctions driven by a deplorable human rights record and evidence of regime involvement in narcotics production and trafficking. In 2010 the country held general elections for parliament and the following year a new civilian government took power, albeit with a strong military influence. Economic reforms initiated by the new government aimed at encouraging foreign investment included the drafting of a new foreign investment law, a labour law and other legislation. Most of the economic sanctions against the military government have been rescinded and with the country's reputation gradually improving, it has received enormous interest from foreign investors from Asia as well as Europe and the United States. Nevertheless, years of mismanagement of the economic, agriculture and education sectors as well as poor infrastructure still need to be addressed.

Until 2010 when a nominal civilian government was established, Myanmar had been ruled continuously by a military regime since March 1962 when the armed forces, led by General **Ne Win**, seized power. At the time, the country was known by its colonial nomenclature of Burma. In September 1998, in response to a popular challenge put down with violence and blood-letting, Ne Win having abdicated formal responsibility in the previous July, the military government transformed itself into the **State Law and Order Restoration Council** (SLORC). In November 1997, SLORC was replaced by the **State Peace and Development Council** (SPDC). The change in nomenclature and in implied orientation did not change the substance of military despotism. Political opposition was ruthlessly repressed, including the use of torture, while the pervasive practice of forced labour led to the country's censure within the International Labour Organization in June 2000. On 18 June 1989, the name of the state was changed from the Socialist Republic of the Union of Burma to Union of Myanmar through the enactment of the Adaptation of Expression law. The English spellings of several regions and cities were officially changed, including the capital Rangoon which was changed to Yangon. In 2008 a new constitution (*see* **Constitution 2008**) was promulgated through a controversial national referendum, and in November 2010 general elections were held for national and regional parliaments for the first time since 1990. The SPDC handed over power to a newly elected government at the end of March 2011 led by former general and prime minister, now president, **Thein Sein**.

Burma was colonized by Britain from the early nineteenth century and was accorded a limited form of self-government only in the late 1930s, when it was separated from the administration of India against a background of nationalist challenge. It was occupied by the Japanese during the Pacific War with the support of Burmese nationalists, who in 1943 were accorded a nominal independence. When it became apparent that the Japanese were going to lose the war, the Burma National Army rebelled against its military mentors in support of the Allied cause. Burma attained full independence in January 1948 after the British Labour Party administration had revised its gradualist timetable in the light of the demonstrable support enjoyed by the **Anti-Fascist People's Freedom League** (AFPFL), the militant nationalist movement led by **Aung San**. Initially self-styled as the Union of Burma, its governments have struggled to overcome the centrifugal political pull of its ethnically diverse population. Geography has combined with ethnicity to obstruct the reach of central power. The majority of the population of Myanmar adhere to Theravada Buddhism, as do some of the ethnic minorities, who also observe **Islam** and Christianity.

The Union of Burma began independence as a parliamentary democracy in inauspicious circumstances. Nationalist leader Aung San had come to an agreement in January 1947 with the British government for the transfer of sovereignty a year later, but in July 1947 he was assassinated together with six cabinet colleagues in a plot mounted by a political rival. Independence went ahead on 4 January 1948 with **U Nu** as prime minister. From independence, Burma was subject to violent internal upheaval as the government in Rangoon was confronted with insurrection by two Communist and a number of ethnic minority insurgencies challenging both the identity and the constitutional arrangements of the new state. The ethnic minorities were distributed in concentrations around the northern perimeter of the country from east to southwest, as well as in the Irrawaddy Delta, and tensions between them and the Burman majority had been inflamed during the Pacific War. These mixed challenges were contained, if not defeated, by the mid-1950s, in part because of the inability of the opponents of the central government to unite among themselves and also because of the success of the Burmese army in pushing them back.

Because of its roots in the nationalist movement against both the British and the Japanese, the army led by General Ne Win displayed a sense of political entitlement which came to affect the future of the country. Violent challenge to the state and its integrity was succeeded by ferocious factional fighting within the ruling political party. It was to repair this situation that in July 1958, the prime minister, U Nu, invited General Ne Win to form a caretaker government and to prepare the country for fresh elections. Power was returned to civilian government in March 1960. With the electoral success of his faction of the AFPFL, U Nu resumed office as prime minister. In March 1962, however, Ne Win mounted a coup in response to concessions by the government to the insurgent ethnic minorities and set up a Revolutionary Council to run the country. Under military rule, the country became committed to an ersatz ideology called the Burmese Way to Socialism, which was a potted version of Marxist and Buddhist formulae. The declared purpose of the undertaking was Burma's development on an autonomous basis. In July 1962 the Revolutionary Council established the **Burma Socialist Programme Party** (BSPP) with the mission to realize the Burmese Way to Socialism. All other parties were abolished, while the BSPP served as the political arm of the army. In 1974 a new constitution was promulgated, the BSPP was opened up to a mass membership and the name of the state was changed to the Socialist Republic of the Union of Burma, with Ne Win in the office of president. Ne Win stepped down in November 1981 but remained in control as chairman of the BSPP. These changes in political form did nothing to arrest a relentless economic decline as the dogma, bureaucracy and corruption of the so-called Burmese Way to Socialism, combined with a policy of international isolation, affected the availability and distribution of basic goods in a country rich with natural resources and once regarded as the ricebowl of Southeast Asia. In addition, the cost of containing the disparate insurgencies which increased in number after the 1962 coup and an invasion out of China by elements of the Burmese Communist Party served to bring the country closer to economic collapse. For a decade and a half, this continuing decline did not lead to any political reaction beyond the ready control of the military. However, acute economic crisis was signalled in

1987, when the government in Rangoon applied to the United Nations for Burma to be accorded the status of 'least-developed country' in order to secure grants in aid.

Burma erupted in political turmoil when the government adopted desperate measures to cope with a deteriorating economy. Demonetization of larger currency notes in circulation in September 1987 provoked student unrest which exploded in demonstrations and violence in March 1988. This challenge was matched by ruthless military repression, which came to a head in August and September. In the interim, Ne Win resigned as chairman of the BSPP in July but failed to stem popular protest which responded to the leadership provided by **Aung San Suu Kyi**, the daughter of national hero Aung San, who had coincidentally returned to the country to nurse her ailing mother. On 18 September 1988 the army chief of staff, General Saw Maung, assumed power on behalf of the military in an incumbency coup marking the culmination of an awesome bloodletting. All state organs were abolished by the new junta, which styled itself the SLORC. The country was placed under martial law but SLORC promised that multi-party elections would be held for a constituent assembly. In the meantime, all references to the Burmese Way to Socialism disappeared from public pronouncements, while the junta sought foreign exchange to buy arms by according foreign entrepreneurs logging and fishing rights. Political parties were allowed to register during 1989. Although more than 200 emerged, only a handful of any significance were formed, above all, the **National League for Democracy** (NLD) led by Aung San Suu Kyi. She was placed under house arrest in July 1989 just prior to the anniversary of the period of bloodletting in 1988. Nonetheless, the NLD won an overwhelming electoral victory at the polls in May 1990 over the **National Unity Party**, which was the political reincarnation of the BSPP. The constituent assembly in the form of a National Convention was not convened until 1993, however, while the position of the NLD was undermined through contrived expulsions, including that of Aung San Suu Kyi, who was kept in incarceration. SLORC's attempt to discredit her nationally and internationally was thwarted when she was awarded the Nobel Peace Prize in October 1991. However, despite almost universal condemnation of its appalling human rights record, the ruling junta held on to power, with Ne Win apparently influential in the background despite his ailing condition.

Senior General Saw Maung stepped down as head of SLORC in April 1992, believed to be suffering from mental disorder, to be succeeded by General **Than Shwe**, who also assumed the office of prime minister. However, Ne Win's close confidant and head of intelligence as well as SLORC's first secretary, General **Khin Nyunt**, was considered his proxy and wielded considerable power in the junta. He inspired the inauguration of the constituent assembly or National Convention in Rangoon, by then known as Yangon, in January 1993, suitably purged of dissident political elements, but the convention was suspended in 1996 following a boycott by the NLD, which labelled it undemocratic. Aung San Suu Kyi was released unexpectedly from detention in July 1995 but without any other political concessions by SLORC. In 2000, she was again placed under house arrest, only to be released again in 2002. During an upcountry tour in 2003 which was met by huge crowds of supporters, her convoy was attacked by a government-backed mob and Aung San Suu Kyi was placed back under house arrest. She would remain in detention until just after general elections in late 2010.

In 2003, Khin Nyunt announced a seven-point '**Roadmap to Democracy**' to guide the country's transition from military rule to a more democratic civilian form of government. The process, which was heavily criticized for its genuflection towards the military, went forward and the National Convention was re-convened in 2004 and a new constitution draft was announced in 2008. In 2005 the government moved the capital from Yangon to a new, specially built capital city in central Myanmar, called **Naypyidaw**. Mass demonstrations led by Buddhist monks in 2007 threatened to interrupt the process, when initial protests against rising costs of living eventually became explicitly anti-government. The protests were violently suppressed amid widespread arrests and heavy international criticism. In May 2008 Cyclone Nargis devastated much of southwestern Myanmar, sparking a humanitarian crisis that was badly handled by the regime which tried unsuccessfully to limit the inflow of international aid and foreign aid workers. The government came in for further criticism for going forward with a nationwide referendum on the 2008 constitution despite the destruction and massive loss of life in the disaster. The constitution was approved amid widespread international criticism. A new name for the country was adopted, the Republic of the Union of Myanmar, along with a new national flag. Subsequently, the government announced that democratic elections would be held the next year and political parties were allowed to register. The NLD, in protest at electoral rules and the continued detention of political prisoners including Aung San Suu Kyi, announced it would boycott the elections. Countrywide elections were held in November 2010 with the **Union Solidarity and Development Party** (USDP), led by retired members of the military, winning an overwhelming majority, although there were widespread allegations of intimidation and electoral fraud. Since the handover of power from the SPDC to the new government led by former general Thein Sein, Myanmar's leadership has embarked on a major reform drive. Although the motives behind the reforms continue to be debated, the government has opened up the economy, repealed repressive laws governing civil society, and pursued peace processes with the majority of ethnic insurgents. Aung San Suu Kyi, released from house arrest and apparently persuaded of the sincerity of the reforms, joined the political process. In by-elections in 2012, her NLD party handily defeated the USDP and became the largest opposition party in parliament, and for the first time Aung San Suu Kyi assumed a role as an elected politician.

An ability to reinforce power at the centre has been matched with an increasing assertion of state power against dissident ethnic minorities. The revolt of northern Wa tribesmen against ethnic Chinese dominance of the Communist Party in the late 1980s enabled the Yangon government to exercise greater control over the flow of opium and military supplies to rebel minorities. Such control has been facilitated by effective cooperation with the government in Beijing, which has been a major source of arms transfers but in return for access to intelligence facilities in the Andaman Sea. In October 1993 a ceasefire was concluded with the **Kachin** Independence Army, regarded as the most significant of the insurgent groupings fighting against the government, which was formalized in February 1994. This accord meant that the armed forces could concentrate their efforts against the **Karen** and the **Shan** rebels to great military effect. By 1996, the government in Yangon had effectively turned the tide of battle against the country's ethnic insurgencies, although armed resistance has been sustained by the Karen and Shan minorities among other smaller groups. In 2009 though, the ceasefires appeared to unravel as the government attempted to force the groups to convert their armed wings to army control and to join the political process, a move most of the groups resisted. After March 2011 the civilian government embarked on a peace drive which has resulted in ceasefire agreements and ongoing peace negotiations with most of the ethnic minority groups. The exception is the Kachin, who in 2011 returned to armed struggle.

In foreign relations, Burma was an early advocate of non-alignment, being represented at the historic **Asian–African Conference** in Bandung in 1955 and at the founding conference of the Non-Aligned Movement in Belgrade in 1961. Indeed, a passionate anti-colonialism had prevented membership of the Commonwealth in advance of the arrangement made to accommodate India, which as an independent republic could not pledge loyalty to the British Crown. The military regime which assumed power in 1962 maintained the same commitment to non-alignment which complemented the aims of the Burmese Way to Socialism. The commitment did not prevent the development of a close association with northern neighbour China. That relationship was never allowed to become unduly deferential, however. During the period of the Cultural Revolution, Burma displayed a testy independence in response to evident intimidation. In September 1979 at the summit meeting in Havana, Burma withdrew from the Non-Aligned Movement on the ground that it had ceased to be neutral enough under Cuba's chairmanship, which claimed a special relationship for the Soviet Union. However, international reaction to SLORC's violation of human rights, especially against its Muslim minority, caused the government in Yangon to revise its view by the time of the Non-Aligned Summit in Jakarta in September 1992. Repressive action in 1992 against the Muslim **Rohingya** minority in Arakan Province bordering Bangladesh drew condemnation from Islamic states, which Myanmar sought to counter by securing readmission to the Non-Aligned Movement. Myanmar's Rohingya problem flared again in 2012 when widespread violence against the Rohingya was triggered in Rakhine state.

Myanmar has been able to attract China's support as both an arms supplier and a patron of a kind, which was willing to help contain international criticism of its brutal repressive regime in return for extensive economic opportunities. China has also developed communication facilities which will enable direct physical access from its borders to the Indian Ocean while an extensive Chinese business/migrant presence has been established in upper Myanmar. The government of Thailand had been the most active among **ASEAN** (Association of Southeast Asian Nations) states in practising the association's policy of **Constructive Engagement**, viewed as more appropriate than one of shunning the Yangon regime. In consequence, a Myanmar delegation was invited by the Thai government to attend as guests at the annual meeting of ASEAN's foreign ministers held in Bangkok in July 1994. Equivalent status was accorded in July 1995 in Brunei when Myanmar's foreign minister signed ASEAN's **Treaty of Amity and Cooperation** and at the **Bangkok Summit** in December 1995, attended by Prime Minister Than Shwe. Singapore had also been forthcoming with a visit to Yangon by its prime minister, **Goh Chok Tong**, in March 1994. His appearance in the capital marked only the second visit by a head of government since SLORC assumed power. The prime minister of Laos had visited the country in 1992. Despite the release of Aung San Suu Kyi, western countries continued to treat Myanmar as a political outcast. Myanmar joined the **ASEAN Regional Forum** in August 1996 and ASEAN in July 1997 but its membership gave rise to difficulties between the Association and some of its dialogue partners. For example, the European Union has until recently denied visas to senior members of the military junta, and refused to engage in multilateral meetings until a compromise agreement with the EU in August 2000. Through the 1990s and 2000s, Myanmar was subject to harsh economic sanctions by western countries in response to its human rights record against political opponents and ethnic minorities. Outrage over the crackdown on the 2007 protests sparked an expansion of sanctions against the government. Likewise, the government's pedestrian response to the Cyclone Nargis disaster led France and the United States to agitate for the invocation of the Right to Protect in order to force the delivery of aid into the country, and a crisis was only averted after the intervention of ASEAN's secretary-general, **Surin Pitsuwan**. While Western governments and the UN were highly critical of the 2008 referendum and the openness of the 2010 elections, the reform agenda of Thein Sein has brought the new government a new international standing. Many of the economic sanctions have been repealed or reduced and international leaders have been flocking to the country to meet both Thein Sein and Aung San Suu Kyi, who was able to leave the country for the first time since the late 1980s.

The military government in Burma and then Myanmar ruled without consent but retained its position because of a caste-like sense of identity and loyalty among the officer corps and a system of patronage which ensures that commands to rank-and-file troops to fire on unarmed demonstrators are obeyed without dissent. Power struggles, however, were not absent. In March 2002, General Ne Win and members of his family were arrested in connection with a supposed coup attempt. Ne Win died under house arrest in December 2002. Two years later, General Khin Nyunt, then prime minister and head of intelligence, was placed under house arrest and his intelligence apparatus dismantled, ostensibly on corruption charges, but most saw it as the culmination of a power struggle with Senior General Than Shwe. Following the March 2011 assumption of power of the new government the military has pulled back from a direct public role in politics, although it maintains a strong role behind the scenes, particularly through the involvement of many former military officers in senior levels of government, including the president, one vice-president and the speaker of the lower house of parliament, and the twenty-five per cent block of parliament reserved for military officers, and retains a constitutional right to step in to assume control of the country in a national emergency. While a Constitutional Review Joint Committee was established to consider revisions to the 2008 Constitution authored by the military, its preliminary recommendations, unveiled on 31 January 2014, fell short of expectations, with the only significant proposed change being the creation of a more equitable power-sharing arrangement between the central government and its ethnic-minority-controlled regions. Notably, the committee specifically cautioned against changing Article 59F, which bars individuals from becoming president if their spouses or children hold foreign citizenship. A revision of this article would have paved the way for Aung San Suu Kyi to contest the presidency.

see also: Anti-Fascist People's Freedom League; ASEAN; ASEAN Regional Forum; Asian–African Conference; Aung San; Aung San Suu Kyi; Bangkok Summit; Burma Socialist Programme Party; Constitution 2008; Goh Chok Tong; Insurgencies, Myanmar; Kachin; Karen; Khin Nyunt, General, National League for Democracy; National Unity Party; Naypyidaw; Ne Win, General; Rohingya; Shan; State Law and Order Restoration Council; State Peace and Development Council; Surin Pitsuwan; Than Shwe, Senior General; Thein Sein; Treaty of Amity and Cooperation; U Nu; Union Solidarity and Development Party.

Philippines, Republic of

The Republic of the Philippines was established as an independent state on 4 July 1946 when sovereignty was transferred by the US colonial administration. The US model of democracy was replaced by authoritarian rule under President **Ferdinand Marcos** from 1972 until 1986. Constitutional democracy was restored by President **Corazón Aquino**, who was succeeded in office by **Fidel Ramos** after elections in May 1992. From Corazón Aquino onwards, the tenure of presidential office was restricted to a single six-year term. President **Benigno Simeon Cojuangco Aquino III**, son of Corazón Aquino, was elected to office in June 2010.

The Philippines is made up of an archipelago of some 7,000 islands extending for nearly 1,000 miles from north to south, which are located at the eastern periphery of Southeast Asia and to the south of the People's Republic of China. Its land area is 300,000 square kilometres. Three principal geographic divisions comprise the main northern island of Luzón, on which is located the capital Manila, the central Visayan islands, and the southerly islands of Mindanao and Sulu. The archipelago was given political coherence through Spanish colonial intervention from the late sixteenth century and was named for the crown prince who became Philip II. The Spanish also left a profound religious legacy, with over ninety per cent of the population of some ninety-four million adhering to the Catholic faith. The Spanish were responsible also for containing Islamic settlement to the extreme south of the archipelago. **Islam** is the religious faith of about five per cent of the population, who have a tradition of resistance and rebellion against the government in Manila.

The United States succeeded Spain as the colonial power through military action at the end of the nineteenth century. A commitment to self-government produced a promise of independence in the 1930s which was fulfilled on time despite a cruel and devastating Japanese occupation during the Pacific War. On independence, the Philippines replicated the US constitutional model with an elected presidential system of government constrained in principle by congressional and judicial checks and balances. Two main political organizations, the **Nacionalista Party** and the **Liberal Party**, contended for office and spoils but did not represent fundamental alternatives. In effect, the two parties served as vehicles for advancing and enriching competing provincial-based elite groups whose power rested on a network of local and personal loyalties. Politics involved the alignment and realignment of these fractious elite groups which switched promiscuously from party to party for electoral advantage. That pattern of politics changed in September 1972 when Ferdinand Marcos, elected in November 1965 and re-elected in November 1969, declared martial law in order to overcome the constitutional limitation of two presidential terms. He concentrated power at the centre at the expense of provincial elites with the exception of cronies from his home base of Ilocos Norte. Initially, law and order visibly improved and bureaucratic corruption was reduced while land reform measures were begun. In the event, adverse economic factors precipitated by the energy crisis together with a gross abuse of personal power and financial mismanagement led to decline and disillusionment as all political and legal institutions were rendered impotent. Martial law was ended formally in January 1981 but without significant political change. Political decay was accelerated after the assassination in August 1983 of President Marcos' principal opponent, **Benigno Aquino**, at Manila airport on his return from exile in the United States. Political change was precipitated by a snap presidential election in February 1986 in which Marcos was challenged by Corazón Aquino, Benigno Aquino's widow. Against a background of charges of electoral fraud, the defence minister, **Juan Ponce Enrile**, and deputy chief of staff of the Armed forces, Fidel Ramos, led a military mutiny. That mutiny inspired a popular demonstration in central Manila against Marcos and in favour of

Corazón Aquino. With the refusal of the security forces to act against civilians, the United States intervened to persuade Marcos and his notorious wife, **Imelda Marcos**, to leave the country on 25 February for exile in Hawaii.

Corazón Aquino was declared president and set about restoring a legitimate constitutional structure. The previous US model was reinstated in slightly modified form with a bicameral congress but with provision for a single presidential term of six years. The new constitution was approved with an overwhelming vote in favour in a national referendum in February 1987, while candidates endorsed by Corazón Aquino won a decisive majority in congressional elections in May. Corazón Aquino faced a series of major political challenges during her tenure. First, she was confronted by a series of abortive coups by a group of alienated army officers who felt that as they were responsible for the fall of Marcos, the armed forces should be the political beneficiaries. Her chief of staff and then defence minister, Fidel Ramos, remained loyal and mobilized military support for constitutional government, which came also from the United States. Second, she was opposed by the Communist Party of the Philippines, which had made great strides as a result of Marcos' years of misrule. Its leadership, which miscalculated popular support for a return to constitutional government, also felt cheated by Corazón Aquino's political success and sought to sustain a military challenge in the rural areas where poverty was most acute. Finally, she had to contend with rumbling Muslim rebellion in the southern islands which had been precipitated by the declaration of martial law in 1972. In the event, Corazón Aquino saw out her tenure and was succeeded through the ballot box in May 1992, when Fidel Ramos was elected with only 23.6 per cent of the vote, less than one million more than his nearest rival in a contest against five other candidates. Corazón Aquino's presidency was not marked by the regeneration of the Philippines, which failed to demonstrate the vigorous economic growth exhibited by its regional partners. She became chief executive with a great opportunity to provide decisive political leadership. However, the very qualities of non-worldliness which made her such a potent opponent of Marcos failed to equip her for the responsibilities of high office, while the prominence of her family in the decision-making process further reduced national confidence. Corazón Aquino restored constitutional government but in so doing enabled a reversion rather than a reform of the political process. Fidel Ramos assumed office in June 1992 without generating the same political expectations and was also not faced with the same challenges that encumbered Corazón Aquino. His political party *Lakas ng Edsa* or Edsa Struggle – recalling the site of the mutiny of February 1986 – was very much a personal following, formed only in 1991 (*see* **EDSA**; ***Lakas*–NUCD**). Nonetheless, he was able to work with Congress in which he commanded a majority only in the House of Representatives and also demonstrated early success in overcoming military dissidence. He acted to neutralize the persistent Communist challenge through persuading Congress to legalize the party, while Indonesia's good offices, specifically those of Ali Alatas, Indonesian foreign minister and chairman of the Organization of Islamic Conference, were employed to begin negotiations over regional autonomy with Muslim separatists. Where Aquino had, in 1989, created the Autonomous Region of Muslim Mindanao (ARMM), pursuant to the provisions of the 1987 constitution, Ramos went further in negotiating Joint Ceasefire Ground Rules in 1994 between the Philippines government and the **Moro National Liberation Front** (MNLF) and eventually, a Final Peace Agreement in 1996. The former granted concessions (such as the right for MNLF members to bear arms in thirteen provinces) in return for peace, while the latter set in motion a two-part process involving the creation of a Special Zone of Peace and Development (SZOPAD), the absorption of MNLF elements into the Philippine National Police (PNP), and the establishment of a Regional Executive Council and Legislative Assembly. Talks with the **Moro Islamic Liberation Front** (MILF), a radical faction which broke away from the MNLF following the **Tripoli Agreement of 1976**, were less successful, with a vague Agreement for the General Cessation of Hostilities only signed in 1997. At the same time, another splinter group was formed by Abdurajik

Abubakar Janjalani, a cleric who had fought with the mujahidin in Afghanistan, and members of the MNLF who were disappointed by the new arrangements and who wished to resume armed conflict. **Abu Sayyaf Group** (ASG) was established in 1991 and carried out bombings within the Philippines until 1998, when Abdurajik was killed by the PNP. His younger brother, Khadaffy Janjalani, subsequently took control, and the group resumed its activities with kidnappings and assaults from 2000.

Under Fidel Ramos, modest economic improvement was demonstrated with continuing support from multilateral agencies but without transforming the poverty-stricken condition of the majority of the population dependent on remittances from family members working overseas. The elite-driven and fractious nature of Philippine politics served to obstruct economic reform, especially over land tenure. Political realignment within Congress occurred in reaction to proposed tax legislation intended to strengthen the resources of central government. President Ramos also attracted strong opposition from his predecessor when it was suspected that he had an interest in amending the constitution to permit him a second term of office. Although the Philippines was afflicted by the regional economic crisis from the middle of 1997, its limited degree of development and restrictions on international borrowing softened its impact. Economic difficulty, however, served to influence the presidential campaign in 1998, which was marked by the breakdown of the ruling coalition. Incumbent vice-president, **Joseph Estrada**, posed as the populist champion of the poor and secured a landslide victory over Jose de Venecia, the speaker of the lower house and the candidate of the ruling party. Venecia's electoral partner, **Gloria Macapagal-Arroyo**, was elected vice-president. The promise of President Estrada's victory soured by the turn of the new millennium as the managerialism of Fidel Ramos was succeeded by a reversion to traditional patron–client politics. In January 2000, finance secretary Edgardo Espiritu resigned in a protest against corruption and cronyism. In February 2000, Estrada dismissed his justice secretary, Serafin Cuevas, ostensibly over a decision to pardon a murderer but in reality over decisions against the business interests of close associates. Charges of corruption and cronyism and failings of leadership provided the background to Estrada's reversal of a declared policy of amending the constitution. His proposal for removing provisions barring foreigners from owning land and controlling key industries in the interests of economic development had met with strong opposition on grounds that it could serve as a precedent for securing a second term of presidential office. The diminishing popularity of President Estrada was compounded by the failure of his hardline policy against Muslim separatists in the south of the country who reacted with a campaign of kidnapping and violence. In April 2000, Estrada provocatively declared an 'all-out war' against the MILF, nullifying the Ramos administration's 1997 Ceasefire Agreement during which an airport and fishing port had been completed in General Santos City, Mindanao, accompanied by a rise in tuna exports, the region's primary export. The MILF called a *Jihad* in response to Estrada's offensive later that year, and withdrew from all talks under the peace process. In the same month, the ASG expanded its operations to Malaysia by seizing twenty-one tourists from a resort on Sipadan and holding them on Jolo, forcing Estrada to cut short a visit to China and cancel a trip to Europe to deal with the situation. In the subsequent months, despite intensified military offensives, the ASG continued to seize both Filipino and foreign hostages, killing several of them along with captured Filipino soldiers and negotiators. The protracted crisis placed the ASG on the international radar and the group admitted links to Al-Qaeda on 15 October 2001.

In October 2000, allegations of cronyism (Estrada was alleged to have received up to 545 million pesos in proceeds from *jueteng*, a form of illegal gambling, as well as 130 million pesos in misappropriated taxes, among other charges) were cast Estrada's way by hitherto close friend, Governor Luis Singson, and Senate minority leader Teofisto Guingona Jr. Several members of the political elite, including former presidents Aquino and Ramos, along with Archbishop

Jaime Sin, called for Estrada's resignation, while members of Congress left the ruling party, and several Cabinet ministers, including Vice-President Macapagal-Arroyo, resigned as Estrada's impeachment trial began. On 17 January 2001, following a vote by eleven of the senators on the jury (who came to be known under an acronym of their names as 'Joe's cohorts') not to examine an envelope of key evidence, Senate president Aquilino Pimentel Jr and the eleven prosecutors in the case resigned from their posts and left the proceedings. The developments, televised live, incensed a growing crowd that gathered outside the EDSA shrine (built to commemorate the **People Power** Revolution of 1986, thus giving this demonstration its name, '**EDSA II**'), and by 19 January the PNP and the Armed Forces of the Philippines (AFP) withdrew their support for Estrada and joined the protests. The next day, Macapagal-Arroyo was sworn in as president in front of the crowd at EDSA by the chief justice, Hilario Davide, Jr, despite doubts over the constitutionality of this move. Estrada's trial continued from April 2001 to September 2007 when he was sentenced to *Reclusion Perpetua* (though his co-accused were acquitted), and he filed an appeal. He was granted exclusive clemency by President Macapagal-Arroyo in October 2007, bringing the trial to an end.

Gloria Macapagal-Arroyo's presidency was first challenged by Estrada supporters who staged the 'EDSA III' demonstrations upon his arrest in April 2001. Macapagal-Arroyo declared a state of rebellion in response, and the protests were put down by the AFP and PNP. EDSA again became a focal point of revolt on 27 July 2003 when 321 AFP soldiers, known as the 'Bagong Kaputineros', occupied the Oakwood Premier Ayala Centre between EDSA and Makati Avenue in Makati City, Metro Manila. The mutiny, which ended with an agreement that same day, was carried out to demand reform of the AFP. Further challenges emerged during Macapagal-Arroyo's second term from 2004 to 2010. An alleged *coup d'état* was exposed on 24 February 2006, to which she responded with warrantless arrests and the seizure of private institutions in control of public utilities. Lessons were suspended nationwide through the Department of Education, leftists were arrested and charged, while the office of the *Daily Tribune*, which had been critical of the administration, was raided. Another rebellion was staged on 29 November 2007 by several officials detained in the Oakwood mutiny who walked out of their trials and took control of the Peninsula Manila Hotel for six hours. Despite these challenges, the administration garnered considerable praise for its economic management. President Macapagal-Arroyo, formerly an economics lecturer, undertook a reform agenda that contributed to an average growth rate of 4.5 per cent during her tenure, higher than the three preceding administrations. The *peso* also became East Asia's best performing currency in 2005–6, and Asia's best performing currency in 2007, strengthening by nineteen per cent that year. Macapagal-Arroyo is also credited with granting amnesty to the long-persecuted members of the Communist Party of the Philippines, the **New People's Army**, the **National Democratic Front** (an umbrella Communist organization) and other rebel groups. Stains on Macapagal-Arroyo's record include a spate of extrajudicial political killings from 2006 to 2007, with the death toll of twenty-three journalists (among others killed) second only to Iraq; a seventeen-year high of 12.5 per cent inflation in 2008; and a drastic rise in inequality, with the number of poor Filipinos increasing by 3.8 million between 2003 and 2006.

Several controversies dogged Macapagal-Arroyo's presidency. The first was regarding the constitutionality of her terms in office. Macapagal-Arroyo's direct installation in 2001, in the absence of an election, raised legal concerns. Her re-election in 2004, too, was initially seen as unlawful, but upheld on the grounds that while the constitution bars a president from re-election, a president who has succeeded the incumbent for not more than four years may be elected. Macapagal-Arroyo was later accused of vote tampering, and this formed the basis of the first of four impeachment complaints in 2005. Several additional allegations, including counts of corruption, extrajudicial killings, torture and illegal arrests, also surfaced. Macapagal-Arroyo's use of emergency powers was called into question as well. Following the attempted coup in 2006, her warrantless arrests and seizure of private institutions were declared illegal by the Supreme Court. The **Maguindanao Massacre** of fifty-seven people in November 2009 prompted her to place the province under martial law, suspending the writ of *habeas corpus* for the first time since 1972. Following the expiration of her presidential term at the May 2010 general elections, Macapagal-Arroyo was returned to Congress as representative of the second district of Pampanga in a landslide victory – only the second president after Jose Laurel to seek lower office after the presidency. In November 2011, however, she was arrested while confined in St Luke's Medical Centre on charges of electoral sabotage. Her husband and son are also implicated in the allegations.

Benigno Simeon Cojuangco Aquino III, son of Benigno Aquino Jr and Corazón Aquino, and chairman of the Liberal Party, was sworn into office in June 2010. Popular support for Benigno Aquino III, also known by the nickname 'Noynoy', grew after the death of his mother, former president Corazón Aquino in August 2009. The former senator and deputy speaker of the House of Representatives, known for several reform bills targeted at the police, the courts and property valuation, among other areas, replaced Mar Roxas as the Liberal Party's standard bearer and defeated his closest contender – none other than Joseph Estrada – by more than five million votes, becoming the third-youngest elected president of the Philippines. Upon entering office, Aquino initiated education reform, established a Truth Commission to investigate allegations against Gloria Macapagal-Arroyo and reversed unconstitutional midnight appointments by Macapagal-Arroyo before the presidential transition. Within three months of Aquino's inauguration, the **Manila Hostage Crisis**, in which a former PNP officer hijacked a bus with twenty-five Hong Kong tourists in a bid for reinstatement, took place in front of the Quirino Grandstand where he was sworn in. Aquino, who then held responsibility for direct supervision of the PNP, took full responsibility for the outcome of the crisis, which led to eight fatalities. Aquino managed to consolidate his position at the May 2013 mid-term elections which saw his Liberal Party win nine out of twelve Senate seats, make substantial gains in the lower house of Congress, and retain its control of nearly half of the available gubernatorial seats. That election also saw former president Joseph Estrada return to Philippine politics by winning the mayoral elections for Manila.

The MILF announced in 2011 – two years after the suspension of military operations by the Macapagal-Arroyo administration in 2009 – that it would no longer seek secession from the Philippines. Prior to that, the Memorandum of Agreement on the Muslim Ancestral Domain, which had been finalized between the government and the MILF, and would have given limited autonomy to 700 villages within a newly created Bangsamoro Judicial Entity, was blocked and declared unconstitutional by the Supreme Court. Aquino resumed peace talks with the MILF leadership after the announcement, though rogue factions continued to launch sporadic attacks against the AFP, such as the killing of nineteen soldiers at Al-Barka, Basilan, in October 2011. Finally, a new agreement on limited autonomy was reached with the **Framework Agreement on the Bangsamoro**, signed in October 2012 after extended discussions, and Aquino made a landmark visit to the MILF headquarters in Sultan Kudarat, Mindanao, in February 2013. This subsequently paved the way for a landmark **Comprehensive Agreement on the Bangsamoro** (CAB). Perceiving that the framework agreement threatened to leave them out in the cold, disgruntled MNLF rebels overwhelmed five coastal villages in Zamboanga and seized nearly 200 hostages. The fighting that ensued when the Philippine military dispatched forces there displaced thousands.

On the foreign policy front, the presidency of Fidel Ramos had marked a major discontinuity in relations with the United States, which withdrew its military presence completely in November 1992. After independence, the former colonial power had been accorded sovereign rights over extensive military base facilities through a treaty in 1947. In 1951 the two countries also entered into a mutual security treaty which constituted an American guarantee in the context of the Cold War. The US military presence became a controversial factor in domestic politics made acute by Washington's support for Marcos' regime until virtually the last possible moment when he was discarded. Nationalist agitation against the US military presence revived during Corazón Aquino's tenure. Negotiations for an agreement to phase out that presence by the end of the decade failed because the nationalist card was employed by members of the Senate with presidential ambitions. The prospect of the end of the US military presence after nearly a century removed any obstacle to the Philippines joining the Non-Aligned Movement in September 1992. The Republic had been a founder of **ASEAN** (Association of Southeast Asian Nations) in August 1967 but differences with Malaysia over the **Philippines' Claim to Sabah** soured the relationship and enthusiasm for ASEAN. Less than convincing offers to drop the claim were treated sceptically in Kuala Lumpur until Fidel Ramos announced in September 1992 that it would no longer be pursued. An improvement in relations was marked by Fidel Ramos' official visit to Kuala Lumpur in January 1993, the first by a Philippine president since 1968. Nevertheless, while the claim remained dormant, it was never really abandoned by Manila. In 2013, the matter surfaced yet again when militants linked to the self-proclaimed sultan of Sulu, Jamalul Kiram III, launched an audacious raid on **Lahad Datu** in Sabah in an attempt to reclaim the territory for the Sulu sultanate by force. The resulting standoff ended with a massive Malaysian military operation to flush out the militants while the Philippines government issued nervous calls for restraint on both sides.

Membership of ASEAN has come to be of increasing importance to the Philippines with its changing relationship with the United States. In December 1987 the ASEAN heads of government persisted in holding a third meeting at their **Manila Summit** in order to demonstrate solidarity with Corazón Aquino, who had nearly been toppled by a coup attempt. The Philippines has long asserted sovereignty over a number of the Spratly Islands in the **South China Sea** which lie to its west. In July 1992 at a meeting of its foreign ministers in Manila, ASEAN served as a vehicle for a **Declaration on the South China Sea** calling on claimants to jurisdiction to settle disputes by peaceful means. That declaration did not inhibit China from seizing a reef near the Philippines island of Palawan in February 1995; nor Malaysia from seizing two others in 1999. The military weakness of the Philippines in the face of China's maritime assertiveness prompted a reconsideration of relations with its main treaty partner. In May 1999, the Philippines Senate approved a Visiting Forces Agreement with the United States. In February 2000, the first large-scale joint military exercise was conducted with American forces. The Philippines had embarked on a US$8.7 billion military modernization programme but its implementation has been delayed by a lack of funds.

The Sipadan hostage crisis, when the ASG occupied a dive resort and took twenty-one hostages, became the trigger for Washington's first direct military involvement in the Philippines for counterterrorism purposes since foreign troops were banned in the 1987 constitution. The Macapagal-Arroyo administration cited the 1951 Mutual Defence Treaty to provide a legal basis for Exercise Balikatan 02–1, in which an initial deployment of 650 troops arrived in January 2002 for joint operations with the AFP. In addition, the United States extended US$93 million in military aid to the Philippines, and US$55 million in development aid for Mindanao. On Macapagal-Arroyo's insistence, the US contingent largely served an advisory function: 500 of the troops were support/maintenance personnel while the remaining 150 special forces members took on training and advisory roles, some accompanying AFP units on Basilan. These figures were scaled up in 2003 following the death of a US special forces soldier in a Zamboanga bombing the previous October, reaching a peak of 350 special forces troops, 400 support personnel, 1,000 marines and a 1,300-strong naval force, authorized to play a frontline combat role against the estimated 500 ASG fighters in Jolo.

The Philippines' relations with China fluctuated during this period of closer military collaboration with the United States. In 1996, following the resolution of the Mischief Reef dispute in 1994–5, the two nations agreed to cooperation and consensus regarding disputes and joint developments in the South China Sea, later affirmed by the Joint Statement on the Framework of Cooperation in the Twenty-First Century, signed in 2000. The goodwill continued with the signing of the **Declaration on the Conduct of Parties in the South China Sea** (DOC) in 2002, between China and ASEAN. In 2004, however, the Macapagal-Arroyo administration undertook controversial joint explorations with China in parts of the South China Sea then also contested by Vietnam and China, under the Joint Marine Seismic Undertaking (JMSU). Strong domestic opposition arose, not only because Macapagal-Arroyo was perceived as having reneged on the terms of the DOC, and hence broken ranks with ASEAN, but also because the enterprise was seen as an opportunity for further corruption and resource manipulation on the part of the administration. Relations with China began to sour in 2007 when a bill which defined the Philippines' territorial baselines to include the Spratly Islands passed two readings in the House of Representatives. Other ASEAN nations, including Vietnam and Brunei, subsequently submitted rival claims over various landforms in the South China Sea, and tensions escalated. In April 2012, the Philippines Navy detained and boarded eight Chinese fishing vessels in the South China Sea, in what came to be known as the **Scarborough Shoal** standoff. Attempts to arrest the fishermen were blocked by Chinese maritime surveillance ships. Heated reactions to the incident included calls to boycott Chinese goods sold in the Philippines, cyber-attacks on the websites of the University of the Philippines, the *Philippine Star* and even the *Official Gazette*, as well as stricter sanctions on Philippine fruit exports to China, and the suspension of Chinese tours to the Philippines. In May 2012, the United States expressed support for the Philippines in the standoff, with several senators describing China's claims as 'illegal' and 'provocative', and US Secretary of State Hillary Clinton using the Philippines' preferred name for the South China Sea: the West Philippine Sea. Disputes over the Spratlys and Scarborough Shoal remain unresolved. Despite popular sensitivities towards foreign troops in the country, escalating tensions in the South China Sea have further prompted Manila to negotiate a larger US presence in order to deter Chinese aggression. In March 2014, Manila officially filed a memorandum with the UN International Tribunal on the Law of the Sea (ITLOS) to pressure China to clarify its claims in the waters of the South China Sea by asking the Tribunal to decide if China's historical nine-dash line claim has a legal basis under the UN Convention on the Law of the Sea (UNCLOS).

see also: Abu Sayyaf Group; APEC; Aquino, Benigno; Aquino III, Benigno Simeon Cojuangco; Aquino, Corazón; ASEAN; Comprehensive Agreement on the Bangsamoro; Declaration on the Conduct of Parties in the South China Sea; Declaration on the South China Sea (ASEAN) 1992; EDSA; EDSA II; Enrile, Juan Ponce; Estrada, Joseph; Framework Agreement on the Bangsamoro; Islam; Lahad Datu Crisis; *Lakas*–NUCD; Liberal Party; Macapagal-Arroyo, Gloria; Maguindanao Massacre; Manila Hostage Crisis; Manila Summit 1987; Marcos, Ferdinand; Marcos, Imelda; Moro Islamic Liberation Front; Moro National Liberation Front; Nacionalista Party; National Democratic Front; New People's Army; People Power; Philippines' Claim to Sabah; Philippines–US Security Treaty 1951; Ramos, Fidel; Scarborough Shoal Dispute; South China Sea; Subic Bay Naval Base.

Singapore, Republic of

The island-state of Singapore, with a land area of just over 600 square kilometres, is located at the southern tip of peninsular Malaysia. It is separated from Malaysia by the Strait of Johor but is joined to the mainland by a causeway carrying road and rail traffic as well as by a road bridge that was opened in 1998. The **Singapore Strait** to the south separates the republic from the Riau Islands of Indonesia. It has a population of around five million people, of whom over three million are citizens. Three-quarters of the citizen population are ethnic Chinese of migrant origin. Some fifteen per cent are ethnic Malay, many with links across the **Strait of Johor** from whose sultan the British pro-consul Sir Stamford Raffles acquired the island in 1819.

Singapore has become an exemplar of post-colonial Asian modernization and achievement, especially under the dynamic leadership of **Lee Kuan Yew**, who served as its prime minister from June 1959 until November 1990. The island is a model of urban planning and design, with remarkable accomplishments in public housing and environmental provision as well as in technological achievement. Astounding economic success beyond a traditional role as a regional trading entrepôt has taken place within a stable and authoritarian political system in which a mandatory democracy to the advantage of the ruling **People's Action Party** (PAP) has not provided opportunity for effective opposition. That form of democracy is based on an informal social contract whereby authoritarian government is accepted in return for material advantages. Recent years however, have seen growing popular resentment translate into notable gains for the political opposition, principally the **Workers' Party** (WP).

Singapore had been separated from Britain's local colonial domain after the Pacific War partly because of its strategic importance as a military base. It acquired self-governing status in 1959 concurrent with the electoral success of the PAP, which has been continuously in power ever since. The leadership of that party judged then that Singapore did not have any future as an independent entity and persuaded Malaya's prime minister, **Tunku Abdul Rahman**, to include it within a wider federation of Malaysia, which was established in September 1963. Singapore's tenure within Malaysia was stormy and brief because of the attempt by the PAP (seen as a Chinese party) to become a part of the federal political establishment. On 9 August 1965 against a background of rising racial tension, Singapore formally separated from Malaysia to become an independent republic. That enforced independence, at a time when Indonesia was still engaged in active **Confrontation** against Malaysia, gave rise to an acute vulnerability which has become part of the political culture of the state. An initial abrasiveness of tone in foreign policy has been succeeded over time by a greater moderation based on national accomplishment and a more assured regional place within **ASEAN** (Association of Southeast Asian Nations), but an underlying sense of vulnerability pervades the calculations of the political elite. That fear has translated into a recurrent practice of mobilizing the population, who are told that the world does not owe them a living and that the material advantages they now enjoy cannot be taken for granted. Order and stability have in consequence been given a higher priority than political freedoms, justified on the ground that Singapore's prosperity depends much on the confidence reposed in the state by foreign investors whose flow of capital has been responsible for successful economic development based on export-led growth.

Initially, the PAP had faced political challenge from a radical left-wing faction which split off in 1961 in opposition to membership of Malaysia. The ***Barisan Sosialis*** (Socialist Front) then withdrew from parliamentary politics, leaving the field to the PAP until the early 1980s. In October 1981, however, a by-election was won by **J. B. Jeyaretnam** representing the WP, which had been a Communist front in the late 1950s.

In general elections in 1984, he retained his seat, while **Chiam See Tong** from the Singapore Democratic Party was also successful at the expense of the PAP, which suffered an adverse voting swing of over twelve per cent. Generational change and a resentment of high-handedness by government had led to a growing measure of political alienation. That voting trend against the PAP was sustained marginally in elections in September 1988 and again in August 1991, when the PAP was led by the prime minister, **Goh Chok Tong**, who had succeeded Lee Kuan Yew in November 1990. An unprecedented four seats were lost to opposition members in 1991. Moreover, in elections for a president with reserve powers in August 1993, the incremental voting trend against the PAP continued when an unknown candidate secured more than forty per cent against Ong Teng Cheong, who had resigned from the office of deputy prime minister in order to stand. Tension between President Ong Teng Cheong and members of the Cabinet over the interpretation of his responsibilities and remit led him to stand down at the end of his term. He was succeeded in August 1999 by S. R. Nathan, a former intelligence chief and diplomat, who eventually served two terms unopposed.

The 1997 'Singapore 21' plan seemed to mark a shift towards consultative politics, building on the work of the Feedback Unit – renamed Reaching Everyone for Active Citizenry at Home, or REACH, in 2006 – established by Goh Chok Tong, who was then deputy prime minister, in 1985. 'Singapore 21' worked to document and synthesize the concerns of 6,000 Singaporeans of various income-groups, across all sectors, and became the basis of a 'Singapore 21 Vision' which the republic adopted as a broad blueprint to tackle anticipated challenges of the twenty-first century. Its focus on aspects of the Singaporean identity also reflected a growing awareness of Singapore's lack of a coherent national ethos, and Goh's desire to strengthen what he termed the 'heartware' of the nation. In 2002, the 'Remaking Singapore' dialogue chaired by the minister of state for national development, Vivian Balakrishnan, continued this trend, but was seen as a step further in focusing on proposals to relax current government regulations in different areas. A notable product of this 2002 effort was the creation of the School of the Arts, established in 2008. Goh confirmed perceptions of himself as an open-minded leader the following year, 2003, in an interview with *Time* magazine, in which he announced that his government had begun to employ homosexuals in public service even though homosexual acts remain an offence in Singapore.

Challenges Goh faced in the latter half of his term included the 2001 terrorist plots against Singapore embassies and the 2003 Severe Acute Respiratory Syndrome (SARS) outbreak. The former involved a plan by Al-Qaeda-linked regional terror group ***Jemaah Islamiyah*** to bomb the diplomatic missions of the United States, Australia, the United Kingdom and Israel in Singapore – foiled by an Internal Security Division operation in December 2001 with fifteen conspirators detained within the month and another twenty-six over the subsequent years of investigation. The latter involved the spread of the SARS epidemic to Singapore in March 2003 via three Singaporeans who had contracted it in Hong Kong, to which Goh's administration responded with a slew of national prevention and control measures such as the closure of schools and public places, and intensive healthcare provision.

By the turn of the century, the question of leadership and political change arose in the domestic political arena as the post-independence generation, or 'post-65ers', had come of age without direct experience of the difficulties faced by their parents and grandparents. Prime Minister Goh Chok Tong left a moderate political imprint on Singapore, distinguishing himself from Lee Kuan Yew primarily through the projection of a 'softer' stance at home and abroad, rather than by significant policy developments. In the eyes of many, he was largely in the shadow of his illustrious predecessor, who remained in the Cabinet with the rank of senior minister and assumed the title of Minister Mentor. Goh was succeeded by Lee's brilliant and dynamic elder son, Lee Hsien Loong, in August 2004. Among Lee Hsien Loong's first policy initiatives were the introduction of a five-day work week, and two-month paid maternity leave for mothers of newborn children, both announced at the National Day Rally on the same day as his swearing-in at the Istana. Within the year, Lee also announced proposals for two Integrated Resorts (holiday resorts with casinos) at Marina Bay and Sentosa respectively. This was seen by many as an open endorsement of gambling in the city-state, as well as a prelude to related undesirable activity such as money laundering and organized crime, and several religious and social-welfare groups openly criticized the project. Lee acknowledged these concerns but went forward with the announcement in April 2005 that the government had chosen to approve the proposals, albeit with social safeguards to limit problem gambling, and took full responsibility for the outcome of the decision. Ahead of Lee's first general election in 2006, the government announced a S$2.6 billion 'Progress Package' that distributed budget surpluses from the preceding years to all Singaporeans, in the form of cash handouts, pension increases, public housing rebates and educational funds – to be implemented in the same month as the elections. Lee led the PAP to win eighty-two out of eighty-four seats with an overall vote-share of 66.6 per cent. The PAP, however, failed to capture the two single-member constituency opposition strongholds – Hougang, defended by WP secretary-general, **Low Thia Khiang**, and Potong Pasir, defended by Chiam See Tong – despite this being a special assignment for Senior Minister Goh Chok Tong. The PAP also saw its vote-share dip island-wide and its overall majority fall by over eight per cent. On the other hand, the WP was the best-performing opposition party with an increased vote-share of over thirteen per cent.

The onset of the global financial crisis at the end of 2007 provided a stiff challenge for Lee and his ministers. In December 2007, Lee relinquished the important post of minister of finance, which he held concurrently, to Tharman Shanmugaratnam, who had been the chief executive of the Monetary Authority of Singapore prior to entering politics. Though Singapore became the first Asian country to enter technical recession after growth fell for two successive quarters in 2008, Tharman's handling of the financial situation ensured a speedy recovery for the republic and he was appointed chairman of the international monetary and financial committee at the International Monetary Fund in March 2011. At the same time, a series of delays and malfunctions on the Mass Rapid Transit System called into question the capacity and integrity of the public transport system, resulting in a change of transport ministers. More significant leadership changes were to come after the 2011 general election. Held in May that year, the election took place against a backdrop of increasing popular resentment over rising costs of living, influx of foreign workers, a growing income gap which led to harsh criticism of the high salaries of cabinet ministers during the financial crisis that left the common man reeling, and the perceived practice of pork-barrel politics through overt promises of housing development and amenity enhancement for PAP-held wards. The landmark election result returned an opposition slate in a group representation constituency (GRC) for the first time, and saw a 6.46 per cent swing against the PAP to its lowest vote-share since independence, at sixty per cent. While Lee Kuan Yew and Goh Chok Tong retained their parliamentary seats for their respective constituencies, both stepped down from the cabinet. PAP candidates who lost included the minister of foreign affairs, George Yeo, and two other junior cabinet ministers. In the presidential elections that followed, a former deputy prime minister, Tony Tan Keng Yam, was elected by a narrow margin of less than one per cent. The 2011 election was held amidst the loosening of previous constraints on the opposition, including reducing the number of GRCs, increasing the number of non-constituency and nominated members of parliament, and legalizing internet campaigning. Two by-elections were subsequently held in 2012, with the PAP losing them both to the resurgent WP. With these electoral outcomes, it has become clear that Singapore has entered a new era where a restive segment of the population, born after 1965 and brought up in prosperity, have no memory of the trials and triumphs of Lee Kuan Yew's generation nor do they feel any obligation to support the new generation of PAP leaders. While becoming an increasingly high-technology business and communications hub Singapore has also reached the level of a mature economy with a growth rate plateauing at around two to three per cent per year, and an ageing population dependent on immigration to maintain its natural increase.

Internationally, Singapore has enjoyed an influence out of proportion to its minuscule scale and limited population. This has owed much to a reputation for excellence and also to the intellectual calibre of its first prime minister, Lee Kuan Yew, who remains an international statesman *par excellence*. Independence coincided with tense relationships with its closest neighbours, Malaysia and Indonesia. Those relationships have never been easy, especially with Malaysia with which a structural tension obtains expressed in periodic open antagonism, most noticeable when both **Mahathir Mohamad** and Lee Kuan Yew served in office either side of the causeway. Those tensions have been contained up to a point through common membership and interest in ASEAN but Singapore has continually looked beyond the Association, exemplified by its initiative in promoting the **ASEAN Regional Forum** (ARF) and the **Asia–Europe Meeting** (ASEM). Singapore's foreign policy has been directed to preventing the dominance regionally of any state that might be able to challenge its independence. To that end, its leaders have been keen to sustain the regional security engagement of the United States. In 1990, it entered into a memorandum of understanding for America's use of military facilities on the island. And with its withdrawal from the Philippines in 1992, the US naval logistics command headquarters was relocated to Singapore. In November 1998, an additional memorandum of understanding was concluded under which the United States was offered the use of the new Changi naval base for its aircraft carriers. That security relationship has withstood differences over political values, exemplified in the controversy over the caning of an American teenager for vandalism in 1994. Singapore was an active diplomatic adversary of Vietnam within ASEAN during the Cambodian conflict but with the end of the Cold War and the **International Conference on Cambodia** in Paris in October 1991, its policy towards Indochina was transformed, exemplified by its support for Vietnam's membership of ASEAN. However, strong resistance was mounted to Cambodia's early membership after the violent coup in July 1997 in Phnom Penh that displaced the coalition government set up under the Paris agreement. Relations with China have steadily progressed, especially after communism had ceased to generate political concerns and to be closely associated in Asia with the Chinese, who are the majority community in Singapore. Diplomatic relations were established in October 1990 but Singapore's enthusiasm for economic cooperation with China soured somewhat after a joint venture to set up a model township in Suzhou, near Shanghai, foundered because the local authority failed to keep to contractual undertakings. Moreover, Lee Kuan Yew was not inhibited in admonishing China in March 1996 when the government in Beijing attempted to intimidate Taiwan's electorate through live-firing missile exercises. Within its own region of Southeast Asia, Singapore is viewed with a mixture of respect and resentment because its remarkable economic accomplishments have been realized by a majority Chinese population who have succeeded in adapting a traditional entrepôt role to the conditions of modern globalization. Its political culture, however, registers an abiding sense of vulnerability, compensated for by an annual defence budget of over US$4 billion and the most technologically advanced armed forces in the region.

From 2000 Singapore's foreign policy became more international after it became a non-permanent member of the UN Security Council, for a two-year term. Following the terrorist attacks on the United States in September 2001, Singapore joined in the American-led war on terror, which acquired a regional dimension against the Southeast Asian-based JI. The JI had planned attacks against western targets in Singapore, Malaysia and Indonesia and bombed nightclubs in Bali and hotels in Jakarta (*see* **Terrorism in Southeast Asia**). Singapore supported the US-led invasion of Afghanistan in October 2001 and subsequently of Iraq in 2003, with logistical and medical assistance groups. Singapore also joined in anti-piracy patrols of the Gulf of Aden and Somalia with international task forces and UN peacekeeping forces in East Timor when it became independent in 2002.

Multilateral cooperation was reinforced with regional organizations such as the ASEAN Plus Three (China, Japan and South Korea) begun in 1998, ASEAN Plus Six (including India, Australia and New Zealand), and the **East Asia Summit** (including Russia and the United States) in 2011. Singapore was at the forefront of efforts to conclude free trade agreements and economic partnerships with all the dialogue partners of ASEAN, as well as advancing the cause of the **Trans-Pacific Partnership**. Spreading its economic wings, Singapore embarked on joint industrial parks and towns in China, India and Vietnam as well as other ASEAN neighbours. Enlarging its defence network Singapore entered into strategic partnerships with the United States, India and China (with its ASEAN partners), while promoting an informal grouping of defence ministers of ASEAN which eventually became the **ASEAN Defence Ministers' Meeting** Plus. Singapore's military cooperation with the United States, France and Australia, expanded with the stationing in Singapore of aircraft and equipment for training exercises, while Singapore also sent troops for exercises in ASEAN countries and India.

see also: Abdul Rahman, Tunku; APEC; ASEAN; ASEAN Defence Ministers' Meeting; ASEAN Regional Forum; Asia–Europe Meeting; *Barisan Sosialis*; Chiam See Tong; Confrontation; East Asia Summit; Goh Chok Tong; International Conference on Cambodia; *Jemaah Islamiyah*; Jeyaretnam, J. B.; Lee Hsien Loong; Lee Kuan Yew; Low Thia Khiang; People's Action Party; Singapore Strait; Johor, Strait of; Terrorism in Southeast Asia; Workers' Party; Yeo, George.

Thailand, Kingdom of

The Kingdom of Thailand, once known as Siam, is situated in the centre of the mainland of Southeast Asia with a land area of some 500,000 square kilometres. It is the only regional state not to have been subject to European colonialism. Thailand is a constitutional monarchy where the reigning King **Bhumibol Adulyadej** has exercised a unique personal authority over various political interests.

To Thailand's west and north lie Myanmar, Laos is to its north and east, Cambodia is to its east and it shares a southern border with Malaysia. Thailand does not have a direct frontier with the People's Republic of China but is separated from it by only narrow stretches of territory extending from Myanmar and Laos, which touch to its extreme north. Thailand has a population of almost seventy million, primarily composed of ethnic T'ai whose religion is the Theravada branch of **Buddhism**. In addition to tribal minorities, such as the **Hmong** in northern provinces, there is a significant concentration of Malay-Muslims (*see* **Islam**) in the southern provinces bordering Malaysia, where armed resistance movements continue to operate. The largest minority is that of ethnic Chinese, who comprise some ten per cent of the population. A considerable proportion, however, have intermarried into Thai families with a notable degree of cultural assimilation (*see* **Chinese Communities in Southeast Asia**).

The origins of the Thai state date from the tenth century, when ethnic T'ai migrated from southwest China towards the central plain then under the control of the Cambodian empire based around Angkor. The current Thai state dates from the eighteenth century when King Rama I sited his capital at Bangkok and founded the Chakri dynasty, which is represented by its ninth incumbent, Bhumibol Adulyadej. From the mid-nineteenth century, modernizing Chakri monarchs opened the country to commercial contact with the west, with the rice trade as the staple basis for economic development. Western skills were drawn on to develop the machinery of state, which over time had the effect of creating tensions between the monarchy and an emerging military-bureaucratic class. In 1932 the absolute monarchy was overthrown by a military coup to be replaced by a constitutional monarchy. There have been nineteen coups in the country since then. Following the events of 1932, two principal internal conflicts have dominated the political life of the country. One was within the armed forces, including the police, for the dominant position; this was resolved in 1957 when Marshal **Sarit Thanarat** seized power on behalf of the army. More protracted has been the problem of establishing a political format acceptable to all competing interests, including the armed forces.

The issue of political format has tested the stability of the state on numerous occasions, with recurrent acts of military intervention serving as the vehicle of political change. After the Pacific War, during which Thailand was allied with Japan, constitutional government of a kind alternated with direct military rule. Thai constitutionalism however, has constantly been subject to the tolerance of the military, who have removed or attempted to remove elected governments on several occasions since the end of the Pacific War. The ability of the military to impose their will was facilitated during the 1960s and into the 1970s by the **Vietnam War**, to which Thailand was a party, as well as by the active insurgent role up to the end of the 1970s played by the Communist Party of Thailand. Moreover, Vietnam's invasion of Cambodia and the ensuing third phase of the **Indochina Wars** during the 1980s also served to maintain the political centrality of the armed forces.

The political pre-eminence of the military began to be challenged from the early 1970s as a consequence of successful economic development, which was accompanied by social change foreshadowed by student activism. In addition, King Bhumibol, who had acquired considerable popular respect for his commitment to rural development, employed the aura of monarchy in the interest of democratization. Violent military reaction to student protest in October 1973 led to the removal of the military regime and its succession by a raucous democratic interlude which was brought to an end by decisive military intervention in October 1976. The tempestuous politics of the mid-1970s concurrent with the Communist victories in Indochina alarmed the king, who lent his weight to a period of more benign military rule in the 1980s under the leadership of the army commander and prime minister, **Prem Tinsulanonda**. Two abortive military coups in 1981 and 1985 failed to arrest the gradual return to constitutionalism concurrent with remarkable economic development by the end of the 1980s. In 1991, the military successfully removed the elected government of **Chatichai Choonhavan**, but appointed a civilian caretaker prime minister, **Anand Panyarachun**, under pressure from the king. Massive vote-buying in the rural areas led to a victory by military-affiliated political parties during the elections of March 1992, intended to return the country to full civilian rule. The appointment of former army commander-in-chief, General **Suchinda Kraprayoon**, as unelected prime minister provoked violent uproar in Bangkok led by the opposition *Palang Dharma* (Moral Force) Party, which only subsided with royal intervention and Suchinda's resignation. Anand Panyarachun was reappointed acting prime minister over a technocratic government. Elections in September 1992 produced a new civilian-based coalition with **Chuan Leekpai**, the leader of the **Democrat Party**, as prime minister. The return to civilian rule marked a notable, if temporary, decline in the prerogative political outlook of the armed forces. Political parties outside of the capital have tended to be fleeting constellations of personal and regional interests bound together in the main by considerations of patronage and not by coherent programmes linked to distinctive constituencies. After the 1991 coup, three new political parties were created. Five disappeared, while others splintered and regrouped. The frustrations of coalition government were exemplified by the experience of the administration headed by Chuan Leekpai, which was thwarted in attempting to secure democratic amendments to the constitution imposed by the military after 1991. His success in January 1995 in securing constitutional amendments in the interest of greater democratization was followed by loss of office through elections in July 1995, which were precipitated by the defection of *Palang Dharma*. A new seven-party coalition with the ***Chart Thai* Party** at its core and **Banharn Silpa-archa** as prime minister was formed without any threat of military intervention. That coalition collapsed and then lost power in elections in November 1996 to be succeeded by a six-party counterpart headed by former army commander, **Chavalit Yongchaiyuth**, leader of the **New Aspiration Party**. The onset of economic crisis following the dramatic floating of the currency in July 1997 precipitated the fall of his government and the emergence of a new political alignment with the Democrat Party at its core. Chuan Leekpai assumed high office for the second time in November 1997 with royal and military support. Initial success in coping with economic adversity gave way to intra-coalition tensions by the turn of the century. Elections to replace the appointed senate of soldiers and businessmen were held on 4 March 2000. Seventy-eight of the 200 winning candidates were then rejected by the election commission over allegations of malpractice. By that juncture, the Democrat Party had lost national standing partly through the decision to decorate Field Marshal **Thanom Kittikachorn**, a disgraced former military dictator. The decline in the political fortunes of the Democrat Party lent significance to the rising electoral challenge of the ***Thai Rak Thai* Party** (TRT) founded by **Thaksin Shinawatra** in 1998. Thaksin, a noted businessman and former deputy superintendent in the police, with a staunch following in the northeast of the country, had previously served as foreign minister and deputy prime minister under the Chuan, Banharn and Chavalit administrations, as well as, briefly, leader of *Palang Dharma*. Competing for the first time in the January 2001 elections – the first to be held under the 1997 constitution – Thaksin's TRT promised universal access to healthcare and extensive rural development, and carried 248 of 500 elected seats in the National Assembly. Though TRT only required three more seats to form a government, Thaksin chose to form a coalition with *Chart Thai* (which had won forty-one seats) and the New Aspiration Party (thirty-six seats), and merged TRT with *Seritham* Party (fourteen seats). He went on to be the first elected prime minister of Thailand to complete a full term in office. It was also during his term that a power struggle was triggered between the traditional middle class Bangkok-based elite and royalists on the one hand, and the rural masses, Thaksin's support base, on the other.

Thaksin's administration, which consisted of his *Palang Dharma* allies, former student demonstrators from the 1973 protests and academics, received praise for policies which targeted rural poverty, the drug trade and public health, driven by a strong recovery from the 1997–8 **Asian Financial Crisis** that allowed the country to repay its debts to the IMF two years ahead of schedule. The means which delivered these excellent outcomes, however, were often controversial. For example, Thaksin's legalization of Thailand's underground lottery system, under the Government Lottery Office, allowed lottery sales of up to seventy billion baht to be used for rural social projects but was seen as a profit-making initiative and the root of social problems in the urban areas. Especially controversial was the 'War on Drugs', initially declared by King Bhumibol on the eve of his birthday in 2002. Having found measures such as border controls and educational campaigns ineffective, Thaksin launched a national effort in January 2003 to exterminate drug abuse in three months. This involved rewarding and punishing officials based on their ability to meet provincial arrest and seizure targets, and led to the creation of at least 2,800 'death squads' mandated to carry out extrajudicial killings of suspected drug abusers and traders. A total of 2,604 resultant murders were recorded – not all of which could be linked conclusively to drug crimes. While the Narcotics Control Board widely publicized the policy's effectiveness in reducing drug consumption, advocacy groups such as Human Rights Watch held that many were accused on false charges, while serial drug users and traders continued despite the government's best efforts. In addition to these criticisms, the Thaksin administration was accused of 'policy corruption', a term used to describe the diversion of state funding to companies linked to the Shinawatra family through infrastructure or liberalization policies. These emerged as central issues following Thaksin's re-election in 2005, which saw the highest voter turnout in Thai history. Soon after the TRT carried 374 seats, opposition politicians led by **Sondhi Limthongkul** of the **People's Alliance for Democracy** (PAD), also a popular talk-show host, alleged abuses of power by the administration. The sale of the Shinawatra family's stake in Shin Corporation to Temasek Holdings (owned by the Government of Singapore) for seventy-three billion baht in January 2006 provided further fodder for his opponents. Protests took place daily outside Government House, compelling Thaksin to dissolve parliament on 24 February 2006. The ensuing snap elections of April 2006 were widely boycotted, and though TRT again won a technical majority, gaining 462 seats, the Constitutional Court invalidated the results in May 2006. By this time, there had been two impeachment attempts against Thaksin, launched by a group of twenty-eight senators and the Thai university students' network, respectively. Thaksin stepped down as prime minister following an audience with King Bhumibol on 4 April 2006, and appointed Chidchai Wannasathit of the TRT as caretaker prime minister in his stead. Non-parliamentary players soon became involved. After nullifying the results of the April elections, the Court ordered fresh elections to be held in October, and called on the Electoral Commission to resign. Upon the Commissioners' refusal, on the grounds of their constitutional independence, the Criminal Courts jailed them and removed them from their posts in July 2006. In the same month, despite earlier assurances in May that the army would not take advantage of the political upheaval, up to 100 army officials close to Thaksin were reassigned by the military high command, and by August tank movements were reported near Bangkok, prompting fears of a coup. President of the Privy Council and former general, Prem Tinsulanonda, heightened tensions further when he suggested in July that the Thai military owed greater allegiance to the King than to the government. Protestors on the streets took sides in what came to be seen as a pro-Thaksin or pro-Monarchy standoff – a view promoted by Sondhi – with divisions exacerbated by claims that Thaksin had insulted the King, and Thaksin's own comments that extra-parliamentary organizations were seeking to overthrow the rule of law.

The Royal Thai Army, led by General **Sonthi Boonyaratglin**, removed Thaksin's government in a swift coup d'état on the evening of 19 September 2006, marking Thailand's first non-constitutional change of government in fifteen years. By the time Thaksin, who was attending a meeting of the UN General Assembly, announced a state of emergency by telephone from New York and attempted to transfer Sonthi from his post as army commander, both the deputy prime minister, Chidchai Wannasathit, and the defence minister, Thammarak Isaragura na Ayuthaya, had been arrested, and national radio and TV networks taken off air. Approaching midnight, the army-led Council for Democratic Reform (CDR) issued two statements declaring the coup successful, and promised to return power to the people. Nevertheless, a third statement in the early hours of 20 September dissolved the cabinet, both houses of parliament and the Constitutional Court, and suspended the constitution. Martial law was declared nationwide. As a result of the coup, elections scheduled for 15 October did not take place. The CDR, representing all branches of the army and police, declared King Bhumibol head of state, granted General Sonthi the powers of a premier, gave itself the role of parliament and created a new National Police Commission under a police general, Kowit Wattana. It then ordered fifty-eight prominent civilians, many of whom were academics, to serve as advisors in various capacities, though most denied having been informed of their appointments and later chose to refuse their positions. The CDR also released an interim constitution in September 2006, renaming itself the Council of National Security (CNS), and appointed former deputy president of the Supreme Court, Nam Yimyaem, to lead a committee investigating allegations against the Thaksin administration. In October 2006, General **Surayud Chulanont**, former supreme commander of the army, was appointed to high office. The CNS reserved a powerful executive role.

The 2006 coup deeply polarized Thai society and precipitated a political crisis pitting supporters of Thaksin against the royalists, sending convulsions across the country. From January 2007, specific charges by the Financial Institutions Development Fund and the attorney general were brought against Thaksin, who was residing in the UK, under an Assets Examination Committee selected by the junta. In June, Prime Minister Surayud declared that he would personally guarantee Thaksin's safety if the latter returned to Thailand. Thaksin, who had by this time purchased Manchester City Football Club, eventually arrived in Bangkok in February 2008, and pleaded not guilty to charges of criminal corruption in March. A month-long return to the UK was granted by the courts, but from June 2008 Thaksin's travel requests were denied, and arrest warrants issued when Thaksin subsequently skipped bail to attend the 2008 Summer Olympics in Beijing. Arrest warrants were also issued for Thaksin's wife Potjaman, who was found guilty of violating stock-trading and land sale laws in July, but had left the country with her husband. Thaksin was officially found guilty of abusing his power as prime minister in October 2008, and both Thaksin's and Potjaman's visas were revoked by the UK.

On 19 August 2007, Thai voters approved a newly drafted constitution in a referendum, after the junta banned public criticism and threatened not to relinquish power if the referendum was not passed. The new Constitutional Tribunal then found the TRT guilty of bribing two smaller parties to cooperate in the 2006 elections, and dissolved it; party executives, including Thaksin, were banned from politics for five years. TRT reformulated itself into the **People's Power Party** (PPP) to contest the December 2007 elections, the first general election since the coup, under the leadership of **Samak Sundaravej** and managed to win 233 out of 480 parliamentary seats, going on to form the government via the vehicle of an alliance with five smaller parties. PPP's victory precipitated a round of protests by the PAD which culminated in the movement seizing Government House. In September, Samak was forced to resign after the Constitutional Court found him guilty of being paid to appear on a cooking programme after he came to power. Samak was replaced as PPP leader by party vice-president, **Somchai Wongsawat**, Thaksin's brother-in-law. Somchai's appointment prompted an escalation of protest and violence leading to the PAD's seizure of the government's temporary offices at Don Muang Airport and the closure of Suvarnabhumi Airport. The PPP and two coalition partners were subsequently dissolved and its leaders barred from politics for five years after being found guilty of electoral fraud. Power then switched hands to the Democrat Party and party leader **Abhisit Vejjajiva**, through a parliamentary vote in December 2008 which was helped by several Thaksin loyalists who were persuaded to change their allegiances. Meanwhile, pro-Thaksin followers of the PPP formed the ***Pheu Thai* Party** in September 2008.

Thailand's tumultuous politics persisted under the Democrat government when the **United Front for Democracy Against Dictatorship** (UDD) opposed Abhisit's appointment and thrust Thailand into a state of paralysis. Mass protests were mobilized in Bangkok and Pattaya in 2009, the latter the site of an **ASEAN** (Association of Southeast Asian Nations) summit and **East Asia Summit** which Thailand was hosting. These protests proved an embarrassment for the Thai government which had to postpone the Pattaya meeting and see to the evacuation of delegates who included senior officials and ministers from regional states. A new round of protests in March and April 2010 resulted in heavy UDD casualties, including more than fifty deaths. At the July 2011 elections, the opposition *Pheu Thai* Party won a landslide victory under the leadership of **Yingluck Shinawatra**, youngest sister of Thaksin. This victory and Yingluck's successful defeat of a no-confidence vote in late 2012 enabled Thaksin to continue exercising a measure of influence over Thai politics. Nevertheless, Yingluck was no mere surrogate, and of her own accord laboured to improve relations with the military that were strained considerably during her brother's tenure, her initiatives included the addition of military officers from Internal Security Operations Command to the Prime Minister's Office.

Parliamentary debate over a proposed amnesty bill crafted to provide amnesty for criminal offences committed by both sides of the political divide triggered a new round of protests and violence in October 2013. Anti-Thaksin forces rallied against the bill behind former deputy prime minister, Suthep Thaugsuban (himself under investigation for alleged offences that would have been absolved under the proposed bill), on grounds that its passage would have paved the way for Thaksin's return to Thailand. Anti-Thaksin sentiments soon turned against the Yingluck government, accusing it of corruption, and calling for her resignation and the formation of a nebulous 'People's Council' to lead the government in the interim. In the circumstances, the prime minister responded by dissolving Parliament and calling snap elections, scheduled for 2 February 2014. The run-up to polling day saw some of the bloodiest protests in recent Thai history even as the Election Commission advised a postponement of the polls and the opposition Democrat Party ominously declared its intention to boycott the election. When the Democrat Party last boycotted elections, in 2006, they triggered a chain of events that led to a military coup and a backroom deal that led to its formation of a minority government. The disputed general election went ahead on 2 February despite the less than fortuitous circumstances and attempts by anti-government protestors, who by then had coalesced into the People's Democratic Reform Council, to disrupt polling. Even then, the protestors were able to force polling to be rescheduled in several Bangkok districts as well as in the southern provinces when they succeeded in shutting down numerous polling stations, in so doing complicating an already contentious situation. In the event, the results of the elections were nullified by the Constitutional Court a month later on grounds that twenty-eight of 375 wards were prevented by anti-government protestors from holding a ballot, leaving the country without a functioning government. Equally bizarre was the court order that no force could be used to remove protestors against the government, even in the event that the business of running the government was being obstructed. Meanwhile, the caretaker prime minister, Yingluck Shinawatra, faced charges of negligence and malfeasance for her role in approving a rice-pledging scheme introduced in 2011, when the government purchased rice from farmers at inflated prices in a move to shore up rural incomes. The Constitutional Court subsequently found her guilty of abuse of power for a deceptively routine act of transferring a bureaucrat, and forced her resignation on 7 May.

In the early hours of 20 May, army general Prayuth Chan-ocha declared martial law in a move to quell escalating unrest. Several days later, while leaders of the former *Pheu Thai* government and the anti-Thaksin People's Democratic Reform Committee were locked in a conclave organized by the military to discuss the political impasse, a coup was launched, the nineteenth since 1932. Four days later, coup leader Prayuth sought and received royal endorsement in the form of a royal decree announced at a ceremony where King Bhumibol was absent. This was followed by the detention of leading political and public opinion leaders, and the imposition of a public curfew. Assurances were given by coup leaders that political reform and elections would follow, but no timeline was given.

For many years, the monarchy has stood as a pillar of stability in contrast with the mercurial quality of partisan politics in Thailand. Yet even the monarchy has not been able to escape the tumultuous tides of political change currently engulfing Thailand. The role of King Bhumibol as political mediator in the conservative democratic interest has waned and will not necessarily be sustained should he be succeeded by his only son and phlegmatic crown prince, **Maha Vajiralongkorn**. Partly as a consequence of ill health, King Bhumibol's role during the political crisis following the 2006 coup was noticeably muted, although his part during the coup itself has been the subject of much speculation, with many taking the view that such an event would not have transpired without the King's knowledge, if not tacit consent. Such suspicions were reinforced when the King appointed interim prime minister, Surayud Chulanont, and senior member of the CNS, Chalit Pukbhasuk, to the Privy Council in 2008 and 2011 respectively, and when Queen Sirikit presided over the cremation of a PAD protestor killed during demonstrations in October 2008. Given the state of the King's health, attention has shifted to heir apparent, Crown Prince Maha. Eccentricities aside, the Crown Prince does not give the impression of sharing his father's sense of duty and is not as well regarded by the Thai people, most of whom prefer Princess Maha Chakri Sirindhorn. This has raised questions regarding the future relationship between the throne and the state which is likely to become increasingly pertinent given increasing popular scrutiny of *lèse majesté* legislation in Thailand. Moreover, against the backdrop of a society polarized between pro- and anti-Thaksin camps, the Crown Prince's close relationship with the former prime minister has alienated him from his father's closest allies.

An additional threat to stability in Thailand is an ongoing ethnic Malay insurgency in the southern border provinces of the country. After a decade or so of relative calm, political violence in the south erupted in January 2004 when militants launched an audacious raid on an arms depot in the province of Narathiwat. This ushered in a new cycle of insurgent violence that has witnessed more than 5,000 deaths. The southern Thailand Insurgency remains premised on an ethnic Malay struggle against discrimination and injustices, and for minority recognition. It has however taken on an increasingly religious colour as the Muslim insurgents make more frequent reference to Islam as a motivating factor (*see* **Insurgency, Southern Provinces**). While the Thai government has embarked on several parallel dialogue tracks facilitated either by neighbouring states or European NGOs these have generated little traction, not least because of the evident reluctance of the Thai government to come to terms with consequences of several early policy missteps that resulted in the deaths of locals and further alienation of the Malay community.

Further afield, Thailand's geographic location and historical experience have moulded a foreign policy outlook of signal consistency over time. Thailand was a beneficiary of Anglo-French imperialist competition whereby the two European states found it politic to have an interposing buffer between their respective colonies in Burma and Indochina. Before colonial intervention in mainland Southeast Asia, Thailand had experienced armed invasion from Burma as well as competition from Vietnam for influence in the trans-Mekong zone. Suspicion of both close and near neighbours survived the end of colonialism, while during the Pacific War Thailand enjoyed Japanese support in prosecuting irredentist claims against Burma, Laos, Cambodia and Malaya. After the Pacific War, Thailand secured international rehabilitation with US support. Prime international concern came to focus on Indochina, where the restored French colonial position was subject to strong challenge from the Communist Party of Vietnam, perceived as a more fearsome historical enemy. Independent Burma, subject to ethnic minority rebellion, was a lesser priority. Indeed, Thai military support was provided for **Karen** and **Shan** rebels close to the common border.

Fear of a resurgent Communist Vietnam with dominion over Laos and Cambodia was reinforced with the advent of a Communist China in 1949. Concurrently, US containment policy served both the domestic and foreign policy interests of the postwar Thai military regime through diplomatic, material and security support. Thai troops participated in the Korean War under the United Nations flag and its government signed the US-inspired **Manila Pact**, the Southeast Asia Collective Defence Treaty, in September 1954. In February 1955 Thailand contributed further to this attempt to shore up the non-Communist position in the region by providing the headquarters of **SEATO** (Southeast Asia Treaty Organization) which served as an institutional base for the Manila Pact until dismantled in 1977. Thailand remained assertively anti-Communist until the fall of Indochina in 1975, sending troops to Vietnam and permitting US aircraft to bomb North Vietnam from its airfields. In addition, Thailand cooperated with Malaysia and the Philippines in **ASA** (Association of Southeast Asia), and more vigorously in **ASEAN** (Association of Southeast Asian Nations). With the Communist victories following US disengagement, though, diplomatic relations were established with the People's Republic of China and successor governments in Indochina.

Thailand began to exploit growing antagonism between China and Vietnam, and between Vietnam and Cambodia, to maintain a physical buffer in Indochina and eliminate external patronage for the Communist Party of Thailand. When Vietnam invaded Cambodia in December 1978, Thailand, with its ASEAN partners, mobilized international opinion in its strategic interest and gave territorial asylum to Cambodian resistance insurgents. Particular support was provided for the ousted **Khmer Rouge**, who were supplied with equipment from China. Pressure on Vietnam during the 1980s culminated in a political settlement of the Cambodian conflict at the **International Conference on Cambodia** in Paris in October 1991, facilitated by the end of the Cold War. Thailand progressively repaired relations with Vietnam and endorsed the outcome of elections in Cambodia conducted in May 1993 under United Nations auspices (*see* **UNTAC**) but its military establishment sustained its links with the Khmer Rouge for reasons of financial advantage and also of geopolitical insurance lest the government in Phnom Penh come under Vietnamese influence. These links disintegrated with the Khmer Rouge, while correct rather than close ties have been maintained with the government in Phnom Penh.

With the end of the Cold War and the Cambodian conflict, the civilian government of Thailand engaged more vigorously in regional multilateral dialogue with ASEAN at its core. It reconciled with Vietnam and welcomed it into the Association. It also sought to modify, albeit without success, the Association's rule of non-interference in the domestic affairs of regional partners where domestic circumstances spill over borders with an adverse effect. In that respect, frustration was experienced in trying to promote a working relationship with the military regime in Myanmar through a policy of so-called **Constructive Engagement** intended partly to counter Myanmar's close ties with China. Geography and history have combined also to sustain a traditional strategic perspective towards the trans-Mekong of Indochina required as a buffer if it cannot be dominated. Defence cooperation has been sustained with the United

States and with Singapore, in particular, among ASEAN states.

Cambodia has emerged as Thailand's most pressing foreign policy concern in recent years as their **Preah Vihear Temple Dispute** erupted into hostilities in 2008. Relations between the two countries soured further during 2009–11 marked by the mutual withdrawal of ambassadors, a move initiated by Bangkok in retaliation for the Cambodian government's appointment of Thaksin as economic advisor. Thai and Cambodian military presences in the disputed area have been scaled back since the advent of the Yingluck Shinawatra government, as both parties await an impending International Court of Justice clarification of its 1962 ruling which awarded the temple but not the adjoining land to Cambodia. In the south, Thailand maintains stable though at times uneasy cooperation with Malaysia, whose role in the management of the insurgency in the southern provinces is critical.

In December 2003, Thailand was accorded 'major non-NATO ally' status by the United States in recognition of its deployment of Thai medical and engineering units to both Afghanistan and Iraq. At the same time, relations with China have also deepened. Thailand's chairmanship of ASEAN in 2008–9 came under heavy scrutiny and criticism after Bangkok was forced to change the location of the fourth East Asia Summit (EAS) from Bangkok to Chiang Mai in October 2008 because of political unrest in the capital. After several other postponements, including the cancellation of the rescheduled April 2009 meeting in Pattaya when protestors seized the premises forcing the emergency evacuation of delegates to the embarrassment of the Thai hosts, the EAS eventually met in October 2009 in Cha-am and Hua Hin.

see also: Abhisit Vejjajiva; Anand Panyarachun; ASA; ASEAN; Asian Financial Crisis 1997–8; Banharn Silpa-archa; Buddhism; Bhumibol Adulyadej; Chavalit Yongchaiyuth, General; *Chart Thai* Party; Chatichai Choonhavan; Chinese Communities in Southeast Asia; Chuan Leekpai; Constructive Engagement; Democrat Party; East Asia Summit; Hmong; Indochina Wars; Insurgency, Southern Provinces; International Conference on Cambodia, Paris 1991; Islam; Karen; Khmer Rouge; Maha Vajiralongkorn, Prince; Manila Pact 1954; New Aspiration Party; Overseas Chinese; People's Alliance for Democracy; People's Power Party; *Pheu Thai* Party; Preah Vihear Temple Dispute; Prem Tinsulanonda, General; Samak Sundaravej; Sarit Thanarat, Field Marshal; SEATO; Shan; Somchai Wongsawat; Sondhi Limthongkul; Sonthi Boonyaratglin, General; Suchinda Kraprayoon, General; Surayud Chulanont, General; *Thai Rak Thai* Party; Thaksin Shinawatra; Thanom Kittikachorn, Field Marshal; Thammasat University Massacre 1976; United Front for Democracy Against Dictatorship; UNTAC; Vietnam War; Yingluck Shinawatra.

Timor-Leste, Democratic Republic of

The Democratic Republic of Timor-Leste, formerly East Timor, is a country in the eastern region of Southeast Asia, whose capital city Dili is situated on its northern coast. Its geographic territory includes the nearby islands of Autouro and Jaco and the Oecusse district, a coastal enclave in West Timor. Timor-Leste was a Portuguese colony since the early sixteenth century. Indonesian interest in East Timor was generated by radical political change in Portugal in April 1974, which paved the way for accelerated decolonization in the country's overseas possessions, including East Timor. Within East Timor, political activity and ferment followed which aroused concern in Jakarta at the prospect of sharing a common border with a radical state at the margin of a fissiparous archipelago. That concern was reinforced with the emergence of the ***Fretilin*** (derived from the Portuguese for Revolutionary Front for an Independent East Timor) demanding early and complete self-rule. Indonesian attempts to sponsor a client political party in favour of integration with the neighbouring republic served to heighten political tension, which culminated in an inept and unsuccessful coup attempt in August 1975. By mid-September, *Fretilin* had established control in the administrative capital, Dili, and had crushed all opposition except along the border with Indonesian West Timor. The outbreak of civil war disrupted Portuguese plans for orderly decolonization and prompted the retreat of its officials to the neighbouring island of Atauro.

Indonesian calculations were made in the context of revolutionary Communist success in Indochina in April 1975. Sensitive to the attitude of western aid donors, Indonesia sought to control East Timor through the vehicle of a collective police action under the aegis of formal Portuguese sovereignty. After the failure of this initiative and the evident consolidation of *Fretilin* control, more direct action was undertaken, employing Indonesian forces in an insurgent role, ostensibly as volunteers on behalf of its domestic opponents in East Timor. *Fretilin* proclaimed the independence of the Democratic Republic of East Timor on 28 November 1975. The next day, its Indonesian-backed adversaries were mobilized to declare East Timor an integral part of Indonesia. A formal declaration of support followed on 1 December from Indonesia's foreign minister, **Adam Malik**, who announced that the solution to the conflict lay on the battlefield. Decisive military intervention by so-called 'volunteers on behalf of East Timorese brothers' began on 7 December, delayed by the presence in Jakarta of US President Gerald Ford accompanied by Secretary of State Henry Kissinger. The intervention was a less than competent military action in the face of vigorous resistance, but the balance of forces and the absence of any external support for *Fretilin* put the incorporation of the eastern half of the island within Indonesia beyond any doubt. The human costs of the brutal annexation were heavy. Out of an original population of some 650,000, an estimated 100,000 inhabitants died as a direct or indirect result of the invasion and consequent pacification operations. The management of political integration was expedited within several months through a spurious process of self-determination, culminating in a formal act of incorporation of East Timor as the twenty-seventh province of the Republic of Indonesia on 17 July 1976.

Within East Timor, armed resistance to Indonesian authority continued on a limited scale, encouraged by the refusal of the international community through the United Nations to endorse the annexation. Despite concentrating development efforts in East Timor and transplanting Indonesia's educational system to the territory, political alienation persisted. President **Suharto** declared East Timor an open province at the end of 1988 which was a preliminary to a visit to its predominantly Catholic population by Pope John Paul II in October 1989. That visit was marked by public demonstrations suppressed by security forces, an episode repeated when the US ambassador, John Monjo, travelled to Dili in January 1990. The failure of Indonesia to integrate East Timor in a national sense was displayed conspicuously on 12 November 1991, when a political protest at a memorial service for two East Timorese killed by the security forces was mercilessly crushed by force with great loss of life. The massacre aroused international outrage which was mitigated by the measures taken by the Indonesian government to inquire into the bloody episode, ostensibly to punish and reprimand those soldiers responsible.

A striking feature of East Timorese resistance to Jakarta's rule was the activism of a younger generation educated in the Indonesian medium for whom the original act of annexation was probably beyond their clear recollection. *Fretilin* suffered a major blow in November 1992 when its military commander, **Jose 'Xanana' Gusmão**, was captured. He was sentenced to life imprisonment, which was subsequently commuted to twenty years. Despite international pressure, President Suharto's government refused to negotiate on the issue of its sovereign jurisdiction. That position was maintained initially following Suharto's resignation in May 1998 against a background of acute economic crisis and the succession of the vice-president, **B. J. Habibie**. On 27 January 1999, partly in response to the prospect of Australia withdrawing recognition of Indonesia's jurisdiction, President Habibie made an astounding offer to the people of East Timor, apparently without consulting his foreign ministry or armed forces. They were offered a choice between extensive autonomy and complete independence. This announcement came as a great shock to the armed forces, in particular, which had not only governed East Timor as a private fiefdom but had also incurred heavy casualties in the process. In the event, an agreement was reached in May 1999 between Indonesia, Portugal (as the former colonial power) and the secretary-general of the United Nations, whereby a referendum in East Timor would be supervised by an unarmed UN mission with security the exclusive responsibility of the Indonesian authorities. By that juncture, Indonesia's forces in the territory had begun to set up an armed militia in an attempt to intimidate the population into voting against independence.

The United Nations Assistance Mission in East Timor (UNAMET) organized the referendum against a background of rising violence. The referendum was held on 30 August 1999 in which 78.5 per cent of registered voters opted for independence. The result was declared in early September and was met with orchestrated violence and a scorched-earth policy on the part of the armed militia, taking the territory into barbarism which seemed beyond the competence of the armed forces leadership in Jakarta to control. Unable to arrest the decline into violence, the UN mission was obliged to withdraw but a visit by representatives of the Security Council recommended the deployment of an international force to restore law and order. The weight of international opinion, and importantly Indonesia's vulnerability to economic pressure, persuaded President Habibie that a United Nations-sanctioned force be permitted to enter the territory, formally a province of the republic. That force was authorized by the UN Security Council on 15 September. The International Force East Timor (INTERFET), under Australian command and with the major contribution from Australia, began its initial deployment on 20 September. A firm response to initial encounters with the armed militia coming across the border with Indonesian West Timor soon led to effective pacification. On 19 October 1999, Indonesia's **People's Consultative Assembly** ratified the result of the referendum in East Timor, while Gusmão, who had been released from arrest, returned to Dili on 22 October to a rapturous welcome as the prospective state's political leader. Australia's lead role in the international force had caused tensions with Indonesia and had aroused criticism within **ASEAN** (Association of Southeast Asian Nations). On 25 October 1999, the United Nations Security Council voted to replace INTERFET with a United Nations Transitional Administration for East Timor (UNTAET), including a military component under a Philippine commander with an Australian deputy (*see* **United Nations: East Timor 1999–2002**). The transfer of military responsibilities from INTERFET to the United Nations Peacekeeping Force took place on 23 February 2000. On 11 December 1999, the first meeting of the National Consultative Council of East Timor convened in Dili with the responsibility to make policy recommendations to UNTAET, which was expected to exercise the equivalent of trusteeship over the territory for up to three years before independence was assumed. In mid-December 1999, an international donors' meeting in Tokyo pledged US$520 million in reconstruction aid for the devastated nascent state whose basic infrastructure had to be rebuilt from scratch. In March 2000, President **Abdurrahman Wahid** visited Dili during which he apologized for Indonesia's brutal twenty-four year occupation. By the first anniversary of the referendum, the UN had begun to create basic institutions and had established security, except along the border with West Timor penetrated still by the armed militia. In September 2000, they murdered three UN refugee workers in West Timor. Independence was finally declared on 20 May 2002.

While a hard-fought independence was finally achieved, stability remained elusive as sporadic violence and widespread unrest threatened. In 2006, a conflict within the military polarized by claims of regional discrimination presaged a renewed crisis which culminated in an attempted assassination, a coup, and the eventual resignation of Prime Minister **Mari Alkatiri**. **José Ramos-Horta** succeeded Alkatiri as prime minister (*see* **Timor-Leste Crisis 2006**). Upon the request of the Timor-Leste government, Australia led an international military force, called 'Operation Astute' and which included forces from Malaysia, New Zealand and Portugal, to help return stability to the country. In August 2006, the United Nations also established an Integrated Mission in Timor-Leste (UNMIT) via United Nations Security Council Resolution 1704 to aid the country to consolidate stability, facilitate national reconciliation and foster social cohesion. On 11 February 2008, rebel Timorese soldiers led by Alfredo Reinado, former military major of the Timor-Leste Defence Force (F-FDTL) organized an assassination attempt on the lives of the two Nobel laureates, Ramos-Horta and Gusmão. While both leaders survived the attack, rebel leader Alfredo Reinado was killed. Following the attack, Gusmão instituted a forty-eight hour state of emergency while Ramos-Horta was flown to Darwin for treatment and recovery. The state of emergency was subsequently extended another three weeks and upon Ramos-Horta's recovery he gave a press conference urging remaining rebels to surrender. Despite security concerns, elections in July 2012 proceeded relatively peacefully. While the election was won by the **National Congress for Timorese Reconstruction**, it failed to secure a majority and a coalition government was formed, resulting in the creation of a massive fifty-seven member cabinet, the largest in Southeast Asia.

Throughout the difficult early years of independence, Timor-Leste continued to maintain good relations with its neighbours, particularly Indonesia, which despite their past turbulent relations became Timor-Leste's largest trading partner. Timor-Leste continues to push for membership in ASEAN after being accorded observer status in 2002, but its attempts have been obstructed by several members of the organization on the grounds that granting membership to them at this point could further compromise already stuttering efforts at broader regional integration, not to mention the struggle that the newly independent state would have to fulfil the obligations that came with membership. Nevertheless, Timor-Leste's submission of an application for ASEAN membership was made at the 2011 ASEAN summit in Jakarta, and was warmly received by Indonesia. Timor-Leste also maintains close political and trade ties with Australia and enjoys good relations with the Philippines, Portugal and the United States.

see also: Alkatiri, Mari; ASEAN; East Timor Crisis; *Fretilin*; Gusmão, José 'Xanana'; Habibie, B. J.; Malik, Adam; National Congress for Timorese Reconstruction; People's Consultative Assembly; Ramos-Horta, José; Suharto; Sukarno; Timor-Leste Crisis 2006; United Nations: East Timor 1999–2002; Wahid, Abdurrahman.

Vietnam, Socialist Republic of

The Socialist Republic of Vietnam was established on 2 July 1976 through the formal unification of the country, which had been effectively joined through *force majeure* at the end of April 1975. The title of the reunified state registered its political identity subject to the monopoly power of the Communist Party, which had been formed in 1930 as the Communist Party of Indochina when the country was under French colonial rule. That party in a changing nomenclature had led the nationalist movement in an armed struggle for independence from the end of the Pacific War. A Democratic Republic of Vietnam had been proclaimed in Hanoi by the Communist leader, **Ho Chi Minh**, on 2 September 1945 following the **August Revolution** but was displaced by the restoration of French rule. The French were obliged to abdicate their position after July 1954 when an international conference, leading to the **Geneva Agreements on Indochina**, endorsed a ceasefire agreement with a temporary division of the country along the line of the seventeenth parallel of latitude. That division hardened into a political boundary which endured for over twenty years. The Democratic Republic of Vietnam succeeded to power north of the line of division, while a US-backed State (subsequently Republic) of Vietnam assumed the administration to its south. The challenge of communist insurgency in the south of the country in the early 1960s led to progressive military intervention by the United States, including the aerial bombardment of the north. The failure of the United States to impose a political solution by military means and growing domestic opposition to the loss of blood and treasure led to the **Paris Peace Agreements** in January 1973. US military withdrawal followed soon after and a military offensive launched by the northern army in March 1975 paved the way to final military victory with the fall of Saigon on 30 April 1975.

Vietnam is located in the mainland of Southeast Asia and comprises an elongated territory of nearly 330,000 square kilometres which resembles a pole with baskets at either end. It shares its northern border with the People's Republic of China and its western borders with Laos and Cambodia. To its east and south, Vietnam is bounded by the **South China Sea** whose islands have been the subject of contested jurisdiction, especially with China. The Vietnamese people, who number some ninety million, are in the main ethnically homogeneous. There are hill tribe minorities and a sizeable Cambodian community in the south as well as an ethnic Chinese community of migrant origins. An autonomous Vietnamese polity located in southern China and northern Vietnam dates from the third century and the basis of Vietnamese statehood came to be centred on the Red River delta. Vietnamese history has comprised a dual process. On the one hand, struggle against and resistance to Chinese hegemony, while assuming its cultural and religious traditions, has served to define national identity. Concurrently, a movement southwards through pioneer settlement took place at the expense of weaker kingdoms. That movement, which gave rise to two competing economic centres in the Red River and Mekong River deltas, provided Vietnam with a precarious unity, which after consolidation in the early nineteenth century was overtaken by French colonial rule which expanded to the whole of Indochina. The French facilitated Vietnamese territorial expansion, while the military struggle from the end of the Pacific War reinforced a geopolitical prerogative on the part of the Communist Party expressed in the concept of a special relationship with Laos and Cambodia (*see* **Treaty of Friendship and Cooperation**). A reunited Vietnam sought to assert that relationship with Cambodia in the context of a revival of antagonism with China from the mid-1970s. An invasion of Cambodia provoked by cross-border military incursions by the **Khmer Rouge** government in Phnom Penh was followed by a punitive intervention by Chinese forces into northern Vietnam. Vietnam was then confronted by an alignment of China, the United States, Japan and **ASEAN** (Association of Southeast Asian Nations) which through a division of labour in isolating it diplomatically and imposing sanctions was able to impose a breaking strain on its government and society. When it became apparent that countervailing support from the Soviet Union was likely to be withdrawn, Vietnam adjusted by changing its domestic and international policies in a radical way.

On unification in 1976, Vietnam had embarked dogmatically on the creation of a socialist state but within a short time was embroiled in conflict over Cambodia. The economic condition of the country became parlous and the position of the ruling Communist Party was placed in some jeopardy. In December 1986, at its sixth national congress, a policy of ***Doi Moi*** (economic renovation) was adopted which took the form of a commitment to market-driven economics. A liberal investment law soon followed as well as a more accommodating attitude over Cambodia, with a settlement reached through United Nations involvement in October 1991. Relations were restored with China and developed with the states of ASEAN, while the United States phased out a long-standing trade and investment embargo which was finally withdrawn in February 1994. Continuing progress in accounting for Americans Missing-In-Action (MIA) during the **Vietnam War** produced an agreement in May 1994 to set up liaison offices in respective capital cities. Diplomatic relations were established in August 1995 and an American ambassador, who was a former prisoner of war in Vietnam, took up residence in May 1996. Although the memories of war continue to cast a shadow over the relationship, William Cohen, America's defence secretary, visited Hanoi in March 2000 where he stated that the United States had resolved to move forward with Vietnam 'in a manner that serves our mutual interests in regional stability, security and stability'.

Vietnam made signal economic advances during the 1990s, exemplified in success in controlling inflation and in moving from a rice deficit country to the world's third largest exporter of rice within a period of five years. Foreign investment was attracted from Taiwan, Hong Kong and Japan. By the turn of the century, however, and despite an increase in foreign investments especially into construction and heavy industry, the momentum of economic reform had been retarded as a consequence of bureaucratic impediments and corruption but, above all, by the failure of the ruling Communist Party to embrace the spirit of *Doi Moi*. Its narrow interpretation of the maxim that development will follow 'a market-based, but socialism-driven structure of economic development' suggested a loss of nerve on the part of a leadership fearful of social and political change represented euphemistically as 'peaceful evolution'. The result has been a discernible outflow of foreign investment, and economic growth has failed to keep pace with a rising population and unemployment. In an attempt to stem the tide, the Vietnamese government concluded a major trade agreement with the United States in July 2000 shortly after relaxing regulations on private enterprise and foreign investment. From 2000 to 2006 however, Vietnam's reforms delivered a steady economic growth-rate of around seven per cent, increasing year-on-year and far outperforming its neighbours. This growth was largely propelled by a strong global appetite for Vietnam's agricultural and commodities exports (total exports amounted to seventy per cent of Vietnam's GDP), with export revenues rising across 2000–12. By 2012, Vietnam was a net exporter for the first time in twenty years, and poverty had also declined such that Vietnam's relative poverty rate fell below that of China and the Philippines. Nevertheless, growth began to slow again in 2012 as a result of subpar performances of inefficient **State Owned Enterprises** (SOE). Though 500–600 SOEs were initially targeted for privatization by 2015, only a small handful were actually restructured each year, and by 2012, SOEs as a whole continued to account for up to thirty per cent of the nation's GDP. The SOEs also commanded US$33.3 billion in capital despite accounting for less than one per cent of Vietnam's total number of enterprises. Another burgeoning problem was resource management. Despite being the third-largest oil producer in Southeast Asia, and devoting the entirety of its natural gas production to the domestic market, falling production from 2004 and the failure to diversify energy sources led to Vietnam becoming a net oil importer in 2011. These problems were compounded by soaring inflation.

Vietnam's commitment to economic reform stands in contradiction to the ruling party's determination not to permit any fundamental change to the political system. The Communist Party refuses to allow the formation of any other political organization and has exercised tight repressive control over Buddhist and Christian associations. A critical factor in the judgement of the party leadership has been the examples of China and Singapore, where capitalism and economic liberalization have co-existed relatively effectively with strong central rule. Furthermore, the circumstances of the assumption of Communist rule and its nature has meant that there is no alternative locus of political activity other than the armed forces, which have been integrated with the party in classical manner. Traditionally, the Communist Party has maintained a remarkable measure of internal cohesion despite factional differences. For example, the death of Ho Chi Minh in 1969 did not give rise to a visible power struggle. Also, the party has never experienced Soviet-style purges, nor has it had to cope with the kind of popular protest confronted by its Chinese counterpart in June 1989. More recently, however, a power struggle between the prime minister, **Nguyen Tan Dung**, and president, **Truong Tan Sang**, has eroded this monolithic image. The former, a political scion of both conservative and reformist factions of parliament, assumed his office – ranked third-highest in the country – in 2006 and was re-elected in 2011, winning 470 out of 500 votes cast, while the latter, a former party secretary for Ho Chi Minh City, ascended to both the presidency and chairmanship of Vietnam's Council for National Defence and Security in 2011, becoming the second-highest official after **Nguyen Phu Trong**, general secretary of the Communist Party. In August 2012, banking tycoon Nguyen Duc Kien, co-founder of Vietnam's fourth-biggest lender, the Asia Commercial Bank, known to be close to Dung, was arrested and charged with financial crimes. Two months later, Trong announced a Politburo decision to adopt discipline against one of its members (widely believed to be Dung), while in November, member of parliament Duong Trung Quoc publicly called on Prime Minister Nguyen Tan Dung to resign over his handling of the economy – and especially the beleaguered banking sector. Charges of widespread nepotism also surfaced, alongside criticism of Dung's relatives' rapid rise to various public and private sector posts. The Vietnam Chamber of Commerce and Industry reported in 2012 that fifty per cent of businessmen admitted to bribing officials to secure contracts, placing the actual proportion far higher in all likelihood. As these investigations were taking place, the Central Steering Committee for Anti-Corruption was taken from Dung's oversight and placed under Trong, while the fast-rising Nguyen Ba Thanh, party secretary of Danang, was appointed to head a new party mechanism mandated to reduce graft, the Central Internal Affairs Commission. Finally, Dung was widely blamed by social media pundits for perpetuating a widening income gap that undermined the Communist Party's commitment to equality, until dissent was curbed to some degree by the arrests and jail sentences of fourteen democracy activists and bloggers, on the grounds of subverting the state, in early 2013. The arrests, however, could barely paper over the fact that civil society activism has been gradually growing in Vietnam. Particularly noteworthy in that regard was the formation of Group 72, comprising intellectuals and former senior officials, including a former minister for justice, which established a Civil Society Forum in September 2013 that called for wide-ranging political reforms and the reduction of the power of the Communist Party of Vietnam.

Vietnam may have given up its revolutionary identity as an outpost of socialism, which was proclaimed with unification in 1976, but it has yet to adjust politically to a postwar world driven by the forces of globalization. It has adjusted, of necessity, to an adverse strategic environment. In armed struggle against France and the United States, it attracted Chinese and Soviet support. That from the former was always problematic, exemplified by Beijing's toleration of the division of Vietnam in 1954. Sino-Vietnamese tensions became open after Sino–US rapprochement in the early 1970s and culminated in a limited punitive invasion in February 1979 in retaliation for Vietnam's invasion and occupation of Cambodia. The Soviet Union sustained Vietnam during the conflict over Cambodia during the first half of the 1980s but became an unreliable partner even before the end of the Cold War. The disintegration of the Soviet Union in December 1991 was a profound political shock to the leadership of a party whose greatest luminary had served part of his political apprenticeship in Moscow. Vietnam was obliged to cope unaided with the transformation in its strategic circumstances by appeasing China over Cambodia, from which it withdrew its forces from 1989. After the **International Conference on Cambodia** in Paris in 1991, a process of Sino–Vietnamese rapprochement was set in train with a meeting of party and state leaders in Beijing in November 1991. A working relationship has been based in part in a common interest in upholding the hegemony of their respective Communist Parties. Vietnam was able to accede to ASEAN's **Treaty of Amity and Cooperation** in July 1992, which gave it observer status at the annual meetings of the Association's foreign ministers. It was admitted to ASEAN as the first Communist member in July 1995 and hosted the sixth summit meeting of the Association in Hanoi in 1998.

A major foreign policy challenge for Vietnam is its relationship with a resurgent China, with which it has a testy relationship because of contention over islands and maritime space in the **South China Sea**. Vietnam is also in contention over some of the Spratly Islands in the South China Sea with ASEAN partners, Malaysia and the Philippines. Progress has been made, however, in demarcating the common land border between Vietnam and China. The Land Border Agreement signed in December 1999 concluded negotiations begun in October 1992, and confirmed an unmistakable shift in Vietnam's attitude towards its northern neighbour – a Sino–Vietnamese Joint Declaration issued earlier that year had already reaffirmed ties of cooperation between the two. This agreement was followed in 2000 by a Joint Statement for Comprehensive Cooperation and the Agreement on Borders in the Gulf of Tonkin, which covered both land and maritime rights, which resolved the **Tonkin Gulf Dispute** between the two countries. At the same time, Vietnam has expanded its relations with old ally Russia, albeit in less direct terms. A 'strategic partnership' was announced in March 2001 following the first visit to Vietnam by a Russian head of state, President Vladimir Putin. Vietnamese politicians then visited Russia yearly, while Putin visited Vietnam again in November 2006 and President Dmitry Medvedev visited in October 2010. Though fewer bilateral deals materialized, Vietnam has been a strong advocate of a Russian presence in the region.

Vietnam assumed chairmanship of ASEAN in 2010, and strengthened the organization's mechanism for defence cooperation by inaugurating the **ASEAN Defence Ministers' Meeting** Plus in October that year. Under Vietnam's tenure, ASEAN also launched the ASEAN Socio-Cultural Community (ASCC) and the ASEAN Children's and Women's Commission (ACWC), besides formally extending permanent membership status in the **East Asia Summit** (EAS) to the United States and Russia. From 2009 to 2012, Vietnam also took over as coordinator for the ASEAN–China 'dialogue relationship' that began in 1991, hosting the thirteenth ASEAN–China Summit in Hanoi in October 2010. At this summit, a new and wide-ranging Plan of Action for the ASEAN–China partnership, covering policies from 2011 to 2015, was unveiled. Nevertheless tensions surfaced soon after, over China's increasingly aggressive stance over its territorial claims in the South China Sea. In May 2011, Chinese fishing boats cut the cables of a Vietnamese seismic survey vessel. This occurred again in November 2012, prompting protests on Vietnamese broadsheets and in the streets of Ho Chi Minh and Hanoi. In June 2012, Vietnam introduced the 'Vietnamese Law of the Sea', which described the Paracel Islands as being within Vietnamese jurisdiction, and established a fishery bureau with the authority to patrol the area and investigate intruding vessels. In response, Hainan province (under whose territorial waters China had circumscribed the Paracel islands) reaffirmed China's stand with new regulations on maritime security, and authorized border police to board or seize foreign ships with effect from January 2013. The seventh conference on ASEAN–China People-to-People Friendship Organizations, held in Hanoi in August 2012, did little to quell the friction. Bilateral relations with China reached a new low on 27 May when a Vietnamese fishing boat sank after colliding with a Chinese vessel following a standoff near a controversial oil rig that China had moved to waters near the disputed Paracel Islands claimed by both countries.

see also: ASEAN; ASEAN Defence Ministers' Meeting; *Doi Moi*; Domino Theory; East Asia Summit; Geneva Agreements on Indochina 1954; Ho Chi Minh; International Conference on Cambodia; Khmer Rouge; Nguyen Phu Trong; Nguyen Tan Dung; Paris Peace Agreements 1973; South China Sea; State Owned Enterprise Reform; Tonkin Gulf Dispute; Treaty of Amity and Cooperation; Treaty of Friendship and Cooperation; Truong Tan Sang; Vietnam War.

A

Abangan (Indonesia)

Abangan is the term applied to rural Javanese who acknowledge an adherence to Islam but order their lives according to precepts and practices drawn from animist and Hindu–Buddhist values. The distinguishing feature of *Abangan* culture is its syncretic quality expressed partly in a refusal to define identity with exclusive reference to Islam by contrast with the alternative ***Santri*** tradition. That refusal assumed political significance prior to the proclamation of Indonesia's independence in August 1945 when an attempt was made to impose a constitutional obligation on all professing Muslims to observe *shari'a* (Islamic) law. That Islamic initiative was frustrated by Indonesia's first president, **Sukarno**, who insisted on religious pluralism expressed through the pre-eminent of five principles, ***Pancasila***, which he enunciated and which became the philosophical bases of the post-colonial republic. *Pancasila* served to protect *Abangan* cultural identity and was entrenched in the constitution during the rule of President **Suharto**. The distinction between *Abangan* and *Santri* became blurred from around the seventh decade of the twentieth century with rapid economic development and urbanization, which has provided a social context within which a burgeoning Islam has become increasingly assertive.

see also: Islam; *Pancasila*; *Santri*; Suharto; Sukarno.

Abdul Rahman, Tunku (Malaya/Malaysia)

Tunku Abdul Rahman was the first prime minister of Malaya and then Malaysia. In 1951, after Dato Onn bin Jafar had lost the confidence of **UMNO** (United Malays National Organization) because of his wish to permit access to members of other communities, the Tunku (as he was generally known) became its president. In this role, he forged a viable coalition, the **Alliance Party**, with Chinese and Indian communal political parties and played the leading part in negotiating the independence of the Federation of Malaya in 1957 and then in promoting the wider Federation of Malaysia which was formed in 1963. He successfully surmounted Indonesia's **Confrontation** of the new Federation but was unable to overcome intercommunal tensions aggravated by Singapore's membership. He took the fateful decision to cast Singapore out of the Federation in August 1965 but communal tensions mounted because the Malays believed that their political birthright was being compromised by the growing economic imbalance with the Chinese. The **May 13 Racial Riots** in the wake of general elections in May 1969, in which UMNO lost ground, made the Tunku's position politically untenable; he stepped down from office in 1970 in favour of his deputy, **Tun Abdul Razak**.

Tunku Abdul Rahman was born in 1903 to a Thai mother as one of forty-five children of Sultan Abdul Hamid of the state of Kedah, then part of Thailand. As a student of law in England who took many years to be called to the bar, he claimed a reputation for fast women, fast cars and not-so-fast horses. His easy-going style was carried over into his political career but it concealed a steely firmness of mind which he demonstrated in the **Baling Talks** with **Chin Peng**, the leader of the Communist Party of Malaya. After leaving high office, the Tunku served during the 1970s as head of the Islamic Secretariat in Saudi Arabia. In later life, he turned his hand to journalism, acting as the liberal conscience of a country which under the leadership of **Mahathir Mohamad** became increasingly authoritarian in its politics. He died on 6 December 1990 at the age of 87.

see also: Alliance Party; Baling Talks 1955; Chin Peng; Confrontation; Mahathir Mohamad, Tun; May 13 Racial Riots 1969; Razak, Tun Abdul; UMNO.

Abdul Rahman Yakub, Tun (Malaysia)

Tun Abdul Rahman Yakub was chief minister of Malaysia's north Bornean state of Sarawak from July 1970 until March 1981. In April 1981 he assumed the office of state governor, which he gave up in 1985 out of frustration with the political constraints of his constitutional role. Tun Yakub was born on 3 January 1928 in Bintulu, Sarawak. He was educated at the University of Southampton in England and went on to qualify as a barrister at Lincoln's Inn in London in 1959. He began his career in the Sarawak government's legal service and played an instrumental role in building Muslim Malay–Melanau political organization on the former British colony's entry into Malaysia. His initial period in politics was at the federal level and he held the portfolios of land and mines and of education during the 1960s. During his tenure as chief minister, he consolidated the position in Sarawak of the ruling ***Barisan Nasional*** (National Front) federal coalition, which was formed during the early 1970s. His exit from active political life expressed itself in a quarrel with his nephew, **Abdul Taib Mahmud**, who had succeeded him as chief minister in 1981. After his failure to unseat his nephew in state elections in 1987, Tun Yakub retired from politics.

see also: Barisan Nasional; Taib Mahmud, Datuk Patinggi Abdul.

Abdullah, Zaini (Indonesia)

Zaini Abdullah is the current governor of the special Indonesian province of Aceh. Zaini was born in Pidie, Aceh, on 24 April 1940. A medical doctor by profession, he graduated from the University of North Sumatra in Medan. He was formerly a key member of the **Aceh Independence Movement** (GAM or *Gerakan Aceh Merdeka*) and was elected alongside former GAM guerrilla commander, Muzakir Manaf, at the 2012 elections. These were the second democratic elections held in Aceh since the Helsinki Peace Accord between GAM and the Government of the Republic of Indonesia in 2005. Running on a platform focused on anti-corruption and the introduction of *shari'a* law, Zaini managed to secure fifty-six per cent of the vote on the way to defeating incumbent **Irwandy Yusuf**, also a former GAM member, and two other candidates. Since 1976, Zaini had held key leadership positions within GAM while in exile in Sweden, including foreign and health minister. Together with GAM president, Hasan di Tiro, and prime minister, Malik Mahmud, Zaini was arrested in June 2004 in Stockholm by Swedish police, under pressure from the Indonesian government, for crimes against the Indonesian state. They were subsequently released on grounds of insufficient evidence. Meanwhile, the Swedish government denied Indonesian requests that the three be extradited to stand trial in Indonesia. Following the August 2005 Helsinki Peace Accord and the disbanding of GAM, Zaini played an instrumental role in the formation of *Partai Aceh* (PA). A split soon occurred within the community of former GAM separatists which saw two prominent leaders, Irwandy Yusuf and Malik Mahmud, contest the gubernatorial elections on different tickets in 2006. Factionalism resurfaced in the buildup to the 2012 elections when Zaini tried to have incumbent Irwandy Yusuf disqualified from running. In retaliation, Irwandy accused Zaini's *Partai Aceh* of using violence and intimidation against his opponents.

see also: Aceh Independence Movement; Yusuf, Irwandy.

Abhisit Vejjajiva (Thailand)

Abhisit Vejjajiva was Thailand's twenty-seventh prime minister. He led a government closely aligned to establishment interests and the military, a stance which was unpopular with a large segment of the population. Mass protests under his rule resulted in a military crackdown and some of the worst civil violence Bangkok has ever seen.

Abhisit was born on 3 August 1964 in Newcastle-upon-Tyne, UK, to an elite Bangkok family. He attended school in Bangkok and later at Eton College in the UK. He went on to earn a bachelor's degree in philosophy, politics and economics at Oxford University. He was then briefly a lecturer at Chulachomklao Royal Military Academy in Nakhon Nayok, Thailand. He returned to Oxford University to study for a master's degree in economics and later studied law at Ramkhamhaeng University in Bangkok. He then taught economics at Thammasat

University in Bangkok. Abhisit entered politics by joining the **Democrat Party**, and was elected to Parliament for Bangkok in 1992. He would be re-elected in 1995 and 1996. From 1992 to 1994, Abhisit was spokesman for the **Chuan Leekpai** government, and would remain as spokesman for the party during its period in opposition from 1995 to 1997. He was a minister to the Prime Minister's Office during the second Chuan Leekpai government, 1997–2001. Abhisit was elected as a party list candidate for the Democrat Party in 2001, 2005 and 2007. Abhisit became the Democrat Party leader in 2005 following the resignation of Banyat Bantadtan as a result of the massive defeat of the democrats by the ***Thai Rak Thai* Party** (TRT) in the 2005 general elections. As the Democrat Party was the leading opposition party, Abhisit also became the leader of the opposition in the parliament from 2005 to 2006, and again in 2008. Abhisit became prime minister of Thailand in 2008 following the dissolution of the **People's Power Party** (PPP). The Democrat Party was defeated by the ***Pheu Thai* Party** in the July 2011 elections, placing Abhisit again in the role of leader of the opposition.

Abhisit was perceived as young and cosmopolitan, with a reputation for being above the sleaze and corruption that characterizes much of Thai politics thanks to his criticism of corrupt practices and cronyism. Yet his legitimacy has been criticized due to his inability to win either of the general elections during his tenure as party leader from 2005. His selection as prime minister in 2005 was brought about through backroom deals between the army commander, **Anupong Paochinda**, and a renegade faction of the dissolved PPP led by Newin Chidchob. The Democrat Party's decision to lead a boycott together with two smaller parties of the 2006 snap elections called by **Thaksin Shinawatra** precipitated a constitutional crisis that led to the September 2006 coup. Still, the Democrat Party gained little politically from the coup, remaining in opposition following the election victory of the PPP, a reincarnation of the TRT, in December 2007. Following the Constitutional Court's decision to disqualify PPP leader **Samak Sundaravej** in September 2008, the Democrats were again blocked from forming a government by a parliamentary vote which chose **Somchai Wongsawat** of the PPP as Samak's replacement. During the same period the democratic credentials of the Democrat Party were questioned due to their seeming support for the six-month protest movement of the **People's Alliance for Democracy** (PAD) against the elected PPP governments. Abhisit and the Democrats only achieved power through a parliamentary vote following a Constitutional Court decision to disqualify and dissolve the PPP in December 2008.

Although he led the opposition to the government of Prime Minister Thaksin Shinawatra, Abhisit publicly opposed the 2006 coup which ousted Thaksin and the TRT. On attaining high office, however, Abhisit's policies largely mirrored the populist polices of his predecessor. Abhisit's term as prime minister was marked by attempts to deal with the global economic crisis and rapidly escalating domestic political pressure. By siding with the elite establishment and backed by the military, Abhisit and the Democrat Party placed themselves in direct opposition to the mass appeal of Thaksin that coalesced around the **United Front for Democracy Against Dictatorship** (UDD), the so-called 'red shirts', and the Thaksin-aligned PPP and its successor, the *Pheu Thai* Party. Abhisit's apparent association with the military and the establishment became more overt through the escalation of responses to growing red shirt protests in 2009 and 2010. Abhisit came to rely increasingly on emergency decrees and military force to suppress protests, which led to limited violence in April 2009 and much wider violence in April–May 2010 that resulted in at least ninety-one deaths on both sides. The protests had a severe economic impact, especially in Bangkok, and polarized the country. The Democrat Party was defeated by the *Pheu Thai* Party in general elections in July 2011, although Abhisit was re-elected. In December 2012, Abhisit was charged with murder for the death of a taxi driver during the 2010 political violence in which he authorized military suppression of red shirt protestors.

see also: Anupong Paochinda, General; Chuan Leekpai; Democrat Party; People's Alliance for Democracy; People's Power Party; *Pheu Thai* Party; Samak Sundaravej; Somchai

Wongsawat; *Thai Rak Thai* Party; Thaksin Shinawatra; United Front for Democracy Against Dictatorship.

ABIM (Malaysia)

ABIM is an acronym drawn from *Angkatan Belia Islam Malaysia*, which translates as Islamic Youth Movement of Malaysia. It was set up in 1971 on the campus of the University of Malaya as a vehicle of Islamic revivalism (*see* ***Dakwah***). ABIM represented an expression of political as well as religious dissent against a Malay-Muslim-dominated government, which had allegedly compromised the political birthright of the indigenous Malays to the advantage of non-Malays, especially the Chinese. The leading role in ABIM's early years was played by **Anwar Ibrahim**, then a student of Malay studies, who exercised a truly charismatic influence on his fellow students. In December 1974, he was detained for twenty-two months for leading a demonstration against peasant poverty in the state of Kedah. ABIM was for a time regarded as the youth wing of the principal Malay opposition ***Parti Islam Se-Malaysia*** (PAS) and some of its members campaigned for PAS in the 1978 elections. It lost national standing as an agent of Islamic resurgence when Anwar Ibrahim joined **UMNO** (United Malays National Organization) shortly before general elections in April 1982. Though Anwar retained his ABIM intellectual links, the party itself toned down its political engagement significantly under new leadership, while resources and energy were refocused to education. ABIM abandoned its quietist disposition at the height of the reform movement that began with Anwar's unceremonious dismissal in September 1998 when the organization joined in the chorus of civil society voices that agitated for political reform in Malaysia. This rediscovery of its activist roots led to the brief detention of several ABIM leaders, including the president, Ahmad Azam Abdul Rahman. During this time, many ABIM members also formally joined opposition political parties, primarily PAS, which already had among its leadership ranks compatriots of Anwar's from his ABIM days, and ***Parti Keadilan Rakyat*** (PKR). The election of Yusri Mohamad as ABIM president in 2005 marked the introduction of a new era in ABIM's history, as Yusri and his new team of leaders came from a generation that did not idolize Anwar to the extent of their predecessors. Yusri also sought to realign ABIM by moving it away from excessive political activism to focus more on social work and *Dakwah*.

see also: Anwar Ibrahim; *Dakwah*; Islam; *Parti Islam Se-Malaysia*; *Parti Keadilan Rakyat*; UMNO.

ABRI (Indonesia)

ABRI is an acronym drawn from *Angkatan Bersenjata Indonesia* which translates as armed forces of the Republic of Indonesia. Indonesia's armed forces, which include the army, navy, air force and police, have long enjoyed a central place in the political and business life of the country and served as the power-base for President **Suharto** during his extended rule. As a serving general, he assumed their leadership during a coup attempt in October 1965 and with military support seized political control in March 1966. Within the armed forces, the army has occupied the dominant position. It draws its tradition from Japanese military culture, inculcated during the Pacific War occupation, and from the experience of national revolution against the Dutch. With the political downfall of President Suharto in May 1998, the national standing and morale of the armed forces was diminished as its record of human rights abuses was publicized. In an attempt to cleanse its sullied reputation, ABRI changed its name to *Tentara Nasional Indonesia* (Indonesia's National Army) in April 1999.

ABRI's origins may be traced back to 5 October 1945 when President **Sukarno** inaugurated the People's Security Army under the initial command of an Indonesian officer from the former Dutch colonial army. That leadership was soon challenged by Indonesians who had been trained in Japanese paramilitary organizations, such as the ***Peta***. By mid-November, leadership had passed to Sudirman, a former *Peta* battalion commander, who distinguished himself in directing guerrilla resistance against the Dutch in the closing stages of the revolutionary war, despite being terminally ill with tuberculosis. The formative moment in the development of the political culture of the armed forces occurred in December 1948 when the Dutch occupied the revolutionary capital of Yogyakarta. The civilian government headed by President Sukarno surrendered, while the army opted to continue resistance by irregular warfare. From this juncture, the military took the view that politics was too serious a matter to be left exclusively in the charge of civilians who had abdicated their responsibility at a time of gravest national peril. Moreover, independence was depicted as having been achieved primarily through armed struggle and not the diplomacy of irresolute politicians. The armed forces represented themselves as the legitimate guardians of the state.

After independence, this prerogative view was confirmed for the leadership of the armed forces by the political instability and economic failings of parliamentary democracy during the 1950s. During this period, the army chief of staff, General **Abdul Haris Nasution**, formulated a theory of the 'Middle Way' to justify a political role for the military. Although the armed forces were instrumental in helping President Sukarno to establish the authoritarian political system of **Guided Democracy** in July 1959, they were neutralized by his manipulative skills. In the wake of an abortive coup in October 1965 (*see* ***Gestapu***), the armed forces reasserted themselves and seized power in March 1966 under the leadership of then Lieutenant General Suharto. Indonesia reverted to the form of constitutionalism with parliamentary and presidential elections revived from the early 1970s but ABRI's right to a prerogative place in political life on account of its ***Dwi Fungsi*** (or dual role) was embodied in legislation in 1982. The special place of the armed forces was acknowledged also by allocating them 100 seats in the Parliament of 500 members, justified in addition by a denial of their right to vote.

In April 1995, ABRI's parliamentary representation was reduced to seventy-five seats. This reduction was justified ostensibly with reference to Indonesia's democratic progress. It was interpreted, however, as an indication of a rising tension between the military establishment and President Suharto, which had showed itself first in February 1988 with the premature removal from office of armed forces commander, General **L. B. Murdani**. Suharto's determination to rule independently of the armed forces as well as his toleration of the extensive business activities of his family caused a progressive alienation. This alienation was aggravated in December 1990 when the president encouraged the formation of an Association of Indonesian Muslim Intellectuals (ICMI) in apparent emulation of the practice of the late President Sukarno of mobilizing countervailing political support against the armed forces. Up to his resignation in May 1998, Suharto dominated the armed forces by controlling the promotion of its most senior officers with ABRI commanders drawn from the ranks of former personal aides. General Wiranto, his last nominee as ABRI commander, endorsed the transfer of executive authority to Vice-President **B. J. Habibie**. An initial working relationship gave way to political tension, especially from January 1999 after President Habibie had offered the people of East Timor the choice between autonomy within Indonesia or full independence, without reference to the armed forces, which had an emotional stake in the territory because of casualties incurred in counterinsurgency and also because of their guardian role in upholding the integrity of the Republic.

The armed forces were obliged to tolerate a further reduction of their parliamentary representation to thirty-eight seats prior to elections in June 1999. They withheld support for President Habibie's bid to retain high office and did not try to obstruct the election of **Abdurrahman Wahid** as president in the following October. His appointment of Professor Juwono Sudarsono as the first civilian minister of defence for several decades indicated the president's determination to reduce the political role of the armed forces. Tension became manifest between the president and General Wiranto, appointed coordinating minister for political and security affairs, especially after President Wahid endorsed the right of a national commission of enquiry into human rights violations in East Timor to hold him and other senior officers accountable. General Wiranto was suspended from cabinet office in February 2000 (resigning formally in May). By then, the concept of *Dwi Fungsi* had lost credibility and the armed forces had lost the cohesive capability to mount a coup, but a significant vestigial influence in politics and business remained. In April 2000, Admiral Widodo announced the armed forces were out of politics and wanted to concentrate on their professional role. The **People's Consultative Assembly** further decreed that year that in order to facilitate this reorientation, the police force would be separated out of the armed forces and would operate independently in the realm of public security and order while the TNI's mandate would be restricted to that of a defence force. The TNI's political role has since been further diminished by legislation that has been passed to end the appointment of military and police personnel in parliament, to compel it to divest its business interests, and to strengthen civilian control over the budgetary and procurement process. Nevertheless, while democratization has facilitated the passage of legislation such as the 2004 armed forces law that reinforces civilian supremacy and respect for human rights, the latitude that the Indonesian armed forces still enjoy continues to be a bone of contention in the country. This includes a culture of impunity within the armed forces and weak military courts, as well as the continued existence of anachronistic vestiges of the Suharto era such as the controversial territorial command structure, which was previously used to protect the interests of ***Golkar***, and is still given to abuse of political interests and to illegal business. Furthermore, while the military has been forced to sell off some of its businesses, and others have succumbed to business failure, it still retains sizeable profit-generating enterprises, ranging from ownership of buildings and other properties to foundations and cooperatives.

see also: Dwi Fungsi; *Gestapu*; *Golkar*; Guided Democracy; Habibie, B. J.; Murdani, L. B., General; Nasution, Abdul Haris; People's Consultative Assembly; *Peta*; Suharto; Sukarno; *Supersemar*; Wahid, Abdurrahman.

Abu Sayyaf Group (ASG) (Philippines)

Abu Sayyaf, which means 'father of the swordsmith', is a militant Muslim group which seeks a separate Islamic state in the southern Philippines. The Abu Sayyaf Group (ASG) was established in 1991 on the island of Basilan by Abdurajik Abubakar Janjalani after he had returned from a period of religious study in Saudi Arabia and Libya sponsored by the **Moro National Liberation Front** (MNLF). His movement is opposed to any accommodation with the Philippines government over Muslim political autonomy and has declared its intention to drive Christian inhabitants from the southern islands of the republic by acts of force which were first undertaken during 1992. He attracted a constituency of politically discontented and radical younger Muslims, including disaffected members of the MNLF, whose numbers grew from 100 to over 500. Initially engaging in kidnappings, bombings and grenade attacks, the ASG achieved international notoriety in April 1995 for a daring surprise sea-borne raid by some 200 armed men on the small predominantly Christian town of Ipil on the southwest tip of the island of Mindanao. In the course of the raid, which devastated the commercial district, the town's seven banks were robbed and fifty-three residents were killed. The raiders then fled into the jungle with hostages, many of whom were hacked to death with knives. The ASG is believed to be stiffened by Filipino Muslims with military experience gained in Afghanistan and to have received financial support from external Islamic sources. It has been linked to the international terrorist network implicated in the bombing of the World Trade Center in New York in 1993 and in a plot to kill the Pope during his visit to the Philippines in January 1995. In a second raid in April 1995, ASG insurgents attacked the coastal town of Tungawan located about twelve miles southeast of Ipil. At the end of 1998, Abdurajik Janjalani was killed in a gun battle outside of the provincial capital of Isabela. Since his death and under the leadership of his brother Khaddafi, the ASG has degenerated into a quasi-criminal organization engaging in kidnapping and hostage-taking justified by outlandish political demands, such as the release of Ramzi Yousef who was convicted of masterminding the bombing in 1993 of the World Trade Center in New York. A group of about fifty Filipino hostages were seized from two schools on the island of Basilan in March 2000, two of whom were beheaded. In late April that year, a group of twenty-one foreign and local tourists were seized from the Malaysian-held resort island of **Sipadan** and taken by boat to the Philippine island of Jolo. In August, Jeffrey Schilling, an American Muslim convert, was abducted after reportedly visiting the group. Recurrent assaults by units of the armed forces failed to dislodge the insurgents from their jungle redoubt only forty minutes' drive from Jolo town. Hostages were released in batches in return for millions of dollars in ransom. In September, following the seizure of a further three hostages from Malaysia, President Estrada ordered a military operation against the ASG. By April 2001, all hostages except one were released or successfully rescued. Not long after in May, two resorts were raided resulting in two deaths and twenty hostages taken, including three Americans, two of whom later died. In June, ASG gunmen seized a hotel and a church in Lamitan town. Some hostages were killed and others ransomed when the group eventually escaped despite the presence of an army cordon. ASG was also believed to have masterminded a bombing at Davao International Airport in 2003, which killed twenty-one people, and the sinking of *SuperFerry 14* in February the following year, which killed 116 people (*see* **Terrorism in Southeast Asia**). In April 2004, one of the group's key leaders, Hamsiraji Sali, was killed in a gun battle with government forces in Basilan. A day later, fifty prisoners including suspected ASG members managed to escape from a jail in the southern Philippines. ASG has been unrelenting with their high-profile kidnappings because of lucrative ransoms they have managed to secure. Frequent clashes with military units highlight the ability of the ASG to mount attacks despite government claims that counter-insurgency operations are making headway, while several instances of militants managing to escape security cordons indicate incompetence on the part of some Philippine military units.

see also: Moro National Liberation Front; Sipadan–Ligatan; Terrorism in Southeast Asia.

Aceh Independence Movement (Indonesia)

The Aceh Independence Movement (*Gerakan Aceh Merdeka* or GAM) was a separatist organization, which was set up on 4 December 1976 by Hasan di Tiro, an American-educated expatriate businessman who had resided in exile in Sweden since 1979. He returned to Indonesia in 2008 and died in 2010.

Aceh is the northernmost province of Sumatra whose population shares a strong Islamic historical identity going back to a powerful seventeenth-century sultanate from which di Tiro claimed descent. It was the last part of the Indonesian archipelago to fall to Dutch colonial rule, which was not effectively consolidated until the early years of the twentieth century. Although an active source of resistance to the return of the Dutch after the Pacific War, on Indonesia's independence Aceh became a seat of the Muslim-inspired rebellion known as ***Darul Islam***, which challenged the unity of the Republic over the next decade, partly in reaction to the new republic merging Aceh into the province of North Sumatra. The source of political alienation, which formed the context to di Tiro's separatist initiative, was Jakarta's failure to honour a promise of provincial autonomy in 1959 and the meagre returns to Aceh from the exploitation of the rich Arun offshore oil and natural gas fields. The Aceh Independence Movement had only a limited impact until the late 1980s when a government clampdown on marijuana growing by army deserters against a context of economic and religious discontent provoked a surge of local dissent with armed attacks mounted on police posts. The limited rebellion was sufficiently crushed by mid-1991 that the government political party ***Golkar*** was able to assert its dominance in the province in parliamentary elections in June 1992. By then, however, several hundred young Acehnese had received military training in Libya. The underlying resentment towards Jakarta and demand for independence came to a head again after the political downfall of President **Suharto** in May 1998 and gained momentum after the seeming precedent of a referendum in East Timor in August 1999. It was reinforced by the indiscriminate nature of military repression, which had been responsible for the loss of some 5,000 lives from the early 1990s. Moreover, statements by **Abdurrahman Wahid**, before and even after he became president, that he supported a corresponding vote in Aceh aroused strong political expectations within the disaffected province. He subsequently ruled out independence as an option in any referendum, partly under pressure from the armed forces (*see* **ABRI**), leading to a political impasse between the government in Jakarta and the separatists in Aceh. The strength of support for independence within Aceh was demonstrated in November 1999 when over 500,000 protesters converged on the province's capital, Banda Aceh, to demand a referendum. The independence movement, led militarily within Aceh by Abdullah Syafie, claimed at its height to have around 1,000 men under arms supplied by sympathizers in Malaysia and Thailand. At the time, the prospect of Indonesia's balkanization alarmed the country's regional partners and major Asia-Pacific powers who have lent their support to the government in Jakarta for the continued integrity of the Republic after the independence of East Timor. President Abdurrahman Wahid played on the popular desire for peace within the province by offering a range of concessions, including a much greater share of natural-gas revenues and latitude in applying Islamic law as well as countenancing a human rights trial of soldiers charged with murdering students at an Islamic school in July 1999, who were found guilty in mid-May 2000. On 12 May, after several months of secret negotiations, a ceasefire described as a humanitarian pause was signed in Davos, Switzerland, between a representative of the Indonesian government and of the faction loyal to Hasan di Tiro. However, under pressure from its parliament, Jakarta refused recognition of the insurgents, who maintained their demand for independence. The ceasefire, renewed in August, failed to end recurrent violence in the province. By 2002 Indonesian forces deployed in Aceh were reported to number 30,000. Military operations also intensified, leading to high casualty rates, including considerable numbers of civilians. A second ceasefire was brokered in December 2002 but lasted only a few months. In 2003, the military presence increased to 50,000, and corruption and war profiteering were rampant within military units in Aceh. A third ceasefire was declared unilaterally by GAM two days after the December 2004 tsunami that devastated the province, in order to facilitate humanitarian operations. Both parties eventually signed a peace agreement in February 2005, bringing an end to a thirty-year-old conflict. GAM's military was disbanded by the end of the year. The peace agreement allowed for the establishment of Aceh-based political parties, a major concession from the Indonesian government. In the event, two former GAM members, **Irwandy Yusuf** and **Zaini Abdullah**, went on to win gubernatorial elections in 2006 and 2012 respectively.

see also: Abdullah, Zaini; ABRI; *Darul Islam*; *Golkar*; Islam; Suharto; Wahid, Abdurrahman; Yusuf, Irwandy.

ADMM (ASEAN Defence Ministers' Meeting) (Brunei/Cambodia/Indonesia/Malaysia/Myanmar/Laos/Philippines/Singapore/Thailand/Vietnam)

The ADMM, established in 2006, is the first region-wide defence forum that brings together the defence ministers of ASEAN member states annually to discuss and exchange views on defence and security challenges in the region. Prior to this, defence cooperation in the region took place only on a bilateral basis. The initiative was prompted by concerns over the lack of an effective multilateral response mechanism to deal with a variety of transnational security challenges. The ADMM seeks to enhance transparency and promote greater understanding of the different security challenges, culture, norms and political pressures between **ASEAN** member states. Moving beyond confidence-building measures, the ADMM places its emphasis on practical areas of cooperation. It produces three-year work programmes which guide cooperation in defence and security issues in the region. These include activities in areas such as promoting defence and security co-operation, conflict prevention and resolution, and norms setting and sharing. The first three-year work programme (2008–10) was adopted at the second ADMM in Singapore in 2007.

Since its inception, intra-ASEAN cooperation in the area of defence has grown, particularly with regards to disaster relief and humanitarian assistance, through the adoption of concept papers such as the Concept Paper on the Use of ASEAN Military Assets and Capabilities in Humanitarian Assistance and Disaster Relief and the Concept Paper on the Establishment of ASEAN Defence Industry Collaboration. At the sixth ADMM in Phnom Penh in May 2012, the defence ministers signed the Joint Declaration on Enhancing ASEAN Unity for a Harmonized and Secure Community, which highlighted the success of the first Humanitarian Assistance and Disaster Relief (HADR) table-top exercise hosted by Singapore and Indonesia in 2011, as well as reaffirming their commitment to the ASEAN Political-Security Community by 2015. In 2010, ASEAN established the ADMM-Plus out of the ADMM process. The ADMM-Plus was formally tabled as a Concept Paper at the second ADMM in Singapore in 2007, with the objective of promoting and strengthening engagement with ASEAN dialogue partners on defence and security issues through triennial meetings and consultations of defence ministers of member states. The dialogue partners in this process are Australia, India, Japan, New Zealand, the People's Republic of China, the Republic of Korea, Russia and the United States. The inaugural ADMM-Plus was convened in Hanoi, Vietnam, on 12 October 2010. In addition to being a forum for building informal contacts, confidence building and developing norms of behaviour, there was a specific focus on five areas of immediate cooperation – disaster relief, counterterrorism, peacekeeping, maritime security and military medicine. The ASEAN Defence Senior Officials' Meeting Plus (ADSOM Plus) and numerous Experts' Working Groups (EWGs) were established to implement the decisions made at the ministerial meetings.

Given perennial regional concerns that Southeast Asia remains susceptible to external power rivalry, the ADMM-Plus serves as a mechanism that entrenches the central role of ASEAN in regional defence and security matters. Yet, despite willingness for dialogue, it is still unclear what the ADMM-Plus can achieve when it comes to longstanding security issues. While it provides platforms for defence ministers to discuss bilateral conflicts or military competition on the sidelines of these meetings, it is unlikely that the ADMM-Plus process would be able to deal comprehensively with traditional threats and issues such as the **South China Sea** disputes or the Korean Peninsula. At the sixth ADMM in Phnom Penh on 29 May 2012, it was agreed that the interval of the ADMM-Plus meetings would be shortened from every three years to two years from 2013 onwards.

see also: ASEAN; South China Sea.

ADMM-Plus (Brunei/Cambodia/Indonesia/Malaysia/Myanmar/Laos/Philippines/Singapore/Thailand/Vietnam) *see* **ADMM**.

AFTA (Association of Southeast Asian Nations Free Trade Area) 1993– (Brunei/Cambodia/Indonesia/Laos/Malaysia/Myanmar/Philippines/Singapore/Thailand/Vietnam)

At the fourth meeting of heads of government of **ASEAN** held in Singapore in January 1992, an agreement was reached on establishing a free trade area with effective tariff reductions ranging from five to zero per cent during a fifteen-year period beginning from 1 January 1993. ASEAN had been established with an ostensible prime commitment to economic cooperation, which had not been realized that far. Political co-operation had taken pride of place, especially during the course of the Cambodian conflict during the 1980s. With its resolution as an international problem and the attendant marginalization of ASEAN as a diplomatic community, its members became conscious of the need for corporate renewal. This concern coincided with a collective fear of global trading blocs as well as with a contrasting opportunity of being able to benefit from a potential single market, then of over 300 million people.

The notion of a free trade area had been suggested by Thailand in September 1991 and was approved in principle the next month at a meeting of ASEAN's economic ministers in Malaysia. The initiative to establish an AFTA marked an attempt to repair the Association's failure to raise intramural trade beyond around fifteen per cent. The main mechanism chosen was the Common Effective Preferential Tariff (CEPT) Scheme. In January 1992, fifteen groups of manufactured goods and processed agricultural products were initially identified for inclusion in the scheme of accelerated tariff reductions. A meeting of economic ministers convened in Manila in October that year, which reached agreement on trying to expedite the process of tariff reduction. A new target of five to eight years was set for lowering tariffs to twenty per cent before realizing the goal of a maximum of five per cent by the end of the fifteen-year implementation period. At issue for ASEAN at the outset was how to overcome the persisting problem of reconciling the conflicting economic interests of member states reflected in their different tariff levels. By October 1993, at a subsequent meeting of economics ministers, it was evident that the CEPT Scheme had stalled. It was agreed to re-launch it, with all members (with the exception of Brunei) beginning tariff cuts from January 1994. In July 1995, despite reservations on the part of Indonesia and the Philippines, ASEAN's foreign ministers supported the reduction of the time-frame for implementing tariff cuts of from five to zero per cent to eight years. Vietnam, which joined the Association in that month, was granted a dispensation to defer its obligations under AFTA until 2006.

At the **Bangkok ASEAN Summit** in December 1995, it was agreed to reduce all intramural tariff barriers under the CEPT Scheme by 2003. Despite the impact of regional economic adversity from mid-1997, the **Hanoi ASEAN Summit** in December 1998 sanctioned an advance by one year to 2002 for tariff reductions to between five and zero per cent, with more recent members, including Vietnam, Myanmar and Laos, which had joined in July 1997, given a dispensation up to 2008 and Cambodia, which joined in April 1999, up to 2010. At an informal summit in Manila in November 1999, the target date for the final elimination of all duties was advanced from 2015 to 2010 for Brunei, Indonesia, Malaysia, the Philippines and Thailand, while the remaining members had their target advanced from 2018 to 2015. Despite general scepticism that has obtained about the Association's ability to keep to its declared target dates for tariff reductions, member states have made significant progress in the lowering of intra-regional tariffs. The ASEAN Six, comprising Singapore, Malaysia, Indonesia, Brunei, Thailand and the Philippines, have managed to bring down more than ninety-nine per cent of the products in the CEPT Inclusion List to the five to zero per cent tariff range. Meanwhile the newer member states have also moved eighty per cent of their products into their CEPT Inclusion List (IL) in line with their respective CPET commitments and sixty per cent of these products have been brought down to the five to zero per cent tariff range. As of 2012, sixty-four per cent of the IL products of the ASEAN Six had no tariffs. Consequently, the average tariff for the ASEAN Six under the CEPT Scheme had been reduced from 12.76 per cent to 1.51 per cent from 1993 to 2012. The following are the AFTAs that have been concluded: the ASEAN–Australia–New Zealand FTA was established in February 2009; the ASEAN–China FTA was signed in November 2002 and came into effect in January 2010; the ASEAN–India FTA was signed in October 2003 and the final agreement was reached in August 2009; the ASEAN–Korea FTA was proposed in October 2003 and negotiations began from 2005 onwards; and the agreement establishing the ASEAN–Japan Comprehensive Economic Partnership was signed in 2008.

see also: ASEAN; Bangkok Summit (ASEAN) 1995; Hanoi Summit (ASEAN) 1998; Singapore Summit (ASEAN) 1992.

Ahmadiyah (Indonesia)

The *Ahmadiyah* is a movement which was founded in Muslim India in 1889. Its founder, Mirza Ghulam Ahmad (d. 1908), is believed to be a divine reformer, the promised messiah and the Imam Mahdi, a prophesied redeemer of Islam. While the *Ahmadiyah* shares many core beliefs with other schools of the Islamic faith, they depart in other critical ways, most notably in their understanding of the nature of the death of Jesus and the finality of the prophethood of Muhammad. As most Ahmadis believe Mirza Ghulam Ahmad to be a revealed prophet who succeeded and yet remains subordinate to Muhammad, many mainstream Muslims do not accept Ahmadis as fellow believers. These also consider Mirza Ghulam Ahmad a heretic.

The roots of the *Ahmadiyah* movement in Indonesia are traceable to the 1920s when three young scholars, Abubakar Ayyub, Ahmad Nuruddin and Zaini Dahlan, set out to India to further their religious studies. They initially made acquaintance with the Lahore *Ahmadiyah* Movement but subsequently made a trip to Qadian to accept formal tutelage (*bay'ah*) with Mirza Basyiruddin Mahmud Ahmad, the second successor and son of Mirza Ghulam Ahmad. In 1925, Mirza Basyiruddin sent a delegate, Maulana Rahmat Ali, to the East Indies to promote *Ahmadiyah* teachings. He visited Aceh, Padang and Jakarta, where he was warmly received. Though Indonesia's main Muslim organizations ***Nahdlatul Ulama*** (NU), ***Muhammadiyah*** and ***Masyumi*** decreed *Ahmadiyah* to be deviant, the latter faced little open hostility from mainstream Indonesian Muslims. In fact, the Indonesian government declared *Ahmadiyah* a lawful organization in 1953. As the *Ahmadiyah* evolved in Indonesia, it split into two groups that mirrored the factions of its parent movement in India, with the half a million strong *Jama'ah Ahmadiyah Indonesia* (JAI or Muslim *Ahmadiyah* Community) aligned with the *Ahmadiyah* Muslim Community and the more obscure *Ahmadiyah* Lahore aligned with the Lahore *Ahmadiyah* Movement.

Indonesia's tolerance of the *Ahmadiyah* diminished in 1980 when the ***Majelis Ulama Indonesia*** (MUI or Indonesian Ulama Council), created in 1975 by President **Suharto**, issued a *fatwa* (decree) declaring the *Ahmadiyah* as deviant and outside of Islam. This view was further reinforced by the Blasphemy Law (*Undang-undang Penistaan Agama*) No. 1/PNPS/1965, which prohibits any persons from speaking about, participating in or supporting interpretations of a religion that deviates from the central teachings of that religion. The Blasphemy Law, which was enacted by President **Sukarno** and implemented by Suharto, is bound by article 156(a) of the criminal code, which subjects perpetrators to a maximum five-year jail term. Prohibitions on the Ahmadiyah were further reinforced when it was banned by the Organization of the Islamic Conference (OIC) in December 1985.

The *Ahmadiyah* enjoyed a temporary respite under President **Abdurrahman Wahid**, an advocate of interfaith dialogue and understanding, who invited Mirza Tahir Ahmad, the fourth successor and grandson of Mirza Ghulam Ahmad, to visit Jakarta. However, under President **Susilo Bambang Yudhoyono**, the MUI re-issued its *fatwa* declaring the *Ahmadiyah* deviant in 2005. Unlike the fallout from its previous *fatwa*, this time sporadic acts of violence against Ahmadis followed. The situation worsened in 2008, when the minister of religious affairs, the attorney general, and the minister of the interior collectively issued a joint ministerial decree declaring the *Ahmadiyah* to be deviant and in violation of the Blasphemy Law, and decreed that for as long as the Ahmadis considered themselves Muslims they were to discontinue the promulgation of their beliefs or risk persecution to the fullest extent of the law. On 28 January 2011, members of ***Front Pembela Islam*** (Islamic Defenders Front, FPI) attacked an *Ahmadiyah* mosque in Makassar and forced the congregation to evacuate the premises before destroying their property. While President Yudhoyono had called for a full investigation of the incident, his failure to repudiate statements which justified the persecution of the *Ahmadiyah* elicited strong criticism by human rights groups worldwide. In February 2011, about 1,500 people disrupted an *Ahmadiyah* service in Banten and viciously attacked and killed three Ahmadis in the presence of police who stood by and watched. The horrific killings were captured on film and circulated through YouTube, leading to further widespread criticism of the Indonesian government. For what was deemed as the imposition of severe limitations on religious liberties, the United Nations Human Rights Council (UNHRC) has requested that Indonesia amend or revoke laws and regulations that impinge on religious freedom. They argued that these were a violation of the International Covenant on Civil and Political Rights ratified by

Indonesia in 2006, and most importantly, contradicted the 1945 constitution of Indonesia which guarantees religious freedom for all.

see also: Front Pembela Islam; Majelis Ulama Indonesia; Masyumi; Muhammadiyah; Nahdlatul Ulama; Suharto; Sukarno; Wahid, Abdurrahman; Yudhoyono, Susilo Bambang.

Aljunied Group Representation Constituency (Singapore)

The Group Representation Constituency (GRC) is a form of electoral division whereby a team of three to six members of parliament (MP) consisting of at least one representative each of Indian and Malay ethnicity are voted into parliament together. The Aljunied Group Representation Constituency (GRC) is the first and only GRC that has been won and controlled by an opposition party in Singapore since the GRC system was introduced at the 1988 general election. At the 2011 general election, the **Workers' Party** (WP) led by secretary-general **Low Thia Khiang** unseated a powerful PAP team in Aljunied GRC after winning fifty-four per cent of the votes, securing a comfortable margin of more than nine per cent. This brought an extra five elected seats in Parliament for the WP, in addition to the one that they held for Hougang Single-Member Constituency (SMC). WP's victory in Aljunied GRC also led to the retirement of three senior PAP politicians from office including the minister of foreign affairs, **George Yeo**, and Singapore's first female full minister, Lim Hwee Hua, who previously was a minister in the Prime Minister's Office. The ruling **People's Action Party** (PAP) has continued to maintain that this system is important to ensure that minority groups are adequately represented in parliament. Nevertheless, the GRC system has attracted criticism for being an obstacle for small opposition parties who wish to chip away at the PAP's stranglehold on power, as well as being a vehicle through which fresh PAP candidates can enter parliament without having to secure their own mandates, as would be the case in a single-seat system.

see also: Low Thia Khiang; People's Action Party; Workers' Party; Yeo, George.

Alkatiri, Mari (Timor-Leste)

Mari Alkatiri was the first prime minister of the Democratic Republic of Timor-Leste and is currently the secretary-general of the Revolutionary Front for an Independent East Timor (***Fretilin***). Born in 1949 in then Portuguese Timor, Alkatiri is a descendant of Yemeni settlers as well as a practising Muslim, unlike most of his counterparts in the *Fretilin* leadership who are Roman Catholic. After receiving primary and high school education in Dili, Alkatiri pursued his university degree in Angola where he graduated as a surveyor from the Angolan School of Geography. Returning to Dili, he started work as a chartered surveyor.

Alkatiri became politically active at the fairly young age of twenty. Together with others, he established the Movement for the Liberation of East Timor, an underground resistance movement calling for independence from Portuguese rule. He then moved on to establish a political party, The Timorese Social Democratic Association (ASDT), which later became part of *Fretilin*. Upon the unilateral declaration of independence of the Democratic Republic of East Timor in November 1975, he was appointed minister of state for political affairs on 1 December 1975. Two days later, he left with other *Fretilin* leaders, to embark on a trip around Africa to gather international support for their new nation-state. However, on 7 December, Indonesian forces moved into Dili and this marked the start of a twenty-four year exile for Alkatiri, who was offered sanctuary by the Mozambique government. While in exile, he pursued another degree in law at the Eduardo Mondlane University in Maputo and went on to work as a lecturer in international law for a decade at the University of Mozambique. In 1977, Alkatiri replaced **José Ramos-Horta**, as the minister for foreign affairs for the external delegation, appointed by the government-in-exile.

A reserved figure who unlike his peer **José 'Xanana' Gusmão**, had not experienced Timor-Leste's independence struggle first-hand, Alkatiri returned to Dili and led *Fretilin* to win Timor-Leste's first elections in August 2001. He was sworn in as prime minister in May 2002. As prime minister, Alkatiri's relationship with Gusmão was rocky and the source of much inter-elite friction that threatened to further destabilize the fragile new government. The differences between them go beyond temperament and style, and lie in their different ideological leanings and political beliefs about the role of *Fretilin* in the new state, given its past as the beacon of the independence movement. Alkatiri resigned in June 2006 under heavy domestic pressure, accepting his share of responsibility in a crisis that had led to widespread violence and at least thirty deaths. He had also been accused of complicity in arming fighters to eliminate political opponents of his government, a charge he has denied.

Under Alkatiri's leadership, *Fretilin* won the greatest number of seats at the 2007 parliamentary elections but was denied the responsibility of forming the government after lengthy political talks with the **National Congress for Timorese Reconstruction** (CNRT) failed to yield conclusive results. President Ramos-Horta then announced that 'Xanana' Gusmão would be appointed prime minister and would lead a CNRT coalition that excluded *Fretilin*. Alkatiri denounced this as unconstitutional and encouraged *Fretilin*'s supporters to embark on a campaign of civil disobedience.

see also: *Fretilin*; Gusmão, José 'Xanana'; National Congress for Timorese Reconstruction; Ramos-Horta, José.

Alliance Party (Malaya/Malaysia)

The Alliance Party was the name adopted by the governing intercommunal coalition which assumed the administration of Malaya on independence in August 1957. The Alliance remained continuously in power after the formation of the Federation of Malaysia in September 1963 until superseded in June 1974 by a larger intercommunal arrangement, the ***Barisan Nasional*** (National Front), based on the same political model and of which it has been the core. The Alliance emerged out of a pact between **UMNO** (United Malays National Organization) led by **Tunku Abdul Rahman** and the Malayan (subsequently **Malaysian**) **Chinese Association** (MCA) to contest elections for the municipality of Kuala Lumpur in 1952 in competition with the multicommunal Independence of Malaya Party (IMP). At issue was the appropriate political format for a communally divided society. The British colonial power had made the grant of independence contingent on a working relationship among the Malay, Chinese and Indian communities, ideally within the framework of a single political organization. Indeed, during the **Emergency 1948–60**, they had set up a Communities Liaison Committee on an intercommunal basis. The IMP proved to be an abortive attempt to realize the ideal of a truly multiracial party. The electoral success of the pact between UMNO and the MCA demonstrated the prospect of an alternative arrangement, whereby exclusively communal parties through inter-elite bargaining and accommodations about political prerogatives and economic advantage could sustain government on a harmonious basis. When the first federal-wide elections were held in July 1955, the initial pact had evolved into an institutionalized undertaking with the additional participation of the Malayan (subsequently **Malaysian**) **Indian Congress** (MIC). The Alliance went on to win fifty-one out of the fifty-two seats, proving itself to be the legitimate representative to negotiate the independence of Malaya from Britain. The Alliance model in which UMNO was the dominant partner was expanded from the early 1970s after elections in May 1969 in which the ruling coalition suffered a major reverse followed by racial violence. Coalition building at state level in northern Borneo, Penang and Perak led on to an arrangement at federal level initially with ***Parti Islam Se-Malaysia***, which came into effect in January 1973. *Barisan Nasional* as the successor of the Alliance was registered formally as a political party on 1 June 1974.

see also: Abdul Rahman, Tunku; *Barisan Nasional*; Emergency 1948–60; Malaysian Chinese Association; Malaysian Indian Congress; *Parti Islam Se-Malaysia*; UMNO.

Al-Ma'unah (Malaysia)

Al-Ma'unah or *Persaudaraan Ilmu Dalam Al-Ma'unah* (Brotherhood of Al-Ma-unah Inner Power) was a fringe Malaysian Islamic martial arts group that engaged in militant activities. At its height it claimed a membership of over 1,000.

On 2 July 2000, using stolen military uniforms, members of the group managed to break into several Malaysian army reserve camps and made away with weapons and ammunition. They later went into hiding in Bukit Jenalik in Sauk, Perak. During a standoff with security forces after their hideout was discovered, the radical group managed to take two police officers, one soldier and one civilian hostage. Among the demands made by the militants was the immediate resignation of the prime minister, **Mahathir Mohamad**, the appointment of an Islamic scholar to replace him, and the implementation of stricter Islamic law in Malaysia. After a four-day standoff, the militants surrendered, but not before torturing their hostages and eventually killing two of them. One *Al-Ma'unah* member was also killed during the firefight. While *Al-Ma'unah* gained notoriety for their part in the Sauk siege, the group also sought to inflict damage on the Batu Caves, a site revered by Malaysia's Hindus, and also various breweries, but with little success. The group was eventually charged with treason against the Malaysian king. Its leader, Mohamed Amin Mohamed Razali, and his three deputies were all sentenced to death, while other members received various jail sentences.
see also: Mahathir Mohamad.

Ambalat (Indonesia/Malaysia)

The territory of Ambalat is a sea block in the Celebes Sea, off the coast of Borneo. It is located east of Kalimantan, Indonesia, and south of the eastern tip of Sabah, Malaysia, and is thus claimed by both countries. Measuring around 15,000 square kilometres, sovereignty issues have been complicated by the reported presence of natural gas and oil deposits. It is estimated that the Ambalat blocks could hold as much as 764 million barrels of oil and 1.4 trillion cubic feet of gas. According to the Indonesian government, the territories are referred to as Ambalat and East Ambalat blocks, while the Malaysians refer to them as blocks ND6 and ND7.

The Ambalat dispute is deeply rooted in its history. The ownership of the area itself had been unclear since colonial times, when Britain administered the Malay Peninsula and North Borneo while the Dutch controlled the Indonesian Archipelago, also known as the Dutch East Indies. Concomitantly, the Celebes Sea became a contested area when the colonial powers left. Jakarta claims that Ambalat is part of the Bulungan sultanate, which became part of Indonesia upon independence in 1945. Malaysia's claim is based on its own controversial 1979 map and the 2002 International Court of Justice (ICJ) judgement which awarded the nearby Islands of Sipadan and Ligitan to Malaysia. From the 1990s to the mid-2000s, a flurry of oil exploration concessions were awarded to various oil companies, likely as a way for the countries to demonstrate ownership over the region as well as to reap its economic benefits. Indonesia awarded the concession for the Bukat block – also an area between East Kalimantan and Ambalat – to the Italian oil and gas company ENI in 1988, and later in 1999 gave the same company the concession for the Ambalat block. Indonesia also gave the American oil company Unocal an exploration licence for Ambalat in December 2004. The dispute over Ambalat heightened in February 2005 when Malaysia began issuing exploration licenses to its national oil company Petronas in partnership with Royal Dutch/Shell Group for two deep-water oil concessions which included ND6 and ND7. This later led to military skirmishes between the two countries and aroused public anger in Indonesia.

At the height of the Ambalat dispute, the Indonesian Directorate General of Sea Transport proceeded to construct a twenty-metre lighthouse on Karang Unarang, an atoll located within the Ambalat waters which only appears at low tide. From Jakarta's perspective, the lighthouse was built on the premise that Karang Unarang was located within its waters. In February 2005, Malaysia proceeded to issue an exploration licence to Royal Dutch Shell Group. That same month also witnessed the Malaysian naval police arrest Indonesians who were working on the construction of the Karang Unarang lighthouse. Indonesia immediately responded with protests and dispatched naval vessels and fighter planes to patrol the disputed zone, threatening to militarize the situation and escalate tension with Malaysia. In retaliation, Malaysia sent gunboats and harassed Indonesians in the area. The events were widely reported in the Indonesian media, leading to protests in front of the Malaysian Embassy in Jakarta. President **Susilo Bambang Yudhoyono** stressed that Indonesia would not compromise its sovereignty and Vice-President Yusuf Kalla even threatened to wage war over the claims. Malaysia responded by sending the Royal Malaysian Navy and Marine police vessels to reinforce security in Sabah and Sarawak. Eventually Hasan Wirajuda and Syed Hamid Albar, then foreign ministers of Indonesia and Malaysia respectively, met to resolve the conflict in Jakarta on 5 March 2005. Following the meeting, both issued statements that committed their governments to restraint and peaceful resolution of the conflict.

see also: Yudhoyono, Susilo Bambang.

Anand Panyarachun (Thailand)

Anand Panyarachun served with distinction as interim prime minister of Thailand on two occasions during 1991–2. He was born in Bangkok on 9 August 1932 and received his secondary and higher education in England, graduating in law from Cambridge University in 1955. He then entered the Thai Ministry of Foreign Affairs, serving in later years as ambassador to the United States and then permanent representative to the United Nations. He returned to Thailand in 1976 with a reputation as a skilful diplomat to become permanent secretary (head) of the Ministry of Foreign Affairs but fell victim to the political purge by the military following a bloody coup in October 1976. During 1977–8, Anand served as ambassador to West Germany, resigning from the foreign service in 1979 to go into private business. In February 1991 a military coup removed the government of **Chatichai Choonhavan**. In March, Anand was persuaded by King **Bhumibol Adulyadej** to accept the post of interim prime minister until fresh elections were held. His mainly technocratic administration took a number of important and successful economic initiatives and enjoyed considerable popular support, in great part because of Anand's reputation for ability and integrity. He relinquished office with the elections in March 1992 but was asked by the king to resume it again after political violence in May, which was precipitated by the non-elected, retired general, **Suchinda Kraprayoon**, taking over as prime minister. Anand returned to high office in June 1992 and held it until elections in September produced a coalition government led by **Chuan Leekpai**. During his second and more limited tenure, Anand acted with royal and popular approval to circumscribe the powers and privileges of the military establishment.

In 1996 Anand was elected a member of the Constitution Drafting Assembly and appointed chairman of the drafting committee. He oversaw the drafting of what came to be called the **People's Constitution 1997**. The constitution would later be abrogated following the 2006 military coup supported by Anand. Anand also served from March 2005 as chairman of the National Reconciliation Commission tasked with exploring options for re-establishing peace in the restive southern provinces. Anand had become a fierce critic of the government of **Thaksin Shinawatra** and his handling of the southern unrest, particularly the imposition of the state of emergency decree. Although critical of Thaksin's handling of the situation, Anand refused to submit the NRC's final report, waiting instead for the results of the 2006 legislative elections. The recommendations were finally submitted on 5 June 2006, but were rejected by **Prem Tinsulanonda**, president of the Privy Council.

see also: Bhumibol Adulyadej; Chatichai Choonhavan; Chuan Leekpai; People's Constitution 1997; Prem Tinsulanonda, General; Suchinda Kraprayoon, General; Thaksin Shinawatra.

Ananda Mahidol, King (Thailand)

King Ananda Mahidol succeeded to the Thai throne in March 1935 following the abdication and exile of his uncle King Prajadhipok, who had conceded the end of the absolute monarchy in 1932. Born in 1925, he was then nine years old and at school in Lausanne. Apart from a brief visit to Bangkok in 1938, he remained in

Switzerland until after the end of the Pacific War, returning to Thailand in December 1945 with his younger brother **Bhumibol Adulyadej**. At the time, Thailand was adjusting to the end of a discredited collaborationist military rule and the introduction of civilian politics with **Pridi Phanomyong**, who had opposed the Japanese, as prime minister. On the morning of 9 June 1946, however, King Ananda was found shot dead in his bed in the Grand Palace in Bangkok. The initial official explanation was that the death had been an accident; the king and his brother had been known to play with guns. Rumours of regicide in order to create a republic prompted Prime Minister Pridi to appoint an official commission into the fatality but public unrest was unabated, aggravated by economic problems and corrupt practices. Ultimately, the death of the king served as a pretext for a military coup in November 1947 which restored to power the wartime leader Field Marshal **Phibul Songkram**. With the change of regime, further investigation of the death led to a prolonged trial and then the execution in 1955 of two royal pages and a friend of Pridi, which confirmed public suspicion of a plot. King Ananda was succeeded in June 1946 by his brother Bhumibol; the circumstances of his death have never been satisfactorily explained and have remained a forbidden topic in Thailand.

see also: Bhumibol Adulyadej; Phibul Songkram, Field Marshal; Pridi Phanomyong.

Angkatan Perpaduan Ummah (Malaysia)

Angkatan Perpaduan Ummah, which translates as Muslim Unity Front, was an electoral coalition which was formed by opposition Malay parties in June 1990 in the wake of the split within **UMNO** (United Malays National Organization) that occurred during 1987 when **Tengku Razaleigh Hamzah** unsuccessfully challenged **Mahathir Mohamad** for the leadership. The coalition comprised ***Parti Islam Se-Malaysia*** (PAS), ***Semangat '46***, *Berjasa* and another minor grouping, *Parti Nasional Muslimin Malaysia*. The Muslim Unity Front contested concurrent federal and state elections in October 1990 but was successful only in the state of Kelantan, where it won all thirty-nine seats in the legislature. It formed the state government but under the effective control of PAS and this was repeated after elections in April 1995. The Front provided an electoral vehicle of convenience for disparate political interests, but by 1996, tensions between the coalition partners reached breaking point over the division of political spoils and PAS's policy of Islamization. *Semangat '46* was formally dissolved in October 1996 and its members were admitted *en bloc* into UMNO, which marked the effective end of the Muslim Unity Front.

see also: Mahathir Mohamad, Tun; *Parti Islam Se-Malaysia*; Razaleigh Hamzah, Tengku; *Semangat '46*; UMNO.

Anglo-Malayan/Malaysian Defence Agreement 1957–71 (Malaya/Malaysia/Singapore)

A commitment by Britain to the external defence of Malaya in return for which it was granted the right to maintain military forces 'for the fulfilment of Commonwealth and international obligations' came into effect on 12 October 1957. In April 1959, through an exchange of letters with the government of Malaya, Australia and New Zealand formally associated themselves with those articles in the agreement which provided for the stationing of Commonwealth forces. The terms of the agreement were extended to all the territories of the enlarged Federation of Malaysia in an undertaking in November 1961, which came into effect from 16 September 1963. That extension of commitment was successfully tested during Indonesia's **Confrontation** of Malaysia during 1963–6. It was expanded to include Singapore, despite the island's separation from the Federation in August 1965. A meeting in London in April 1971 between representatives of Britain, Australia, New Zealand, Malaysia and Singapore reached an accord on the termination of the agreement on 1 November 1971. It was succeeded by the **Five Power Defence Arrangements** in which the explicit commitment to the external defence of the two Southeast Asian states was replaced by a provision for consultation only.

see also: Confrontation; Five Power Defence Arrangements (FPDA) 1971–.

Anti-Fascist People's Freedom League (AFPFL) (Burma/Myanmar)

The Anti-Fascist People's Freedom League (AFPFL) was a political organization set up in 1944 by the nationalist leader, **Aung San**. It was intended initially to challenge Japanese occupation in the context of changing military fortunes in the Pacific War but then became the vehicle for nationalist opposition to British plans for postwar Burma. Britain's political accommodation with the AFPFL paved the way for negotiations for independence which were concluded harmoniously in January 1947. In elections in April 1947, the AFPFL won 172 of the non-communal seats and thereby demonstrated its political dominance. It formed the first government after independence in January 1948 with **U Nu** as prime minister, Aung San having been assassinated in July 1947. Over the next decade as the country faced turbulence from ethnic-minority and Communist rebellion, the AFPFL proceeded to fragment. In April 1958 it split into two factions, with U Nu leading the majority alignment. It was then that the prime minister turned to General **Ne Win** to request that the army assume a caretaker role, which lasted for two years. U Nu's so-called 'clean' faction won elections held in February 1960 but the AFPFL government was removed with the military coup in March 1962 which also made the party illegal.

see also: Aung San; Ne Win, General; U Nu.

Anupong Paochinda, General (Thailand)

General Anupong Paochinda was commander-in-chief of the Royal Thai Army from October 2007 to December 2010 during a period of political turmoil in the country. He was a member of the junta that carried out a coup against the government of **Thaksin Shinawatra** in September 2006 and oversaw security operations during violent political protests in Bangkok in 2009 and 2010.

Anupong was born in Bangkok on 10 October 1949. He completed his primary schooling in Bangkok in 1965 and joined Class 10 of the Armed Forces Academies Preparatory School, graduating in 1967. He attended the Chulachomklao Royal Military Academy, graduating with Class 21 in 1972. Anupong received a degree in political science from Ramkhamhaeng University in 1993 and completed master's degrees at the National Defence College and the Institute of Development Administration in 2004. After rising through the ranks, Anupong eventually commanded the 21st Infantry Battalion, a unit responsible for protection of the royal family. He later commanded the 1st Infantry Division, a key unit based in Bangkok. At the time of the 2006 coup, Anupong was in command of the important Bangkok-based 1st Area Army. He was selected by the junta's Council of Ministers to succeed **Sonthi Boonyaratglin** as army commander on 19 September 2007, and confirmed in the appointment by the king on 1 October 2007. Anupong inherited an army which had been thrust back into politics by the 2006 coup. His forces were criticized during the 2008–10 political turmoil for seemingly supporting the elite establishment. Anupong declined to use force against the **People's Alliance for Democracy** protesting against the pro-Thaksin **People's Power Party** (PPP) governments of **Samak Sundaravej** and **Somchai Wongsawat**. Anupong brokered a **Democrat Party**-led government with military and establishment backing following the dissolution of the PPP. Under Anupong, Thai soldiers suppressed red shirt protestors in April 2009 and then launched two violent crackdowns on mass protests in Bangkok in April and May 2010. Anupong played an active role in counterinsurgency operations in the restive southern provinces, reducing the levels of violence during his command of the army. A staunch monarchist, Anupong retired from the army on 30 September 2010 and was appointed Privy Councillor. Following the 22 May 2014 coup, Anupong was appointed advisor for security to the military government.

see also: Democrat Party; People's Alliance for Democracy; People's Power Party; Samak Sundaravej; Somchai Wongsawat; Sonthi Boonyaratglin, General; Thaksin Shinawatra.

Anwar Ibrahim (Malaysia)

An immensely charismatic politician with a cerebral persona, Anwar Ibrahim is currently *de facto* leader of the Malaysian opposition coalition, ***Pakatan Rakyat*** (PR). He was elected deputy president of **UMNO** in November 1993 and appointed deputy prime minister of Malaysia a month later, and served in those positions until September 1998 when he was dismissed against a context of economic adversity and political differences with Prime Minister **Mahathir Mohamad**.

Anwar Ibrahim was born on 10 August 1947 in Bukit Mertajam and was educated at the University of Malaya in the late 1960s where he read Malay Studies. He became the charismatic leader of **ABIM**, the Islamic Youth movement, which he founded in 1971 and which posed a radical challenge to the UMNO-dominated government. In 1974, Anwar was detained for leading a protest in support of rice farmers in the state of Kedah. It came as a great surprise, therefore, when he announced that he was joining UMNO to stand as a parliamentary candidate in general elections in April 1982. His Islamic credentials and close association with Prime Minister Mahathir Mohamad were judged to have been important factors in helping to fend off the electoral challenge of the opposition ***Parti Islam Se-Malaysia*** (PAS). With electoral success, he was appointed a junior minister in the Prime Minister's Office. In September 1982, Anwar was elected a vice-president of UMNO and head of the party's youth wing. He then rose steadily in government, assuming in succession the youth, culture and sport; agriculture; and education portfolios. During the power struggle within UMNO in 1987 in which Mahathir was challenged by **Tengku Razaleigh Hamzah**, Anwar remained fiercely loyal to the prime minister, who triumphed over his political adversary. In March 1991, after the resignation of the incumbent **Daim Zainuddin**, he was appointed minister of finance. Although he entered politics from an Islamic base, Anwar Ibrahim advocated religious pluralism in a Malaysian society divided along racial–religious lines. Prior to the onset of economic adversity in the late 1990s, Anwar Ibrahim was widely regarded as the Mahathir's chosen successor. However, his perceived challenge to Mahathir at a time of economic difficulty prompted the prime minister to act to destroy politically his younger protégé in order to try to salvage his own historical reputation.

After mounting a campaign for political reform, Anwar was detained under the now-defunct Internal Security Act and assaulted in custody, which provoked anti-government protests and international criticism. He was then charged with corruption and sexual misconduct. Anwar pleaded not guilty claiming that he was the victim of a political conspiracy, while his cause was taken up by his wife Wan Azizah Ismail who founded the *Parti Keadilan Nasional* (National Justice Party) – which later became ***Parti Keadilan Rakyat*** (People's Justice Party or PKR) – in his support. In April 1999, Anwar was found guilty of four charges of corruption (abuse of power) and sentenced to six years' imprisonment, which precipitated public disorder in Kuala Lumpur. Anwar was also found guilty of sodomy in August 2000 and sentenced to nine years in prison, but the conviction was overturned by the Federal Court in 2004 and Anwar was released. As he was banned from joining politics for five years following his release, he took on teaching positions in Oxford, Johns Hopkins and Georgetown universities. Anwar returned to politics when his ban from public office expired in April 2008, just one month after Malaysia's twelfth general elections. In August that year he was returned to parliament after a landslide victory at a by-election for the seat of Permatang Pauh. His return to politics was not short of controversy: in 2008, Anwar was again facing sodomy charges. A two-year trial began in 2010 and ended with an acquittal.

Since his dismissal from government, Anwar has played an instrumental role in opposition politics. In 1999, his cause was taken up by a reinvigorated opposition movement leading to significant gains against the incumbent ***Barisan Nasional*** (National Front, BN) in federal elections that year. In 2008, Anwar was the linchpin for an opposition alliance featuring the **Democratic Action Party** (DAP), PAS and PKR that managed to deny the BN a two-thirds parliamentary majority for the first time in Malaysian history. In 2013, Anwar led the three parties, which had by then formally coalesced into the PR coalition, to an unprecedented fifty-one per cent of the popular vote and eighty-nine parliamentary seats.

Anwar's successful 2004 appeal against his sodomy conviction was overturned in March 2014 and he was subsequently sentenced to five years' imprisonment, pending appeal. This latest move has been viewed in many quarters as a politically motivated gambit on the part of the incumbent regime in response to rumours in early 2014 that Anwar would contest a state by-election in Selangor so as to eventually assume the post of chief minister of the opposition-held state, Malaysia's richest and most industrialized, from where he not only would have access to state coffers but also to the Conference of Rulers comprising Malaysia's nine sultans and four governors.

see also: ABIM; *Barisan Nasional*; Daim Zanuddin, Tun; Democratic Action Party; Mahathir Mohamad, Tun; *Pakatan Rakyat*; *Parti Islam Se-Malaysia*; *Parti Keadilan Rakyat*; Razaleigh Hamzah, Tengku; UMNO.

APEC (Asia-Pacific Economic Cooperation) 1989– (Brunei/Indonesia/Malaysia/Philippines/Singapore/Thailand/Vietnam)

APEC is an organization of twenty-one member economies set up in November 1989 as a result of an Australian initiative with the object of promoting freer multilateral trade and investment within Asia-Pacific. That initiative was prompted by concern over lack of progress in the Uruguay Round of the General Agreement on Tariffs and Trade (GATT) and the prospect of exclusive trade blocs developing in North America and Europe. For that reason, all members of **ASEAN** (Association of Southeast Asian Nations) joined APEC at the outset, but with mixed feelings over the extent to which the association might have its separate regional identity diluted as a consequence. Indeed, it was in January 1992, not long after APEC's formation, that ASEAN's heads of governments decided to establish a free trade area, known as **AFTA**, for members of the association. Although APEC was represented initially as a loose consultative body, its members agreed in September 1992 to set up a small permanent secretariat in Singapore. That sign of institutionalization may well have prompted Malaysia's prime minister, **Mahathir Mohamad**, to propose an alternative East Asian Economic Grouping at the end of the year, subsequently modified to an East Asian Economic Caucus (EAEC).

The character of APEC changed as a result of an initiative by US President Bill Clinton in July 1993 to hold a meeting of APEC's political leaders following a scheduled ministerial meeting in Seattle in November. His grandiose scheme to use APEC as the prime vehicle for creating a so-called 'New Pacific Community' was greeted without enthusiasm by ASEAN governments, while Mahathir took particular offence and boycotted the meeting. In the event, the summit passed off without incident but failed to rise above declaratory commitments on trade liberalization. However, it did mark a qualitative change in the structure and intended role of APEC because President **Suharto** agreed to host a second summit in Indonesia in the following year which has set an annual pattern. In Bogor in November 1994, the members of APEC agreed on a two-step approach to free and open trade and investment in the region by 2020. Much of the impetus for an accord on general principles came from the host government of President Suharto, which saw the occasion as an opportunity to demonstrate the international standing of Indonesia while chair of the Non-Aligned Movement. Once again, the only openly discordant note was struck by Prime Minister Mahathir, who attended the meeting but issued reservations to the effect that his government would commit itself to trade liberalization on a unilateral basis only at a pace and capacity commensurate with Malaysia's level of development. Private reservations about the pace of trade liberalization are more widely shared within ASEAN because of concerns about the vulnerability of national markets to seemingly unfair competition. At Osaka in November 1995, the Bogor Action Agenda was reaffirmed but also qualified by provision for flexibility 'in the liberalization and facilitation process' to take account of the different levels of development and diverse circumstances in APEC economies. The meeting in Vancouver in November 1997 was dominated by the **Asian Financial Crisis** and revealed the limitations of APEC whose leaders acknowledged the central role of the International Monetary Fund. Plans were made for liberalizing trade in nine sectors but there was an impasse at the meeting in Kuala Lumpur in November 1998 over fast-track liberalization. The meeting in 1997 had admitted Peru, Russia and Vietnam to membership but also imposed a ten-year moratorium on new entries. By the end of the century, in addition to the seven ASEAN states listed above, the members of APEC were Australia, Canada, Chile, China, Hong Kong, Japan, South Korea, Mexico, New Zealand, Papua New Guinea, Peru, Russia, Taiwan and the United States.

The 2001 meeting in China was dominated by discussions on the war on terror, and commitments were made to enhance counterterrorism cooperation. This was significant, as it was the first time APEC explicitly dealt with a non-economic issue. Furthermore, the Shanghai Accord which clarified APEC's roadmap towards achieving free trade and investment goals was adopted. Representation of Taiwan in APEC has remained an issue, as Beijing rejected Taiwan's choice of former vice-president Li Yuan-zu, and in response, the government of Taiwan refused to select another representative and boycotted the 2001 meeting. Following 2001, meetings in subsequent years focused on achieving sustainable and equitable growth so as to reduce economic disparities by meeting the Bogor Goals of trade and investment liberalization, enhancement of human security, and promoting good governance and a knowledge-based society. At the 2004 Santiago meeting, the Santiago Initiative for Expanded Trade in APEC was launched, and it had the aim of capacity building of all member state economies so as to implement trade liberalization. In the 2006 Hanoi meeting, support for the Doha Development Round remained a top priority. The 2001 target which aimed to achieve a five per cent reduction in trade transaction costs by 2006 was reached, and therefore the next Trade Facilitation Action Plan (TFAP II) was endorsed, which targeted a further five per cent reduction of trade transaction costs in the APEC region by 2010. The 2007 meeting stressed the need for a successful conclusion of the WTO Doha Round, and to address the challenges of climate change through the adoption of the Declaration on Climate Change, Energy Security and Clean Development, which set an APEC-wide target for reducing energy intensity by at least twenty-five per cent by 2030. Discussions on prospects for a Free Trade Area of the Asia-Pacific were inconclusive. The 2008 meeting concentrated mainly on the global financial crisis at the time.

APEC's experience has also revealed some of the weaknesses of voluntary cooperation among countries with diverse economies and at various developmental levels. While cooperation has brought down barriers to trade and investment, there remains a lack of liberalization of 'sensitive sectors' such as agriculture. In addition to this, APEC's response to the 1997–8 Asian Financial Crisis was limited. Furthermore, the role of APEC is increasingly being challenged due to the proliferation of bilateral Free Trade Agreements (FTAs) and sub-regional forms of economic cooperation in response to the impasse at the WTO rounds. There are several countries seeking membership in APEC, such as India, Pakistan, Bangladesh, Sri Lanka, Macau, Mongolia, Laos, Cambodia, Costa Rica, Colombia, Panama and Ecuador.

see also: AFTA; ASEAN; Asian Financial Crisis 1997–8; Mahathir Mohamad, Tun; Suharto.

Aquino, Benigno (Philippines)

Benigno (popularly known as Ninoy) Aquino was the most prominent and effective opposition leader during the first decade of President **Ferdinand Marcos'** authoritarian rule. He was imprisoned on the introduction of martial law in September 1972 and remained in detention until the end of the decade, when he was allowed to travel to the United States for heart surgery. After recovery, he remained in the United States as a rallying point for political dissent. He returned to the Philippines in August 1983, driven by a concern to sustain his political appeal and encouraged by evidence that Marcos was mortally ill. Aquino arrived at Manila airport on 21 August and was taken off the plane by armed members of the Aviation Security Command, one of whom shot him in the head as he was being led down stairs from the exit to the runway and a waiting car (*see* **Ver, General Fabian**). His blatant murder served to transform the political condition of the Philippines by arousing great popular anger against President Marcos and his regime. The assassination marked a political turning point which led directly to the collapse of Marcos' rule following fraudulent elections in February 1986.

Benigno Aquino was born on 27 November 1932 into an elite landowning family from Tarlac Province, north of Manila. His father had been a member of the prewar Senate and controversially the speaker of the Legislative Assembly set up under the Japanese occupation. Aquino first made his mark as a journalist for the *Manila Times* at the age of seventeen when he covered the Korean War. Then, after qualifying as a lawyer, he married Corazón Cojuangco, a member of an immensely wealthy Sino-Philippine family (*see* **Corazón Aquino**). He entered politics in 1955 and secured election as Mayor of Tarlac but was then disqualified for being below the minimum age of twenty-three. Two years later, he successfully contested the office of vice-governor of the province and became governor at the age of twenty-seven when the incumbent joined the national cabinet. Over the next five years, Aquino acquired a national reputation as a capable administrator. In 1967 he stood successfully for the Senate but was obliged to win a court case to hold on to his seat because he had reached the minimum age of thirty-five only on taking the oath of office after the elections had taken place. In the Senate, Aquino became a vigorous opponent of Marcos, who had been president for two years. He was returned to the Senate for a second term in 1971 and was regarded as the politician most likely to succeed Marcos, who was permitted to serve only two terms under the constitution. In September 1972 Marcos declared martial law in an attempt to retain power. Aquino was then arrested and charged with murder and the illegal possession of firearms; he was ultimately sentenced to death by a military tribunal. In the event, he was executed in cold blood because his return to the Philippines in 1983 constituted a direct political threat to the decaying Marcos regime. Ironically, that execution served only to accelerate that decay.

see also: Aquino, Corazón; Marcos, Ferdinand; Ver, General Fabian.

Aquino III, Benigno Simeon Cojuangco (Philippines)

Benigno Simeon Cojuangco Aquino, III is the fifteenth president of the Republic of the Philippines. He is the son of the late political activist and senator, **Benigno Aquino**, and former president **Corazón Aquino**. Aquino comes from a long line of politicians. His great grandfather served in the Malolos Congress while his grandfather served in the Philippine Congress. His father was elected senator in 1967 and became a vocal critic of the administration of **Ferdinand Marcos**.

Aquino graduated from the Ateneo de Manila University with a Bachelor's Degree in Economics. After graduation, he joined his family in exile in the United States. When his father was assassinated in 1983, Aquino returned to the Philippines. He was later elected as congressman for Tarlac province. Aquino was re-elected several times, and in 2007 won a seat in the Senate. Amidst popular dissatisfaction with the administration of **Gloria Macapagal-Arroyo**, Aquino ran for presidency in 2010, announcing his candidature a month after his mother's death. Aquino capitalized on this popular dissatisfaction by reviving memories of the first **EDSA** revolution that overthrew Marcos and was swept into power in the May election by a landslide. At the onset of his administration, Aquino announced that anti-corruption would evolve to become a major preoccupation. Since then, he has stood firm in his anti-corruption advocacy, deriding his predecessor and declaring that her policies had not only increased corruption in the country, but also aggravated the poverty and hardship which Filipinos were experiencing. Beyond the rhetoric however, results from his first years in office have not been convincing. After bringing Aquino into power, popular sentiment has started to gravitate away from the president as a result of growing frustration at his inability to implement more substantive policies to address challenges inherited from the previous government. Such was the extent of popular disillusionment that the epithet 'Noynoying' – in reference to Aquino's nickname 'Noynoy' – was coined by the media to describe the Aquino administration's foot-dragging. The early months of Aquino's tenure also saw him confronted with the **Manila Hostage Crisis**, which resulted in the death of eight tourists from Hong Kong. Controversially, while he took responsibility for the incident and expressed regret that it happened, he has maintained that the Philippines did not need to apologize for it. With the **Moro Islamic Liberation Front** (MILF), Aquino pushed for the signing of a major peace deal, for which a framework peace agreement was eventually agreed in October 2012. Aquino followed this up with a landmark visit to the MILF stronghold in Sultan Kudarat, the first Philippine president to make a peaceful visit to a MILF camp.

On the foreign policy front, a major challenge for Aquino has been the escalation of tensions with China over competing claims in the **South China Sea**. Tensions became particularly acute when both parties claimed territorial jurisdiction over **Scarborough Shoal**. Under pressure from domestic constituencies and intent on portraying an image of strength, Aquino firmly expressed that the Shoal was part of Philippine territory and called on the United States and the international community to support its claim. China reacted to this escalation by curtailing the import of bananas from the Philippines as well as reducing the number of Chinese tourists headed to the archipelago. As a consequence of these pressures, Aquino was forced to soften his administration's stance on the issue and focus on behind-the-scenes negotiations both bilaterally and as part of the **ASEAN** effort to achieve a Code of Conduct on the South China Sea in accordance with the aspiration of the **Declaration on the Conduct of Parties in the South China Sea** (DOC).

see also: Aquino, Benigno; Aquino, Corazón; ASEAN; Declaration on the Conduct of Parties in the South China Sea (ASEAN) 2002; EDSA; Macapagal-Arroyo, Gloria; Manila Hostage Crisis; Marcos, Ferdinand; Moro Islamic Liberation Front; Scarborough Shoal Dispute; South China Sea.

Aquino, Corazón (Philippines)

Corazón Aquino was president of the Philippines from February 1986 until June 1992, when she gave up office without seeking re-election. She was born on 25 January 1933 into the extremely wealthy landowning Cojuangco family from Tarlac Province. She entered politics as a result of personal tragedy: her husband **Benigno Aquino** – whom she married in 1954 and by whom she had four children – had been murdered at Manila airport in August 1983 on his return from exile in the United States. As an aggrieved widow, she became politically active in challenging President **Ferdinand Marcos**, whom she held personally responsible for her husband's fate. When Marcos announced a snap election in late 1985, Corazón Aquino was persuaded to stand against him. That election was fraudulently conducted and provoked a military rebellion. The rebellion was on the point of being crushed when Church leaders mobilized massive popular support in Manila in Corazón Aquino's name (*see* **EDSA**; **Jaime Sin**). This display of so-called 'People Power' together with US encouragement persuaded Marcos to go into exile. Corazón Aquino succeeded him as the first female president of the republic.

As a political leader, Corazón Aquino suffered from the defects of her qualities. As the saintly widow of Benigno Aquino, she represented moral virtue. Indeed, the very lack of political experience and taint seemed to qualify her for high office. But in office, moral strength was translated into political weakness and indecisiveness. Corazón Aquino's prime achievement was in restoring constitutional democracy but she was never able to capitalize on her national standing to contain the political contention which followed, and which obstructed any attempt to address deep-seated economic and social problems. Buffeted from both right and left, Corazón Aquino sought to lead through conciliation, which exposed her to charges of weakness and encouraged military challenges. The most serious of these took place in December 1989, when she was saved from political overthrow only by US military intervention. By that juncture, the high promise of her assumption of office had gone sour as she became identified with vacillation and drift. Moreover, her personal credibility had been tainted by the financial malpractices of members of her family. She salvaged some of her initial reputation, however, when she kept her word in not seeking a second term of presidential office through exploiting the letter of the constitution. Moreover, she was able to play an important role in determining the identity of her successor through public support for **Fidel Ramos**, who as chief of staff of the armed forces and then minister of defence had acted loyally to obstruct military coups against her. Out of office, Corazón Aquino avoided political activity with the important exception of defending her democratic legacy against attempts by presidents Fidel Ramos and **Joseph Estrada** to change the constitution for possible personal advantage.

In 2000 Corazón Aquino lent her voice to growing calls for the resignation of the president, Joseph Estrada, because of allegations of corruption. Attempts to impeach President Estrada were unsuccessful, but he was eventually ousted by popular revolt in January 2001, in a reprise of the 1986 EDSA revolution that removed Ferdinand Marcos. Corazón Aquino initially supported the ascendency of **Gloria Macapagal-Arroyo** to the presidency, but later led massive demonstrations against her for rigging the 2004 presidential elections. In the 2007 senatorial elections, Corazón Aquino actively campaigned for her son, **Benigno Aquino III**. In December 2008, Corazón Aquino publicly expressed regret for her role in ousting Joseph Estrada and apologized to the former president. She was diagnosed with colon cancer that year, and died on 1 August 2009. Her son was elected president of the Philippines almost a year later, and sworn into office in June 2010.

see also: Aquino, Benigno; Aquino III, Benigno Simeon Cojuangco; EDSA; Estrada, Joseph; Macapagal-Arroyo, Gloria; Marcos, Ferdinand; Ramos, Fidel; Sin, Cardinal Jaime.

Archipelago Declaration 1957 (Indonesia)

On 13 December 1957 Indonesia's government unilaterally extended the breadth of its territorial waters from three to twelve nautical miles. Concurrently, it asserted the right to establish a system of linked straight baselines around the archipelago connecting the outermost points of its outermost islands. This claim to the same quality of jurisdiction over waters surrounding and intersecting the island constituents of the republic as applied to its territory was pressed by Professor Mochtar Kusumaatmadja at successive United Nations Conferences on the Law of the Sea from 1958. Indonesia's claim was conceded at the conclusion of the Third Conference in November 1982 and incorporated in the UN Convention on the Law of the Sea in return for rights of maritime passage through the archipelago also incorporated in the convention. In October 1999, in an indication of a renewed interest in protecting Indonesia's archipelagic interests, President **Abdurrahman Wahid** appointed a minister with special responsibility for maritime exploration, in addition to a minister of communications, to his cabinet.

see also: Wahid, Abdurrahman.

Article 11 Coalition (Malaysia)

The Article 11 Coalition brings together thirteen Malaysian civil society groups which seek to defend the rights of non-Muslims especially on issues related to religious freedom and conversion (*see* **Lina Joy Issue**). Although Malaysia has both secular and *shari'a* legal systems that run in parallel, the legal process is nevertheless viewed as biased against non-Muslims on religious matters. Cases such as that of Moorthy Abdullah in 2005 exemplified the concerns of the coalition: Moorthy was an army corporal who allegedly converted to Islam and later passed away. His wife, Sharmala, however, maintained that he was still a Hindu and hence should have a Hindu funeral. Her claim was rejected by the *Shari'a* Court which then proceeded with a Muslim burial without Moorthy's wife's consent. The civil court refused to intervene on the grounds that it could not overrule decisions made by the *Shari'a* Court. At the same time, because the *Shari'a* Court had no jurisdiction to hear non-Muslim cases, Sharmala was effectively left with no legal recourse. Named after Article 11 in the federal constitution which guarantees the freedom of religion, the coalition aims to promote awareness and advocate respect for constitutional guarantees of equal protection for every person in a multicultural Malaysia. Activities which the coalition has engaged in mostly take the form of public forums, public education, and legal advice and assistance. Predictably, the activities of the coalition have drawn the ire of Muslim civil society groups and organizations that see them as a threat to the position of Islam in the country, several of which have rallied to form groups such as an Anti-Article 11 Coalition and ***Pembela***.

see also: Lina Joy Issue; *Pembela*.

ASA (Association of Southeast Asia) 1961–7 (Malaya/Malaysia/Philippines/Thailand)

The Association of Southeast Asia (ASA) was a short-lived experiment in regional cooperation established on 31 July 1961 in Bangkok between the governments of Malaya, the Philippines and Thailand. It was intended to offer an alternative approach to security to that provided by military alliances and especially by the ill-regarded **SEATO** (Southeast Asia Treaty Organization). Its underlying rationale was that economic progress provided the foundation for political stability and the best guarantee for political independence. ASA foundered within two years without significant practical achievement, primarily because of a territorial dispute between the Philippines and Malaya over the **Philippines' Claim to Sabah**, a northern Borneo territory. The dispute was aggravated at ASA's expense because of the concurrent challenge of **Confrontation** by Indonesia, supported by the Philippines, to the legitimacy of Malaya's constitutional successor Malaysia. ASA was revived temporarily in March 1966 as Confrontation waned but was superseded in the following year, in a concession to Indonesia, by the new **ASEAN** (Association of Southeast Asian Nations). ASEAN adopted the institutional structure and also the approach to security pioneered without success by ASA.

see also: ASEAN; Confrontation; Philippines' Claim to Sabah; SEATO.

ASEAN (Association of Southeast Asian Nations) 1967– (Brunei/Cambodia/Indonesia/Laos/Malaysia/Myanmar/Philippines/Singapore/Thailand/Vietnam)

The Association of Southeast Asian Nations (ASEAN) was established on 8 August 1967 at a meeting in Bangkok of the foreign ministers of Indonesia, the Philippines, Singapore and Thailand and the deputy prime minister of Malaysia. Brunei joined in January 1984, Vietnam was admitted in July 1995, while Myanmar and Laos entered in July 1997 but Cambodia's membership was delayed until April 1999. Although bound by common Cold War concerns, the initial objective of the founding members was to locate regional reconciliation (in the wake of Indonesia's **Confrontation** of Malaysia) within an institutionalized structure of relations. Under the terms of the **Bangkok Declaration 1967**, ASEAN's prime formal purpose was to promote economic and social cooperation but its underlying undeclared goal was political cooperation. That cooperation has expressed itself in an intramural practice of conflict avoidance and management and in a role as a diplomatic community on regional issues. The founding Declaration also indicated a prerogative aspiration to manage regional order, which was registered in a declaratory commitment by its foreign ministers in Kuala Lumpur in November 1971 to make Southeast Asia a **ZOPFAN** (Zone of Peace, Freedom and Neutrality). That aspiration has not been realized, in important part because of the absence of a shared strategic perspective among member governments.

A meagre performance in economic cooperation, an aversion to formal defence cooperation and only limited political cooperation made up the sum of ASEAN's record until the success of revolutionary communism in Indochina during 1975. Moreover, the viability of the Association had been tested in the late 1960s by the revival of the **Philippines' Claim to Sabah**, a part of Malaysia. Its members responded to political change in Indochina by closing ranks and convening the first meeting of heads of government at the **Bali Summit** in February 1976. A formal commitment to political cooperation was expressed in a **Declaration of ASEAN Concord**, while provision for a norms-based regional order and for dispute settlement was contained in a **Treaty of Amity and Cooperation**. Defence cooperation under ASEAN's aegis was ruled out but sanctioned on a primarily bilateral basis outside of the walls of the Association. A second **Kuala Lumpur Summit** in August 1977 failed to generate an anticipated economic cooperation but attracted the presence of the prime ministers of Australia, New Zealand and Japan who began a practice of ASEAN Post-Ministerial Conferences with dialogue partners, which has become institutionalized. Political cooperation among member governments was effectively displayed in the wake of Vietnam's invasion of Kampuchea (Cambodia) in December 1978. By employing their regional credentials and highlighting the sanctity of national sovereignty, the ASEAN states were able to deny legitimacy to the government conveyed into Phnom Penh by Vietnam's occupying army. During the 1980s, they attracted strong voting support in the General Assembly of the United Nations for an annual resolution calling for Vietnam's military withdrawal from Cambodia, which materialized from September 1989.

With the end of the Cold War and the attendant resolution of the Cambodian conflict as an international problem, ASEAN was faced with a new and uncertain strategic environment distinguished by a change in the pattern of international alignments that had sustained its collective diplomacy against Vietnam. To meet this challenge, a meeting of ASEAN's foreign ministers together with those from the United States, China, Russia and other regional states in Singapore in July 1993 agreed to inaugurate the **ASEAN Regional Forum** (ARF) as a wider vehicle for addressing security issues, which held its first working session in Bangkok in July 1994. ASEAN's successful ARF initiative demonstrated the political standing of the Association in the wake of the Cambodian conflict but it also indicated an abdication from a prerogative attitude to managing regional order based on excluding major powers from a superintending role. The Singapore Summit also saw a commitment to establishing an **AFTA** (ASEAN Free Trade Area) as well as an agreement to hold formal meetings of heads of government every three years.

Although ASEAN's foreign ministers were able to issue a **Declaration on the South China Sea** in Manila in July 1992, which called for peaceful resolution of jurisdictional disputes, the end of the Cold War and the attendant enlargement of the Association generated intramural discord as well as problems in external relations. Vietnam's entry in July 1995 was regarded as an historic reconciliation and uncontroversial. However, the entry of Myanmar in July 1997 attracted strong criticism from Western states because of Myanmar's deplorable human rights record with, for example, a disruption of dialogue with the states of the European Union. Additional controversy arose over the membership of Cambodia, which had also been expected to join in July 1997 close to the thirtieth anniversary of ASEAN's foundation. A bloody coup in Phnom Penh to the political advantage of the second prime minister, **Hun Sen**, just days before entry led the foreign ministers to defer Cambodia's membership. That issue proved to be contentious at the sixth **Hanoi Summit** in December 1998 and served to exemplify the greater difficulty in managing consensus within the enlarged Association. In the event, Cambodia was admitted to ASEAN in April 1999. The **Asian Financial Crisis** further compounded the disarray in the Association when it led to the overthrow of Indonesian president Suharto, leaving ASEAN without a natural political leader. Indeed, Indonesia's contribution to ASEAN had been a conspicuous rejection of past hegemonic ambitions and a willingness to defer to the strategic priorities of other members, exemplified in the case of Thailand during the Cambodian conflict, in the interests of regional harmony.

ASEAN is an intergovernmental body without aspirations to political integration of the kind associated with the European Union. A permanent secretariat was set up in Jakarta in June 1976 with limited service functions. The title of its principal administrative officer was secretary-general of the ASEAN Secretariat, *not* of ASEAN, for over a decade and a half until redesignated secretary-general of ASEAN at the Singapore Summit in January 1992. Until 2000, ASEAN's principal organ had been an annual meeting of foreign ministers serviced by a prior meeting of senior officials. At the fourth summit in Singapore in 1992, the Association agreed to regularize summit meetings every three years. In 1995, they decided to add an informal summit in each of the two years between summits. At the fourth informal summit in 2002, ASEAN leaders agreed to meet annually and to do away with the distinction between formal and informal summits. Concurrent with this evolution was the gradual increase in frequency and number of summits with non-ASEAN leaders through arrangements such as ASEAN Plus One, ASEAN Plus Three (APT), and more recently, the **East Asia Summit**.

During the ASEAN Summit in 2000, the ASEAN heads of state launched the Initiative for ASEAN Integration (IAI) with the objectives of Narrowing the Development Gap (NDG) and accelerating the economic integration of the relatively new members of ASEAN, namely Cambodia, Laos, Vietnam and Myanmar. With four ASEAN members involved in the **South China Sea** territorial and maritime disputes with China, ASEAN has played an active role in encouraging a common approach to peacefully resolve the disputes in accordance with international law. In November 2002, the foreign ministers of the ten ASEAN member countries and China signed the **Declaration on the Conduct of Parties in the South China Sea** (DOC), pledging to find a peaceful and durable solution for disputes among them in the South China Sea. Hopes for effective implementation of the DOC diminished as China and some Southeast Asian claimant states pressed their claims incrementally through a combination of juridical manoeuvring, militarization and nationalistic posturing. Given the circumstances, regional diplomacy was handicapped, culminating in the impasse of 2012, when the Association embarrassingly failed to reach a consensus for a joint statement for the first time in its history at the July ministerial meeting in Phnom Penh.

At the ninth ASEAN summit in October 2003, the ASEAN leaders signed the Declaration of ASEAN Concord II (or Bali Concord II) expressing their commitment to establish an **ASEAN Community**. The ASEAN Community, envisaged for implementation in 2020, is to be founded on three mutually reinforcing pillars: (1) an ASEAN Security Community for political and security cooperation, (2) an ASEAN Economic Community for economic integration, and (3) an ASEAN Socio-Cultural Community for socio-cultural cooperation. In 2004, the ASEAN **Vientiane Action Plan** (VAP) was established at the tenth ASEAN summit, and focused on deepening regional integration and narrowing the development gap between the ten member countries. The VAP was later replaced by the Roadmap for an ASEAN Community. During the twelfth ASEAN summit, ASEAN leaders decided to accelerate the establishment of the ASEAN Community, bringing the deadline forward from 2020 to 2015 and signing the Cebu Declaration on the Acceleration of the Establishment of an ASEAN Community by 2015. As part of the initiative of an ASEAN Economic Community, ASEAN has established a raft of bilateral free trade agreements with key dialogue partners.

The rise of regional giants China and India prompted the Association to aspire to greater cohesion. In the event, the **ASEAN Charter** was tabled in 2005 and entered into force in 2008, and conferred on the Association a legal personality. The ASEAN Charter codifies ASEAN principles, norms and rules, and provides the legal and institutional framework for achieving the goal of an ASEAN community. While the previous role of the secretary-general was to merely serve as a coordinating office devoid of substantive powers, the enactment of the Charter provided for the expansion of the secretariat's administrative mandate and of the role of the secretary-general who could now speak on behalf of ASEAN. The Charter further changed the schedule for the annual ASEAN chairmanship to run for the calendar year rather than the previous practice of starting at mid-year for twelve months. This change however necessitated that the Thai government hold its position as the chair for an unprecedented period of eighteen months from mid-2008 to the end of 2009 in order to synchronize the schedule. In 2006, the ASEAN Defence Ministers' Meeting (**ADMM**) was inaugurated as part of the aspiration for the creation of an ASEAN Security Community. In 2010, an ADMM-Plus process was initiated to allow the ADMM to engage with ASEAN dialogue partners on defence issues.

see also: ADMM; AFTA; ASEAN Charter; ASEAN Community; ASEAN Regional Forum; Asian Financial Crisis 1997–8; Bali Summit 1976; Bangkok Declaration 1967; Confrontation; Declaration of ASEAN Concord 1976; Declaration on the Conduct of Parties in the South China Sea (ASEAN) 2002; Declaration on the South China Sea (ASEAN) 1992; East Asia Summit; Hanoi Summit 1998; Hun Sen; Kuala Lumpur Summit 1977; Philippines' Claim to Sabah; South China Sea; Treaty of Amity and Cooperation 1976; Vientiane Action Plan; ZOPFAN.

ASEAN Charter (Charter of the Association of Southeast Asian Nations) (Brunei/Cambodia/Indonesia/Laos/Malaysia/Myanmar/Philippines/Singapore/Thailand/Vietnam)

The ASEAN Charter is a legally binding agreement signed by the ten **ASEAN** member states that codifies ASEAN principles, norms and rules, and provides the legal and institutional framework for achieving the goal of an ASEAN community.

The proposal for the Charter was formally tabled at the **Kuala Lumpur Summit** of ASEAN (the eleventh ASEAN summit) in December 2005. The decision was taken in Kuala Lumpur to establish an Eminent Persons Group (EPG) consisting of distinguished and respected statesmen, with the mandate of making recommendations for the Charter. They would do so through meetings and consultation with various stakeholders such as the business community, members of parliament, academics and civil society. The EPG submitted their recommendations to the ASEAN leaders at the **Cebu Summit** (twelfth ASEAN summit). A High Level Task Force (HLTF) set up at the summit and consisting of senior government officials, was tasked to draft the Charter. A much watered-down version from that proposed by the EPG was subsequently signed by ASEAN leaders in November 2007 at the thirteenth ASEAN summit. Within a year, all ten members ratified the agreement and the Charter entered into force on 15 December 2008.

A major issue that provided the impetus for the Charter was the matter of member states' non-compliance with rules, decisions and agreements. The prioritization of self-interest over regional collective interests and therefore, ASEAN's history of members not honouring agreements has meant that economic integration has been slow despite the numerous agreements that have been signed and ratified. Given the strong aversion towards the development of any supranational enforcement mechanism, ASEAN agreements have often been characterized by the use of vague terms such as 'promoting' or 'encouraging' that fail to define clearly practical rules on matters of cooperation. They have also been declarations of intent rather than cooperation on implementation on such agreements. The Charter was seen as a mechanism to address the ineffectiveness of a consensual approach and hence the EPG's recommendation to abolish it in favour of decision by majority rule; this provision was however later dropped in a compromise in exchange for having a human rights body instead, due to strong opposition from newer member states such as Vietnam and Cambodia.

There is no gainsaying that the ASEAN Charter reflected the organization's lofty aspirations. Under the Charter, ASEAN would acquire a legal personality distinct from that of its member states. People would be at the centre in the community-building process. There would be increased commitment to democratic accountability and the protection of human rights, which includes the establishment of an ASEAN human rights body. A greater role would also be given to foreign ministers who would form an ASEAN Coordinating Council (ACC) charged with preparation for meetings and implementation of decisions. But for all that is said, the Charter only tells us the intentions laid out by its signatories. In practical terms, what has actually been achieved or can be achieved remains bound by the principles of consensus and consultation that continue to characterize decision-making within ASEAN. In particular, the inclusion of the goal of promoting sovereignty-transcending norms of democracy and protecting human rights appears to run directly counter to ASEAN's much cherished norm of non-interference and state sovereignty. ASEAN had been under considerable internal and international pressure to take a proactive approach in promoting democracy, good governance and human rights. But this new agenda of democracy, driven largely by the Philippines and Indonesia, is not shared by all members. In fact, pursuing this lofty objective could potentially undermine regional unity which has hitherto been predicated on the mutual respect for sovereignty and non-interference in each other's internal affairs. Equally surprising was the proposal to establish an ASEAN human rights body given that the many ASEAN members are possessed of a longstanding aversion to the notion of universal human rights, deeming it to be a Western idea that is incompatible with 'Asian values'. Paradoxically, the decision to go ahead with the signing of the Charter despite the Myanmar junta's bloody repression of demonstrations led by Buddhist monks two months before the signing of the Charter in September 2007 (*see* **Saffron Revolution**), dealt a huge blow to ASEAN credibility, and in particular to their professed objectives to strengthen democracy, enhance good governance and the rule of law, and to promote human rights and fundamental freedoms. While as a collective they issued a strong statement condemning the violent clampdown, the acquiescence to Myanmar's protest over a scheduled briefing by Ibrahim Gambari, UN envoy to Myanmar, betrayed the persistence of the longstanding ASEAN norms of non-interference.

see also: ASEAN; Cebu Summit; Kuala Lumpur Summit; Saffron Revolution.

ASEAN Community (Brunei/Cambodia/Indonesia/Laos/Malaysia/Myanmar/Philippines/Singapore/Thailand/Vietnam)

At the **Bali Summit** in Indonesia on 7 October 2003, the leaders of the ten **ASEAN** (Association of Southeast Asian Nations) member countries signed the **Declaration of ASEAN Concord II** (or Bali Concord II), declaring their intention to establish an ASEAN Community.

In recent years, ASEAN member countries have felt increasingly threatened by the intrusive economic and political assertiveness of extra-regional powers. In response, ASEAN leaders have registered the need to act collectively to gain better bargaining power on economic and political issues. In addition to external pressures, intra-regional issues which involve the security of the region such as cross-border tensions, terrorism and illegal migration have also prompted leaders to seek further consolidation and enhancement of cooperation between them in order to ensure economic and social stability in the region, as well as peaceful and progressive national development. The leaders acknowledged that sustainable economic development required a secure political environment based on a strong foundation of mutual interests generated by economic cooperation and political solidarity.

The ASEAN Community, envisaged for implementation in 2020, is to be founded on three pillars: (1) an ASEAN Security Community or ASC for political and security cooperation, (2) an ASEAN Economic Community or AEC for economic integration, and (3) an ASEAN Socio-Cultural Community or ASCC for socio-cultural cooperation. These three pillars are envisaged to be closely intertwined and mutually reinforcing to ensure durable peace, stability and prosperity in the region.

The framework to achieve an ASEAN Community has been drawn up to address each individual pillar. The ASC is envisaged to ensure peaceful processes are employed in the settlement of intra-regional differences. The ASC is also expected to address transboundary maritime issues and concerns in a holistic, integrated and comprehensive manner. On the other hand, the AEC will seek to create a stable and highly competitive ASEAN economic region with free flow of goods, services, investment and capital; equitable economic development; and reduced poverty and socio-economic disparities. The AEC will also establish ASEAN as a single market and production base, increasing ASEAN's strength in the global supply chain. Last but not least, the ASCC will aim to foster cooperation in social development targeted at raising the standard of living of disadvantaged groups and rural populations. The ASCC will also address issues in the work force, public health, promotion of ASEAN's diverse cultural heritage and fostering regional identity, population growth, unemployment, environmental degradation and transboundary pollution.

Conscious that accelerated establishment of an ASEAN Community will reinforce ASEAN's centrality and strength in charting the regional architecture, at the twelfth ASEAN summit ASEAN leaders decided to accelerate the establishment of an ASEAN Community, bringing the deadline forward from 2020 to 2015. Concomitantly, the Roadmap for an ASEAN Community (2009–15) consisting of the ASEAN Political-Security Community Blueprint, the ASEAN Economic Community Blueprint, the ASEAN Socio-Cultural Community Blueprint, and the IAI Work Plan 2 (2009–15), was drafted to replace the **Vientiane Action Plan**.

see also: ASEAN; Bali Summit 2003; Declaration of ASEAN Concord II 2003; Vientiane Action Plan 2004.

ASEAN Regional Forum (ARF) 1994–

(Brunei/Cambodia/Indonesia/Laos/Malaysia/Myanmar/Philippines/Singapore/Thailand/Timor-Leste/Vietnam)

The ASEAN Regional Forum (ARF) is an institution for multilateral security dialogue with the participation of twenty-seven states which was established at the initiative of **ASEAN** (Association of Southeast Asian Nations) during the annual meeting of its foreign ministers held in Singapore in July 1993. Its prime function is confidence-building and not conventional defence cooperation. At its **Singapore Summit** in January 1992, ASEAN's heads of government had agreed that security dialogue beyond conventional regional bounds could be undertaken through the vehicle of the Post-Ministerial Conference (PMC). This conference, which convenes immediately after the annual meeting of foreign ministers, then involved seven dialogue partners: Australia, Canada, the European Union, Japan, New Zealand, South Korea and the United States. At Singapore's initiative and with backing from its regional partners, an unprecedented meeting of senior officials from ASEAN states and their dialogue partners was convened on the island in May 1993. It was agreed to invite the foreign ministers of China, Russia, Vietnam, Laos and Papua New Guinea (the latter three as signatories of ASEAN's **Treaty of Amity and Cooperation**) to a special meeting in Singapore in July 1993 concurrent with that of ASEAN's foreign ministers and their dialogue partners. The declared purpose was 'for ASEAN and its dialogue partners to work with other regional states to evolve a predictable and constructive pattern of relationships in Asia-Pacific'. However, the more practical purposes were to encourage the post-Cold War regional security commitment of the United States and the international good citizenship of an irredentist China.

At the inaugural dinner meeting in July, it was decided that the ARF would convene formally in Bangkok in July 1994, to be preceded by a meeting of senior officials. At the first working session, only three hours were allocated for substantive discussion but it was agreed to reconvene the Forum on an annual basis and to endorse the purposes and principles of ASEAN's Treaty of Amity and Cooperation as a code of conduct for regional relations. At the second session in Brunei in August 1995, a 'Concept Paper' was endorsed in the Chairman's Statement, which affirmed that the ARF should adopt an evolutionary approach at a pace comfortable to all participants moving in stages from the promotion of confidence-building, development of preventive diplomacy and elaboration of approaches to conflict; the latter a concession to China's objection to conflict resolution. Apart from its annual meetings of senior officials and foreign ministers, the ARF works through inter-sessional meetings, the most important of which is the Inter-Sessional Support Group on Confidence Building which reports to the annual working meeting. At its annual meeting in Kuala Lumpur in July 1997, the ARF agreed to address preventive diplomacy where it overlapped with confidence-building but the outcome has been a cosmetic exercise, while confidence-building measures have not progressed significantly. Nonetheless, the ARF has maintained a cordial tone, which has been reflective of an underlying accommodation between the United States and China. The title of the security dialogue is indicative of the diplomatic centrality of ASEAN, which has been concerned to uphold its international standing with the establishment of a structure of relations involving all the major powers. Despite objections from some Western states to ASEAN's claim to be the 'prime driving force' of the ARF as iterated in the concept paper, rivals of the United States such as China, India and Russia have supported ASEAN's diplomatic assertiveness. The annual sessions of the ARF are held in the capital where ASEAN's annual meeting of foreign ministers convenes and are chaired by the appropriate incumbent, while all inter-sessional meetings are co-chaired by an ASEAN member. In addition to all ASEAN states, the participants in the ARF comprise: Australia, Bangladesh, Canada, China, European Union, India, Japan, Mongolia, New Zealand, North Korea, Pakistan, Papua New Guinea (observer), Russia, South Korea, Sri Lanka, Timor-Leste and the United States.

At the 2000 ARF meeting held in Thailand, a call was made for all states to sign and ratify the Comprehensive Nuclear Test Ban Treaty (CTBT) and accede to the Treaty on Non-Proliferation of Nuclear Weapons (NPT). Discussions were also initiated on transnational crime, piracy, illegal immigration, and illicit trafficking in small arms and light weapons. In the 2001 meeting in Vietnam, focus was mainly on developments in the **South China Sea**, with consultations between ASEAN and China to develop a Code of Conduct being welcomed. The ministers encouraged the development of Confidence Building Measures (CBMs) in the area, and for disputes to be resolved by peaceful means in accordance with the recognized principles of international law as well as to ensure the freedom of navigation in the area. The 2002 ARF meeting in Brunei Darussalam discussed the impact of the September 11 attacks on the security environment and ratification of relevant conventions and protocols relating to terrorism. Other regional issues were also discussed such as tensions between India and Pakistan, the situation in Korea and the reconstruction efforts in Afghanistan.

In Cambodia in 2003, discussions were focused on urging the Democratic Republic of Korea (DPRK) to resume cooperation with the International Atomic Energy Agency (IAEA) and to reverse its decision to withdraw from the NPT. Subsequent annual ARF meetings rehashed discussions on familiar issues such as terrorism, disarmament, disaster relief and transnational crime without any major breakthrough agreement. In June 2004, ASEAN established the ARF Unit at the ASEAN Secretariat so as to enhance the role of the ARF Chair as well as function as a depositary and registry by providing administrative support to the ARF.

see also: ASEAN; Singapore Summit; South China Sea; Treaty of Amity and Cooperation.

Asia–Europe Meeting (ASEM) 1996–

(Brunei/Cambodia/Indonesia/Laos/Malaysia/Myanmar/Philippines/Singapore/Thailand/Vietnam)

The Asia–Europe Meeting was established at a meeting of heads of government in Bangkok in March 1996 where it was agreed to continue the inter-governmental dialogue on a biannual basis. The initiative came from Singapore's prime minister, **Goh Chok Tong**, who was conscious of the lack of a third structure of global dialogue to that between the United States and Europe and the United States and Asia. He was also keen to encourage greater European investment and a greater political interest in the region to counter the influence of China and the United States. He received ready support from ASEAN partners, especially Malaysia whose prime minister, **Mahathir Mohamad**, recognized a correspondence between the Asian composition of the dialogue, including China, Japan and South Korea as well as **ASEAN** (Association of Southeast Asian Nations) states, and his proposal for an East Asian Economic Caucus. In that respect, the distinguishing feature of ASEM was the absence of the United States, which had staked a claim to the leadership of **APEC** at a meeting of heads of government on Blake Island in 1993. At its first working session, the buoyancy of the Asian economic situation provided a nexus for dialogue, but in London in 1998 economic adversity interposed to weaken it. ASEAN membership was initially limited with a line drawn after the admission of Vietnam, partly to avoid controversy over Myanmar.

Four defining features of ASEM are informality, multi-dimensionality (i.e. equal weight is accorded to political, economic and socio-cultural dimensions), emphasis on equal partnership, and dual focus on high-level and people-to-people exchange. ASEM has three main pillars: the political pillar; the economic pillar; and the social, cultural and educational pillar. Under the political pillar, key issues discussed include counterterrorism, environmental issues, migration and more sensitive issues like human rights. At the third ASEM foreign ministers meeting held in China in 2001, it was decided that an informal, ad hoc consultative mechanism enabling ASEM officials to exchange views on significant international events should be held before sessions of the United Nations General Assembly. Under the economic pillar, issues discussed include trade facilitation and trade security, investment issues, information and communication technology, and regionalism and multilateralism. As a result, certain initiatives have been adopted, such as the Trade Facilitation Action Plan (TFAP) aimed at the reduction and removal of non-tariff barriers to trade between the two regions; the Investment Promotion Action Plan (IPAP) to promote two-way investment flows between Europe and Asia; the ASEM Trade Pledge expressing the common resolve of all ASEM partners to resist any protectionist pressures; the ASEM Trust Fund which provides technical advice and training to assist with policy reform in both the financial and social sectors in countries affected by financial crises; and the Asia–Europe Business Forum (AEBF) which provides the opportunity for the private sector to review issues related to trade and provide input to the official dialogue. Under the social, cultural and educational pillar, the Asia–Europe Foundation (ASEF) was founded, and is the sole ASEM institution in existence. Its mandate is to promote cultural, intellectual and people-to-people exchanges between Europe and Asia.

ASEM saw its first significant expansion during the fifth ASEM summit held in 2004 in Vietnam, where ten new EU members (Cyprus, Czech Republic, Estonia, Hungary, Latvia, Lithuania, Malta, Poland, Slovakia and Slovenia) and three new ASEAN countries (Cambodia, Laos and Myanmar) became official members of ASEM. The second round of enlargement occurred in 2007 where Bulgaria, India, Mongolia, Pakistan, Romania and the ASEAN Secretariat joined. In October 2010 three more members (Australia, New Zealand and Russia) joined, and two years later in Vientiane, Laos, Bangladesh, Norway and Switzerland joined, thereby increasing the total ASEM membership to fifty-one partners.

see also: APEC; ASEAN; Goh Chok Tong; Mahathir Mohamad, Tun.

Asian–African Conference, Bandung 1955 (Indonesia)

An unprecedented conference of representatives from twenty-nine Asian and African states took place on 18–24 April 1955 in the Indonesian city of Bandung. The initiative for calling the meeting rested with Indonesia's prime minister, Ali Sastroamijoyo, who raised the idea at a gathering of five Asian prime ministers in Colombo in April 1954 at a time of growing international concern about the prospect of US military intervention in Indochina. A key factor in convening the conference was the opportunity seen by India's prime minister, Jawaharl al Nehru, of using the occasion to welcome the People's Republic of China into the comity of Asian and African states. In the event, Sino–Indian tensions were exposed by the conference but the occasion was significant for being the first time that post-colonial states

had come together to register their own international agenda. Colonialism in all its manifestations was denounced as an evil. The Bandung Conference gave its name to a new spirit of international conciliation in the context of the Cold War and to that extent was a stage in the emergence of the Non-Aligned Movement. The initiative failed to assume institutionalized form. Moreover, the participation of China excluded the Asian–African undertaking from the mainstream of non-alignment, while an attempt to convene a second meeting in Algeria in June 1965 with a greater African participation had to be called off because of the military coup which brought Colonel Boumedienne to power. The so-called Afro-Asian Movement was accordingly discredited, while President **Sukarno** of Indonesia was more interested in convening a conference of what he termed 'New Emerging Forces'. Nonetheless, the Bandung Conference enjoys an honoured place in Indonesia's history and in 1985 President **Suharto** convened a thirtieth anniversary meeting as a way of registering his country's restored international standing.
see also: Suharto; Sukarno.

Asian Financial Crisis 1997–8

(Indonesia/Malaysia/Thailand)

Originating in Thailand but spreading to regional countries such as Indonesia, Malaysia, South Korea and the Philippines through the contagion effect, the Asian financial crisis of 1997–8 was one of the most severe economic crises to affect the developing world since the 1982 debt crisis. The crisis can be attributed to a number of causes, including the mismanagement of banks and financial institutions in the region, corruption and crony capitalism, policy missteps by governments at the onset of the crisis, financial panic and political uncertainty, and poorly designed international rescue programmes.

Prior to the crisis, East and Southeast Asian economies had been experiencing a decade of unprecedented economic growth, which led pundits to proclaim that an 'Asian economic miracle' was shaping the post-Cold War order in the region. This growth was undergirded by a boom in international lending and large-scale foreign capital inflows into regional financial systems in response to high interest rates. Underlying this economic growth however, were structural deficiencies that were compounded by corruption and nepotism, and which resulted in capital inflows being short-term. As a consequence, once the Thai economy started wavering, foreign funds were quickly withdrawn first from Thailand, and then increasingly, from several other key Southeast Asian economies. While the crisis reflected existing underlying problems in the Asian economies at the macro-economic and micro-economic levels in the financial sector, the severity of the crisis is attributed to speculation and panic which led to large capital outflows.

The swift outflow of capital led to a massive reduction in productivity and slowdown of economic activity. This in turn resulted in the implosion of local stock and currency markets, and the increase of state debt in the affected countries. In fact, it was estimated at the time that several regional stock markets lost over seventy per cent of their value, and their currency depreciated against the US dollar by the same amount. In response to the rapid devaluation of their currencies, Thailand, Malaysia and Indonesia each floated their respective currencies on the international market and imposed capital controls to decrease the outflow of speculative money. Yet the initial implementation of monetary policy reform was tepid, and it was only with further devaluation that implementation of more serious monetary tightening measures escalated.

Indonesia was the hardest hit by the crisis and sought large-scale financial assistance from the International Monetary Fund (IMF). However, the Indonesian government failed to enforce these IMF programmes as a corrupt and authoritarian regime overlooked most of its commitments until the severe deterioration of economic conditions led to a full-fledged collapse of the rupiah. Thailand tried to discourage capital outflows with the introduction of limited capital controls and also requested IMF financial assistance. It carried out further major restructuring in response to conditions set by the fund. However assistance from the IMF had a deleterious effect. In effect, the IMF's contractionary measures – such as imposed fiscal restraint through higher taxes, lower public spending and privatization – all but signalled to creditors an impending crisis, thereby accelerating the outflow of foreign investments. On the other hand, Malaysia refused help from the IMF and responded to the crisis by adopting a strong capital control policy and a fixed exchange rate regime in order to stabilize the exchange rate and boost the financial sector. As a result of long and difficult negotiations with the IMF and the relative ineffectiveness of IMF programmes in alleviating the economic conditions, a regional response was sought. Members of ASEAN Plus Three agreed to set up a mainly bilateral currency swap scheme, known as the **Chiang Mai Initiative**, in 2000 in order to be able to handle more effectively and with greater preparedness any future financial crisis. Other initiatives launched in response to the crisis included a regional economic surveillance mechanism, a regional liquidity support arrangement and an Asian bond markets initiative.

Apart from severe economic and financial dislocation, the crisis also had severe social and political consequences in affected countries. These consequences were most profound in Indonesia, where the financial crisis precipitated a political crisis that culminated in a series of bloody riots in May 1998 and ultimately, the resignation of President **Suharto** after more than three decades of authoritarian rule. Thailand too, suffered a change in government, while in Malaysia, Prime Minister **Mahathir Mohamad** faced the sternest test to his legitimacy when the crisis catalysed a domestic reform movement that rallied around the sacked deputy prime minister, **Anwar Ibrahim**. The Asian financial crisis also exposed institutional weaknesses of **ASEAN** (Association of Southeast Asian Nations). In the early months of the crisis ASEAN dismissed the initial signs as simply a domestic problem and played no role in devising a regional response to provide assistance to the affected member states, thereby failing to provide effective regional leadership.

see also: Anwar Ibrahim; ASEAN; Chiang Mai Initiative; Mahathir Mohamad, Tun; Suharto.

August Revolution 1945 (Vietnam)

The August Revolution describes the seizure of power in Hanoi on 19 August 1945 by armed units of the Communist-led **Viet Minh** in the wake of Japan's surrender four days before. Although short-lived, this seizure of power marked the beginning of a national revolution which was not fully realized until April 1975. Japan's military occupation of Indochina from 1940 did not displace French colonial administration, which remained subject to the nominal authority of the government in Vichy. The reversal of its military fortunes prompted the Japanese to remove the French administration by force on 9 March 1945 and to sponsor independence in Indochina, in the case of Vietnam under the leadership of Emperor **Bao Dai**. Japan's surrender to the Allies on 15 August created a political vacuum which the Viet Minh filled. On 25 August they secured Bao Dai's abdication and his acceptance of the post of supreme political adviser in a provisional government established on 28 August. The Communist leader **Ho Chi Minh** reached Hanoi on 30 August and proclaimed the independence of the Democratic Republic of Vietnam on 2 September. His statement included extracts from the US declaration of independence in an abortive attempt to attract international recognition, while the French set about trying to restore their colonial position. Viet Minh rule was displaced from 9 September as Chinese troops began occupying Vietnam down to the sixteenth parallel of latitude under an agreement among the Allies to take the surrender of Japanese forces. On 28 February 1946 a Sino-French treaty provided for the return of French troops. Britain had assumed responsibility for the surrender of Japanese troops south of the sixteenth parallel. Its local commander, General Gracey, faced with the Viet Minh challenge, armed French prisoners of war and thus enabled it to be contained. French troops returned to the south in October 1945. Negotiations between the Viet Minh and the French broke down at the end of 1946 and armed conflict ensued in two stages until the unification of Vietnam in April 1975.

see also: Bao Dai; Ho Chi Minh; Viet Minh.

Aung San (Burma/Myanmar)

Aung San is the acknowledged father of Burmese nationalism whose life was cut short by assassination in July 1947 before independence was obtained from Britain. He was born in 1915 in Magwe district and rose to prominence as a radical nationalist student leader in Rangoon during the 1930s. In 1939 he founded the Communist Party of Burma and the next year left the country by ship with the intention of making contact with the Communist Party of China. He arrived in Japanese-occupied Amoy from where he was sent to Tokyo to enjoy the patronage of the military government. In 1941 Aung San returned secretly to Burma to recruit contemporaries for military training in Japan. Aung San led twenty-eight comrades out of an initial thirty back to Burma with the Japanese army when it invaded the country from Thailand in December 1941. Aung San proceeded to establish the Burma Independence Army, which fought alongside the Japanese. Political tensions arose, however, when it became evident to the Burmese nationalists that the independence granted by the Japanese in August 1943 was spurious. Links were then established with the Allies and in March 1945 the reorganized Burma National Army under Aung San declared war against the Japanese, attracting recognition from the Supreme Allied Commander in Southeast Asia, Lord Louis Mountbatten (*see* **Southeast Asia Command**). After the end of hostilities, Aung San led the **Anti-Fascist People's Freedom League** (AFPFL) in the political struggle for independence stiffened by a paramilitary force. In this role, he came to enjoy the support of Mountbatten, who used his influential position to urge the British government to make concessions to the young nationalist leader. On 27 January 1947 Aung San signed an agreement in London with the prime minister, Clement Attlee, which promised full independence within a year. Despite acute factional divisions within the Burmese nationalist movement as well as the competing interests of apprehensive ethnic minorities, Aung San appeared to enjoy sufficient confidence to set up a viable Union of Burma with a federal constitution. On the morning of 19 July 1947, however, while the provisional cabinet was in session, a group of armed men burst into the room and sprayed it with machine-gun bullets. Aung San, then only thirty-two, was killed together with six of his ministerial colleagues. He had been murdered on the instructions of a political rival, U Saw, who was subsequently tried, convicted and hanged. Aung San was succeeded by his deputy **U Nu**, who negotiated the eventual independence of Burma on 4 January 1948. Aung San has since been revered as the outstanding figure in the pantheon of Burmese nationalism, a status which has helped his daughter, **Aung San Suu Kyi**, in her political resistance against the ruling military government.

see also: Anti-Fascist People's Freedom League; Aung San Suu Kyi; Nu, U; Southeast Asia Command 1943–6.

Aung San Suu Kyi (Myanmar)

Aung San Suu Kyi is the general secretary of the **National League for Democracy** (NLD), and the most credible opposition leader to challenge military rule in Myanmar (Burma) since its establishment in 1962. Aung San Suu Kyi is the daughter of the legendary leader and martyr of Burma's independence movement, **Aung San**. He was assassinated in July 1947 when she was only two years old, having been born on 19 June 1945. She left Burma at the age of fifteen to study abroad and eventually married a British citizen and settled in Oxford. Aung San Suu Kyi returned to Burma in April 1988 to nurse her ailing mother. By then, popular unrest against the military regime established by General **Ne Win** had gained strong momentum. She quickly assumed a leading role in political challenge, attracting support because of her lineage and personal qualities. After a bloody confrontation on the streets in August and September 1988, the military reasserted control but also promised free elections. Aung San Suu Kyi and supporters then formed the NLD, which became the foremost opposition party attracting widespread popular backing. She became its main asset, able to mobilize tens of thousands in rallies against the martial law regime. On 19 July 1989, the anniversary of her father's death, celebrated as Martyr's Day, she cancelled marches and a rally because of the prospect of another bloodletting. The next day, Aung San Suu Kyi was placed under house arrest for 'endangering the state' and thousands of her party members were arrested. She then embarked on a hunger strike which raised the political temperature for a time. The NLD achieved an overwhelming victory in elections called by the military regime in May 1990 while Aung San Suu Kyi remained incarcerated. The ruling **State Law and Order Restoration Council** (SLORC) set up in September 1988 refused to accept the outcome of the elections and agreed to release Aung San Suu Kyi only if she gave up her political beliefs and left the country, which she refused to do. In September 1991 Aung San Suu Kyi was awarded the Nobel Peace prize for her non-violent struggle for democracy and human rights. She was allowed limited family visits and in February 1994 was permitted to receive a visit from US Congressman William Richardson. But the effective head of Burma's military junta, Lieutenant General **Khin Nyunt**, refused to provide an indication of her likely release after describing Aung San Suu Kyi's attitude as negative and counter-productive. Richardson was refused a second visit in May 1995. Therefore it was with some surprise that Aung San Suu Kyi was released from detention on 10 July 1995. No conditions were imposed formally on her release. However, her English husband Michael Aris, terminally ill with cancer, was refused a visa to visit her in Yangon in early 1999. He died in March that year. In July 1999, she was denounced in the official press as a traitor who should be driven out of the country. She remained a symbol of the lack of legitimacy of the military regime. In April 2000, in a videotape delivered to the United Nations Human Rights Commission, she maintained that government oppression had worsened. In September 2000, she was forcibly detained and returned to house arrest in Rangoon after attempting to leave the capital to visit NLD party workers.

Aung San Suu Kyi was released from house arrest in 2002 and embarked on a hugely popular tour of upper Myanmar where she attracted large crowds of supporters. On 3 May 2003 her convoy was attacked by a mob believed engineered by the military rulers in the northwestern town of Depayin, Sagaing Division. She was able to escape, but was arrested by the military, initially imprisoned in Yangon's Insein prison, and later moved to house arrest in September 2003. During this time, Aung San Suu Kyi was allowed what proved to be a futile meeting with NLD members in 2007. During the same year Aung San Suu Kyi made an appearance at the gate of her house to accept the blessings of monks during the **Saffron Revolution**. In 2009, Aung San Suu Kyi was sentenced to three years at hard labour for allegedly violating the terms of her house arrest by harbouring an American man who swam across Inya Lake in Yangon to her house uninvited and was arrested leaving three days later. Commuted to eighteen months of continued house arrest, the sentence effectively barred her from participating in elections scheduled for November 2010.

On 13 November 2010, six days after national general elections, Aung San Suu Kyi was released after spending a total of fifteen years under house arrest. Following her release there has been unprecedented cooperation between herself and her party with the newly elected government including several discussions with former general and president, **Thein Sein**. In November 2011, Aung San Suu Kyi and the NLD announced their intention to re-register the party and participate in by-elections scheduled for April 2012. Over this period she met with a series of international leaders, including US Secretary of State Hillary Clinton in December 2011 and British Prime Minister David Cameron in April 2012. After the by-election of 1 April 2012, Aung San Suu Kyi was elected as a member of parliament from Kawhmu township in Yangon Division along with forty-three other NLD candidates who had won seats out of the forty-five contested. Initially protesting a required oath of loyalty to the **2008 Constitution** as a prerequisite to sitting in parliament, Aung San Suu Kyi and other elected members of her party eventually reversed their decision and were sworn into office on 2 May, making the NLD the largest opposition party in parliament. In June 2012, Aung San Suu Kyi made her first trip outside the country in twenty-one years and finally received her Nobel Peace Prize in Norway on 16 June 2012. In September 2012, she travelled to the United States where she met President

Barack Obama and other political leaders from both parties. She also toured the country to meet with Myanmar exile communities. In parliament she has taken an active role as a lawmaker and moral leader of the opposition. She has recently come in for some criticism for her seeming lack of willingness to speak out on ethnic riots in the western portion of the country between the Buddhist Rakhine and Muslim **Rohingya** minorities. In June 2013, Aung San Suu Kyi declared an intention to run for the presidency. This pits her against constitutional restrictions that prevent anyone with a foreign spouse from running for president, as well as a twenty-five per cent military bloc in the parliament which could forestall attempts at constitutional revision.

see also: Aung San; Constitution 2008; Khin Nyunt, General; National League for Democracy; Ne Win, General; Rohingya; Saffron Revolution; State Law and Order Restoration Council; Thein Sein.

Azahari, A. M. (Brunei)

A. M. Azahari was the leader of the **People's Party** (*Partai Rakyat*) of Brunei, which has been banned in the sultanate since it mounted a revolt in December 1962. He was born on the island of Labuan in 1928 of Arab-Malay parents. During the Japanese occupation, he was sent to study veterinary science in Indonesia. He participated in the national revolution against the Dutch, returning to Brunei in 1952. He then became involved in a series of unsuccessful business ventures before turning to politics in 1956. He founded the People's Party, which was modelled on a radical Malayan equivalent and attracted considerable support from among Brunei Malays. In April 1962 as a nominated member of the **Legislative Council**, he failed to secure passage of a motion seeking to restore Brunei's sovereignty over northern Borneo. He then went into exile to Johor Bahru in Malaya where he campaigned against Brunei's membership of the proposed Federation of Malaysia. He was in the Philippines in December 1962 at the time of the Brunei Revolt and took refuge in the Indonesian Embassy after its failure. He was not allocated any public role during Indonesia's **Confrontation** of Malaysia. He is believed to have resided in the Indonesian town of Bogor, constrained by the government of Jakarta from engaging in political activity, especially after Brunei became independent and a member of **ASEAN** (Association of Southeast Asian Nations) in January 1984.

see also: ASEAN; Brunei Revolt 1962; Confrontation; Legislative Council; People's Party.

B

Ba'asyir, Abu Bakar (Indonesia)

Abu Bakar Ba'asyir is a Muslim cleric who was born in Jombang, East Java on 17 August 1938 and educated at Al-Irsyad University in Solo, Central Java. His early days as an activist began with the Islamic Students Association in Solo, the Al-Irsyad Youth Organization, the Indonesian Islamic Youth Movement and the Student Da'wah Organization. He was also the leader of the ***Majelis Mujahidin Indonesia***, an umbrella organization for Indonesian Islamist groups. In 1972 he co-founded the Al-Mukmin Islamist boarding school in Ngruki, Central Java. The school has since gained notoriety for producing considerable numbers of Islamic extremists, to the extent that the International Crisis Group has described it as the 'Ivy League' for recruits for the notorious terrorist organization, ***Jemaah Islamiyah*** (JI).

Ba'asyir actively supported the ***Darul Islam*** revolt in the early 1960s for the establishment of an Islamic state in Indonesia. He was imprisoned without trial from 1978 to 1982 and exiled from Indonesia in 1993 by the **Suharto** government for agitating for the implementation of *shari'a* law and non-recognition of the Indonesian national ideology, ***Pancasila***. Ba'asyir fled to Malaysia, where he took refuge for seventeen years before returning after the demise of the New Order in 1998 to renew his call for *shari'a*. During his exile in Malaysia, he is alleged to have co-founded JI. Ba'asyir is widely believed to be the spiritual leader and ideological godfather of JI and to have links with Al-Qaeda. However there has been no public evidence implicating him in terrorist attacks undertaken by JI, and Ba'asyir himself has denied the existence of the organization, dubiously contending instead that the 2002 Bali bombings were the work of American and Israeli intelligence. Nevertheless, Ba'asyir remains on the United Nation's list of international terrorists. In 2003 he was acquitted of terrorism charges linked to a series of church bombings in December 2000 in Java and Sumatra, but convicted on immigration violations and sentenced to three years imprisonment, which was later reduced to twenty months. In October 2004 he was again arrested and charged with involvement in the 2003 Marriott Hotel bomb attacks and sentenced to two and a half years of imprisonment. In 2008, Ba'asyir announced his intention to establish a new Islamic group in Indonesia, *Jemaah Ansharut Tauhid*. The group has since 2012 been labelled a foreign terrorist organization by the American government. In 2010, Ba'asyir was charged with involvement in the plotting of terrorist attacks and military training in Aceh. He denied the charges, of inciting others to commit terrorism, levelled against him. In June 2011 Ba'asyir was convicted of coordinating, financing and supporting a jihadi training camp and was sentenced to fifteen years in prison. Though this was later reduced to nine years upon appeal, the Supreme Court rejected the appeal, annulled the reduced sentence and reinstated the original fifteen-year sentence of imprisonment which he is currently serving. He continues however to preach and speak from prison with impunity.

see also: Darul Islam; Jemaah Islamiyah; Majelis Mujahidin Indonesia; Pancasila; Suharto.

Badawi, Tun Abdullah Ahmad (Malaysia)

Abdullah Ahmad Badawi was appointed prime minister of Malaysia on 31 October 2003 and served in that office until 1 April 2009 when he was unceremoniously forced to resign. 'Pak Lah', as Badawi is affectionately known, was born in Penang on 26 November 1939 and was educated at the University of Malaya. His grandfather was instrumental in the formation of ***Parti Islam Se-Malaysia*** while his father was a major figure in **UMNO** (United Malays National Organization). Badawi was first elected to Parliament in 1974 and was appointed a minister in the prime minister's department in 1982. He served subsequently as minister of education and of defence but was dismissed from the cabinet in

1987 because of his identification with a dissident wing within UMNO led by former minister of trade and industry, **Tengku Razaleigh Hamzah**. Badawi did not sever his formal affiliation to UMNO and was a successful parliamentary candidate in its interest in October 1990. Moreover, he demonstrated his personal standing within UMNO by securing election to one of the three senior posts of party vice-president but behind his main rival **Anwar Ibrahim**, who was promoted from education to finance on Badawi's return to the cabinet as foreign minister in March 1991. Following the dismissal of Anwar Ibrahim, Badawi was elevated unopposed to the position of deputy president of UMNO and deputy prime minister in May 2000. In a move that surprised some, Prime Minister **Mahathir Mohamad** appointed Badawi as his successor, purportedly for his conservatism rather than dynamism.

As prime minister, Badawi sought to differentiate his administration from that of his predecessors by projecting a softer image and a reformist agenda predicated on Islamic principles, which he described as '*Islam Hadhari*' (Civilizational Islam), and by having a retinue of young, dynamic policy advisors, led by his son-in-law Khairy Jamaluddin, known as the 'fourth floor boys'. He won a resounding mandate at the 2004 general election, which consisted of a successful campaign to wrest back the state of Terengganu from opposition hands and make significant inroads into the opposition stronghold of Kelantan. Badawi's softer, more engaging approach, however, had the deleterious effect of raising expectations, ultimately to levels that Badawi himself could not meet. Despite starting with some relatively high-profile cases, his anti-corruption campaign soon came under heavy criticism for lack of transparency. Similarly, his propensity for consensus building translated into policy inertia as frustration at the slow pace of reform mounted. Even more calamitous for Badawi was the swift deterioration of his relationship with his erstwhile benefactor, Mahathir Mohamad, which was triggered by his attempts to bring to an end major business and infrastructure projects he inherited from his predecessor. Mahathir launched a series of online missives against Badawi (Mahathir had accused Badawi of curtailing press freedom by obstructing publication of his commentaries on Badawi's policies), followed by unrelenting public statements expressing his disappointment at Badawi's decisions. Already facing an opposition rejuvenated by Anwar Ibrahim, Mahathir's unyielding attacks cast a dark shadow over Badawi's leadership of ***Barisan Nasional*** (National Front, BN) into national polls in March 2008. In the event, the elections proved a major setback for the ruling coalition, which lost control of four state legislatures and their customary two-thirds parliamentary majority. For Mahathir, the poor performance at the polls occasioned a call for Badawi's resignation that was echoed in several quarters within UMNO, including by Mahathir's son, Mukhriz Mahathir. Matters escalated with Mahathir going to the extreme of resigning from UMNO, and declaring that he would only rejoin the party after Badawi resigned. Meanwhile, parliamentarians from a BN component party, the Sabah Progressive Party, attempted to table a no-confidence vote in June 2008 against the besieged prime minister. Despite public proclamations of support from his deputy prime minister **Najib Tun Razak**, Badawi was heavily criticized and forced under pressure to take responsibility for the results of the March 2008 elections by resigning from the presidency of UMNO and as prime minister of Malaysia.

Abdullah Badawi's first wife, Endon Mahmood, passed away in October 2005. He remarried in June 2007. Badawi's son-in-law, Khairy Jamaluddin, is currently leader of the youth movement of UMNO and a cabinet minister, and rising star in the party. Khairy also became a target of personal attacks by Mahathir Mohamad during Badawi's tenure in office.

see also: Anwar Ibrahim, Datuk Seri; *Barisan Nasional*; Mahathir Mohamad, Tun; Najib Tun Razak, Datuk Seri Mohamad; *Parti Islam Se-Malaysia*; Razaleigh Hamzah, Tengku; UMNO.

Bali Summit (ASEAN) 1976 (Indonesia/Malaysia/Philippines/Singapore/Thailand)

The first meeting of heads of government of **ASEAN** (Association of Southeast Asian Nations) took place on the island of Bali in February 1976. It was significant as a display of solidarity and collective nerve in the close wake of the success of revolutionary Communism in Indochina and also because it registered a political role for ASEAN after nearly a decade of unconvincing claims of interest in only economic and social cooperation. That role was defined in the Declaration of ASEAN Concord 1976 whose objectives and principles were designed to promote political stability within member states and also within Southeast Asia. The declaration reaffirmed a commitment to a regional **ZOPFAN** (Zone of Peace, Freedom and Neutrality). In addition, the member governments concluded a **Treaty of Amity and Cooperation** which included machinery for regional dispute settlement and made provision for accession to it by non-members. To that extent, the treaty represented a political opening to the revolutionary states of Indochina and an attempt to interest them in a common code of conduct as a basis for regional order. The initial response was negative and it was only after the end of the Cold War and the formal settlement of the Cambodian conflict that Vietnam and Laos indicated a willingness to adhere to the treaty, which occurred at an ASEAN ministerial meeting in Manila in July 1992. The Bali Summit was significant also for an agreement to establish a secretariat to be based in Jakarta as well as for excluding defence cooperation from within the Association.

see also: ASEAN; Declaration of ASEAN Concord 1976; Treaty of Amity and Cooperation; ZOPFAN.

Bali Summit (ASEAN) 2003 (Brunei/Cambodia/Indonesia/Laos/Malaysia/Myanmar/Philippines/Singapore/Thailand/Vietnam)

The ninth meeting of the heads of government of **ASEAN** (Association of Southeast Asian Nations) convened in Bali, Indonesia, on 7–8 October 2003. The most significant outcome of the summit was the adoption of the **Declaration of ASEAN Concord II** (or Bali Concord II) in which ASEAN leaders agreed to establish an **ASEAN Community** by the year 2020. The ASEAN Community would rest on three pillars: an ASEAN Security Community (ASC), an ASEAN Economic Community (AEC), and an ASEAN Socio-Cultural Community. The ASC concept, proposed by Indonesia at the summit, was not designed to be a framework for military cooperation or alliance, nor was it a departure from ASEAN's existing security arrangements. Rather, it was a reaffirmation of the principles of non-interference and consensual decision-making in a new international environment defined by the rise of China and India as well as the emergence of non-traditional security threats such as pandemics and terrorism.

The venue of the summit was also symbolic for two reasons. First, Bali was the site of a large-scale terrorist bombing in October 2002. ASEAN leaders as well as the leaders of China, India, Japan and South Korea had gathered amidst tight security as an expression of faith and confidence in Indonesia's counter-terrorism efforts. Second, Bali was also the venue of the first ASEAN Summit (**Bali Summit 1976**) where the **Treaty of Amity and Cooperation** (TAC) was codified, thereby establishing the norms of non-interference and peaceful resolution of disputes that has anchored ASEAN diplomacy since. China and India, two of ASEAN's major dialogue partners, acceded to the TAC on the sidelines of the 2003 summit.

see also: ASEAN; Bali Summit (ASEAN) 1976; Declaration of ASEAN Concord II 2003; Treaty of Amity and Cooperation.

Bali Summit (ASEAN) 2011 (Brunei/Cambodia/Indonesia/Laos/Malaysia/Myanmar/Philippines/Singapore/Thailand/Vietnam)

The nineteenth meeting of heads of government of **ASEAN** convened in Bali, Indonesia from 14 to 19 November 2011. The main focus of the meeting was to inject greater impetus into ASEAN's community-building process. It was also intended to be a showcase of ASEAN solidarity amidst growing signs of discord and a widening economic gap in the region. To that end, ASEAN leaders adopted the **Declaration of ASEAN Concord III** (or Bali Concord III) which aims to develop a common ASEAN position on global issues so that a more coordinated approach will allow ASEAN to better respond to new challenges the region will face in the future. Also notable at the Summit was the decision to accede to Myanmar's request to hold the chairmanship of ASEAN in 2014, as ASEAN leaders were persuaded by the positive steps that Myanmar had hitherto taken in terms of political reform. The **East Asia Summit** (EAS) that followed witnessed formal American and Russian participation for the first time. In the buildup to the EAS, US President Barack Obama had hinted that Washington would like to see the **South China Sea** disputes raised at the Summit for discussion. This was however firmly rejected by the Chinese premier, Wen Jiabao, prior to the summit, insisting that the dispute should be addressed through bilateral consultations and warning against foreign involvement.

see also: ASEAN; Declaration of ASEAN Concord III 2011; East Asia Summit; South China Sea.

Baling Talks 1955 (Malaya/Malaysia)

A meeting was held in December 1955 in the Malayan town of Baling close to the Thai border at the initiative of **Chin Peng**, the leader of the Communist Party of Malaya, which had mounted an armed insurrection from 1948. He had offered to negotiate with **Tunku Abdul Rahman**, chief minister of Malaya, and **David Marshall**, chief minister of Singapore, both of whom owed their positions to general elections. Tunku Abdul Rahman had declared an amnesty for all insurgents but the talks failed because Chin Peng's demand that the Communist Party be made legal was rejected. His initiative reflected the international Communist reorientation to peaceful coexistence as well as the slackening momentum of the insurgency. The **Emergency**, as it was generally known, continued officially until 1960, even though Malaya became fully independent in 1957 and Singapore self-governing in 1959. The insurgency continued in sporadic form beyond 1960, but the Baling Talks marked a turning point after which the Communist challenge lost its initial force.

see also: Chin Peng; Emergency 1948–60; Marshall, David; Rahman, Tunku Abdul.

Bandar Seri Begawan Summit (ASEAN) April 2013 (Brunei/Cambodia/Indonesia/Laos/Malaysia/Myanmar/Philippines/Singapore/Thailand/Vietnam)

The twenty-second **ASEAN** summit was held in Brunei Darussalam on 24–25 April 2013. Cognizant of the controversy surrounding competing **South China Sea** claims and the deleterious effect they had on ASEAN meetings the previous year (*see* **Phnom Penh Summit November 2012**), as ASEAN chair Brunei sought to prioritize the demonstration of ASEAN unity above all else at this summit. To that end, much stress was given to the need to deepen cooperation in political, security, economic and socio-cultural areas, as captured in the summit theme of 'Our People, Our Future Together'. One notable absentee at the meeting was Malaysian prime minister **Najib Tun Razak** who was preparing for a major general election. He was replaced by the president of the Malaysian Senate, Tan Sri Abu Zahar Ujang, who assumed the role of the prime minister's special representative. Much effort was made to ensure that all member states reaffirmed the collective commitments under the **Declaration on the Conduct of Parties in the South China Sea** (DOC), which they did. ASEAN leaders also expressed support for continued engagement with China in implementing the DOC in a full and effective manner. While the South China Sea dominated proceedings, ASEAN leaders also discussed denuclearization of the Korean Peninsula and reaffirmed commitments to preserve Southeast Asia as a nuclear weapons-free zone.

see also: ASEAN; Declaration on the Conduct of Parties in the South China Sea (ASEAN) 2002; Najib Tun Razak, Datuk Seri Mohamad; Phnom Penh Summit (ASEAN) November 2012; South China Sea.

Bandar Seri Begawan Summit (ASEAN) October 2013 (Brunei/Cambodia/Indonesia/Laos/Malaysia/Myanmar/Philippines/Singapore/Thailand/Vietnam)

The twenty-third ASEAN summit was held in Brunei Darussalam on 9–10 October 2013 with discussions on the progress towards the 2015 objective of establishing an ASEAN Community set as the meeting's priority. Nevertheless, the **South China Sea** disputes predictably dominated the agenda. The commencement of formal consultations between ASEAN and China on the development of the Code Of Conduct (COC) in the South China Sea were welcomed during the summit. These had taken the form of the ASEAN–China Senior Officials Meeting on the Implementation of the DOC and the 9th ASEAN–China Joint Working Group on the Implementation of the DOC which were held in China on 14–15 September 2013. The summit was notable for the absence of the American president, Barack Obama, due to the crisis in Washington following the US government's shutdown. President Obama was represented by his secretary of state, John Kerry.

The twenty-third ASEAN summit also saw the ASEAN Chair transferred to Myanmar, which assumed leadership of ASEAN for the first time on 1 January 2014. Myanmar joined ASEAN in 1997 and was to have assumed the chair in 2006 but was blocked from doing so by strong international pressure against its poor human rights record.

see also: Declaration on the Conduct of Parties in the South China Sea (ASEAN) 2002; South China Sea.

Bandung Conference 1955 (Indonesia) *see* **Asian–African Conference, Bandung 1955**.

Bangkok Declaration (ASEAN) 1967 (Indonesia/Malaysia/Philippines/Singapore/Thailand)

The founding document of **ASEAN** (Association of Southeast Asian Nations) was promulgated in the Thai capital on 8 August 1967. The Bangkok Declaration's prime formal commitment was to accelerate economic growth, social progress and cultural development in the region. However, a proprietary aspiration in the preamble affirmed 'that the countries of Southeast Asia share a primary responsibility for strengthening the economic and social stability of the region and ensuring their peaceful progressive national development, and that they are determined to ensure their stability and security from external interference in any form or manifestation in order to preserve their national identities in accordance with the ideals and aspirations of their peoples'. That proprietary aspiration with security in mind was given formal content in a declaration by ASEAN's foreign ministers in November 1971 to secure the recognition and respect for Southeast Asia as a ZOPFAN – a Zone of Peace, Freedom and Neutrality. The commitment to a ZOPFAN was reaffirmed in the Declaration of ASEAN Concord at its first summit (**Bali Summit 1976**) but the goal has never been realized in practical terms.

see also: ASEAN; Bali Summit 1976; Declaration of ASEAN Concord 1976; ZOPFAN.

Bangkok Summit (ASEAN) 1995 (Brunei/Cambodia/Indonesia/Laos/Malaysia/Myanmar/Philippines/Singapore/Thailand/Vietnam)

The fifth meeting of **ASEAN**'s heads of government convened in the Thai capital in mid-December 1995. The meeting was notable for the attendance of the prime minister of Vietnam as the representative of the first Communist member following his country's entry in the previous July. Present also were the heads of government of Cambodia and Laos, with observer status, and that of Myanmar as a guest, making it the first occasion at which all ten Southeast Asian governments had been so represented. A corresponding commitment was made to enlarge the Association to include all the states of Southeast Asia by the year 2000. An accord was reached on removing all tariff barriers within the ASEAN Free Trade Area (**AFTA**) by 2003 and a treaty was concluded

with the object of establishing a Southeast Asia Nuclear Weapon-Free Zone, also known as SEANWFZ.
see also: AFTA; ASEAN.

Banharn Silpa-archa (Thailand)

Banharn Silpa-archa was prime minister of Thailand between July 1995 and November 1996. He led the ***Chart Thai* Party** (Thai National Party) to victory with the largest number of seats in elections in July 1995 and formed a seven-party coalition, which broke up over political spoils in September 1996 and lost office after elections in November 1996. Banharn Silpa-archa was born on 20 July 1932 in Suphanburi in central Thailand of Chinese immigrant parents. He was educated initially at Bangkok Business College and started working life as an office boy. He entered politics as a member of the municipal assembly for Suphanburi in 1974 at the inception of the *Chart Thai* Party, which was partly based on provincial business networks. Banharn had already established a strong local base through public benefaction using wealth accumulated from his success in the construction industry. He rose quickly to the office of deputy secretary-general of his party and entered the national parliament in its interest in 1976. He held a number of ministerial appointments during the 1980s, including the agriculture, communications and finance portfolios, and enjoyed a reputation as a political fixer and an exponent of 'money politics'. Banharn was the subject of an inconclusive investigation by an anti-corruption committee after his party was removed from government by a military coup in 1991. He sought to demonstrate a seriousness of mind by studying law but, in office, was accused of plagiarizing his master's thesis. He took over the leadership of the *Chart Thai* Party in May 1994 after the resignation of a caretaker leader who had assumed the position following the defection of former prime minister **Chatichai Choonhavan**. After a significant electoral setback in November 1996, Banharn took his party into opposition but then negotiated its entry into a coalition government headed by **Chuan Leekpai**, which was formed in November 1997. In January 2008 he reneged on a pledge never to join a government led by **Thaksin Shinawatra** because of corruption and announced that his *Chart Thai* Party would join in coalition with the **People's Power Party**, a successor to Thaksin's dissolved ***Thai Rak Thai* Party**. The *Chart Thai* Party was dissolved by the Constitutional Court on 2 December 2008 and Banharn was barred from politics for five years. Still an influential political fixer, Banharn has operated by proxy, forming the ***Chart Pattana* Party** (Thai National Development Party) with non-executive members of his former party chaired by his younger brother, Chumpol Silpa-archa. The party joined the **Democrat Party**-led government of **Abhisit Vejjajiva**.
see also: Abhisit Vejjajiva; *Chart Pattana* Party; *Chart Thai* Party; Chatichai Choonhavan; Chuan Leekpai; Democrat Party; People's Power Party; *Thai Rak Thai* Party; Thaksin Shinawatra.

Bank Bumiputera Crisis (Malaysia)

In September 1984 Malaysia's minister of finance, **Daim Zainuddin**, announced that Petronas, the national oil company, had assumed financial responsibility for Bank Bumiputera, the country's largest bank, in a multi-million dollar rescue operation. Bank Bumiputera had been created as a prime vehicle for promoting the **New Economic Policy** launched at the beginning of the 1970s in order to redress the balance of material advantage between the indigenous Malays (***Bumiputra***) and the non-Malays of migrant origin. Bank Bumiputera had established a subsidiary company in Hong Kong called Bumiputera Malaysia Finance Ltd. This subsidiary engaged in speculative involvement in the territory's property market between 1979 and 1983 through loans to the Chinese-owned Carrian Group of companies, whose chairman was George Tan. These loans were placed in serious jeopardy with the collapse of the property market and the Carrian Group, which exposed not only Bumiputera Malaysia Finance Ltd but the parent Bank Bumiputera. The consequence was effectively to wipe out its total capital and reserves. The issue became a national scandal because the nature of the speculative involvement, through a Hong Kong Chinese company, had violated the spirit and purpose of the New Economic Policy. It also gave rise to accusations that the abortive undertaking was riddled with personal and political corruption; two deaths in Hong Kong in suspicious circumstances were linked to the episode. Criminal proceedings in Hong Kong continued into the 1990s without giving rise to a satisfactory account of the episode or to an adequate explanation of its Malaysian dimension, involving **UMNO** (United Malays National Organization) and its leadership.

see also: *Bumiputra*; Daim Zainuddin; New Economic Policy; UMNO.

Bao Dai, Emperor (Vietnam)

Bao Dai was the last emperor of Annam, the central part of Vietnam, which became a French protectorate in 1874. Although never more than a figurehead, he was of political significance from 1940 until 1955 because of his successive collaboration with the Japanese, the **Viet Minh**, the French and finally the anti-Communist nationalists who deposed him. His genuine attempts at political reform never bore fruit. Bao Dai was born in Hue, in October 1913, the son of the Emperor Khai Din, and ascended the throne in January 1926 on the death of his father. He was denied a political role by the French but in March 1945 proclaimed Vietnam's independence under Japanese auspices. With their surrender to the allies and the **August Revolution**, he was persuaded to abdicate in favour of a provisional government set up by the Communist-led Viet Minh, headed by **Ho Chi Minh**, in which he accepted the nominal role of supreme counsellor. He left Vietnam in March 1946, initially for Hong Kong, with the restoration of French rule. Bao Dai returned to Vietnam encouraged by French assurances. On 8 March 1949, he entered into an exchange of letters (known as the **Elysée Agreement**) with French President Vincent Auriol, which restored him as head of state of a nominally independent Vietnam. This attempt to demonstrate a semblance of independence failed to stem the political and military advance of the Viet Minh. In June 1954, following the French defeat at the Battle of **Dien Bien Phu**, he called on the anti-Communist exile **Ngo Dinh Diem** to form a government, which he did in the southern half of a Vietnam partitioned by the **Geneva Agreements on Indochina** of July 1954. With US backing, Diem organized a referendum in October 1955, which deposed Bao Dai and established the Republic of Vietnam. He left the country soon after to spend the remainder of his life in exile, mainly in the south of France where he earned a reputation as a playboy. He died in Paris on 31 July 1997.

see also: August Revolution 1945; Diem, Ngo Dinh; Dien Bien Phu, Battle of, 1954; Elysée Agreement 1949; Geneva Agreements on Indochina 1954; Ho Chi Minh; Viet Minh.

Barisan Alternatif (BA) (Malaysia)

The Malay term *Barisan Alternatif* (Alternative Front) was the name of an electoral pact set up in June 1999 to challenge the ***Barisan Nasional*** (National Front, BN) in federal and state elections, which were held in the following November. It comprised ***Parti Islam Se-Malaysia*** (PAS) and the Democratic Action Party (DAP), both well-established, the newly established *Parti Keadilan Nasional* (National Justice Party) and the minor *Parti Rakyat Malaysia* (PRM, Malaysian People's Party). The significance of the pact was the attempt to appeal across racial bounds in the manner of the BN. In the event, only PAS made a major electoral impact by increasing its federal parliamentary strength from seven to twenty-seven seats as well as gaining control of the Terengganu state legislature. The DAP increased its federal representation from nine to ten, while *Parti Keadilan Nasional* won five seats. *Parti Rakyat Malaysia* failed to win any seats. Despite this mixed electoral showing and fundamental differences between PAS and the DAP over the issue of Malaysia becoming an Islamic state, the *Barisan Alternatif* held together as an opposition replica of the ruling coalition.

However the ideological differences proved to be too great, and DAP withdrew from the pact in September 2001. By the 2004 general election, *Barisan Alternatif* consisted of only two parties: ***Parti Keadilan Rakyat*** (People's Justice Party) – the result of a merger between *Parti Keadilan Nasional* and PRM – and PAS, and managed to win only eight parliamentary seats and the state legislature of Kelantan. Their loss was partly attributable to Malaysia's newly appointed prime minister, **Abdullah Badawi**, who was seen as a positive symbol of change in the country's politics, as well as PAS' insistence on furthering their divisive Islamic state agenda. *Barisan Alternatif* was succeeded by the ***Pakatan Rakyat*** coalition, formed shortly after the 2008 general election.

see also: Badawi, Tun Abdullah Ahmad; *Barisan Nasional*; Democratic Action Party; *Parti Islam Se-Malaysia; Pakatan Rakyat; Parti Keadilan Rakyat.*

***Barisan Nasional* (BN)** (Malaysia)

The Malay term *Barisan Nasional* (National Front, BN) is the name of the ruling federal coalition in Malaysia. The coalition is constituted on an inter-communal basis but subject to Maláy dominance, which is reflected in the distribution of Cabinet portfolios. The BN is the direct successor to the **Alliance Party** coalition, which formed the first government of Malaya before independence in August 1957. The Alliance was also an inter-communal coalition comprising the politically predominant **UMNO** (United Malays National Organization), the Malayan (subsequently **Malaysian) Chinese Association** (MCA) and the Malayan (subsequently **Malaysian) Indian Congress** (MIC). The rationale of coalition politics is that bargaining and compromise at the elite level serve to ensure the exercise of collective power, the control of patronage and racial peace.

The BN employs the same inter-communal governing model but on a far more extensive coalition basis, with up to fourteen parties contesting general elections under its banner since its formation. Its origins are to be found in the electoral reverse suffered by UMNO in May 1969, which was followed by inter-communal violence in the **May 13 Racial Riots**. Prime Minister **Tun Abdul Razak** employed the device of a wider coalition to entrench the position of UMNO and to ensure political stability. In February 1972, the primarily non-Malay ***Gerakan Rakyat Malaysia*** Party, which provided the state government on the island of Penang, was brought into the Alliance federal structure, to be followed in April by a coalition arrangement at the state level in Perak between the Alliance and the Indian-led People's Progressive Party. More significant, however, was the agreement in September 1972 between the ruling Alliance and ***Parti Islam Se-Malaysia*** (PAS), the principal Malay opposition party, to establish coalition governments at both state and federal levels. That coalition was constituted formally on 1 January 1973. The BN was registered as a political party on 1 June 1974 and went on to secure a resounding electoral success in August.

The BN survived a major crisis in December 1977 when PAS was expelled after a revolt within the Kelantan state legislature against a chief minister appointed by the federal government. That expulsion was not permitted to undermine the political centrality of the national coalition, which was extended to Malaysian Borneo. Despite reverses in state elections, continuous success at the polls has been demonstrated at the federal level from 1978, the first election after the expulsion of PAS. The BN enjoyed comfortable political success in the 1990s; in April 1995 it was returned to office with 162 seats in a federal Parliament of 192, although in the subsequent November 1999 elections, that number was reduced to 148 seats in a Parliament of 193. The 1999 elections also saw PAS securing control of the state legislature in Terengganu, while holding on to Kelantan which it had retained since 1990.

In the 2004 general election, helmed by **Abdullah Badawi**, the BN performed exceptionally well, winning 198 of the 219 parliamentary seats. However, the coalition's performances have taken a tumble in recent times. In 2008 they won only 140 out of the 222 parliamentary seats, the first time the BN lost its two-thirds parliamentary majority, precipitating Badawi's resignation. In 2013 their majority dipped further to 133 of the 222 parliamentary seats with MCA accounting for most of the seats lost. The BN has also not governed the states of Selangor and Penang since 2008.

Among the reasons for the BN's poor performance in recent times was the resurgence of a more united opposition coalition and the weaknesses of its non-Malay component parties, especially the MCA and MIC, which are viewed in their respective communities as having become too subservient to UMNO. There has also emerged within UMNO's fringes a view that the BN could do without the deadweight of these considerably weakened component allies. However, the BN still wields significant strength in the Borneo states of Sabah and Sarawak, which together accounted for more than one-third of the coalition's parliamentary seats won in the 2008 and 2013 elections.

see also: Alliance Party; Badawi, Tun Abdullah Ahmad; Malaysian Chinese Association; Malaysian Indian Congress; May 13 Racial Riots; *Parti Islam Se-Malaysia*; Razak, Tun Abdul; UMNO.

Barisan Revolusi Nasional (Thailand)

The *Barisan Revolusi Nasional* or BRN is one of the oldest armed insurgent groups operating in Thailand's Malay-majority southern provinces. It was formed in the early 1960s by Haji Abdul Karim bin Hassan, a headmaster of a traditional Islamic boarding school in Narathiwat. Although the BRN drew its support from a network of traditional Islamic schools in Thailand's three Malay-speaking southern border provinces, Karim himself was heavily influenced by the brand of socialism espoused by Indonesia's founding president, **Sukarno**. So closely aligned was the BRN to Sukarno's ideals, Karim was known to have voiced support for Indonesia's policy of **Confrontation** against Malaysia. The BRN established a loose pact with the Communist Party of Malaya in the early 1960s and built up its own armed wing in 1968. Even though it attempted to reach out to Islamic countries in the Middle East, the BRN's embracing of socialist ideals alienated the movement from more conservative Muslim elements. By the early 1980s, differences within the BRN led to the creation of two separate factions, BRN-Coordinate under Haji Amin Tohmeena and BRN-Congress. In the face of increasing pressure from more effective Thai counterinsurgency activities which had the attendant effect of weakening the southern insurgency, both factions were forced to withdraw from open confrontation with the Thai government in the 1990s. It is believed that during this time the BRN-Coordinate managed to recruit a new generation of militants to their cause, allowing them to resume armed conflict in the region at the turn of the century when the government of **Thaksin Shinawatra** came to power. The nature of their recruitment and mobilization strategy however, designed to prevent penetration, has meant that this new generation of insurgents do not follow a readily identifiable chain of command, and so their attacks have taken on a decentralized character without any overarching leadership. This was evident from the inability of self-proclaimed BRN-Coordinate leaders to restrain violence after entering into talks with the Thai government on several occasions since 2006. Therefore, the extent to which BRN elements exercise control over the ongoing insurgency in the southern provinces is unclear (*see*: Insurgency, Southern Provinces).

see also: Confrontation; Insurgency, Southern Provinces; Sukarno; Thaksin Shinawatra.

Barisan Revolusi Nasional-Coordinate (Thailand) *see* ***Barisan Revolusi Nasional***.

Barisan Sosialis (Singapore)

The *Barisan Sosialis* (a Malay term meaning Socialist Front) was a radical left-wing party, which was established in July 1961 as a result of a split within Singapore's ruling **People's Action Party** (PAP). At issue was the prospect of the self-governing island becoming part of a new Federation of Malaysia, comprising also Malaya and British territories in north Borneo, which had been proposed by Malaya's prime minister, **Tunku Abdul Rahman**, in May 1961. That proposal was welcomed by Singapore's prime minister, **Lee Kuan Yew**, and his cabinet colleagues but was denounced as a neo-colonialist plot by a left-wing faction within the PAP. Thirteen parliamentary dissidents crossed the floor of the house to jeopardize the PAP's working majority and to precipitate a major political crisis.

For a short period, the *Barisan Sosialis* gave the impression of being an alternative government in waiting with the capability of thwarting the Malaysia project. However, through political intimidation and the support of conservative opposition parties, the PAP maintained itself in office until after the formation of Malaysia on

16 September 1963. Elections were held in Singapore a week later in which the PAP was returned to office with thirty-seven out of fifty-one seats, which marked a loss of only six seats from its political triumph in May 1959. The *Barisan Sosialis* retained its thirteen seats but failed to make a significant political impact, especially after Singapore became independent in August 1965 on its separation from Malaysia. The PAP increased its seats to forty-nine by the next elections in April 1968 through winning a series of by-elections caused by the resignation of *Barisan Sosialis* members. The party then ceased to function as a credible political entity when it decided to boycott the polls and the PAP won all fifty-eight seats in an enlarged Parliament. From then on, it maintained a vestigial existence; for example, nominating only four candidates without success in elections in September 1988. After those elections, its long-standing leader, Lee Siew Choh, took a place in the Parliament as a 'non-constituency MP' with restricted voting rights as one of two defeated candidates with the highest number of votes. However, the *Barisan Sosialis* failed to nominate candidates in subsequent elections in September 1991 and January 1997 and has ceased to be of any political relevance.

see also: Abdul Rahman, Tunku; Lee Kuan Yew; People's Action Party.

Bersih (Malaysia)

Bersih, which stands for the Coalition of Free and Fair Elections, is a collection of civil society groups and organizations which advocate electoral reform in Malaysia. Since November 2007 when the coalition successfully organized the first of a series of major street demonstrations, *Bersih* has entered the Malaysian political lexicon to describe their rallies as well.

The first *Bersih* rally was held on 10 November 2007, and has been seen as a major contributor to the massive gains made by the opposition ***Pakatan Rakyat*** coalition in the March 2008 general election. The organizers had targeted 100,000 demonstrators, but attendees were estimated to be about 20,000, of which 245 were later detained by the authorities. A heavy police presence diverted the march from the original destination of Dataran Merdeka to the National Palace, where the organizers handed a memorandum to the king of Malaysia. Although the number of participants was small compared to later *Bersih* rallies, it was nevertheless regarded as a success due to the political impact it had on the general election a few months later. The original *Bersih* rally also seemed to have emboldened other non-governmental organizations to take to the streets. Within the same month, another public rally took place, this time organized by **Hindraf** (Hindu Rights Action Force) over alleged injustices against Hindus. The second *Bersih* rally, aptly named *Bersih* 2.0, took place in July 2011, and gained more support than its predecessor. Estimates put the number of demonstrators at around 30,000, although the organizers claimed 50,000 attended. Around 1,600 protestors were arrested and later released. This time, **UMNO** (United Malays National Organization) attempted to counter with a simultaneous rally of their own at a nearby venue, but their turnout was negligible. The buildup to *Bersih* 2.0 was a contentious affair. Aware of the devastating effect of the first *Bersih* rally on their political fortunes, the incumbent government moved quickly to respond once they received word that a second *Bersih* rally was being planned. Attempts to stop the rally from proceeding ranged from intimidation to persuasion to the spread of disinformation. A heavy downpour on the day itself did not deter a turnout much larger than the first *Bersih* rally. Following *Bersih* 2.0, the ***Barisan Nasional*** (National Front) government announced the creation of a non-partisan parliamentary select committee to look into the demands for electoral reform. The third *Bersih* rally was held less than a year later on 28 April 2012 and an estimated 100,000 people took part. The number of arrests made, about 500, was however much smaller. Despite Prime Minister **Najib Razak**'s attempt to assuage civil society groups with pledges of reform and the repeal of the internal security act, *Bersih* 3.0 brought out the largest crowd of the *Bersih* series of rallies calling for the government not only to make good on pledges of reform, but to do so in time for the 2013 general election. The increased number of demonstrators at *Bersih* 3.0

was indicative of growing dissatisfaction towards the government, as well as growing opposition momentum.

Although *Bersih* claims to be apolitical, it is closely associated with opposition political parties that obviously stand to benefit from *Bersih*'s demands for a more transparent electoral system. Led by **Anwar Ibrahim**, opposition parties seized upon the opportunity *Bersih* presented to mobilize popular sentiments against the incumbent government. Aside from opposition political leaders, *Bersih* catapulted several personalities to the status of household names. *Bersih* leader Ambiga Sreenevasan and the popular Malay literary figure A. Samad Said became well-known political activists due to their prominent roles during these rallies. Another development that the *Bersih* rallies unveiled was the increasingly crucial role that internet social networks such as Facebook and Twitter played in social mobilization.

see also: Anwar Ibrahim; *Barisan Nasional*; Hindraf; Najib Tun Razak, Datuk Seri Mohamad; *Pakatan Rakyat*; UMNO.

Bhumibol Adulyadej, King (Thailand)

King Bhumibol Adulyadej is the reigning constitutional monarch of Thailand, the world's longest-ruling monarch, and the longest-lived member of a dynasty which was founded in 1782 by King Rama I. He has exercised a remarkable political influence by augmenting the traditional aura of the throne through an exemplary personal life. He became king on 9 June 1946 after the still unexplained death of his elder brother, **Ananda Mahidol**, from a gunshot wound. Bhumibol was then nineteen; he had been born on 5 December 1927 in Boston, Massachusetts, where his father, Prince Mahidol, was studying medicine. Ananda had ascended to the throne following the abdication of his uncle King Prajadhipok in 1935 in the wake of the coup that abolished absolute monarchy. Both brothers lived in Switzerland, except for a brief visit to Thailand in 1938, until their return in December 1945. After his accession, King Bhumibol went to live again in Switzerland to return to Bangkok in 1950 for his coronation as Rama IX of the Chakri dynasty. By then, Thailand had reverted to military rule for which the monarchy served as a compliant symbol despite an underlying tension which was a legacy of the coup of 1932.

After Field Marshal **Sarit Thanarat** seized power from Field Marshal **Phibul Songkram** in 1957, a conscious policy was adopted of grooming the young king for a national role by exposing him and other members of the royal family to popular contact through an extensive range of ceremonial and civic duties. He took a special interest in rural development and social welfare and began to speak out on constitutional matters after Sarit's death in 1963 when the successor military government lost its authority. King Bhumibol first demonstrated his political facility and authority in October 1973 in reaction to bloodshed in the streets when university students demonstrated against military rule. He intervened to end the violence and was responsible for the prime minister, **Thanom Kittikachorn**, and deputy prime minister, **Praphas Charusathien**, going into exile, which paved the way for a democratic political interlude. The king endorsed democracy but as a conservative became alarmed at the breakdown in public order coincident with the success of revolutionary communism in Indochina in 1975, which resulted in the Laotian monarchy being overthrown. A right-wing assault on students protesting at the return of exiled prime minister Thanom resulted in the **Thammasat University Massacre** on 6 October 1976; this provided the pretext for a military coup, which installed a nominee of the king as prime minister. The king came down on the side of political conservatism and lost popularity as a consequence. With the return to military rule, Thailand began to experiment with a series of constitutions over which the role of the armed forces was centrally at issue. In this chequered process, the king played a cautious part, being careful not to tarnish the throne by too close an association with political life.

During the 1980s King Bhumibol supported the non-elected administration of General **Prem Tinsulanonda** without loss of popular respect because it conducted itself with regard for the virtues of good government. When the elected government of **Chatichai Choonhavan** was overthrown by a military coup in February 1991, he indicated his mild disapproval. In May 1992 popular demonstrations against the unelected retired general **Suchinda Kraprayoon** assuming the office of prime minister were dispersed by the military with great loss of life. After initial hesitation, the king intervened personally to defuse the crisis, which was brought to an end with Suchinda's resignation and fresh elections in September, which produced a democratically elected prime minister, **Chuan Leekpai**. By that intervention, the king restored his political standing and that of the Thai monarchy. In late 1997, during a devastating economic crisis, he let it be known that he was opposed to military intervention and in favour of democratic political change. In December 2002, King Bhumibol called for a 'war on drugs' to arrest the upsurge in substance abuse cases across the country, following which Prime Minister **Thaksin Shinawatra** launched a controversial campaign against such illicit activity in January 2003. The campaign led to more than 2,000 deaths and drew heavy international and domestic criticism. Even so, King Bhumibol openly endorsed Thaksin's heavy-handed approach, suggesting that otherwise the casualty figures from substance abuse would have been much higher. Notwithstanding his endorsement on this occasion, the relationship between King Bhumibol and Prime Minister Thaksin was for the most part a tense one. Thaksin's surging popularity, demonstrated in the election results of 2001 and 2005 when his ***Thai Rak Thai* Party** won landslide victories, unnerved a royal palace concerned about the rise of an alternative centre to which popular sentiments gravitated. Indeed, Thaksin's growing personal stature among the masses was seen to be a direct challenge to the king, to whom the Thai people traditionally turned for succour and leadership. In the event, King Bhumibol was believed to have given his tacit approval of the 2006 coup that removed Thaksin. This stemmed from suggestions that he had received a briefing from privy councillors on their plan to stage a coup, and later granted a special audience to Privy Council president, Prem Tinsulanonda, on the day of the coup. Throughout the political crisis that followed, King Bhumibol's role came under heavy scrutiny and criticism, especially in the international media. The fact that he later appointed coup plotters **Surayud Chulanont**, the interim prime minister, and Air Chief Marshal Chalit Pukbhasuk to the Privy Council only further fanned the flames of suspicion of his role. In June 2006, King Bhumibol celebrated the sixtieth anniversary of his reign, making him the longest-reigning monarch in Thailand.

King Bhumibol is protected by *lèse majesté* laws that sanction the incarceration of critics of Thai royalty for periods between three and fifteen years. However in 2005, King Bhumibol openly called for criticism of the king to be permitted, and for him to be alerted to his mistakes. Heeding the king's call, critics began speaking out, but this merely led to a sharp rise in *lèse majesté* prosecutions from five to six per year prior to 2005 to 478 cases in 2010.

King Bhumibol and his consort Queen Sirikit have four children, three daughters and one son, Crown Prince **Maha Vajiralongkorn**, who has one daughter by his official wife. Prince Vajiralongkorn is the heir apparent but he does not command the reverence and respect enjoyed by his father. The king's highly respected second daughter, Princess Sirindhorn, who is not married, was elevated to the status of an heir presumptive on his fiftieth birthday in December 1977. Despite the many accomplishments of his reign and his sustained reputation, King Bhumibol has not been able to assure the future of the Chakri dynasty. He has a history of cardiac problems which required angioplasty treatment on two occasions during 1995. In September 2009, King Bhumibol was admitted to hospital for flu and pneumonia. He also suffers from lumbar spinal stenosis, and was hospitalized in July 2006, October 2007 and September 2009. In November 2011, the King was diagnosed with diverticulitis and received further treatment for the condition in January 2012. His failing health has meant that he can only observe the latest events in Thailand's unfolding political crisis silently from the sidelines. King Bhumibol was absent from the ceremony which endorsed the military coup of 22 May 2014.

see also: Ananda Mahidol; Chatichai Choonhavan; Chuan Leekpai; Maha Vajiralongkorn,

Prince; Phibul Songkram, Field Marshal; Praphas Charusathien, Field Marshal; Prem Tinsulanonda, General; Sarit Thanarat, Field Marshal; Suchinda Kraprayoon, General; Surayud Chulanont, General; Thammasat University Massacre 1976; *Thai Rak Thai* Party; Thaksin Shinawatra; Thanin Kraivichian; Thanom Kittikachorn, Field Marshal.

Boat People (Vietnam)

The term Boat People has been associated with more than one million refugees who fled from Vietnam in the wake of the Communist seizure of power in the southern half of the country in April 1975. Initially, the exodus was composed of indigenous Vietnamese linked in some way with the defeated Saigon administration who had reason to fear the retribution of the revolutionary government. They left in small boats and undertook perilous journeys across the **South China Sea**, braving the elements and pirates to make landfall in particular in Thailand, Malaysia and Indonesia as well as travelling in a northeasterly direction to reach Hong Kong when the prevailing winds blew that way. The composition of the Boat People changed over the years, however. For example, as the Socialist Republic of Vietnam applied economic dogma in agriculture and directed urban dwellers to new economic zones in the countryside in the late 1970s, Boat People came to be driven by a determination to seek a better life, often to join relatives in the United States and Australia. Then in the late 1970s, with a marked deterioration in Sino-Vietnamese relations which was expressed in discrimination against the Chinese community, Vietnamese of ethnic Chinese identity increasingly made up the flow of Boat People coming from both north and south of the country. That flow was aggravated with Vietnam's invasion of Cambodia in December 1978 and the People's Republic of China's retaliatory military intervention in Vietnam in February 1979.

During the course of the 1980s, however, the flow of Boat People was sustained by economic circumstances in the main, which coincided with a decline in global compassion for their condition. The growing refusal of western governments to accept economic refugees led to a slowing down in the rate of their movement from camps in Southeast Asia to final destinations. The issue of economic refugees from Vietnam came to a head during the late 1980s in Hong Kong, whose camps harboured at one stage over 60,000 refugees, some of whom had travelled overland via China. The solution to the problem of the Boat People came about as a function of Vietnam embarking on market-driven economics followed by concessions over the Cambodian conflict. Under the terms of a comprehensive plan of action agreed in 1989, Vietnam accepted the involuntary repatriation of economic refugees from Hong Kong while the United Nations High Commission for Refugees applied increasing pressure on the population of the Hong Kong camps to return. By the early 1990s, only a handful of Boat People continued to arrive in the territory, with matching figures for Southeast Asian landfalls. In February 1994 the United Nations High Commission for Refugees announced that Vietnamese people would no longer be automatically eligible for consideration as political refugees, which meant that all those resident in camps could be returned home under international law. By 1995, after the United States had lifted its trade and investment embargo against Vietnam, the number of refugees remaining in camps amounted to around 40,000, half of whom were in Hong Kong. In January 1996, the United Nations High Commission for Refugees announced that it would halt funding for all Boat People in first asylum camps by the following July, while Vietnam agreed to speed up repatriation. In the special case of Hong Kong, China urged that all Vietnamese refugees be repatriated before it resumed sovereignty in July 1997, by which time only a remnant were left in one holding camp. In January 1998, the Hong Kong Special Administrative Region abolished the port of first asylum policy, which had applied for the past nineteen years, while the last holding camp was closed in May 2000 with some 1,400 remaining refugees being offered local identity cards.

see also: South China Sea; Vietnam War.

Boediono (Indonesia)

Boediono was vice-president of Indonesia during the second presidential term of **Susilo Bambang Yudhoyono**. He was born on 25 February 1943 in East Java and received his higher education from Gadjah Mada University before leaving to study at the University of Western Australia. He graduated in 1967 with an economics degree and received his master's degree in 1972 from Monash University. Boediono completed his doctoral degree from the Wharton School of the University of Pennsylvania in 1979.

Boediono began his career as Director III in Bank Indonesia, the Central Bank of Indonesia from 1996 to 1997. During this period he was also a professor teaching economics at Gajah Mada University. Subsequently, from 1997 to 1998, he assumed the post of Director I of Bank Indonesia, being in charge of operations and monetary policy. Boediono worked closely with the economist Mubyarto to propound concepts regarding 'the people's economy' and formulated policies that focused on the poor. Known primarily as a brilliant economist, Boediono entered politics late in his career when he was appointed state minister of national planning and development in 1998. In 2001, President **Megawati Sukarnoputri** appointed Boediono as minister of finance. Under his leadership the economy grew by four per cent during 2001–2 as it recovered from the financial meltdown at the end of the last decade. In 2005, President Yudhoyono appointed Boediono as coordinating minister for the economy. In 2008 Boediono was elected governor of Bank Indonesia. He resigned from this post in 2009 to become Yudhoyono's running mate in the latter's successful 2009 presidential re-election campaign. Boediono became embroiled in controversy in 2012 when efforts were made to impeach him on the grounds that he should be held accountable for the controversial US$696.8 million bailout of Bank Century (currently named Bank Mutiara) in 2008, when he was the governor of Indonesia's central bank. However, according to Indonesia's ambiguous constitutional legislation governing investigations into the actions of 'special citizens', any move to impeach Boediono will require the support of two-thirds of the **People's Consultative Assembly**, a sizeable task given that Yudhoyono's ***Partai Demokrat*** and its allies command more than a third of the house.

see also: Megawati Sukarnoputri; *Partai Demokrat*; People's Consultative Assembly; Yudhoyono, Susilo Bambang.

Bolkiah, Sultan Hassanal (Brunei)

Sultan Hassanal Bolkiah is the twenty-ninth absolute ruler of the Sultanate of Brunei. He was born on 15 July 1946 and succeeded his father Sultan Omar Ali Saifuddin in October 1967 when Sultan Omar abdicated the throne in order to thwart British attempts to promote greater democratization. At the time, Hassanal Bolkiah was only a few weeks from graduating from the Royal Military Academy at Sandhurst. He was crowned as Head of State in August 1968. For nearly twenty years, however, until the former sultan's death in 1986, he was overshadowed by his domineering father, from whom he became progressively estranged. Brunei assumed full independence in January 1984 following which a cabinet system of government was established with the sultan as prime minister. In that role, Hassanal Bolkiah consolidated his position, assuming also the portfolio of minister of defence after the death of his father. Hassanal Bolkiah has acquired notoriety by becoming known as one of the richest men in the world, exemplified by his private collection of 500 Rolls Royce cars. Since the death of his father, however, he has adopted a more serious frame of mind, exhibiting greater interest in the business of government of the oil-rich state. He was obliged to assume the additional portfolio of finance minister in February 1997 following the resignation of his brother, Prince Jefri. In August 1998, against a background of economic adversity and fraternal tensions, the sultan had his eldest son, Prince Billah, invested as crown prince in order to assure the succession.

In 2001, the sultan sued his brother, Prince Jefri Bolkiah for embezzling $20.7 billion from the Brunei Investment Authority (BIA) for personal expenses. The sultan however dropped these charges in London's High Court in February 2006. Though original charges against Prince Jefri had been settled, further complications led him to appeal to the Privy Council in London. The Council ruled against him, and in 2008 an arrest warrant was issued against him in London, but he has since claimed to have reconciled with the sultan and settled matters privately.

In a rare move towards political reform, an appointed parliament (also known as the **Legislative Council**), which had been suspended since independence in 1984, was reconvened in 2004. The 2004 amendment to the country's constitution called for a forty-five seat Legislative Council with fifteen elected members, though no timeframe for an election was announced. In September 2005, the Sultan appointed twenty-nine members to the Legislative Council, but further increased the size of the Council to thirty-three members in June 2011. However, the Legislative Council is only invested with advisory powers, and nothing in the constitution could be deemed to derogate from the prerogative of the sultan. In the 2004 constitutional amendment, the sultan conferred upon himself the equivalent of papal infallibility, with the clause: 'His Majesty the Sultan . . . can do no wrong in either his personal or any official capacity'. The amendment not only removed checks on the sultan and granted him complete immunity, but also broadened his powers, for instance, with the clause that the sultan alone has the right to amend the constitution. The sultan has four sons and six daughters with his first wife Queen Saleha and his second wife, Queen Mariam. In 2003, he stripped his second wife of all her royal titles and divorced her, and married Queen Azrinaz Mazhar Hakim in August 2005.

Notwithstanding the sultan's recent moves to consolidate power, at issue is whether this absolutist political system, whose form (***Melayu Islam Beraja***, meaning Malay Islamic Monarchy) is an anachronism within Southeast Asia, can be maintained over time. Hassanal Bolkiah is also head of religion of Brunei. From that position, the absolute monarch passed a controversial edict on the implementation of *shari'a* law in March 2014.

see also: Legislative Council; *Melayu Islam Beraja*.

Bouasone Bouphavanh (Laos)

Bouasone Bouphavanh was prime minister of the People's Democratic Republic of Laos from 2006 to 2010. Bouasone was born in Salavan province in 1954. A student activist in Vientiane in 1975 and key protest organizer against the royalist regime of **Souvanna Phouma**, he attended the Communist Party Institute in Moscow from 1986 to 1990. He was later considered a protégé of former party leader and prime minister, **Khamtay Siphandon**. Bouasone is widely seen to be a key member of a new generation of leaders in the **Lao People's Revolutionary Party** (LPRP) whose political and strategic outlook have been shown to be less constrained by the traditional ties to Vietnam and more open to China. At the same time, the start of Bouasone's premiership also coincided with plans to overhaul the Lao economy, increase foreign investments and open a stock exchange. Bouasone unexpectedly resigned as prime minister in 2010 and was removed from the Politburo during the Ninth Congress of the LPRP a year later. Bouasone was replaced as prime minister by **Thongsing Thammavong**. His sudden resignation and fall from grace raised many questions that remain unanswered.

see also: Khamtay Siphandon; Lao People's Revolutionary Party; Souvanna Phouma, Prince; Thongsing Thammavong.

Brevié Line (Cambodia/Vietnam)

The Brevié Line is a delimitation drawn on a map in 1939 to differentiate administrative and police responsibilities over offshore islands between Cochin China (southern Vietnam) and Cambodia, then both subject to French control. Named after Jules Brevié, a governor-general of Indochina, the line extended into the Gulf of Siam from the land border between the two territories without confirming sovereign jurisdiction. The line was recognized as a maritime boundary in 1967 after negotiations between the government of Cambodia and representatives of the Democratic Republic of (North) Vietnam and the **National Liberation Front of South Vietnam**. It became a matter of contention after the **Khmer Rouge** assumed power in Cambodia in April 1975. Talks with Vietnam in May 1976 broke down over the proposal by its government to modify the line so as to redefine the configuration of territorial waters to permit easier access to the Vietnamese island of Phu Quoc. The status of the line remains unclear in the wake of the settlement of the Cambodian conflict at the **International Conference on Cambodia** in Paris in October 1991. Although relations between Phnom Penh and Hanoi have been repaired, an underlying historical tension has prevented any conclusive agreement on the definition and demarcation of territorial waters.

see also: International Conference on Cambodia, Paris 1991; Khmer Rouge; National Liberation Front of South Vietnam.

Brunei Revolt 1962 (Brunei)

An abortive uprising was staged in the British-protected sultanate of Brunei on 8 December 1962 by members of the opposition **People's Party** (*Partai Ra'ayat*) led by A. M. Azahari. The People's Party had won an overwhelming majority of elective seats in the first general elections to the **Legislative Council** in August 1962 on a platform of opposition to Brunei joining the projected Federation of Malaysia. Expressing a local irredentism, Azahari had called for the establishment of a state of North Borneo (to include adjacent Sarawak and Sabah). Frustrated in its attempt to have the Legislative Council convened, the clandestine military wing of the People's Party – the self-styled North Borneo National Army – made an attempt to seize power. The sultan called on British military support under a treaty of 1959; troops were dispatched from Singapore and put down the revolt within a matter of days. Since then, a state of emergency has been in force in the sultanate. The constitution has remained suspended and the People's Party proscribed. Azahari's absence from Brunei at the time of the uprising suggests an ill-planned exercise, although material support and training is believed to have been provided from Indonesian Borneo. He had enjoyed close political associations with President **Sukarno**'s Indonesia where he found asylum and diplomatic support after the uprising had failed. Domestically, the Brunei Revolt arrested political development in the sultanate. Internationally, it provided the pretext for Indonesia's policy of **Confrontation** of Malaysia with support proffered for the so-called state of North Borneo. The revolt almost certainly was a factor in the decision by Sultan Sir Omar Ali Saifuddin in July 1963 not to take Brunei into Malaysia.

see also: Azahari, A. M.; Confrontation; People's Party; Sukarno.

Buddhism (Cambodia/Laos/Myanmar/Thailand/Vietnam)

The Buddhist faith in Southeast Asia is identified primarily with countries of the mainland part of the region. It draws its name from the philosopher Gautama Buddha, who lived in the sixth century in Nepal. His personal revelation came from an attempt to transcend the constraints of Hinduism based on a continuing cycle of life, death and reincarnation. He claimed to have found the secret to *nirvana* or personal salvation from the suffering of life through renouncing all worldly possessions and desires and by total immersion in meditation, not through worship of any deity. His example lives on in the regime of saffron-robed monks who eat only one meal a day provided by benefactors who fill their bowls at the roadside.

Buddhism came to Southeast Asia through two routes and has taken two forms. Mahayana Buddhism (the greater vehicle) is to be found primarily in Vietnam, where it was brought from India via China. Theravada Buddhism (the lesser vehicle) is believed to have penetrated Myanmar (Burma), Thailand, Laos and Cambodia from India via Sri Lanka (formerly Ceylon). Although Buddhism is a religious philosophy which renounces the material world, its clergy and adherents have been directly involved in political activity. In Burma and Cambodia before the Pacific War, Buddhism served as a vehicle for expressing nationalist sentiment against the colonial powers. In South Vietnam in 1963, Buddhist agitation against the government of the Catholic **Ngo Dinh Diem** was an important factor in US support being withdrawn and a military coup being mounted during which he was killed. In Thailand, the *Palang Dharma* (Moral Force) Party led by retired general **Chamlong Srimuang**, which challenged military rule on the streets of Bangkok in May 1992, has been closely identified with the *Santi Asoke* Buddhist sect. In September 1998, Buddhist monks were in the forefront of a mass protest outside the US embassy in Phnom Penh against Prime Minister **Hun Sen** whose **Cambodian People's Party** had secured victory in general elections in the previous July. Buddhist monks were also at the forefront of widespread anti-government demonstrations in Myanmar in August 2007 in what has come to be called the **Saffron Revolution**. Although Buddhism stresses peace and harmony, the political cultures of countries in mainland Southeast Asia have not been informed by its ethics and political violence has been commonplace. Against the backdrop of political liberalization under the government of President **Thein Sein**, Buddhist aggression, inflamed by the radical teachings of the popular monk Ashin Wirathu, has been directed at Rohingya Muslims in 2012–13. On the other hand, Buddhist monks have frequently been victims in Thailand's southern border provinces where a Malay-Muslim insurgency rages.

see also: Cambodian People's Party; Chamlong Srimuang, General; Diem, Ngo Dinh; Hun Sen; Insurgency, Southern Provinces; Saffron Revolution; Thein Sein.

Bumiputra (Malaysia)

Bumiputra is a Malay term which translates as sons of the soil or indigenous people. In practice, the term has been applied exclusively to the Malays and not the *orang asli* (aborigines) whose settlement predates them. *Bumiputra* entered the vocabulary of Malaysian politics with a vengeance after racial violence in the **May 13 Racial Riots** 1969. That violence, which followed an electoral rebuff to **UMNO** (United Malays National Organization), was interpreted as a strong indication that the principal Malay party was losing its traditional constituency. To counter this trend, in 1970 the Malay-dominated government introduced a **New Economic Policy** whose objective was to redress the balance of economic advantage in favour of the *Bumiputra* or Malays. Underlying the affirmative action was a Malay anxiety that they would lose their political birthright to the non-Malays of migrant origin, especially the Chinese, unless control of the economy was radically revised. Communal prerogative in economic affairs was demonstrated from then on by financial and trade portfolios being held exclusively by Malay ministers, by the redistribution of corporate wealth and by the allocation of educational scholarships and access to government-controlled employment. The allocation of shares in publicly listed companies in order to give Malays a greater stake in corporate wealth has been controversial, with recurrent charges of corrupt practice. The equivalent term in Indonesia is *Pribumi*.

see also: Bank Bumiputera Crisis; May 13 Racial Riots 1969; New Economic Policy; *Pribumi*; UMNO.

Burma Socialist Programme Party (BSPP) (Burma/Myanmar)

On 2 March 1962 a military-based Revolutionary Council led by General **Ne Win** seized power in Burma. The Revolutionary Council then published an ideological document entitled the 'Burmese Way to Socialism', which sought to justify the coup against the democratically elected government and to chart the future course of the state. On 4 July the Revolutionary Council announced the establishment of a new Burma Socialist Programme Party or BSPP (*Lanzin* in Burmese) charged with the task of guiding the country along the so-called way to socialism. All other parties were declared illegal. Comprising initially members of the Revolutionary Council only, the BSPP was modelled on Communist counterparts but, in effect, served as a political instrument at the personal disposal of Ne Win and his clients in the armed forces for only as long as it was necessary.

The BSPP was changed from a cadre to a mass party in 1971; membership became essential for any kind of preferment in society. Of the one million full and candidate members, over half were drawn from serving or retired military or police, while around eighty per cent of the active armed forces belonged to the patronage network. A new constitution promulgated in January 1974, which inaugurated the Socialist

Republic of Burma, made no difference to the power structure with which Ne Win through the armed forces controlled the BSPP and its mass organizations. For example, Ne Win stepped down as head of state in November 1981 but continued as chairman of the BSPP. In the meantime, through a dogmatic and highly bureaucratized system of economic planning compounded by an isolationist foreign policy, the Burmese people experienced a steady decline in their standard of living. The party and the army, however, maintained a position of privilege, generating a growing popular alienation which came to a head in the late 1980s.

Popular dissent began to manifest itself in a politically significant way from September 1987 after an arbitrary act of demonetization to cope with economic collapse removed some eighty per cent of banknotes in circulation. In March 1988 a clash involving students in a teashop in a Rangoon suburb sparked off sustained protests which were put down by the military with great loss of life. The BSPP convened an extraordinary congress in July at which Ne Win announced his intention to retire as chairman. After a bloody confrontation in the streets of Rangoon in August, the BSPP convened a second extraordinary congress in September at which multiparty elections were promised. Shortly after, the government revealed that all members of the armed forces had given up membership of the BSPP. On 18 September 1988 the minister of defence, General Saw Maung, announced that the military had set up a **State Law and Order Restoration Council** (SLORC) which, in effect, marked the end of the BSPP as the main political instrument of Ne Win's rule.

On 26 September 1988 the BSPP changed its name to the **National Unity Party**. It took part in elections for a constituent assembly in May 1990, losing heavily to the **National League for Democracy** led in effect by an incarcerated **Aung San Suu Kyi**, the daughter of nationalist martyr, **Aung San**. The military authorities refused to recognize the results of the elections and employed SLORC as the principal vehicle for exercising power, having lost all use for the BSPP in its revised form. In November 1997, SLORC was succeeded by the **State Peace and Development Council** (SPDC).

see also: Aung San; Aung San Suu Kyi; National League for Democracy; National Unity Party; Ne Win, General; State Law and Order Restoration Council; State Peace and Development Council.

Buy British Last Policy (Malaysia)

The Buy British Last Policy was an act of open discrimination against the purchase of British goods and services which was first announced by Malaysia's prime minister, Mahathir Mohamad, in October 1981 within three months of his assumption of high office. The Buy British Last Policy was precipitated by the decision of the London Stock Exchange to adjust its rules in order to make 'dawn raids' or surprise takeover bids more difficult to execute. In September 1981 Malaysia's National Investment Corporation, acting through British agents, had secured control of Guthrie, which owned large plantations in the country, by such means. Mahathir construed the decision by the Stock Exchange as a deliberate attempt to frustrate his government's policy of securing control of national assets. He was angered also by the British government's decision to oblige its universities to charge higher fees for overseas students, of whom Malaysians constituted the largest number, as well as resistance to additional flights into London for his country's national airline. In employing the policy, Mahathir was giving public vent to a deep-seated personal resentment arising from his experiences during the colonial period as well as securing political advantage from his open confrontation of Britain.

The Buy British Last Policy was sustained until April 1983 when Mahathir withdrew his directive to government departments which required all contracts with British firms to be scrutinized by his office to see whether or not there was a better alternative source. His change of political heart had been prompted by discussions with Britain's prime minister, Margaret Thatcher, during a visit to London in the previous month. Anglo-Malaysian rapprochement was sealed during a visit to Malaysia by Prime Minister Thatcher in April 1985 but an understanding on aid and trade reached during that visit sowed the seeds for future acrimony between the two governments.

A confidential Anglo-Malaysian memorandum of understanding was concluded in September 1988 for Malaysia's purchase of British defence exports. An earlier draft of that memorandum had linked aid provision and defence sales. The matter became public knowledge in Britain following a report from the National Audit Office in October 1993 which was highly critical of aid provided for a hydroelectric dam on the Pergau River in the state of Kelantan. During the course of an extensive press investigation and hearings by the House of Commons Public Accounts Committee and its Select Committee on Foreign Affairs, the memorandum of understanding was leaked to a British newspaper, to the embarrassment of the two governments. In addition, a report in *The Sunday Times* in February 1994 alleged that a leading British construction company had been involved in negotiating 'special payments' at the highest level in Malaysia in order to secure a contract. The Malaysian government reacted angrily on 25 February 1994 when the deputy prime minister, **Anwar Ibrahim**, announced a boycott of all British companies bidding for official contracts. Malaysia's decision was prompted by the personal fury of Mahathir at allegations of his personal financial impropriety set against a domestic background of political challenges and setbacks after nearly thirteen years in high office. The ban was rescinded in September 1994.

see also: Anwar Ibrahim; Mahathir Mohamad, Tun.

C

Cam Ranh Bay (Vietnam)

Cam Ranh Bay is situated on the central coast of Vietnam some twenty miles to the south of Nha Trang. It provides good natural anchorages and was used in 1905 by the ill-fated Russian fleet on their way to engage the Japanese. It assumed more than local significance from the mid-1960s, when it was developed into a major military logistical facility for both aircraft and naval vessels by the United States, then assuming the prime burden in military confrontation with the Vietnamese Communists. In the **Vietnam War** the base was subject to rocket attack during the **Tet Offensive** in 1968 and was taken over by the government in Hanoi following its ultimate military success in 1975. Soviet interest in replacing the United States as the tenant of the base was resisted by Hanoi until early 1979, when relations with the People's Republic of China had deteriorated dramatically over Cambodia. A **Treaty of Friendship and Cooperation** signed with the Soviet Union in November 1978 provided the basis for the deployment of its aircraft and naval vessels at Cam Ranh Bay from March 1979. That deployment never had a tangible military role; Soviet forces were never engaged in any military action from the base. Intelligence gathering and showing the flag constituted the main purpose of the exercise, which aggravated Vietnamese and Soviet relations with China and caused suspicion within Southeast Asia. The Soviet presence was directly affected by the attempt by Mikhail Gorbachev from his assumption of power in March 1985 to improve relations with both China and the United States.

In January 1990 it was announced in Moscow that, in line with an overall reduction in overseas commitments, the Soviet Union had begun withdrawing most of its aircraft from Cam Ranh Bay from the end of 1989. In October 1990 the Soviet ambassador to Vietnam announced that his country had begun withdrawing its troops from the base. With the collapse of the Soviet Union, Russia assumed responsibility for the residual military presence in Vietnam and it was announced in January 1992 that the last major warship had returned to Vladivostok in December 1991. A vestigial presence of neither military nor political significance has remained which Russia has sought to retain, while the Vietnamese have begun to explore alternative commercial possibilities for the facility. After a visit by Russia's foreign minister in July 1995, it was announced that its fleet would continue to enjoy access to the military base. In October 2010, Vietnamese prime minister **Nguyen Tan Dung** announced that after reconstruction, Cam Ranh Bay would be open for use by foreign naval vessels in 2014.

see also: Nguyen Tan Dung; Tet Offensive 1968; Treaty of Friendship and Cooperation 1978; Vietnam War.

Cambodia National Rescue Party (Cambodia)

The Cambodia National Rescue Party (CNRP) is an electoral alliance formed in October 2012 between the two main opposition parties, the **Sam Rainsy Party** (SRP) and the Human Rights Party (HRP). The CNRP is led by former leader of the SRP, **Sam Rainsy**, who had lived in self-imposed exile in France since 2005 and only returned to Cambodia a week before the polling for the 2013 general elections after receiving a royal pardon from King **Norodom Sihamoni** at the request of the prime minister, **Hun Sen**. Nevertheless, the National Election Commission banned Sam Rainsy from contesting an electoral seat as it deemed his return too late for his inclusion in the polls. In the event, CNRP exceeded expectations on its way to victory in fifty-five out of the 123 National Assembly seats, in the process capturing forty-four per cent of the valid vote. In doing so the CRNP prevented the ruling party from obtaining a two-thirds majority in Parliament. This was a marked improvement from the previous election, when both the SRP and HRP managed to collectively win only twenty-nine seats. The CNRP rejected the victory of the **Cambodian People's Party** (CPP), and called for investigations to be performed by an independent committee into alleged election irregularities, to which Hun Sen has agreed. The ground gained by the CNRP at the 2013 polls have been attributed to a united opposition, the return of Sam Rainsy, and a generational shift in attitudes and voting allegiances as youths cast dissenting votes against the prolonged authoritarian rule of Hun Sen.

see also: Cambodian People's Party; Hun Sen; Sam Rainsy; Sam Rainsy Party; Sihamoni, King Norodom.

Cambodian People's Party (CPP)

(Cambodia)

The CPP is the direct lineal successor of the **Kampuchean People's Revolutionary Party** (KPRP), which was established in January 1979 in the wake of Vietnam's invasion and occupation of Cambodia. The change in nomenclature, together with a disclaimer of Marxist identity and Vietnamese links, took place at an extraordinary congress on 17–18 October 1991 just before the **International Conference on Cambodia** reconvened in Paris. The CPP was a signatory to the political settlement reached in the French capital, which left its administration of Cambodia intact during the transitional period before elections held under **United Nations** auspices. The CPP, headed by **Chea Sim**, president of the National Assembly, and **Hun Sen**, the prime minister, cooperated up to a point with **UNTAC** (United Nations Transitional Authority in Cambodia) but employed its internal security apparatus to intimidate its non-Communist electoral opponents. In the event, it came second with fifty-one seats to **FUNCINPEC** led by Prince **Norodom Ranariddh** with fifty-eight. The CPP contested the outcome vociferously and, for a time, threatened secession in the country's eastern provinces as a gambit to ensure its participation in government. It eventually joined a fragile coalition at the end of October in which Hun Sen assumed the office of second prime minister to Prince Ranariddh, while Chea Sim maintained his National Assembly position.

The coalition government existed more in form than substance and was flawed by the refusal of the CPP to share power within the army, police and the provincial administration where its hold was tightly maintained. Political polarization within the coalition came to a head over the competing ambitions of Hun Sen and Prince Ranariddh and their attempts to recruit defectors from the **Khmer Rouge** for their bitter struggle. In April 1997, Hun Sen engineered the defection to the CPP of sufficient FUNCINPEC members of the National Assembly to overturn its majority. In July 1997, Hun Sen ousted Prince Ranariddh in a bloody coup and established his political dominance, while still holding the office of second prime minister. Hun Sen led the CCP to electoral victory in the July 1998 elections, as it won sixty-four of the 123 seats in the National Assembly. After elections in July 1998, a new coalition government was established in November based on a new power-sharing agreement between the CPP and FUNCINPEC, which barely masked political realities. Hun Sen became the sole prime minister, while Prince Ranariddh assumed the office of president of the National Assembly. By that juncture, the CPP had long shed its Vietnamese provenance and had become a vehicle for the personal political ambitions of Hun Sen.

Hun Sen continued to lead the CPP to victory in seventy-three out of 123 National Assembly seats at the 2003 elections. This was however short of the two-thirds majority required to form a government on its own. In order to overcome this deadlock, the CPP held protracted negotiations with FUNCINPEC and a new coalition government was cobbled together in July 2004. In early 2006, the CPP moved to shed its dependence on FUNCINPEC when it mobilized its majority to amend the constitution in order that the formation of a government required only a simple majority in the National Assembly. In 2008, the CPP won the popular vote by the largest margin since the introduction of democratic elections in the country, on the way to ninety seats. Despite the fact that the CPP secured an outright majority in the National Assembly and Senate, it continued to govern in coalition with the royalist FUNCINPEC, although the influence of the latter has declined steadily since 1998. In 2013 however, the CPP saw its majority erode to sixty-eight seats as it lost considerable ground to the opposition **Cambodia National Rescue Party**.

see also: Cambodia National Rescue Party; Chea Sim; FUNCINPEC; Hun Sen; International Conference on Cambodia, Paris 1991; Khmer Rouge; Kampuchean People's Revolutionary Party; Ranariddh, Prince Norodom; United Nations: Cambodia 1991–3; UNTAC.

Cebu Summit (ASEAN) 2006 (Brunei/Cambodia/Indonesia/Laos/Malaysia/Myanmar/Philippines/Singapore/Thailand/Vietnam)

The twelfth meeting of heads of government of **ASEAN** (Association of Southeast Asian Nations) convened in Cebu, Philippines, from 9 to 15 January 2007. The summit was originally scheduled to be held in December 2006, but the Philippines government postponed it two days before ASEAN leaders were to meet, citing adverse weather disturbance as typhoon Seniang was expected to hit Cebu during that period. Instability in the administration of President **Gloria Macapagal-Arroyo** and growing civil unrest against the government at the time might have also contributed to the government's decision to postpone the summit.

The leaders gathered in January 2007 amidst a heavy security presence in Cebu after three consecutive bombings struck cities in Mindanao only hours after the Summit kicked off. ASEAN leaders signed the Cebu Declaration on the blueprint of an **ASEAN Charter**, endorsing the recommendations of the Eminent Persons Group (EPG). The High Level Task Force (HLTF) was then tasked to draft the charter for submission at the thirteenth ASEAN summit in Singapore in 2007. The Cebu meeting also witnessed the signing of the Cebu Declaration on the Acceleration of the Establishment of an ASEAN Community by 2015 which effectively pushed forward the original deadline by five years. At the second **East Asia Summit** (EAS), special attention was given to cooperation on energy issues including but not limited to energy security, renewable energy, energy efficiency and climate change. To that end, the leaders signed the Cebu Declaration on East Asian Energy Security which aims to enhance regional cooperation in reducing dependence on fossil fuels, improving energy efficiency, mitigating greenhouse gas emissions and encouraging private sector investment, as well as developing open competitive regional and international energy markets. The summit also witnessed the accession of France and Timor-Leste to the **Treaty of Amity and Cooperation**.

see also: ASEAN; ASEAN Charter; East Asia Summit; Macapagal-Arroyo, Gloria; Treaty of Amity and Cooperation.

Cham (Cambodia/Vietnam)

The Cham are a distinct ethno-cultural group to be found in both Cambodia and Vietnam. They trace their origins to the ancient kingdom of Champa once located in central Vietnam, which was overwhelmed and its inhabitants dispersed in the fifteenth century by Vietnam's relentless expansion to the south. By that time, **Islam** had been adopted as the religious faith, which has been more rigorously maintained in the Cambodian diaspora, while a form of Malay has become the common language. Cham in Cambodia, who numbered fewer than 100,000, sustained a distinct identity under French rule which began to be challenged by Prince **Norodom Sihanouk**'s regime. They suffered cruelly from the **Khmer Rouge**, however, who sought to extinguish their separate cultural existence, decimating their communities in the process. Since Vietnam's overthrow of **Pol Pot**'s government, the Cham have maintained a vestigial existence, although a significant number have been accepted as refugees in Malaysia.

see also: Islam; Khmer Rouge; Pol Pot; Sihanouk, King Norodom.

Chamlong Srimuang, General (Thailand)

Chamlong Srimuang played a critical role in mobilizing popular protest against the former army commander-in-chief, General **Suchinda Kraprayoon**, in May 1992 after he had assumed the office of prime minister in Thailand without having stood in general elections in March 1992.

Chamlong Srimuang was born on 5 July 1935 in Thonburi of Chinese immigrant parents and was educated at the Chulachomklao Royal Military Academy, after which he began his career as a signals officer. He served in Vietnam and received postgraduate training in public administration in the United States. He was a prominent member of the **Young Turks** faction of the military, which was responsible for replacing General **Kriangsak Chomanan** with General **Prem Tinsulanonda** as prime minister in 1980. He served as secretary-general to Prem but resigned this post after an abortive coup in April 1981 mounted by his military contemporaries. Chamlong had joined the radical Buddhist *Santi Asoke* sect in 1979 and became an open advocate of its regime of personal self-denial. In 1985, he resigned from the army with the rank of major general and in November stood as an independent candidate in elections for the office of governor of Bangkok, which he won comfortably. In 1988 he established the *Palang Dharma* (Moral Force) Party, which had only limited success in general elections in July. Chamlong won a second term as governor of Bangkok in January 1990 but resigned in January 1992 to stand in national elections in March. His party fared much better this time and after General Suchinda assumed the office of prime minister, Chamlong led the popular confrontation in the streets against the military which resulted in not only great loss of life but in Suchinda's political downfall. Chamlong was re-elected to Parliament in September 1992 and his party became a member of the ruling coalition. Chamlong refused to hold office, however, and announced in January 1993 that he was giving up the leadership of *Palang Dharma*. Nevertheless, he continued to be politically active. In April 1994 he made a crude bid for cabinet office, which was resisted by Prime Minister **Chuan Leekpai**. He then secured re-election as leader of *Palang Dharma* and in October 1994 entered the cabinet as deputy prime minister. He gave up the leadership of his party just before parliamentary elections in July 1995 in favour of **Thaksin Shinawatra**, reflecting the tension between religious and business-oriented factions and also announced his withdrawal from political life. However, in June 1996, he stood unsuccessfully for governor of Bangkok and again announced his retirement from politics. Chamlong remained out of the public eye until 2005 when he led a protest against the initial public offering of Thai Beverage PLC on the Stock Exchange of Thailand. In the same year he rose to prominence and became a key leader in the **People's Alliance for Democracy** (PAD) protesting against the rule of Thaksin Shinawatra which culminated in the September 2006 military coup. Chamlong was rewarded for his role with an appointment to the new parliament. His stance shifted somewhat afterward towards the military, but against the government of **Surayud Chulanont**. Chamlong and the PAD took to the streets again in May 2008 after the elections of December 2007 and the establishment of the **People's Power Party** government. Perceiving the government to be a vehicle for Thaksin's return from exile, Chamlong and the PAD organized demonstrations to urge the ousting of the government. Stepping up the pressure, the PAD seized the Government House compound on 26 August. Although **Samak Sundaravej** resigned as prime minister in early September he was replaced by **Somchai Wongsawat**, Thaksin's brother-in-law. Chamlong was arrested on 4 October on charges of treason, illegal assembly, insurrection and conspiracy, but the insurrection charges were later withdrawn and he was released on bail. Chamlong remained a leader of the PAD, threatening to bring the group back to the streets in 2009 in response to the growing 'red shirt' protest movement against the government of **Abhisit Vejjajiva**. Chamlong has enjoyed a mixed reputation. His role in challenging military autocracy has been acknowledged, but together with a ruthless personal ambition and an authoritarian disposition.

see also: Abhisit Vejjajiva; Chuan Leekpai; Kriangsak Chomanan, General; People's Alliance for Democracy; People's Power Party; Prem Tinsulanonda, General; Samak Sundaravej; Somchai Wongsawat; Suchinda Kraprayoon, General; Surayud Chulanont, General; Thaksin Shinawatra; Young Turks.

Chart Pattana Party (Thailand)

The *Chart Pattana* (National Development) Party was set up in July 1992 as the political vehicle of former prime minister **Chatichai Choonhavan**, who defected from the *Chart Thai* Party of which he had been leader. It enjoyed modest electoral success in September 1992 and was in opposition until December 1994 when it entered the Democrat Party-led coalition but without Chatichai assuming ministerial office. It returned to opposition after elections in July 1995 but then joined the government headed by the New Aspiration Party after elections in November 1996. In November 1997, with a political realignment induced by economic adversity, and after an abortive bid by Chatichai to become prime minister, the **Democrat Party** replaced the New Aspiration Party as the core of the ruling coalition and *Chart Pattana* returned to opposition. Chatichai died in May 1998 but, despite expectations of the party's likely demise, it entered the Democrat-led ruling coalition in October 1998 in the face of some resistance because of its reputation for corruption. After the sweeping victory of the ***Thai Rak Thai* Party** (TRT) in the 2001 elections, *Chart Pattana* joined the coalition government of **Thaksin Shinawatra** in December 2001, but was later dropped in November 2003. Several party members subsequently defected while the party was pressured by Thaksin to merge with TRT before the 2005 elections. TRT was dissolved by the Constitutional Court in May 2007 following the September 2006 military coup that ousted the Thaksin government. In September 2007, members of the *Chart Pattana* faction of TRT merged with the *Ruam Jai Thai* (Thai United) Party to form the *Ruam Jai Thai Chart Pattana* Party. In the 2007 election the party won eight seats in the House of Representatives and became a member of the six-party coalition government led by the Democratic Party's **Abhisit Vejjajiva**. In 2011 the party merged with the *Puea Pandin* Party to form the *Chart Pattana Puea Pandin* Party under Wannarat Channukul. The party won seven seats in the July 2011 elections, a step down from the combined total of forty-one seats held by the two parties before the elections. Following the overwhelming victory of the ***Pheu Thai* Party** in 2011, *Chart Pattana Puea Pandin* joined three others and *Pheu Thai* in a coalition government under **Yingluck Shinawatra**.

see also: Abhisit Vejjajiva; Chatichai Choonhavan; *Chart Thai* Party; Democrat Party; New Aspiration Party; *Pheu Thai* Party; Samak Sundaravej; Somchai Wongsawat; *Thai Rak Thai* Party; Thaksin Shinawatra; Yingluck Shinawatra.

Chart Thai Party (Thailand)

The *Chart Thai* (Thai National) Party served as a junior member of the **Democrat Party**-led ruling coalition which assumed office in November 1997. It had been the core party in government between July 1995 and November 1996, when a poor electoral showing led to a period in opposition. The *Chart Thai* Party has its origins in a military–business family network in direct lineal descent from Field Marshal Pin Choonhavan, a political strongman during the 1950s. It was founded in 1974 by close relatives of Field Marshal Pin, including his son-in-law, General Adireksan, who became its leader. He was succeeded in 1986 by Pin's son, General **Chatichai Choonhavan** who was prime minister between 1988 and 1991. The *Chart Thai* Party has participated in a series of coalition governments since 1975 primarily as a political vehicle for a set of business interests with military links, which have disposed of great wealth in election campaigns. Like virtually all Thai parties, it has experienced recurrent defections from its ranks, including its former leader, Chatichai Choonhavan, who established the ***Chart Pattana* Party** (National Development Party) just before elections in September 1992. Despite factional tensions, the *Chart Thai* Party has sustained its institutional identity. It was led nominally by retired air chief marshal Sombun Rahong until May 1994, when he was succeeded by provincial businessman **Banharn Silpa-archa** who took the party to electoral success in July 1995 when it secured ninety-two seats in a Parliament of 391 and took over the office of prime minister. It lost office in elections in November 1996 but returned to government as a junior partner in November 1997. In coalition, Banharn has retained tight control over the party without assuming ministerial office. *Chart Thai* won forty-one seats in the 2001 elections and formed a coalition government with the largest party, ***Thai Rak Thai* Party** (TRT), led by **Thaksin Shinawatra**. However, during the 2005 elections the party won only twenty-seven seats. Policy conflicts led *Chart Thai* to defect from its coalition with TRT and later, together with the Democrat Party, boycotted the April 2006 elections in an attempt to block TRT from forming a new government. *Chart Thai* participated in the December 2007 election, winning thirty-seven seats, making it the biggest winner after the **People's Power Party** (PPP) and the Democrat Party. In January 2008, *Chart Thai* joined the PPP and five other parties to form a coalition government, only to fall victim to the Constitutional Court's decision on 2 December 2008 to dissolve the party, along with the PPP and Matchima Party, for having violated electoral laws during the 2007 election. Party executives, including Banharn, were banned from politics for five years. Most former *Chart Thai* members of parliament went on to found the *Chart Thai Pattana* (Thai Nation Development) Party.

see also: Banharn Silpa-archa; *Chart Pattana* Party; Chatichai Choonhavan; Democrat Party; People's Power Party; *Thai Rak Thai* Party; Thaksin Shinawatra.

Chatichai Choonhavan, General (Thailand)

Chatichai Choonhavan was a flamboyant political figure who served as prime minister of Thailand from August 1988 until his removal from office through a military coup in February 1991. As leader of the *Chart Thai* **Party** (Thai National Party), with the largest number of members in the Parliament, he succeeded **Prem Tinsulanonda** on his resignation. As the first elected prime minister for twelve years, Chatichai Choonhavan made an immediate impact in foreign policy by softening his country's stance towards Cambodia and Vietnam and announcing his intention of turning Indochina from a battleground into a trading market. In domestic policy he departed from the cautious technocratic culture of his predecessor to provide a more direct business orientation. In the event, his administration's reputation for corrupt practices softened the public response to his overthrow, which was precipitated by suspicion within the military establishment that he intended to purge its serving hierarchy.

Chatichai Choonhavan was born in Bangkok on 5 April 1922. His father was Field Marshal Pin Choonhavan, who was a powerful political figure during the 1950s until displaced by Field Marshal **Sarit Thanarat**. He was educated at the Chulachomklao Royal Military Academy in Bangkok and served with Thai units in Burma and southern China during the Pacific War and also saw action in the Korean War. With his father's political fall, he was sent, in effect, into exile serving as ambassador in Europe and Latin America. After the death of Sarit, he returned to Thailand and worked in the foreign ministry; in 1972 he distinguished himself for his bravery in rescuing Israeli hostages seized by the Palestinian Black September organization. He was a founder member of the *Chart Thai* Party in 1974. As a leading member of that alliance between the military and business, he held a number of government offices including that of foreign minister. Following his removal from power, he spent time in exile in Britain but returned to political life in 1992. He led a defection from the *Chart Thai* Party to form the ***Chart Pattana* Party** (National Development Party), which took part in elections in September 1992 to win sixty seats but without securing membership of the coalition government led by **Chuan Leekpai**. His new party entered the ruling coalition in December 1994 but without Chatichai assuming ministerial office. It returned to opposition after elections in July 1995 but re-entered government after further elections in November 1996, but again without Chatichai. In November 1997, when Prime Minister **Chavalit Yongchaiyuth** was obliged to give up office against a background of economic crisis, Chatichai made an abortive bid to succeed him. He died in May 1998.

see also: Chart Pattana Party; *Chart Thai* Party; Chavalit Yongchaiyuth, General; Chuan Leekpai; Prem Tinsulanonda, General; Sarit Thanarat, Field Marshal.

Chavalit Yongchaiyuth, General
(Thailand)

General Chavalit Yongchaiyuth was prime minister of Thailand between November 1996 and November 1997 when he was obliged to resign office against a background of economic crisis. Chavalit Yongchaiyuth was born on 15 May 1932 in Nonthaburi Province and began his career as a professional soldier on entering the Chulachomklao Royal Military Academy in 1953. He received staff training in Thailand and also at Fort Leavenworth in the United States. He developed strong ideas from Communist defectors about the need to promote rural economic development as a counter to insurgency and was associated with the influential **Democratic Soldiers** faction. He put such ideas into practice when he rose to become army commander-in-chief in 1986. In that position, he indicated clear political ambition but his crude ideological formulations aroused hostility from the royal family, who suspected him of republican leanings. He was never tempted to realize his ambition through direct military means but was attracted by an offer of political preferment by then Prime Minister **Chatichai Choonhavan**. He retired from active command in March 1990 to be directly appointed deputy prime minister and minister of defence. His first spell in politics as an unelected minister proved to be frustrating and in June he resigned from the government, ostensibly because of allegations of corruption by a cabinet colleague. In October 1990 General Chavalit founded the **New Aspiration Party** with military and bureaucratic support. He was out of office when the military coup of February 1991 took place. His party contested the elections held in March 1992 and won seventy-two seats but was not made a member of the governing coalition which nominated the non-elected former army commander, General **Suchinda Kraprayoon**, as prime minister. General Chavalit was not tainted by the bloodshed which occurred in May when mass protests at General Suchinda's appointment took place in Bangkok. In the fresh elections which were held in September 1992, the New Aspiration Party secured only fifty-one seats but was included in the ruling coalition led by **Chuan Leekpai**. After elections in July 1995, he became a deputy prime minister and minister of defence in the ruling coalition formed by **Banharn Silpa-archa** and demonstrated his political influence in September that year when he secured the appointment of his nominee as army commander against the wishes of the retiring incumbent. In elections in November 1996, his New Aspiration Party won 125 seats in Parliament to form a new coalition government under his leadership. That realization of political ambition turned sour within a year as Thailand was confronted with economic adversity, which brought his government down. In opposition, he has been combative but has been unable to live down his close association with economic failure.

Since his resignation as prime minister, Chavalit has continued to exert influence in Thai politics by aligning himself with various political factions and interests at various times. Chavalit led his New Aspiration Party into coalition with the ***Thai Rak Thai* Party** in 2001 in a collaborative venture that eventually transformed into a merger of the two parties. Later, Chavalit was believed to have also played a clandestine role in bringing down the government of **Thaksin Shinawatra** in 2006 and proceeded to establish a close relationship with **Sonthi Limthongkul**, one of the key leaders of the **People's Alliance for Democracy** (PAD). In 2008 however, Chavalit returned to Cabinet as deputy prime minister to Somchai Wongsawat tasked with resolving the crisis between the government and the PAD, only to resign several months later to take partial responsibility for police violence perpetrated against 'yellow shirt' protestors at Parliament Building. He followed this up by controversially suggesting that a military coup was the only way through which order could be restored in the country. In October 2009, Chavalit joined the ***Pheu Thai* Party** as chairman, a move that led to a major falling out between him and his mentor, Privy Council president and former prime minister, **Prem Tinsulanonda**. He subsequently resigned from the *Pheu Thai* Party in April 2011. As deputy prime minister, Chavalit was also tasked with mediating the brewing conflict with Cambodia over the **Preah Vihear** temple dispute but failed to make any headway, and instead came under heavy domestic criticism.

see also: Banharn Silpa-archa; Chatichai Choonhavan, General; Chuan Leekpai; Democratic Soldiers; New Aspiration Party; People's Alliance for Democracy; *Pheu Thai* Party; Preah Vihear Temple Dispute; Prem Tinsulanonda, General; Sonthi Limthongkul; Suchinda Kraprayoon, General; *Thai Rak Thai* Party; Thaksin Shinawatra.

Chea Sim (Cambodia)

Chea Sim became the president of a newly constituted appointed Senate in November 1998. He was born on 15 November 1932 into a peasant family in Svay Rieng Province. His revolutionary activity is believed to date from the early 1950s and two decades later he was secretary of a district committee of the Communist Party of Cambodia under the **Khmer Rouge**. After they came to power in April 1975, he was elected to the National Assembly but then became disaffected and was one of the leaders of a rebellion in eastern Cambodia against Pol Pot's rule. That rebellion provided the Vietnamese with an opportunity to invade through a united front of Cambodians. Chea Sim rose in the hierarchy of the Vietnamese-sponsored **Kampuchean People's Revolutionary Party** (KPRP) as well as holding ministerial portfolios in the **People's Republic of Kampuchea** and the chairmanship of the National Assembly from its establishment in 1981. He has enjoyed a reputation as a party hardliner and asserted his position against the younger, more moderate prime minister, **Hun Sen**. Chea Sim assumed the leadership of the **Cambodian People's Party** (CPP), established in succession to the KPRP when it was set up at an extraordinary congress on 17–18 October 1991, shortly before the **International Conference on Cambodia** was reconvened in Paris. After the formation of a coalition government in October 1993 following elections conducted by the United Nations, he became the president of the National Assembly until November 1998. Although he remains chairman of the CPP, effective power has been assumed by Hun Sen. When King **Norodom Sihanouk** announced his official abdication on 7 October 2004, Chea Sim once again became the acting head of state, having performed this role in 1993, 1994 and 1995. Chea Sim left this position in 14 October 2004 when **Norodom Sihamoni** ascended the throne.

see also: Cambodian People's Party; Hun Sen; International Conference on Cambodia, Paris 1991; Kampuchea, People's Republic of; Kampuchean People's Revolutionary Party; Khmer Rouge; Sihamoni, King Norodom; Sihanouk, King Norodom.

Chiam See Tong (Singapore)

Chiam See Tong is the secretary-general of the Singapore People's Party (SPP) and was the longest-serving opposition member of parliament until his defeat at the 2011 general election.

Born in Singapore on 12 March 1935, Chiam pursued his Bachelor of Science degree in New Zealand (1956–1961) before starting his career as a teacher. In 1972, he went to Inner Temple in London to study law and became a Barrister-at-Law. On his return to Singapore, he worked for two years at Philip Wong & Co (Advocates & Solicitors) before opening his own practice Chiam & Co. in 1976. Chiam See Tong founded the Singapore Democratic Party (SDP) in 1980 and contested and won the Potong Pasir seat in the 1984 general election, marking the start of a twenty-seven year career as a representative for Potong Pasir. He was the head of the SDP until 1993 when he resigned and left the party after infighting within the party leadership when he opposed the preference of the new generation of SDP leaders, led by Chee Soon Juan, to pursue a more confrontational approach towards the **People's Action Party** (PAP). In 1994, Chiam and other disenchanted SDP members formed the current SPP, winning in Potong Pasir again in the 1997 election. Chiam's spearheading of the Singapore Democratic Alliance (SDA) in 2001, which initially brought together four political parties – the National Solidarity Party, the Singapore Justice Party, the Singapore Malay National Organization and Chiam's SPP – reflected his belief that opposition parties in Singapore should work closely together to have a stronger voice in parliament. He was re-elected for Potong Pasir under the SDA banner for another two terms in the 2001 and 2006 elections. However, the SDA failed to make an impression, having only won one seat in Parliament (that of Potong Pasir held by Chiam) since its inception. Just prior to the 2011 elections, Chiam announced that the SPP had decided to pull out of the SDA and he would stand for re-election under the SPP banner instead. In an attempt to capture more seats for the opposition in Parliament, Chiam handed over the reins of the SPP in the contest for the Potong Pasir to his wife, Lina Loh, while he led a team of SPP candidates to contest the election in the Bishan-Toa Payoh Group Representation Constituency. However, the SPP failed to win in both constituencies; Chiam lost his seat in parliament, while the SPP narrowly lost its bastion of Potong Pasir.

Unlike many of his peers in opposition politics, Chiam's political career is notable for the fact that he has managed to avoid having lawsuits brought against him. He is widely respected in Singapore for his dedication to the opposition cause. His popularity increased after 2008, when he refused to retire from opposition politics despite suffering a stroke.
see also: People's Action Party.

Chiang Mai Initiative (Brunei/Cambodia/Indonesia/Laos/Malaysia/Myanmar/Philippines/Singapore/Thailand/Vietnam)

The Chiang Mai Initiative (CMI) was established in May 2000 in the wake of the devastating **Asian Financial Crisis** to serve as a financial safety net for regional currencies. It comprises a network of bilateral currency swap agreements among the central banks of **ASEAN** (Association of Southeast Asian Nations), China, Japan and South Korea to provide greater liquidity. The arrangement was transformed in March 2010 into the Chiang Mai Initiative-Multilateral (CMIM) with pooled resources amounting to US$240 billion. Notwithstanding its potential, the CMIM remains an unused financial mechanism. Despite having the CMI at its disposal in 2008 when it was confronted with a looming crisis, South Korea chose to arrange direct swap lines with China and Japan.
see also: ASEAN; Asian Financial Crisis.

Chin (Myanmar)

The Chin are an indigenous minority group of Tibeto-Myanmar origin who are to be found in a stretch of mountainous terrain extending southwards along Myanmar's borders with India and Bangladesh and then into the heart of the Arakan region. Mixed culturally in attachment to Hindu, Christian and folk religions, the Chin have never assimilated to Buddhism and during the colonial period were recruited by the British into the local army. Their leaders welcomed independence in 1948 but sought political autonomy within the Union of Burma beyond the special territorial division which they were accorded. The Chin, like other ethnic minorities in Myanmar, have long been in a state of armed rebellion against the government in Yangon. They found increasing difficulty in sustaining their military campaign during the 1990s, however, as the ruling **State Law and Order Restoration Council** (SLORC) and its successor, the **State Peace and Development Council** (SPDC), were able to disrupt their lines of logistical support as well as to reinforce their own counterinsurgency capabilities. The Chin remain a target of discrimination, including arbitrary arrests and forced labour, and in a 2011 study by the United Nations Development Programme, Chin state was identified as the poorest region in Myanmar. In May 2012, a ceasefire was signed between the central government and Chin rebels. This was followed by a landmark visit to the Chin capital of Hakha on 20 February 2013, the occasion of the Chin National Day, by President **Thein Sein**. While promises of development were made during that visit and abuses of Chin minorities stopped with the new government, doubts remain if a resolution to the longstanding clash between centre and periphery can be found.
see also: State Peace and Development Council; State Law and Order Restoration Council; Thein Sein.

Chin Peng (Malaya/Malaysia)

Chin Peng, whose real name is Ong Boon Hua, became general secretary of the Communist Party of Malaya in March 1947 in succession to **Loi Tack**, who was revealed as a double agent after he had absconded with party funds. Chin Peng, who was born in Malaya in 1922, had been a wartime guerrilla commander decorated with the OBE by the British for his role against the Japanese. He assumed the leadership of the Communist Party of Malaya at the outset of the Cold War and, when confirmed in office by its central committee in March 1948, the party announced a programme of mass struggle against British imperialism. Under his leadership, an insurrection was launched from June after the colonial government had declared a state of **Emergency** in response to growing acts of Communist violence. By the mid-1950s, that insurrection had been well contained with its fighting remnant regrouped along the border with Thailand. In November 1955 Chin Peng indicated a willingness to negotiate with the elected governments of Malaya and Singapore. The **Baling Talks** with the chief minister of Malaya, **Tunku Abdul Rahman**, and that of Singapore, **David Marshall**, took place near the border with Thailand in the following month but without success. Chin Peng's offer to end the insurrection in return for the legalization of the Communist Party met with a blank refusal. He returned to the jungle but the insurrection continued to lose momentum and the state of Emergency was rescinded in 1960 by the government of an independent Malaya. There were no further confirmed sightings of Chin Peng, who was alternately reported to be in southern Thailand and in China. His voice was heard, however, on the clandestine radio station, the Voice of the Malayan Revolution, whose transmitter was located in southern China. During the 1970s, when the Communist Party of Malaya split into three factions concurrent with a revival of guerrilla activities, he was rumoured to have been replaced as general secretary. On 2 December 1989 Ching Peng appeared in public for the first time since 1955 at a hotel in the southern Thai town of Hat Yai dressed in a business suit and in apparent good health. On behalf of the Communist Party he signed two peace agreements with the governments of Thailand and Malaysia which, in effect, constituted acts of surrender but without indicating the party's disbandment. He then appeared to return to the jungle but in the following decade was known to engage in business in Thailand, and also to give media interviews about his experience as an insurgent leader with a view to publishing his memoirs. Living in exile in Thailand, Chin Peng applied for permission to enter Malaysia at the beginning of 2000. The application was rejected by the Malaysian High Court on 25 July 2005. His subsequent appeal was rejected by the Court of Appeal in June 2008, which upheld the earlier ruling that requested that he present identification papers as proof of citizenship. Chin Peng maintained that his birth certificate had been seized during a police raid in 1948. Chin Peng passed away on 16 September 2013 at the age of ninety.

see also: Abdul Rahman, Tunku; Baling Talks 1955; Emergency 1948–60; Loi Tack; Marshall, David.

Chinese Communities in Southeast Asia

Once known as 'Overseas Chinese', ethnic Chinese communities throughout Southeast Asia make up well over thirty million people of migrant origin who are dispersed disparately across the region. They comprise a majority of the population only in Singapore.

Chinese migration to Southeast Asia was driven by a mixture of push and pull factors and took place in the main from the southern provinces of China precipitated by adverse economic circumstances and political upheaval during the nineteenth century. It was also affected and tied up with colonialist expansion and an attendant demand for supplies of disciplined labour. The Chinese term for such migrants has been *Hua Qiao* (sojourners) indicating the intention of the first waves of migrants to amass sufficient wealth to return to their native villages to retire in comfort and with respect. Up to the 1930s, migration was primarily a male phenomenon and there was a return traffic, but there were not many cases of peasants living in rags and returning with riches. However, with the migration of Chinese women and marriage among Chinese within Southeast Asia, a pattern of permanent settlement began which has been sustained and consolidated with successor generations, so that Chinese communities are an established part of Southeast Asian societies. Of the main concentrations, around nine million reside in Indonesia, eight million in Thailand, over seven million in Malaysia and almost three million in Singapore.

During the colonial period, Chinese migrants distinguished themselves by their industry and acumen and established a strong position in the retail trades in particular, assisted by close-knit kin and dialect associations. Their economic success as well as continuing ties with China and engagement in Chinese politics attracted envy and suspicion. In 1914 Thailand's King Vajiravudh wrote a booklet entitled *The Jews of the East*, which compared Chinese immigrants to insect pests that devour crops and leave fields dry and bare of grain. He attacked the migrant Chinese for their racial loyalty and sense of racial superiority, which stood in the way of their assimilation and transfer of allegiance to their country of residence. Ironically, although Chinese in Thailand rose to over ten per cent of the population, their assimilation has been quite striking, with intermarriage leading to a close identification with Thai culture. Although Chinese distinctiveness has not been erased completely, assimilation has more readily occurred where the local cultures have been receptive. Thus in predominantly Buddhist Thailand and in the predominantly Christian Philippines, for example, the intermarried-Chinese communities have found a social niche that has allowed them to rise to the highest offices in politics. The same cannot be said of Chinese in Indonesia and Malaysia, where clear distinctions have been made and perpetuated that identify Chinese as outsiders in one way or other. Having said that, the situation in Indonesia has improved to a far greater extent than in Malaysia, where this distinction has caused Malaysian Chinese voters to gravitate *en masse* to the opposition.

If the Chinese of Southeast Asia were suspect by indigenous communities because of their attachment to their homeland, that suspicion was made acute after the Pacific War with the establishment of the People's Republic of China as a revolutionary state. Earlier Chinese involvement in Communist insurrection in Malaya and Singapore had made the Chinese susceptible to the charge of being both capitalist and Communist at the same time. Initially, the Communist government in Beijing carried over the *jus sanguinis* policy of its ousted Nationalist predecessor whereby any person of all or partly Chinese parentage was treated as a Chinese citizen. That policy was changed from the mid-1950s, when it began to be realized in Beijing that it was a major obstacle to promoting good state-to-state relations in the region. A landmark Dual Nationality Treaty with Indonesia, negotiated and signed by Prime Minister Zhou Enlai in April 1955, marked a change in formal practice. However, where it has suited Chinese interests, the welfare of overseas Chinese has been employed for political purposes, as in the case of Vietnam in the late 1970s.

The centre of ethnic Chinese achievement in Southeast Asia is the Republic of Singapore, which became independent in August 1965 on its expulsion from the Federation of Malaysia. Singapore's population of just over five million is more than seventy per cent Chinese. Before China gave up its revolutionary mission, the government of Singapore was at great pains to play down any ethnic Chinese identity and indeed chose Malay as the national language. Any depiction of Singapore as a third China after the People's Republic and Taiwan (Republic of China) was strongly resisted. Since China has embarked on the road to economic modernization and with the end of the Cold War, such inhibitions have been discarded. Indeed, with China and communism ceasing to be synonymous, a revival of pride in Chinese cultural identity has taken place, with Singapore being willing to host a World Congress of Overseas Chinese in 1991.

It is important to register that today, the nature of how members of the Chinese communities in Southeast Asia identify with China and with their 'host' country has changed fundamentally. In the first instance, many ethnic Chinese no longer view themselves primarily by ethnic affiliation but by citizenship. Second, ethnic ties have not had a considerable effect on how new generations of Southeast Asian

Chinese relate to their ancestral country. This is perhaps most profoundly evident in Singapore, where many Singaporean Chinese harbour resentment towards the influx of Chinese from the mainland. Indeed, over time, numerous factors have combined to weaken presumed ethnic affiliation. Concomitantly, there have been fewer instances of the scapegoating of the Chinese community for national ills. Nevertheless, despite the fact that large numbers of Chinese in Southeast Asia have either adopted the host nationality or more importantly, were born and raised in their 'host' country, it remains that many are still viewed with envy and suspicion. One reason for this is the fact that the elite of various Southeast Asian Chinese communities are in possession of a disproportionate share of the wealth and economic influence in their host countries.

Choummaly Sayasone (Laos)

Choummaly Sayasone is president of Laos and current general secretary of the **Lao People's Revolutionary Party** (LPRP). He has held both positions since 2006. Choummaly was born in Attapeu in southern Laos on 6 March 1936. He joined the military and fought in the Lao civil war from 1962 to 1975, eventually attaining the rank of lieutenant general. He was elected to the LPRP's Central Committee in 1982 during the third National Congress and became an alternate member of the Politburo and secretary of the secretariat of the Central Committee in 1986. Choummaly became a member of the LPRP's Politburo in 1991, the same year he became minister of defence. He was reelected to the Politburo in 1996 and 2001, and remained minister of defence until 1993. From February 1998 to March 2001 he held the dual positions of minister of defence and vice prime minister. In 2001 he became vice-president of Laos. He was elected general secretary during the LPRP's eighth Congress in March 2006, succeeding **Khamtay Siphandon**. Three months later he succeeded Khamtay as president. He retained his position as general secretary at the ninth Congress in 2011 and in June of that year was re-elected president by the seventh Lao National Assembly. Choummaly's gradual rise to the top of the Communist Party hierarchy suggests he possesses a conservative disposition and is not prone to taking radical policy detours.

see also: Khamtay Siphandon; Lao People's Revolutionary Party.

Chuan Leekpai (Thailand)

Chuan Leekpai was prime minister of Thailand from September 1992 until July 1995 and then, after more than two years in opposition, resumed that high office in November 1997. He was also leader of the **Democrat Party** during this period, only stepping down in 2003.

Chuan Leekpai was the first truly civilian prime minister since the mid-1970s and has maintained a reputation for personal probity and integrity. He came to power through elections in September 1992, which were held in the wake of a bloody confrontation on the streets of Bangkok in the previous May. Civilian demonstrators had challenged the right of former army commander, General **Suchinda Kraprayoon**, to become prime minister without election to Parliament. The Democrat Party secured seventy-nine seats, the largest number in Parliament, and provided the core of a new coalition government.

Chuan Leekpai was born on 28 July 1938 in Trang Province. He studied law at Thammasat University in Bangkok and entered Parliament at the age of thirty-one, when Thailand was still under military rule. He has been a member of parliament continuously ever since and first held government office as deputy minister of justice in 1975. He was speaker of the Lower House during 1986–8 as well as a deputy prime minister between the end of 1989 and August 1990, which is when he became leader of the Democrat Party on the resignation of Bhichai Rattakul. During his first term of high office, Chuan Leekpai ruled at the head of a discordant coalition without demonstrating inspired or decisive leadership. For example, in early 1994, he failed to secure the passage of amendments designed to revise the constitution imposed by the military after they seized power in 1991. This failure indicated his inability then to overcome a structural tension in Thai politics between civilian and military interests. He was also embarrassed by the residual support of the military for the **Khmer Rouge**, despite his government's commitment to good relations with its counterpart in Phnom Penh. He lost office in July 1995 after elections, which had been precipitated by the defection of a coalition partner. The Democrat Party won eighty-six seats compared to ninety-six by the ***Chart Thai* Party**, which provided the core of a new coalition from which the Democrat Party was excluded. Chuan Leekpai returned to high office in November 1997 when **Chavalit Yongchaiyuth** lost national confidence and was obliged to resign as prime minister after the devastating onset of an acute economic crisis. A political realignment allowed Chuan to form a new coalition government, although initially with only a limited parliamentary majority, which was not augmented until October 1998 when the *Chart Pattana* Party joined. There was no resistance from the armed forces to his return to power, while he enjoyed critical support from King **Bhumibol Adulyadej**.

On taking office, he put together a credible economic team that inspired confidence among international financial institutions as well as the approval of the United States. Nevertheless, his conservative economic policies also came under heavy domestic criticism for their elitist nature and neglect of the plight of the common Thai citizen. This brewing antagonism eventually culminated in his defeat by the populist **Thaksin Shinawatra** in elections in 2001. Following his defeat, Chuan remained a senior advisor to the Democrat Party and trenchant critic of Thaksin and the ***Thai Rak Thai* Party**. Chuan was instrumental in the grooming of his protégé, **Abhisit Vejjajiva**, for leadership, and articulated a stout defence of the Democrat Party during the party's dissolution trial in 2010.

see also: Abhisit Vejjajiva; Bhumibol Adulyadej; *Chart Thai* Party; Chavalit Yongchaiyuth, General; Democrat Party; Khmer Rouge; Suchinda Kraprayoon, General; *Thai Rak Thai* Party; Thaksin Shinawatra.

Clark Air Base (Philippines)

Clark Air Base on the island of Luzón was one of the major military facilities to which the United States acquired leasehold title, initially for ninety-nine years, under an agreement concluded with the government of the Philippines on 17 March 1947. That tenure was reduced to twenty-five years under a revised agreement of 16 September 1966. Under a further agreement concluded with the Philippines government on 27 August 1991, designed to extend US tenure at Subic Bay Naval Base for ten years, the United States agreed to transfer jurisdiction over Clark Air Base by September 1992, but by then it had lost its operational value because of the damaging effect of the volcanic eruption of neighbouring Mount Pinatubo. Also, the Philippine Senate repudiated the overall package in September 1991. Clark Air Base had been the site for the only major US tactical air force deployment in Southeast Asia with fighter and airlift wings. It had also been the air logistics centre for all US forces in the western Pacific, while the Crow Valley Weapons Range provided the only facility for live tactical training west of California. The base lost its former military significance with the end of the Cold War and tactical fighter aircraft were withdrawn early in 1991. In June 1991 the volcanic eruption of nearby Mount Pinatubo caused irreparable damage to the base, which was completely evacuated by United States personnel.

see also: Subic Bay Naval Base.

Cobbold Commission 1962 (Malaya/Malaysia)

A commission of inquiry was appointed by the British and Malayan governments on 16 January 1962 to ascertain whether or not the inhabitants of Britain's colonies of Sarawak and North Borneo wished them to become constituent parts of the projected Federation of Malaysia. Comprising five members and chaired by Lord Cobbold, governor of the Bank of England, the commission issued its report in July 1962. Its members concluded that about one-third of the population in each territory strongly favoured an early realization of Malaysia; another third, many of whom favoured the project, had asked for conditions and safeguards of a varying nature; the remaining third was divided between those who insisted on independence before Malaysia was considered and those who strongly preferred British rule to continue. The report had the effect of reinforcing the momentum for the new Federation which enjoyed the explicit support of the Malayan and British governments. At the time, Brunei was a candidate for membership but was not included within the Cobbold Commission's remit.

Cobra Gold Military Exercises (Thailand/Singapore/Indonesia/Malaysia/Philippines)

Cobra Gold is the name given to combined exercises between Thai and US forces which have been held on an annual basis from 1982, with an interruption in 1991. After the end of the **Vietnam War** in April 1975, Thailand moved quickly to distance itself from a close military relationship with the United States. The civilian government brought about the withdrawal of all US military bases and troops by July 1976. However, a military coup in October restored an earlier strategic perspective in Bangkok, which was reinforced after Vietnam's invasion of Cambodia at the end of 1978 in the third phase of the **Indochina Wars**. The exercises, involving troops from both countries, were intended to signal the continued commitment of the United States to the territorial integrity of a Thailand seemingly under threat from an expansionist Vietnam. Following the end of the Cold War and Vietnam's withdrawal from Cambodia, the United States had no compunction in suspending the exercises after the military removed the elected government of **Chatichai Choonhavan** by a coup in February 1991. Political violence in May 1992 by the military in an attempt to hold on to power served to maintain that suspension. The appointment of a civilian prime minister, **Chuan Leekpai**, after elections in September 1992 led to a decision to revive Cobra Gold, which resumed in northern Thailand in May 1993. Since 2000, the Cobra Gold military exercises have expanded to involve the militaries of Indonesia, Malaysia, Australia, Singapore, Philippines, Japan and South Korea, and have had up to twenty observer nations, including Myanmar, invited in 2013. In addition to conventional military exercises, Cobra Gold activities have increasingly emphasized humanitarian and disaster relief operations, drug interdiction and peacekeeping training.

see also: Chatichai Choonhavan, General; Chuan Leekpai; Indochina Wars; Vietnam War.

Communism in Southeast Asia

Communism in Southeast Asia has attained and maintained positions of power only in Vietnam and Laos.

The Communist Party of Vietnam, established originally as the Communist Party of Indochina in 1930, came to power in two stages. In July 1954, after a period of armed revolution from 1945 when it seized power briefly in Hanoi, it formed the government north of the seventeenth parallel of latitude in the name of the *Lao Dong* (Workers Party). It then inspired and supported the insurgency to the south of that latitude led nominally by the **National Liberation Front of South Vietnam**. In April 1975 its armed forces seized power in the southern part of Vietnam, which was formally reunified in July 1976 as the Socialist Republic of Vietnam. At its fourth National Congress in December 1976, the name Communist Party of Vietnam was adopted. The **Lao People's Revolutionary Party**, which was created from the Communist Party of Indochina, consolidated its power in the wake of the Communist victory in Vietnam. In December 1975 it established the Lao People's Democratic Republic, displacing the Kingdom of Laos.

A Communist government came to power in Cambodia in April 1975 through the revolutionary success of the **Khmer Rouge**. In the name of the State of **Democratic Kampuchea**, it achieved notoriety through its brutal and bloodthirsty collectivism. It was overthrown by a Vietnamese invasion in December 1978 and in January 1979 an alternative Marxist regime was established under Vietnamese aegis in the name of the **People's Republic of Kampuchea**. That regime was superseded in September 1993 when a royalist constitution was reinstated in the wake of the political settlement of the Cambodian conflict concluded by an **International Conference on Cambodia** in Paris in October 1991. The former ruling **Kampuchean People's Revolutionary Party** (KPRP), in the name of the **Cambodian People's Party** (CPP), which had repudiated Marxist ideology, then shared power in a coalition government from October 1993.

After mounting a violent coup in July 1997, the CPP consolidated its position, which was validated by elections a year later. The insurgent Khmer Rouge had begun to disintegrate as a fighting force from the establishment of the coalition government and also suffered political defections. With the death of its leader **Pol Pot** in April 1998, it ceased to exist as a viable organization and to inspire the awesome fear that had been generated during its murderous rule between 1975 and 1978.

Elsewhere in Southeast Asia, Communism has come close to seizing power but has experienced declining fortunes from the mid-1960s. Communism in the region has its origins in the colonial connection and through links with overseas Chinese (*see* **Chinese Communities in Southeast Asia**).

The first party to be established was in the Netherlands East Indies where a Dutch Marxist, Franciscus Marie Sneevliet, set up the Indies Social Democratic Association on 9 May 1914. It was transformed into the Communist Party of Indonesia (*Partai Komunis Indonesia*: PKI) on 23 May 1920, the first such organization to be set up in Asia outside of the former Russian empire. Under an indigenous leadership in the mid-1920s the party launched an uprising, which was crushed. It also failed to put its political stamp on the nascent republic through involvement in an abortive uprising, the **Madiun Revolt**, in east Java in 1948. After international recognition of independence in December 1949, a younger generation of cadres led by D. N. Aidit secured a legitimate place for Communism within the parliamentary system by stressing its nationalist credentials. During the period of **Guided Democracy**, the PKI established a close relationship with President **Sukarno** and raised its membership to three million, which made it the largest party outside of China and the Soviet Union. By the mid-1960s, the PKI seemed to be on the threshold of power but an abortive coup (*see* ***Gestapu***) in October 1965, in which it was implicated, provided an opportunity for the armed forces to destroy and outlaw it. The Communist Party of Indonesia has never recovered from that act of repression in which its leadership was liquidated and its membership decimated.

Communism in the Philippines has also had a colonial connection in its provenance. Harrison George, a leader of the Communist Party of the United States, took the initiative to induct Filipinos into the international movement. The Communist Party of the Philippines was founded on 26 August 1930 by Cristanto Evangalista, who was a trade union leader. It began to make an impact during the Japanese occupation when it organized the insurgent *Hukbo ng Bayan Laban sa Hapon*, in abbreviation ***Hukbalahap***, which translates as People's Anti-Japanese Army. Mixed success in harassing the Japanese led to the establishment of local territorial positions of power prior to liberation which were not recognized by the United States. A period of legal struggle followed, with the Democratic Alliance Party serving as an electoral vehicle in April 1946 just before independence. Its six successful candidates were then denied seats in the Congress and its demands for land reform were rejected. The *Hukbalahap* took up armed struggle in January 1950 under the banner of the *Hukbong Mapagpalaya ng Bayan* (People's Liberation Army). During the course of the year a series of military challenges were posed to the government in Manila; these were overcome in October only when virtually the entire party Politburo was arrested in Manila. From that juncture, and with the subsequent surrender of their military commander, Luis Taruc, they went into decline despite the failure of the government to address fundamental economic and social ills.

The Communist Party of the Philippines then degenerated into an armed banditry although a fraternal affiliation of a kind was maintained with the Soviet Union. Under the intellectual guidance of **José María Sisón**, the party was reconstituted at the end of 1968, inspired by Chinese revolutionary experience, when a **New People's Army** was established in March 1969 as its military wing. Adopting a strategic doctrine which exploited the archipelagic condition of the Philippines as well as economic distress in the rural areas, the Communist Party was able to make dramatic gains from the mid-1970s as the rule of President **Ferdinand Marcos** began to decay. The prospect of political victory slipped away after the downfall of President Marcos and his succession by **Corazón Aquino**. A miscalculation of the popular mood followed, and unrealistic demands of the government in Manila were met with military repression, which took its toll of insurgent strength. By 1992 President **Fidel Ramos**, who had succeeded Aquino, felt sufficiently confident to persuade the Congress to make the Communist Party a legal organization. Subject to internal cleavage and a loss of morale from the failure of communism as a practical ideology, the party enjoys only a vestigial existence despite continuing gross inequalities within Philippine society. It continues to be represented by the **National Democratic Front**, whose leadership has been bitterly divided. The movement was dealt a significant blow in March 2014 when its top leaders, Benito Tiamzon and Wilma Austria, were captured.

Chinese influence was more direct and continuous in the case of Communist parties in Malaysia, Singapore and Thailand, although their achievement has been even less than that of comrades in the Philippines. The Chinese Communist Party was instrumental in organizing in Singapore in January 1928 the Nanyang or South Seas Communist Party, which was succeeded in April 1930 by the Communist Party of Malaya, which incorporated Singapore within its revolutionary jurisdiction. The party engaged in trade union agitation but built up its following through anti-Japanese activity in the late 1930s. With the outbreak of the Pacific War, British assistance was provided for military training for the insurgent Malayan People's Anti-Japanese Army, which engaged in jungle warfare after the surrender of Singapore. Only limited demobilization took place after the defeat of the Japanese and peaceful struggle was replaced by armed struggle against the colonial government in June 1948. During the **Emergency** declared by the colonial administration, the Communist Party drew on support almost exclusively from the Chinese community and appeared to have seized the military initiative by 1951, when they assassinated the British High Commissioner, Sir Henry Gurney. However, by that juncture, the balance of military advantage had already begun to turn against the Communist Party, which had sought to revise its militant strategy in order to widen its political appeal. The **Baling Talks** between its leader, **Chin Peng**, and the chief ministers of Malaya and Singapore in December 1955 were inconclusive, because the latter refused to countenance the legality of the party. Chin Peng refused to give up armed struggle, which continued in a sporadic manner from redoubts established along the border with Thailand. The reduction in military activity enabled the independent government of Malaya to announce an end to the Emergency in 1960. The Communist Party was afflicted by splits within its ranks during the late 1960s but revived its military activities at the end of the **Vietnam War** without any political advantage. In Singapore, the Communist movement had been effectively crushed by the time the island became independent in 1965. In December 1989 Chin Peng appeared along the border with Thailand to sign two ceasefire agreements with the Malaysian and Thai authorities, which amounted to a virtual surrender after forty years of fruitless struggle. A Communist movement developed in Sarawak in northern Borneo during the wartime Japanese occupation with a constituency among the Chinese community. It enjoyed a measure of success during Indonesia's **Confrontation** of Malaysia but was crushed after their reconciliation.

The Communist Party of Thailand originated from the same source as the Communist Party of Malaya in the form of a Siam Special Committee, which was set up by the South Seas Communist Party in the late 1920s. Although a full-fledged Thai party was established in July 1929, its first congress is believed to have convened only in 1942 with a predominantly Chinese membership. Significant activity by the party dates only to the 1960s, concurrent with the United States' growing military involvement in Vietnam, with a clandestine radio station, the Voice of the People of Thailand, operating from March 1962. Armed struggle, which began only in August 1965 in the economically deprived northeastern province of Nakhon Phanom, spread during the decade to the north and south of the country. The overthrow of the military regime in October 1973 provided an opportunity for the party to extend its support to a student constituency which was strengthened with the **Thammasat University Massacre** in October 1976 and the return to power of the armed forces. The ranks of the party were augmented by students seeking refuge in the jungles but tension developed between an ethnic Chinese leadership and the younger generation of Thai members. The opportunity to pose a challenge of substance to the government in Bangkok was frustrated by the development of civic action programmes by the armed forces as well as by the alienation that developed between the Vietnamese and Chinese Communists. With the onset of the Cambodian conflict, the Thai Communists were driven out of sanctuaries in Laos and their cause was sacrificed by China to the need to align with Thailand to challenge Vietnam's occupation of Cambodia. From that juncture, the Thai Communist movement began to collapse until it had ceased to exist as a viable entity by the end of the Cold War.

Communism in Burma/Myanmar has had a more indigenous source arising from the Marxist stream of the nationalist movement against the colonial administration. At the end of the Pacific War, Communist rebellion challenged the government in Rangoon together with ethnic-minority uprisings. The party then split into two factions which aligned in time with Moscow and Beijing. The White Flag faction which looked to China was provided with a measure of material support and served as a point of leverage for Beijing but without ever enabling the party to pose an effective military threat. The Burmese army was successful in driving the Communists from the Pegu Yoma heartland in the 1970s and the party continued its insurgency with support from Wa tribesmen in the north adjacent to the border with China. A revolt by these tribesmen in 1989 removed an ethnic Chinese leadership, which had the effect of emasculating the party as a viable political entity.

Communism has enjoyed its greatest success in Indochina. Under the original inspiration and leadership of **Ho Chi Minh** acting for the Comintern, rival revolutionary groupings were amalgamated into the Communist Party of Indochina at a unity conference in Hong Kong in 1930. The Communist Party of Indochina provided the core of the **Viet Minh**, a national front which challenged French rule at the end of the Pacific War in the **August Revolution 1945**. The party divided formally into three national components in 1951, with the *Lao Dong* assuming responsibility for revolution in Vietnam. Corresponding parties were set up for Laos and Cambodia under Vietnamese patronage, but in the case of Cambodia an alternative leadership emerged in the 1960s, which rejected lineal descent from the Communist Party of Indochina and became known as the Khmer Rouge. The ruling parties in Hanoi and Vientiane have maintained their monopoly of power but have been obliged to compromise their socialist doctrine in order to practise market economics. The lead was taken by Vietnam's Communist Party at its sixth national congress when it adopted a policy of ***Doi Moi*** (economic renovation) followed by its Laotian counterpart. Both parties have resisted demands for liberalization and have maintained a tight control over their respective political systems.

see also: Aquino, Corazón; August Revolution 1945; Baling Talks 1955; Cambodian People's Party; Chin Peng; Chinese Communities in Southeast Asia; Confrontation; Democratic Kampuchea; *Doi Moi*; Emergency 1948–60; *Gestapu*; Guided Democracy; Ho Chi Minh; *Hukbalahap* Movement; International Conference on Cambodia, Paris 1991; Kampuchea, People's Republic of; Kampuchean People's Revolutionary Party; Khmer Rouge; *Lao Dong*; Lao People's Revolutionary Party; Madiun Revolt 1948; Marcos, Ferdinand; National Democratic Front; National Liberation Front of South Vietnam; New People's Army; Pol Pot; Ramos, Fidel; Sisón, José María; Sukarno; Thammasat University Massacre 1976; Viet Minh; Vietnam War.

Comprehensive Agreement on the Bangsamoro (CAB) 2014

(Philippines)

Signed between the Government of the Republic of Philippines and the Moro Islamic Liberation Front (MILF) on 27 March 2014, the Comprehensive Agreement on the Bangsamoro (CAB) brings together seventeen years of documents agreed between the two parties, starting from the Agreement for General Cessation of Hostilities, signed in July 1997, and ending with the **Framework Agreement on the Bangsamoro** signed on 15 October 2012. It also includes the critical four annexes that followed on from the Framework Agreement, namely:

1) Annex on Transitional Arrangements and Modalities, signed on 27 February 2013;
2) Annex on Revenue Generation and Wealth Sharing, signed on 13 July 2013;
3) Annex on Power Sharing, signed on 8 December 2013;
4) Annex on Normalization, signed on 25 January 2014.

Together, these documents form the basis of a complete agreement under which a Bangsamoro entity will be created to replace the Autonomous Region of Muslim Mindanao that was formed under the auspices of agreements with the Moro National Liberation Front (MNLF). This Bangsamoro entity would be formed under a transitional authority until elections are held in 2016. The Comprehensive Agreement brings to an end almost three decades of insurgency led by the MILF. In reality though, it remains to be seen if implementation will be a success. Moreover, elements from the MNLF as well as breakaway factions of the MILF have already voiced their rejection of the agreement, as well as their intention to continue armed struggle.

see also: Framework Agreement on the Bangsamoro.

Confrontation (Indonesia/Malaysia)

Confrontation (*Konfrontasi* in Indonesian) was a term first employed by President **Sukarno** in June 1960 to register his country's militant stance towards the Netherlands in pursuing its claim to the western half of the island of New Guinea, now **Irian Jaya**. The term was subsequently employed in January 1963 by Sukarno's foreign minister, **Subandrio**, to register a corresponding stance towards the advent of the Federation of Malaysia, whose legitimacy was thereby challenged. Described by Sukarno as a contest of power in all fields, Confrontation amounted to a practice of coercive diplomacy, employing military measures stopping short of all-out war, which was designed to create a sense of international crisis in order to provoke diplomatic intervention in Indonesia's interest. The campaign of Confrontation to recover West New Guinea from the Dutch, who had retained the territory after according independence to the rest of the Netherlands East Indies, reached a successful conclusion in August 1962. US mediation, driven by fear of Communist advantage, produced a negotiated settlement which provided for the transfer of the territory to Indonesia, via the United Nations' temporary administration in May 1963. In the case of Malaysia (a British-backed Malayan proposal to merge the Federation of Malaya, the self-governing island of Singapore, the British colonies of Sarawak and North Borneo and the British protected Sultanate of Brunei), Confrontation failed in its purpose (*see* **Anglo-Malayan/Malaysian Defence Agreement 1957–71; Brunei Revolt 1962**). Indonesia was not able to press its anti-colonial claim with the same legitimacy as in the case of Irian Jaya and proved unable to mobilize corresponding international support. President Lyndon Johnson did dispatch the US attorney general, Robert Kennedy, to engage in seeming mediation in January 1964 but was not disposed to bring pressure to bear on Malaysia in the way that the late President John F. Kennedy had coerced the Dutch. Britain honoured its treaty commitment and with Australian, New Zealand and Malaysian military support, fended off armed incursions in northern Borneo and peninsular Malaysia and also deterred more substantial military intervention. After the political downfall of Sukarno in 1966, Indonesia became reconciled with Malaysia, with which it established diplomatic relations in August 1967. The term Confrontation disappeared from Indonesia's political lexicon with the consolidation of President **Suharto**'s New Order.

see also: Anglo-Malayan/Malaysian Defence Agreement 1957–71; Brunei Revolt 1962; Irian Jaya; New Order; Subandrio; Suharto; Sukarno.

Constitution 2008 (Myanmar)

Myanmar's 2008 Constitution is the current constitution of the Republic of the Union of Myanmar, approved through a nationwide referendum in May 2008. It replaces the 1974 constitution, which was suspended by the **State Law and Order Restoration Council** (SLORC) when it came to power in 1988. A constitutional convention was convened in 1993 as a prerequisite for a transition to a civilian government. Hampered by government manipulation and the **National League of Democracy**'s (NLD) withdrawal, it moved at a glacial pace and was eventually suspended in 1996. The convention was reconvened in 2004 by the **State Peace and Development Council** (SPDC) with representatives chosen from the government, military, civil society and ethnic minorities, but without the involvement of major opposition figures and parties. In September 2007, the government announced the conclusion of the convention and a set of fundamental principles and basic rules for a new constitution. A final draft of the new constitution was made available to the public on 9 April 2008 and a national referendum was held in May that approved the new constitution, albeit with complaints of government manipulation of the referendum process.

The new constitution came under heavy criticism by opposition parties, ethnic minority leaders, international organizations and Western governments for its preservation of a paramount role for the military in decision-making. The document guarantees the military twenty-five per cent of seats in parliament as well as a strong presence on the ill-defined National Defence and Security Council, an extra-legal group headed by the president and empowered to carry out executive functions without reference to parliament and to assume power in a national emergency. Additional regulations make it difficult for former political prisoners to stand for office and prohibit opposition leader **Aung San Suu Kyi** from assuming high office. For all its controversial points, the constitution holds out the opportunity for collaboration with the opposition and tries to address a number of issues that have emerged since independence, including the complex issue of political autonomy for ethnic minorities, and the distribution of power between the executive, judicial and legislative branches. In 2014, a 109-member parliamentary committee assembled to look into constitutional reform submitted conservative recommendations to the government.

see also: Aung San Suu Kyi; National League for Democracy; State Law and Order Restoration Council; State Peace and Development Council.

Constitutional Crises (Malaysia)

In 1983 and in 1992, the popularly elected government of the Federation of Malaysia came into conflict with the country's constitutional monarchy comprising the king and the other hereditary sultans or rulers of the peninsular Malaysian states. The king, known in Malay as ***Yang di-Pertuan Agong***, serves an elected five-year term of office which rotates among the nine rulers in an agreed order of seniority. The initial conflict was precipitated when a package of constitutional amendments was rushed through the federal parliament in August 1983. The most significant measure provided for any bill to become law automatically fifteen days after it had been presented to the king for his assent, with a corresponding application to states' legislatures and sultans. In addition, the formal right of the king to proclaim a state of emergency was transferred to the prime minister. The particular motive for the legislation was concern on the part of the government at the likely interventionist political role of a future king. An underlying complementary factor was the attitude towards the rulers and the monarchy on the part of Prime Minister **Mahathir Mohamad**, whose social background disposed him against the idea of royal prerogative. The constitutional crisis arose when the king – then the Sultan of Pahang – refused his assent to the package of amendments with unanimous support from all the other hereditary rulers. After a period of political tension, a basis for compromise was reached at the end of the year. In mid-December during the indisposition of the king, who had suffered a stroke, his deputy signed the Constitution (Amendment) Bill on the understanding that a special session of Parliament would be called to introduce new legislation restoring the monarch's right to proclaim a state of emergency on the advice of the prime minister. The right of the king to refuse his assent to any federal legislation was not restored but his power of delay was extended to thirty days in the case of non-money Bills; the states' rulers retained such a right in principle. The compromise package was approved by Parliament in January 1984, with the prime minister judged to have made important concessions.

A second constitutional crisis arose at the end of 1992 when Parliament, in a unanimous and unprecedented measure, approved a motion censuring the Sultan of Johor, and former king, for having (allegedly) assaulted a college field-hockey coach. Parliament convened in a special session in January 1993 and proceeded to amend the constitution so as to remove the immunity from criminal prosecution enjoyed by the hereditary rulers. The rulers initially refused to grant their assent to the legislation as required under the constitution, which prompted a politically inspired press campaign against their self-indulgent lifestyles. Compromise was reached in March when a revised Bill was passed which made provision for a special court to hear criminal cases which might be brought against any of their number. In May 1994 a further constitutional amendment was passed whereby all Acts of Parliament would be deemed to have been assented to by the *Yang di-Pertuan Agong* after thirty days following approval by both houses, even if not formally granted.

see also: Mahathir Mohamad, Tun; *Yang di-Pertuan Agong*.

Constructive Engagement
(Myanmar/Thailand)

Constructive Engagement was a term coined to describe a dual-track policy embarked on by **ASEAN** (Association of Southeast Asian Nations) towards Myanmar in the 1990s and 2000s. The policy was premised on the belief prevalent in ASEAN circles that the best way to change the behaviour of the Myanmar government towards its own people and the international community was through diplomatic engagement and economic inducements. Beyond this, ASEAN was conscious of the need to prevent Myanmar from gravitating strategically, politically and economically towards China. The modus operandi of constructive engagement held closely to the ASEAN way, in which dialogue, consultation, consensus and a strict adherence to non-interference in affairs of member states is critical. On the other hand, the policy came in for much criticism from Western governments and human rights activists that favoured the use of a sanctions regime, which ASEAN viewed as counterproductive, to change the behaviour of the military junta in Myanmar.

Introduced by Thailand in 1991, the policy marked a departure from the international condemnation aimed at Myanmar after the military junta there crushed the 1988 pro-democracy protests and invalidated the results of the 1990 national election. The policy was a part of Thai prime minister **Chatichai Choonhavan**'s vision to establish Thailand as the economic hub of mainland Southeast Asia by strengthening economic relations with former adversaries Laos, Cambodia and Myanmar. Chatichai's policy toward Myanmar was subsequently followed by the governments of **Anand Panyarachun** and **Chuan Leekpai**. Thailand's policy was later adopted by ASEAN as justification for bringing Myanmar into ASEAN in 1997. Over time, certain ASEAN member countries deviated somewhat by openly criticizing the regime. Underlying these criticisms were concerns that the policy allowed Myanmar to shelter behind ASEAN's non-interference principle while it persisted with its hardline approach against its own population. At the same time, ASEAN countries, particularly Thailand and Singapore, continued to invest heavily in the country. While this benefited Myanmar's growing economy, ASEAN also came under criticism from Western governments and rights advocates who claimed that economic investments simply propped up the regime.

When Myanmar's new democratic government took office in March 2011 following elections in late 2010, both sides claimed victory. To a certain degree, Myanmar was able to undertake gradual reforms because it was sheltered by the constructive engagement policy.

However, ASEAN membership and, occasionally, grudging diplomatic protection, could not counterbalance growing Chinese influence in Myanmar nor completely shelter it from the effects of Western sanctions and diplomatic censure.

see also: Anand Panyarachun; ASEAN; Chatichai Choonhavan, General; Chuan Leekpai.

Contemplacion, Flor: Hanging 1995
(Philippines/Singapore)

In March 1995, a diplomatic rift occurred between the governments of the Philippines and Singapore over the execution of Flor Contemplacion, a Filipina domestic helper working in the Republic who had been convicted of murder.

Flor Contemplacion was hanged in Singapore on 17 March 1995. She had been sentenced to death by its High Court in January 1993 for the murder in May 1991 of another Filipina domestic helper, Della Marga, and a four-year-old Singaporean boy in the latter's charge. An appeal led to a further trial in April 1994 which upheld her death sentence, while a further appeal was dismissed in October 1994. In January 1995, President **Fidel Ramos** wrote to President **Ong Teng Cheong** requesting clemency on humanitarian grounds, which was refused in the absence of special circumstances. He wrote again in March, six days before the scheduled hanging, asking for a stay of execution in the light of alleged new evidence forthcoming from another domestic helper but once again his plea was refused, this time on the grounds that the so-called new evidence had no basis in fact. The execution of Flor Contemplacion went ahead as scheduled but aroused an immediate emotional outrage among Filipinos, which had an adverse effect on relations with Singapore. That popular outrage, which was fanned by the press and exploited by opponents of President Ramos in the run-up to mid-term congressional elections in May, caught his government by surprise. In addition to the element of political opportunism, the outrage expressed a strong sense of national guilt and anguish that it was necessary for so many Filipino women to work overseas in trying circumstances in order to support their impoverished families. The government in Manila was charged with not doing enough for such workers, who number around two million, while Flor Contemplacion was portrayed as a heroine and martyr in their cause. Singapore was depicted as arrogant and insensitive in its handling of the case and as not acting as a friendly regional partner.

The Philippines government immediately postponed a visit to Manila by Singapore's prime minister, **Goh Chok Tong**, and also downgraded its representation in the island-state to that of chargé d'affaires, which was reciprocated. President Ramos then set up a special commission to investigate the case and threatened to break off diplomatic relations should it find that Flor Contemplacion had been the victim of injustice. By the end of March, however, President Ramos was making conciliatory noises out of concern at the damage that might be caused both to relations with Singapore and to **ASEAN** (Association of Southeast Asian Nations). Singapore responded by indicating a willingness to accept his proposal for an independent autopsy but in early April the Philippines commission found that Flor Contemplacion had been mistakenly blamed and hanged for the two murders, and that Della Marga had been severely beaten before she died and therefore could have been killed only by a man. President Ramos then acted to contain domestic anger by suspending nine diplomats and labour officials allegedly remiss in their duties in connection with Flor Contemplacion's hanging, including the Ambassador to Singapore. The two governments then agreed to a re-examination of Della Marga's remains by forensic experts of both countries but President Ramos still found it necessary to force the sacrificial resignation of his foreign secretary, Roberto Rómulo, on 17 April, two days before an inconclusive joint autopsy attended by American forensic experts, who supported the initial Singaporean conclusion. Both parties then recognized the value of a cooling-off period before seeking a further fully independent autopsy in a neutral location. That autopsy was not held until after the mid-term congressional elections in May in which President Ramos' coalition overcame the burden of the Flor Contemplacion issue to secure command of the Senate. The diplomatic rift did not affect working relations between Singapore and the Philippines, with the former offering strong support for the latter in its dispute with China over its seizure of Mischief Reef in the **South China Sea**. Tourist traffic and much needed Singaporean investment in the Philippines suffered, however. Moreover, within the Philippines, the making of a film about the life and death of Flor Contemplacion sustained popular interest in the alleged miscarriage of justice. In July 1995, an independent panel of American pathologists examined the remains of Della Marga in the presence of medical observers from the Philippines and Singapore and upheld the original findings of Singapore's pathologists that her death was due to strangulation. Those findings were accepted as final by the government of the Philippines. President Ramos then announced that he had taken steps to normalize ties with Singapore. Singapore's new ambassador to Manila presented his credentials in April 1996.

see also: ASEAN; Goh Chok Tong; Ong Teng Cheong; Ramos, Fidel; South China Sea.

Corregidor Affair 1968 (Philippines/Malaysia)

The Corregidor Affair is the term used to describe an alleged massacre of Filipino Muslims on the island in Manila Bay which was the site of a memorable last stand by Filipino and US troops following Japan's invasion of the Philippines at the outset of the Pacific War. The episode was reported in the Philippine press from 21 March 1968 after a survivor of the alleged massacre presented himself at the residence of the governor of Cavite Province. He claimed to be one of more than 100 young Muslims recruited in the southern Sulu region in 1967 by an air force major who was head of the Civil Affairs Office of the Department of National Defence. Their role was to undergo special forces training in preparation for infiltration into Sabah, which had become part of Malaysia in September 1963 in the face of Philippine objections. It was claimed initially that eleven trainees had been killed by their officers when they mutinied over demands for back-pay. The full facts of the episode have never been established but confirmation of the training programme was indicated when the Malaysian government announced that it had arrested twenty-six Filipinos in possession of small arms and explosives on an island belonging to the Federation some thirty miles to the north of Sabah's mainland early in March 1968. The revelations had the effect of reversing the signal improvement in Malaysian–Philippine relations indicated by the official visit to Kuala Lumpur in January 1968 by President **Ferdinand Marcos**. Malaysian demands that the government in Manila affirm its recognition of the Federation's sovereignty over the territory prompted a revival of the **Philippines' Claim to Sabah** first enunciated in June 1962. The episode led to a suspension of diplomatic relations and imposed a strain on the workings of the recently established **ASEAN** (Association of Southeast Asian Nations) of which Malaysia and the Philippines were founder members. It also served as a factor in aggravating Muslim alienation in the Philippines which erupted into revolt in 1972 (*see* **Moro National Liberation Front**).

see also: ASEAN; Marcos, Ferdinand; Moro National Liberation Front; Philippines' Claim to Sabah.

D

Daim Zainuddin, Tun (Malaysia)

Daim Zainuddin was a senior cabinet minister in the government of Prime Minister **Mahathir Mohamad** and a highly influential corporate figure. Daim was born on 29 April 1938 in the same village in Kedah as Mahathir. He qualified as a lawyer at Lincoln's Inn in London in 1959. He worked for a while in government legal service before entering private business in the late 1960s. He has enjoyed a longstanding close personal relationship with Mahathir, who was instrumental in appointing him to head of government enterprises, including Fleet Holdings, the investment arm of **UMNO** (United Malays National Organization). Daim was elected to the federal Parliament in 1982 when Mahathir first led UMNO and the ruling ***Barisan Nasional*** (National Front) coalition at the polls. As finance minister, he managed the scandal which arose over the **Bank Bumiputera Crisis** and was also responsible for guiding Malaysia through a period of economic recession in the mid-1980s to a spectacular recovery by the early 1990s. He remained an economic adviser to the prime minister after giving up office in 1991.

Daim returned to Cabinet as finance minister of Malaysia for the second time in January 1999. His resumption of high office was precipitated by economic and political crisis. He had returned to the cabinet in June 1998 with the portfolio of minister for special functions in charge of economic development, which was interpreted as an attempt by Prime Minister Mahathir to reduce the influence of the deputy prime minister and finance minister, **Anwar Ibrahim**. After the imposition of exchange controls and the dismissal and arrest of Anwar Ibrahim, Mahathir assumed the finance portfolio but then transferred it to Daim after his ruling coalition was returned to government in elections in November 1999. Dain played a decisive role in the change of Malaysia's economic course in the face of unprecedented adversity. After elections in November 1999, his relationship with Mahathir became temporarily strained over economic appointments and decisions. He retired from all government positions in 2001, at the same time relinquishing his post as UMNO's treasurer. He then moved back to the private sector and became active in consulting for African governments on economic planning. In late 2007, Daim accurately predicted the loss of the state governments in Kedah, Penang and Selangor to the opposition at the March 2008 general election.

see also: Anwar Ibrahim; Bank Bumiputera Crisis; *Barisan Nasional*; Mahathir Mohamad, Tun; UMNO.

Dakwah (Malaysia)

Dakwah is the generic name for an Islamic revivalist movement that arose among younger educated Malays in the wake of inter-communal violence in May 1969. *Dakwah,* which translates literally as to call or invite, is best understood as missionary activity among Muslims. It began in moderate form within Malaysia as a dissenting search for identity and challenge to government spearheaded by **ABIM** (Islamic Youth Movement of Malaysia), which had its origins in the University of Malaya. It assumed a more radical expression through the role of students who, returning from higher education in Britain from the mid-1970s, had been subject to the influence of radical Islamic ideas from Egypt and Pakistan. *Dakwah* so dominated university campuses by the end of the 1970s that the government was obliged to launch its own countervailing programme of Islamization but more in form than in substance. Islamic identity in Malaysia had become well entrenched by the 1990s and in the wake of the economic crisis towards the end of the decade served as a basis for political challenge to the ruling ***Barisan Nasional*** (National Front) coalition. That challenge was effectively mounted by ***Parti Islam se-Malaysia*** as well as ***Parti Keadilan Rakyat***.

see also: ABIM; *Barisan Nasional*; Islam; *Parti Islam se Malaysia; Parti Keadilan Rakyat*.

Darul Islam (Indonesia)

Darul Islam (DI), which translates literally as House of Islam, is the name given to a rebellion launched against the embattled Republic of Indonesia in west Java in 1948 which petered out only in the early 1960s. In west Java, the Hizbullah (a Japanese-inspired Muslim militia) had operated independently of the aspirant republic whose forces had been withdrawn from early 1948 under the terms of the Renville Agreement with the Dutch. DI was set up in March 1948. In August its leader, S. M. Kartosuwirjo, proclaimed *Negara Islam Indonesia*, literally the Islamic State of Indonesia. Because the republic was subject to continuing military pressure from the Dutch, the theologically driven movement was able to extend its presence into central Java. DI refused to acknowledge the authority of the Indonesian state after the transfer of sovereignty from the Dutch in December 1949. Attempts at negotiations were rebuffed and an insurgency was sustained, albeit with decreasing effect, on Java during the 1950s as the army began to bring its power to bear against the movement. Loose affiliates of DI in north Sumatra and south Sulawesi troubled the central government in the context of widespread regional rebellions in the latter part of the decade. These rebellions were broken by the early 1960s with the capture of Kartosuwirjo, who then ordered his followers to lay down their arms. DI activism was however revived in the 1970s through the likes of Abdullah Sungkar and **Abu Bakar Ba'asyir**, who used the *Al-Mukmin* pesantren (Islamic boarding school) in Ngruki, Central Java, which they founded, to recruit a new generation of DI members. This elicited a crackdown by the government of President **Suharto**, and key leaders of DI were imprisoned from 1977 to 1982 on charges of anti-government activities. Sungkar and Ba'asyir fled to Malaysia in 1985 and began recruiting yet another generation of DI followers, which included the children of former DI members, who would later form its offshoot, ***Jemaah Islamiyah***. Some from this generation of DI members, including **Hambali**, were dispatched to fight in Afghanistan during the Soviet invasion. After their return from Afghanistan, these elements thrived in the initial post-Suharto years. They first formed the backbone of *Jemaah Islamiyah*, and following splits and factionalism within the organization, proceeded to splinter off into other groups, some of which like the *Jemaat Anshorut Tauhid* proved far more extreme than their spiritual forebears, the original DI.

see also: Ba'asyir, Abu Bakar; Hambali; Islam; *Jemaah Islamiyah*; Suharto.

Declaration of ASEAN Concord 1976 (Indonesia/Malaysia/Philippines/Singapore/Thailand)

The Declaration of ASEAN Concord was made on 24 February 1976 on the island of Bali at the first meeting of the heads of government of **ASEAN** (Association of Southeast Asian Nations). The **Bali Summit** declaration was significant for registering the political identity and goals of ASEAN nearly a decade after the **Bangkok Declaration 1967** claimed that its prime purposes were economic, social and cultural cooperation. Cooperation in pursuit of political stability was identified as the pre-eminent priority, while common threat was defined with reference to subversion. Security cooperation was excluded from the corporate structure of ASEAN but could be undertaken on 'a non-ASEAN basis'. The open commitment to political cooperation was a direct response to the success of revolutionary Communism in Indochina in April 1975. The declaration brought the commitment in November 1971 to a **ZOPFAN**, a Zone of Peace, Freedom and Neutrality, under the formal aegis of the Association as well as recording the agreement to establish an ASEAN Secretariat.

see also: ASEAN; Bali Summit (ASEAN) 1976; Bangkok Declaration (ASEAN) 1967; ZOPFAN.

Declaration of ASEAN Concord II 2003 (Brunei/Cambodia/Indonesia/Malaysia/Myanmar/Laos/Philippines/Singapore/Thailand/Vietnam)

The Declaration of ASEAN Concord II was signed on the occasion of the **Bali Summit** of **ASEAN** (Association of Southeast Asian Nations) in October 2003. An aspirational document, ASEAN Concord II served to lay the foundations for a more institutionalized ASEAN. Foremost of its stated objectives was the formation of an **ASEAN Community** by 2020 which would be built on enhanced security and political cooperation, economic cooperation, and socio-cultural cooperation. At ASEAN's January 2007 Summit in Cebu, the organization signed an acceleration agreement to bring forward the goal of an ASEAN Community by five years, to 2015.

see also: ASEAN; ASEAN Community; Bali Summit (ASEAN) 2003.

Declaration of ASEAN Concord III 2011 (Brunei/Cambodia/Indonesia/Malaysia/Myanmar/Laos/Philippines/Singapore/Thailand/Vietnam)

In November 2011, leaders of **ASEAN** (Association of Southeast Asian Nations) signed the Declaration of ASEAN Concord III on the occasion of the ASEAN Summit (*see* **Bali Summit 2011**), held in Bali. This third iteration of ASEAN's Bali Concords outlined further measures to strengthen the three pillars of the **ASEAN Community**, as well as the establishment of a coordinating centre to manage humanitarian relief efforts in response to disasters. The main element to Concord III however, was its articulation of ASEAN's outward-focus on the premise of deepened integration and connectivity. This was reflected in the official title of the document: 'Bali Declaration on ASEAN Community in a Global Community of Nations'.

see also: ASEAN; ASEAN Community; Bali Summit (ASEAN) 2011.

Declaration on the Conduct of Parties in the South China Sea (ASEAN) 2002 (Brunei/Cambodia/Indonesia/Malaysia/Myanmar/Laos/Philippines/Singapore/Thailand/Vietnam)

The Declaration on the Conduct of Parties in the South China Sea, known as the DOC, was signed on 4 November 2002 in Phnom Penh, Cambodia, by the foreign ministers of the ten **ASEAN** (Association of Southeast Asian Nations) member countries and China. Signatories to the DOC pledged to find a peaceful and durable solution to differences and disputes among them in the **South China Sea**. Specifically, they committed to the resolution of their territorial and jurisdictional disputes by peaceful means without resorting to the threat or use of force, through friendly consultations and negotiations in accordance with universally recognized principles of international law. The signatories also pledged to exercise self-restraint in the conduct of activities that would complicate or escalate disputes before the peaceful settlement was reached. The DOC was agreed to be the initial step towards a more binding Code of Conduct.

The provisions laid out in the DOC were violated on several occasions, leading to criticisms that it was little more than a political statement. In May 2009, Malaysia and Vietnam made separate and joint submissions to the UN Commission on the Limits of the Continental Shelf, which were later protested by China. China then reacted by tabling its 'nine-dotted line' map outlining its claims to almost the entire South China Sea. Since then, China has relentlessly increased its capacity to exercise control over the South China Sea by expanding the number of vessels active in the area. It has also constructed a naval base at Sanya on Hainan Island. In response to China's actions, Vietnam has modernized its navy and the Philippines announced plans to increase its maritime territorial defence capability with the help of the United States. China has insisted that territorial disputes should not be settled through multilateral discussions, rejecting any involvement of non-claimants. However, ASEAN has argued the legitimacy of outside powers as stakeholders, on grounds that the escalation of any dispute in the area will affect stability and security, not to mention freedom of navigation. Despite these differences, both parties initially set 2012 as the target for the adoption of a more legally binding Code of Conduct, on the occasion of Cambodia's chairmanship of ASEAN. Yet, just three months prior to the ASEAN ministerial meeting in Phnom Penh in July 2012, tensions came to a head with the military standoff between Chinese and Philippine gunboats at **Scarborough Shoal**. The crisis was triggered when the Philippine navy attempted to arrest and detain Chinese fishermen and their vessels for illegally obtaining endangered marine life.

While only four ASEAN members are involved in the South China Sea territorial and maritime boundary disputes with China, ASEAN has been keen to follow a common approach to peacefully resolve the disputes, in particular an approach that would be in accordance with international law and the UN Convention on the Law of the Sea (UNCLOS). Nevertheless, instead of a showcase of ASEAN solidarity, the Phnom Penh meeting amplified differences in approach within ASEAN over the South China Sea dispute, as the foreign ministers of ASEAN member states were not able to come to a consensus on a joint statement over the issue. On this occasion, the Cambodian chair of ASEAN, a beneficiary of extensive Chinese investments, had refused Vietnamese and Philippine requests to include references to their individual disputes with China in the joint communiqué, or offers from other members to provide alternative drafts. Cambodia chose instead to echo to the Chinese position that bilateral disputes should not be discussed in a multilateral setting. Following the failure to achieve consensus, Indonesia's foreign minister, **Marty Natalegawa**, travelled around the capitals of Southeast Asia to smooth out differences and negotiate a common ASEAN position. His shuttle diplomacy resulted in the release of a statement on the 'Six-Point Principles on the South China Sea', which reaffirmed ASEAN's commitment to a peaceful resolution of the dispute. China, in turn, expressed willingness to continue working alongside ASEAN towards the eventual adoption of the Code of Conduct, but no firm timetable has been set for this. Nevertheless, the Philippines' move to seek arbitration on its bilateral territorial dispute with China, threatens to undermine the latter's commitment to the ASEAN process.

see also: ASEAN; Natalegawa, Marty; Phnom Penh Summit (ASEAN) April 2012; Scarborough Shoal Dispute; South China Sea.

Declaration on the South China Sea (ASEAN) 1992 (Brunei/Cambodia/Indonesia/Laos/Malaysia/Myanmar/Philippines/Singapore/Thailand/Vietnam)

At a meeting of ASEAN's foreign ministers in Manila on 22 July 1992, a joint declaration was issued on the South China Sea. Among its members, Malaysia and the Philippines claimed jurisdiction over some of the Spratly Islands in that sea, while Brunei claimed jurisdiction over adjacent maritime space. China, including Taiwan, and Vietnam claimed the entire group. The declaration arose from a Philippine initiative, which was supported by Malaysia in return for Manila withdrawing its candidate for the office of secretary-general of **ASEAN** (Association of Southeast Asian Nations) in favour of that from Kuala Lumpur. ASEAN's interest and apprehension had arisen since 1988 when China had engaged in military action at Vietnam's expense in order to hold some of the Spratly Islands. China had also published a law on its territorial waters and their contiguous areas in February 1992 which proclaimed its maritime rights in a way that suggested a policy of creeping assertiveness. The disturbing effect of the disintegration of the Soviet Union at the end of 1991 and the impending withdrawal of the US military presence from the Philippines later in 1992 on the regional balance of power served to encourage the diplomatic initiative. The declaration emphasized 'the necessity to resolve all sovereignty and jurisdictional issues pertaining to the **South China Sea** by peaceful means, without resort to force' and also urged 'all parties concerned to exercise restraint with the view to creating a positive climate for the eventual resolution of all disputes'. The declaration, which invited all parties concerned to subscribe to the declaration of principles, received a positive response from Vietnam, whose foreign minister attended the Manila meeting as an observer. China responded more equivocally and subsequently seized an additional reef in the Spratly Islands. The declaration had a moderating effect on the issue at the time but without inducing any ASEAN claimants to modify their own positions on sovereignty. The ASEAN governments invoked the declaration in March 1995 in response to China's maritime assertiveness but without any signal effect. The place of the Declaration as the blueprint governing behaviour in the South China Sea has since been superseded by the **Declaration on the Conduct of Parties in the South China Sea** signed in 2002.

see also: ASEAN; Declaration on the Conduct of Parties in the South China Sea (ASEAN) 2002; South China Sea.

Democracy Uprising 1988 (Myanmar)

The 1988 democracy protests were a series of demonstrations and riots against the government of the **Burma Socialist Programme Party** (BSPP). The protests became known as the '8888 Uprising' after the general strike that began on 8 August 1988 and were supported by large segments of the civilian population throughout the country. The protests were a direct response to more than two decades of poor governance under the BSPP led by General **Ne Win** since it was installed after the coup of 1962. Economic mismanagement under the guiding principle of the Burmese Way to Socialism had impoverished the country, resulting in Myanmar's inclusion on the United Nation's list of least-developed countries in December 1987. Anger at the situation was compounded by two unannounced reissues of banknotes in 1985 and 1987 that destroyed the savings of many citizens.

The initial protest occurred on 12 March 1988 in response to the release from police custody of the son of a BSPP official arrested for injuring a student in a scuffle at a teashop. During the ensuing clash with police a student was shot and killed. Angered by the injustice, students rallied at several campuses across Yangon over the next few days. The protests quickly cascaded into calls for the end of one-party rule. Following the brutal killing of a number of students by security forces during a rally on 16 March, unrest intensified across a number of cities. The authorities closed the universities, but demonstrations continued with sympathizers from other walks of life now joining the students. Large-scale demonstrations continued until Ne Win's resignation on 23 July. Nevertheless, when it was announced that his replacement was to be the hugely unpopular Brigadier General Sein Lwin, also known as the 'Butcher of Rangoon' for his role in the shooting of student protestors in 1962, the protests continued. 8 August 1988 was chosen for a nationwide demonstration and general strike for its auspicious numerological significance. The scale of the protests surprised the government as the students were joined by people from all walks of life, including some government workers and members of the military. The military responded by bringing in more troops resulting in running fights in Yangon between protestors and soldiers. Soldiers fired into the crowds as they tried to put down the protests across the country, killing and wounding many. Estimates of casualties from the August demonstrations vary between hundreds to over 10,000 across Myanmar.

Sein Win resigned on 12 August and was succeeded by Maung Maung as president. Correspondingly, some concessions were made. **Aung San Suu Kyi** made her debut on the political scene at this point with a speech at Shwedagon Pagoda in Yangon on 26 August urging non-violence. The Maung Maung government was given until 7 September to resign. The government responded with announcements that peace and security were breaking down, but continued to grant concessions to the protestors, including discussion of elections. The army, alarmed at the possibility of a complete breakdown in government authority, staged a coup on 18 September 1988, ousting Maung Maung and the BSPP government. It also repealed the 1975 Constitution and established the **State Law and Order Restoration Council** (SLORC) under General Saw Maung. Martial law was imposed and the protests violently suppressed with soldiers indiscriminately firing on demonstrators. By the time the army regained control at the end of the month, around 3,000 people had been killed. During the crackdown and the months that followed around 10,000 people fled to insurgent areas along the country's borders and received military training while others continued on to exile in other countries. Many of the student protest leaders were jailed and served lengthy prison terms. Some, after release from prison, would later join the 88 Generation student group, a major organizer of the 2007 anti-government protests.

see also: Aung San Suu Kyi; Burma Socialist Programme Party; Ne Win, General; State Law and Order Restoration Council.

Democrat Party (Thailand)

The Democrat (*Prachathipat*) Party has enjoyed the greatest continuity of any Thai civilian political organization. After holding office twice briefly after the Pacific War and then again briefly in the mid-1970s, it enjoyed more sustained fortunes during the 1990s and into the next century. In general elections in September 1992, it secured seventy-nine seats, the largest number in Parliament. In consequence, its leader, **Chuan Leekpai**, became prime minister of a coalition government. The Democrat Party lost power in July 1995 after elections precipitated by the defection of a coalition partner. Its parliamentary numbers were reduced to eighty-six, six less than its main rival the ***Chart Thai* Party**, which went on to form a new coalition. The Democrat Party returned to government with Chuan again as prime minister in November 1997 after the ruling coalition collapsed because of its failure to cope with the economic crisis.

Its success had followed a period of political turmoil after which the military had been obliged to concede a longstanding popular demand for a democratically elected prime minister. The Democrat Party was established in 1946 as a conservative pro-monarchist parliamentary group in opposition to the government of **Pridi Phanomyong** which had replaced the military dictatorship of **Phibul Songkram**, both men having been party to removing the absolute monarchy in 1932. The Democrat Party leader, Khuang Aphaiwong, became prime minister from November 1947 after a military coup and then again after elections in January 1948, but within two months was obliged to give up office by an assertive military. The Democrat Party drew its support in the main from Bangkok and southern Thailand and stood for liberal constitutionalism rather than for any coherent social programme. During the course of Thailand's fluctuating political evolution, the Democrat Party has seized every opportunity for parliamentary representation. During the democratic interlude which followed the successful student-led challenge to military rule in October 1973, its political fortunes revived. Under the leadership of wartime resistance leader and co-founder **Seni Pramoj**, it initially failed to form a government. In April 1976, however, fresh elections brought the Democrats to office in a shortlived administration headed by Seni, which was then overthrown by a military coup in October. A poor performance in elections in 1979 was succeeded by a much better one in 1983, with continued minority participation in government during the decade until a military coup in February 1991 led on to a further turning point in Thai politics, which after political turbulence in May 1992 saw its return to government in September. The Democrat Party attracted popular support because of its civilian credentials but its parliamentary majority was eroded through stress within the ruling coalition over perquisites of office. It suffered also through the inability of Prime Minister Chuan Leekpai to command the political stage in the face of obstruction of democratic political reforms by the military establishment. On its return to office, the Democratic Party has commanded greater respect because of its degree of success in economic management and also because of its relative freedom from the taint of corruption. However, it has been vulnerable to revived charges of corruption, which have damaged its electoral prospects. In March 2000, Sanan Kachornprasart, party secretary-general and minister of the interior as well as a deputy prime minister, was obliged to resign government offices after being charged by the National Counter Corruption Commission with concealing his assets by falsifying documents relating to a loan. He was found guilty by the Constitutional Court in August 2000, thus reducing his party's electoral prospects. The Democrat Party managed to win 128 seats at the 2001 elections, but this paled in comparison to the ***Thai Rak Thai* Party**'s (TRT) 248 seats. Chuan stepped down from his position as party leader in 2003 and was succeeded by Banyat Bantadtan, a fellow southerner and close aide. The Democrat's Apirak Kosayothin won the Bangkok gubernatorial election in 2004, but the party lost further ground to the TRT in the 2005 general election. In an effort to launch a no confidence vote against the **Thaksin Shinawatra**-led government, the Democrats hoped to secure at least 201 seats but managed only ninety-six. In the wake of this defeat, Banyat resigned and was replaced by **Abhisit Vejjajiva** on 6 March 2005.

The TRT's brand of populist politics posed a formidable challenge to the Democrat Party. But support for Thaksin had also started to wane after revelations that his family had directly profited from the tax-free sale of their stake in Shin Corp to Temasek of Singapore in January 2006. During the ensuing protests led by the **People's Alliance for Democracy** (PAD), several Democrat members of parliament openly joined the movement. Thaksin dissolved Parliament on 24 February 2006 and called for elections. The Democrat Party, on the other hand, backed the PAD in their call for a royally appointed government, which was rejected by King **Bhumibol Adulyadej**. The Democrat Party and their allies then opted to boycott the 2006 elections in April, claiming they were an attempt to divert public attention from the corruption charges against Thaksin. The boycott resulted in a constitutional crisis and new elections were called for October 2006. These were however cancelled when the army seized power on 19 September.

Abhisit initially opposed the coup and the Democrats were found guilty by the Attorney General's Office of bribing other parties to participate in their election boycott. Moves were put in place to dissolve the party, but this was blocked by a tribunal assembled by the military junta, which acquitted the Democrat Party but banned the TRT instead. Abhisit went on to support the junta's 2007 Constitution and together with his party machinery promoted populist policies to challenge TRT's successor, the **People's Power Party** (PPP), in the run-up to the December 2007 elections. The Democrats lost the election, failing to penetrate the PPP's strongholds in central, north and northeastern Thailand, and became the main opposition party. After further agitation from the PAD, again supported by several Democrat parliamentarians, the Constitutional Court dissolved the PPP on 2 December 2008. A new coalition government was formed led by the Democrats, a situation many believed was engineered by army commander and coup co-leader, **Anupong Paochinda**. As part of the machinations, former PPP parliamentarians and their allies crossed over to join the Democrat Party, giving it enough representatives to form a government. Protests by the Thaksin-aligned **United Front for Democracy against Dictatorship** 'red shirt' movement aimed at destabilizing the Democrat-led coalition began to gather pace in early 2009 and turned violent in April, forcing Abhisit to declare a State of Emergency for three days, during which he censored the media and used military force to disperse protestors. Abhisit dissolved Parliament in early 2011 and scheduled general elections for 3 July. The elections saw the Democrats soundly defeated by the ***Pheu Thai* Party**, successor to both the TRT and the PPP, which won an outright majority and appointed **Yingluck Shinawatra** as Prime Minister. Abhisit stepped down as party leader following the defeat, but was re-elected to the post on 6 August 2011. The Democrat Party remained staunch opponents of the *Pheu Thai* Party right up to the May 2014 coup which removed the elected *Pheu Thai* government.

see also: Abhisit Vejjajiva; Anupong Paochinda, General; Bhumibol Adulyadej; *Chart Thai* Party; Chuan Leekpai; People's Power Party; *Pheu Thai* Party; Phibul Songkram, Field Marshal; Pridi Phanomyong; Seni Pramoj; *Thai Rak Thai* Party; Thaksin Shinawatra; United Front for Democracy against Dictatorship; Yingluck Shinawatra.

Democratic Action Party (DAP)
(Malaysia)

The Democratic Action Party (DAP) is the most important non-Malay opposition party in Malaysia. The DAP originated as the peninsular Malaysian branch of Singapore's ruling **People's Action Party** (PAP) while the island was a constituent part of Malaysia. As such, it participated in elections on the mainland in April but secured only one seat out of nine contested. After Singapore separated from Malaysia in August 1965, it became necessary for the PAP branch to assume a different name to avoid deregistration, which it did in March 1966.

The name Democratic Action Party and a commitment to a socialist model of society corresponded closely to the declared political identity of its predecessor. The taint of its origins has never been completely overcome, especially given the abiding structural tension between Malaysia and Singapore. The DAP's constituency is non-communal, in principle, and it puts up Malay electoral candidates. In practice, however, voting support has been drawn primarily from non-Malays and in particular urban Chinese frustrated by the denial of educational and career opportunities to their children because of the preference accorded to Malays under the ***Bumiputra*** policy. The DAP has been outspoken on behalf of the rights of the non-Malays and also in support of civil liberties. It has been a constant thorn in the side of government over constitutionalism, corrupt practices and maladministration. Over the years, the DAP has been subject to recurrent political constraints, with its leading members being detained under the Internal Security Act, as well as being disciplined by the speaker of the federal Parliament for alleged breaches of standing orders. In addition, restrictions have been placed on the circulation of the party's newspaper.

The DAP has been involved in several opposition political coalitions. In 1990, it captured twenty parliamentary seats as part of the *Gagasan Rakyat* coalition together with ***Semangat '46*** and ***Parti Bersatu Sabah***. In 1999, it was part of the ***Barisan Alternatif*** (Alternative Front) but managed to secure only ten seats as Chinese voters were unconvinced of the prudence of political cooperation with ***Parti Islam Se-Malaysia*** (PAS), with which the DAP has a running debate over the matter of the Islamic state, the declared objective of PAS, which was incompatible with the DAP's idea of a pluralistic, democratic and secular society. The 1999 elections also proved very disappointing as several party stalwarts, particularly the secretary-general, **Lim Kit Siang**, and chairman, Karpal Singh, lost their seats. The DAP's fortunes took a turn for the better at the 2004 elections when it won twelve parliamentary seats and regained its position as opposition leader from PAS. The party capitalized on widespread non-Malay frustration and put in strong performances in the last two elections – 2008 and 2013 – as part of the ***Pakatan Rakyat*** (People's Alliance) opposition alliance, which formalized the opposition coalition cobbled together for the 2008 election. In 2008, the DAP won twenty-eight parliamentary seats and together with ***Parti Keadilan Rakyat*** (PKR) and PAS managed to deny the ***Barisan Nasional*** (National Front) a two-thirds majority in Parliament. The DAP was able to secure a majority of the state seats in Penang and formed the state government along with its alliance partners – PAS and PKR. DAP secretary-general, **Lim Guan Eng**, son of Lim Kit Siang, became chief minister. However, in the state of Perak, despite the DAP winning the majority of seats, a PAS assemblyman was appointed as chief minister. In response, Lim Kit Siang issued an initial instruction for all DAP candidates to boycott the swearing-in ceremony, resulting in its cancellation. The ceremony was reinstated only after Lim retracted his instruction and apologized. At the May 2013 elections, the DAP improved its parliamentary representation to thirty-eight seats. However, less than a month prior to the election, the party almost had to contest under the banner of its coalition allies as the Registrar of Societies sought to de-recognize the party's leadership after a technical glitch at party elections led to a miscount. A crisis was averted when the Registrar of Societies permitted the DAP to use its own symbol a few days later.

see also: Barisan Alternatif; Barisan Nasional; Bumiputra; Lim Guan Eng; Lim Kit Siang; *Pakatan Rakyat; Parti Bersatu Sabah; Parti Islam Se-Malaysia; Parti Keadilan Rakyat*; People's Action Party; *Semangat '46*.

Democratic Kampuchea (Cambodia)

The **Khmer Rouge** seized power in Cambodia on 17 April 1975 in the name of the Royal Government of National Unification, which had been proclaimed in the People's Republic of China on 5 May 1970, with Prince **Norodom Sihanouk** as head of state. On 5 January 1976 a new constitution was promulgated in Phnom Penh establishing the State of Democratic Kampuchea, initially with Prince Sihanouk as its head. He resigned on 4 April, to be succeeded by **Khieu Samphan**. On 14 April **Pol Pot** was appointed prime minister but gave up the post between 27 September and 15 October. On 25 December 1978 Vietnamese forces, acting ostensibly as volunteers in support of a Kampuchean National United Front for National Salvation, invaded Cambodia. They ousted the government of Democratic Kampuchea and replaced it on 8 January 1979 with the **People's Republic of Kampuchea**. Representatives of Democratic Kampuchea continued to occupy the Cambodian seat in the United Nations, albeit from 1982 until 1990 as part of a coalition delegation with two non-Communist Khmer factions. From the General Assembly session beginning in 1991, the Cambodian seat was held, in principle, by the **Supreme National Council** comprising representatives of all four Khmer groupings until a coalition government of the restored Kingdom of Cambodia, without Khmer Rouge participation, was established in October 1993. The term Democratic Kampuchea is replete with tragic irony because of the bloody tyranny which marked its tenure.

see also: Democratic Kampuchea, Coalition Government of; Kampuchea, People's Republic of; Khieu Samphan; Khmer Rouge; Pol Pot; Sihanouk, King Norodom; Supreme National Council.

Democratic Kampuchea, Coalition Government of (CGDK) 1982–90

(Cambodia)

At a meeting in Kuala Lumpur in June 1982, sponsored by **ASEAN** (Association of Southeast Asian Nations), representatives of three insurgent Cambodian (Kampuchean) factions challenging Vietnam's occupation agreed to form a coalition government. They comprised the **Khmer Rouge**, led nominally by **Khieu Samphan**, which had retained Cambodia's seat in the United Nations in the name of the ousted government of Democratic Kampuchea, the republican-oriented non-Communist **Khmer People's National Liberation Front** (KPNLF) led by a former prime minister, **Son Sann**, and the royalist **FUNCINPEC** (National United Front for an Independent, Neutral, Peaceful and Cooperative Cambodia) led by the former head of state, Prince **Norodom Sihanouk**. Prince Sihanouk became president, Son Sann became prime minister and Khieu Samphan became vice-president responsible for foreign affairs.

The coalition government did not establish an identifiable territorial seat, while the agreement did not provide for merging the resistance factions. On the contrary, it was stipulated that the coalition partners would retain separate organizational and political identities as well as freedom of operational action. Moreover, the Khmer Rouge insisted on having written into the agreement their proprietary right to the political trademark 'Democratic Kampuchea' and to the United Nations seat should the coalition break up. The accord was an expression of tactical political convenience intended to dilute the bestial identity of Democratic Kampuchea and to refute charges that ASEAN was engaged in an immoral relationship in its diplomatic challenge to Vietnam. The coalition device made it easier to solicit voting support in the United Nations and to justify ASEAN's charge that Vietnam had implanted an illegitimate government in Cambodia. The coalition partners maintained a common diplomatic front over the terms for a political settlement but the relationship among the disparate factions along the Thai border during the 1980s, where they drew on support from concentrations of refugees, was tense, in the main because of unprovoked armed attacks by Khmer Rouge units. Acts of resignation by Prince Sihanouk were justified on that ground, although he insisted on Khmer Rouge participation in a political settlement because of the danger of violent disruption should they be excluded. The coalition changed in nomenclature to the National Government of Cambodia in 1990 as negotiations proceeded between Cambodian factions over the terms of a United Nations peace plan which was approved by an **International Conference on Cambodia** in Paris in October 1991. The so-called coalition lapsed when its members participated in the **Supreme National Council**, which was accorded a symbolic sovereignty so that authority could be delegated to the United Nations to implement the 1991 Paris Peace Agreement. The coalition broke up in discord when the Khmer Rouge refused to participate in elections in May 1993 to elect a Constituent Assembly. It was superseded when the incumbent **Cambodian People's Party** (CPP) joined with FUNCINPEC and the political successor of the KPNLF to form a coalition government in Phnom Penh in October 1993.

see also: Cambodian People's Party; Democratic Kampuchea; FUNCINPEC; International Conference on Cambodia, Paris 1991; Khieu Samphan; Khmer People's National Liberation Front; Khmer Rouge; Sihanouk, King Norodom; Son Sann; Supreme National Council; United Nations: Cambodia 1991–3; UNTAC.

Democratic Soldiers (Thailand)

Democratic Soldiers is the term applied to a group of middle-ranking Thai officers who were influential from the late 1970s in providing a conceptual social basis for the military's claim to political entitlement. More intellectual than the **Young Turks** faction which changed prime ministers in 1980 by switching support from General **Kriangsak Chomanan** to General **Prem Tinsulanonda**, its members were driven by their experience of countering Communist rural insurgency by civic action. Tutored by defectors from the Communist Party of Thailand, they espoused a simplistic state socialism as a way of overcoming rural poverty and a condition of alleged international economic dependence brought about by feckless civilian politicians and Sino-Thai business people. Former Democratic Soldiers sought political expression through the Thai People's Party (*Puang Chon Chao Thai*) which enjoyed a brief period of coalition government from October 1990 until February 1991. In the next elections in March 1992, it secured only one seat and had lost its political identity by the subsequent elections in September that year. Its leader, General Arthit Kamlang-ek, resigned from the party in January 1992 to join another military-based grouping, *Sammakkhi Tham*. By the time of the disintegration of the Thai People's Party, the ideas of the Democratic Soldiers had lost their earlier political immediacy as Communist insurgency had effectively ceased.

see also: Kriangsak Chomanan, General; Prem Tinsulanonda, General; Young Turks.

Demokrasi Terpimpin (Indonesia) *see* Guided Democracy.

Diem, Ngo Dinh (Vietnam)

Ngo Dinh Diem was president of the Republic of (South) Vietnam from its proclamation on 26 October 1955 until his assassination on 2 November 1963. Diem was born on 3 January 1901 in Hue in central Vietnam. His family were traditionally mandarins or public servants and had been Catholic for more than two centuries. After a conventional education which culminated in the study of law at the University of Hanoi, Diem entered the imperial service and so distinguished himself that he was appointed minister of the interior by Emperor **Bao Dai** in 1933 but soon resigned in protest at the constraints imposed on his office by French colonial rule. His nationalist credentials assured, he withdrew from public life in keeping with an early ambition to become a priest. Ngo Dinh Diem was a fervent anti-Communist which was an extension of his religious faith. He refused to join in cooperation with **Ho Chi Minh** and was embittered by the Communists' assassination of his brother Ngo Dinh Khoi, then governor of Quang Nai Province. He also rejected an offer to serve in the government of the former Emperor Bao Dai in the late 1940s under French aegis. He left Vietnam in 1950 and travelled in Japan, Italy, the Philippines, the United States and Belgium, enjoying the hospitality of a network of Catholic associates. He went to France in 1953 and was still there in June 1954 when Bao Dai, influenced by the Eisenhower administration, invited him to become prime minister. He returned to Saigon towards the end of the month in time to oppose the terms of the **Geneva Agreements on Indochina**: the conference concluded its deliberations on 21 July 1954. Diem built up his political position with US support after crushing the criminal Binh Xuyen organization and two religious sects. In October 1955 he held a spurious referendum whose controlled outcome enabled him to remove Bao Dai as head of the State of Vietnam and to have himself appointed as president of the Republic of Vietnam. Committed to celibacy, Diem came under the powerful influence of his brother (and minister of the interior) Ngo Dinh Nhu and his formidable wife. Their authoritarian regime, within which Diem appeared as a remote figure, failed to contain the revival of Communist insurgency by the end of the 1950s. US support began to wane in the wake of Buddhist demonstrations and self-immolations and the Kennedy administration became persuaded to countenance a military coup by dissident army officers. That coup was mounted on 1 November 1963. Diem and his brother were captured and then killed the next day but successive military governments failed to do any better against the Communist insurgency directed from the northern part of the country.

see also: Bao Dai; Geneva Agreements on Indochina 1954; Ho Chi Minh.

Dien Bien Phu, Battle of, 1954 (Vietnam)

Dien Bien Phu (literally seat of the Border County Prefecture) is the name of a valley in northwestern Vietnam close to the border with Laos and the site of the most decisive battle of the First Indochina War between the Communist-led **Viet Minh** and the French colonial army. The battle took the form of a siege of French military positions established in November 1953. It began on 13 March 1954 and culminated fifty-six days later with a Viet Minh victory which sapped the political will of the French government. The site of the battle was fixed by a French determination to force a major test of military strength on the elusive Viet Minh and because the valley was a practical blocking point against incursions into Laos. The military deployment to the valley floor proved to be a fatal blunder. Against expectations and all odds, the Viet Minh had transported heavy artillery to impregnable dominating positions in the surrounding mountains. Superiority in firepower determined the outcome of the battle, which was virtually decided in the first week, presaged by the suicide of the French artillery commander, Colonel Charles Piroth. The final French position surrendered on 7 May 1954 with impeccable timing just one day before an international conference convened in Geneva to address the political future of Indochina.

see also: Geneva Agreements on Indochina 1954; Indochina Wars; Viet Minh.

Do Muoi (Vietnam)

Do Muoi served as general secretary of the Communist Party of Vietnam from June 1991 until December 1997. He was elected to that office at the seventh Party Congress and was re-elected at the eighth Party Congress in June 1996. At the age of eighty, he was replaced as general secretary by the party's Central Committee at its meeting in December 1997 in favour of General **Le Kha Phieu**. Do Muoi remained as an advisor to the Central Committee from 1997 to 2001, when the institution of Advisory Council of the Central Committee was abolished.

Do Muoi was born on 2 February 1917 in an outer district of Hanoi. He worked as a house painter and became involved in nationalist politics in his late teens. Do Muoi joined the original Communist Party of Indochina in 1939. He was arrested by the French authorities and sentenced to ten years' imprisonment in 1941 but escaped in 1945 and was active as a party official and political commissar during the First Indochina War. He then rose steadily within the party hierarchy. In March 1955 he became an alternate member of the central committee and a full member in December 1960. Over the next twenty years, he combined governmental office with party position, rising to vice-premier. Do Muoi was elected an alternate member of the Politburo of the Communist Party at its fourth National Congress in December 1976 and became a full member at its fifth National Congress in December 1986. Over the years, Do Muoi acquired a reputation as a conservative ideologue who only reluctantly agreed to the policy of ***Doi Moi*** (economic renovation) which had been introduced as a matter of political necessity. In June 1988, when he was elected to the office of chairman of the Council of Ministers (the equivalent of prime minister), it was assumed that he had been chosen to balance the reformist zeal of the new general secretary of the party, **Nguyen Van Linh**. In the event, he showed himself to be a pragmatist willing to encourage Vietnam's economic adaptation in order to overcome adverse circumstances.

At the same time, he represented ideological continuity and reaffirmed a commitment to socialism. As general secretary for over six years, Do Muoi stood fast against any concessions to political pluralism and any diminution of the monopoly role of the ruling Communist Party. He was a vocal opponent of General Secretary Le Kha Phieu's leadership, and used his considerable influence as convenor of the ninth National Congress in 2001 to criticize Le, a move which was supported by party stalwarts **Vo Van Kiet** and **Le Duc Anh**.

see also: Doi Moi; Indochina Wars; Le Duc Anh, General; Le Kha Phieu, General; Linh, Nguyen Van; Vo Van Kiet.

Doi Moi (Vietnam)

The term *Doi Moi* means renovation or renewal of the economy. It was promulgated at the sixth National Congress of Vietnam's Communist Party in December 1986 and reconfirmed at the seventh National Congress in June 1991. As a direct consequence of the attendant reforms, the material condition of Vietnam has been transformed with a growing engagement with the international economy. The policy of *Doi Moi* seeks to encourage free market economics while protecting the Communist political system. It was introduced by **Nguyen Van Linh** as a matter of political necessity. The failings of the Communist Party in not fulfilling the promise of the revolution to give the people of Vietnam a better life had brought it into political disrepute and also threatened its regime. *Doi Moi* has been distinguished from *perestroika*, introduced in the former Soviet Union, because the notion of restructuring which it conveyed was regarded in Hanoi as subversive of the leading role of the Communist Party. In consequence, political conservatism induced caution in economic liberalization as hardliners refused to cede ideological ground, which had the effect of retarding the momentum of *Doi Moi* by the turn of the century.

see also: Do Muoi; Linh, Nguyen Van.

Domino Theory (Cambodia/Laos/Vietnam)

Domino Theory served as an underlying rationale for the United States' fateful intervention in Vietnam. In the context of the Cold War and US policy of containing a monolithic international communism, the strategic importance of Indochina was represented in terms of an analogy with a line of standing dominoes which would tumble one by one should the first fall. The theory has been most closely identified with President Dwight D. Eisenhower, who argued at a press conference in Washington on 7 April 1954: 'You have a row of dominoes set up, you knock over the first one, and what will happen to the last one is that it will go over very quickly'. He concluded that if Indochina fell to Communism, the rest of Southeast Asia would go very quickly, with incalculable losses to the free world. That statement was made as French forces, embattled by the Communist-led **Viet Minh** at **Dien Bien Phu**, seemed likely to be overcome in the absence of a military intervention. The US government was not prepared then to risk military intervention in the light of recent experience in Korea; nor was its British ally. In the event, Dien Bien Phu fell to the Viet Minh in the first **Indochina War** in May 1954 and at an international conference on Indochina which convened concurrently in Geneva and concluded its deliberations in the **Geneva Agreements on Indochina** in July, Vietnam became subject to a *de facto* partition with the north in Communist hands. Laos was subject to a measure of partition, while only Cambodia remained intact under a non-Communist government.

A domino effect did not immediately follow but domino theory remained integral to the United States' strategic rationale expressed in the Collective Defence Treaty for Southeast Asia or **Manila Pact** in September 1954 and the establishment of **SEATO** (Southeast Asia Treaty Organization) in February 1955. Domino Theory was based in part on an interpretation in Washington of Cold War circumstances in which Vietnam's Communists were perceived as proxies of a revolutionary China, which was in turn viewed as the Soviet Union's vehicle for expansion in Asia against whom a line had to be drawn and held. Underlying that interpretation was the United States' experience of the outbreak of the Pacific War in which Japan's avenue to spectacular conquest in Southeast Asia from December 1941 had been through Indochina, where access had been secured at French expense. In the event, the forcible unification of Vietnam in April 1975 had a domino effect of a kind, as political accommodation in neighbouring Laos between Communist and non-Communist Parties crumbled in favour of the former by the end of the year. In neighbouring Cambodia, Vietnamese Communist support helped the murderous **Khmer Rouge** come to power but not as subordinates to the ruling party in Hanoi with whom confrontation ensued. To the extent that China backed the Khmer Rouge against Vietnam, a sort of reverse domino effect occurred. Moreover, the success of revolutionary communism in Indochina during 1975, in the wake of ignominious American withdrawal, did not produce any domino effect within the rest of Southeast Asia, which did not succumb to internal Communist challenge. At issue and controversial, however, is the extent to which the United States' ill-fated military intervention, prompted by the reasoning of domino theory, was responsible for 'buying time' against the threat of communism for the states of Southeast Asia beyond Indochina.

see also: Communism in Southeast Asia; Dien Bien Phu; Geneva Agreements on Indochina 1954; Indochina Wars; Khmer Rouge; Manila Pact 1954; SEATO; Viet Minh; Vietnam War.

Dong, Pham Van (Vietnam) *see* Pham Van Dong.

Duan, Le (Vietnam) *see* Le Duan.

Dung, Nguyen Tan (Vietnam)

Nguyen Tan Dung was appointed prime minister of Vietnam in 2006, replacing **Phan Van Khai** as part of a cabinet reshuffle with the objective of revitalizing the country's leadership. He assumed office at the age of fifty-seven, making him the youngest prime minister since Vietnamese unification in 1975. Nguyen Tan Dung was born in 1949 and holds a Bachelor of Law degree in High-Level Political Theory. He joined the Vietnamese army in 1961 when he was twelve during the country's struggle for reunification, and served in the military for two decades. He started off as a medic and was slowly promoted up the ranks to become a major and head of the personnel board of the military command in Kien Giang Province. During his time in the army, he was involved in the Third Indochina War which eventually led to the fall of the **Khmer Rouge** regime in Phnom Penh. After the war, he climbed quickly up the party ranks to become a member of its Politburo in 1996. Prior to his appointment as prime minister, he became first deputy prime minister in 1997 and served as governor of the State Bank of Vietnam from 1998 to 1999.

Coming from the more commercial South, Nguyen Tan Dung has been a strong advocate of Vietnam's liberal economic reforms. Nevertheless, he was heavily criticized at the January 2011 National Congress by a conservative faction led by the newly appointed president, **Truong Tan Sang**, which drew attention to huge losses incurred by **State Owned Enterprises** (SOE) under the supervision of the prime minister. Further attacks were launched against Nguyen Tan Dung at the fourth Plenum (December 2011) and the sixth Plenum (October 2012). Though these attempts to unseat Nguyen ultimately failed, they did signal a reduction in his influence. As a result of these pressures, Nguyen Tan Dung was compelled to publicly accept personal responsibility for the failure of several SOEs.

see also: Khmer Rouge; Phan Van Khai; State Owned Enterprise Reform; Truong Tan Sang.

Dwi Fungsi (Indonesia)

Dwi Fungsi translates as 'Dual Function' and was employed in Indonesia to explain and justify the prerogative position of the armed forces. The term originated in the critical role played by them during the national revolution, especially in the latter stage after the Dutch had captured its political leadership. After independence, that role first received doctrinal expression with the failure of parliamentary democracy and the declaration of martial law in 1957. The army chief of staff, Major General **Abdul Haris Nasution**, devised the notion of a 'middle way', namely, that the armed forces would neither totally disengage from public life nor totally dominate it. In April 1965 at their first national seminar, the armed forces affirmed their dual role as both a military and a socio-political force. After General **Suharto** had established his **New Order** after March 1966, the concept of dual function became a central legitimizing device. The second armed forces seminar in August 1966 and a Ministry of Defence seminar in November gave content to the concept, which was adopted as part of military doctrine. It was accorded formal recognition by the **People's Consultative Assembly** (MPR) in 1978 and then enacted in law in 1982. The claim to a *Dwi Fungsi* has been asserted as a military prerogative and was expressed in the right of the armed forces to hold 100 seats in the 500-member Parliament in return for not voting in national elections. The reduction of that number to seventy-five seats by former president Suharto for the parliament elected in May 1997 indicated his intention to limit the remit of dual function. Following Suharto's resignation in May 1998 and his succession by interim-president Habibie, that number was further reduced to thirty-eight for the parliament elected in June 1999. By that juncture, the reputation and national standing of the armed forces had been diminished and the concept of *Dwi Fungsi* was in disrepute. In August 2000, however, the MPR resolved to extend military representation until 2009.

see also: ABRI; Habibie, B. J.; Nasution, General Abdul Haris; New Order; People's Consultative Assembly; Suharto.

E

East Asia Summit 2005– (Brunei/Cambodia/Indonesia/Laos/Malaysia/Myanmar/Philippines/Singapore/Thailand/Vietnam)

On 14 December 2005, representatives from sixteen countries gathered in Kuala Lumpur, Malaysia, for the inaugural session of the East Asia Summit (EAS). Participants at that first meeting comprised the ten members of **ASEAN** (Association of Southeast Asian Nations), China, Japan and South Korea, as well as Australia, New Zealand and India. As had been the case with China, Japan and Korea, the latter three states were dialogue partners of ASEAN and had either acceded or indicated their willingness to accede to ASEAN's **Treaty of Amity and Cooperation**, which has been the principle document that has governed multilateral institutions such as ASEAN and the **ASEAN Regional Forum** (ARF) in the region. The United States and Russia officially participated in the EAS at the sixth iteration of the meeting in Indonesia in 2011.

Opinions differ, but many regional observers agree that the origins of this summit go back to the 1990 proposal for an East Asian Economic Grouping (EAEG) popularized by former Malaysian prime minister, **Mahathir Mohamad**, but which met with stiff opposition from Japan and the United States. The project was later revived through the ASEAN Plus Three or APT (China, Japan and South Korea) summit of heads of state and government that first met in Kuala Lumpur in December 1997, and eventually found further expression through the creation of the EAS in December 2005. The EAS grew out of the proposal of South Korean president Kim Dae Jung, made at the second APT meeting in Vietnam in November 1998, for the formation of an East Asian Vision Group (EAVG) to explore the prospects for the formation of an East Asian community. Comprising twenty-six civilian experts, the group was tasked to research and recommend concrete measures that the APT could take to increase East Asian regional cooperation. In 2001, the EAVG released findings that proposed the establishment of an East Asia Summit to further regionalism in East Asia. To that end, the EAS was envisaged as a vehicle to build this community and pre-empt or resolve any future regional challenges that may arise.

Initial reactions to the proposal were cautious but positive. While states concerned broadly embraced the EAS idea as a further step to community building in the region, opinions differed over the channels through which this was to be actualized. Some states, such as China, remained inclined towards the APT, and thought the existing APT framework would provide the best means of bringing the EAS to fruition. Concern about Chinese dominance led ASEAN to press for a separate entity altogether. Eventually, a consensus was reached that the EAS would take the form of a separate institution complete with its own summit meeting.

Following the proposals of the EAVG, Prime Minister **Abdullah Badawi** of Malaysia proposed at the APT summit in 2004 to bring about the recommendations for the EAS, and offered to host the first meeting in Kuala Lumpur the following year. In December 2005, the EAS comprising the ten members of ASEAN, China, Japan, South Korean, India, Australia and New Zealand met for the first time alongside the annual ASEAN ministerial meeting in Kuala Lumpur, with Russia also present as observer at the invitation of the Malaysian hosts. At the conclusion of the meeting, the Chairman's Statement and Kuala Lumpur Declaration clarified that the EAS was to be an 'open' forum for dialogue on broad strategic, political and economic issues of common interest and concern with the aim of promoting peace, stability and economic prosperity in East Asia.

The 2006 meeting had to be rescheduled because of a typhoon that struck the Philippines, then the ASEAN chair, while the 2009 meeting was rescheduled because of political unrest in Thailand. Regardless of these disruptions, little of substance has been achieved over seven summits. At the seventh meeting in Phnom Penh, high hopes for further progress in economic integration were dashed when discussions on the topic were sidetracked by differences over the **South China Sea**, while President Barack Obama's absence from the October 2013 Bandar Seri Begawan summit after the US government failed to avert the fiscal cliff proved to be the highlight of that meeting.

see also: ASEAN; ASEAN Regional Forum; Badawi, Abdullah; Mahathir Mohamad, Tun; South China Sea; Treaty of Amity and Cooperation.

EDSA (Epifanio de los Santos Avenue) (Philippines)

Epifanio de los Santos Avenue is a major thoroughfare in Manila. From 23 to 25 February 1986 it was the setting for a remarkable display of popular opposition in support of a military revolt led by **Juan Ponce Enrile** and **Fidel Ramos** against the regime of President **Ferdinand Marcos** in the wake of a fraudulently conducted snap election. Its acronym EDSA was taken as the name for the civilian-supported military revolt whose headquarters in Camp Crame bordered the avenue. After an appeal by Cardinal **Jaime Sin**, the revolt was sustained by an interposing human wall of passive resistance which prevented Marcos loyalists from crushing it by force. The episode, which was critical in **Corazón Aquino** becoming president of the Philippines, has passed into legend as '**People Power**'.

see also: Aquino, Corazón; Enrile, Juan Ponce; Marcos, Ferdinand; People Power; Reform the Armed Forces Movement; Sin, Cardinal Jaime.

EDSA II (Philippines)

EDSA II, otherwise known as Edsa Dos or the EDSA revolution of 2001, refers to the second People's Power revolution that forced a transfer of presidential power in the Philippines. The event lasted for four days and included a peaceful rally at the **EDSA** Shrine, where calls for the overthrow of President **Joseph Estrada** reverberated in a replay of the demonstration of **People Power** that removed President **Ferdinand Marcos** a decade and a half earlier in the original EDSA revolution. Rallies soon broke out elsewhere across the Philippines when it became evident that the impeachment trial of Estrada following corruption charges was losing momentum. The movement led to the installation of the vice-president, **Gloria Macapagal-Arroyo**, as president of the Philippines. Although many critics and purists denounced the revolution as 'mobocracy', the point remains that it was still widely recognized and supported by civil society groups and the international community, thereby lending legitimacy to Macapagal-Arroyo's presidency.

see also: EDSA; Estrada, Joseph; Macapagal-Arroyo, Gloria; Marcos, Ferdinand, People Power.

Elections 1990 (Myanmar)

The 1990 general election in Myanmar was the first multi-party election in the country since 1960. Myanmar had become a one-party state in 1962 following a military coup and the establishment of the **Burma Socialist Programme Party** (BSPP) led by General **Ne Win**, but new elections were promised following nationwide protests in 1988 and the September 1988 coup of the **State Law and Order Restoration Council** (SLORC). The elections would be for a new parliament with 492 seats. Over 200 parties initially registered but ninety-three parties eventually contested the elections, presenting 2,297 candidates. Restrictions were placed on opposition politicians and both **Aung San Suu Kyi**, who was placed under house arrest in July 1989, and former premier **U Nu** remained under house arrest during the campaigning period and the election proper. Restrictions were also placed on public gatherings and political meetings as well as on political literature, although these were frequently defied. When the elections were eventually held on 27 May 1990, the **National League for Democracy** won an overwhelming fifty-eight per cent of the vote and 392 seats in Parliament. The military's **National Unity Party** received twenty-one per cent of the vote but only ten seats. The results were a surprise for the SLORC, which hitherto had been confident its party would win the elections. Myanmar's military rulers initially said they would honour the election results, and in July 1990 announced they would relinquish power once a new constitution was drafted. A new constitution would not be drafted until 2007. By the time elections were announced for 2010, new election laws came into being that annulled the 1990 results.

see also: Aung San Suu Kyi; Burma Socialist Programme Party; National League for Democracy; National Unity Party; Ne Win, General; U Nu.

Elections 2010 (Myanmar)

The general election held in Myanmar on 7 November 2010 was the first in over twenty years and marked a significant shift from military rule to a more democratic form of government. The polls were held for both the upper and lower houses of parliament, as well as parliaments in each of the seven states and seven divisions. Forty political parties registered to contest the election. Some of the parties were sizable enough to compete nationally, while others concentrated on contesting seats in their respective states or divisional parliaments. The military government transformed its mass organization, the Union Solidarity and Development Association, into a political party, the **Union Solidarity and Development Party** (USDP), and a number of senior military officers in the **State Peace and Development Council** (SPDC) resigned their commissions in order to join the party and contest the elections. A number of parties were established along ethnic lines, with the largest, the Shan Nationalities Democratic Party (SNDP), eventually winning the third highest number of seats. The **National League for Democracy** (NLD) boycotted the elections in protest at what they considered to be unreasonable election laws, a flawed constitution and the continued detention of political prisoners.

The final results of the elections were announced on 17 November 2010 with the military-backed USDP predictably winning a landslide. In second place were the **National Unity Party** (NUP), followed by the National Democratic Force (NDF) and the SNDP. The elections were criticized by the United Nations and a number of Western governments amid accusations of vote rigging, intimidation and other forms of electoral fraud, as well as the decision of the government to reject international monitoring. The election was called into further question given the fact that opposition leader **Aung San Suu Kyi** remained under house arrest during that period, although she was released six days after the elections. The SPDC handed power over to the elected government, and parliament was convened for the first time on 30 March 2011.

see also: Aung San Suu Kyi; National League for Democracy; National Unity Party; State Peace and Development Council; Union Solidarity and Development Party.

Elysée Agreement 1949 (Vietnam)

On 8 March 1949 an agreement was reached between the French government and **Bao Dai**, who had abdicated as Emperor of Vietnam in August 1945 in favour of the Communist-controlled **Viet Minh**. The agreement provided for French recognition of the limited independence of the Associated State of Vietnam within the French Union and included the former colony and so-called Republic of Cochin China, which had been accorded a separate constitutional identity in 1946. The agreement took effect in Vietnam with a ceremony in Saigon on 14 June which led on to the formal establishment of the Associated State on 1 July. It was ratified by the French National Assembly on 29 January 1950. The background to the agreement was France's attempt to engage the United States in its military struggle in the First Indochina War to retain its colonial domain in Indochina by representing it as a critical theatre in the global conflict against international Communism. The United States had made its support dependent on France being willing to transfer power to nationalist figures who could provide a credible alternative to the Communists. The result was the so-called Bao Dai solution whereby the former emperor returned from exile to become head of state. It was no coincidence that on 4 February 1950, within days of the ratification by the French National Assembly, the United States extended formal diplomatic recognition to the Associated State of Vietnam as well as to Laos and Cambodia, to which corresponding commitments had been made: Laos on 19 July 1949 and Cambodia on 8 November 1949. A formal request from France for US military aid followed on 16 February 1950; this was approved by President Truman on 1 May to the sum of US$15 million. That commitment marked the beginning of the United States' intervention in what eventually became the **Vietnam War**.

see also: Bao Dai; Indochina Wars; Viet Minh; Vietnam War.

Emergency 1948–60 (Malaya/Malaysia)

The term 'Emergency' was employed to describe the insurrection mounted by the Communist Party of Malaya against the British colonial authorities from 1948. Emergency regulations were promulgated on 18 June 1948 in response to armed attacks against rubber plantations. Those regulations were not rescinded until 31 July 1960. A distinguishing feature of the insurrection was the predominant support provided by the ethnic Chinese community, initially mobilized during the Japanese occupation. Although the colonial authorities were unprepared for the insurrection, the Communist Party was also less than fully ready for armed struggle, feeling obliged to respond to governmental action against its trade union representatives as well as to the call of the Cominform for national liberation revolution. The insurrection reached its peak in 1951 with the assassination of Britain's high commissioner, Sir Henry Gurney. By then, however, the party had admitted the failure of its policy to establish liberated areas and sought to change tack in an attempt to widen its popular base. But it was too late as the security forces had gained the initiative in both the armed struggle and in that for hearts and minds. The Communist guerrillas were driven deeper into the rainforest and from the mid-1950s were obliged to retreat to redoubts along the border with Thailand. Although the Communist Party was able to engage in sporadic military operations after 1960, especially at the end of the Vietnam War in 1975, internal dissension and governmental action effectively confined the insurgency to a nuisance role. On 2 December 1989 in the southern Thai town of Hat Yai, the governments of Thailand and Malaysia and the Communist Party of Malaya issued a joint statement to mark the signing of two peace agreements whereby the three sides would terminate all armed activities. The agreement constituted an act of surrender by the Communist Party of Malaya; it was signed by the party's general secretary, **Chin Peng**, who had not been seen in public since the Baling Talks in 1955.

see also: Baling Talks 1955; Chin Peng.

Enrile, Juan Ponce (Philippines)

Juan Ponce Enrile, as minister of defence, led a military mutiny against President **Ferdinand Marcos** on 22 February 1986 in the wake of fraudulently conducted elections. He was joined in revolt by the deputy chief of staff of the armed forces, **Fidel Ramos**, and encouraged by the head of the Catholic Church, Cardinal **Jaime Sin**. Cardinal Sin's appeal for popular support led to the remarkable political phenomenon of '**People Power**' whereby residents of Manila stood between the military dissidents based in Camp Crame and those units loyal to President Marcos. President Marcos went into exile later that month, to be succeeded by his electoral rival, **Corazón Aquino**, who reappointed Enrile as minister of defence in her first cabinet.

Juan Ponce Enrile was born on 14 February 1924 in Cagayan Province, north of Manila. He had a legal education at the University of the Philippines and in the United States at Harvard University after the Pacific War and began his career as a corporation lawyer. He assumed political office as undersecretary of finance after Ferdinand Marcos became president in January 1966, rising to minister of defence by the turn of the decade. As a close confidant of President Marcos, he helped to mastermind the introduction and management of martial law from 1972. When the promise of Marcos' New Society Movement began to sour, he cultivated a coterie of young military officers, the **Reform the Armed Forces Movement**, ostensibly in the cause of reform but essentially to further his own political ambitions. His act of mutiny in February 1986 was precipitated by fear of his impending arrest.

His tenure as minister of defence under President Aquino was shortlived. Enrile was removed from office in November 1986 after coming into conflict with her over policy towards the insurgent Communist Party, which expressed his personal frustration that Corazón Aquino had been the political beneficiary of the mutiny which he had inspired. He stood as a successful candidate in elections for Senate in May 1987 and was subsequently linked to a series of abortive coups against President Aquino's administration. In February 1990 he was arrested on charges of murder, rebellion and harbouring criminals. Released on bail in March, the charges were dismissed by the Supreme Court in June. Enrile then sought to pursue his presidential ambitions through the vehicle of the revived **Nacionalista Party** but his expectations were dashed with its fragmentation into rival factions. In elections in May 1992, he was successful in his bid for a seat in the House of Representatives on behalf of a Cagayan provincial constituency and then went on to win a Senate seat in May 1995. Enrile held his position as senator until 2001. During this time, he ran as an independent candidate in the 1998 presidential elections, losing to the then vice-president, **Joseph Estrada**. In January 2001, Enrile was among those who voted against the opening of the 'second bank envelope', allegedly containing incriminating evidence against the president, and this vote led to the **EDSA II** movement that eventually ousted President Estrada. Enrile was re-elected to a fourth term as senator that year. In early 2012, Enrile served as the presiding officer of the impeachment of Chief Justice Renato Corona. He was one of twenty senators who voted for the impeachment. As of 2013, Enrile was the oldest senator in Congress at the age of eighty-nine years old.

see also: Aquino, Corazón; EDSA II; Marcos, Ferdinand; Nacionalista Party; People Power; Ramos, Fidel; Reform the Armed Forces Movement; Sin, Jaime.

Estrada, Joseph (Philippines)

Joseph Estrada (known by the nickname *Erap*, a play on a Tagalog word *pare*, meaning friend) was elected the thirteenth president of the Philippines in May 1998 with thirty-nine per cent of the vote, which was a superior performance to that of his predecessor, **Fidel Ramos**, who had secured only twenty-three per cent in the previous election. In May 1992, Joseph Estrada had been elected vice-president but not on the same ticket as Ramos. He had entertained presidential ambitions since entering national politics in 1987 and had registered as a candidate on behalf of his own People's Filipino Party. In March 1992, however, Estrada agreed to stand as the vice-presidential running mate of Eduardo Cojuangco, an alienated cousin of President **Corazón Aquino**, on a ticket representing a combination of old **Nacionalista Party** and **Liberal Party** interests. In the event, Cojuangco came third to Ramos in the presidential contest but Estrada secured thirty-three per cent of the vote to win the vice-presidential election. The constitutional limit of one six-year presidential term put him in an advantageous position to succeed Ramos.

Joseph Estrada was born on 19 April 1937 in the Tondo area of Manila. He became a national celebrity as a young man through his success as a movie actor playing dashing action parts, while his private life mirrored his screen roles. He entered politics in August 1969 when he became mayor of San Juan, which is within the metropolitan limits of Manila, after a long legal battle in which he successfully challenged the initial outcome of the polls. Estrada was detained twice after President **Ferdinand Marcos** introduced martial law in 1972. He subsequently became a member of President Marcos' New Society Movement and secured support for social welfare in his municipality but was not politically disadvantaged by the president's fall from power. He was elected to the Senate in 1987 as one of only two opposition senators together with **Juan Ponce Enrile** and built a political reputation by playing on populist-nationalist issues. He was outspoken in his opposition to US military bases and also called for the repudiation of national debts incurred during Marcos' tenure. As vice-president, he enjoyed an uneasy relationship with President Ramos, with whom he had little in common. However, he was allocated the high-profile office of head of the presidential Anti-Crime

Commission, which attracted extensive media coverage, particularly when he led police raids in virtual reruns of his former movie roles. A major asset in Joseph Estrada's successful presidential bid was his strong reputation as a champion of the interests of the poor. Within eighteen months, however, his popularity had declined significantly. Against a background of economic adversity attributed to inept management, he was accused of benefiting the rich and of returning Philippine politics to corruption and cronyism. Moreover, his abortive attempt to amend the 1987 constitution to allow foreigners to purchase land and to own 100 per cent of investments was represented as having the hidden agenda of permitting himself a second term of office. He has also been subject to domestic and international criticism for his hard line position against the **Moro Islamic Liberation Front** (MILF), which is alleged to have prejudiced peace negotiations.

Estrada's tenure as president was as brief as it was controversial. He was impeached following a corruption scandal that erupted in October 2000 when he was charged with receiving bribes worth millions in order to allow the continuation of an illegal lottery game (*jueteng*) operating throughout the Philippines. These charges were denied by Estrada, who insisted they were politically motivated. In November 2000, the Senate began an impeachment trial, which was however suspended after eleven senators allied with Estrada and blocked admission of evidence. However, this triggered mass demonstrations, known as **EDSA II**, demanding Estrada's resignation. Subsequently, Estrada's cabinet resigned en masse and the security forces withdrew their support too. On 20 January 2001, Estrada was ousted from office by the Supreme Court, the first Philippine president to be impeached, and his vice-president, **Gloria Macapagal-Arroyo**, succeeded him. Estrada was subsequently arrested, initially detained in Quezon City, then later transferred to a military facility in Tanay, Rizal, and finally placed under house arrest until 2007. In September 2007, Estrada was convicted of the charges against him, and consequently sentenced to '*Reclusion Perpetua*' (permanent imprisonment). However, the following month he was granted executive clemency by President Macapagal-Arroyo and released from detention. Estrada made a re-entry into Philippine politics in October 2009, when he announced his candidacy for the May 2010 presidential elections, with the Mayor of Makati City, Jejomar Binay as his running mate. However, he was defeated by Senator **Benigno Aquino III**. Nevertheless, in 2013 Estrada managed to stage a successful return to politics, winning the election for the office of mayor of Manila.

see also: Aquino III, Benigno Simeon Cojuangco; Aquino, Corazón; EDSA II; Enrile, Juan Ponce; Macapagal-Arroyo, Gloria; Marcos, Ferdinand; Moro Islamic Liberation Front; Nacionalista Party; Ramos, Fidel.

Exchange of Letters 2009
(Brunei/Malaysia)

The Exchange of Letters between Brunei Darussalam and Malaysia refers to the agreement signed between Malaysian Prime Minister **Abdullah Badawi** and Brunei's Sultan **Hassanal Bolkiah** on 16 March 2009 that aims to resolve all outstanding bilateral issues, in particular maritime boundaries and border demarcation disputes. The March 2009 agreement was the culmination of thirty-nine rounds of negotiations that began in 1995. Given stable and positive relations between both countries, the resolution of disputes has not been a matter of priority. Nevertheless, these issues acquired greater urgency after a near clash in the disputed maritime waters off Borneo in 2003 following the separate awarding of petroleum-production-sharing contracts by Malaysia and Brunei in the disputed areas.

While the agreement has not been officially published, both governments have issued joint and individual statements on what the Exchange of Letters entails. There are four essential elements to the agreement. First, maritime boundaries, including the continental shelf and exclusive economic zones, were delimited in the disputed waters off Borneo. Importantly, the Exchange of Letters places two oil-rich blocks that were previously claimed by Malaysia within Brunei's maritime zone. According to the 1982 United Nations Convention on the Law of the

Sea (UNCLOS), Brunei thus exercises sovereign jurisdiction over the area. Second, the agreement provides for the establishment of a Commercial Arrangement Area (CAA) within which joint development could be pursued and revenues from oil and gas resources shared. Third, the demarcation of the land boundary in **Limbang** district will be undertaken via a joint survey based on past agreements signed between 1920 and 1939. In areas not covered by previous agreements, the working group will adopt the watershed principle in determining the land boundary. Finally, the agreement assures that residents on both sides of the border enjoy transit rights and access through the maritime area to the north of Limbang.

Former Malaysian Prime Minister **Mahathir Mohamad** openly criticized his successor for signing the agreement, arguing that the lucrative blocks L and M had been used as barter in exchange for Limbang and that this would cost Malaysia a potential loss in earnings of at least US$100 billion. Abdullah Badawi refuted the allegations and argued that the Exchange of Letters allowed for joint commercial development of oil and gas resources, while settling the outstanding border and maritime sovereignty disputes, and hence marked major progress in bilateral relations between the two countries.

see also: Badawi, Tun Abdullah Ahmad; Bolkiah, Sultan Hassanal; Limbang Claim; Mahathir Mohamad, Tun.

F

Five Power Defence Arrangements (FPDA) 1971– (Malaysia/Singapore)

On 15–16 April 1971 representatives of Britain, Australia, New Zealand, Malaysia and Singapore met in London to revise provision for the external defence of the two Southeast Asian states. A joint air defence council was established to manage an integrated air defence system. Agreement was reached also on deploying a joint ANZUK (Australian, New Zealand and United Kingdom) ground force in Singapore and on an Australian air force contribution in Malaysia. Under these arrangements, an obligation to consult in the event of any form of external attack was substituted for the automatic commitment to respond in the **Anglo-Malaysian Defence Agreement**, which was superseded on 1 November 1971 when the arrangements came into effect. The defence arrangements, promoted by the British Conservative government which assumed office in June 1970, modified the decision of its Labour predecessor to disengage militarily from east of Suez by the end of 1971. The original tripartite military structure was denuded during the 1970s. Australia's battalion was withdrawn from Singapore by February 1974. Britain's ground troops left by the end of March 1976, its naval presence having been removed in September 1975. Joint military cooperation through exercises lapsed for a time but was revived from 1980 through an Australian initiative in the wake of Vietnam's invasion of Cambodia and the Soviet invasion of Afghanistan. By 1986 Australia had withdrawn their Mirage fighter squadrons based at Butterworth in Malaysia, though Canberra committed itself to deploying F-18 fighter aircraft for a minimum of sixteen weeks a year on joint exercises and maritime surveillance for a further five years. In December 1986 New Zealand's government gave notice that it would withdraw its military battalion from Singapore by the end of 1989.

The initial arrangements had been predicated on the indivisibility of the defence of Malaysia and Singapore. They were intended as transitional to prevent a power vacuum in the wake of major military disengagement by Britain and to give Malaysia and Singapore time to develop their armed strength. Above all, they were intended to promote strategic confidence between Malaysia and Singapore. Limited military exercises have continued on an annual basis but the signatories have never been required to consult in response to the threat of an external attack against either Malaysia or Singapore. In August 1998, however, against the background of deteriorating relations with Singapore, Malaysia announced that it would not participate in that year's FPDA military exercises, but then resumed participation in April 1999. Also in August 1998, the FPDA Consultative Committee commissioned a policy working group to provide advice to the five defence ministers. While periodically dismissed as a strategic anachronism by its detractors, the FPDA has in recent years sought to maintain its relevance by shifting its focus to more immediate concerns about terrorism, after 2001, and humanitarian assistance and disaster relief after the Boxing Day **Tsunami of 2004**. Concomitantly, the evolution of FPDA exercises in relation to this new mandate has further enhanced interoperability of members' armed forces.

see also: Anglo-Malayan/Malaysian Defence Agreement 1957–71; Tsunami 2004.

Framework Agreement on the Bangsamoro 2012 (Philippines)

On 15 October 2012, the government of the Philippines and leadership of the **Moro Islamic Liberation Front** (MILF) signed a landmark agreement which portends the resolution of a longstanding conflict in the southern Philippines. The treaty was the culmination of political resolve on the part of the administration of **Benign Aquino III** and the MILF, demonstrated in the 'secret meeting' in Tokyo between

President Aquino and MILF chairman, Murad Ibrahim, in July 2011, but also the contribution of an International Monitoring Team (IMT) led by Malaysia which began in 2004. The creation of an IMT was a deliberate attempt on the part of Malaysia to dispel suspicions in the Philippines that its involvement in the peace process was foremost driven by its interest in suppressing any prospect of a revival of the **Philippines' Claim to Sabah**, the East Malaysian state whose ownership has been contested by various Philippines governments since the formation of the Malaysian Federation in 1963. The Framework Agreement paved the way for the eventual signing of the Comprehensive Agreement on the Bangsamoro (CAB) in March 2014. Under the CAB, MILF fighters would surrender their arms and disband their military wing, the Bangsamoro Islamic Armed Forces (BIAF), while the government agrees to a series of power- and resource-sharing arrangements.

Since the outbreak of armed insurgency in the southern Philippine islands of Mindanao and Sulu in the early 1970s, there have been a string of failed agreements between the Philippines government and various Mindanao-based rebel movements, including the **Tripoli Agreement** of 1976, the Final Peace Agreement of 1996, the Agreement on the General Cessation of Hostilities in 1997, the Tripoli Agreement of 2001 and the Memorandum of Agreement on Ancestral Lands of 2008.

see also: Aquino III, Benigno Simeon Cojuangco; Moro Islamic Liberation Front; Philippines' Claim to Sabah; Tripoli Agreement.

Free Papua Movement (Indonesia)

The Free Papua Movement (*Organisasi Papua Merdeka* – OPM) is the name of an indigenous Melanesian insurgency in Irian Jaya, the western half of the island of New Guinea. The OPM has posed only a limited challenge to Indonesian authority since that authority was established under United Nations auspices in May 1963. Resistance to Indonesian rule had been encouraged by the Dutch, who withheld the territory from the transfer of sovereignty over the Netherlands East Indies in 1949. They actively promoted local self-government until persuaded to give up their administration through Indonesian intimidation and US pressure. Violent opposition to Indonesian rule was triggered by its even more heavy-handed colonial nature and the clash of cultures involved.

The roots of organized opposition are to be found in a Papua Youth Movement established in late 1962 by a student, Jakob Prai, who was subsequently arrested but then escaped to join a small core of dissidents. An initial uprising in the central highlands in July 1965 among Dutch-trained militia was put down after two years, but sporadic armed resistance by poorly armed and trained irregulars was sustained with some support from across the border in Papua New Guinea after the eastern half of the island became independent in 1975. A declaration of independence took place under the name of Seth Rumkorem in 1971 but without any evidence of territorial control. The movement has been beset by factionalism through tribal divisions and many of its leaders have been either killed or driven into exile. The OPM has never attracted the kind of international support mobilized in the case of ***Fretilin*** in East Timor, while the government in Port Moresby has placed good relations with Jakarta before any sense of shared Melanesian identity. A continuing source of local grievance and alienation sustaining separatist sentiment in Irian Jaya has been Indonesia's encouragement of migration from more densely populated islands, interpreted as an attempt to change the demographic character and political balance of the territory. In June 1995, a regional military commander admitted that elements of the so-called Security Disturbance Group were active along the border with Papua New Guinea. The arrest, torture and murder of civilians near the Freeport–McMoran mining complex has attracted the condemnation of Indonesia's Human Rights Commission. In January 1996, a unit from the Free Papua Movement led by Kelly Kwalik seized and held hostage a group of Westerners and Indonesians engaged on a scientific expedition, in an attempt to secure political recognition and a withdrawal of Indonesian forces. The hostages were not released until May in a military operation with fatalities among them and the OPM. Popular support within Irian Jaya for the OPM was stimulated by the political downfall of President **Suharto** in

May 1998, with demonstrations and violent confrontations with security forces in the capital Jayapura in July as well as representations in Jakarta. More significant was the example of a referendum in East Timor in August 1999 in which the vast majority of voters opted for independence. In December 1999, in emulation of a popular protest in Aceh, around 10,000 supporters of the OPM assembled in the provincial capital for a ceremonial hoisting of the flag of the separatist movement to mark the anniversary of its formation. While President **Abdurrahman Wahid** was amenable to granting autonomy to the region and to a name change from Irian Jaya to West Papua, the rebels demanded nothing less than complete independence via secession. To that end, they also rejected Jakarta's overtures of economic development and continue to sustain their low-intensity armed insurgency against the Indonesian military which includes the taking of foreign hostages.

see also: Fretilin; Irian Jaya; Suharto; Wahid, Abdurrahman.

Fretilin (Timor-Leste)

Fretilin is an acronym derived from *Frente Revolucionária do Timor-Leste Independente*, the Portuguese term for the Revolutionary Front for an Independent East Timor. This political movement was established in its original form in East Timor's administrative capital, Dili, in May 1974 in the wake of the revolutionary Armed Forces Movement in Lisbon which committed Portugal to independence for all of its overseas possessions. *Fretilin* was established by a seminary-trained mestizo elite of intellectuals and civil servants with links to left-wing groups in both Portugal and its African colonies. The title *Fretilin* was devised in August 1974 to replace that of the more innocuous Timorese Social Democratic Association. *Fretilin* possessed an intentional acronymic similarity to *Frelimo* in Mozambique and the radical rhetoric of its leadership alarmed the military government in Indonesia, which ruled the western half of the island of Timor. Indonesia's sponsorship of competing political groups encouraged a seizure of power by its clients in August 1975 which was crushed by *Fretilin* loyalists among Timorese soldiers in the Portuguese garrison. By mid-September, *Fretilin* was in control of Dili and had eliminated all opposition except along the border with West Timor. An Indonesian attempt to intervene through the vehicle of a multinational force failed because of a lack of Australian and Portuguese cooperation. When Portugal conceded Indonesia's right to be a principal party to the conflict, *Fretilin* asserted a unilateral independence for the territory on 28 November 1975. Timorese clients of Indonesia then declared the integration of the territory into the republic. A brutal invasion by Indonesia, ostensibly by volunteers, followed on 7 December, delayed briefly by a visit to Jakarta by US President Gerald Ford. East Timor was formally integrated into Indonesia as the twenty-seventh province of the republic on 17 July 1976 after a bloody war in which an estimated 100,000 Timorese died.

Despite the lack of external military assistance and the repressive rule by Indonesia's army, *Fretilin*'s military arm sustained a sporadic resistance that appeared to have run its course by the end of the 1980s. A massacre of its youthful supporters at a funeral demonstration at a cemetery in Dili in November 1991 aroused international outrage but also thinned the ranks of the movement. A further blow followed in November 1992 when, **José 'Xanana' Gusmão**, the commander of *Fretilin*'s military arm, was captured on the outskirts of Dili. He was sentenced to life imprisonment in May 1993, which was commuted to twenty years in the following August. *Fretilin*'s cause received international backing in November 1996 when East Timor's most prominent dissidents, Bishop Carlos Belo of Dili and **José Ramos Horta**, the movement's official observer at the United Nations, jointly received the Nobel Peace Prize. Resistance to Indonesia's rule intensified during 1997, culminating in Indonesian troops storming the campus of the university in Dili. A national convention of East Timorese exiles met in Portugal in April 1998 to establish a National Council of the Timorese Resistance and elected Gusmão as president and Ramos-Horta as vice-president of its political committee. In June 1998, in the wake of the resignation of President **Suharto**, interim-president **B. J. Habibie** offered the territory a special autonomous status within

Indonesia, which was rejected by Gusmão who called for a referendum on independence. In an unanticipated reversal of policy in January 1999, Indonesia offered East Timor the choice between independence and autonomy. The next month Gusmão was released from prison into house arrest and began to take part in negotiations that led to an agreement to hold a referendum under UN auspices in the following August. Despite brutal intimidation by local militia organized and armed by Indonesia's army, the outcome of the referendum was overwhelmingly in favour of independence. International pressure and domestic political change, rather than action by *Fretilin*, persuaded Indonesia to permit the deployment of an international peacekeeping force sanctioned by the UN and to endorse the result of the referendum that showed seventy-eight per cent of voters favoured independence. Gusmão returned to East Timor in October and Ramos-Horta in December 1999. That month, the first meeting of the National Consultative Council convened in Dili with *Fretilin* representatives in the majority.

East Timor held its first parliamentary election in August 2001 where *Fretilin* won fifty-five seats of eighty-eight in the Constituent Assembly. Gusmão became president of East Timor on 14 April 2001 and was able to secure full independence on 19 May 2002. This however ushered in a period of chronic instability which culminated in bloody street battles following the dismissal of a third of military personnel by *Fretilin*'s prime minister, **Mari Alkatiri**, in June 2006. Following this, Alkatiri himself was forced to resign but returned to contest the 2007 elections under the banner of *Fretilin*. Though *Fretilin* won the most seats held by a single party, it was forced into the position of opposition by a coalition led by Gusmão's **National Congress for Timorese Reconstruction** (CNRT). Despite sporadic violence and threats of legal action by *Fretilin*, the CNRT-led coalition remained in power through the 2012 elections, which again saw *Fretilin* reprise its role as the main opposition.

see also: Alkatiri, Mari; Gusmão, José 'Xanana'; Habibie, B. J.; National Congress for Timorese Reconstruction; Ramos-Horta, José; Suharto.

Friendship Bridge (Laos/Thailand)

The Thai–Lao Friendship Bridge connects Nong Khai, Thailand with Vientiane prefecture, Laos. The 1,170-metre bridge was opened in April 1994, making it the first bridge across the lower Mekong linking Thailand and Laos. The US$30 million bridge was funded by Australian government development aid and built by Australian companies for Laos. The bridge marked a further normalizing of relations between Vientiane and Bangkok after almost two decades of animosity over ideology and border demarcation disputes, with the latter resulting in a brief **Thai–Lao Border War** in 1987–8. The bridge is part AH12 of the Asia Highway Network linking China and Southeast Asia through Laos. A rail line was added to the bridge in 2010 connecting Laos with the Thai rail network, but only extending 3.5 kilometres to the Tha Nalaeng Railway Station with plans to connect it to Vientiane nine kilometres away.

The bridge was later joined by a second Friendship Bridge linking Savannakhet in southern Laos with Mukdahan in Thailand in January 2007, and a third Friendship Bridge linking Thakhek in the central Khammouane Province with Thailand's Nakhon Phanom province in November 2011. A fourth bridge linking Houayxay in northern Bokeo province with Chiang Khong in Thailand's northern Chiang Rai province was completed in 2013. The bridges are important infrastructural support for the Lao economy as they link it not only to the Thai economy, but also position Laos at the crossroads of Thailand, Vietnam and China. A direct result of these linkages was the lifting of most restrictions on foreign trade and investment in Laos. A proposed high-speed rail link from China to Thailand via Laos, however, threatens to make the bridge redundant.

see also: Thai–Lao Border War 1987–8.

Front Pembela Islam (Indonesia)

Front Pembela Islam or the Islamic Defender's Front (FPI) is an Islamic vigilante group established in 1998 by Misbahul Alam, a preacher from ***Nahdlatul Ulama***, and Muhammad Rizieq Syihab, a Jakarta-born, Saudi-educated Islamic scholar of Arab-Betawi descent.

FPI is based in central Java, and since its formation has managed to build a network across the Indonesian archipelago. Although led by *habib* (preachers of prophetic lineage) who are well respected in their communities, the membership of FPI comprises mostly Muslims with little education and from the lower strata of society. Like many radical Muslim groups in Indonesia, FPI aspires to transform Indonesia into an Islamic state with *shari'a* as its centrepiece, and to oppose the influx of Western morals and values into the country. To that end, FPI's ideology is twofold: to revise the Indonesian constitution such that it would include references to *shari'a*, and to enjoin good and forbid evil (based on scriptural edict of *Amr Ma'ruf Nahy Munkar*).

Since its formation, FPI has gained notoriety for its moral policing activities. In 1999, 4,000 FPI members broke into the regional government office of Jakarta demanding that all nightspots be shut down during the fasting month of *ramadhan*. The fact that the police chief agreed to the FPI's terms further emboldened the organization, and from 1999 until late 2002 when its paramilitary wing was disbanded, FPI vigilantes launched frequent attacks on enterprises deemed 'un-Islamic', such as brothels, bars, gambling halls and massage parlours. Moreover, while its initial raids were limited to the *ramadhan* period, they were later expanded to clashes with local residents, security officials and the police.

The popularity of FPI has fluctuated, reaching its apex immediately after the September 11 attacks when it managed to mobilize 10,000 demonstrators to protest against the American invasion of Afghanistan. The 2002 Bali bombings however, diminished the popularity of radical Muslim groups in Indonesia considerably. Between October 2002 and November 2003, Rizieq was arrested and either jailed or placed under house arrest frequently, yet the organization's moral policing activities continued. In an attempt to improve organizational discipline, the leadership of FPI tightened its recruitment process in 2004 in order to weed out opportunists who used the organization's religious agenda for material gain. In December 2004, FPI was among the first groups to enter Aceh in the aftermath of the **2004 Tsunami** to provide humanitarian assistance. Its moral policing activities nevertheless picked up pace in 2008 when FPI members attacked members of the National Alliance for the Freedom of Faith in a confrontation that led to Rizieq being arrested yet again. In early 2011, FPI was involved in the brutalization of three ***Ahmadiyah*** followers who were beaten to death. This was followed by attacks on a *Shi'a* boarding school in East Java and churches in Aceh in 2012. In yet another demonstration of their impunity, FPI successfully forced the relocation of the venue of the Miss World beauty pageant from Jakarta to Bali in August 2013 by threatening to disrupt the 'unIslamic' event.

see also: Ahmadiyah; Nahdlatul Ulama; Tsunami 2004.

Fuad, Tun Mohammad (Donald Stephens) (Malaysia)

Mohammad Fuad, who was born in Kudat in 1920 as Donald Stephens of an Australian father and a Kadazan ethnic group mother, was the first chief minister of Sabah on its incorporation into Malaysia in September 1963. A successful businessman who owned a local newspaper, he entered politics in the early 1960s, drawing on Kadazan support initially to oppose membership of the Federation of Malaysia. Converted to its cause, in part by the **Philippines' Claim to Sabah**, he became a defender of Sabah's rights as chief minister but was eased from office in December 1964 in exchange for the post of federal minister for Sabah affairs, which he held for only nine months, giving up political life shortly after. He became high commissioner to Australia in 1968 and in 1971 converted to Islam, taking the name Mohammad Fuad. He served as Sabah's head of state for nearly two years from September 1973 and then resigned in July 1975 to assume the leadership of a new intercommunal party *Berjaya* (Sabah People's Union), set up with federal support in June 1975 in challenge to the ruling **United Sabah National Organization** (USNO) led by the chief minister, Tun **Mustapha Harun**. He led *Berjaya* to electoral victory in April 1976 and again became chief minister but held office for only fifty-three days. On 6 June he was killed, together with four of his ministers as well as his son, when the light aircraft in which he was travelling crashed into the sea on its approach to Kota Kinabalu airport.

see also: Mustapha bin Datuk Harun, Tun; Philippines' Claim to Sabah; United Sabah National Organization.

FUNCINPEC (Cambodia)

FUNCINPEC is an acronym derived from *Front uni national pour un Cambodge indépendant, neutre, pacifique et coopératif*, the French term for the National United Front for an Independent, Neutral, Peaceful and Cooperative Cambodia, which was established in March 1981 by Prince **Norodom Sihanouk** with a presence on the Thai border. This resistance movement to challenge Vietnam's occupation of Cambodia was encouraged in particular by ASEAN (Association of Southeast Asian Nations) states which were concerned at the prominence of the Khmer Rouge's role. In June 1982 FUNCINPEC joined with another non-Communist movement, the **Khmer People's National Liberation Front** (KPNLF) and the **Khmer Rouge** in a so-called **Coalition Government of Democratic Kampuchea** (CGDK) with Prince Sihanouk as its head. That coalition maintained an uneasy coexistence until the **International Conference on Cambodia** in Paris reached agreement in October 1991. In the intra-Cambodian negotiations leading to the establishment of a symbolically sovereign **Supreme National Council**, Prince Sihanouk gave up his leadership of FUNCINPEC in order to head the new council, to be succeeded by his son Prince **Norodom Ranariddh**. Prince Ranariddh led FUNCINPEC in the elections conducted in Cambodia in May 1993 by the United Nations and secured a plurality of the seats in the Constituent Assembly. As leader of FUNCINPEC, Prince Ranariddh became first prime minister in the coalition government formed in Phnom Penh at the end of October 1993.

Tensions and cleavages emerged with FUNCINPEC, as the practice of coalition government confirmed the political dominance of the **Cambodian People's Party** (CPP), which had been put in power by the Vietnamese but had come second in the 1993 elections. Those tensions and cleavages were manifested openly with the dismissal of FUNCINPEC member, **Sam Rainsy**, as finance minister in October 1994 and from the National Assembly in June 1995. They were manifest also with the arrest and exile of former foreign minister, Prince Norodom Sirivudh, who was the party's secretary-general, at the end of the year. In April 1996, four FUNCINPEC National Assembly members defected to the CPP overturning the former's narrow majority in the latter's favour. Tension between the two parties rose with competing negotiations with the Khmer Rouge. Those tensions came to a head when the second prime minister, **Hun Sen**, mounted a successful coup in July 1997 to oust Prince Ranariddh, who had fled abroad. Elections were held in July 1998, monitored by international observers, in which FUNCINPEC participated. In the event, it took second place behind the CPP which won a plurality of seats but insufficient to form a government. After extensive negotiations, FUNCINPEC joined in a coalition government headed by Hun Sen in the following November. Prince Ranariddh accepted the post of chairman of the National Assembly and, by implication, the subordinate position of FUNCINPEC in Cambodian politics. Since then, FUNCINPEC's influence in Cambodian politics has diminished considerably. In July 2004, FUNCINPEC and the CPP concluded lengthy negotiations for a power-sharing agreement that again saw the former assuming a subordinate role. In March 2006, the National Assembly amended the constitution to enable the passing of bills with a simple majority, thereby negating the need for a two-thirds majority, and by extension, the utility of a coalition government. After Norodom Ranariddh was dismissed from the party leadership in October 2006 for dereliction of duties, he left to form the Norodom Ranariddh party while Keo Puth Rasmeyand, son-in-law of former King Norodom Sihanouk, took over the reins of leadership in FUNCINPEC. Norodom Ranariddh and FUNCINPEC soon became embroiled in a legal battle which proved an unnecessary distraction. Against this backdrop, FUNCINPEC performed poorly at the 2008 National Assembly elections, winning only two seats compared to the CPP's landslide victory of ninety seats. FUNCINPEC was forced to concede its position as the second largest party in the National Assembly when the **Sam Rainsy Party** outdid it by winning twenty-six seats on its way to becoming the main opposition party.

Following the 2008 elections, the CPP and FUNCINPEC once again entered into a coalition government, though by then the latter had clearly lost any capacity to influence policy in any meaningful manner. In April 2010, FUNCINPEC and the Nationalist Party (formerly the Norodom Ranariddh Party) formally agreed to form a political alliance ahead of the 2012 commune elections and 2013 national elections. In March 2013, Princess Norodom Arun Reaksmey, youngest daughter of Norodom Sihanouk, was appointed party president. Even so, FUNCINPEC continues to be plagued by internal discord, with factions loyal to either Norodom Ranariddh or Hun Sen. In January 2008 ten FUNCINPEC officials holding ministerial and state secretarial rank defected to the CPP. This was followed by another defection of six senior officials to the CPP in February 2009. At the 2013 elections, FUNCINPEC failed to win any seats and was all but eclipsed by the newly formed **Cambodia National Rescue Party** as the opposition party of consequence. Nevertheless its leader, Princess Reaksmey, became the first female to lead a Cambodian political party into elections.

see also: Cambodia National Rescue Party; Cambodian People's Party; Democratic Kampuchea, Coalition Government of; Hun Sen; International Conference on Cambodia, Paris 1991; Khmer People's National Liberation Front; Khmer Rouge; Ranariddh, Prince Norodom; Sihanouk, King Norodom; Supreme National Council.

G

Geneva Agreements on Indochina 1954 (Cambodia/Laos/Vietnam)

The Geneva Agreements on Indochina comprise a set of accords which were intended to restore peace and confirm the sovereign independence of Cambodia, Laos and Vietnam. They were concluded at an international conference between 8 May and 21 July in Geneva. Indochina had been subject to violent conflict from the end of the Pacific War when the **Viet Minh** took the lead in challenging the restoration of French colonial rule throughout the peninsula in the **August Revolution of 1945**. The Viet Minh, headed by **Ho Chi Minh**, had declared the independence of the Democratic Republic of Vietnam in Hanoi on 2 September 1945. Limited political concessions by France as well as US military assistance failed to stem Communist insurgent success. By the end of 1953, French political will had virtually drained away as the colonial conflict and its costs became matters of domestic political contention.

At a meeting of the foreign ministers of the United States, the Soviet Union, Britain and France in Berlin in February 1954, it was agreed that Indochina would be placed on the agenda of a forthcoming international conference in Geneva which had been arranged to address the question of Korea. The Korean phase of the conference was inconclusive. Moreover, the negotiating position of the French was dramatically weakened by the fall of its military fortress in the **Battle of Dien Bien Phu** to Viet Minh forces on 7 May 1954, the day before the Indochina phase of the conference was due to begin. Representatives attended from France, the United States, the Soviet Union, the People's Republic of China, Britain, the Democratic Republic of Vietnam, the French-backed State of Vietnam, and the kingdoms of Laos and Cambodia. The conference was chaired jointly by Anthony Eden and Vyacheslav Molotov, the foreign ministers of Britain and the Soviet Union, who rejected a request by the Democratic Republic of Vietnam that representatives from self-styled Laotian and Cambodian resistance governments also be permitted to participate. That decision indicated Soviet and Chinese interest in avoiding contention with the United States. This consideration was also important in arriving at a line of demarcation in Vietnam which did not reflect the full extent of Communist military success. The Viet Minh were thus constrained by their external allies into accepting an accommodation that compromised their political interests.

The Geneva Agreements took the principal form of three accords on the cessation of hostilities in Vietnam, Laos and Cambodia and a final declaration on restoring peace in Indochina. The armistice agreements for Vietnam and Laos were signed between representatives of the French and Viet Minh high commands, while that for Cambodia was signed between military representatives of the Royal government and the Viet Minh. A declaration by the French government affirmed a willingness to withdraw all of its troops from Indochina at the request of the peninsular governments concerned. The provisions for Vietnam were the most important, and the failure to implement them led on to further conflict over the unification of the country which was not resolved until the end of the **Vietnam War** in 1975. A provisional line of demarcation was established along the seventeenth parallel of latitude, on either side of which the two contending sides were to withdraw and regroup their forces. After two years, elections were to be held to determine the political future of the country, conducted by an international commission for supervision and control comprising India, Poland and Canada, with prior responsibility for overseeing the workings of the ceasefire agreements. The ceasefire agreements for Laos and Cambodia made provision for the withdrawal of foreign forces and recognized a single governmental authority in each case but in the case of Laos took account of the separate control by Viet

Minh-stiffened insurgents of two provinces adjacent to Vietnam.

The Final Declaration of the Conference, which was not a signed document, encompassed provisions for ceasefire and political order for all three countries, spelling out their political and electoral obligations and the role of international supervision. A formal treaty commitment was not undertaken, only a series of expressions of assent and reservations by the nine representatives on all of the accords, including the Final Declaration. One reason why the Final Declaration of the Conference was not signed was the resistance of the United States, which resented the confirmation of Communist victory as well as the Communist Chinese presence. The US secretary of state, John Foster Dulles, boycotted the conference proceedings after initial participation. The United States took note of the accords and promised to refrain from the threat of force to disturb them, but maintained that elections set for July 1956 should be supervised by the United Nations. That stand encouraged the Vietnamese government to the south of the seventeenth parallel to refuse to comply with the provision for national elections.

The Geneva Agreements provided, in effect, for an interlude between two phases of violent conflict in Indochina. They had the unintended consequence of dividing Vietnam into two parts, reflecting in international recognition the pattern of Cold War alignments. The cessation of hostilities broke down when the Democratic Republic of Vietnam (re-established in Hanoi after July 1954) revived its military challenge. In December 1960 the **National Liberation Front of South Vietnam** (NLF) was set up as a vehicle for reunifying Vietnam on Communist terms. In the case of Laos, the two provinces under insurgent control were never integrated under the authority of a central government until the Communists assumed power in December 1975 in the wake of the victory in April 1975 of their counterparts in Vietnam. It was only in Cambodia that the accord reached at Geneva was implemented with endorsement by the International Commission for Supervision and Control of the conduct and outcome of general elections in 1955. Prince **Norodom Sihanouk**'s political order, established by those elections, was overthrown in 1970.

see also: August Revolution 1945; Dien Bien Phu, Battle of, 1954; Geneva Agreements on Laos 1962; Ho Chi Minh; Indochina Wars; National Liberation Front of South Vietnam; Sihanouk, King Norodom; Viet Minh; Vietnam War.

Geneva Agreements on Laos 1962
(Laos)

On 23 July 1962 an international conference in Geneva attended by fourteen governments reached agreements on political unity and neutralization for Laos. The earlier **Geneva Agreements on Indochina** of July 1954 had failed to bring peace to the country. Laos had not been subject to partition like Vietnam but national integration had been frustrated because the Communist ***Pathet Lao***, stiffened by Vietnamese counterparts, had withheld the administration of Phong Saly and Sam Neua provinces from the royal government in Vientiane. Polarization between Laotian factions aligned competitively with Vietnam, and with Thailand and the United States prevented national unity by consensus during the rest of the 1950s. A coup in August 1960 by a young paratroop officer, Captain Kong Le, which established an ostensibly neutral government under Prince **Souvanna Phouma**, served only to extend political fragmentation. By this stage, the second phase of the **Indochina Wars** had begun with Vietnam as the main prize. Laos became of increasing importance to the resolution of that conflict because its eastern uplands made up the critical section of the **Ho Chi Minh Trail**.

By 1961, Laos existed as a state in international legal fiction only as three politico-military groupings with external supporters contended for power. At that juncture, a diplomatic initiative by the Soviet Union attracted US interest because of common fears that an escalation of internal conflict would lead to wider confrontation. Agreement on a ceasefire made possible the international conference which convened in Geneva in May 1961. It took until June 1962, however, for a preliminary accord to be concluded between the leaders of the contending factions. A formal agreement on establishing a tripartite coalition and on neutralizing Laos was eventually signed on 23 July 1962. That settlement broke down beyond repair by 1964 and neutralization came to exist only on paper. In the event, competitive military intervention confirmed Laos' role as a subordinate theatre of the **Vietnam War** whose eventual outcome determined its political identity by the end of 1975.

see also: Geneva Agreements on Indochina 1954; Ho Chi Minh Trail; Indochina Wars; *Pathet Lao*; Souvanna Phouma, Prince; Vietnam War.

Gerakan Rakyat Malaysia (Malaysia)

Gerakan Rakyat Malaysia translates from Malay as the Malaysian People's Movement and is most commonly known as *Gerakan*. The party was founded on the island of Penang on 25 March 1968 in the main by intellectually minded Chinese opposition politicians and university teachers as a multiracial and democratic socialist party. In the elections of May 1969, whose outcome provoked the **May 13 Racial Riots**, *Gerakan* won eight seats in the federal Parliament and secured control of the state government in Penang. After an internal split, the party began to cooperate politically with the **Alliance Party** coalition government, which became a formal arrangement in February 1972 further consolidated with the establishment of the *Barisan Nasional* (National Front) in June 1974. *Gerakan* has maintained its multiracial platform but over the years has become primarily a vehicle for urban middle-class Chinese who lack confidence in the **Malaysian Chinese Association** (MCA) to represent their interests within the ruling coalition. This has frequently resulted in strained relations between the two Chinese-based parties, particularly in Chinese-majority state of Penang.

In April 1995, *Gerakan* increased its share to seven seats compared to thirty won by the MCA. In November 1999, it won six seats compared to twenty-nine by the MCA. Its share of seats increased to ten in the 2004 elections before taking a significant dent in the 2008 and 2013 elections, with only two and one seats respectively. The poor showing was a direct result of the erosion of its influence among its core constituency as well as the increased popularity of the **Democratic Action Party** among Chinese voters.

see also: Alliance Party; *Barisan Nasional*; Democratic Action Party; Malaysian Chinese Association; May 13 Racial Riots 1969.

Gerindra (Indonesia)

Gerakan Indonesia Raya (*Gerindra* or The Great Indonesia Movement Party) is an Indonesian political party founded on 6 February 2008 and registered with the Ministry of Justice and Human Rights on 26 February 2008. On 16 October 2008, the party nominated **Prabowo Subianto**, who had earlier resigned from the ***Golkar*** party, as its presidential candidate for the 2009 presidential election. In possession of a strong personality and eloquent in English, Prabowo Subianto was a former army general with the special forces and was also married to President **Suharto**'s daughter.

Among the most controversial figures in contemporary Indonesian politics, Prabowo's military career has come under immense scrutiny for allegations that he had sanctioned human rights abuses. His tour in East Timor in the late 1970s earned him accolades and swift promotion, but he also came under heavy criticism when soldiers from his special forces units were tried over a series of abductions and tortures during President Suharto's rule. In May 1998, Prabowo was dismissed by Indonesian military commander General Wiranto for his alleged involvement in the disappearance of pro-democracy activists. After leaving the military, Prabowo joined his brother and billionaire businessman, Hashim Djojohadikusumo, to build a lucrative business empire. Hashim was also among the early founders of *Gerindra*, coining the party's name and bankrolling its television and media campaigns that were aimed not only at providing visibility for the party, but also to influence public perceptions of Prabowo, which were often negative as a result of his alleged role in human rights violations during his service in the Indonesian military. *Gerindra* participated in its first legislative election on 9 April 2009 and won 4.5 per cent of the vote on the way to securing twenty-six seats in the People's Representative Council. Prabowo Subianto subsequently joined former president **Megawati Sukarnoputri**, head of the ***Partai Demokrasi Indonesia–Perjuangan*** (Indonesian Democratic Party of Struggle, PDI–P) as her vice-presidential running mate for the 2009 presidential elections on the understanding that she would support a future presidential bid. The pair gained 26.8 per cent of the vote against incumbent **Susilo Bambang Yudhoyono** and Boediono's 60.8 per cent victory and filed a rejection of the results on account of electoral violations.

In November 2011 Prabowo confirmed his intent to join the 2014 presidential race on the back of the increasing popularity of *Gerindra*. This was confirmed in March 2012 when *Gerindra* officially nominated Prabowo as its presidential candidate. Of the parties that contested the April 2014 elections, *Gerindra* registered the largest improvement when its share of the popular vote rose from 4.5 per cent in 2009 to twelve per cent. It has since entered into coalition with *Golkar*, ***Partai Keadilan Sejahtera*** (PKS), ***Partai Amanat Nasional*** (PAN), and ***Partai Persatuan Pembangunan*** (PPP).

see also: Golkar; Megawati Sukarnoputri; *Partai Amanat Nasional*; *Partai Demokrasi Indonesia–Perjuangan*; *Partai Keadilan Sejahtera*; *Partai Persatuan Pembangunan*; Prabowo Subianto; Suharto; Yudhoyono, Susilo Bambang.

Gestapu (Indonesia)

Gestapu is an acronym in Indonesian taken from *Gerakan September Tiga Puluh* (Thirtieth of September Movement). The acronym represents a deliberate attempt to tar an abortive coup with the brush of Nazi-German symbolism. That abortive coup was mounted primarily in the capital Jakarta in the early hours of 1 October 1965 against a background of rising political tension. A group of dissident army and air force officers led nominally by a battalion commander from President **Sukarno**'s palace guard arranged the abduction of six of the country's most senior generals, including the army commander, Lieutenant General Achmad Yani. They were taken to Halim Air Base outside the capital where those not killed during their abduction were murdered at the Crocodile Hole and all the bodies thrown down a well. The coup group then broadcast the names of members of a Revolutionary Council set up ostensibly to forestall a plot by the US Central Intelligence Agency (CIA). The council announced that it would carry out the policies of President Sukarno, who was safe under its protection. Major General **Suharto**, then head of Kostrad, the army's strategic reserve based in west Java, was not on the abduction list. He assumed command and overcame the coup group within two days.

The Communist Party of Indonesia was implicated in the abortive coup and its members and presumed supporters soon became the object of physical attack by security forces and Muslim militants with at least 100,000 fatalities. President Sukarno was politically discredited also, because of his patronage of the Communists, his presence at the coup headquarters at Halim Air Base, his failure to denounce the murder of the generals, and his description of the coup attempt as an internal affair of the army. The outcome of the abortive coup was a fundamental change in the structure of the political system at the expense of the Communists and President Sukarno and to the advantage of the armed forces as a corporate entity. Their political dominance was asserted on 11 March 1966 when President Sukarno was obliged to transfer executive authority to Suharto, by then promoted to lieutenant general (*see* ***Supersemar***). The next day, the Communist Party of Indonesia was declared an illegal organization.

In August 2013, a critically acclaimed film, *The Act of Killing*, was released which detailed the role of gangsters mobilized by the Indonesian military to root out and massacre suspected Communists and leftists in Medan, North Sumatra, during that troublesome period in 1965.

see also: Guided Democracy; Suharto; Sukarno; *Supersemar*.

Ghazali Shafie, Tun Mohamad (Malaysia)

Ghazali Shafie, popularly known as 'King Ghaz', transferred from a career in the civil service to political office in the wake of communal violence in the **May 13 Racial Riots** in 1969. He served in turn as minister for special functions and then concurrently as minister of information, minister of home affairs and finally foreign minister of Malaysia. He held the last office from July 1981 until July 1984 in **Mahathir Mohamad**'s first administration and then retired from active politics.

Ghazali Shafie was born in Kuala Lipis on 22 March 1922 and was educated at Raffles College in Singapore. During the Japanese occupation, he played a role in the British-inspired clandestine resistance. After the Pacific War, he studied law at the University of Wales in Aberystwyth and then spent a year at the London School of Economics. On his return to Malaya, he joined the civil service and then went abroad for training to prepare for a senior position in the country's fledgling Foreign Ministry. On independence in August 1957, he became deputy secretary of the ministry of external affairs. In 1958 he assumed the office of permanent secretary, subsequently secretary-general, which he held without interruption until 1970. During that period, he played a key role in advising on foreign policy both over the formation of Malaysia and in countering Indonesia's **Confrontation** of the wider federation during 1963–6. As a flamboyant politician during the 1970s, he acquired a reputation as an ambitious man. After the death of the prime minister, Tun **Abdul Razak**, who was succeeded by Tun **Hussein Onn**, with Mahathir Mohamad becoming deputy prime minister, he used his powers of detention as minister of home affairs to assert his position against political rivals. Mahathir held on to office and when he became prime minister in July 1981, Ghazali Shafie was shifted to the less-powerful portfolio of foreign affairs. As foreign minister, he played an active part in **ASEAN**'s collective diplomacy during the early years of the Cambodian conflict. 'King Ghaz' retired to a corporate career in 1984. He passed away in January 2010.

see also: ASEAN; Hussein Onn, Tun; Mahathir Mohamad, Tun; May 13 Racial Riots 1969; Razak, Tun Abdul.

Giap, General Vo Nguyen (Vietnam)

General Giap is regarded as the founding father of the People's Army of Vietnam. He achieved renown as his country's leading military thinker and as the architect of historic victories against France and the United States in the **Indochina Wars** and the **Vietnam War**. General Giap was born in August 1911 to a peasant family in a village in Quang Binh Province north of Hue. A nationalist in his teens, he was detained in 1930 by the French colonial authorities for leading a student protest. He graduated in law from Hanoi University in 1937 and in political economy the following year, by which time he had joined the Communist Party of Indochina founded by **Ho Chi Minh**. Following the outbreak of the Second World War in 1939, he evaded police arrest and made his way to southern China, where he first met the Vietnamese Communist leader. Giap's wife and child remained in Hanoi, both dying in prison. He returned to the border region of Vietnam early in 1941 as one of Ho's closest advisers, with responsibility for training a fledgling guerrilla army. In May 1941 he participated in establishing the **Viet Minh** (League for the Independence of Vietnam) which nominally led the nationalist struggle against French colonial rule. After the proclamation of the Democratic Republic of Vietnam in Hanoi in September 1945, Giap became minister of the interior as well as commander-in-chief of the armed forces and then minister of defence in 1947. He always upheld the primacy of politics in war. He displayed logistical genius at the **Battle of Dien Bien Phu** in 1954, planning the decisive deployment of heavy artillery in the mountains surrounding the valley where the French had established their military positions.

After that dramatic victory, the partition of Vietnam and the establishment of a Communist government north of the seventeenth parallel of latitude, Giap led its armed forces continuously against the government in Saigon and US military intervention until final victory and national unification in 1975. He gave up his post as commander-in-chief in 1976 and was removed as minister of defence in 1980 and then from the Politburo in 1982, possibly for opposing the invasion of Cambodia. He retained office as deputy prime minister to which he was appointed in 1979 until leaving office in August 1991, but devoted much of his time to a commission responsible for training scientists and technicians. When Vietnam and China began to engage in serious rapprochement in the late 1980s, General Giap played a role in the personal diplomacy. In September 1989 he led the Vietnamese delegation to the Asian Games in Beijing, the highest-ranking Vietnamese to visit the Chinese capital openly for over a decade. He also played a personal role in reconciliation with the United States through participation in historical seminars in Hanoi on the Vietnam War. Giap passed away on 4 October 2013, a celebrated Vietnamese war hero.

see also: August Revolution 1945; Dien Bien Phu, Battle of, 1954; Ho Chi Minh; Indochina Wars; Viet Minh; Vietnam War.

Goh Chok Tong (Singapore)

Goh Chok Tong succeeded **Lee Kuan Yew** as prime minister of Singapore on 28 November 1990. Goh was born on 20 May 1941 in Singapore; he read economics at the University of Singapore and then entered the government's Economic Planning Unit. In 1969, after postgraduate studies at Williams College in the United States, he was seconded to Neptune Oriental Lines as planning and projects manager, rising to managing director in 1973. He was persuaded to enter politics by Finance Minister Hon Sui Sen, and stood successfully as a candidate for the ruling **People's Action Party** (PAP) in the parliamentary elections of December 1976. Goh was appointed senior minister of state in the Ministry of Defence in September 1977 and then minister for trade and industry in March 1979. As a leading member of the second generation of politicians whom Lee Kuan Yew was training to succeed the founding fathers of the republic, he was also given experience in the portfolios of health and defence.

After general elections in December 1984 in which there was a notable swing against the ruling party, Goh was made first deputy prime minister, having been picked by his cabinet colleagues, although Lee Kuan Yew let it be known that he had not been his first choice. Goh succeeded Lee in November 1990 after a long apprenticeship. His predecessor remained in the cabinet with the office of senior minister, also retaining initially the post of secretary-general of the PAP. Goh was distinguished from Lee by his softer political style, more in tune with the aspirations of a younger, more affluent generation of Singaporeans. At the same time however, he represented a continuity of philosophy based on the shared conviction of the essential vulnerability of the island-state and the need to demonstrate resoluteness of mind and action. He led the PAP to resounding electoral victories in 1991, 1997 and 2001, in which the party won 61 per cent, 65 per cent and 75 per cent of the popular vote, respectively. Under his steady-handed leadership Singapore weathered the storms of the **Asian Financial Crisis** of 1997–8 and the Severe Acute Respiratory Syndrome (SARS) epidemic in 2003.

Following the 2001 general election, Goh Chok Tong announced his intention to relinquish office, which he did on 12 August 2004 and was succeeded by **Lee Hsien Loong**, eldest son of Lee Kuan Yew. Shortly afterwards, Goh assumed the post of chairman of the Monetary Authority of Singapore, while concurrently serving as senior minister in the cabinet. In the 2006 election Goh Chok Tong was tasked with helping the PAP win back the two opposition wards of Hougang and Potong Pasir. In the event, the PAP was unsuccessful, and the seats were retained by opposition politicians **Low Thia Khiang** and **Chiam See Tong**. In January 2011, Goh announced that he would seek re-election to Parliament at the 2011 elections. However, the Marine Parade Group Representation Constituency (GRC) that he had helmed since 1988 proved one of the most hotly contested battles of the election. Goh barely managed to avert an upset, eventually leading his team to victory with 56.6 per cent of the vote. In May that year, he announced his retirement from cabinet. He was nevertheless given the title emeritus senior minister, and continues to play an active role especially in the area of foreign relations pertaining to China and the Middle East.

see also: Asian Financial Crisis 1997–8; Chiam See Tong; Lee Hsien Loong; Lee Kuan Yew; Low Thia Khiang; People's Action Party.

Goh Keng Swee (Singapore)

Goh Keng Swee was active as a leading political figure in Singapore for twenty-five years, playing a key role in promoting both the island-state's economic development and its defence capability. He was born in Malacca on 6 October 1918 and was educated at Raffles College in Singapore and, after the Pacific War, in England at the London School of Economics, returning to join the local civil service. In London, he was a founder and first chairman of the nationalist Malayan Forum, whose alumni included **Lee Kuan Yew** and Tun **Abdul Razak**. He resigned from the civil service to stand as a candidate for the **People's Action Party** (PAP) in May 1959 and was appointed minister of finance in the government formed after its electoral victory. On Singapore's expulsion from the Federation of Malaysia in August 1965, he was the first defence minister in the independent state and then became deputy prime minister in 1972, a post which he held until he retired from politics in 1984. He enjoyed the reputation of being one of the few intellectual peers of Lee Kuan Yew. In retirement, he served for a time as deputy chairman of the Monetary Authority of Singapore, an economic adviser to the government of China, head of the Racecourse Totalisator Board and deputy chairman of the Government of Singapore Investment Corporation. Since suffering strokes in 1999 and 2000, Goh had been in ill health. He died on 14 May 2010 at the age of ninety-one years, and was laid to rest with a state funeral.

see also: Lee Kuan Yew; People's Action Party; Razak, Tun Abdul.

Golkar (Indonesia)

Golkar is an acronym drawn from the Indonesian *Golongan Karya*, meaning Functional Groups. *Golkar* is a political organization, which was employed primarily to generate electoral support for the administration of President **Suharto**. It was established in October 1964 by senior army officers under the extended acronym of *Sekber Golkar* from *Sekretariat Bersama Golongan Karya* (Joint Secretariat of Functional Groups). Their object was to use the organization to counter the influence of the Communist Party within the National Front set up by President **Sukarno** as a vehicle for mass mobilization in his own political interest. *Sekber Golkar* failed to make any political showing and was then overtaken by events with the abortive coup (*see* ***Gestapu***) of October 1965 and its far-reaching political consequences. Nothing was heard of the organization until 1971 when it was revived to serve the electoral interests of the Suharto administration, which had made a formal commitment to constitutionalism.

Golkar was rehabilitated in 1971 for the specific purpose of demonstrating electoral support for President Suharto's rule without risking a change of government. *Golkar* was first so employed in elections in July 1971 and secured 62.8 per cent of the vote with the evident support of the armed forces and the civil service. That figure was raised to 64.3 per cent in May 1977 and approximately held in May 1982. In April 1987 *Golkar* received a somewhat embarrassing 72.9 per cent of the vote, which was reduced to sixty-eight per cent in elections in June 1992. In parliamentary elections in May 1997, it polled seventy-four per cent of the vote and secured 325 of the 425 elective seats. This overwhelming majority served to provide a mandate for President Suharto's successful bid for a seventh consecutive term of office in March 1998. *Golkar*'s political fortunes waned dramatically with President Suharto's resignation in the following May against a background of economic crisis. Interim-president **B. J. Habibie** led the much discredited party into fresh parliamentary elections in June 1999 in which *Golkar* secured 20.9 per cent of the vote with 120 seats behind the ***Partai Demokrasi Indonesia–Perjuangan*** (PDI–P), which secured 37.4 per cent and 154 seats. Moreover, after a banking scandal over financing his campaign and resentment over his handling of East Timor and evident divisions within the party, Habibie withdrew from the presidential contest within the **People's Consultative Assembly** (MPR) in October 1999, which was won by **Abdurrahman Wahid**. However, a number of members of the liberal wing of *Golkar* were included in the new cabinet announced at the end of the month, while Akbar Tanjung became parliament speaker. In 2001 *Golkar* was successful in its bid to have President Wahid replaced by **Megawati**

Sukarnoputri through a special session of the MPR.

The party continues to be of political consequence in spite of its previous association with the **New Order** regime. *Golkar* has been represented in all cabinets since the fall of Suharto, and thus has never been in opposition since its founding. In 2004 *Golkar* won the biggest share of the vote in both the parliamentary and local elections. In September of the same year, **Yusuf Kalla** became vice-president to **Susilo Bambang Yudhoyono**, cementing *Golkar*'s ties to the administration and role as kingmaker. Under current party chairman, Abdurrizal Bakrie, *Golkar* managed to secure about fifteen per cent of the vote at the 2014 legislative election, making it the second largest party to the PDI–P in the Indonesian Parliament. The party has also lent its support to **Prabowo Subianto**'s bid for the presidency.

see also: Gestapu; Habibie, B. J.; Kalla, Yusuf; Megawati Sukarnoputri; *Partai Demokrasi Indonesia– Perjuangan*; People's Consultative Assembly; Prabowo Subianto; Suharto; Sukarno; Wahid, Abdurrahman; Yudhoyono, Susilo Bambang.

Guided Democracy (Indonesia)

Guided Democracy is the name for the authoritarian political system inaugurated by decree by President **Sukarno** on 5 July 1959 when he dissolved the elected Constituent Assembly and reinstated the independence constitution of 1945. Known in Indonesian as *Demokrasi Terpimpin*, its inauguration marked the final failure of Indonesia to practise parliamentary democracy against a tempestuous background of political and military factionalism, religious and regional dissension and economic decline. Guided Democracy gave rise to a myriad of radical and romantic political symbols which Sukarno wielded to his short-term advantage to the neglect of economic priorities. Although Guided Democracy was represented as an authentically Indonesian alternative to an alien political tradition, it was an intensely competitive system. The personal dominance of President Sukarno barely masked the bitter contention between the conservative armed forces and the radical Communist Party. Sukarno's political balancing act between the two rivals came to an end after an abortive coup (*see* ***Gestapu***) in October 1965 which discredited him and the Communist Party. A military initiative in March 1966 led by Lieutenant General **Suharto** which removed Sukarno from effective power and also proscribed the Communist Party marked the dissolution of Guided Democracy and its replacement by a more constructive developmental authoritarianism.

see also: Gestapu; Suharto; Sukarno.

Gulf of Tonkin Incident 1964 (Vietnam) *see* **Tonkin Gulf Incident 1964**.

Gusmão, José 'Xanana' (Timor-Leste)

José 'Xanana' (Alexandre) Gusmão was leader of East Timorese resistance to Indonesian rule and is currently prime minister of Timor-Leste. He had previously also been president at independence.

Gusmão was born in 1946 in Dili and was educated at a Jesuit seminary. He then worked in the Department of Forestry and Agriculture during Portuguese rule until 1974. After Indonesia's invasion in December 1975, he rose to prominence as a ***Fretilin*** resistance leader. He succeeded Nicolau Lobato as commander of its military wing in 1979 and helped to sustain its armed struggle against superior odds during the 1980s. He was captured in Dili in 1992 and sentenced to life imprisonment in the following year, which was subsequently commuted to twenty years. In April 1998, he was elected as president of the National Council for Maubere (East Timorese) Resistance at a convention of exiles in Portugal. After the overthrow of President **Suharto** in May 1998, he became the interlocutor for the East Timorese cause and was released into house arrest in February 1999 in the month after the decision by President **B. J. Habibie** to permit the East Timorese to choose between autonomy within Indonesia or full independence. He returned to East Timor in October 1999, after the United Nations-sanctioned International Force for East Timor had begun to restore order following the orchestrated anarchy in the wake of the UN-conducted referendum in which the vast majority of voters had opted for independence.

The National Council of Timorese Resistance formerly known as the National Council of Maubere Resistance, elected Gusmão to lead the movement in 2000. Gusmão was also speaker of the National Council from November 2000 to April 2001. The National Council was a body comprising various groups ranging from political parties, civil society movements and religious organizations that were involved in charting the future of East Timor during its transitional phase. Gusmão contested the country's first presidential elections as an independent candidate and won with a large majority. He was sworn in as president of the Democratic Republic of Timor-Leste on 20 May 2002 for a five-year term. When his presidential term ended Gusmão entered party politics as leader of the **National Congress for Timorese Reconstruction** (CNRT) party, campaigning in the 2007 legislative elections. Having performed significantly at the polls, CNRT was able to form an alliance with three other major parties, and collectively it was known as the Alliance with Parliamentary Majority (AMP). The AMP was able to secure more than half the seats in Parliament and on 8 August 2007 Gusmão was sworn in as the fourth prime minister of Timor-Leste, concurrently holding the defence portfolio as well. On 11 February 2008, Gusmão's motorcade was attacked just hours after rebels had shot and wounded President **José Ramos-Horta** but he escaped unharmed.

Gusmão is a mild-mannered man with a poetic disposition and considerable personal appeal. In May 2000, he published his autobiography entitled *To Resist Is to Win* and was also the main narrator of the film *A Hero's Journey* also known as *Where the Sun Rises*. The film was a 2006 documentary detailing nearly two-and-a-half years of East Timor's resistance against the occupying Indonesian forces and its current tryst with independence and the challenges that lie ahead for this young country.

see also: Fretilin; Habibie, B. J.; National Congress for Timorese Reconstruction; Ramos-Horta, José; Suharto; United Nations: East Timor 1999–2002; Wahid, Abdurrahman.

H

Habibie, B. J. (Indonesia/Timor-Leste)
Dr B. J. Habibie became president of Indonesia on 21 May 1998 on the resignation of President **Suharto** against a background of economic crisis and political turbulence. As vice-president, elected by the **People's Consultative Assembly** (MPR) in the previous March, he succeeded to high office for the remainder of the presidential term under article eight of Indonesia's constitution. As a protégé and close confidant of former president Suharto, he represented political continuity as a symbol of a discredited order. Nonetheless, he did not abdicate presidential ambitions. He pursued them through promoting a liberal agenda whereby political prisoners were released and freedom of the press was restored. He authorized fresh parliamentary and presidential elections but failed to overcome the political taint of the Suharto era, which was demonstrated in the poor performance of ***Golkar***, the government's party in parliamentary elections in June 1999. He lost the support of the armed forces through his seemingly precipitate willingness to countenance the independence of East Timor in an offer of a referendum made unexpectedly in January 1999. A scandal over campaign financing further diminished his presidential chances, while he was opposed by a liberal faction within his own party. In the event, he withdrew from the presidential contest and gave up office on 20 October 1999 when the MPR elected **Abdurrahman Wahid**.

Bacharuddin Jusuf Habibie was born on 25 June 1936 in Pare-Pare in south Sulawesi. He was educated at the Technical University in Bandung and then at the Technical University in Aachen, Germany, from which he graduated with a doctorate in engineering. He became a member of the faculty and then director for research and development for Messerschmitt, the German aircraft corporation. He was well known to President Suharto through a family connection established during a military posting in Sulawesi. Indeed, Suharto took the personal initiative to bring Habibie back to Indonesia in 1974, where he worked initially for Pertamina, the state oil corporation. In 1978, he was appointed minister of state for research and technology, holding that portfolio continuously until becoming vice-president in 1998. In that portfolio, he made a dubious mark by establishing an aircraft manufacturing industry in Bandung as part of a grand design to make Indonesia a regional centre of modern technology. In this costly and unsuccessful enterprise, he enjoyed President Suharto's full backing. Habibie began to engage in political activities from December 1990 when, again with Suharto's support, he was instrumental in establishing ICMI (Association of Indonesian Muslim Intellectuals) as a counter to the influence of the armed forces. In 1998 he was hand-picked by President Suharto in a political initiative interpreted as an attempt to ensure that his running mate was not a credible successor. Habibie had by then secured a reputation for eccentricity in economic judgements as well as displaying an excessively egocentric disposition. When Suharto reluctantly resigned on 20 May 1998, Habibie as stipulated by the 1945 constitution was sworn into the office of the president on 21 May 1998. Habibie courted controversy very early on in office when he was quoted in a newspaper article as describing Singapore as a 'little red dot', a term that is today an epithet for the country. While he was expected to function as a reformist, Habibie's policies seemed to be an extension of the Suharto regime's. The cabinet which he headed, while known as the Development Reform Cabinet, continued to seek the patronage of former members of Suharto's cabinet and the highly criticized Indonesian military. Habibie's only attempt at reform seemed to be in keeping the authority of the governor of the Central Bank independent and including **Hamzah Haz** of ***Partai Persatuan Pembangunan*** (United Development Party, PPP) in his cabinet. Hamzah Haz now leads the PPP and he was also the ninth vice-president of Indonesia under President **Megawati Sukarnoputri**. However, it was

Habibie's initiative in suggesting the possibility of an independent East Timor – which materialized on 20 May 2002 ending nearly twenty-seven years of Indonesian occupation – that had far-reaching consequences. Habibie was not just instrumental in the referendum that lead to East Timor's independence but also in bringing about some form of stability in the chaotic economy of Indonesia that was greatly impaired by the **Asian Financial Crisis** and the political turmoil that gripped the country just before Suharto's resignation. Habibie continues to contribute to Indonesian policy matters through his think tank, the Habibie Centre.

see also: Asian Financial Crisis 1997–8; *Golkar*; Haz, Hamzah; Megawati Sukarnoputri; *Partai Persatuan Pembangunan*; People's Consultative Assembly; Suharto; Wahid, Abdurrahman.

Hadi Awang, Abdul (Malaysia)

The current president of ***Parti Islam Se-Malaysia*** (PAS), Abdul Hadi Awang was born in 1947 in the northern Malay state of Terengganu. He holds bachelor and master's degrees in *shari'a* from the Islamic University of Madinah and Al-Azhar University, respectively.

Abdul Hadi's political activism began when he led the youth movement of PAS in his home state of Terengganu. In 1977, he was elected onto the PAS Central Executive Committee. He was also concurrently leader of the Terengganu chapter of the Islamic Youth Movement of Malaysia (**ABIM**). Abdul Hadi is known to be a firebrand Islamic preacher and prolific author, and has regularly criticized the religious credentials of the Muslim leaders of **UMNO** (United Malays National Organization). Indeed, he gained notoriety in 1981 for his comments about UMNO, now famously known in Malaysia's lexicon of politics as the *Amanat Haji Hadi* (Edict of Haji Hadi), where he alleged that UMNO perpetuated unIslamic rule and called for a *jihad* against them. At the same time, Abdul Hadi was equally critical of the leadership of the main PAS party in the late 1970s, which many from the youth movement saw to be drifting away from true Islamic teachings. In 1982, Abdul Hadi helped to usher in clerical rule in PAS, and in 1989 he became the party's deputy president. He was briefly chief minister of Terengganu when PAS managed to wrest the state assembly from UMNO at the 1999 general election. UMNO regained the state at the 2004 elections. Following the sudden death of Fadzil Noor in 2002, Abdul Hadi was appointed party president.

In PAS circles, Abdul Hadi is known to be an advocate of conservative interpretations and positions on religious matters, and was the chief architect of the party's controversial Islamic State Document published at the end of 2003. He is frequently also associated with the issue of the implementation of *hudud* (the Islamic penal code) in Malaysia, which he has championed persistently. Nevertheless, political pragmatism and the growing fortunes of the opposition ***Pakatan Rakyat*** (People's Alliance) coalition, central to his party's aspirations to national leadership, has seen him temper his conservatism.

see also: ABIM; *Pakatan Rakyat*; *Parti Islam Se-Malaysia*; UMNO.

Hambali (Riduan Isamuddin) (Indonesia)

Riduan Isamuddin, better known as Hambali, was born on 4 April 1964 in West Java, Indonesia. He is the former operational leader of the Indonesian terrorist organization, ***Jemaah Islamiyah*** (JI), and had served as its main link to Al-Qaeda. From 2003 to 2005, Hambali was believed to have been third in command in Al-Qaeda. He is currently detained in Guantanamo Bay, Cuba.

Hambali joined the *jihad* against the Soviet Union in Afghanistan from 1987 to 1990, and it was during this time that he was believed to have met Osama bin Laden personally. Hambali remained in Afghanistan after the Soviet withdrawal and only returned to Malaysia in 1991, where he met the two co-founders of JI, **Abu Bakar Ba'asyir** and Abdullah Sungkar. During this time he travelled around Southeast Asia promoting militant extremism and cultivating relationships between JI and other Islamist groups. In mid-1991 he travelled from Malaysia to the Philippines as a Muslim missionary, and sojourned at Camp Abu Bakar, then the headquarters of the **Moro Islamic Liberation Front**. To covertly facilitate terrorist activities, Hambali formed *Konsojaya* in June 1994, purportedly a trading company involved in palm oil trade between Malaysia and Afghanistan but which in actual fact served as a conduit for the movement of funds. It was with Hambali's prompting that JI began entertaining a vision not only to transform Indonesia into an Islamic state governed by *shari'a*, but also the expansion of this vision across Southeast Asia towards the goal of the formation of a regional Islamic caliphate. Following the fall of President **Suharto** in 1998, Hambali returned to Indonesia where he could organize more freely, and where brewing communal tensions offered opportunities for his followers to rise in the defence of Islam. In 1998, Hambali was appointed leader of JI's regional group which encompassed Malaysia and Singapore. Following the 2000 Christmas Eve bombings, Hambali became a fugitive and fled to Malaysia with his wife, Noralwizah Lee Abdullah.

In 2000, Hambali went underground and started a wave of church bombings in Indonesia. He is alleged to be responsible for several terrorist attacks, including the bombing of churches in December 2000 and subsequent bombings in the Philippines, as well as the Marriott Hotel attacks in Jakarta. Intelligence agencies and police from Indonesia, Malaysia and the United States, as well as testimony by those arrested for the October 2002 bombings in Bali, identified Hambali as the mastermind behind those attacks and the one who secured US$36,000 to finance the operation (*see* **Terrorism in Southeast Asia**). He was captured by a joint operation between the Thai police and the CIA in Ayudhya, Thailand. At the time of his arrest, Hambali was the most wanted man in Southeast Asia.

see also: Ba'asyir, Abu Bakar; *Jemaah Islamiyah*; Moro Islamic Liberation Front; Terrorism in Southeast Asia.

Hanoi Summit (ASEAN) 1998

(Brunei/Cambodia/Indonesia/Laos/ Malaysia/Myanmar/Philippines/ Singapore/Thailand/Vietnam)

The sixth meeting of **ASEAN**'s heads of government convened in the Vietnamese capital in mid-December 1998. The venue of the meeting was significant as further evidence of reconciliation between Vietnam and those founding members of ASEAN (Association of Southeast Asian Nations), which had challenged its invasion and occupation of Cambodia. The declared purpose of the meeting was to devise a corporate strategy that would enable ASEAN's governments to address the regional economic crisis whose devastating impact had diminished the standing of the Association. To that end, a Hanoi Plan of Action was promulgated in an attempt to strengthen regional cooperation but without any tangible effect on economic circumstances. In the event, the main business of the meeting was the problem of Cambodia's membership, which had been postponed in July 1997 after a violent coup in Phnom Penh displacing the first prime minister, Prince **Norodom Ranariddh**, to the political advantage of the second prime minister, **Hun Sen**, who attended the Hanoi meeting as an observer. Vietnam used its position as host to press for Cambodia's immediate entry and was supported by Indonesia and Malaysia, while the Philippines, Singapore and Thailand insisted that its entry be delayed until the coalition government formed in the previous month headed by Hun Sen demonstrated its durability. Vietnam's prime minister, **Phan Van Khai**, had his way in announcing that a consensus had been reached on Cambodia's membership and that a ceremony to mark its entry would take place in Hanoi at an unspecified date. That ceremony took place in April 1999.

see also: ASEAN; Hun Sen; Phan Van Khai; Ranariddh, Prince Norodom.

Hanoi Summit (ASEAN) April 2010

(Brunei/Cambodia/Indonesia/Laos/ Malaysia/Myanmar/Philippines/ Singapore/Thailand/Vietnam)

The sixteenth meeting of heads of government of **ASEAN** (Association of Southeast Asian Nations) convened in the capital of Vietnam on 8 and 9 April 2010. The focus of the agenda revolved around the concept of ASEAN Connectivity, and in particular a Master Plan scheduled for submission at the next summit at the end of the year. ASEAN leaders agreed that

while the importance of developing ASEAN's external relations should continue to be emphasized, it was nevertheless crucial to enhance intra-ASEAN connectivity and improve on existing communication and infrastructure frameworks so as to deepen integration. Prior to the summit proper, attempts were made by the Vietnamese chair to push for a common approach in dealing with China on the **South China Sea** territorial disputes, where Vietnam was a claimant along with several other ASEAN states. Nevertheless, the issue was only mentioned in passing due to a lack of consensus, while the focus of the discussion remained very much on strengthening action in economic areas of cooperation.
see also: ASEAN; South China Sea.

Hanoi Summit (ASEAN) October 2010 (Brunei/Cambodia/Indonesia/Laos/Malaysia/Myanmar/Philippines/Singapore/Thailand/Vietnam)

The seventeenth meeting of heads of government of **ASEAN** (Association of Southeast Asian Nations) convened in the capital of Vietnam from 28 to 30 October 2010. The main business of the meeting was to endorse the Master Plan on ASEAN Connectivity which aims to boost physical connectivity, institutional connectivity and people-to-people connectivity within the region, thereby facilitating the building of the **ASEAN Community**. However, it remains to be seen whether this new concept of connectivity can bridge the growing division within the regional organization between the maritime Southeast Asia states (the original members) and those newer members in mainland Southeast Asia. The latter – Myanmar, Cambodia, Laos and, to a lesser extent, Vietnam and Thailand – have, with their growing infrastructural linkages, investment and trade, and even political ties with China, developed into something of a greater Mekong region that threatens to diminish the relative importance of ASEAN and its community-building efforts. These long-term concerns notwithstanding, the Hanoi Summit was overshadowed by the China–Japan dispute over the Diaoyu/Senkaku islands. A scheduled bilateral meeting between leaders of both countries on the sidelines of the summit was cancelled by China after it accused Japan of unilaterally raising the issue at the concurrent fifth **East Asia Summit** (EAS). ASEAN's meetings with its dialogue partners in Hanoi also marked the first time that the United States and Russia participated in the EAS, where they were represented by their respective foreign ministers.
see also: ASEAN; ASEAN Community; East Asia Summit.

Harris Mohamad Salleh, Datuk (Malaysia)

Datuk Harris Mohamad Salleh was chief minister of Sabah from June 1976 until April 1985. He had been instrumental in helping to form *Berjaya* (the Malay acronym for the Sabah People's Union) in July 1975 as a challenge to the government of Chief Minister Tun **Mustapha Harun** but gave up the leadership to Tun **Mohammad Fuad** on his resignation as head of state. He became deputy chief minister to Tun Mohammad Fuad after *Berjaya* won the state elections in April 1976 but then succeeded Fuad after his death in an air crash in June. Datuk Harris was born in Brunei on 4 November 1930 and initially received only a secondary education. He worked as a teacher, a government clerk and then as an assistant district officer, which gave him the opportunity to pursue a qualification in public administration at the University of Melbourne. His career blossomed as political opportunities opened up with decolonization and Sabah's membership of Malaysia. He was vice-president of the **United Sabah National Organization** (USNO) led by Tun Mustapha and held a number of senior cabinet portfolios until his resignation in July 1975. His defection from USNO was encouraged by the federal government, which had become alarmed at Tun Mustapha's separatist disposition. As chief minister, he failed to live up to expectations of good government generated by his initial criticism of Tun Mustapha's administration and was neglectful of non-Muslim interests. In February 1985 a new party was formed in Sabah based on an alliance of Christian Kadazans and Chinese. This ***Parti Bersatu Sabah*** (Sabah United Party) was carried

to office by the same kind of popular wave which had benefited *Berjaya* nearly ten years previously. After his electoral defeat, Datuk Harris retired from political life.
see also: Fuad, Tun Mohammad; Mustapha bin Datuk Harun, Tun; *Parti Bersatu Sabah*; United Sabah National Organization.

Hatta, Mohammad (Indonesia)

Mohammad Hatta, who proclaimed the independence of Indonesia jointly with **Sukarno** on 17 August 1945, was the republic's first vice-president. He played a critical role in the concurrent office of prime minister from January 1948 in guiding the embryonic state during the struggle for independence from the Dutch during which he also articulated the ideal of an 'independent and active' foreign policy for the republic. He led the Republic of Indonesia's delegation at the Round Table Conference in The Hague from August 1949, which concluded with an agreement on independence in the following December. After independence, he continued as prime minister of the United States of Indonesia until its replacement by a unitary republic in August 1950. His attempt to steer Indonesia in the direction of economic development was thwarted by the political radicalism of President Sukarno. He resigned as vice-president in July 1956 out of a sense of frustration. Although he continued to command wide respect, he never again held public office.

Mohammad Hatta was born in western Sumatra on 12 August 1902. As a young man, he was exposed to Islamic modernism, while as a student of economics in Rotterdam he was attracted to Marxist ideas and became an active nationalist. On his return to the then Netherlands East Indies in 1932, he came into conflict with the colonial authorities who sent him into internal exile in West New Guinea and Banda. He cooperated with the Japanese during their occupation in the nationalist cause, advocating negotiation as the prime means of its fulfilment. Toward the end of his life, Mohammad Hatta was drawn into an abortive attempt by a Javanese mystic, Sawito Kartwibowo, to persuade President **Suharto** to give up power on the ground that he had abused it. Mohammad Hatta, who died in 1980, was never able to translate his ideal role as the social and political conscience of Indonesia into practical politics.
see also: Suharto; Sukarno.

Haz, Hamzah (Indonesia)

Hamzah Haz served as the ninth vice-president of Indonesia from 2001 to 2004 under the government of **Megawati Sukarnoputri**. He is also the current leader of the ***Partai Persatuan Pembangunan*** (United Development Party, PPP).

Haz was born on 15 February 1940. Prior to pursuing a political career, Haz worked as a newspaper journalist in Borneo and later taught economics at the Tanjungpura University. His political career began in 1968 as a member of the West Kalimantan provincial parliament. Subsequently, he moved to Jakarta and in 1971 became a member of parliament as a representative from ***Nahdlatul Ulama***. In 1973 he joined the PPP. Haz served as minister for investment from 1998 to 1999 in the **B. J. Habibie** government. He later resigned this post in order to lead the PPP in the 1999 presidential elections. In 1999 he ran for vice-president but was defeated by Megawati. Later that year he joined the cabinet of President **Abdurrahman Wahid**, and was appointed minister for people's welfare, only to resign two months later amidst allegations of corruption and graft levelled at him by none other than the president himself. Following President Wahid's impeachment in 2001, Haz defeated **Susilo Bambang Yudhoyono** and Akbar Tanjung to become Megawati's vice-president despite having publicly announced several years earlier that a woman should not lead the world's largest Muslim nation. In 2004 Haz ran for the presidential elections as a PPP candidate, along with running mate Agum Gumelar. The pair received only three per cent of the total vote, and Haz finished last among five presidential candidates.

Haz is known to be close to Islamist groups in Indonesia which form his support base. In the past, he has publicly associated himself with **Abu Bakar Ba'asyir**, the spiritual leader of ***Jemaah Islamiyah*** who is currently serving time for financing terrorist activities. Up until the 2002 Bali bombings, Haz had also consistently denied the presence of a terrorist network in

Indonesia, or that Ba'asyir was party to terrorist activities. In line with Ba'asyir's rhetoric, Haz condemned the American invasion of Iraq on the grounds that it violated the human rights of Iraqis. For this, he was criticized as an opportunist who legitimized extremism in Indonesia in exchange for political support.

see also: Ba'asyir, Abu Bakar; Habibie, B. J.; *Jemaah Islamiyah*; Megawati Sukarnoputri; *Nahdlatul Ulama*; *Partai Persatuan Pembangunan*; Wahid, Abdurrahman; Yudhoyono, Susilo Bambang.

Heng Samrin (Cambodia)

Heng Samrin came to international attention when he was appointed from obscurity as president of the National United Front for National Salvation in whose name Cambodia was invaded by Vietnam in December 1978. In January 1979 he became president of the ruling People's Revolutionary Council of the **People's Republic of Kampuchea** and in the following month, president of the Council of State. Heng Samrin has served as a political frontman without a power base of his own. He is believed to have been born in 1934 in Prey Veng Province but apart from an association with **Khmer Rouge** insurgency, little more is known of his early life. Between 1976 and 1978 he was a political commissar and commander of the Khmer Rouge's fourth infantry division deployed in the eastern region. In May 1978 Heng Samrin was involved in that region's rebellion against **Pol Pot**'s leadership, finding refuge in Vietnam where he was given a political role. He became general secretary of the ruling **Kampuchean People's Revolutionary Party**'s Central Committee in December 1981 after Vietnam's initial nominee had proved unreliable. He remained in that position for nearly a decade until a political settlement came into sight, although real leadership was shared between Prime Minister **Hun Sen** and the speaker of parliament, **Chea Sim**. With the adoption of the title State of Cambodia in place of People's Republic of Kampuchea in April 1989, Heng Samrin's role began to diminish. In October 1991 the Kampuchean People's Revolutionary Party changed its name to the **Cambodian People's Party** (CPP), dropping Heng Samrin as general secretary for Chea Sim. He was replaced as head of state by Prince **Norodom Sihanouk** when he returned to Cambodia in November 1991, enjoying no more than a nominal role as honorary president of the CPP.

see also: Cambodian People's Party; Chea Sim; Hun Sen; Kampuchea, People's Republic of; Kampuchean People's Revolutionary Party; Khmer Rouge; Pol Pot; Sihanouk, King Norodom.

Hertogh, Maria: Riots 1950 (Singapore)

Maria Hertogh was a Dutch girl who had been given over by her parents at the age of four to a local foster mother for safekeeping just prior to Japan's occupation of the Netherlands East Indies. After the end of the Pacific War, her parents located their daughter in Malaya where she was living as a Muslim and speaking only Malay. They commenced proceedings in Singapore's High Court to regain custody but in the meantime their daughter was married to a Malay. The decision of the court to revoke the marriage, the removal of the girl to a Roman Catholic convent and from there to the Netherlands, and then a Malay newspaper's publication of her photograph in the convent sparked off violent demonstrations in Singapore by Malays in December 1950. They felt aggrieved that their faith had been publicly insulted. Violence was directed primarily against Europeans and Eurasians, leaving sixteen people dead.

Herzog Affair 1986 (Malaysia/Singapore)

An official visit to Singapore in November 1986 by President Chaim Herzog of Israel prompted diplomatic protests from the governments of Brunei, Indonesia and Malaysia. In addition, Indonesia and Malaysia withdrew their heads of mission for the duration of the visit. Greatest strain occurred in the relationship between Singapore and Malaysia, whose prime minister, **Mahathir Mohamad**, interpreted the visit as a personal slight. It had been announced, without consultation or notice, coincident with his public denunciations of Zionism provoked by allegations in the *Asian Wall Street Journal* that his finance minister had been manipulating the stock market. Singapore's invitation was also resented because it touched Mahathir's political authority, then subject to challenge by rivals within **UMNO** (United Malays National Organization). Mahathir's evident displeasure provided an opportunity for an *ad hoc* coalition of political forces to agitate against the visit, with the ulterior motive of embarrassing Malaysia's prime minister. In Singapore, Malaysian ministerial and journalistic protests were treated as a test of national sovereignty, while the willingness of the Malay-Muslim community of Singapore to take their lead from Malaysia in opposing the Israeli president's visit caused serious concern. In the event, the domestic repercussions of the affair in both states brought home to their respective prime ministers that they could not afford to allow the quarrel to fester. After an apology of a kind from Prime Minister **Lee Kuan Yew**, and despite a revival of tension because of a remark about the role of Malays in the republic's armed forces by their defence minister, **Lee Hsien Loong** (the prime minister's elder son), serious attempts were made to repair relations. Lee Kuan Yew and Mahathir talked in October 1987 at the Commonwealth heads of government meeting in Vancouver and set in train a process of reconciliation, expressed in subsequent agreements on the sale of water and gas by Malaysia to Singapore and in defence cooperation. Symbolic reconciliation was marked in July 1988 by the first official visit to Singapore by a reigning king of Malaysia. In October 1993 a brief visit to Singapore by Israeli Prime Minister Yitzhak Rabin, which followed on a stopover in Indonesia, passed off without comment from Malaysia, while Lee Kuan Yew paid his first visit to Israel in May 1994.

see also: Lee Hsien Loong; Lee Kuan Yew; Mahathir Mohamad, Tun; UMNO.

Hindraf (Hindu Rights Action Force)

(Malaysia)

The Hindu Rights Action Force, better known as Hindraf, is a loose coalition of some thirty Hindu-based non-governmental organizations with varying objectives and goals working largely among the Indian-Hindu minority population in Malaysia. Its leadership consists mostly of ethnic Indian lawyers such as the brothers Ponnusamy Uthayakumar and Ponnusamy Waythamoorthy. Established in early 2006, Hindraf's stated aims were to improve the socio-economic position of ethnic Indians and to protect their cultural practices. The impetus for the creation of Hindraf came from increasing encroachment by the Muslim-dominated Malaysian government into ethnic Indian cultural and religious space. Foremost was the alarming acceleration of demolition of Hindu temples and shrines during the government of **Abdullah Badawi**. Many of these temples and shrines were built during the era of British colonial administration without permits or licenses. In the course of redevelopment, the lands these religious sites were situated on were being requisitioned, and they were being demolished in the process. The Indian community had also been outraged at how the widow of a deceased decorated soldier was denied access to her husband's body and the right to give him a Hindu funeral after the *shari'a* court ruled that he had died a Muslim. Percolating beneath these tensions was a general dissatisfaction towards the **Malaysian Indian Congress** (MIC), the ethnic Indian party in the ruling ***Barisan Nasional*** (National Front, BN) coalition, for failing to defend the community's interests or improve the socio-economic position of ethnic Indians.

While it was initially not regarded as a significant political movement, the widening support that Hindraf received for its campaigns against the demolition of Hindu temples across Malaysia increasingly placed it in the spotlight. Hindraf organized its biggest demonstration in Kuala Lumpur on 25 November 2007 after it was clear that its campaigns against the continued demolition of Hindu temples had been futile. Prior to the planned demonstration, Hindraf filed a first-of-its-kind class action suit against the British government in London on 31 August. The lawsuit demanded reparations amounting to £1 million for every Indian Malaysian on grounds that the then-colonial government had brought them to Malaya as contract labourers, 'exploited' them for 150 years, and then failed to accord them sufficient protection in the British-drafted Federal Constitution as an under-class ethnic minority in a Malay-Muslim dominated Malaysia.

The aim of the demonstration in November was to deliver a 100,000-signature petition to the British high commissioner, asking that the Queen of England appoint a Queen's Counsel to represent their case. The protest was met with tear gas and water cannons. 136 individuals were arrested and the petition never got through to the high commissioner. In December, several prominent Hindraf activists were arrested on charges of sedition while five leaders were detained under the Internal Security Act. Nevertheless, together with the ***Bersih*** demonstrations, the Hindraf protest set in motion events that culminated in the significant erosion of support for the incumbent BN coalition government at the 2008 pools. After repeated warnings, Hindraf was banned by the Malaysian government on 15 October 2008. The ban was lifted by Prime Minister **Najib Razak** in 2013, in anticipation of impending elections. By then, internal friction within Hindraf had become acrimonious factionalism. Waythamoorthy took his faction into the BN weeks prior to the 2013 election in a move condemned by his older brother, Uthayakumar. Sidelined within the BN by the MIC, Waythamoorthy resigned from his cabinet position in February 2014.

see also: Badawi, Tun Abdullah Ahmad; *Barisan Nasional*; *Bersih*; Malaysian Indian Congress; Najib Tun Razak, Datuk Seri Mohamad.

Hizbut Tahrir Indonesia (Indonesia)

The Indonesian Party of Liberation or Hizbut Tahrir Indonesia (HTI) is the Indonesian chapter of Hizbut Tahrir, a transnational Islamist movement founded in 1953 in Jerusalem by Taqiyyuddin Nabhani, an Azharite scholar who was once a judge in the Islamic court in Palestine. Hizbut Tahrir's main objective is to re-establish the Islamic caliphate system based on the principle of *Amr Ma'ruf Nahy Munkar* (enjoining the good and forbidding the evil). Unlike many other Muslim organizations who prioritize spiritual, social, educational and welfare issues, Hizbut Tahrir is explicit in its political goals, and views itself primarily as a political organization. It is, in its own words, 'political in activity, Islamic in ideology'. While Hizbut Tahrir is openly anti-Western and engages directly in very confrontational discourse and rhetoric, it publicly disavows violence and terrorism as a means to achieving its ends.

The HTI is arguably the largest national chapter of Hizbut Tahrir, claiming to cover all thirty-three provinces in Indonesia with a membership in the hundreds of thousands. While HTI subscribes to the ultimate objective of a global caliphate, it views the way forward in Indonesia to be the conversion of the country into an Islamic state. To that end, HTI has outlined a three-step process: education of cadre, community engagement and power acquisition through *nusrah* (seeking assistance) from key stakeholders in the government, military and judiciary. HTI mainly targets its recruitment at tertiary education students and professionals. HTI's roots in Indonesia can be traced to the *Al-Ghazali* pesantren (Islamic boarding school) run by Abdullah bin Nuh, where he hosted a Hizbut Tahrir leader from Australia in 1982. As HTI grew, it operated through a shadow structure behind a range of Muslim organizations and religious classes in mosques in Bogor. Such was the secrecy behind the movement in these early years that group leaders themselves did not know about the existence of HTI until 1987. Throughout the **New Order** period, HTI remained an underground organization, focusing its activities on study circles, youth programmes, and outreach events in selected mosques and private residences. The group produced *the Al-Islam* Bulletin, which was later renamed *As-Salam* Bulletin when its main meeting venue changed from the Standard Chartered building in Jakarta to the *As-Salam Waqf* Foundation, which served as the main vehicle for propagating the group's ideas. Following the end of the New Order, HTI came to the fore officially in 2000. That same year, it organized its inaugural Khilafah conference which was attended by 5,000 HTI activists.

see also: New Order.

Hmong (Laos)

The Hmong are an ethnic minority identified with mountain settlement in Laos who were known at one time by the pejorative *Meo* (savage). Because of clan rivalries, Hmong were to be found on both sides of the internal conflict which afflicted Laos for three decades after the end of the Pacific War (*see* **Indochina Wars**; **Vietnam War**). The Hmong are not indigenous to Laos but migrated from southern China from the early nineteenth century; they have been identified with slash-and-burn agriculture and the cultivation of opium. A French-inspired attempt to administer the Hmong in 1938 led to the split within the minority which enabled both the ***Pathet Lao*** and the Royal Lao government to recruit them for their military purposes. Many thousands of Hmong were recruited into a fighting force by General Vang Pao, who was funded by the US Central Intelligence Agency (CIA). The Hmong bore the brunt of the United States's efforts in Laos to prevent the takeover of the country by the *Pathet Lao* and the interdiction of North Vietnamese supply lines to its forces in South Vietnam. As many as twenty per cent of the Hmong died as a result of the war. After the *Pathet Lao* achieved power in 1975, many Hmong fled the country to Thailand.

A Hmong resistance has festered since the 1970s especially in the central province of Kiang Khouang. Almost forgotten in the West, small bands of Hmong fighters and their families have subsisted on assistance from exile groups in Thailand, France, Australia and the United States. Many of these groups have aligned themselves to General Vang Pai, who lived in the United States until his death in January 2011. Vientiane has largely been unsympathetic to demands for Hmong political autonomy, instead seeking to assimilate them into mainstream Lao society along with the many Hmong who chose to side with the *Pathet Lao* during the war, including current president of the National Assembly and Politburo member, Pany Yathotu. In December 2009, Thailand repatriated the last of the Hmong refugees to Laos in a move aimed at putting an end to a remaining sticking point in Bangkok's relations with Vientiane.

see also: Indochina Wars; *Pathet Lao*; Vietnam War.

Ho Chi Minh (Vietnam)

Ho Chi Minh is a legendary figure in Vietnamese and international communism. As a thinker, he combined an attachment to Marxist principles with a fervent nationalist commitment. As a revolutionary leader, he was distinguished as a practitioner rather than as a theoretician. In his later years, he was portrayed as an ascetic and benign father figure as a role model for the Vietnamese people. For youthful dissenters in the west during the **Vietnam War**, he served as a symbol of revolutionary dedication to a just cause. Ho Chi Minh was born Nguyen Tat Thanh in Nghe An Province in central Vietnam on 19 May 1890. His father was an official at the imperial court in Hue who had also worked as an itinerant teacher. Ho is believed to have been expelled from the French Lycée at Vinh as a teenager for nationalist activities. In September 1911 he began work as a mess boy on a French liner, so beginning a long period of travel outside of Vietnam. During the First World War he settled in France, where he began to involve himself in the Vietnamese nationalist cause, taking the name Nguyen Ai Quoc (Nguyen the Patriot). In 1920, influenced by Lenin's writings, Ho became a founder member of the French Communist Party. He went to Moscow in the early 1920s and began to work for the Comintern, whose agent he became in Southeast Asia later in the decade. It was in this capacity that in 1930 he reconciled competing factions to establish the Communist Party of Indochina whose direct lineal successor is the ruling Communist Party of Vietnam. In May 1941 he set up the **Viet Minh** (League of the Independence of Vietnam) which was a Communist-led national united front which successfully challenged French colonial rule after the end of the Pacific War in the **August Revolution 1945**. Ho Chi Minh took the full pseudonym (meaning Ho who brings enlightenment) to avoid arrest on entering China in 1942. Ho engaged in fruitless negotiations with France in 1946 and then led the Viet Minh to victory in the First **Indochina War**, which secured the country north of the seventeenth parallel for Communist Party rule in 1954. He inspired the insurgent challenge to the government in Saigon after 1960 but did not live to see

Vietnam's unification. He died on 2 September 1969 at the age of seventy-nine. His party colleagues announced his death as having occurred a day later because they did not want it known that he had passed away on the anniversary of national independence, which he had declared in Hanoi on 2 September 1945.
see also: August Revolution 1945; Indochina Wars; Viet Minh; Vietnam War.

Ho Chi Minh Trail (Vietnam)

The Ho Chi Minh Trail was the name given in the west to the network of infiltration routes extending from North Vietnam through Southern Laos and Eastern Cambodia into the highlands of South Vietnam which bypassed the effective political boundary of the seventeenth parallel of latitude created by the **Geneva Agreements on Indochina in 1954**. These routes were employed from the early 1960s during the **Vietnam War** by the People's Liberation Army to channel personnel and supplies first to the southern insurgency and then to the conventional military challenge to the government in Saigon, which was defeated in April 1975. The trail ran through mountainous and jungle terrain and took a heavy toll on the flow of North Vietnamese forces who were subjected to military interdiction on their way south. In February 2000, Prime Minister **Phan Van Khai** approved a plan to turn part of the trail into a 1,690-kilometre modern highway linking northern and southern parts of Vietnam.
see also: Geneva Agreements on Indochina 1954; Indochina Wars; Phan Van Khai; Vietnam War.

Horsburgh Lighthouse (Malaysia/Singapore)

The Horsburgh Lighthouse is situated on the tiny island of Pedra Branca (White Rock), also known in Malay as Pulau Batu Puteh. The island is located at the eastern entrance to the **Singapore Strait** between the opposite coasts of Malaysia and Indonesia. The lighthouse was constructed by the British Straits Settlements colonial administration in 1850 and began operating a year later. The lighthouse has always been administered and maintained from Singapore, even though it is located some eighteen nautical miles beyond the republic's territorial waters limit of three miles. The basis for the republic's jurisdiction over the island as well as adjacent waters and seabed is a series of treaties between the East India Company and the Sultanate of Johor and an Anglo-Dutch Treaty of 1824 which demarcated colonial dominion.

Singapore's jurisdiction over Pedra Branca has been the subject of dispute by the government of Malaysia. A claim was first signalled in December 1979 when Malaysia published a map including the island within its territorial waters. Singapore responded with a protest note. It has been argued in Kuala Lumpur that although the lighthouse had been built and operated from Singapore, it was not a sufficient basis for ownership of the island, which was part of the domain of Johor inherited by Malaysia. The dispute became a matter of public contention from the late 1980s when fishing vessels from Johor were discouraged from sailing close to the island. In September 1991 the chief minister of Johor endorsed the claim publicly. There was an abortive attempt in 1992 by members of the youth wing of the opposition ***Parti Islam Se-Malaysia*** to plant the Malaysian flag on the island. In September 1994 at a meeting in Malaysia, prime ministers **Mahathir Mohamad** and **Goh Chok Tong** agreed to resolve the dispute through reference to a third party, including the International Court of Justice (ICJ). In 1998, both states agreed on a Special Agreement that that was required in order to submit the dispute over Pedra Branca to the ICJ. This Special Agreement was subsequently signed in February 2003 and formally notified in July of the same year. The argument put forward by the Malaysian side was that Singapore's claim was at all times consistent with that of a lighthouse administrator littoral state, and not an exercise of sovereignty. The Foreign Counsel for Malaysia also opposed Singapore's claims that its conduct on the island went completely unopposed by arguing that there had been no open conduct of a *titre de souverain* to be opposed. The Singapore counsels defended this claim by pointing out the many other non-lighthouse related activities that had been conducted, which included having reclamation plans for the island, installing military communication equipment, and investigating shipwrecks in the waters around the island from 1920 to 1979. Crucially, Singapore also produced a letter dated in 1953 from the Sultanate of Johor which stated that that the island was not owned by Johor, but Malaysia refuted this evidence by denying the legal standing of the letter as it was sent by a minor official who had no authority to disown the island. On 23 May 2008 the ICJ announced its decision regarding the dispute and awarded the island to Singapore, while sovereignty over the nearby cluster of features called Middle Rocks was awarded to Malaysia. The reasoning behind the judgement was that although the island of Pedra Branca was originally within the territorial domain of the Sultanate of Johor, the 1953 letter demonstrated the relinquishment of sovereignty over the island to Singapore. The Court also decided that the activities conducted by Singapore around the island could be interpreted as conduct of a *titre de souverain*. Though the decision is binding, Malaysia has signalled its intention to appeal.

see also: Goh Chok Tong; Mahathir Mohamad; *Parti Islam Se-Malaysia*; Singapore Strait.

Hua Hin Summit (ASEAN) February 2009 (Brunei/Cambodia/Indonesia/Laos/Malaysia/Myanmar/Philippines/Singapore/Thailand/Vietnam)

The fourteenth meeting of heads of government of **ASEAN** (Association of Southeast Asian Nations) convened in Cha-am and Hua Hin, Thailand, from 26 February to 1 March 2009. The meeting was initially scheduled to be held in December 2008, but was postponed due to a political crisis in Thailand. This gathering marked the first Summit under the new **ASEAN Charter**, which came into force on 15 December 2008. ASEAN leaders signed the Cha-am Hua Hin Declaration on the Roadmap for the ASEAN Community (2009–15) and adopted the ASEAN Political–Security Community (APSC) Blueprint. The APSC Blueprint emphasizes ASEAN's commitment to the promotion of good governance, democracy, protection and promotion of human rights, humanitarian assistance and development of confidence building measures. It further stresses the continued importance of the **Treaty of Amity and Cooperation** and the implementation of the **Declaration on the Conduct of Parties in the South China Sea**.

While the ASEAN summit was held successfully, the subsequent ASEAN Plus Three and East Asia summits hosted in the resort town of Pattaya in April were abruptly cancelled after protestors forced their way into the summit venue, demanding the resignation of Thai prime minister **Abhisit Vejjajiva**. Some of the ASEAN leaders at the meeting had to be evacuated from the site by helicopter, while the leaders of the Plus Three countries were obstructed from travelling to the summit venue. Abhisit declared a state of emergency in Chonburi Province where Pattaya is located, which was only lifted after all the ASEAN leaders and leaders of the dialogue partners had left Pattaya. The breach of security and subsequent cancellation of the meeting was an embarrassment for Abhisit's government, which was locked in a political tussle with supporters of the ousted former prime minister, **Thaksin Shinawatra**. The deeply divided country had seen four prime ministers sworn in in just over fifteen months, with none able to bridge the bitter divide between Thailand's military and business elite on the one hand, and the rural majority who formed the backbone of Thaksin's support on the other.

see also: Abhisit Vejjajiva; ASEAN; ASEAN Charter; Declaration on the Conduct of Parties in the South China Sea (ASEAN) 2002; Thaksin Shinawatra; Treaty of Amity and Cooperation.

Hua Hin Summit (ASEAN) October 2009 (Brunei/Cambodia/Indonesia/Laos/Malaysia/Myanmar/Philippines/Singapore/Thailand/Vietnam)

The fifteenth meeting of heads of government of **ASEAN** (Association of Southeast Asian Nations) convened in Cha-am and Hua Hin, Thailand, from 23 to 25 October 2009. In view of what transpired in February, security measures were put in place around the meeting venues to ensure that there was no repeat of the mayhem which had caused the abrupt cancellation of the previous ASEAN summit.

During this meeting, ASEAN leaders formally inaugurated the ASEAN Intergovernmental Commission on Human Rights as a new principal organ of ASEAN. They also endorsed the Terms of Reference that had been drafted by the High Level Panel on an ASEAN Human Rights Body and submitted to the ASEAN ministerial meeting in February 2009. Also on the agenda was the matter of how to enhance intra-regional connectivity that would facilitate and expedite the development of an **ASEAN Community** that was both competitive yet strongly linked to the rest of the world. To that end, the leaders agreed to a statement calling for the establishment of an ASEAN High Level Task Force (HLTF) to work out an ASEAN Master Plan on regional connectivity for submission at the seventeenth ASEAN summit. The summit also witnessed the accession of the United States to ASEAN's **Treaty of Amity and Cooperation**, which paved the way for Washington's participation in the **East Asia Summit**.

see also: ASEAN; ASEAN Community; East Asia Summit; Treaty of Amity and Cooperation.

***Hukbalahap* Movement** (Philippines)

Hukbalahap is a contraction of the Tagalog term *Hukbo ng Bayan laban sa Hapon*, which translates as People's Anti-Japanese Army. The *Huk* Movement, as it became known, had its origins in the establishment in March 1942 of an anti-Japanese resistance by a group of Communist and Socialist Union leaders, who had organized armed uprisings by tenant farmers in central and south Luzón during the 1930s. Consolidating their position during the Pacific War, they sought to engage in electoral politics after its conclusion, backing the Democratic Alliance in opposition to established parties which had collaborated with the Japanese. Despite notable success in central and southern Luzón the new congress elected in April 1946 refused to seat the Democratic Alliance candidates.

Frustrated in their attempt to act through the political process, the *Huk* Movement resorted to military action, confronting the private armies of landlords as well as government forces. Full-scale rebellion was signalled in February 1950 when the movement changed its name to *Hukbong Mapagpalaya ng Bayan* (People's Liberation Army) and called for the overthrow of the government in Manila. At their peak, the *Huks* claimed a following of 30,000 armed insurgents and were able to take temporary charge of the provincial capitals in Central Luzón, giving the impression of imminent revolutionary success.

The revolutionary challenge from the *Huks* was ended after **Ramón Magsaysay** was appointed secretary of national defence in August 1950. The capture of the entire Communist Politburo during raids in Manila in October was critical in this development. Magsaysay was able to revive the morale of a dispirited army with US backing as well as detaching peasant support from the insurgents through a skilful combination of personal public relations and governmental benefaction in the rural areas. Magsaysay, who went on to become president in 1953 with US assistance, conveyed a charismatic appeal which the urban intellectual leadership of the peasant insurgency could not match. By 1954 the *Huk* Movement had been crushed and reduced to a desultory banditry which remained until it was revived in a different form and with a different leadership from the late 1960s.

see also: Magsaysay, Ramón.

Hun Sen (Cambodia)

Hun Sen became prime minister of the Kingdom of Cambodia in October 1998 as head of a revamped coalition government dominated by his **Cambodian People's Party** (CPP), which had secured a plurality of seats in elections in the previous July. Hun Sen's assumption of high office reflected the effective balance of power in the country, which had been evident from July 1997 when he had mounted a violent coup displacing his senior partner in a coalition government established in October 1993.

Hun Sen was born on 4 April 1952 in Kompong Cham Province into a peasant family. He joined the **Khmer Rouge** in 1970 after Prince **Norodom Sihanouk** had been overthrown by a right-wing coup. With their seizure of power in April 1975, he rose in the military hierarchy of the country's eastern zone to become a deputy regimental commander but defected to Vietnam in 1977 as an internecine purge spread within the Cambodian revolutionary party. He became a member of the central committee of the Kampuchean National Front for National Salvation, which served as Vietnam's vehicle for invading Cambodia in December 1978. Hun Sen was made foreign minister of the **People's Republic of Kampuchea** on its establishment in January 1979 and deputy prime minister in June 1981. From an untutored base, Hun Sen demonstrated a growing aptitude for political organization but also became involved in factional rivalries with an older generation of party cadres. He was appointed prime minister in January 1985 but gave up his concurrent office of foreign minister between December 1986 and December 1987. He then resumed the additional foreign affairs portfolio to lead negotiations with Prince Norodom Sihanouk which paved the way to the **International Conference on Cambodia** in Paris in 1989 and then to an eventual settlement of the Cambodian conflict, also in Paris, in October 1991. In April 1989, the **People's Republic of Kampuchea** had been renamed the State of Cambodia with Hun Sen continuing as prime minister. Early in October 1991, the ruling **Kampuchean People's Revolutionary Party** was renamed the CPP and Hun Sen led its campaign in UN-supervised elections in May 1993. The party was bitterly disappointed at coming second in those elections to **FUNCINPEC** (the National United Front for an Independent, Neutral, Peaceful and Cooperative Cambodia) headed by Prince **Norodom Ranariddh**. A threat of force served to give the CPP a place in a coalition government in which Hun Sen became second prime minister to Prince Ranariddh. The political partnership was strained from the outset over the issue of power-sharing, while Hun Sen displayed great skill in marginalizing Prince Ranariddh and his allies as well as considerable ruthlessness in deploying intimidating violence against all opponents. On becoming sole prime minister in 1998, he also assumed the office of president of the Throne Council, which has the responsibility for authorizing monarchical succession.

An adroit politician, Hun Sen employed strategies of both co-option and coercion to consolidate power. To that end, he managed to divide and factionalize the royalist FUNCINPEC, resulting in the collapse of the royalist vote in 1998 which has been in decline since. At the same time, Hun Sen could also connect with ordinary citizens, a skill his political opponent **Sam Rainsy** could not match. He led the CPP to victory in the July 2003 general elections and was re-elected as prime minister by the National Assembly following the coalition government formed in mid-2004 by CPP and FUNCINPEC. He was re-elected in July 2008 following a landslide victory. The tide started to turn from then however, and by 2013 he saw his majority reduced significantly by a reinvigorated opposition that coalesced in the form of the **Cambodia National Rescue Party** which managed to win fifty-five seats on the back of widespread public discontent. This was followed by popular demonstrations calling for his resignation. Nevertheless, after twenty-eight years in power, Hun Sen remains the longest-serving elected leader in Southeast Asia and continues to demonstrate a keen sense of self-preservation, wielding unparalleled power in Cambodian politics.

see also: Cambodia National Rescue Party; Cambodian People's Party; FUNCINPEC; International Conference on Cambodia, Paris 1989; Kampuchea, People's Republic of; Kampuchean People's Revolutionary Party; Khmer Rouge; Ranariddh, Prince Norodom; Sam Rainsy; Sihanouk, King Norodom.

Hussein Onn, Tun (Malaysia)

Hussein Onn was Malaysia's third prime minister and held office from January 1976 until July 1981. He was a reluctant politician who was persuaded to return to public life by his brother-in-law, Tun **Abdul Razak**, whom he succeeded into high office following Razak's death from leukaemia. Hussein Onn was born on 12 February 1922, the son of a Johor state official. Trained as a soldier, he served in the Indian army during the Second World War. After the hostilities, he joined with his father, Dato Onn bin Ja'afar, then chief minister of Johor, in founding **UMNO** (United Malays National Organization) to challenge Britain's **Malayan Union Proposal**. When his father was rejected by UMNO for attempting to make it multiracial, Hussein Onn withdrew from active politics out of a sense of filial piety and took up the study and practice of law. He returned to public life after the **May 13 Racial Riots 1969**, when Malaysia had experienced unprecedented racial violence, and held ministerial office for only five years before becoming prime minister. His tenure was not marked by strong government or imaginative leadership. He was responsible for appointing Mahathir Mohamad as his deputy prime minister, which precipitated a period of intra-party strife. He gave up office in July 1981 because of ill health but regretted his successor's style of government and openly indicated his support for an alternative splinter party which challenged UMNO for the leadership of the Malay community. He died on 28 May 1990 at the age of sixty-eight, retaining intact his reputation as an honest politician.

see also: Mahathir Mohamad, Tun; Malayan Union Proposal 1946; May 13 Racial Riots 1969; Razak, Tun Abdul; UMNO.

I

Ieng Sary (Cambodia)

Ieng Sary was a deputy prime minister in the government of **Democratic Kampuchea** between 1975 and 1978. He had been a leading figure in the **Khmer Rouge** until the withdrawal of Chinese support after the **International Conference on Cambodia in Paris** in October 1991 led to his political demotion.

The early life of Ieng Sary is obscure, with his date of birth probably in the second half of the 1920s and his place of birth in Tra Vinh Province in southern Vietnam. He is believed to have befriended Saloth Sar, later **Pol Pot**, when they were both students at the Lycée Sisowath in Phnom Penh at the end of the war. Like Pol Pot, he secured a government scholarship to study in France, where he arrived in October 1950 and where formative social bonding and political commitment took place. His wife, Ieng Thirith, was the sister of Pol Pot's wife, Khieu Ponnary. On his return to Cambodia in the mid-1950s, Ieng Sary became a teacher and an active participant in clandestine revolutionary activity. In September 1960 he was present at a secret meeting of the Communist Party of Cambodia which set it on the road to revolutionary struggle and at which he was elected to its Central Committee. In May 1963, after his name had been included in a list of subversives announced by Prince **Norodom Sihanouk**, together with Pol Pot he left the capital for the forests of eastern Cambodia. His movements until 1971 are not well known but he is believed to have assumed responsibility for contacts with both Vietnamese and Chinese Communist parties. In August 1971 his presence was announced in Beijing, ostensibly as special envoy from the liberated area of Cambodia, but he acted as watchdog to Prince Norodom Sihanouk, who was then head of a government in exile. He accompanied Prince Sihanouk on visits abroad, in particular to the Non-Aligned Conference in Algeria and to the liberated area of Cambodia in 1973. Known as 'Brother Three' in the Khmer Rouge hierarchy, he held high office with responsibility for foreign affairs during the period of Khmer Rouge rule; in the negotiations with Thailand he demonstrated a clear preference for the finer qualities of life, including expensive cigars and brandy. He escaped from Phnom Penh by train to Thailand before the city was occupied by the Vietnamese in January 1979. He travelled on to Beijing and was subsequently for a time a member of the Democratic Kampuchean delegation at the United Nations, being confirmed as deputy prime minister in charge of foreign affairs for the government in exile at the end of 1979. After the formation of the tripartite **Coalition Government of Democratic Kampuchea** (CGDK) in June 1982, he gave up formal responsibility for foreign affairs to his Khmer Rouge colleague, **Khieu Samphan**. He ceased to hold any official position within the Khmer Rouge hierarchy but established a personal stronghold in the gem-rich Pailin district in Western Cambodia.

In August 1996, Ieng Sary defected to the government in Phnom Penh and was granted an amnesty by King Norodom Sihanouk in the following month from the death sentence passed on him *in absentia* in August 1979 for his complicity in mass murder. His defection, together with the forces under his command, marked the effective disintegration of the Khmer Rouge. He integrated those forces nominally into the Cambodian army in November 1996 and returned to Phnom Penh in November 1997 for a meeting with the second prime minister, **Hun Sen**, which was his first visit to the capital for nearly eighteen years. He continued to run Pailin like a private fiefdom generating a substantial income from gambling, prostitution and the sale of precious stones and hardwoods.

In November 2007, Ieng Sary was arrested in Phnom Penh following a warrant from the Cambodia Tribunal for war crimes and crimes against humanity. Upon his arrest, Ieng Sary refused to cooperate with the court, insisting that he had been pardoned by King Norodom Sihanouk. However, the UN tribunal ruled that the pardon did not override its indictment against him. His wife Ieng Thirith was also arrested alongside him for crimes against humanity, but was later judged mentally unfit to stand trial. On 16 December 2009, the tribunal officially charged Ieng Sary with genocide for his involvement in the activities of the Pol Pot regime. He was tried in 2011 alongside Nuon Chea, the Khmer Rouge's chief ideologist, and Khieu Samphan, an ex-head of state, by the Extraordinary Chambers in the Court of Cambodia (*see* **Khmer Rouge Trials**). Ieng Sary denied any wrongdoing and claimed that Pol Pot was the sole architect of the party's strategy and tactics. On 4 March 2013, Ieng Sary was removed from his holding cell for health reasons. On 14 March, he passed away at the age of eighty-seven in Phnom Penh, before his trial for involvement in the Khmer Rouge could be brought to a verdict. His son Ieng Vuth is the deputy governor of Pailin.

see also: Democratic Kampuchea; Democratic Kampuchea, Coalition Government of; Hun Sen; International Conference on Cambodia, Paris 1991; Khieu Samphan; Khmer Rouge; Khmer Rouge Trials; Pol Pot; Sihanouk, King Norodom.

Indochina Wars (Cambodia/Laos/Vietnam)

Three successive wars of international significance have afflicted the three states of Indochina, Cambodia, Laos and Vietnam, between 1946 and 1991.

The First Indochina War took place primarily between French forces seeking to restore colonial dominion and the insurgent Democratic Republic of Vietnam, which had been declared an independent state by the legendary Communist leader, **Ho Chi Minh**, on 2 September 1945 following the **August Revolution**. It was triggered by a dispute over control of customs in the port of Haiphong in November 1946 following the failure of a conference in Fontainebleau in the previous summer to resolve political differences. The escalating violence which spread to Laos and Cambodia became a major factor in the Cold War, with the formation in October 1949 of the People's Republic of China, seen by the United States as the aggressive ally of the Soviet Union. China provided military support for the fraternal Communist movement across a common border, while corresponding assistance for France came from the United States. The war culminated in France's defeat in May 1954 in the **Battle of Dien Bien Phu**, which destroyed the political will of the government in Paris. The Communist victory coincided with the opening of an international conference on Indochina, which resulted in the **Geneva Agreements on Indochina** (July 1954) to demarcate Vietnam provisionally along the line of the seventeenth parallel of latitude prior to countrywide elections two years later. The Communist Democratic Republic of Vietnam assumed power north of that line; the residual State of Vietnam to its south came under the control of an anti-Communist government headed by a returned exile, **Ngo Dinh Diem**, who enjoyed the support of the United States for his decision not to take part in countrywide elections.

Both Laos and Cambodia were accorded an intact independence under royal governments, although two Laotian provinces bordering Vietnam remained effectively under the control of the insurgent ***Pathet Lao*** which was, in effect, a branch of the Vietnamese Communist movement.

The Second Indochina War was very much a continuation of the first. At issue was the unity and political identity of a divided Vietnam, but again Laos and Cambodia were drawn into the fray. Although a northern-inspired insurgency had revived in the south from the late 1950s, the lines of conflict became clearly drawn from 20 December 1960 with the establishment of the **National Liberation Front of South Vietnam** (NLF) which was the irredentist vehicle of the northern Communist government. Cold War considerations dominated the conflict. The United States, committed to containing international Communism, became increasingly involved in military support of the government in Saigon from the mid to late 1960s until its forces were shouldering the main responsibility for the war. Aerial bombardment of the north and the deployment of half a million combat troops failed to break a military stalemate. The ability of the Vietnamese Communists to launch a series of coordinated attacks on urban centres at the end of January 1968 produced a devastating political impact within the United States. The historic **Tet Offensive** demonstrated to an American public sickened by continuing heavy casualties in the **Vietnam War** that a military solution was unlikely, which convinced President Lyndon Johnson of the need to enter into negotiations, which began formally in Paris in January 1969. By this juncture, Laos and Cambodia had become part of the theatre of war as the Vietnamese Communists used their territories to transship troops and supplies along the **Ho Chi Minh Trail** from the north to battlefields in the south. Johnson's successor, President Richard Nixon, began a process of military disengagement facilitated by a rapprochement with China. After the failure of a major offensive by the Communist forces across the seventeenth parallel of latitude in March 1972 in an abortive attempt to break the military stalemate, negotiations led to the **Paris Peace Agreements** in January 1973. The United States agreed to withdraw all of its forces in return for the repatriation of prisoners of war but without removing the Saigon government, which had been a longstanding demand of the National Liberation Front of South Vietnam (NLF). A weakened southern government resisted for just over two years until overwhelmed by a northern military attack, the Ban Me Thuot Offensive, launched in March 1975, which culminated in the seizure of Saigon at the end of April and the effective unification of the country under Communist rule. Formal unification as the Socialist Republic of Vietnam occurred in July 1976. A corresponding peace agreement for Laos, the **Vientiane Agreement on the Restoration of Peace and Reconciliation in Laos**, was concluded in February 1973. The military victory in Saigon at the end of April 1975, however, led to the political collapse of the ostensibly neutral government in Vientiane, with the Communist *Pathet Lao* removing the monarchy to establish the Laotian People's Democratic Republic at the end of the year. In Cambodia, the head of state, Prince **Norodom Sihanouk**, had been removed in a right-wing coup in March 1970 which received US support. A civil war followed in which Vietnamese military intervention to protect lines of communication served as the initial vanguard for the eventual victory in mid-April 1975 of the politically fundamentalist **Khmer Rouge** insurgents. Their state of so-called **Democratic Kampuchea**, headed by the notorious **Pol Pot**, rejected the concept of a special relationship with Vietnam and subsequently engaged it in armed confrontation, which provoked a full-scale war from the end of 1978.

The Third Indochina War began in December 1978 when Vietnamese forces invaded and occupied Cambodia. The conflict registered the radical revision of international alignments arising from Sino-Soviet antagonism and Sino-US rapprochement. Relations between former allies Vietnam and China had deteriorated, with the former resentful of the act of betrayal of the latter in coming to terms with their US adversary. For its part, China came to view Vietnam as the willing proxy for the interests of its Soviet antagonist, to which Vietnam had turned through a **Treaty of Friendship and Cooperation** in November 1978 for countervailing support. The paranoid Khmer Rouge regime had earlier aligned itself with China, which convinced the government in Hanoi that Vietnam was being trapped in a strategic vice from which it had to break free. Vietnam overwhelmed Khmer Rouge military resistance, driving their forces to the Thai border. A **People's Republic of Kampuchea** was established in January 1979 but failed to attract international recognition other than from the Soviet Union and its allies. Moreover, China launched a punitive military expedition into northern Vietnam in February 1979. Vietnam's stalwart military defence was not sufficient to diminish the political significance of China's action, which pointed up the permanent geopolitical relationship between the two neighbouring countries. Vietnam was then obliged to face an international alignment comprising China, the United States and the members of **ASEAN** (Association of Southeast Asian Nations) which together brought military, economic and diplomatic pressure to bear on Vietnam. The alignment was also responsible for mobilizing Cambodian military resistance to Vietnam's occupation and the government in Phnom Penh, making it possible in particular for the Khmer

Rouge to regenerate as a fighting machine. The failure to crush an externally supported Cambodian insurgency together with economic failure and the loss of Soviet patronage eventually obliged Vietnam to accept a United Nations political settlement endorsed at the **International Conference on Cambodia, Paris 1991** (October). It had withdrawn its main force units from Cambodia by September 1989 and had left the government implanted there to fend for itself in part through a reversion in nomenclature to the State of Cambodia. Vietnam's military intervention in Cambodia was of major international significance in the context of the so-called Second Cold War, which reached its peak with the Soviet invasion of Afghanistan. The settlement of the Cambodian conflict as an international problem was a direct consequence of the end of the Cold War, which required Vietnam to come to terms with China in the absence of access to any credible source of external countervailing power. Within Cambodia, the United Nations was able to conduct countrywide elections which produced a coalition government in October 1993.

see also: ASEAN; August Revolution 1945; Democratic Kampuchea; Diem, Ngo Dinh; Dien Bien Phu, Battle of, 1954; Geneva Agreements on Indochina 1954; Geneva Agreements on Laos 1962; Ho Chi Minh; Ho Chi Minh Trail; International Conferences on Cambodia, New York 1981, Paris 1989, 1991; Kampuchea, People's Republic of; Khmer Rouge; National Liberation Front of South Vietnam; Paris Peace Agreements 1973; *Pathet Lao*; Pol Pot; Sihanouk, King Norodom; Tet Offensive 1968; Treaty of Friendship and Cooperation 1978; Vientiane Agreement on the Restoration of Peace and Reconciliation in Laos 1973; Vietnam War.

Insurgencies, Myanmar (Myanmar)

Civil war, both ethnically based and ideological, afflicted Myanmar (Burma) soon after independence in January 1948 and remains an important issue in Myanmar politics. On 31 January 1949, the **Karen** under the Karen National Union (KNU) rebelled against the government of Prime Minister **U Nu** and were soon joined by Karen soldiers, who mutinied *en masse*, and a number of other ethnic armed political organizations representing Mon, **Kachin**, Karenni and Pa-O minorities. U Nu was already fighting a civil war against demobilized members of the Burma Independence Army (BIA) known as the People's Volunteer Organization (PVO) and armed elements of the Burmese Communist Party (BCP) in central Burma, as well as the 'Red Flag' faction of the BCP, Rakhine nationalists and Muslim **Rohingya** in the west. Three battalions of the Burmese army also mutinied and joined the insurgency. The ethnic insurgencies were fuelled in part by disaffection due to harsh retaliation against their communities by largely Burman military formations for their assistance to the Allies during the Pacific War and fears of fair treatment in an independent Burma. By 1950 the Karen, occasionally in cooperation with the BCP and PVO, had seized most of lower Burma and had very nearly taken Yangon (Rangoon). Although the Karen were pushed back, that they had almost seized the capital made sure counter-insurgency remained at the forefront of policy during the U Nu years and later under military rule.

U Nu's government, however, was able to secure foreign assistance, which allowed for the reorganization and expansion of the army under the ambitious general **Ne Win** to deal with the myriad threats. The insurgents were hampered by their diverse causes and ideologies, and the personalities of some of their leaders made it difficult to organize a common front. Several attempts were made, but each alliance proved temporary. The reformed Burmese army under General Ne Win's direction began to slowly push the insurgents back from Yangon and other major population centres throughout the 1950s into areas along the northern and eastern borders. The chronic lack of unity even within insurgent groups became apparent when in 1958 several groups split with some returning to the legal fold while others continued to resist.

Other forces, however, were causing discontent among ethnic groups that had hitherto remained loyal to the government, particularly in the northern **Shan** States which had largely remained under the authority of local leaders, or *sawbwa*, following independence. An invasion out of southern China by the Kuomintang (KMT) in 1950 retreating from the victorious Communist People's Liberation Army forced the army to enter the Shan States, declare martial law and place Shan leaders under military administration. In 1958–9, the traditional *sawbwa* handed their formal power over to the government, giving the central government much more sway in the region. Dissatisfaction with expanding central rule, in contradiction, some saw, to the spirit of the 1947 **Panglong Agreement**, together with discontent over the army's behaviour in Shan State prompted Shan politicians to agitate for a new formally federal system of government. In 1961, a combined operation by the Burmese military and units of the Chinese People's Liberation Army forced the KMT out of Shan State and into Thailand where they set up enclaves along the border.

The largely Christian Kachin were also becoming increasingly uncomfortable with U Nu's attempts in 1960–1 to have Buddhism declared the state religion. A June 1961 majority vote by delegates from several ethnic groups for federalism sparked resistance from Burman political parties, especially the ruling **Anti-Fascist People's Freedom League** (AFPFL), but U Nu announced it would be considered if proposed democratically and agreed to formally discuss a new federal constitution with Shan leaders. This became the declared reason for the military coup of 2 March 1962 that installed Ne Win as leader of the country and eventually installed the **Burma Socialist Programme Party** (BSPP). Since then, prevention of the breakup of the Union became paramount in military thought.

During the 1960s numerous new ethnic insurgencies broke out across the country, particularly in the north. The Kachin, already upset by U Nu's attempts to have Buddhism declared the state religion, became alarmed at Ne Win's rejection of their right to secede, and rose up under the leadership of the Kachin Independence Organization (KIO). The Shan too rebelled and formed several different insurgent organizations that fought each other almost as much as the Burmese Army, many of which also became involved in the opium and heroin trade in Burma–Laos–Thai tri-border region that became known as the Golden Triangle. The narcotics trade would become a highly lucrative business through which groups could buy weapons and supplies to fight, but it also amplified corruption in ethnic political organizations as well as the government. Many of the local militias set up by the government in Shan State in the 1960s to fight the insurgents were allowed to trade in opium, with several, most notably Khun Sa and Lo Hsing Han, turning on the regime and forming their own ostensibly nationalist organizations that concentrated more on the opium business than fighting the government.

During the 1960s China began to provide covert aid to Burma's Communist movement, especially after 1966 and the Cultural Revolution in China. The BCP was suffering at the time from leadership disputes which resulted in a major purge of pro-Soviet members. At the same time that the BCP seemed to be imploding, the Burmese army launched a new offensive against the group's base areas in central Myanmar using a new doctrine – 'The Four Cuts' – to cut off supplies, funds, intelligence and recruits needed by the insurgents. Following the defeat of the BCP in central Burma this strategy would be used to evict the KNU from the Irrawaddy Delta region and would remain a core counterinsurgency doctrine for Myanmar's military to the present day.

While the BCP was imploding inside the country, China's stepped-up support for the BCP leaders in southwest China in the 1960s led to the organization's reorganization which culminated in an 'invasion' of Burma by the BCP's new army on New Year's Day 1968. Equipped with new Chinese weapons and advised by a number of Chinese Red Guard volunteers, the BCP's sizeable military managed to seize an area in Myanmar's northern Shan State that it would largely maintain until 1989, when ethnic tensions within the BCP exploded in a mutiny that would split the organization into three different insurgent organizations along ethnic lines, the largest of which would become the United Wa State Army (UWSA).

In eastern Myanmar, a loose stalemate existed throughout much of the 1970s and into the early 1980s. Fighting settled down to a seasonal affair with campaigns in the dry season followed by relative calm during the rainy season. The Karen and Mon were funding their insurgencies through the taxation of the large black market trade between Thailand and Myanmar that flourished because of the BSPP's isolationist policies. An ethnic alliance was finally achieved in 1976 with the establishment of the National Democratic Front (NDF) under the leadership of KNU chairman Saw Bo Mya and based at KNU headquarters at Manerplaw near the Thai border. Under Bo Mya, the KNU, and to an extent the thirteen-member NDF would become anti-Communist in outlook, although an alliance was eventually agreed with the BCP in the mid-1980s. The NDF, however, lacked outside support and there was little cooperation militarily, but the alliance did result in the abandonment of demands for independence in favour of a federal union as a common goal. In 1984, the Burmese army paid renewed attention to the war in eastern Burma, launching several successful offensives against the KNU's tax gates and cutting much of its financial support. At the same time attitudes in Thailand began to change from seeing the insurgencies as a useful buffer against a traditional enemy, to a desire for increased economic interaction that became **Chatichai Choonhavan**'s 1991 **Constructive Engagement** policy. This resulted in dwindling support for the KNU and other ethnic insurgencies on the kingdom's western border and a further loss of revenue and logistic support. During the 1988 demonstrations the ethnic groups surprisingly failed to seize the initiative allowing the army to reinforce units in population centres that would later put down the uprisings. Following the crackdown, tens of thousands of Burmese fled to the border areas, especially to the area under the KNU where some were supplied with weapons and given military training, coalescing into the All Burma Students Democratic Front (ABSDF). Although their numbers would dwindle in ensuing years, the ABSDF continues to operate in eastern Myanmar. From 1988 to 1994, Manerplaw became the headquarters of not only the KNU and the NDF, but also much of the pro-democracy political opposition.

Facing not only ethnic insurgencies but also an internationally supported democracy movement by 1989, the regime sought to buttress its strength. In 1989–90, General **Khin Nyunt** went to northeastern Myanmar to negotiate with the new groups formed following the collapse of the BCP. He was able to negotiate ceasefire agreements with former BCP groups by offering business concessions while holding out the promise of a political solution some time in the future after a new constitution was implemented. In the same way a ceasefire was agreed with the powerful KIO in 1994. Disaffection between Karen Buddhist rank and file and their largely Christian leadership was exploited by Khin Nyunt's intelligence apparatus, resulting in a mutiny in the KNU's armed wing and the formation of the Democratic Karen Buddhist Army (DKBA). With their new allies in the DKBA, the Myanmar army forced the KNU to abandon Manerplaw in January 1995, a move that also dispersed the NDF and the democratic political forces based there. In January 1996, the **State Law and Order Restoration Council** (SLORC) were also able to convince Khun Sa to surrender his forces in Shan State, though several more nationalist-inclined officers split off to continue the fight as the Shan State Army. In 2009, as the country gravitated towards political openness, the **State Peace and Development Council** (SPDC) demanded that all ceasefire groups convert their armed wings into Border Guard Forces (BGF) as a component of the Myanmar army; their political wings would be allowed to form political parties. Ethnic leaders opposed the idea, believing that without their weapons they would have no leverage over the regime. While several smaller groups were compelled to join the BGF, the only sizeable group to join was the DKBA. This led to rising tensions between the central government and ceasefire groups, most of whom were based along the border with China. One group, the Myanmar National Democratic Alliance Army of ethnic Kokang along the China border, was eliminated through a rapid offensive in 2009 that not only reinforced the government's demands, but also resulted in increased tensions with China over a possible renewed civil war. The UWSA and its allies, however, steadfastly refused to join the scheme.

Still the KNU fought on, waging a guerrilla war that continued until a peace process was begun with the democratically elected government in 2012. The Shan State Army also entered into peace negotiations with the government in 2012, although one other Shan group, the Shan State Army (North) continues to resist by means of arms. The UWSA and other former BCP groups continued to refuse to join the BGF after the elections, but have agreed to work together with the new government to resolve differences. The government of President **Thein Sein** has made overtures to most of the other insurgent groups and former ceasefire organizations, and peace processes are ongoing with most of them. The major exception is the KIO, which after an increase in tensions over development projects and the political future of Kachin State, took up arms again in June 2011.

see also: Anti-Fascist People's Freedom League; Burma Socialist Programme Party; Chatichai Choonhavan, General; Constructive Engagement; Kachin; Karen; Khin Nyunt, General; Ne Win, General; Panglong Agreement; Rohingya; Shan; State Law and Order Restoration Council; State Peace and Development Council; Thein Sein; U Nu.

Insurgency, Southern Provinces (Thailand)

Thailand's southernmost region has experienced continual violence of varied intensity since the 1960s. Most of the violence has been the result of political alienation and a feeling among local Malay-Muslims of persecution by the majority Thai Buddhist government. The three southernmost provinces of Yala, Pattani and Narathiwat together with four bordering districts of Songkhla province have Malay-Muslim majority populations. Muslims constitute four to eight per cent of Thailand's population of around fifty-six million. More than half of their number live in the four southern provinces of Pattani, Narathiwat, Satun and Yala where their ancestors had been converted to Islam from the end of the twelfth century before coming under Thai domination from the early seventeenth century. That domination had extended to the four northern provinces of present-day peninsular Malaysia which were incorporated within the British colonial domain in a treaty of 1909. The Muslims of southern Thailand were therefore separated from their coreligionists by a political boundary not of their own making.

Muslim political alienation in Thailand dates from the late 1930s. A policy of Buddhist cultural assimilation pursued from Bangkok by the government of **Phibul Songkram** generated a flow of refugees into Malaya. Ironically, the four northern provinces of the Malay Peninsula were reincorporated into Thailand by Japan for the duration of the Pacific War. Muslim separatist sentiment was stirred after the war by the success of Malay nationalism to the south. Muslim organizations to promote separatism were set up both in southern Thailand and northern Malaya. A revolt of a kind was launched in southern Thailand in 1948 but it was effectively crushed, especially given Anglo-Thai cooperation prompted by the insurgency waged by the Communist Party of Malaya. Muslim cultural alienation was sustained as a result of both administrative heavy-handedness and neglect, especially in lack of provision of economic opportunity. Throughout the 1970s and into the 1980s the preeminent militant organization was the **Patani United Liberation Organization** (PULO). Established in 1968, its formation represented the frustration of a younger generation of Thai Muslims. International support for PULO took the form of Syrian and Libyan sympathies in the United Nations as well as informal representation before the Organization of the Islamic Conference. Popular support within Thailand for PULO and allied organizations has tended to vary with the administrative competence of local military commanders in the south but has never posed a major challenge to the authority of the government in Bangkok. While PULO claimed responsibility for sporadic attacks in the 1990s, including the bombing of a railway station in the southern town of Hat Yai in 1992, a string of arson attacks on schools in the south in 1993, and the bombing of a bridge between Hat Yai and Chana railway stations in 1994, the government's amnesty policy significantly eroded its support base during this period. The emergence of opportunities for Muslim political representation in the form of the *Santiparb* (Peace) Party and the Wadah faction of the ***Thai Rak Thai* Party** further undermined the credibility of PULO.

In the early 2000s there were indications that the accommodation reached with Muslim elites was fraying and the violence that had been largely reduced to manageable levels of banditry was growing and becoming more sophisticated. Still, Thailand was unprepared for the January 2004 attack on an army camp and theft of weapons that signalled the insurgency had been rekindled. Instead of the largely secular PULO, the new insurgents employed religious rhetoric. It remains a largely secretive movement with no readily identifiable senior leadership, nor any specific demands. Indications are that the PULO has taken a far less prominent role, with some suggesting it has given way to the *Barisan Revolusi Nasional-Coordinate* (BRN-C, *see* ***Barisan Revolusi Nasional***), an organization that had only a small presence during the 1970s and 1980s. Solutions to the violence remain elusive as negotiations between the government and the insurgents are hampered by unclear lines of responsibility on the insurgent side, as well as conflicting intentions of the civil and military parts of the Thai government. This was exacerbated following the 2006 coup when the military took on a much more prominent, but less conciliatory role in the negotiations. Early missteps by the government of **Thaksin Shinawatra** were reversed somewhat by an influx of troops, and large-scale cordon and search operations by the Thai army in 2008 reduced the number of violent incidents. The insurgents, however, have adapted and the number of incidents as well as their lethality began to climb again in 2010 as conciliatory gestures have been met with studied hostility. Overall, the latest wave of insurgency has seen much more serious levels of violence and far wider support from the populace than earlier periods of unrest. While several attempts have been made at initiating dialogue towards a resolution of the conflict, including a process facilitated by the Malaysian government, these have been hampered by the questionable authority of insurgent 'representatives' and the doubtful commitment of the Thai security officials involved in these processes, not to mention the lack of coordination among the Thai government agencies involved.

see also: *Barisan Revolusi Nasional*; Patani United Liberation Organization; Phibul Songkram, Field Marshal; *Thai Rak Thai* Party; Thaksin Shinawatra.

International Conference on Cambodia, New York 1981

(Cambodia)

In July 1981 an international conference on Kampuchea (as Cambodia was then known) convened in New York under the auspices of the secretary-general of the United Nations. The meeting was a diplomatic success of a kind for **ASEAN** (Association of Southeast Asian Nations), which had pressed for it from 1979 in the wake of Vietnam's invasion of Cambodia (*see* **Indochina Wars**). That success was one of form rather than of substance, however, because of the absence in particular of representation from Vietnam and the Soviet Union. Their governments had objected to the ousted **Khmer Rouge** regime occupying the Cambodian seat in the world organization in place of the incumbent administration in Phnom Penh. The conference convened, therefore, as a group of states opposed to Vietnam's position rather than as a forum for negotiations. Moreover, its sessions exposed major differences of interest between ASEAN and the People's Republic of China over terms for a political settlement. An ASEAN proposal for an interim administration before elections to be conducted under United Nations supervision foundered on the rock of Chinese opposition with tacit US support. In the event, the conference reiterated bland General Assembly resolutions, while a semblance of institutional continuity was maintained through the mediatory role of its Austrian chairman but without any tangible result. A decade would have to pass together with a change in strategic context before the Cambodian conflict became susceptible to solution through an international conference. Ironically, the formula adopted for a political settlement at the **International Conference on Cambodia** in Paris in October

1991 was much the same as that rejected in New York in July 1981.

see also: ASEAN; Indochina Wars; International Conferences on Cambodia, Paris 1989, 1991; Khmer Rouge.

International Conference on Cambodia, Paris 1989 (Cambodia)

At French initiative, a second international conference on Cambodia convened in Paris at the end of July 1989 with Indonesia as co-chairman. Unlike the **International Conference on Cambodia** held in New York in July 1981, it was attended by all the internal and external parties to the conflict as well as the foreign ministers of all permanent members of the United Nations Security Council and a representative of the secretary-general. The conference had been preceded by a series of abortive negotiations among Cambodian and regional parties in the previous year. The incentive for organizing a meeting in Paris had been the announcement in April 1989 by the governments of Hanoi, Vientiane and Phnom Penh that all Vietnamese troops would be withdrawn from Cambodia by the end of September that year, irrespective of a political solution. The conference devolved into four working committees. The first was charged with drawing up ceasefire terms and defining the mandate of an international control mechanism or institution to oversee a settlement. The second was required to construct a system of guarantees for the neutrality and independence of Cambodia. The third was set the task of working out arrangements for repatriating refugees from the Thai border. Finally, an *ad hoc* committee consisting of France, Indonesia and the four Cambodian factions was established to address the internal aspects of the conflict, including provision for power-sharing prior to internationally supervised elections, which would mark the final stage of political settlement. The four committees concluded their deliberations on 28 August without constructive outcome and the conference suspended its deliberations in the absence of the foreign ministers of the permanent members of the United Nations Security Council (with the exception of France). Several problems obstructed a successful outcome, including the role of the United Nations in supervision and control of the process of settlement. Primarily at issue, however, was the failure of the Cambodian parties and their external patrons to reach an accord on the status and composition of an interim administration for the period between a political accord and the outcome of general elections to decide the future of the country. The incumbent administration in Phnom Penh refused to be dismantled and to tolerate the **Khmer Rouge** as a legitimate party to a settlement. The failure in August 1989 indicated that those changes in international relations marking the end of the Cold War had not had sufficient regional effect to enable the Cambodian conflict to be resolved.

see also: Indochina Wars; International Conferences on Cambodia, New York 1981, Paris 1991; Khmer Rouge.

International Conference on Cambodia, Paris 1991 (Cambodia)

The International Conference on Cambodia in Paris, which had suspended its deliberations in August 1989, reconvened in Paris on 21 October 1991 and two days later approved a comprehensive political settlement which was signed by nineteen governments as well as by four Cambodian factions. The Final Act of the conference comprised three documents:

1 An Agreement on a Comprehensive Political Settlement of the Cambodia Conflict together with five annexes dealing with (a) the mandate of **UNTAC** (United Nations Transitional Authority in Cambodia); (b) withdrawal, ceasefire and related measures; (c) elections; (d) repatriation of Cambodian refugees and displaced persons; and (e) principles for a new constitution for Cambodia.
2 An Agreement concerning the sovereignty, independence, territorial integrity, and inviolability, neutrality and national unity of Cambodia.
3 A Declaration on rehabilitation and reconstruction of Cambodia.

The road back to Paris following the abortive conference in 1989 had been pioneered through an initiative by US Congressman Stephen Solarz to overcome the persisting obstacle of power-sharing through having the United Nations assume the transitional administration of Cambodia before the outcome of general elections. The government of Australia took up this proposal and commissioned a feasibility study of the peacekeeping exercise. The plan then attracted the serious attention of the permanent members of the United Nations Security Council whose officials drafted a framework agreement which was adopted at the end of August 1990. The persisting deadlock over power-sharing was addressed through the vehicle of a **Supreme National Council** on which all Cambodian factions would be represented. The Council, envisaged as a symbol and repository of Cambodian sovereignty rather than as a government, would authorize a ring-holding role for the United Nations. Executive powers would be delegated to UNTAC comprising civilian and military components with responsibility for supervising key ministries and conducting elections in a secure and neutral environment. In the event, this framework agreement provided the basis for the accord reached in October 1991.

The course of preliminary negotiations was chequered. **Khmer Rouge** participation in a political settlement was accepted at the first meeting of the Supreme National Council in Indonesia in September 1990. However, serious disagreement persisted over the role of UNTAC, the status of the incumbent government in Phnom Penh, provision for demobilization and disarmament of contending Cambodian forces, and the chair of the Council. A political breakthrough occurred at the end of June 1991 as a direct consequence of an improvement in relations between the People's Republic of China and Vietnam whose antagonism had been at the heart of the Cambodian conflict from the outset. In effect, an enfeebled and vulnerable Vietnam had been obliged to defer to Chinese priorities in Indochina and withdrew its longstanding patronage of the government which it had imposed by its force of arms in January 1979. As a result of an initiative by Prince **Norodom Sihanouk**, sanctioned by China, the process of negotiations was accelerated. Within less than four months, outstanding issues such as a ceasefire, demobilization and disarmament of contending forces were resolved, making possible the final accord in Paris. Although the incumbent government in Phnom Penh was not dismantled in advance of general elections, a power-sharing arrangement of a kind was worked out in cooperation between the Supreme National Council chaired by Prince Sihanouk and the United Nations preliminary to general elections scheduled for early 1993. At the time, the peacekeeping operation was the most ambitious and difficult undertaken since the UN's formation in 1945. It ran into major difficulty from June 1992, when the Khmer Rouge refused to cooperate in the critical second phase which required the warring factions to regroup their forces into cantonments for disarmament. Elections were conducted, nonetheless, in May 1993 without notable disruption and were endorsed by the United Nations Security Council as free and fair. A new constitution was ratified on 21 September which ended, in effect, the UN mandate as recommended by the Paris conference.

see also: Indochina Wars; International Conferences on Cambodia, New York 1981, Paris 1989; Khmer Rouge; Sihanouk, King Norodom; Supreme National Council; United Nations: Cambodia 1991–3; UNTAC.

Irian Jaya (Indonesia)

Irian Jaya is the Indonesian name for the western half of the island of New Guinea. This mountainous territory with a population of less than two million became an object of contention between Indonesia and the Netherlands for more than a decade after the republic attained independence in 1949. Indonesia's administration has been in place since May 1963 but has been resisted by a local insurgency known as the **Free Papua Movement** or OPM (*Organisasi Papua Merdeka*). Although of limited military significance, it has attracted sympathy and support from fellow Melanesians in neighbouring Papua New Guinea.

At the time of Indonesia's proclamation of independence, the western half of New Guinea was part of the Netherlands East Indies. During negotiations at The Hague in 1949 over the transfer of sovereignty, the Dutch insisted on retaining control of the territory, subject to further talks within a year. These talks proved to be inconclusive and the dispute which followed strained the post-colonial relationship. President **Sukarno** took the major initiative in prosecuting the nationalist claim through a practice of coercive diplomacy self-styled as Confrontation. The dispute was resolved eventually through US diplomatic intervention from a concern that further denial of Indonesia's claim would provoke its adherence to the Communist camp. An agreement between Indonesia and the Netherlands was concluded on 15 August 1962. It provided for an initial transfer of administration to United Nations authority from 1 October 1962 and then an ultimate transfer to Indonesia from 1 May 1963. In addition, it was stipulated that an 'act of free choice' with United Nations advice, assistance and participation would take place before the end of 1969 in order to determine whether or not the inhabitants wished to remain subject to Indonesian jurisdiction. That exercise took place in July and August 1969 but was conspicuously a form of political stage management.

Nonetheless, the United Nations endorsed the transfer of the territory, which was incorporated into the Republic as its twenty-sixth province on 17 September 1968. Indonesia's jurisdiction has not been matched by popular acceptance. Indigenous resentment of its rule has been aggravated by Jakarta's policy of transmigration whereby around 200,000 settlers, primarily from overcrowded Java, have been dispatched to the province, while the local population has felt discriminated against in employment opportunities. Moreover, human rights abuses by the armed forces have also alienated the indigenous people. Organized resistance has been mounted by the OPM but with limited effect. The momentum of separatism revived with the political downfall of President **Suharto** in May 1998. Demonstrations in favour of independence were mounted in Jakarta as well as within Irian Jaya where violent clashes with security forces occurred. Developments in East Timor, where a referendum offering a choice between autonomy and independence was held in August 1999, encouraged demands for comparable treatment. In December 1999, over 10,000 pro-independence supporters demonstrated in the central square of the province's capital Jayapura, where they raised the separatist Morning Star flag. Such protests have not brought any substantive concessions from the government in Jakarta concerned to uphold the integrity of Indonesia, after East Timor, as well as to retain control of Irian Jaya's rich natural resources. During a visit to the province in January 2000, President **Abdurrahman Wahid** was only prepared to offer autonomous status and a change in the name of the province to West Papua. He reiterated that position at a meeting in Jakarta with members of a delegation from the province in May 2000. In June 2000, a people's congress in Jayapura resolved that West Papua was sovereign and independent but without formally declaring independence. On 1 January 2002, the government of **Megawati Sukarnoputri** allocated a set of unprecedented autonomy measures to Irian Jaya. Its name was changed to Papua, and the provincial flag was allowed to fly alongside, but lower than, the Indonesian national flag. A key concession according to Jakarta was that the Papuan provincial government would be allowed to retain seventy per cent of revenue from oil and gas production and eighty per cent from other mineral and forestry activity which is worth hundreds of millions of dollars annually. However, while there would be greater autonomy at multiple levels, defence, foreign affairs, finance, internal and judicial affairs would remain in Jakarta's jurisdiction. This gesture was rejected by the Papuan Presidium Council (PDP) and the OPM on grounds that it did not deal with issues of human rights violations and Papuans were not consulted. The day after, PDP leader Theys Eluay was found dead. Indonesian soldiers were eventually tried and convicted of his murder though it was unclear who issued the instructions.

In February 2003, the province was split into two. The Indonesian government declared the westernmost part of the island to be a separate province and named it West Irian Jaya (*Irian Jaya Barat*) whilst the rest of the province retained the name Irian Jaya. However, in November 2004, the Indonesian judiciary came to a consensus that the split violated Papua's autonomy and declared the move unconstitutional. In April 2007 Irian Jaya was renamed Papua and West Irian Jaya came to be known as West Papua. The change in name was both a symbolic and a political move by the Indonesian government, which had always preferred the name Irian. In September 2007 representatives from Papua's indigenous political organizations, including the OPM, established an umbrella body known as the West Papua National Coalition for Liberation (WPNCL) to pressure Jakarta to renegotiate the terms of the 2001 special autonomy provisions. In October 2011 the vice-president's office established the Unit to Accelerate Development in Papua and West Papua, to focus on economic development. The committee includes members who were previously involved in the peace talks over Aceh.

Papua continues to suffer not just political marginalization but also economic hardship. In October 2011, 8,000 workers at a copper and gold mine owned by US company Freeport-McMoran in the eastern province of Papua went on a three-month strike for better salaries. Papuans have also been victims of Indonesian police and military brutality. The military closely monitors activists and politicians, and any form of dissidence has never been tolerated. In 2010 the military was forced to admit that men caught on video torturing Papuan villagers were members of its special forces. In October 2011 security forces clamped down on a Papuan Congress meeting, resulting in the arrest of more than 300 Papuans. At the end of the violent crackdown three men were killed and more than ninety were injured, while some Papuan leaders were charged with treason.

see also: Free Papua Movement; Megawati Sukarnoputri; Suharto; Sukarno; United Nations: Irian Jaya 1962–9; Wahid, Abdurrahman.

Iskandar Development Region (Malaysia/Singapore)

The Iskandar Development Region or IDR (also known as Iskandar Development Zone and Iskandar Malaysia) is Malaysia's largest growth corridor and measures 2,217 square kilometres. It is located in the southern Malaysian state of Johor. Mooted in 2005 and launched in 2006, the idea behind the project was to turn the area into a southern development region, contributing to the goal of raising the per capita income in Malaysia to US$15,000 by the year 2020. Named after the late Sultan of Johor, Sultan Iskandar, the region also houses Johor's new administrative capital in Nusajaya. Aside from Nusajaya, other flagship zones are Johor Bahru City which forms the central business district as well as the state capital of Johor, Western Gate Development which focuses on logistics, production and manufacturing, Eastern Gate Development which emphasizes heavy industries and logistics, and Senai-Skudai where the airport is located. The region is also home to several international schools, as well as medical facilities, theme parks and residences. As of 2012, the government of Malaysia had invested M$6.3 billion into IDR. IDR has also drawn significant foreign direct investment into the country, particularly from Singapore which borders it, and this is seen as a major avenue through which sound bilateral relations between Malaysia and Singapore have been sustained through business and investment synergies and mutual economic interests.

Islam (Brunei/Cambodia/Indonesia/Malaysia/Myanmar/Philippines/Singapore/Thailand)

The Islamic faith requires complete submission to the will and obedience to the law of a single god. Its adherents believe that the precepts of their faith were revealed in the seventh century AD to his messenger, the Prophet Muhammad, who incorporated them into the *Qur'an* to provide a comprehensive and superior way of life. Islam did not take root within Southeast Asia until around the beginning of the fourteenth century, when port cities began to adopt the *Sunni* faith of Arab and Indian maritime traders. This conversion extended northwards through the Malay Peninsula into southern Thailand and south and east through the northern coasts of the Indonesian archipelago and then northwards from Borneo to the island of Luzón in the

Philippines. In the case of Myanmar, Islam spread to the Arakan region overland from India.

Islam became identified with state power in Southeast Asia from the fifteenth century shortly after the foundation of the trading empire of Malacca based on the west coast of the Malay Peninsula. But after the fall of Malacca to the Portuguese in the early sixteenth century, its adherents dispersed to other parts of the Indonesian archipelago where their faith became most deeply accepted among coastal trading communities. In Java, Islam was later adopted by local princes to underpin their mystical power but primarily as a cultural veneer on entrenched animist and Hindu–Buddhist beliefs whose syncretic legacy is to be found in eastern and central parts of the island. The Islamic faith was also employed to mobilize opposition to Dutch colonial control.

Within Southeast Asia, the most significant Islamic communities are to be found in Indonesia, Malaysia and Brunei.

In *Indonesia*, Muslims number around eighty-seven per cent of a population of some 260 million but do not constitute a homogeneous community. A division between devout (***Santri***) and nominal (***Abangan***) adherents of the faith is a consequence of the uneven pattern of conversion. Islam played an important part in the rise of nationalism against the Dutch but attempts to promote an Islamic state were denied before the proclamation of independence in August 1945. The authorized state philosophy ***Pancasila*** enjoins all Indonesians to believe in a single deity but accords them the right to believe in any god of their own choosing. It was conceived in June 1945 by President **Sukarno** to prevent the political pretensions of Islam from provoking civil strife and was accorded an even greater political sanctity by President **Suharto**. From independence, Islam was not accorded a special status but has been one of several recognized faiths under the auspices of the ministry of religious affairs. After independence, the government of Jakarta faced insurgent challenge from the ***Darul Islam*** movement based primarily in northern Sumatra and western Java. The movement appeared to have been quelled by the 1960s, yet its factions have managed to resurface over the years in various guises, including as clandestine militant organizations such as ***Jemaah Islamiyah***. Under the rule of President Suharto, a policy of draining Islam of political content was pursued, especially after its global resurgence had been highlighted by the revolution in Iran. All Muslim political parties were grouped within one umbrella organization, the ***Partai Persatuan Pembangunan*** (United Development Party, PPP), which has been obliged to acknowledge *Pancasila* as its sole ideology. Personal devotion to Islam has increased, however, in response to the materialism unleashed by successful economic development. President Suharto encouraged the formation of the Association of Indonesian Muslim Intellectuals or ICMI as an instrument to counter the influence of the armed forces and to generate greater support for his retention of high office. Under the leadership of **B. J. Habibie**, ICMI served as the political vehicle of modern Islam with a nationalist economic agenda. Islam took on a more conspicuous, albeit diverse, political expression after Habibie, as vice-president, succeeded Suharto in May 1998. In the event, a so-called central axis of Muslim-based parties collaborated to deny the presidency to **Megawati Sukarnoputri**, regarded as a representative of Christian and secular forces. The beneficiary of this manoeuvre was **Abdurrahman Wahid**, the leader of the Muslim-based ***Partai Kebangkitan Bangsa*** (National Awakening Party, PKB) and also of the ***Nahdlatul Ulama***, whose commitment to religious pluralism and opposition to an Islamic state made him the natural political partner of Megawati, who became vice-president. He has sought to keep political Islam to the margins of public life. However, sectarian violence between Muslims and Christians caused considerable loss of life and devastation in the Moluccan Islands and also in Sulawesi and Lombok. In Aceh, in north Sumatra, an independence movement driven by Islamic priorities has long been engaged in insurgency but concluded a ceasefire with the government in Jakarta in May 2000.

The 2004 general election saw the participation of several political parties that rallied around the banner of Islam. These included the ***Partai Bulan Bintang*** (Crescent Star Party, PBB), which won 2.6 per cent of the vote, and ***Partai Keadilan Sejahtera*** (Prosperous Justice Party, PKS), which won a commendable 7.3 per cent. Collectively, Muslim-based parties captured about thirty per cent of the overall vote. By 2009 however, the support for Muslim parties plummeted, with only PKS registering a small increase in its vote share to 7.9 per cent. Heavy losses suffered by the other Islamic parties illustrated the fact that while personal piety was on the rise in Indonesia, most Indonesian Muslims preferred either secular or more moderate Islamic parties. Nevertheless, Islamic parties enjoyed a surprising upsurge of support at the 2014 polls, when all but the PKS improved their share of the popular vote. This upturn in support however, had less to do with the ideological appeal of these parties than their ability to tailor their campaigns to appeal to specific constituencies. Beyond party politics, Islam continues to play an important role in the civil society sphere. This is evident from the growing influence of groups such as the ***Majelis Mujahidin Indonesia***, ***Front Pembela Islam*** and **Hizbut Tahrir Indonesia** at one end of the spectrum, and *Jaringan Islam Liberal* (Liberal Islam Network) at the other.

In *Malaysia*, Islam provides a common orthodoxy for more than half of the population of around twenty million. Adherents are concentrated mainly in the Malay Peninsula with only a minority position in Sarawak and Sabah. Islam has been the official religion since independence and is an essential criterion for defining identity on the part of indigenous Malays, who have long felt their political birthright threatened by the large and commercially successful ethnic-Chinese community of migrant origin. Malay and not Islamic symbolism, however, served as the vehicle for nationalist assertion after the Pacific War in response to a British attempt to create a common citizenship to include Chinese and Indians and to dethrone the Malay sultans. In political life, Islam has been associated primarily with Malay opposition to **UMNO** (United Malays National Organization), which has governed in coalition with Chinese- and Indian-based parties since before independence. Malaysia also experienced the effects of Islamic resurgence from the 1970s as economic modernization disturbed the values and orientation of a younger generation of Malays, especially from a rural environment. UMNO has sought to harness Islam by championing its virtues and causes and for a time accommodating the opposition ***Parti Islam Se-Malaysia*** (PAS) within the ruling coalition. Over time, Islam has become central to national political and cultural life because of the need of UMNO to compensate for a vulnerability arising from its longstanding practice of intercommunal coalition politics. The revivalist *Al-Arqam* movement was banned in Malaysia in August 1994 and disbanded formally in the following November. PAS was able to mount a political challenge to UMNO in the wake of the political crisis generated by the dismissal from office, detention, trial and imprisonment of former deputy prime minister, **Anwar Ibrahim**. It demonstrated its electoral appeal in November 1999 not only on the basis of its Islamic credentials among the rural Malays but also from the example of probity in the public and personal lives of its leadership. Although PAS is committed to establishing an Islamic state, it found it politic to enter into an opposition alliance with the primarily ethnic-Chinese **Democratic Action Party** in recognition of the fact that to achieve political power in Malaysia, the support of the non-Malay and non-Islamic communities is required. In July 2000, members of an Islamic cult, ***Al-Ma'unah*** (Brotherhood of Inner Power) raided two military arms depots and seized heavy weapons. Anti-terrorist commandos then overran their jungle camp. It was around this time that Malaysian security forces uncovered another organization, ***Kumpulan Militan Malaysia***, which purportedly was planning terrorist attacks in the country.

Within the political sphere, PAS performed poorly in the 2004 elections. Nevertheless, Prime Minister **Abdullah Badawi**'s inability to capitalize on this mandate and PAS's own internal shift towards a more inclusivist and reformist register led to the turning of tables in 2008, when PAS joined in the ***Pakatan Rakyat*** (People's Alliance) coalition to severely dent the ruling coalition's legitimacy. Among the issues for which PAS won accolades from non-Muslims was the party's support for minority rights and opposition to attempts by the Malaysian government to ban the use of the word *Allah* in Malay translations of the bible. Nevertheless, in the wake of the party's failure to improve its performance in the 2013 polls, conservative leaders within PAS have reversed their position on the matter.

In *Brunei*, Islam is the faith of some 270,000 Malays out of a population of around 400,000. Brunei is unique in Southeast Asia as the sole ruling monarchy. Sultan **Hassanal Bolkiah** is the head of the faith combining temporal and spiritual powers in one person in the classical Muslim tradition. The authoritarian system which pivots on a materially self-indulgent royal family has been rationalized as a ***Melayu Islam Beraja*** (Malay Islamic Monarchy) in an attempt to perpetuate a regional political anachronism. In a conscious attempt also to fend off external Islamic influences, the government rules on the basis of *shari'a* and has introduced a superficial austerity by banning the sale of alcohol and preventing the celebration of the religious festivals of other faiths, such as Christmas. Proselytization has also been curtailed, leading to some measure of disquiet among follows of minority religions in the country. Unlike the experience of Indonesia and Malaysia, Brunei has never faced political challenge through the vehicle of Islam.

Islam is in a minority position in Cambodia, Myanmar, the Philippines, Singapore and Thailand. With the exceptions of Cambodia and Singapore, heightened ethno-religious identity in the face of discrimination by the dominant culture has led to abortive separatist violence which has been met with repressive reaction.

The **Cham** Muslim minority in *Cambodia* are the displaced survivors of the Kingdom of Champa (once located in central Vietnam), which was extinguished by the drive southwards of the Vietnamese in the fifteenth century. They enjoyed a tolerated existence after independence until they became victims of civil war and the bestiality of the **Khmer Rouge** during the 1970s. A significant number escaped as refugees to Malaysia; since the downfall of the Khmer Rouge regime in 1979, the Cambodian Cham have virtually disappeared as a separate community. Today, Cham Muslims are able to practice their religion openly and have similar voting rights to all other Khmer citizens. However, after the September 11 terrorist attacks in the United States, authorities have become more wary of foreign groups such as the Wahhabi from Saudi Arabia and Tabligh Jamaat from South Asia. The arrest of three foreign Muslims in Cambodia on terrorism charges in May 2003 has reinforced fears within the Cambodian leadership about the threat of terrorism.

Muslim separatist activity has not enjoyed any success in *Myanmar* despite participation in challenges to the central government with other ethnic minority groups after independence in 1948. Since the advent of rule by the military **State Law and Order Restoration Council** (SLORC) in September 1988, the **Rohingya** minority in Arakan has been driven in tens of thousands as refugees into neighbouring Bangladesh. For generations, the Rohingya minority group has demanded recognition of citizenship, as currently they are trapped in camps on the borders of Myanmar with no rights to travel nor access to education or other privileges accorded to a citizen. Most of them claim to have lived in the country for generations but have no proper documentation to support their claim. In June 2012, violence between majority Rakhine Buddhists and minority Rohingya Muslims left thousands of homes destroyed, 200 people killed and more than 115,000 people displaced.

In *Thailand*, Muslims number around five to six million out of a population of seventy million. The vast majority are concentrated in the four southern provinces of Narathiwat, Pattani, Satun and Yala, close to the northern border of Malaysia which was determined by Anglo-Thai agreement in 1909. Muslim alienation had been generated by a policy of Buddhist cultural assimilation by Bangkok in the late 1930s and then the success of Malay nationalism across the southern border after the Pacific War, while malign administration also made a continuous contribution. Armed separatism has been a recurrent activity from the late 1940s with the best-known exponent being the **Patani United Liberation Organization** (PULO). Apart from sporadic bombings in Bangkok and the south of the country, the challenge to central government had hitherto been limited. This changed when a new cycle of violence erupted in the early 2000s that severely undermined the credibility of the central government. Policy missteps by the government of **Thaksin Shinawatra** in response to renewed violence, including the killing of more than eighty Muslims after a demonstration in the southern province of Narathiwat in October 2004, further compounded the crisis in legitimacy, as trust between the Muslim community in the southern provinces and the central government eroded considerably. Armed groups such as *Barisan Revolusi Nasional-Coordinate* (*see* ***Barisan Revolusi Nasional***) took advantage of the situation and mobilized further armed resistance using religious language and metaphors. In March 2005, a National Reconciliation Commission was set up for discussions with Muslim leaders to end conflict but to no avail. Despite several further attempts at dialogue, the violence continues unabated.

In the *Philippines*, Muslims number around nine million out of a population of some ninety-six million. They are concentrated in the southern islands of Basilan, Mindanao, Palawan, Sulu and Tawi Tawi. Subject to religious and administrative discrimination under Spanish colonial rule, the Muslims have long been a deprived community. Political alienation became acute after the Pacific War. Christian settlers moved south to appropriate Muslim land and transformed the demographic pattern. Political alienation was expressed organizationally by the **Moro National Liberation Front** (MNLF) which began armed struggle against the government of President **Ferdinand Marcos** in 1972 after it had declared martial law. Violent conflict reached a peak in the mid-1970s, but has diminished ever since a provisional settlement was negotiated through the good offices of Colonel Gadaffi of Libya in 1976 and the Marcos government began to play on tribal divisions within the Muslim community. A political solution remained elusive for two decades, while a split developed in the Muslim separatist movement, giving rise to the **Moro Islamic Liberation Front** (MILF). In 1996, with Indonesia in the role of broker, the MNLF agreed to a cessation of armed struggle in return for the establishment of an Autonomous Region of Muslim Mindanao with its leader, **Nur Misuari**, as its governor together with a key role in a Southern Philippines Council for Peace and Development. The MILF together with the insurgent **Abu Sayyaf Group** continued with Islamic rebellion in support of a separate state. The Abu Sayyaf Group has degenerated, however, into a criminal organization noted for armed abduction of hostages for ransom, especially after the seizure of tourists from Malaysian Borneo in April 2000. The Philippines became an important front in regional counterterrorism efforts after camps in the southern Philippines were found to be training *Jemaah Islamiyah* operatives. With the assistance of the United States, many these camps were eradicated by 2005. More recently, a **Comprehensive Agreement on the Bangsamoro** between the Philippines government and MILF was signed leading to the creation of an autonomous political entity known as Bangsamoro.

In *Singapore*, with an overwhelming Chinese majority, the Muslim community of around 800,000 has close links with peninsular Malaysia. Their political orientation was pointed up by reaction to the visit to the republic by Israel's president, Chaim Herzog, in 1986. At one time, they were excluded from national service but greater efforts have been made by the government to promote their integration. In Singapore, Muslim affairs are governed by Administration of Muslim Law Act (AMLA) which led to the formation of MUIS, the Islamic body of Muslims in Singapore. Although the government is secular, there are religious bodies like *shari'a* courts to handle Muslim affairs under the Islamic laws. Although relations between the government and the Muslim community soured in the early 2000s due to disagreement over the management of madrasahs and a ban on the headscarf in schools, relations have improved. Most Muslim organizations have steered away from politics and have worked closely with the government to improve the lives of Muslims in the country.

While the vast majority of Muslims in Southeast Asia are of *Sunni* persuasion, numbers of *Shi'a* Muslims have gradually increased, in part as a result of the successful outreach undertaken by numerous Iranian cultural centres established in the region's capitals, with the possible exception of Malaysia, where adherence to the *Shi'a* schools is officially illegal.

see also: Abangan; Abu Sayyaf; *Al-Ma'unah*; Anwar Ibrahim; Badawi, Tun Abdullah; *Barisan Revolusi Nasional*; Bolkiah, Sultan Hassanal; Cham; *Darul Islam*; Democratic Action Party; *Front Pembela Islam*; Habibie, B. J.; Herzog Affair; Hizbut Tahrir Indonesia; *Jemaah Islamiyah*; Khmer Rouge; *Kumpulan Militan Malaysia*; *Majelis Mujahidin Indonesia*; Marcos, Ferdinand; Megawati Sukarnoputri; *Melayu Islam Beraja*; Moro Islamic Liberation Front; Moro National Liberation Front; *Nahdlatul Ulama*; Nur Misuari; *Pakatan Rakyat*; *Pancasila*; *Partai Bulan Bintang*; *Partai Keadilan Sejahtera*; *Partai Kebangkitan Bangsa*; *Partai Persatuan Pembangunan*; *Parti Islam Se-Malaysia*; Patani United Liberation Organization; Rohingya; *Santri*; State Law and Order Restoration Council; Suharto; Sukarno; Thaksin Shinawatra; UMNO; United Development Party; Wahid, Abdurrahman.

J

Jakarta Conference on Cambodia 1970 (Cambodia/Indonesia)

The government of Indonesia convened an international conference on Cambodia in Jakarta on 16 May 1970. It acted out of concern for the possible impact on national security of the extension of the **Vietnam War** to Cambodia after the deposition of its head of state, Prince **Norodom Sihanouk**, in March 1970. The motivation was complex, however. Some military officers sought to exploit the conflict by transferring a stock of outmoded rifles to Cambodia in return for the United States replacing them with modern weapons. In addition, a proposal to dispatch an expeditionary force to help the vulnerable **Lon Nol** government was put to President **Suharto**. Suharto had a special interest in Cambodia, viewed previously as a model non-aligned state which he had visited for that very reason during his first overseas tour in 1968. However, his foreign minister, **Adam Malik**, persuaded Suharto of the risks of any military involvement and of the greater political utility of a conference which could demonstrate Indonesia's resumption of an independent and active foreign policy.

The conference, which was called with the approval of the secretary-general of the United Nations, was intended as a representative Asian diplomatic gathering. A major obstacle was Indonesia being identified with demands for the withdrawal of foreign troops and the restoration of Cambodia's neutrality, which appeared to endorse the authority of Lon Nol. In the event, the Jakarta Conference convened as a partisan assembly, attended only by western-aligned states. Communist invitees refused to participate, as did notable Asian neutrals such as India and Burma. Moreover, military incursions into Cambodia at the beginning of May by combined US and South Vietnamese units constituted a major political embarrassment. The conference was called 'to find a constructive formula on how to stop the deteriorating situation in Cambodia and restore peace and security to that country' but failed to accomplish anything. A pious resolution calling for the withdrawal of all foreign troops was placed in the charge of a three-man mission from Indonesia, Malaysia and Japan, which then engaged in a fruitless perambulation to solicit cooperation from members of the Security Council of the United Nations.

see also: Malik, Adam; Nol, Lon; Sihanouk, King Norodom; Suharto; Vietnam War.

Jakarta Summit (ASEAN) 2011 (Brunei/Cambodia/Indonesia/Laos/Malaysia/Myanmar/Philippines/Singapore/Thailand/Vietnam)

The eighteenth meeting of heads of government of **ASEAN** (Association of Southeast Asian Nations) convened in the capital of Indonesia on 7–8 May 2011. The leaders gathered to deliberate an agenda focused on efforts to expedite and strengthen economic integration. Most importantly, a joint statement was issued on an 'ASEAN Community in a Global Community of Nations', where members agreed to work towards achieving a common platform and position on global issues and challenges beyond 2015. The leaders directed their foreign ministers to work out a declaration, which would be endorsed at the nineteenth ASEAN summit in Bali later in the year. Also on the agenda was Myanmar's bid for the grouping's chairmanship in 2014, a request that put the regional grouping under an uncomfortable spotlight given widespread criticism from ASEAN's US and EU dialogue partners of Myanmar's human rights record. Also at issue at the summit was Timor-Leste's application for ASEAN membership. The leaders postponed the decision to later in the year while the ASEAN Coordinating Council made up of foreign ministers was given the responsibility of evaluating the issue and providing recommendations. Nevertheless, it was clear that Timor-Leste's membership application would not enjoy unanimous support within ASEAN.

The Summit was however overshadowed by the ongoing border conflict between Cambodia and Thailand. Thailand's prime minister, **Abhisit Vejjajiva**, and his Cambodian counterpart, **Hun Sen**, exchanged sharp remarks and issued separate press statements that indicated little progress had been made towards resolution of the dispute. The summit ended without resolving the border skirmishes around the **Preah Vihear Temple** that had by then cost eighteen lives. As ASEAN chair, Indonesia agreed to mediate talks between Thailand and Cambodia. The dispute worryingly highlighted the apparent inability of ASEAN to deal with internal conflicts and disagreements despite its lofty declaratory goals. Other ASEAN members expressed concern that such incidents and disunity would undermine the region's potential and derail efforts to achieve an ASEAN Community by 2015.

see also: Abhisit Vejjajiva; ASEAN; ASEAN Community; Hun Sen; Preah Vihear Temple Dispute.

Jatuporn Prompan (Thailand)

Jatuporn Prompan is one of the key leaders of the **United Front for Democracy Against Dictatorship** (UDD) and a former member of parliament for the ***Pheu Thai* Party**. Born in Surat Thani on 5 October 1965, Jatuporn studied at Ramkhamhaeng University in Bangkok, graduating with a bachelor's degree in political science. While at university he was politically active during the May 1992 pro-democracy uprising that followed the crackdown on demonstrators at the Democracy Monument in central Bangkok. In 1996, Jatuporn joined the *Palang Dharma* Party, but defected to the ***Thai Rak Thai* Party** (TRT) two years later. As he was not a party executive, Jatuporn was not banned from politics after the dissolution of TRT following the 2006 coup. During the 2007 parliamentary elections, Jatuporn ran for a seat under the **People's Power Party** (PPP). He retained his parliamentary seat after the 2008 dissolution of the PPP, moving to the *Pheu Thai* Party. At the same time, he became an active member of the UDD and quickly became a key leader of the movement. Jatuporn helped lead the 'red shirts' through the protests in April 2009 and later during their occupation of the Democracy Monument area and the central commercial district in March through May 2010. Jatuporn surrendered together with other 'red shirt' leaders when the military cracked down on protests on 19 May 2010, and was subsequently jailed on terrorism charges. He stood for election as a *Pheu Thai* candidate in the July 2011 elections, and although he won a seat, was disqualified as he was still incarcerated. The Election Commission eventually endorsed his status as a member of parliament and he was released on bail in August 2011. The Commission then revised its approval in November 2011, and in May 2012, the Constitutional Court ruled that Jatuporn was ineligible.

see also: People's Power Party; *Pheu Thai* Party; *Thai Rak Thai* Party; United Front for Democracy Against Dictatorship.

Jemaah Islamiyah (Indonesia/Malaysia/Philippines/Singapore)

Jemaah Islamiyah (JI) is an Islamic organization which was responsible for a number of terrorist attacks in Indonesia. JI was formed in Malaysia in January 1993 by two Indonesian clerics, Abdullah Sungkar and **Abu Bakar Ba'asyir**. The organization's ideology is salafist and extremist in that it believes national governments to be illegitimate, and that their violent overthrow is necessary towards the ultimate objective of reviving a pristine form of Islam and establishing a regional Islamic state or caliphate in Southeast Asia.

JI's roots can be traced to the ***Darul Islam*** (DI), a separatist Islamist organization that waged an armed insurgency in Indonesia in the 1950s and 1960s with the objective of establishing an Islamic state in the country. JI was formed when Sungkar and Ba'asyir broke away from DI as a result of differences with Ajengan Masduki, then chief of DI. While in Malaysia, where they had gone to escape persecution from Indonesian authorities, Sungkar and Ba'asyir expanded their network of like-minded activists from Malaysia, Singapore and the Philippines through the establishment of training camps and some Islamic boarding schools. Following the demise of the **New Order** and advent of democratization in Indonesia, both returned to Indonesia to capitalize on new opportunities afforded by the expanded political space. Sungkar died in 1999 however, and was succeeded by Ba'asyir as JI's spiritual head. The ideology of JI is captured in its handbook, PUPJI or *Pedoman Umum Perjuangan Al-Jama'ah Al-Islamiyah*, which translates to *The General Guide for the Struggle of Al-Jama'ah Al-Islamiyah*. Ba'asyir has always denied the existence of JI, or his position within the organization, despite overwhelming evidence to the contrary provided in the testimony of numerous JI members, including defectors.

Though Sungkar was believed to have communicated with Osama bin Laden, it is Ba'asyir who is seen to be the ideologue behind the ideas of suicide bombings and attacks on the 'far enemy', which echo Al-Qaeda ideology. The organization's activities were initially limited to Indonesia, but after September 11, the focus shifted to attacking Western interests in the region. While plans to conduct violent operations in Singapore were foiled, JI succeeded in gaining a foothold in the southern Philippines through collaboration with like-minded groups, and was behind several attacks in Indonesia. The first attack linked back to JI was the Medan church bombings in May 2000. That same year, JI also attempted to assassinate the Philippine ambassador to Indonesia as well as President **Megawati Sukarnoputri**. This was followed by its most lethal attack, the bombings in Bali in October 2002. Other attacks traceable to JI or JI splinter groups are the JW Marriot Hotel bombing in 2003, the Australian Embassy bombing in 2004, the second Bali bombing in 2005 and the twin attacks on the JW Marriot Hotel and Ritz-Carlton Hotel in 2009 (*see* **Terrorism in Southeast Asia**). The 2002 bombings in Bali, however, sowed the seeds of schism within JI between hardliners who believed that violence was the only means to achieve their objectives, and others who were increasingly alarmed at the cost in Muslim casualties. This schism eventually manifested itself in the emergence of hardline splinter groups on the one hand, and the intensification of proselytization and outreach on the other, on the part of those more reticent towards indiscriminate violence.

At the same time, JI has also come under increasing pressure from the Indonesian police. Prominent figures such as **Hambali**, Abu Dujana, Azahari Husin, Noordin Top and Dulmatin have either been killed or captured. The ideological underpinnings of the group have also been crippled by outspoken defectors such as Nasir Abas, who has written a series of books refuting JI's extremist ideology, and Abu Rusydan. Abu Bakar Ba'asyir is currently serving a fifteen-year prison sentence for supporting a training camp for violent extremism.

see also: Ba'asyir, Abu Bakar; *Darul Islam*; Hambali; Megawati Sukarnoputri; New Order; Terrorism in Southeast Asia.

Jeyaretnam, J. B. (Singapore)

Benjamin Jeyaretnam became the first opposition Member of Parliament in Singapore for over a decade when, standing for the **Workers' Party** (WP), he defeated the **People's Action Party** (PAP) candidate in a by-election on 31 October 1981. He was born in 1926 in Jaffna, Ceylon (now Sri Lanka), and trained as a lawyer in London. As a loquacious opposition member of parliament, he became a thorn in the flesh of Prime Minister **Lee Kuan Yew**, who appeared determined to drive him from political life. Jeyaretnam was returned to Parliament in 1984 but in 1986 he was found guilty of making a false declaration of his party's accounts and fined a sum which disqualified him from holding a legislative seat until November 1991. He was also disbarred from legal practice. In October 1988 the judicial committee of the Privy Council ruled that he had been wrongly disbarred and that the court decision was 'a grievous injustice'. The WP won a single seat in the general election in August 1991, but Jeyaretnam did not take the opportunity to stand in a by-election in December 1992 after his disqualification had expired, and he lost political credibility as a consequence. However, in January 1997, he stood again for election, this time with party colleagues in the five-member group representation constituency of Cheng San. The WP ran the PAP sufficiently close for J. B. Jeyaretnam, as its secretary-general, to assume the third opposition seat in the Parliament as a Non-Constituency Member of Parliament (NCMP) without voting rights. In the following August, he was tried before the High Court on the charge of having defamed Prime Minister **Goh Chok Tong** and ten other senior members of the PAP in remarks made at an election rally for fellow WP candidate Tang Liang Hong, who subsequently fled Singapore. In September, the court found in favour of the prime minister but awarded damages of S$20,000, only one-tenth of that demanded and imposed only sixty per cent of the costs on Jeyaretnam. On appeal in July 1998, the damages were increased to S$100,000 and full costs imposed. In the following October, Jeyaretnam agreed to pay the damages in instalments to avoid bankruptcy proceedings and prejudicing his parliamentary status. In his declining years, and despite attracting a measure of public sympathy, he has ceased to be a thorn in the flesh of the government. In May 2000, he was declared bankrupt by the High Court for failing to keep up payments for damages in another libel case.

Since undischarged bankrupts are banned from serving in Parliament, he was stripped of his NCMP seat in 2001, and was also disbarred. He was not eligible to take part in an election until he had cleared all his debts and was therefore unable to stand as a candidate in the 2001 general elections. Subsequently, in October 2001, Jeyaretnam resigned from his position of secretary-general of the WP and was replaced by **Low Thia Khiang**. Tensions between Jeyaretnam and Low emerged as the former accused the latter and the party of not helping him pay off his debts, and shortly afterwards Jeyaretnam left the WP. In May 2004, Jeyaretnam was sued for libel and defamation by Prime Minister **Lee Hsien Loong** and other prominent PAP politicians. In October 2004, Jeyaretnam appealed for an early discharge from bankruptcy so as to contest the next general election, on the grounds that he wanted another chance to contribute to society. Jeyaretnam was discharged from bankruptcy in May 2007 after paying S$233,255.78 and was reinstated to the bar in September that year. In June 2008, Jeyaretnam founded the Reform Party of which he became the secretary-general. In September 2008 Jeyaretnam passed away due to heart failure at the age of eighty-two. Following his death, his son Kenneth Jeyaretnam took over the leadership of the Reform Party.

see also: Goh Chok Tong; Lee Hsien Loong; Lee Kuan Yew; Low Thia Khiang; People's Action Party; Workers' Party.

Johor, Strait of (Malaysia/Singapore)

The Strait of Johor separates peninsular Malaysia from Singapore. Maritime traffic cannot pass through it because of the road and rail links across a causeway linking the two states. The strait varies in width from between three-quarters of a mile to two miles; the boundary between the two states has its origins in a treaty of 1824 between the British East India Company and the Sultan of Johor from whom Sir Stamford Raffles acquired Singapore in 1819. That treaty ceded to the company and its successors 'the island of Singapore, situated in the **Straits of Malacca**, together with the adjacent seas, straits and islets, to the extent of ten geographical miles from the coast'. A subsequent treaty of 1828 retroceded some islets and areas of territorial water within three nautical miles of the Johor coast and also employed the principle of an imaginary line following the centre of the deep-water channel in the strait to establish the maritime boundary which still obtains. In March 1994 the governments of Singapore and Malaysia signed an agreement to build a second land-link to the west of the existing causeway. That bridge was opened in April 1998.

In 2003, Malaysia sought to build a bridge across the strait in order to replace the existing causeway to ease congestion in Johor Bahru, and allow free flow of water between both sides of the strait which would consequently allow ships to pass. However, negotiations with Singapore regarding this were not successful. In August 2003, Malaysia announced that it was going ahead with a plan to build a bridge that would join up with Singapore's half of the existing causeway. However, plans to build this bridge were called off in 2006. The area is also a source of contention due to Singapore's land reclamation projects on its northeastern islands.

see also: Malacca Strait; Singapore Strait.

K

Kachin (Myanmar)

The Kachin are a minority tribal group of Tibeto-Burman linguistic affiliation who inhabit the northeastern uplands of Myanmar adjacent to India and the People's Republic of China. They have been party to rebellion against the Myanmar central government since the early 1960s. Before independence, their sense of separate cultural identity was reinforced by the influence of Christian missionaries and by recruitment into the colonial army. Their leaders agreed to join the Burmese state through the **Panglong Agreement** in 1947 and supported the central government for the first ten years of independence. However, after the first assumption of power by the military led by General **Ne Win**, they launched a rebellion under the auspices of the Kachin Independence Organization which in time forged cooperative links with eleven other dissident ethnic minorities within a National Democratic Front. The Kachin rebellion was sustained over three decades but lost its momentum when the central government was able to interdict their sources of material support. On 1 October 1993 a peace agreement was signed between the Kachin leader, Major General Zau Mai, and Myanmar's intelligence chief, Lieutenant General **Khin Nyunt**. The agreement was reinforced at a further meeting in 1994, seemingly bringing to an end to this insurgent challenge to the government. After seventeen years, the ceasefire was broken when government forces attacked a Kachin Independence Army (KIA) post in 2011. The attack presaged a sustained offensive by the Myanmar army in Kachin state, including the use of air strikes for this first time in Myanmar's history of internal conflicts, resulting in countless deaths and the displacement of more than 75,000 Kachin from their homelands as the military advanced towards the KIA headquarters in Laiza, bordering China. The KIA, the armed wing of the Kachin Independence Organization (KIO) and the largest rebel army in Myanmar, continues to wage insurgency even as political representatives participate in talks with the government on a nationwide ceasefire agreement.

see also: Insurgencies, Myanmar; Khin Nyunt, General; Ne Win, General; Panglong Agreement 1947.

Kalla, Yusuf (Indonesia)

Yusuf Kalla is an Indonesian politician and businessman who was the tenth vice-president of Indonesia during the period from 2004 to 2009. Kalla was born on 15 May 1942 in Wantampone, South Sulawesi. He attended the University of Hasanuddin in Makassar and in 1967 graduated from its economics faculty. In 1977 he graduated from INSEAD in Fontainebleau, France. Prior to embarking on a political career, Kalla was a prominent student activist. He served as chair of the South Sulawesi branch of the Indonesian Muslim Students' Association, KAMMI, and later headed the Makassar branch of the Islamic Students' Association, HMI, from 1965 to 1966.

Kalla's early political career began with membership in the Regional People's Representative Council. With the establishment of ***Golkar*** in 1965 he joined the party and chaired the youth division of its Makassar branch. In 1968 he left politics to become CEO of his family's business, NV Hadji Kalla. He returned to politics in 1982 as a member of *Golkar*'s advisory board and of the **People's Consultative Assembly** until 1987.

In 1999 Kalla became the minister of industry and trade in the government of President **Abdurrahman Wahid**. However, he was removed from this position within six months over charges of corruption. Following Wahid's dismissal in 2001, President **Megawati Sukarnoputri** appointed Kalla coordinating minister of people's welfare. Kalla was also involved in conflict resolution in Sulawesi. He facilitated negotiations which culminated in the signing of the Malino Declaration in December 2001 which ended a three-year interreligious conflict in Poso.

In 2002 he oversaw the resolution of the **Maluku Violence** with the signing of the Malino II Declaration. In 2003 Kalla was announced as *Golkar*'s candidate for the 2004 presidential election, but he later withdrew to accept the offer to become running mate of ***Partai Demokrat*** leader and presidential candidate **Susilo Bambang Yudhoyono**. Kalla's non-Javanese background was seen as an electoral asset for the Javanese Yudhoyono, allowing him to diversify his appeal. On 20 September 2004, the pair won with sixty per cent of the vote, and Kalla was appointed vice-president. On the back of this success, Kalla ran for the position of chairman of *Golkar*, which he secured via election in 19 December 2004. Kalla contested the 2009 presidential elections under *Golkar*'s banner and finished with 12.4 per cent of the vote. Touted as an effective administrator, Kalla was chosen by presidential hopeful **Joko Widodo** to be his running mate for the July 2014 presidential election.

see also: Golkar, Maluku Violence 1999–2002; Megawati Sukarnoputri; *Partai Demokrat*; People's Consultative Assembly; Wahid, Abdurrahman; Widodo, Joko; Yudhoyono, Susilo Bambang.

Kampuchea, People's Republic of (PRK) (Cambodia)

The People's Republic of Kampuchea (PRK) was proclaimed on 8 January 1979, the day after Phnom Penh fell to Vietnamese forces acting on behalf of a so-called Kampuchean National United Front for National Salvation (KNUFNS). The new state was very much a Vietnamese creation. Its leading personnel comprised a mixture of **Khmer Rouge** defectors, survivors of the terror between 1975 and 1978 who had served both the **Lon Nol** and **Norodom Sihanouk** regimes, as well as Cambodian Communists long in political communion with Vietnam. A constitution was promulgated in June 1981 in which the PRK was described as an independent sovereign state moving step by step towards socialism. Elections were held only once, in May 1981, when 117 seats in the National Assembly were contested by 148 KNUFNS members. Power was exercised by the leadership of the **Kampuchean People's Revolutionary Party** (KPRP), the only political organization permitted. The administration was built up with Vietnamese advisers, but by the end of the 1980s with the withdrawal of Vietnam's main force units, the PRK had become relatively autonomous, albeit politically isolated and fragile. It enjoyed very limited diplomatic recognition, primarily from Vietnam and its political friends, and failed to secure United Nations endorsement. In April 1989, in an attempt to attract international sympathy, the name of the PRK was changed to the State of Kampuchea, readily transliterated as Cambodia. The country's national flag, national anthem and coat of arms were altered to remove any offending political symbolism, while Buddhism was re-established as the national religion. In October 1991 the ruling party changed its name to the **Cambodian People's Party** (CPP) and also discarded its Marxist political identity. The People's Republic of Kampuchea was effectively superseded on 21 September 1993 when a new constitution was ratified which re-established the Kingdom of Cambodia.

see also: Cambodian People's Party; Kampuchean People's Revolutionary Party; Khmer Rouge; Nol, Lon; Sihanouk, King Norodom.

Kampuchean People's Revolutionary Party (KPRP) (Cambodia)

The Kampuchean People's Revolutionary Party (KPRP) was the ruling and sole legal party in the **People's Republic of Kampuchea** (PRK) established on 8 January 1979. The party's existence was revealed only at its claimed fourth Congress in May 1981. The date of its foundation was given as 1951 in order to demonstrate a direct lineal descent from the Vietnamese-dominated Communist Party of Indochina founded by **Ho Chi Minh** in 1930. Its first secretary-general was Pen Sovan, who was replaced by **Heng Samrin** in December 1981. His role (held concurrently with that of head of state) was primarily ceremonial. Two dominant political figures have been Politburo members, **Hun Sen** and **Chea Sim**, who were, respectively, prime minister and chairman of the National

Assembly. On 17–18 October 1991, just prior to the reconvening of the **International Conference on Cambodia in Paris**, the KPRP held an extraordinary congress. In a dramatic initiative, the word 'revolutionary' was dropped from the party's name and in translation the word 'Cambodian' was substituted for 'Kampuchean'. Heng Samrin was removed as formal leader in favour of Chea Sim and an exclusive Marxism was repudiated for political pluralism, while Prince **Norodom Sihanouk** was endorsed as head of state in succession to Heng Samrin. The change in nomenclature and the decision to opt for a multi-party system and political realignment in order to be identified with Prince Sihanouk served to demonstrate the shallow political base of the party and the extent to which it had been a creation of the Vietnamese invasion and a career vehicle for its leadership. The **Cambodian People's Party** (CPP) took part in elections in May 1993 conducted under United Nations auspices, securing second place overall, and then joined a coalition government in October in which Hun Sen became second prime minister. Prime Minister Hun Sen continues to lead the party to electoral victories, including ninety seats in the 2008 elections where it won the popular vote by the biggest margin ever for a National Assembly in Cambodian politics, and sixty-eight seats in 2013.

see also: Cambodian People's Party; Chea Sim; Heng Samrin; Ho Chi Minh; Hun Sen; International Conference on Cambodia, Paris 1991; Kampuchea, People's Republic of; Sihanouk, King Norodom.

Karen (Myanmar)

The Karen are a substantial but less than homogeneous ethnic minority in Myanmar who have long resisted domination by the central government through armed struggle. Numbering some seven million, the Karen are concentrated from south of Mandalay in three mixed geographic zones of deltas, mountain ranges and plateaux which extend in a south-easterly direction parallel to the border with Thailand. The separate identity of the Karen was strengthened during British rule when a good number were converted to various denominations of Christianity and also recruited into the ranks of the colonial army. Karen were involved in helping to crush an anti-colonial rebellion in the early 1930s and in conducting armed resistance against the Japanese in 1942 to cover the British retreat into India. Ethnic Burmans within the Japanese-sponsored Burma Independence Army took a savage revenge against the Karen civilian population, which left a bitter legacy of political alienation after independence in 1948.

In February 1947 a meeting in Panglong between the provisional central government and representatives of a number of ethnic minorities came to an agreement on the constitutional basis of a federal Union of Burma. The Karen, organized in the Karen National Union (KNU), rejected this accord and boycotted elections to a constituent assembly in April 1947. Independence in January 1948 was followed by civil war in which the Karen played a major role in challenging central authority. By January 1949, the Karen rebellion had penetrated the northern suburbs of the capital and posed an acute threat to the integrity of Burma, until August 1950 when good fortune enabled a unit of the national army to eliminate two of their key leaders. The Karen were pushed back into their traditional areas of settlement but have continued to resist the central government since the early 1950s. The KNU has continued to demand political autonomy within a multi-minority National Democratic Front, which in 1988 transformed itself into the Democratic Alliance of Burma with dissident student and religious groups who had been alienated by the bloody repression of the military regime. An opposition National Coalition Government of the Union of Burma was established in December 1990 in the town of Manerplaw (close to the Thai border) which housed the headquarters of the KNU. Manerplaw had been under recurrent attack by the Myanmar army and in 1992 its troops advanced to within six miles of the town before being repulsed with heavy casualties. The Karen position crumbled in December 1994 with the defection of a Buddhist faction which allied with the Yangon government. Manerplaw fell in January 1995 after being held by the Karen for forty-seven years, forcing the Karen to retreat to their new base in Mu Aye Pu (Pu Bo Mya Plaw) on the Thai border. The KNU entered into talks with the Yangon authorities from December 1995 but they failed to produce an accord and collapsed in January 1997. Fighting then resumed, which was spearheaded by the disaffected Democratic Karen Buddhist Army, giving rise to a flow of refugees into Thailand and a further deterioration of the Karen position. In October 1999, a Karen splinter group, known as God's Army, seized Myanmar's Embassy in Bangkok and then negotiated their release by helicopter to the Thai border. In January 2000, the same splinter group seized Ratchaburi hospital on Thailand's western border in an attempt to stop the Thai army from shelling its positions and also to secure permission for its unarmed fighters to receive medical treatment. In the event, the hospital was stormed by Thai commandos who killed all the Karen insurgents and released all hostages. The net effect was to turn Thai public sentiment against the Karens. The KNU, which denounced the hospital seizure, then announced the removal from military command of General Bo Mya, its long-time leader. A verbal agreement for a ceasefire reached in 2003 between Karen leaders and Lieutenant General **Khin Nyun**t broke down a year later after the latter's fall from grace in the junta. Since then, the Myanmar military has continued its offensive against Karen villages. Beset by factionalism and the death of General Bo Mya in 2006, the KNU has struggled to fend off these offensives.

In January 2012, following years of pressure and sanctions by the international community, the Myanmar government signed a ceasefire with the KNU, following talks held between the two parties in Hpa-an. The KNU released a list of demands to be satisfied in order for a peace agreement to be reached, which called for security guarantees, provision of basic services to underdeveloped regions, land reform, an end to the forced labour of civilians, a release of prisoners and an effective mechanism to monitor the truce. Although major offensives in the Karen State have decreased following the ceasefire, Myanmar's military still maintains a large troop presence in the state. In February 2013, KNU general secretary Padoh Kwe Htoo stated that the KNU did not support the **2008 Constitution** as it provided no guarantees for ethnic minorities, democracy or people's rights, and therefore discounted the possibility of the KNU being registered as a political party to contest elections. In March 2013 it was reported that the Myanmar army was grabbing land in the Karen state for development projects despite the ceasefire agreement, and in the process were displacing Karen communities. The Karen National Liberation Army (KNLA), the armed wing of the KNU, is increasingly isolated, as many other ethnic rebel groups have signed ceasefire deals with the ruling military junta over the past decade. The KNLA has been significantly weakened as a result of the counter-insurgency campaign led by the Myanmar Army and its numbers have reduced to 5,000 from a peak of 14,000.

see also: Constitution 2008; Insurgencies, Myanmar; Khin Nyunt, General.

Kaysone Phomvihan (Laos)

Kaysone Phomvihan was the most powerful figure in the Laotian Communist movement from its formation at the end of the Pacific War for almost half a century. He was born on 13 December 1920 near the southern town of Savannakhet to a Laotian mother and a Vietnamese father who was an official in the French colonial administration. His parents sent him to be educated in Hanoi, where he studied law and also became drawn into the anti-colonial movement which was subject to the strong influence of the Communist Party of Indochina (and subsequently of Vietnam) which he joined. At the end of the Pacific War, the party dispatched him back to his home town in an abortive attempt to seize power from the Japanese in order to pre-empt the return of the French.

In his political career, Kaysone appeared guided by the judgement that independence for landlocked Laos could be secured only through the patronage of the Communist Party of Vietnam. In January 1949 he founded a fighting unit which was the precursor of the Lao People's Liberation Army. In August 1950 he became minister of national defence in the Vietnamese-sponsored Lao Resistance government, more commonly known as ***Pathet Lao*** (translated as Lao Nation or State). This so-called government failed to secure representation at the conference leading to the **Geneva Agreements on Indochina** in 1954, which recognized the independence of the Kingdom of Laos from France. Kaysone then devoted his organizational skills to challenging the Royal government in Vientiane, serving as general secretary of the clandestine **Lao People's Revolutionary Party** (LPRP) founded in March 1955. The open instrument of challenge was the ***Neo Lao Hak Sat*** (Lao Patriotic Front) led nominally by Prince **Souphanouvong** but with Kaysone always in a commanding position able to draw on Vietnamese military stiffening. The political future of Laos was determined by the outcome of revolutionary struggle in neighbouring Vietnam. The fall of Saigon in April 1975 led to a progressive collapse of the coalition government in Vientiane by the end of the year. On 2 December 1975 the monarchy was abolished and the Lao People's Democratic Republic was proclaimed with Kaysone Phomvihan as prime minister. He combined the office with that of general secretary of the LPRP.

Initially, Kaysone followed Vietnamese doctrine and practice in managing the economy which led to a dramatic failure in performance. He also allied Laos with Vietnam in the conflict over Cambodia in the third of the **Indochina Wars**, early in the course of which relations with the People's Republic of China became strained, while those with the Soviet Union were reinforced. Under Kaysone's leadership and again following Vietnam's lead, Laos changed economic course and adopted market-driven principles, while retaining an authoritarian political system. Correspondingly, relations were repaired with China and improved with Thailand and the United States. With the end of the Cold War, Laos under Kaysone still acknowledged a special relationship with Vietnam but sought a more balanced international position to compensate for the loss of support from both Vietnam and the former Soviet Union. Despite the fluctuations of policy which distinguished his rule, Kaysone never appeared to be subject to serious political challenge. At the fifth Congress of the LPRP in March 1991, the Secretariat was abolished and Kaysone was elected to a new office of party president. In August 1991, with the promulgation of a new constitution, he gave up the office of prime minister for that of president. On his death on 21 November 1992, his offices were shared out among senior colleagues. Prime Minister **Khamtay Siphandon** became party leader, while **Nouhak Phoumsavan** became head of state.

see also: Geneva Agreements on Indochina 1954; Geneva Agreements on Laos 1962; Indochina Wars; Khamtay Siphandon; Lao People's Revolutionary Party; *Neo Lao Hak Sat*; Nouhak Phoumsavan; *Pathet Lao*; Souphanouvong.

Khamtay Siphandon (Laos)

Khamtay Siphandon became head of state in February 1998 concurrently with his tenure as chairman of the **Lao People's Revolutionary Party** (LPRP), which he had assumed in November 1992 on the death of **Kaysone Phomvihan**. He had been a close associate of Kaysone for over three decades, having succeeded him as head of the ***Pathet Lao*** in 1962.

Khamtay was born on 8 February 1924 in Champassak Province. He worked as a postman under French rule but became involved in revolutionary nationalism under Vietnamese sponsorship at the end of the Pacific War. By the late 1940s, he had made his mark as a political cadre and military leader. He attended the meeting in August 1950 of the Free Laos Front, which gave the name *Pathet Lao* to the pro-Communist insurgency against the government in Vientiane. He became a member of the central committee of the Lao People's (subsequently Revolutionary) Party in 1957 and following on his military leadership of the *Pathet Lao* in 1962, he was appointed commander-in-chief of the Lao People's Liberation Army in 1966. He became a member of the Politburo of the LPRP in 1972 and played a leading role in the seizure of power during 1975. After the creation of the Lao People's Democratic Republic, Khamtay was appointed minister of defence and deputy prime minister. By the early 1990s, he had risen to third place in the Politburo and in August 1991 succeeded Kaysone as prime minister. He gave up that office on becoming head of state in succession to **Nouhak Phoumsavan**. Khamtay remained president of Laos from 24 February 1998 until 8 June 2006. In June 2006 Khamtay resigned and was officially replaced by former vice-president, **Choummaly Sayasone**. In March 2006, he had stepped down as head of the Communist Party and had also left the Politburo.

see also: Choummaly Sayasone; Kaysone Phomvihan; Lao People's Revolutionary Party; Nouhak Phoumsavan; *Pathet Lao*.

Khieu Samphan (Cambodia)

Khieu Samphan has been the best-known intellectual voice among the **Khmer Rouge** as well as acting as their official representative and spokesman with consistent servile loyalty to **Pol Pot**'s leadership.

Khieu Samphan is believed to have been born in 1931 in Svay Rieng Province, the son of a local judge. He was a promising student and won a scholarship to study economics in Paris, where he became secretary-general of the Communist-dominated Union of Cambodian Students. In 1959 he was awarded a doctorate for his thesis on Cambodia's economy that advocated an autonomy from market capitalism which corresponded to policies implemented by the Khmer Rouge when they were in power. On his return to Cambodia, he entered left-wing journalism and was subsequently elected to the National Assembly in 1962 and again in 1966, where he acquired a popular reputation for political integrity and incorruptibility. He was co-opted into government by Prince **Norodom Sihanouk** but broke with him and in 1967 fled the capital with two other dissident colleagues to join Pol Pot in the jungle. Khieu Samphan did not make a public reappearance until 1973 after the deposition of Prince Sihanouk. Khieu Samphan was then commander-in-chief of the Khmer Liberation Armed Forces, despite a lack of military experience. After the Khmer Rouge seized power, he succeeded Prince Sihanouk as head of state in April 1976 and survived in that position until the Vietnamese invasion in December 1978. He was evacuated through Beijing and assumed a major diplomatic role on behalf of the ousted government of so-called **Democratic Kampuchea**, which still retained the Cambodian seat in the United Nations. When the **Coalition Government of Democratic Kampuchea** (CGDK) was formed in June 1982 with non-Communist participation under Prince Sihanouk's leadership, he became vice-president in charge of foreign affairs. In August 1985 he assumed formal responsibility for the Democratic Kampuchean faction on the ostensible retirement of Pol Pot. In that role, he took part in negotiations which led ultimately to a political settlement for Cambodia under United Nations auspices reached at the **International Conference on Cambodia** in Paris in October 1991. He became the senior Khmer Rouge representative on the **Supreme National Council**, returning to Cambodia in the following month, when he was almost lynched by a mob organized by the incumbent government. As a member of that Council, he registered Khmer Rouge obstructionism to implementing the Paris accords and in April 1993 withdrew from Phnom Penh as an act of defiance before general elections which were boycotted by the Khmer Rouge.

With the successful conduct of those elections in May and the formation of a coalition government in October, from which the Khmer Rouge were excluded, Khieu Samphan made an abortive attempt to secure an advisory place for his faction. He refused to return to Phnom Penh on the grounds that adequate provision could not be made for his protection. In July 1994, he was named prime minister in a provisional government proclaimed by the Khmer Rouge and served as its nominal leader. In July 1997, he was involved in abortive negotiations with representatives of Cambodia's first prime minister, **Norodom Ranariddh**, which precipitated a successful coup mounted by second prime minister **Hun Sen** the following month. Although Pol Pot died in April 1998, Khieu Samphan only surrendered to the authorities in Phnom Penh in December that year. He was flown in a helicopter to the capital where he was received by Prime Minister Hun Sen, who initially promised him an amnesty in return for pledging allegiance to his government. Nevertheless Khieu Samphan was arrested by the Cambodia tribunal in November 2007 and charged with crimes against humanity and war crimes, including against groups of Vietnamese and Cham at the **Khmer Rouge Trials**. In April 2008 he made his first appearance at Cambodia's genocide tribunal, with the defence that as the head of the state he was not directly responsible for the genocide. In May 2013, Khieu Samphan expressed remorse for the atrocities committed by the Khmer Rouge regime.

see also: Democratic Kampuchea, Coalition Government of; Hun Sen; International Conference on Cambodia, Paris 1991; Khmer Rouge; Khmer Rouge Trials; Pol Pot; Ranariddh, Prince Norodom; Sihanouk, King Norodom; Supreme National Council.

Khin Nyunt, General (Myanmar)

Lieutenant General Khin Nyunt was Myanmar's prime minister from 2003 until his arrest in 2004. He was a crucial figure in Myanmar's transition to democracy and the opening of the economy to foreign direct investment. He is credited for formulating the seven-step '**Roadmap to Democracy**' that guided Myanmar through the **2010 elections** and the formation of a semi-civilian democracy in March 2011.

Khin Nyunt was born on 11 October 1939 in Kyauktan, Yangon division, and after dropping out of Yankin College in the 1950s, graduated as part of the twenty-fifth batch of the Officer's Training School in 1960. He began his career in the infantry and rose to become a tactical operations officer in the 44th Light Infantry Division in 1982 before moving to military intelligence. In 1983, he was appointed as head of the Directorate of Defence Services Intelligence, an organization with a secret police role collecting intelligence on both the civilian population and the military, thus giving Khin Nyunt his source of power. Khin Nyunt became Secretary-1 of the **State Law and Order Restoration Council** (SLORC) from its formation in 1988, and assumed the same role in the **State Peace and Development Council** (SPDC) that replaced the SLORC in November 1997. This position made him number three in the military junta. He is believed to have been the primary influence in managing the country's burgeoning relationship with the People's Republic of China as well as responsible for sustaining military pressure against dissident ethnic minorities, such as the **Kachin**. In late 1992 he reportedly overcame attempts to remove him by a group of military officers opposed to his policy of closer relations with China. Khin Nyunt was chief negotiator for the ceasefire agreements between the junta and ethnic groups in the 1990s and normalization of relations with China and Thailand. He was also an important figure in leading Myanmar into **ASEAN** (Association of Southeast Asian Nations) in 1997. Until shortly before his arrest in 2004, Khin Nyunt was widely considered to be the most powerful man in the country due to his pervasive intelligence network, albeit still deferential to his patron, **Ne Win**. That position appeared to have been consolidated with the establishment in September 1998 of a political affairs committee with Khin Nyunt as its chairman.

Dependent on continuing support from an ailing Ne Win in the face of resentment towards his role by mainstream field commanders, Khin Nyunt's position became somewhat precarious after the arrest of Ne Win in March 2002, the result of an alleged coup plot to overthrow the government. On 25 August 2003, he was appointed prime minister of Myanmar and soon after announced the 'Roadmap to Democracy', which provided a blueprint for the country's transition from military rule to a democracy, albeit with military influence. He also oversaw the reconvening of the National Convention which eventually drafted Myanmar's **2008 Constitution**. On 18 October 2004, Khin Nyunt was placed under house arrest for a term of forty-four years on corruption charges and his intelligence apparatus largely dismantled with many of its officers receiving lengthy prison terms on corruption charges. This act removed a potential challenger to **Than Shwe** and cemented his grip on power. The military government is believed to have continued to consult Khin Nyunt on foreign policy and ethnic minority issues. Khin Nyunt was released from house arrest on 12 January 2012 by order of President **Thein Sein**.

see also: Constitution 2008; Elections 2010; Roadmap to Democracy; State Law and Order Restoration Council; State Peace and Development Council; Than Shwe, Senior General; Thein Sein.

Khmer People's National Liberation Front (KPNLF) (Cambodia)

The Khmer People's National Liberation Front (KPNLF) was a non-Communist resistance organization set up in October 1979 in order to challenge the government imposed in Cambodia by Vietnamese force of arms in January 1979. The principal role in its formation was played by **Son Sann**, who had served as prime minister under Prince **Norodom Sihanouk**. The KPNLF drew support from an educated constituency of a republican disposition which had supported the overthrow of Prince Sihanouk in 1970. In June 1982 it joined in a so-called **Coalition Government of Democratic Kampuchea** (CGDK) with the **Khmer Rouge** and Prince Sihanouk's **FUNCINPEC** (National United Front for an Independent, Neutral, Peaceful and Cooperative Cambodia) in which Son Sann was named prime minister. The KPNLF suffered from problems of divided leadership and lack of internal cohesion and also enjoyed mixed military fortunes. Despite misgivings about direct negotiations with the government in Phnom Penh, the KPNLF became a party to the dialogue, initially at regional level, which led on to the United Nations-sponsored peace accord concluded at the **International Conference on Cambodia** in Paris in October 1991. When the United Nations presence in Cambodia charged with conducting elections began to register political parties (*see* **UNTAC**), the KPNLF changed its name to the Buddhist Liberal Democratic Party (BLDP). It participated in those elections in May 1993, winning ten seats in a Constituent Assembly of 120 members and then secured minimal representation in the coalition government established at the end of October 1993.

In 1995, there emerged internal dissension within the BLDP caused by conflict between two politicians: Son Sann and Ian Mouly. Differences between the two politicians were settled through a power-sharing agreement after the 1993 elections, where Sann would remain as head of the party, while Mouly would get the party's only cabinet position as minister of information. However, this arrangement did not last for long as tensions re-emerged in 1995, leading to Sann's faction announcing that Mouly had been ousted from the BLDP, to which the Mouly faction retaliated by claiming that it was Sann who had been ousted from the party. On 9 July, 1995, Mouly summoned a special congress of the BLDP in order to select a new leadership. Due to the non-attendance of Sann and his supporters, Mouly was elected unanimously by the congress. However, shortly after the congress was held, the BLDP was dissolved in 1997. In 1998, Mouly's faction formed the Buddhist Liberal Party, while Sann's supporters created the Son Sann party. Yet, both these parties failed to win a single seat in the 1998 National Assembly elections.

see also: Democratic Kampuchea, Coalition Government of; FUNCINPEC; International Conference on Cambodia, Paris 1991; Khmer Rouge; Sihanouk, King Norodom; Son Sann; United Nations: Cambodia 1991–3; UNTAC.

Khmer Republic (Cambodia)

The Khmer Republic was proclaimed in Phnom Penh on 9 October 1970 in succession to the monarchy which had been terminated with the overthrow of Prince **Norodom Sihanouk** in March 1970. The Khmer Republic, which was inspired by Marshal **Lon Nol**, who led the coup against Prince Sihanouk, lasted only until 17 April 1975, when the **Khmer Rouge** seized power. The Khmer Republic was distinguished by feckless political leadership and corrupt practices which led to an initial popular welcome to the end of the civil war won by the Khmer Rouge.

see also: Khmer Rouge; Nol, Lon; Sihanouk, King Norodom.

Khmer Rouge (Cambodia)

The pejorative term Khmer Rouge (Red Cambodians) was originally applied to the country's Communist movement in the 1960s by the head of state, Prince **Norodom Sihanouk**, to differentiate them from the right-wing Khmer Bleu. That movement had by then become dominated by an indigenous intellectual leadership which had been converted to Marxism while students together in Paris. By the late 1960s, it had mounted an insurgency which exploited rural discontent. In March 1970 Prince Sihanouk was overthrown by a right-wing coup while out of the country. In exile in the People's Republic of China, he joined a united front with his Communist adversaries against the government in Phnom Penh headed by General **Lon Nol**. The term Khmer Rouge stuck, nonetheless. Its revolutionary army, initially spearheaded by Vietnamese intervention, achieved military victory in April 1975. A reign of collectivist terror was then launched under the leadership of party leader **Pol Pot** in an attempt to create an ideal socialist society, which led to up to one million deaths. All members of the Lon Nol administration and army were executed. The cities were emptied of their populations, who were set to work in agricultural communes, many to die from malnutrition and disease. Family life was abolished and the Buddhist religion erased. Economic failure aggravated a paranoid tendency expressed in intra-party purges against alleged Vietnamese agents, while armed raids were conducted across the eastern border. In December 1978 invading Vietnamese forces drove the Khmer Rouge from Cambodia. Provided with territorial sanctuary by Thailand and military supplies by China, the Khmer Rouge were revived and able to launch an insurgency against the government installed in Phnom Penh by Vietnam in January 1979. In June 1982 the Khmer Rouge joined in a fragile **Coalition Government of Democratic Kampuchea** (CGDK) with two non-Communist Cambodian factions in a united challenge to Vietnam's military occupation and the Phnom Penh government under the nominal leadership of Prince Sihanouk. As a party to that coalition, they engaged in negotiations which culminated in a political settlement for Cambodia at the **International Conference on Cambodia** in Paris in October 1991. Although a signatory to the Paris accord, the Khmer Rouge refused to accept its military provisions and then boycotted the elections, which were held in May 1993 without significant disruption. The elections led to a new coalition government in October 1993 between the two non-Communist factions and the prior incumbent administration in Phnom Penh. The Khmer Rouge then sought an advisory position within the new government, while continuing their insurgency. The Phnom Penh government conducted armed operations against Khmer Rouge base camps in the north and west of the country in early 1994 but after initial successes experienced military reverses at heavy cost. The effect was to demonstrate the military resilience of the Khmer Rouge, leaving them with greater territorial control. The Khmer Rouge maintained a coherent political identity and a viable military organization with a younger generation of commanders assuming leadership roles. Although Pol Pot formally retired from all leadership positions in September 1985, informed sources maintained that he continued in overall control of the Khmer Rouge. In July 1994, the Khmer Rouge proclaimed a provisional government headed ostensibly by **Khieu Samphan** in reaction to their being outlawed by Cambodia's parliament.

Although able initially to resist military challenge by the government in Phnom Penh, the Khmer Rouge failed to demonstrate an ability to challenge its national power. Moreover, it began to experience a revival of self-destructive internal strife, which led on to its effective disintegration as a viable political–military entity, signalled first by the defection of **Ieng Sary** in August 1996. Moreover, the two rival first and second prime ministers in Phnom Penh competed to inspire further defections. It was in this context in June 1997, that Pol Pot ordered the murder of former defence minister, **Son Sen**, his wife and sixteen members of his family. Pol Pot then fled into the jungle with a small band of loyalists with other Khmer Rouge leaders as hostages. Pol Pot was captured by **Ta Mok**, the one-time chief of staff, and returned to the redoubt of Anlong Veng where, in July 1997, he was sentenced to life imprisonment by a 'people's court' for the murder of Son Sen. The trial was witnessed by an American journalist, Nate Thayer, who interviewed an unrepentant Pol Pot in October 1997. Pol Pot died in April 1998 in a remote jungle retreat, apparently from a heart attack, although his body was cremated before a post-mortem examination could be conducted. Desultory armed confrontation continued between government forces and Khmer Rouge bands but several hundred insurgents surrendered nominally to the government in a ceremony near the Thai border in December

1998, leaving just a small number led by Ta Mok under arms. At the end of the month, Khmer Rouge leaders, Khieu Samphan and Nuon Chea, were flown by helicopter to Phnom Penh where they were met by **Hun Sen** who received their pledge of allegiance to his government. The surrender of the last main fighting units and of the political leaders brought an effective end to over three decades of civil war, which had drawn Cambodia into a living hell. Ta Mok was captured in March 1999. In May, security forces apprehended Kang Kek Leu, alias Duch, the commandant of the notorious prison and interrogation centre, **Tuol Sleng**. They were both charged with genocide in September 1999 but their trial was delayed by a dispute with the United Nations over the composition of the judicial tribunal and the appointment of prosecutors, which was resolved through a compromise agreement in May 2000 (*see* **Khmer Rouge Trials**). The Khmer Rouge period in Cambodian history was a murderous experience; its historical lesson is that evil practice may be readily justified in the name of a noble ideal. A significant remnant of the Khmer Rouge now live unmolested in the town of Pailin to the southwest of Battambang, which is a centre of gem-trading, gambling and prostitution.

see also: Democratic Kampuchea, Coalition Government of; Hun Sen; Ieng Sary; International Conference on Cambodia, Paris 1991; Khieu Samphan; Khmer Rouge Trials; Nol, Lon; Pol Pot; Sihanouk, King Norodom; Son Sen; Ta Mok; Tuol Sleng; United Nations: Cambodia 1991–3.

Khmer Rouge Trials (Cambodia)

The Khmer Rouge Trials represent a series of trials of key figures in the **Khmer Rouge** regime (1975–9), prosecuted for grave human rights violations including genocide, and are conducted by a UN-backed war crimes tribunal consisting of both Cambodian and international judges. Conservative estimates put the number of deaths during the Khmer Rouge regime at 1.7 million, almost twenty-five per cent of the population at that time. However, serious attempts to hold them accountable were not made for almost two decades after the atrocities had taken place due to domestic political circumstances, the weakness of the Cambodian judiciary (the legal sector was emasculated during the reign of the Khmer Rouge for whom trained lawyers were a prime target), as well as lack of international interest in international law and human rights during the Cold War. This mood shifted in the 1990s, when the international community and the UN became increasingly concerned with massive human rights violations in the former Yugoslavia and Rwanda.

The origins of the Khmer Rouge Tribunal (KRT) have its roots in the royal pardon of **Ieng Sary**, the former deputy prime minister for foreign affairs who had earlier been given the death sentence *in absentia* by a Cambodian court in September 1996. His pardon attracted the attention of the UN Commission on Human Rights (UNCHR), which suggested that a KRT be created and modelled after the international tribunal established for the former Yugoslavia. In 1997, the Cambodian government formally requested UN assistance to establish a court to try senior leaders of the Khmer Rouge. Negotiations between Cambodia and the UN began on the establishment of the KRT.

The process of establishing a judicial procedure and forum for trying the Khmer Rouge was fraught with difficulties and controversy. From the outset, the composition and juridical scope of the tribunal became a matter of considerable contest. Harbouring reticence towards the Cambodian judiciary's skill and capability to repel political interference, UN negotiators concluded that international participation on the panel was absolutely essential. On the other hand, Prime Minister **Hun Sen** had insisted that Cambodians made up the majority of the court, and the role of international personnel be restricted to the provision of assistance. It took six years for a compromise to be reached between both parties. In June 2003, the Extraordinary Chambers in the Courts of Cambodia (ECCC), which constituted the KRT, were established.

The KRT itself was battered with criticism even before investigations began. For a start, the inclusion of Cambodian officials in the KRT came under attack from detractors who argued it was weighted in favour of the Cambodian government and hence the officials would inevitably be the thin end of a wedge of government interference. Many observers also cast aspersions on Hun Sen's role, alleging that his intentions for the KRT were not so much for justice and reconciliation for the Cambodian people, but more for personal gain – to establish himself as the leader who would bring peace to the conflict-ridden nation. Negotiations between the UN and Cambodia over the crimes to be included were to cover three major categories – genocide, war crimes and crimes against humanity. There were differences, however, as to what constituted these crimes, in particular, whether what the Khmer Rouge did amounted to genocide. A bigger controversy that complicated negotiations and continues to act as a constraint on the trials today pertains to the prosecution of perpetrators involved in the human rights abuses of the Khmer Rouge regime. During the negotiations, Hun Sen had rejected an initial international expert report that put the figure at between twenty to thirty persons. Instead, he wanted the KRT to focus exclusively on the most senior leaders of the Khmer Rouge regime, arguing that actions taken to prosecute former low-ranking members of the Khmer Rouge, who had been re-integrated into the society, could lead to civil unrest and violence. This led to the provision regarding the scope of jurisdiction of the tribunal, that allows the prosecution only of '(s)enior leaders of Democratic Kampuchea' and '(t)hose believed to be most responsible for grave violations of national and international law'. The ambiguity of the legal wording should not be a surprise given that some of the elite members of the ruling **Cambodian People's Party** (CPP), including Hun Sen himself, had been mid-level Khmer Rouge officials.

Notwithstanding the obstacles to its formation enumerated above, the KRT successfully completed its first case in February 2012, giving a life sentence to Duch, who had been in charge of running a notorious prison and was thus held responsible for some 15,000 deaths. Attention then shifted to its second case against four senior Khmer Rouge leaders – 'Brother Number Two' Nuon Chea, former head of state **Khieu Samphan**, Ieng Sary (now deceased) and his wife Ieng Thirith, a former social action minister. All four were accused of genocide, crimes against humanity and war crimes during the 1970s. It remains to be seen though, if any of the four will live long enough to be convicted. Given their ill health and advanced age – indeed, Ieng Thirith's trial has already been suspended for reasons of dementia – the fact that they have pleaded not guilty means that legal proceedings are likely to be complex and long-drawn.

A second challenge pertains to cases three and four involving mid-level Khmer Rouge military commanders who have been identified by the international co-prosecutor as being responsible for the deaths of tens of thousands of people – many more than Duch was accused of. In a surprising and puzzling move, the judges announced that the cases being investigated have been closed without even bringing in the suspects for questioning. This has heightened suspicion that the outcomes have already been pre-determined, or that the tribunal has caved in to political pressures. The Cambodian government has made clear repeatedly that it does not want the tribunal to move on with the third and fourth cases. Attempts to investigate mid-level Khmer Rouge officials have met strong resistance and opposition, leading to the resignation of two international judges from the court within a span of six months in 2011–12.

see also: Cambodian People's Party; Hun Sen; Ieng Sary; Khieu Samphan; Khmer Rouge.

Kiet, Vo Van (Vietnam) *see* Vo Van Kiet.

Konfrontasi (Indonesia/Malaysia) *see* Confrontation.

Kriangsak Chomanan, General (Thailand)

General Kriangsak Chomanan held the office of prime minister of Thailand from November 1977 until February 1980. In the wake of a coup that removed Prime Minister Thanin Kraivichian, he was appointed as a compromise candidate of the military with the conditional support of the **Young Turks** faction. He initiated a policy of reconciliation with Vietnam and Laos and then authorized its reverse in response to the challenge posed by Vietnam's occupation of Cambodia from December 1978 in the third phase of the **Indochina Wars**. He was obliged to resign office in favour of the army commander, General **Prem Tinsulanonda**, after losing the support of young military officers represented in Parliament. Kriangsak Chomanan was born in 1917 and educated at Chulachomklao Royal Military Academy and the American Army Staff College. He saw service during the Korean War and by the 1970s had assumed a series of senior staff posts. In October 1977 he held the honorific office of Supreme Commander of the Armed Forces. He was the first prime minister drawn from the ranks of the military in forty-six years who had not previously been a first army area commander and commander-in-chief of the army. After losing office, he stood successfully for Parliament in August 1981 but was implicated in an abortive military coup in September 1985 and was placed under arrest. He was granted bail in February 1986 and went on trial in 1987. He benefited from a general amnesty in 1988 and has ceased to play any part in public life, with the exception of assisting in restoring relations with Laos.

see also: Indochina Wars; Prem Tinsulanonda, General; Young Turks.

Kuala Lumpur Declaration 1971
(Indonesia/Malaysia/Philippines/ Singapore/Thailand)

A meeting of foreign ministers of **ASEAN** (Association of Southeast Asian Nations) states in Kuala Lumpur issued a declaration on 27 November 1971 which expressed their governments' determination 'to exert initially necessary efforts to secure the recognition of, and respect for, Southeast Asia as a Zone of Peace, Freedom and Neutrality (**ZOPFAN**), free from any form or manner of interference by outside Powers'. The meeting had been arranged at the United Nations in New York at the beginning of October in the expectation that the People's Republic of China would assume China's seat in place of Taiwan. The realization that such a change would have an impact in Southeast Asia brought the five representatives to the Malaysian capital to find an acceptable formula for regional order. At issue was whether to endorse an earlier Malaysian proposal that Southeast Asia be neutralized with guarantees from major powers. Indonesia, in particular, took exception to this prescription, which appeared to accord virtual policing rights to extra-regional states. The final declaration reflected Indonesia's priority that regional order should be managed on an autonomous basis rather than be determined through the intervening role of external powers. Accordingly, only lip service was paid to the desirability of neutralization. In November 1971 ASEAN was not yet ready to declare a corporate political role. Consequently, the foreign ministers met on an *ad hoc* basis and not in a corporate capacity. In February 1976, however, at the **Bali Summit**, the first meeting of heads of government of ASEAN, the Kuala Lumpur Declaration was incorporated in the **Declaration of ASEAN Concord** which registered political goals. Subsequently the formula for a ZOPFAN became a part of the common declaratory policy of ASEAN but without any practical operational utility, despite the measure of success in December 1995 in concluding a treaty on a regional nuclear weapon-free zone.

see also: ASEAN; Bali Summit (ASEAN) 1976; Declaration of ASEAN Concord 1976; ZOPFAN.

Kuala Lumpur Summit (ASEAN) 1977
(Indonesia/Malaysia/Philippines/ Singapore/Thailand)

The tenth anniversary of the formation of **ASEAN** (Association of Southeast Asian Nations) was celebrated with a meeting of heads of government in the Malaysian capital on 3–4 August 1977. Although the first summit had taken place only in February 1976, the meeting was convened in order to reaffirm the corporate solidarity of ASEAN within a Southeast Asia which had not long partly fallen prey to successful revolutionary forces. In addition, there was some expectation that proposals for trade liberalization among members which had proven abortive at the 1976 **Bali Summit** might be revived. In the event, little of substance was achieved by way of new forms of economic cooperation, while a Thai initiative for greater security cooperation came to naught. ASEAN did achieve an important measure of diplomatic success, however. Any disappointment experienced at Vietnam's refusal to be represented at the inaugural ceremony was more than compensated for by the presence in Kuala Lumpur of the prime ministers of Japan, Australia and New Zealand, who took part in post-Summit discussions with their ASEAN counterparts. Of special significance was the presence of Japan's prime minister, Takeo Fukuda, indicating a major Japanese reappraisal of ASEAN. The Kuala Lumpur Summit provided the opportunity for Japan to communicate its visible approval of ASEAN. Moreover, it inaugurated a wider process of institutionalized dialogue between ASEAN as a corporate entity and industrialized states which served to enhance the Association's international standing. The practice of wider dialogue was initiated in September 1977 with a meeting in Manila with a US delegation led by an Under-Secretary of State for Economic Affairs.

see also: ASEAN; Bali Summit (ASEAN) 1976.

Kuala Lumpur Summit (ASEAN) 2005 (Brunei/Cambodia/Indonesia/Laos/Malaysia/Myanmar/Philippines/Singapore/Thailand/Vietnam)

The eleventh meeting of heads of government of **ASEAN** (Association of Southeast Asian Nations) convened in the capital of Malaysia on 12–14 December 2005. The Summit was most notable for the signing of the Kuala Lumpur Declaration on the Establishment of the **ASEAN Charter**, a document that sought not only to codify ASEAN norms, rules and values but also accord ASEAN a legal personality separate from the member states. It was agreed that an Eminent Persons Group (EPG) consisting of distinguished and respected statesmen would be established with the mandate of making recommendations on the contents of the Charter. ASEAN leaders also agreed that a High Level Task Force would be established to draft the ASEAN Charter based on the Kuala Lumpur Declaration as well as the recommendations of the EPG. The Summit also witnessed the accession of Mongolia, Australia and New Zealand to the **Treaty of Amity and Cooperation**. In the case of the latter two states, this paved the way for their membership in the **East Asia Summit** (EAS). The meeting of leaders at the inaugural EAS also convened in Kuala Lumpur on 14 December. The EAS, to be held annually, brought ASEAN leaders together with the heads of government of Australia, China, India, Japan, New Zealand and South Korea. It was envisaged to complement the ASEAN Plus Three process in strengthening cooperation in a broad range of issues in the region.

see also: ASEAN; ASEAN Charter; East Asia Summit; Treaty of Amity and Cooperation.

Kukrit Pramoj (Thailand)

Kukrit Pramoj was prime minister of Thailand between March 1975 and April 1976 during the democratic interlude after the student-inspired removal of the military regime in 1973. He led a minority government as head of the progressive Social Action Party (*Kit Sangkhom*). In January 1976 he dissolved Parliament; in elections in April he lost his seat in a Bangkok constituency which contained a high proportion of military voters. Kukrit Pramoj was born in Bangkok on 20 April 1911 into a junior branch of the royal family and was the younger brother of former prime minister **Seni Pramoj**. He completed his higher education in England at Queen's College, Oxford, and on his return to Thailand made an initial career in the Ministry of Finance. After the Pacific War, he became active in the **Democrat Party** and then made a reputation as the publisher of the newspaper *Siam Rath* (Thai State). After the fall of the military regime in 1973, he was instrumental in helping to form the liberal conservative Social Action Party, which remained a continuing factor in Thai politics after Kukrit ceased to be prime minister. He stayed in politics on losing high office but played only an elder statesman role, being especially critical of military intervention and opposed to the unelected prime minister, **Prem Tinsulanonda**, who initially took that position when army commander. He gave up the leadership of the Social Action Party in December 1985

to the foreign minister, Siddhi Savetsila, to retire from public life. He died on 9 October 1995 aged eighty-four.
see also: Democrat Party; Prem Tinsulanonda, General; Seni Pramoj.

Kumpulan Militan Malaysia (Malaysia)

In August 2001, investigation into a botched bombing attempt at a shopping mall in Jakarta uncovered information on an underground militant group known then as *Kumpulan Mujahidin Malaysia* (KMM). In a move that puzzled even Malaysia's security agencies who continued using the term *'Mujahidin'*, newspaper reports on the KMM started soon after the discovery of the group to refer to it as *Kumpulan 'Militan' Malaysia*.

The KMM is an underground militant Muslim group which sought to overthrow the government of Malaysia and to create an Islamic state to span from the Philippines to Indonesia. While there have been purported linkages with ***Jemaah Islamiyah*** (JI), the extent and substance of these links remain murky. According to authorities in Singapore, a JI member was supposed to have assisted the KMM to purchase a boat for activities in Indonesia, while the KMM allegedly aided JI in obtaining ammonium nitrate. Investigations revealed that the KMM was formed on 12 October 1995 by Zainon Ismail, and had its roots in *Halaqah Pakindo*, a clandestine movement formed in 1986 as an alumni association for Malaysian graduates from religious institutions in Pakistan, India and Indonesia. The government later disclosed that eight of the ten alleged KMM members detained in an August 2001 raid were members of the youth wing of ***Parti Islam Se-Malaysia***, including Nik Adli Abdul Aziz, the son of **Nik Aziz Nik Mat**. Nik Adli was allegedly elected leader of the KMM at a meeting of twelve senior members in Kampung Seri Aman, Puchong, in early 1999, though it was later contended by the government that real leadership came from **Abu Bakar Ba'asyir** and **Hambali**, the notorious spiritual and operational leaders of the Indonesia-based JI. According to government investigations and allegedly Nik Adli's own confession, the religious teacher had made frequent trips to Afghanistan. This confession formed the basis of government allegations that Nik Adli was active in the Mujahidin resistance in Afghanistan during the era of the Afghan–Soviet war, and upon his return evidently maintained connections with 'key leaders of radical groups in the region'. To date however, these allegations have not been conclusively proven.
see also: Ba'asyir, Abu Bakar; Hambali; *Jemaah Islamiyah*; Nik Aziz Abdul Nik Mat; *Parti Islam Se-Malaysia*.

Kumpulan Mujahidin Malaysia (Malaysia) *see* ***Kumpulan Militan Malaysia***.

Kwam Wang Mai (Thailand) *see* **New Aspiration Party**.

L

Laban ng Demokratikong Pilipino (LDP) (Philippines)

Laban ng Demokratikong Pilipino (LDP), the Philippine Democratic Struggle, is a coalition of political groups whose origins lie in the formation in 1978 of *Lakas ng Bayan* (*Laban*), the People's Struggle Movement, by the late **Benigno Aquino**, while in detention. In 1983, after his assassination, *Laban* was merged with the *Partido Demokratiko Pilipino* (Philippine Democratic Party – PDP) as PDP–*Laban* by José Cojuangco, the younger brother of **Corazón Aquino**. It served as the vehicle for the challenge to President **Ferdinand Marcos** by Corazón Aquino, who ran for election in February 1986 under its banner. After her success, it became the governing party but was joined in a wider coalition in June 1988 to become the LDP. The enlarged grouping began to fracture, as it was employed as an instrument for the presidential ambitions of the speaker of the House of Representatives, Ramon Mitra. The LDP secured seventeen seats in the Senate and eighty-nine seats in the House of Representatives in the legislative elections in May 1992, making it the largest party in Congress. But with Ramon Mitra's failure in the concurrent race for president, it progressively lost sixty-four of its members through defection to ***Lakas*–NUCD**, the party of President **Fidel Ramos**. Ramos had himself left the LDP after it had failed to nominate him for the presidency. The party revived during 1994 as popular alienation from President Ramos over his taxation policy prompted political realignments in Congress. The LDP then moved from opposition into a coalition with Ramos' *Lakas*–NUCD to contest mid-term elections in May 1995. Success in that venture reinforced the congressional position of the LDP. In February 1996, the LDP broke with *Lakas*–NUCD, ostensibly over taxation policy but driven by the presidential aspirations of its leader in the Senate, Edgardo Angara. In October, it forced a change in the Senate presidency in order to pre-empt the tabling of a constitutional amendment, which would have permitted Ramos to stand for a second term. In June 1997, however, the LDP merged with the Struggle of the Nationalist Filipino Masses (LMMP) headed by Vice-President Joseph Estrada, which served as the vehicle for his successful bid for presidential office in May 1998. Angara stood as the LMMP's unsuccessful candidate for vice-president but was appointed agriculture minister in the new administration.

When Estrada became president, LMMP became the ruling coalition but its hold on Congress ended with the ouster of Estrada. Subsequently, it was planned that the LDP would form the core of the main opposition coalition, the *Koalisyon ng Nagkakaisang Pilipino* (KNP). However, by 2004, the party was divided into two factions, led by party president Edgardo 'Sonny' Angara who supported the presidential candidacy of party outsider Fernando Poe Jr and by party secretary-general Agapito Aquino who supported Senator Panfilo Lacson's candidacy. The split became institutional when the Commission on Elections (COMELEC) intervened. Subsequently, Lacson ran under the LDP–Aquino Wing and Poe under the LDP–Angara Wing which would later take on the KNP name. During the campaign period there were numerous unification talks between the two factions. Unification however failed to materialize as neither Poe nor Lacson were prepared to concede their presidential ambitions to the other. Eventually, Lacson only gained 10.8 per cent of the vote while Poe won 36.5 per cent, coming second to **Gloria Macapagal-Arroyo,** who won forty per cent. In the May 2007 general election the LDP won two seats, and in the 2010 general election LDP was part of the **Liberal Party**-led coalition which came into power. In the 2013 Senate elections, LDP candidate Angara was successfully elected.

see also: Aquino, Benigno; Aquino, Corazón; Estrada, Joseph; *Lakas*–NUCD; Liberal Party; Macapagal-Arroyo, Gloria; Marcos, Ferdinand; Ramos, Fidel.

Lahad Datu Crisis 2013 (Malaysia/Philippines)

Lahad Datu is a coastal town in the northeast of the East Malaysian state of Sabah, in Borneo, which has remained an object of a Philippine sovereignty claim since its incorporation into the Malaysian federation in 1963.

On 9 February 2012, an armed group numbering more than 100 followers of the presumptive sultan of Sulu Jamalul Kiram III, led by his brother Azinmudie Kiram, landed undetected at the village of Tanduau on the shores of Lahad Datu. Calling themselves members of the Royal Army of Sulu, this militia was evidently dispatched by Jamalul Kiram, one of at least two claimants to the defunct Sultanate of Sulu and North Borneo, to advance his claim to ownership over the territory of Sabah on grounds that the East Malaysian state was historically part of the Sulu sultanate. Malaysian security forces responded to this incursion by surrounding Tanduau and giving the Sulu militia three weeks to withdraw. On his part, President **Benigno Aquino III** attempted to negotiate an extension to the Malaysian deadline for the militants to return to the Philippines even as he echoed Malaysian calls for the militia to stand down. In the face of recalcitrance on the part of the Sulu militia, Malaysian security forces launched a major offensive which included air strikes and mortar fire on 5 March. Military operations continued for several days, resulting in more than sixty casualties and 150 arrests.

At the heart of events at Lahad Datu was the unresolved **Philippines' Claim to Sabah**. Located nearer Manila than Kuala Lumpur, Sabah was historically a gift from the sultan of Brunei to the sultan of Sulu in 1685 for the latter's assistance in quelling a rebellion. In 1878, the British North Borneo Company leased Sabah from the Sulu sultanate in return for a sum of money to be paid in perpetuity. In 1885, Spain renounced its claims over Borneo in exchange for British recognition of its control of the Sulu archipelago. Sabah became a crown colony in 1946 after the British North Borneo Company ceded its lease to the British government, and together with Sarawak and Singapore in 1963, it became a part of the Federation of Malaysia. In 1962, heir to the Sulu sultanate, Esmail Kiram, surrendered his territories to the government of **Diosdado Macapagal**. When the Federation of Malaysia was formed in 1963, the Philippines government rejected the inclusion of Sabah on the grounds that sovereignty over the territory belonged to Manila. In December 1967, President **Ferdinand Marcos** approved a plan to use Moro militants to infiltrate Sabah in order to foment instability and press Manila's claims to the territory. 'Operation Merdeka', as it was called, was later abandoned when the Moro militants rejected the prospect of fighting their ethnic kin in Sabah and withdrew their commitment to the operation. This led to their massacre in the infamous **Corregidor Affair** in order to cover up the operation. The fact that the Malaysian government continues to pay an annual sum to the sultan of Sulu has been interpreted by Filipinos as an acknowledgement that Sabah was leased, and not ceded, to Britain, and by extension, Malaysia. On its part, the Malaysian government has never officially acknowledged this payment and views the acts of the Sulu militia as an incursion onto Malaysia's sovereign territory. The Philippines government has never officially disavowed its claim to Sabah, although in recent years it has chosen not to pursue the issue in favour of better relations with Malaysia.

see also: Aquino III, Benigno Simeon Cojuangco; Corregidor Affair 1968; Macapagal, Diosdado; Marcos, Ferdinand; Philippines' Claim to Sabah.

Lakas–CMD (Philippines)

Lakas–CMD is a mixed acronym for the ruling coalition in the Philippines during the incumbency of President **Fidel Ramos**, which was built on the earlier *Lakas*–NUCD party. *Lakas* is the shortened form for *Lakas ng Edsa* (People's Power Party), harking back to the overthrow of **Ferdinand Marcos** in 1986 (*see* **EDSA**; **People Power**), while NUCD stands for National Union of Christian Democrats.

Lakas was formed in December 1991 as the vehicle for the presidential ambitions of former defence minister Fidel Ramos, who had left the ***Laban ng Demokratikong Pilipino*** (LDP) after he had failed to secure its nomination. It formed a partnership with the minor liberal–centre NUCD headed by **Corazón Aquino**'s foreign minister, Raul Manglapus. Fidel Ramos stood under its banner in May 1992 to win the presidential elections with 23.6 per cent of the vote. *Lakas*–NUCD failed to make much of a showing in the elections to Congress. It subsequently attracted the largest number of members to its parliamentary ranks through defections from other parties but without any deep political loyalty. Opposition within Congress was overcome through a pact with the LDP to contest mid-term elections in May 1995. Success in nine out of twelve seats in the Senate and in the House of Representatives enabled President Ramos to claim a fresh mandate for his economic reform programme, but *Lakas*–NUCD remained in a minority position in the Congress. That minority position was exposed again when its coalition with LDP broke up in February 1996. In December 1997, after a failed attempt to secure a second term, Ramos endorsed Jose de Venecia, speaker of the House of Representatives, as his party's preferred presidential candidate. In May 1998, Venecia polled well behind the successful **Joseph Estrada**. A significant consolation for *Lakas*–NUCD was the election of its candidate **Gloria Macapagal-Arroyo** to the office of vice-president.

In 2004, *Lakas*–NUCD transformed into the *Lakas*–Christian Muslim Democrats (*Lakas*–CMD) to champion both Christian–Muslim democracy as well as a parliamentary form of government. It contested the 2004 elections as a member of the K-4 coalition represented by Macapagal-Arroyo's candidature. Factionalism was rife within the party however, with heavyweights Macapagal-Arroyo, Fidel Ramos and Jose de Venecia all commanding their own support base. This led to frequent acrimonious internal party exchanges, including calls for President Arroyo's resignation. In May 2009 *Lakas*–CMD officially merged with *Kabalikat ng Malayang Pilipino* (KAMPI), established in 1998 to support Macapagal-Arroyo's abortive presidential bid and revived by her husband Jose Miguel after she came to power, to form the largest national political party at the May 2010 polls against the objections of Ramos and de Venecia. *Lakas*–CMD–KAMPI's inability to win at the 2010 presidential elections led to massive defections to the **Liberal Party** and the National Unity Party.

see also: Aquino, Corazón; EDSA; Estrada, Joseph; *Laban ng Demokratikong Pilipino;* Liberal Party; Macapagal-Arroyo, Gloria; Marcos, Ferdinand; People Power; Ramos, Fidel.

***Lakas*–NUCD** (Philippines) *see* ***Lakas*–CMD**.

Lanzin (Burma/Myanmar) *see* **Burma Socialist Programme Party**.

Lao Dong (Vietnam)

Dang Lao Dong Viet Nam (Vietnam Workers Party) was the name adopted by the Communist Party of Indochina in February 1951 when separate revolutionary parties were concurrently established for Laos and Cambodia, partly in order to accommodate nationalist feelings in the peninsula. The term *Lao Dong* continued to be employed by the party during the course of the **Vietnam War** against France and the United States. After formal unification of the country in July 1976, the title Communist Party of Vietnam was adopted in replacement at its fourth National Congress in December that year. It incorporated also the People's Revolutionary Party which had been established in southern Vietnam in 1962 as a branch of the northern organization.

see also: Communism in Southeast Asia; Indochina Wars; Provisional Revolutionary Government of the Republic of South Vietnam PRG 1969–76; Vietnam War.

Lao Patriotic Front (Laos) *see Neo Lao Hak Sat.*

Lao People's Revolutionary Party (Laos)

The Lao People's Revolutionary Party (LPRP) is the title adopted by the ruling Communist Party in Laos. It traces its origins in direct lineal descent to the Communist Party of Indochina set up by **Ho Chi Minh** in 1930 and has always modelled itself on its Vietnamese mentor. When the Communist Party of Indochina was dissolved in 1951, successor parties for the three Indochinese states were established but in the case of Laos took the initial form of a committee for the preparation of the party. The Lao People's Party was subsequently set up in March 1955 as the clandestine core organization within the ***Neo Lao Hak Sat*** (Lao Patriotic Front) designed to attract popular support for the ***Pathet Lao*** (Lao Nation or State) revolutionary movement. At the second Congress of the party in 1972, its name was changed to Lao People's Revolutionary Party, which was revealed after the Communists had consolidated their seizure of power in December 1975 and proclaimed the Lao People's Democratic Republic. The distinguishing feature of the party, apart from its monopoly political role, has been the continuity in high office of a limited number of members whose association dates from the initial struggle against French rule at the end of the Pacific War. **Kaysone Phomvihan** served as its leader from the formation of the Lao People's Party in 1955 until his death in November 1992. He was succeeded by **Khamtay Siphandon**, also a veteran party member, who had followed Kaysone as commander of the *Pathet Lao* armed forces and as prime minister in August 1991. In February 1998, he exchanged the office of prime minister for that of head of state, while continuing as party chairman. In the 2002 National Assembly elections the LPRP won 108 of the 109 seats. Since 2006, the LPRP has been led by **Choummaly Sayasone**. In the April 2006 National Assembly elections, the LPRP won 113 of the 115 seats. In the April 2011 National Assembly elections the LPRP won 128 of the 132 seats.

see also: Choummaly Sayasone; Ho Chi Minh; Kaysone Phomvihan; Khamtay Siphandon; *Neo Lao Hak Sat*; *Pathet Lao*.

Laskar Jihad (Indonesia)

Laskar Jihad or Warriors of *Jihad* was an Islamist anti-Christian militia established in January 2000 by Jaafar Umar Thalib, an Indonesian of Arab-Madurese descent, who fought with the Afghan Mujahidin in the late 1980s and studied in the Mawdudi Institute in Lahore. Laskar Jihad shared many of the ideals of Islamic revival and struggle against Western cultural influences that defined Islamist organizations the world over, though its focus of attention was confined to Indonesia, which it aimed to convert into an Islamic state. *Laskar Jihad* gained notoriety for violence against Christians. Under Jaafar Umar Thalib, *Laskar Jihad* declared a *jihad* against Christians during the period of **Maluku Violence** between 1999 and 2002, and managed to dispatch a 10,000 strong militia to Ambon under the pretext of providing humanitarian assistance. Despite instructions from President **Abdurrahman Wahid** that they were not to be permitted entry, the militia managed to gain access into Ambon through alleged complicity of the security forces. In some cases these militia even managed to acquire weapons from sympathizers within the Indonesian army and police. Aside from Ambon, *Laskar Jihad* was also reported to have been involved in violence in Sulawesi, and was also known for its periodic raids on places they deemed 'un-Islamic,' such as brothels and nightclubs. The group was eventually disbanded in 2002 soon after the Bali bombings (*see* **Terrorism in Southeast Asia**).

see also: Maluku Violence 1999–2002; Terrorism in Southeast Asia; Wahid, Abdurrahman.

Le Duan (Vietnam)

Le Duan held the office of general secretary of the Communist Party of Vietnam from September 1960 until his death in July 1986 and was its most important leader after the death of **Ho Chi Minh** in 1969. He was born in 1908 in Quang Tri Province, where his father was a railway clerk. Twenty years later, he joined Ho Chi Minh's revolutionary movement and in 1930 became a founding member of the Communist Party of Indochina. He spent ten of the next fifteen years in prison, including the period of the Pacific War. After his release in 1945, he assumed responsibility for organizing revolutionary activity in the south of the country where he remained until after the **Geneva Agreements on Indochina in 1954**. He was brought to Hanoi in 1957 to join the Politburo and after Ho Chi Minh's death presided effectively over a collective leadership and the revolutionary struggle which culminated in the unification of

Vietnam in 1975. That success was followed by bitter years. Le Duan is believed to have been responsible for the dogmatic application of socialist economic doctrine as well as implicated in the ill-fated military intervention into Cambodia which together brought Vietnam virtually to its knees. He was also identified with the country's alignment with the Soviet Union (the **Treaty of Friendship and Cooperation 1978**) which aggravated relations with the People's Republic of China. After he died in July 1986, he was succeeded initially by another reputed hardliner **Truong Chinh**. But in December, at the Communist Party's sixth National Congress, Vietnam embarked on a radical reversal of the economic policy associated with his leadership, with **Nguyen Van Linh** appointed as a reformist general secretary.

see also: Geneva Agreements on Indochina 1954; Ho Chi Minh; Linh, Nguyen Van; Treaty of Friendship and Cooperation 1978; Truong Chinh; Vietnam War.

Le Duc Anh, General (Vietnam)

General Le Duc Anh was president of the Socialist Republic of Vietnam between September 1992 and September 1997. On his election by the National Assembly, he was the second-ranking member of the Politburo of the ruling Communist Party, which indicated his national political standing. Le Duc Anh was born near the central Vietnamese city of Hue in 1920. He was a factory worker as a young man, joining the Communist Party in his late teens and then pursuing a military career during the long period of armed struggle. He held the rank of lieutenant general at the time of unification in 1975 and in 1980 became vice-minister of defence, having played a key role in the invasion of Cambodia. Le Duc Anh was admitted to the Politburo in 1981 and became minister of defence in 1986. He assumed a special responsibility for managing relations with the People's Republic of China. He was the first senior party official to make an official visit to China after key changes in the leadership following the seventh National Congress in June 1991. In November 1993 he was also the first president of Vietnam to visit China since **Ho Chi Minh** in 1959. His election as president was interpreted as an assurance to the party faithful that economic reform would not be allowed to infect the conservative Communist political system.

In mid-November 1996, he was hospitalized after a major stroke. His illness coincided with factional infighting within the party between a reformist camp led by **Vo Van Kiet** which wanted to liberalize the Vietnamese economy and a conservative camp which advocated a socialist-oriented market economy. Though reformists were at a numerical disadvantage at the time of Le's illness, the change of political leadership weakened the conservatives. However, under party leader **Do Muoi**, the conservative camp gained momentum. They were further reinvigorated by Le's recovery in April 1997. Le Duc Anh stepped down as president shortly afterwards, in September 1997, and was succeeded by **Tran Duc Luong**. Subsequently, he became an advisor to the party's Central Committee from 1997 to 2001.

see also: Do Muoi; Ho Chi Minh; Nguyen Phu Trong; Tran Duc Luong; Vo Van Kiet.

Le Duc Tho (Vietnam)

Le Duc Tho was a senior member of the Communist Party of Vietnam who is best known for his role in leading the negotiations for the **Paris Peace Agreements** which ended the United States' military intervention in the **Vietnam War** and also for turning down the joint award of the Nobel Peace Prize with Henry Kissinger. He was born in Mam Ha Province on 14 October 1911, the son of an official in the French colonial administration. Inducted into the anti-French revolutionary movement as a teenager, he was a founder member of the Communist Party of Indochina and spent many years in the 1930s and early 1940s in French prisons. He was released in time to join **Ho Chi Minh** for the declaration of Vietnam's independence in Hanoi in September 1945 following the **August Revolution** and the beginning of military confrontation with France in the first of the **Indochina Wars**. By the early 1950s he had become a member of the Politburo of the Communist Party. In that capacity, he held a special responsibility for its southern branch and proved to be a guardian of ideological rectitude, especially after unification in 1975. He is believed to have been jointly

responsible for Vietnam's decision to invade Cambodia in December 1978 and also for resisting the pace of economic reform intended to overcome the country's attendant international isolation. He was obliged to step down from the Politburo at the Communist Party's sixth National Congress in December 1986 but continued to exercise political influence. His death at the age of seventy-nine on 13 October 1990 is believed to have paved the way for a softening of Vietnam's position on Cambodia and a greater concentration on internal priorities.
see also: August Revolution 1945; Ho Chi Minh; Indochina Wars; Paris Peace Agreements 1973; Vietnam War.

Le Kha Phieu, General (Vietnam)

General Le Kha Phieu, then senior political commissar in the armed forces, was elected general secretary of the Communist Party of Vietnam in December 1997. He was born on 27 December 1931 in Thanh Hoa province. He joined the Communist Party in 1949 and took part in the military struggle against the French. He graduated from the military college and subsequently transferred into the army's political wing receiving his higher military education in the Soviet Union. He spent his army career as a political officer and saw service in Cambodia between 1984 and 1988. He was elected to the party's Central Committee in June 1991 and to its Politburo in January 1994, joining its inner-core Standing Board in July 1996. He has been identified as a hardline conservative with misgivings about the political implications of market-based economic reforms. However, he held the middle ground in the debate about their continued pace in the face of economic adversity during the late 1990s. He has also been publicly identified as a strong opponent of corruption. Le Kha Phieu remained the general secretary of the Communist Party of Vietnam until April 2001, when he was unable to muster the patronage and support required to gain re-election.

Lee Hsien Loong (Singapore)

Lee Hsien Loong assumed the office of prime minister of Singapore on 12 August 2004 after the retirement of **Goh Chok Tong**. His rise in the military and politics has been nothing short of meteoric – he was promoted to the rank of brigadier general at the age of thirty-one years and became deputy prime minister at the age of thirty-eight years.

Lee Hsien Loong was born on 10 February 1952 in Singapore and educated in England and the United States; in mathematics and computer sciences at the University of Cambridge and in public administration at Harvard University on scholarships awarded to him as a serving officer in Singapore's armed forces. His intellectual attainment at university was distinguished. In September 1984, shortly after having been promoted to the rank of brigadier general, he retired from military service and stood successfully as a parliamentary candidate for the ruling **People's Action Party** (PAP). Within two years, Lee had become minister for trade and industry, acquiring a reputation for administrative ability and also for an abrasive assertiveness in the style of his father, **Lee Kuan Yew**, in the process. His position as heir apparent to Goh Chok Tong was placed in doubt with the announcement in November 1992 that he was suffering from cancer of the lymphatic system and that he was temporarily relinquishing his trade and industry portfolio. The next month, however, he was elected first assistant secretary-general of the PAP when Goh Chok Tong succeeded Lee Kuan Yew as secretary-general. In December 1993, as part of a Cabinet reshuffle, Prime Minister Goh Chok Tong confirmed Lee Hsien Loong's position as sole deputy prime minister and also that he was in full remission from cancer. He was appointed to oversee the Ministry of Trade and Industry from January 1994 and from mid-1994 the Ministry of Defence, without holding either portfolio. The return to Cabinet in August 1995 of Tony Tan as deputy prime minister and minister of defence revived speculation about Lee's health and his political future. In the event, such speculation proved to be ill-founded. Lee Hsien Loong assumed a vigorous role in managing Singapore's response to the economic crisis in the late 1990s. In December 1997, he was appointed chairman of its Monetary Authority. He had also begun to assume a more appropriate public persona for advancing his political career. In 2001, Lee was appointed minister of finance. He became Singapore's third prime minister in August 2004. A month prior to assuming high office, Lee made an official visit to Taiwan and was castigated by the government of the People's Republic of China. In response, Lee reiterated Singapore's longstanding One-China policy.

During his term as prime minister, Lee Hsien Loong has passed several novel policies such as the controversial construction of two Integrated Resorts (IRs) with casinos, which was a matter of considerable debate behind closed Cabinet doors, the five-day work week, and increased paid maternity leave to two months in response to the declining national birth rate. At the same time, Lee's tenure has been defined by a considerable softening of the PAP's approach to governance. Lee adopted a more consultative style not only within the government but also through active engagement with the population, the latter of which was at least in part prompted by the party's declining popularity. This has been most recently expressed in the launch of his 'National Conversation' initiative that was premised on focused group discussions with various segments of the Singapore population in order to both elicit feedback and convey the logic behind unpopular government policies.

In his first election at the helm, Lee led the PAP to a landslide victory in 2006, winning eighty-two of eighty-four seats, including thirty-seven uncontested seats, and 66.6 per cent of the popular vote. At the time however, Lee was criticized by the opposition for attempting to buy support through his policy of budget surplus redistribution to the sum of S$2.6 billion just three months before the election in May. In May 2010, Lee Hsien Loong instituted several electoral reforms including reducing the number of group representation constituencies (GRC), increasing the number of non-constituency members of parliament and nominated members of parliament, and legalizing internet campaigning. Despite these piecemeal attempts to liberalize the political sphere, the PAP delivered its worst electoral performance since independence at the 2011 general election, when it managed to capture only 60.1 per cent of the total vote and lost six seats to the opposition in the process. Notably, the PAP also lost the **Aljunied Group Representation Constituency** (GRC) to the **Workers' Party**, making it the first time a GRC had fallen into opposition hands. In 2006 and 2010, Lee Hsien Loong launched two successful defamation lawsuits against the *Far East Economic Review* and the *International Herald Tribune* respectively. In June 2011, Lee Hsien Loong was appointed as the chairman of the Government of Singapore Investment Corporation (GIC). His current wife, Ho Ching, is chief executive officer of Temasek Holdings, an investment company owned by the Government of Singapore.

see also: Aljunied Group Representation Constituency; Goh Chok Tong; Lee Kuan Yew; People's Action Party; Workers' Party.

Lee Kuan Yew (Singapore)

Lee Kuan Yew was prime minister of Singapore from June 1959 until November 1990, when he relinquished that office voluntarily. He has enjoyed an international reputation as a politician and statesman of singular intellectual ability and fearsome personality. His principal legacy is the remarkable economic achievement and environmental quality of Singapore, which under his leadership was transformed from a declining regional entrepôt into a renowned international centre for manufacturing, technology and financial services. As a politician, he has commanded more respect than affection. He has been guided by the conviction that Singapore is afflicted by an innate vulnerability and that its government's margin for error is minimal. He has been an unrepentant elitist believing in the virtues of good government and civic discipline, which in Singapore's case are said to require limiting western-style democracy.

Lee Kuan Yew was born in Singapore on 16 September 1923 to a Straits Chinese family. He received his secondary education at Raffles Institution. During the Japanese occupation, he worked for a time as a cable editor for a propaganda agency. At the end of hostilities, he made himself useful to the returning British military authorities by procuring supplies and in return secured passage on a troopship to Britain where he had obtained a place to study law at the London School of Economics. Lee found postwar London a trying place and moved to Cambridge, where he studied law at Fitzwilliam House with great distinction. He completed his professional legal studies at the Middle Temple in London and became involved in the Malayan Forum, a political club comprising students from Malaya and Singapore who sought an early end to colonial rule.

On returning to Singapore, Lee entered legal practice and his skill as an advocate took him into politics through becoming an adviser to a number of radical trade unions subject to Communist influence. In November 1954 he played a leading role in founding the **People's Action Party** (PAP), a self-styled democratic socialist body committed to the political union of Singapore and Malaya. Lee Kuan Yew bid deliberately for the Chinese-educated vote in an island whose population was then more than three-quarters ethnic Chinese and won election as one of three PAP members in 1955. He also skilfully played the anti-colonial card and secured support from the Communist Party of Malaya while fending off their control of the PAP, of which he was secretary-general. In May 1959 Lee led the PAP to an impressive victory at the polls, becoming in June prime minister of a self-governing but not fully independent Singapore. One of his early successes was to convince Malaya's prime minister, **Tunku Abdul Rahman**, of the urgent need to proceed with a political merger, albeit in a wider context incorporating British North Borneo. The terms of union for a Federation of Malaysia announced in 1961 provoked a split within the PAP, with a left-wing faction moving into opposition as the ***Barisan Sosialis*** (Socialist Front). Lee's government held on to office with the support of right-wing opponents and won the day politically through successfully managing a referendum on Singapore's entry into Malaysia. On the formation of the new federation in September 1963, which had been opposed externally by Indonesia, Lee led his truncated party to a second victory at the polls.

Singapore's membership of Malaysia was shortlived. The island with its Chinese majority had been accepted into the new federation only as a matter of political necessity. In April 1964 the PAP contested nine constituencies in elections in mainland Malaya in an attempt to attract the vote of the ethnic Chinese and secure a place in the federal Cabinet. Although the PAP won only one seat, Lee Kuan Yew continued to press his party's claim to be more representative of the interests of the non-Malays than the peninsular Chinese **Alliance Party** partners of the **UMNO** (United Malays National Organization). His perceived headstrong approach, including speeches in the federal legislature, provoked racial tension which Tunku Abdul Rahman decided could be contained only by Singapore's separation from Malaysia, which took place in August 1965. Lee's public expression of disappointment was tearful, but he was quick to recover and he and his cabinet colleagues demonstrated remarkable resoluteness and resilience as they tackled the unanticipated problem of governing an independent Singapore.

Deprived of a natural hinterland, Singapore under Lee's leadership set out to extend national economic horizons by transcending the island-state's regional environment to make the world its marketplace. In that endeavour, his success has been quite remarkable. Lee Kuan Yew has been distinguished among politicians by always thinking ahead, driven in Singapore's context by an acute sense of the innate vulnerability of the island because of its scale, locale, predominantly ethnic Chinese identity and economic role. He began to make provision for orderly political succession early on by promoting a second generation of leadership. Concern that they were not steeled sufficiently in political combativeness reinforced a natural intolerance towards organized dissent. When he gave up office as prime minister, he remained in cabinet as senior minister (from 1990 to 2004) and minister mentor (2004–2011) and also held on for a time to the post of secretary-general of the PAP. Immediately after stepping down from high office, he continued to assert influence in decision-making and politics through informal cabinet sessions which he chaired, and through some of his public comments. However, after his elder son and deputy prime minister, **Lee Hsien Loong**, had been diagnosed as suffering from cancer of the lymphatic system, he resigned as secretary-general of the PAP in favour of **Goh Chok Tong** and took more of a political backseat. In May 2011, he announced his retirement from the Cabinet. He currently holds the position of senior advisor to the Government of Singapore Investment Corporation. In September 2008, Lee underwent successful treatment for abnormal heart rhythm (atrial flutter). In September 2010 he was hospitalized for a chest infection; and subsequently at eighty-eight years, he was diagnosed with peripheral neuropathy. His wife and confidante, Kwa Geok Choo, passed away at the age of eighty-nine in October 2010 following a long illness.

A dynamic and cerebral figure who seldom pulled his punches, Lee has held strong and oftentimes controversial views on a range of issues. Referring to politics in the island-state, he has suggested on occasion that a one-man one-vote system may not be the best for Singapore, and that Muslim communities were difficult to integrate into society because of their strict observance of religious mores. A firm believer in social Darwinism, Lee has frequently articulated the view that marriage should involve partners of equal intellectual standing as the intellect of children is presumed to be considerably influenced by those of their parents. On the basis of this assumption, policies have been formulated in Singapore to facilitate marital union between graduates.

Regionally within Southeast Asia, Lee Kuan Yew played an important part in helping to consolidate the viability of **ASEAN** (Association of Southeast Asian Nations). Initially suspicious of the Association as an Indonesian vehicle for regional dominance, he soon recognized its utility as a diplomatic community which could protect Singapore's interests through encouraging the habit of bureaucratic and ministerial consultation. More widely in Asia, he has enjoyed the confidence of governments both in Beijing and Taiwan and after his retirement as prime minister travelled on invitation to Vietnam, where his advice on economic development had been eagerly sought. As an international statesman, Singapore has provided a limited base for Lee Kuan Yew's talents. In his later years, Lee Kuan Yew has been a vigorous advocate of authoritarian 'good government' as a visible alternative to the failings of Western liberal democracy. In September 1998, on his seventy-fifth birthday, he published the first volume of his memoirs dealing with his life experience up to separation in 1965. Its appearance served to aggravate relations with Malaysia, and especially with Malaysia's prime minister, **Mahathir Mohamad**, with whom he has a testy relationship. The second volume of his memoirs was published in 2000. After Malaysia's watershed 2008 election, Lee made a visit to Malaysia the following year where he met both government and opposition leaders, including a face-to-face meeting with ***Parti Islam Se-Malaysia*** spiritual leader **Nik Aziz Nik Mat**.

Though retired from Singapore politics and in poor health, Lee continues to be viewed as an international statesman of considerable stature, and his views on world affairs, particularly on China and the future of US–China relations, continue to be widely sought.

see also: Abdul Rahman, Tunku; Alliance Party; ASEAN; *Barisan Sosialis*; Goh Chok Tong; Lee Hsien Loong; Mahathir Mohamad, Tun; Nik Abdul Aziz Nik Mat; People's Action Party; UMNO.

Legislative Council (Brunei)

The Legislative Council is a unicameral semi-elected parliamentary body of Brunei Darussalam and currently possesses only consultative powers. It was introduced and provided for in Brunei's 1959 Constitution, which also permitted half of the council to comprise elected representatives. However, the council was temporarily suspended after the **Brunei Revolt** of 1962, during which a state of emergency was declared. The British re-opened the Legislative Council in 1965. This time, instead of a semi-elected Parliament, all the members of Brunei's Legislative Council were to be appointed by the sultan. Upon independence from Britain in 1984, the Legislative Council was abolished. Since then, the sultan has ruled by emergency decree, assisted by the Council of Ministers and the Privy Council.

Rather unexpectedly, the Legislative Council was reconvened on 25 September 2004 with twenty-one members appointed by the sultan. The newly reconvened council subsequently voted and passed a constitutional amendment that would increase its size to forty-five members, fifteen of whom would be directly elected by the people as district representatives while the rest would be appointed by the sultan. As yet, no date has been set for the new amendment to take effect, or for elections to take place. In September 2005, the sultan dissolved Parliament and an enlarged Legislative Council comprising thirty members was reconvened. Five of the members had been indirectly elected by village and sub-district heads.

The mandate of the Legislative Council has largely been restricted to discussion of and debate over the yearly national budget. Political parties are hoping that the election of the fifteen members will signal the start of political reforms that will gradually allow them greater involvement in government. Independent observers, however, have noted that significant reforms are still lacking, and the space available for political contestation remains limited. The majority of the council members will continue to be appointed by the sultan, and candidates running for the few elected seats will be prescreened. Furthermore, the sultan does not require approval from the Legislative Council to pass laws, thus ensuring that the council's influence remains limited.
see also: Brunei Revolt 1962.

Liberal Party (Philippines) *see* ***Partido Liberal ng Pilipinas*.**

Lim Guan Eng (Malaysia)

Lim Guan Eng is secretary-general of the **Democratic Action Party** (DAP). He has been the chief minister of the Malaysian state of Penang since March 2008, after the twelfth general election. Lim was a certified accountant before entering politics. He is also son of DAP stalwart **Lim Kit Siang**. His wife, Betty Chew, is a DAP assemblywoman for the state of Malacca.

A graduate of Monash University in Australia, Lim first became a member of parliament in 1986 for Kota Melaka, and was re-elected to the same seat on three occasions. Lim has courted controversy through his political career, and has been painted as a Chinese chauvinist by the Malay right-wing daily, *Utusan Malaysia*. Lim was also detained twice by government authorities. In 1987, he was detained with other prominent opposition political figures under the internal security act during Operation Lalang, a crackdown on opposition politicians, academics and activists for allegedly stoking racial tension. He was released a year and a half later, in April 1989. In 1994, Lim was arrested following his vocal criticism of the Malaysian government's handling of an alleged statutory rape involving Penang's former chief minister, Rahim Thamby Chik. He was subsequently sentenced to eighteen months' imprisonment but served only twelve months. In 2011, Lim ran afoul of the Johor state government when he remarked that Singaporeans travelling to the southern Malaysian state risked being kidnapped. He was later forced to publicly apologize to the sultan of Johor for the remark. Controversy has also surrounded his leadership within the DAP. Although Lim has been secretary-general since 2004, both he and his wife were surprisingly voted out of the party's state committee in Malacca in 2005. However, the party's constitution permits him to retain a seat in the committee by virtue of his position as secretary-general.
see also: Democratic Action Party; Lim Kit Siang.

Lim Kit Siang (Malaysia)

Lim Kit Siang was the leader of the opposition **Democratic Action Party** (DAP) for over thirty years until his resignation in December 1999 following his failure to hold both state and federal seats in elections in the previous month. He had also been leader of the federal parliamentary opposition and in that role was the most vocal critic of the ruling ***Barisan Nasional*** (National Front) coalition.

Lim was born on 20 February 1941 in Batu Pahat in the state of Johor. After finishing his secondary education in 1959, he worked as a temporary teacher and then as a journalist in Singapore. He returned to Malaysia after Singapore had been expelled from the Federation to work for the *Rocket*, the newspaper of the newly registered DAP. Lim Kit Siang was first elected to the federal Parliament for a Malacca constituency in May 1969 but was detained for almost a year and a half under the Internal Security Act after the **May 13 Racial Riots** that followed the elections. He returned to active politics after October 1970 and also stood successfully for the DAP for the Malacca state legislature. During the 1970s Lim Kit Siang found time to pursue a career as a lawyer, qualifying from Lincoln's Inn in London in 1977. He spent a second period in detention from October 1987, when Prime Minister **Mahathir Mohamad** seized the opportunity to detain a large number of political opponents in response to a rise in racial tension over the issue of Chinese education. He was made subject to a two-year detention order in December 1987 together with his son, **Lim Guan Eng**. In April 1989 Lim Kit Siang and his son became the last of 106 people detained without trial in October 1987 to be released. In June 1999, he took the DAP into the ***Barisan Alternatif*** (Alternative Front), an inter-racial electoral pact. In the elections in the following November, his party improved its federal position marginally, while his personal political standing was diminished with his failure at the polls. In 2004 Lim Kit Siang refused re-appointment as chairman of the DAP and was subsequently succeeded by Karpal Singh. That year, he was successfully elected a member of Parliament for Ipoh Timur, a seat he also defended successfully in the 2008 election, and became the opposition leader in Parliament while his son became secretary-general of the DAP. In the 2013 elections, Lim Kit Siang caused an upset when he resoundingly defeated Johor's chief minister, Abdul Ghani Othman, for a parliamentary seat from the state.

A senior figure in opposition politics in Malaysia, Lim Kit Siang has been a vocal opponent of forces aiming to introduce Islamic strictures in Malaysia at the expense of the non-Muslim minority. In 2001, he stood at the forefront of the 'No to 929' campaign launched to challenge Prime Minister Mahathir's claim that Malaysia was already an Islamic state. Likewise, he has frequently been at loggerheads with leaders from the Islamic opposition party ***Parti Islam Se-Malaysia*** (PAS) over the latter's objectives of the creation of an Islamic state in Malaysia, including the implementation of the Islamic *hudud* penal code.

see also: Barisan Alternatif; Barisan Nasional; Democratic Action Party; Lim Guan Eng; Mahathir Mohamad, Tun; May 13 Racial Riots 1969; *Parti Islam Se-Malaysia.*

Lim Yew Hock (Malaya/Malaysia/Singapore)

Lim Yew Hock served as chief minister of Singapore between June 1956 and June 1959 before the colony acquired self-governing status. He was born in 1914 in Singapore and from a lowly occupation as a clerk moved into politics through the trade union movement. As secretary-general of the Singapore Clerical and Administrative Workers Union, he was nominated to the Legislative Council in 1948. As president of the Singapore Labour Party in 1949, he went on to form the Labour Front coalition to participate in elections to the more representative Legislative Assembly in 1955. He succeeded **David Marshall** as chief minister in June 1956 against a background of Communist-inspired political violence and went on to reach an understanding with the British government for Singapore's self-rule. His wider coalition, the Singapore People's Alliance, lost to the **People's Action Party** (PAP) in 1959 and Lim Yew Hock lost his parliamentary seat in elections in 1963. He moved to Kuala Lumpur under the patronage of Malaysia's prime minister, **Tunku Abdul Rahman**, and became high commissioner to Australia but was obliged to resign in embarrassing circumstances. Lim Yew Hock then converted to Islam and moved to Saudi Arabia as an official of the Islamic Conference, dying there in November 1984.

see also: Abdul Rahman, Tunku; Marshall, David; People's Action Party.

Limbang Claim (Brunei/Malaysia)

Limbang is a tongue of territory under the jurisdiction of the Malaysian state of Sarawak in northern Borneo which interposes between the two enclaves of land that comprise the Sultanate of Brunei. Limbang had at one time been a constituent part of Brunei but had been annexed in March 1890 by Sarawak, then under the rule of Raja Charles Brooke. That final dismemberment of the once extensive Brunei state has long rankled with its ruling royal family because it occurred after British protection had been established in 1888. In the wake of some acrimony over Brunei's decision not to merge with Malaysia, Sultan Sir Omar Ali Saifuddin revived the claim to Limbang in the late 1960s. Although relations between Brunei and Malaysia improved substantially from the late 1970s and especially after the sultanate became independent and joined **ASEAN** (Association of Southeast Asian Nations) in January 1984, the claim has not been withdrawn. In 1986 a meeting in Brunei between Sultan **Hassanal Bolkiah** and Prime Minister **Mahathir Mohamad**, prompted press speculation about the retrocession of Limbang in return for financial compensation. In April 1994, a joint commission involving the foreign ministers of Brunei and Malaysia agreed to address the Limbang claim through bilateral dialogue and not through litigation but without making any headway towards resolving the dispute.

The signing of the **Exchange of Letters** between Prime Minister **Abdullah Badawi** and Sultan Hassanal Bolkiah in March 2009 signalled that both parties had reached an agreement on Limbang as part of the resolution of a series of disputes. In April 2010, Prime Minister Badawi revealed that the Exchange of Letters settled the issue of sovereignty of the area in dispute, whereby sovereign rights to the resources in the disputed area belonged to Brunei. This provoked acrimonious accusations by former prime minister, Mahathir Mohamed, that his successor was 'signing away' Malaysia's rights over hydrocarbon resources in the area, specifically in Blocks L and M, in exchange for Brunei giving up its claim over Limbang.

see also: ASEAN; Badawi, Tun Abdullah; Bolkiah, Sultan Hassanal; Exchange of Letters; Mahathir Mohamad, Tun.

Lina Joy Issue (Malaysia)

The Lina Joy Issue concerns an attempt by a Malaysian, Azalina Jailani, to have her change of religion reflected in her official papers but which eventually escalated into a constitutional controversy regarding religious freedom in Malaysia.

In 1998, Azalina Jailani chose to leave the Muslim faith in order to become a Christian. She changed her name to Lina Joy, although her official papers still indicated her religion as 'Islam'. As Malaysia has a parallel legal system of secular and *shari'a* law, where the latter governs the private lives of Muslims, Lina Joy had to secure the *Shari'a* Court's approval to officially change her religion. Her applications to the *Shari'a* Court however were rejected on grounds that Muslims were not permitted to leave the faith. Attempts to appeal to the High Court and Court of Appeals also failed. Joy's final recourse was to bring her case before Malaysia's Federal Court, the highest court in the land, where she filed a suit in 2006. In May 2007, the panel of three judges delivered a verdict against her by two to one. The decision was based on the court's position that a person who wished to renounce his or her religion must do so according to the practices and laws of the particular religion, and only when the respective religious authorities had approved the apostasy would a change of religion be recognized. At the same time the sole dissenting judge, a non-Muslim, expressed the view that this interpretation was discriminatory and unconstitutional.

Although Article 11 of Malaysia's constitution allows for freedom of religion, it appears that the right of Malaysian Muslims to exercise this freedom was dependent on the Islamic religious courts. In this regard, the Lina Joy case highlighted the predicament of Muslims who wished to convert to other religions. The case also underlines the complexity of the parallel legal system, which seems to blur the spheres of jurisdiction between the *shari'a* and secular courts. Outside of the courtrooms, the publicity surrounding the case led conservative Muslims on the one hand and non-Muslims on the other to mobilize for and against Lina Joy's right to leave Islam and become a Christian, giving rise to groups such as ***Pembela*** and the **Article 11 Coalition**.

see also: Article 11 Coalition; *Pembela*.

Linh, Nguyen Van (Vietnam)

Nguyen Van Linh held the office of general secretary of the Communist Party of Vietnam from its sixth National Congress in December 1986 until its seventh National Congress in June 1991. In that office, he was responsible for promoting the policy of ***Doi Moi*** (economic renovation) as well as initiating Vietnam's military withdrawal from Cambodia. His

appointment to succeed **Truong Chinh** came as a surprise. Nguyen Van Linh had suffered politically in the late 1970s for his resistance to doctrinaire economic policies for southern Vietnam, losing his Politburo seat in 1982 as a consequence. Nguyen Van Linh was born in Hanoi on 1 July 1915 with the original name of Nguyen Van Cuc which was changed to avoid arrest by the South Vietnamese authorities after 1954. He grew up in the south of the country where he joined the revolutionary movement as a young man. He was imprisoned by the French and spent the Pacific War years in incarceration. After the war, he worked under party luminary **Le Duan**, rising to direct the Central Office for South Vietnam (COSVN) which was the headquarters for Communist revolutionary activity against the Saigon administration. After Vietnam's unification, he was made a member of the party's Politburo and headed its committee for Ho Chi Minh City (formerly Saigon). He fell out of political favour from the late 1970s for his objections to so-called socialist reconstruction in the south. Shortly after losing his Politburo seat, he was returned as party chief in Ho Chi Minh City and then extraordinarily reinstated to the Politburo in July 1985 without the sanction of a party congress when it had become evident that without economic reform, Vietnam faced a major crisis. In retirement, he was an outspoken critic of inefficiency and corruption. He died on 27 April 1998 aged eighty-seven.
see also: Doi Moi; Le Duan; Truong Chinh; Vietnam War.

Loi Tack (Malaya/Malaysia)

Loi Tack was general secretary of the Communist Party of Malaya between 1939 and 1947. He disappeared with its funds after having served as a prime source of intelligence for British Special Branch in Singapore. Although posing as a Chinese, he was born in Vietnam and had worked for French Intelligence in Indochina. British Special Branch had arranged for him to move to Singapore in the early 1930s ostensibly as a representative of the Comintern. He worked for the Japanese during the occupation and organized the liquidation of leading Communist Party members in an ambush in the Batu Caves outside of Kuala Lumpur in September 1942. After the war, he resumed his work for British Intelligence until he came under suspicion in March 1947, leaving first for Hong Kong and then on to Thailand, where he was assassinated, probably by a Communist hit squad.
see also: Emergency 1948–60.

Lon Nol (Cambodia) *see* **Nol, Lon.**

Low Thia Khiang (Singapore)

Low Thia Khiang is the secretary-general of the **Workers' Party** (WP) and a member of parliament (MP) for **Aljunied Group Representation Constituency** (GRC) in Singapore. Born in 1956 in Singapore, he graduated from Nanyang University with a Bachelor of Arts degree in 1980 and a Bachelor of Arts (Honours) degree from the National University of Singapore in 1981. Upon his graduation, he pursued a Diploma in Education at the Institute of Education in Singapore and began his career as a teacher. He subsequently left the profession to start his own business. Low joined the WP in 1982. In 1991, he became an MP after winning the Hougang single-member constituency seat at the 1991 general election. He was re-elected for a further three terms and remained the MP for Hougang for almost two decades, from 1991 to 2011. Low succeeded **J. B. Jeyaretnam** as the secretary-general of the WP in 2001, and initiated a renewal process in the party, successfully recruiting younger candidates for subsequent elections. At the 2011 general election, Low led a team of five candidates to victory in Aljunied GRC against the incumbent **People's Action Party** (PAP) by a margin of more than nine per cent. Low has been credited with the transformation of the image of the party, which resulted in the coming of age of a new generation of leaders with impressive professional qualifications. He also moved the party away from the tradition of robust ideological confrontation with the PAP under his predecessor to a more focused strategy of engagement on local issues.
see also: Aljunied Group Representation Constituency; Jeyaretnam, J. B.; People's Action Party; Workers' Party.

Luong, Tran Duc (Vietnam)

Tran Duc Loung was elected president of Vietnam in September 1997. He was born on 5 May 1937 in Quang Ngai Province. He trained as a geologist and also studied economic management in Moscow. He rose to the post of general director of the Mining and Geology General Department in 1982. He was then made an alternative member of the Central Committee of the Communist Party. He became a full member in 1986 and a deputy prime minister in the following year with industrial and technological responsibilities. He held that position until being elevated to presidential office but was elected to the party's Politburo in 1996. He then became a standing member of the Politburo during its eighth National Assembly Convocation, and deputy to the tenth and eleventh national assemblies. Without military experience and a personal power base, he was regarded as a compromise choice for president without strong views either for or against economic reform. Tran Duc Luong was re-elected in 2002. In June 2006, he announced his resignation and was succeeded by **Nguyen Minh Triet**.

see also: Nguyen Minh Triet.

M

Macapagal, Diosdado (Philippines)

Diosdado Macapagal was president of the Philippines between January 1961 and January 1965, having served for the previous four years as vice-president. He was born on 28 September 1910 into a peasant family in Pampanga Province and in his youth had ambitions to become an actor. A benefactor financed his legal education at Santo Tomas University in Manila, after which he went into a United States law firm. After the Pacific War he served in his country's foreign service where he developed an interest in reclaiming territory which had once been part of the domain of the Sultanate of Sulu and had then been incorporated into British North Borneo. He entered politics in 1949, winning a place in the House of Representatives on behalf of the **Liberal Party**. He established himself as a fine orator and was skilful at securing financial support for agriculture and rural health projects. In 1957 he was elected as vice-president to Carlos García from the **Nacionalista Party**, who treated him as a non-person. Macapagal exploited his humble origins and exposed governmental graft and corruption to succeed to highest office in 1961 aided by strong United States support. As president, he failed to make a real impact on fundamental economic and social ills, giving considerable attention to rousing nationalist feelings as a distraction. He changed the date of the anniversary of national independence from 4 July, when sovereignty had been transferred from the United States in 1946, to 12 June, when Emilio Aguinaldo had declared independence from Spain in 1898. He also prosecuted the **Philippines' Claim to Sabah** and in the process challenged the formation of Malaysia in company with President **Sukarno**'s Indonesia (*see* **Confrontation**). As an alternative, he proposed the formation of a confederation called in acronym **Maphilindo** (comprising the first parts of the names of Malaya, the Philippines and Indonesia) but this foundered from the outset. He was defeated in his attempt to retain office by **Ferdinand Marcos**, who had defected from the Liberal Party to the Nacionalista Party after Macapagal had reneged on a promise to stand down from the presidency after only one term. He died on 21 April 1997.

see also: Confrontation; Liberal Party; Maphilindo; Marcos, Ferdinand; Nacionalista Party; Philippines' Claim to Sabah; Sukarno.

Macapagal-Arroyo, Gloria (Philippines)

Gloria Macapagal-Arroyo was sworn in to the presidency of the Philippines after the impeachment of her predecessor, **Joseph Estrada**. She was the second female president of the Philippines. Gloria Macapagal-Arroyo was born in Manila on 5 April 1947 and is the daughter of the late president, **Diosdado Macapagal**. She was educated at the Ateneo de Manila and at Georgetown University in Washington, where she was a contemporary of President Bill Clinton. She returned home to take a doctorate in economics at the University of the Philippines after which she pursued an academic career. She was drawn to politics through her opposition to the late president, **Ferdinand Marcos**. After his overthrow in 1986, she received junior office in the government of President **Corazón Aquino**. She stood successfully for the Senate in June 1992, where she established a reputation for championing economic reform legislation. As senator, Arroyo filed 400 bills, and in addition to that authored or sponsored approximately fifty-five laws. Among the more prominent of these are the Anti-Sexual Harassment Law and the Indigenous People's Rights Law. She also established her own party as a vehicle for pursuing presidential ambitions but judged such a bid premature and settled successfully for vice-presidential office. As vice-president to President **Joseph Estrada**, Arroyo skilfully reconciled collective responsibility with her evident role as a focus of opposition to a president who had failed to live up to his populist promise. After impeachment proceedings against

President Estrada for corruption led to a second People's Power revolution (known as **EDSA II**) and ultimately to his removal in 2001, Arroyo was appointed president. She would later win her own mandate for the presidency at the 2004 election.

As an economist, Arroyo focused heavily on economic policy during her administration, especially rural development. During her presidency which ended in 2010, growth in the Philippines averaged a commendable five per cent annually, a figure that exceeded what her predecessors managed to achieve. At the same time, however, according to various reports from international organizations, poverty levels in the country had also increased. Her term was also marked by high rates of corruption, and at one point, she was also accused of electoral fraud. Yet, unlike her predecessor whose populist brand of politics posed a direct challenge to established institutions of the Philippines state, President Arroyo utilized 'pork barrel politics' to placate the church, the military and Congress in order to reinforce her position against a rumoured possible coup.

During the 2010 elections, she ran for Congress, winning a seat representing her province of Pampanga. In November 2011, Arroyo was arrested for electoral fraud and soon after (medical reasons being cited), she was placed under hospital arrest at the Veterans Memorial Medical Centre in Quezon City. She has since been granted bail and is awaiting trial for electoral fraud and plunder.

see also: Aquino, Corazón; EDSA II; Estrada, Joseph; Macapagal, Diosdado; Marcos, Ferdinand.

Madiun Revolt 1948 (Indonesia)

Madiun is a town in east Java where in late September 1948 armed clashes between dissident military units and forces loyal to the government of the revolutionary Republic of Indonesia escalated into an uprising on the part of the Communist Party of Indonesia. The uprising, which received retrospective endorsement from Moscow Radio, was crushed by the end of the month and the principal leaders of the party were killed. A factor in the uprising had been the disguised return to Indonesia in early August 1948 of Musso, the prewar Communist leader, who was believed to have been in exile in the Soviet Union. His return and resumption of party leadership encouraged the radical left-wing of the nationalist movement to challenge the policy of the Republican government of seeking independence from the Dutch by diplomacy rather than by armed struggle. They attracted support from irregular forces resentful of a programme of rationalization intended to ensure central military control as well as of the terms of an agreement with the Dutch reached in January 1948. In the event, Musso found himself drawn into an abortive physical challenge to the government of the republic at a time when it was still subject to acute menace from the Dutch. The Communist Party was accordingly discredited with its leadership eliminated, but the embryonic republic attracted favourable interest in Washington, where foreign policy had come to be dictated by Cold War priorities. Madiun marked a turning point in Indonesia's national revolution, leaving not only a legacy of political bitterness but one of communal hatred. Armed confrontation in the villages around Madiun tended to correspond with a fundamental cultural–religious division in Java between observant Muslims (***Santri***) and those who combined a nominal observance of Islam with attachment to Hindu–Buddhism and mystical practices (***Abangan***). That division, with a repetition of bloodletting, was revealed again after the abortive coup (*see* ***Gestapu***) in Indonesia in October 1965. A notable party to and casualty of the uprising, besides Musso, was Amir Syarifuddin, a former socialist party prime minister, who was captured and executed in December 1948 by republican forces.

see also: Abangan; Gestapu; Islam; *Santri.*

Magsaysay, Ramón (Philippines)

Ramón Magsaysay was president of the Philippines from January 1953 until his premature death in an air crash on 16 March 1957 on the island of Cebu. He was a man of considerable personal magnetism whose honesty and close affinity with the mass of the people as well as a reputation for having been instrumental in crushing the '*Huk*' (***Hukbalahap* Movement**) insurgency made him a national hero and then

a martyr. Ramón Magsaysay was born in 1907 in Zimbales Province into a wealthy family of part Chinese descent. He was an indifferent student and became a bus mechanic before taking over the management of the bus company. During the Japanese occupation, he joined a US-led guerrilla group and at the end of the war was made provincial military governor. He stood successfully for Congress in 1946 and made a name for himself as a lobbyist in Washington on behalf of Filipino war veterans. This activity brought Magsaysay to the attention of Colonel Edward Landsdale of the US Central Intelligence Agency who saw him as the ideal candidate to lead the fight against the Communist insurgency in the Philippines. Through Landsdale's intervention with the US State Department, President Elpidio Quirino was persuaded to appoint Magsaysay as secretary of national defence in August 1950. In that office, he became identified with land reform and clean elections and received the credit for the collapse of the insurgency, which failed for a variety of reasons without any fundamental change to the Philippine pattern of land tenure. With US funding and public relations support, Magsaysay won a landslide victory in contesting the presidency against the incumbent Quirino in 1953. This moment of glory was followed by several years of political anti-climax until his death, as he never came to grips with fundamental problems of governance and administration which required more than public relations for their solution.
see also: Hukbalahap Movement.

Maguindanao Massacre 2009
(Philippines)

The Maguindanao Massacre refers to an incident that took place in the southern Philippine province of Maguindanao in which fifty-eight people were killed in a politically motivated slaughter. On 23 November 2009, vice-mayor of Buluan in Maguidanao, Esmael Mangudadatu, invited journalists to cover the filing of his candidacy for the Maguindanao gubernatorial elections with the Commission on Elections in the provincial office at Shariff Aguak. A convoy of six vehicles carrying thirty-seven journalists, several lawyers and relatives of Mangudadatu started their ill-fated journey to the provincial office in the morning that day. Along the way, the convoy was set upon by around 100 armed men who abducted and massacred those in the convoy. Several individuals who happened to be travelling along the same route were mistaken to be members of the convoy and were also killed. In gruesome deeds, many of the women, including Mangudadatu's wife, aunt and sister, were raped, mutilated, beheaded and dumped in a shallow grave. In a text message sent just before she was killed, Mangudadatu's wife was able to identify those who stopped the convoy, including a son of rival politician and incumbent Maguindanao governor, Andal Ampatuan Sr. Ampatuan was later identified as the mastermind of the massacre. Both father and son and other identified attackers were later charged with the murders. The trial is still ongoing, and has been stalled by the troubling disappearance and murder of several key witnesses.

Maha Vajiralongkorn, Prince
(Thailand)

Maha Vajiralongkorn is the only son of King **Bhumibol Adulyadej** and Queen Sirikit. He was born on 28 July 1952 in Bangkok and was invested as Crown Prince in December 1972, thus making him heir apparent. His early education was in England and Australia; and from January 1972, he attended the Royal Military College, Duntroon, in Canberra for four years. He went on to the Royal Thai Army Command and General Staff College during 1977–8 and then trained as a pilot. He also received advanced military training at the United States Army Institute at Fort Bragg as well as spending a year at the Royal College of Defence Studies in London. In 1988 he was promoted to the rank of lieutenant general as commander of the King's Own Bodyguard Regiment. His role in Thailand has been primarily ceremonial and has not involved him in political life in the manner of his father, whom he has represented at home and abroad. He has yet to command the kind of popular regard enjoyed by King Bhumibol. As the king has advanced in years, the issue of royal succession has become a matter of deep political concern because of the stabilizing influence of the current monarch. With the king's advanced age and poor health causing his hospitalization in 2009, much speculation now surrounds his succession. A combination of several factors, including the current king's enormous personal prestige, the lack of a precedent for royal succession during the modern era (King Bhumibol having been on the throne since 1946), and changing sentiment about the role of the institution in the twenty-first century suggest that the transition will be difficult. Though the designated male heir to the throne is the crown prince, the succession is unlikely to be smooth due to his unpopularity and lack of the moral authority that his king father possesses. Though public dislike of the prince is not outspoken due to the *lèse majesté* law (which deems criticism of the royal family as a punishable offence), it was nevertheless evident from online chatter that negative sentiments were only heightened following a 2007 scandal where the prince was filmed with his topless third wife at a birthday party held for his dog. Such incidents typically associated with the crown prince stand in contrast to the virtues associated with King Bhumibol. His questionable legitimacy also remains a matter of concern for monarchists and royalists who are engaged in a debilitating political struggle with former prime minister **Thaksin Shinawatra**, whom the crown prince is known to be close to.

see also: Bhumibol Adulyadej, King; Thaksin Shinawatra.

Mahathir Mohamad, Tun (Malaysia)

Mahathir Mohamad was Malaysia's longest serving prime minister, having held office from July 1981 to October 2003. He has left his political mark on Malaysia as a strong, testy-minded, and successful leader with combative qualities and an authoritarian disposition determined to bend all independent institutions to his will. When in power, he also assumed a strident role as a spokesman for post-colonial states revealing a deep resentment of British attitudes and policies. Though retired, he continues to exercise a considerable degree of influence in Malaysian politics.

Mahathir Mohamad was born on 20 December 1925 in Alor Setar, Kedah. His father was a schoolteacher who had migrated from southern India. He qualified in medicine at the University of Malaya, then located in Singapore. Mahathir entered politics in April 1964 as a Member of Parliament for UMNO (**United Malays National Organization**). He was expelled from the party in July 1969 after losing his seat in elections in May and then writing a bitterly critical letter to the prime minister, **Tunku Abdul Rahman**, accusing him of betraying the Malay community. In the political wilderness, he wrote a controversial book entitled *The Malay Dilemma*, which addressed the economic backwardness of the indigenous people. Mahathir was readmitted to UMNO after **Tun Abdul Razak** became prime minister. He was re-elected to Parliament in August 1974 and then appointed minister of education. In March 1976, after **Hussein Onn** had succeeded Tun Razak as prime minister, he appointed Mahathir as deputy prime minister.

On assuming high office, Mahathir sought to transform the national work ethic, encouraging his countrymen to look east to Japan for economic example. He led UMNO to resounding electoral victories in April 1982 and August 1986 but his strong-minded style of leadership together with scandal in public life provoked dissension within the party. In April 1987 he was challenged for UMNO's leadership by **Tengku Razaleigh Hamzah**, minister for trade and industry, and retained office only by a narrow margin of forty-three votes. In February 1988, after a High Court decision declaring UMNO to be an illegal organization because some of its branches were not validly registered, Mahathir set up UMNO *Baru* (New UMNO) with majority support in Parliament. Faced with a major political challenge by an alternative Malay party, *Semangat '46* (Spirit of 1946), headed by Tengku Razaleigh, he consolidated his leadership by taking UMNO to a further victory in general elections in October 1990, retaining a two-thirds majority for the ***Barisan Nasional*** (National Front, BN) coalition in which UMNO was the dominant party. In late 1997, differences over economic policy against the backdrop of the

Asian Financial Crisis reinforced a growing personal rivalry between Mahathir and his hitherto protégé and deputy prime minister, **Anwar Ibrahim**, who had risen meteorically through UMNO ranks. Matters came to a head after the political downfall of President **Suharto** of Indonesia when Mahathir concluded Anwar was trying to force him from office and that his historical reputation as a successful economic modernizer would be placed in jeopardy. In September 1998, Mahathir dismissed Anwar from government office and also had him removed as deputy president and as a member of UMNO. He was then detained and charged with abuse of power in connection with allegations of sodomy on which he was subsequently tried and convicted. Anwar was sentenced to six years' imprisonment – only to be released in 2004 when the court decision was overturned – and Malaysian politics was thrown into turmoil. In the event, Mahathir led the BN to an overwhelming federal electoral victory in November 1999. On forming his new cabinet, Mahathir announced that it would be his last term of office.

Mahathir's penchant for the dramatic was evident at the 2002 UMNO General Assembly when he tearfully announced his resignation as prime minister to the surprise of assembled party leaders and the audience. Following the expression of widespread support for his continued leadership, he postponed his retirement to October 2003 in order to enable a smooth transition of office to his handpicked successor, **Abdullah Ahmad Badawi**. Rejecting an invitation to stay on in cabinet, Mahathir took on the role of senior advisor to flagship Malaysian companies such as Proton and Petronas. He also returned to the social and political commentary he had engaged in as a medical student, using the *nom de guerre* 'Che Det'.

Despite having handpicked Badawi as his successor, their relationship soon broke down, and in 2005 he became his successor's fiercest and most caustic critic. Such was the acrimony, in 2006 Mahathir even sought election as a local UMNO divisional representative to the party general assembly with the explicit purpose of catalysing opposition to Badawi. In 2008, UMNO lost its two-thirds parliamentary majority at the general election and Mahathir resigned from the party, declaring that he would only rejoin if Badawi resigned or was removed. Mahathir returned to the party fold upon Prime Minister Badawi's replacement in 2009 by **Najib Tun Razak**, a move which he publicly advocated. Nevertheless, though less acerbic in his criticisms of Najib, Mahathir's support for the incumbent was in many ways equivocal.

In foreign policy, Mahathir gained notoriety during the early 1980s by denigrating the Commonwealth and by his **Buy British Last Policy**, prompted by a belief that the former colonial power had deliberately acted against Malaysia's interests. He enhanced Malaysia's standing by promoting South–South cooperation and took a strong stand on the Palestinian issue in which his anti-Zionism was at times difficult to distinguish from anti-Semitism. He has enjoyed an uneasy position within **ASEAN** (Association of Southeast Asian Nations), creating tension within the Association by his proposal for an East Asian Economic Caucus which was put forward publicly without consultation. His anger at US President Bill Clinton's neglect of his proposal led him to boycott an informal summit of Asian-Pacific leaders called by the president in Seattle in November 1993 at the end of an **Asia-Pacific Economic Cooperation** (APEC) ministerial meeting.

In February 1994 Mahathir announced that British firms would cease to be eligible to bid for Malaysian government contracts because of allegations in the British press of his financial impropriety. The ban, which was rescinded in September 1994, was a matter of some embarrassment to his ASEAN partners. Among Southeast Asian leaders, Mahathir was prominent in arguing that China did not represent a threat to regional security, while the presence of the United States was unnecessarily intrusive. He consistently employed the rhetoric of 'Asian values' in opposition to Western interference in the region. Mahathir's relationship with Australia was also marked with tensions, as in 2003 when he sarcastically accused Australia's prime minister, John Howard, of attempting to be America's 'Deputy Sheriff' in the Pacific region. Mahathir has been a vocal critic of Washington's Middle East policy and viscerally opposed the invasion of Iraq in 2003, which he decried as an expression of an American war against Muslims.

Mahathir remains an active and visible political figure in his retirement, and is most remembered for leading Malaysia's ascent to be a global player. Nevertheless, given his recent close affiliation with right-wing pro-Malay groups, Mahathir has also become something of a divisive figure in Malaysian society. He has recently had health problems, undergoing a bypass operation in 2007 and receiving treatment for a chest infection in 2010.

see also: Abdul Rahman, Tunku; Anwar Ibrahim; ASEAN; Badawi, Tun Abdullah Ahmad; *Barisan Nasional*; Buy British Last Policy; Constitutional Crises; Hussein Onn, Tun; Najib Tun Razak, Datuk Seri Mohamad; *Parti Islam Se-Malaysia*; Razak, Tun Abdul; Razaleigh Hamzah, Tengku; Suharto; UMNO; *Yang di-Pertuan Agong*.

Majelis Mujahidin Indonesia

(Indonesia)

Majelis Mujahidin Indonesia (MMI or the Indonesian Mujahidin Council) was established in 2000 as an Islamist umbrella organization purportedly aiming to unite Islamist activist groups with a radical bent such as ***Jemaah Islamiyah*** (JI), ***Front Pembela Islam*** (FPI) and ***Hizbut Tahrir Indonesia*** (HTI). While there are significant operational and ideological differences among its constituent groups, the members of the MMI shared in common their desire for the creation of an Islamic state in post-**Suharto** Indonesia. Although it is not a militant Islamist organization, MMI did accept such groups into its fold. Along the way, the nomenclature of MMI has evolved to become The Council of Mujahidin for Islamic Law Enforcement, as reflected in its current official website and Facebook page. It is currently led by Muhammad Thalib.

The origins of MMI can be traced to the activism of Irfan Awwas, a radical cleric and member of ***Darul Islam***, who published a wide range of semi-clandestine bulletins in Yogyakarta in the 1980s. Another key figure in MMI is **Abu Bakar Ba'asyir**, who spearheaded the inaugural Mujahidin Congress in August 2001 and who served as the *Amir al-Mujahidin* (Commander of the Mujahidin). Despite its radical origins, one of its most notable contributions was its activism in the wake of the **2004 Tsunami**, where MMI members helped in aid distribution and spiritual relief for survivors as well as the more morbid task of disposing of dead bodies. While the ideology of MMI was clearly radical, it also condemned the 2005 Bali bombings and distanced itself from the extreme faction of JI which perpetrated the attacks. Instead, MMI took the position that while it opposed the Indonesian government's support for the United States' policies in Iraq and Afghanistan, it also opposed the killing of innocent Indonesian Muslims through such attacks. On the other hand, MMI was also involved in attacks against ***Ahmadiyah*** mosques in 2007, after a *fatwa* issued by ***Majelis Ulama Indonesia*** (Indonesian Ulama Council) declared the *Ahmadiyah* to be heretics. In 2008, Abu Bakar Ba'asyir resigned from his position in MMI after infighting within MMI, and formed *Jamaah Ansarut Tauhid* (JAT or the Supporters of Monotheism Group).

see also: Ahmadiyah; Ba'asyir, Abu Bakar; *Darul Islam*; *Front Pembela Islam*; *Hizbut Tahrir Indonesia*; *Jemaah Islamiyah*; *Majelis Ulama Indonesia*; Tsunami 2004.

Majelis Ulama Indonesia

(Indonesia)

The Indonesian Ulama Council, or in Indonesian, *Majelis Ulama Indonesia* (MUI), was established in 1975 by President **Suharto** to serve as a bridge between the government and Indonesia's large Muslim population. Specifically, MUI has been a source of *fatwas* (religious edicts) as well as advice and commentary on contemporary social issues affecting Indonesian Muslims. The Council claims a membership comprising all major Muslim organizations in Indonesia, including the ***Nahdlatul Ulama*** and ***Muhammadiyah***. Two groups that represent alternative streams of the Muslim faith, the *Ahlul Bait Indonesia* (*Shi'a*) and *Jemaat Ahmadiyah Indonesia* (***Ahmadiyah***), lie outside its fold. Because of its close association with the state, its source of financial support, MUI is sometimes viewed as an instrument of the ruling regime. To that effect, it has been criticized for issuing *fatwas* that appear to legitimize government policies, such as in the case of mandatory birth control and the use of money derived from the sale of lottery tickets. Other MUI *fatwas* have been controversial for their effect on social cohesion, such as the 2005 *fatwa* declaring that secularism, pluralism and liberalism were against the teachings of Islam, and the 2008 *fatwa* against the *Ahmadiyah* sect.

see also: Ahmadiyah; Muhammadiyah; Nahdlatul Ulama; Suharto.

Malacca Strait (Indonesia/Malaysia/Singapore)

The Malacca Strait is located between the eastern coast of the Indonesian island of Sumatra and the western coasts of Thailand and peninsular Malaysia. It extends for more than 500 miles to join up with the **Singapore Strait**, which is located south of the island-state and the south-eastern tip of peninsular Malaysia and north of Indonesia's Riau Islands. Together the linked straits extend for some 600 miles and have provided the shortest and most important maritime passage between the Indian and Pacific Oceans since the Suez Canal was opened in 1869. The straits are constricted and heavily congested and had experienced a number of serious collisions and groundings involving oil tankers before a traffic separation scheme was instituted in 1977. Close to where the Malacca and Singapore straits merge, the land width narrows to 3.2 miles and the navigable channel reduces to 1.8 miles. Indonesia had extended the breadth of its territorial waters to twelve miles in a historic **Archipelago Declaration** in December 1957 (subsequently enacted in law in February 1960) so extending its jurisdiction in the Malacca Strait. In August 1969 Malaysia followed suit. On 17 March 1970 a treaty was concluded which delimited the territorial sea boundary between Indonesia and Malaysia in the Malacca Strait, south of One Fathom Bank, reflecting the improved bilateral relationship since the end of **Confrontation**. Maritime cooperation continued with both safety of navigation and security in mind. On 16 November 1971, in response to a Japanese attempt to institutionalize international responsibility for safety of navigation through the linked straits, the governments of Indonesia, Malaysia and Singapore issued a dissenting joint declaration. That declaration maintained that safety of navigation was the exclusive responsibility of the three coastal states. Controversy arose from a part of the statement, to which Singapore only took note, by which Indonesia and Malaysia challenged the customary legal status of passage through the linked straits. This attempt to substitute a regime of innocent for that of free passage was resolved ultimately during the course of the Third United Nations Conference on the Law of the Sea and embodied in the Convention promulgated on 10 December 1982. In that Convention, the linked straits of Malacca and Singapore were to be encompassed by a new regime of transit passage applying to all straits used for international navigation. As a preliminary to this accord, the three coastal states had come to an agreement on 24 February 1977 on provision for safety of navigation incorporating a traffic separation scheme which received international recognition. However, by the early 1990s, a series of collisions in the Malacca Strait with loss of life and spillage of oil had led to calls by Malaysia and Indonesia that the self-policing traffic separation scheme should be replaced by a new regime corresponding to that employed in trans-oceanic canals. An additional hazard to navigation, life and property has been the growing incidence of piracy. Cooperation between the three littoral states however had brought the problem of piracy under control by 2004.

In comparison, cooperation to battle the threat of maritime terrorism in the Strait proved more difficult given sensitivities towards external power involvement. This came primarily in the form of American interest in countering the threat of **Terrorism in Southeast Asia** in the wake of the events of September 11. In that regard, an American offer to increase its naval presence in the region was not well received by Indonesia and Malaysia. In 2004, the United States proposed the Regional Maritime Security Initiative, which would allow US special forces to provide security patrols in the Malacca Strait.

This was once again rejected by Indonesia and Malaysia, although both eventually consented to a scaled-down version of the proposal. Meanwhile, cooperation between the three littoral states progressed further with the inception of the **Malacca Strait Patrol** in 2004 and the 'Eyes in the Sky' programme in 2005. Nevertheless, the potential effectiveness of these initiatives was dampened by residual mistrust among the participating states, exemplified for instance in how air patrols were prohibited from going within three miles of each other's borders, thus limiting the scope of intelligence sharing.
see also: Archipelago Declaration 1957; Confrontation; Malacca Strait Patrol; Singapore Strait; Terrorism in Southeast Asia.

Malacca Strait Patrol (Indonesia/Malaysia/Singapore/Thailand)

The Malacca Strait Patrol (MSP) is a set of practical cooperative security measures undertaken by the four littoral states – Indonesia, Malaysia, Singapore and Thailand – in an effort to maintain the security of the **Malacca Strait**. It consists of two initiatives – MALSINDO and Eyes in the Sky (EiS). The MSP initiative recognizes the urgency of multilateral cooperation among the littoral states that would be significantly affected in the event the security of shipping lanes was undermined.

In 2004, and against the backdrop of concerns that American unilateralism might translate to military intervention in the Malacca Strait, Indonesia proposed trilateral coordinated naval patrols involving Malaysia and Singapore. These patrols, codenamed MALSINDO, were subsequently launched by the chiefs of armed forces of Indonesia, Malaysia and Singapore in July 2004 after the initial Indonesian proposal was accepted by the other two littoral states. Thailand joined the initiative in 2008. The EiS initiative was launched in September 2005 to augment surveillance efforts by providing coordinated air surveillance over the Strait through the deployment of maritime patrol aircraft from the four littoral states. The collective efforts of the MSP were further bolstered in 2006 with the formation of the Intelligence Exchange Group (IEG) to support the sea and air patrols through the use of the internet-based Malacca Strait Patrols Information System which enhances shared situation awareness and facilitates cooperation in terms of a collective response. The initiation of the MSP was the first time that the littoral states of Southeast Asia committed to coordinated patrols in a multilateral rather than bilateral setting. The success of the initiative is all the more remarkable given that cooperation between these littoral states had hitherto been hampered by **ASEAN** (Association of Southeast Asian Nations) norms which emphasize sovereignty and non-interference, and the historical suspicions each has harboured towards the other.
see also: ASEAN; Malacca Strait.

Malayan Union Proposal 1946 (Malaya/Malaysia)

The Malayan Union was an abortive scheme for constitutional change in Malaya promulgated by Britain on 1 April 1946. Restricted territorially to the Malay Peninsula (that is including Penang but excluding Singapore), it entailed transferring the formal sovereignty of the sultans or rulers of the Malay states to the British Crown and establishing a common citizenship to the advantage of ethnic Chinese and Indian residents of migrant origin. The initial objectives were political integration of a plural society and the rationalization of colonial administration within a unitary form of government. However, the coercive manner in which the rulers were relieved of sovereign status confirmed for the indigenous Malays that their political birthright was at serious risk. The scheme provoked an unprecedented expression of Malay nationalism but not a demand for independence from colonial rule, given the growing threat from the predominantly ethnic Chinese Communist Party of Malaya. In March 1946 a Pan Malayan Malay Congress was convened in Kuala Lumpur in a protest which led on to the formation in May of **UMNO** (United Malays National Organization), the first effective Malay political party. Led by Onn bin Ja'afar, a senior civil servant from Johor, it campaigned successfully for the Malayan Union to be rescinded, touching a British political nerve at the prospect of mass

violence of the kind in train in neighbouring Indonesia. The Malayan Union was set aside on 25 July 1946 in favour of a Federation of Malaya under colonial aegis with the position of the rulers restored and citizenship made more difficult for non-Malays to acquire. Sovereignty was transferred ultimately to an independent Federation of Malaya (still excluding Singapore) on 31 August 1957.
see also: UMNO.

Malaysian Chinese Association (MCA) (Malaya/Malaysia)

The Malaysian Chinese Association (MCA) was established originally in 1949 as the Malayan Chinese Association, ostensibly as a welfare organization to counter the appeal of Communist insurgency among the Chinese community. In February 1952 its Selangor branch took a historic political initiative by entering into an electoral pact with the local branch of **UMNO** (United Malays National Organization) in contesting municipal elections in Kuala Lumpur. Success in this enterprise paved the way for partnership with UMNO and the Malayan (subsequently **Malaysian**) **Indian Congress** (MIC) in federal elections in July 1955. This intercommunal **Alliance Party** provided the political model for a ruling coalition which has been continuously in power since before independence.

The MCA has always occupied the role of principal communal partner of UMNO within the ruling coalition which in the early 1970s became known as the ***Barisan Nasional*** (National Front, BN). That position has never reflected its true standing within the Chinese community. The MCA has been primarily identified with a wealthy elite prominent within Chinese chambers of commerce who have been content to appease Malay political partners in a narrow economic interest. As such, it has found it difficult to command a majority of the Chinese vote in competition with the opposition **Democratic Action Party** (DAP), which attracts lower-income support. The MCA has always suffered from never having been able to satisfy adequately its senior political partner and its communal constituency at the same time. A humiliating electoral failure in May 1969 was a factor in a political crisis brought to a head by the **May 13 Racial Riots**. In its wake, and with the introduction of a **New Economic Policy** designed to revise the balance of advantage in the Malay interest, the MCA was downgraded as a political partner. While it had to give up key economic portfolios in Cabinet, the primarily Chinese-based ***Gerakan Rakyat Malaysia*** (Malaysian People's Movement) was brought into the ruling coalition. The problem for the MCA from that juncture has been that the more its leaders have attempted to cultivate the separate interests of the Chinese community, the greater the political alienation exhibited by UMNO. For example, after a period of internal factionalism, an attempt to take up the emotive issue of Chinese education led in October 1987 to the detention of eight party members. The MCA has survived politically because its place in politics and government serves UMNO's interests and also because Malaysia has prospered since the mid-1970s. The New Economic Policy has caused alienation among the Chinese community but they have also shared in the fruits of development. During the 1980s, the MCA did little more than hold its own politically, however, because of the contradiction in representing Chinese interests, while at the same time subordinating those interests to Malay priorities. In national elections in October 1990, the MCA marginally improved its position by winning eighteen seats in the 180-member federal Parliament compared to seventeen seats in 1986 in a 177-member chamber. In April 1995, however, it made a major political breakthrough in securing a majority of Chinese votes at the expense of the DAP. The MCA won thirty seats out of thirty-four contested in the federal Parliament, its best ever electoral performance. The number was reduced to twenty-nine in elections in November 1999.

Since 1999, factionalism has taken the party to the brink of collapse. The party's problems were compounded by widening disconnect with the ethnic Chinese grassroots, eroding its support base considerably. Chronic internal discord was triggered by the retirement of Deputy President Lim Ah Lek in 1999. Lim's retirement was followed by a series of leadership tussles which were only interrupted by a cosmetic show of unity on the eve of the 2004 election, which nevertheless saw a strong performance by MCA. In the event, it proved to be a pyrrhic victory, and persistent myopic factionalism took its toll at the 2008 general election, when a groundswell of opposition against MCA's impotence within the BN and the party's inability to surmount factional politics led to significant losses, as it managed to secure a meagre fifteen parliamentary seats. Rather than recede, factionalism intensified. In 2011, the MCA General Assembly endorsed a cryptic resolution to decline government posts if the party performed badly in the forthcoming elections. In the event, the 2013 election saw MCA's worst ever performance. Consequently, for the first time since independence there are no MCA ministers in the Malaysian Cabinet. The 2013 election was also the first time that a sitting president (Chua Soi Lek) of the MCA, the second largest party in the BN, was omitted from the coalition's candidate list.

see also: Alliance Party; *Barisan Nasional*; Democratic Action Party; *Gerakan Rakyat Malaysia*; Malaysian Indian Congress; May 13 Racial Riots 1969; New Economic Policy; UMNO.

Malaysian Indian Congress (MIC) (Malaya/Malaysia)

The Malaysian Indian Congress (MIC), formerly the Malayan Indian Congress, is one of the core communal components of the ***Barisan Nasional*** (National Front) ruling coalition. The MIC was founded in 1946 to represent peninsular Malayan residents of sub-continental origin. Its initial orientation was as much Indian as Malayan with the name taken from the Indian National Congress. A leftist disposition was discarded with the onset of the **Emergency** in 1948. After the success of Malay–Chinese political cooperation in municipal elections in Kuala Lumpur in 1952, the MIC participated within the tripartite intercommunal **Alliance Party**, which won every seat but one in national elections the following year. The MIC has always been the most junior partner in this successful governing relationship, which was carried over with the formation of the Federation of Malaysia in 1963 and then in the wider *Barisan Nasional* (National Front, BN) in the early 1970s. Indians comprise only slightly over seven per cent of the population of peninsular Malaysia and their geographic distribution means that they command very few natural constituencies, leaving the MIC to secure representation through receiving a small quota of state and federal seats as well as minimal representation in the cabinet. Indian political influence is limited also because of Hindu–Muslim divisions and because Indian rural workers in the rubber industry have never felt that their interests have been represented by the small group of business people and professionals of Tamil origin who have always dominated the MIC.

The MIC's claim to represent the Indian community in Malaysia was severely undermined in 2007 when the **Hindu Rights Action Force** (Hindraf) led a massive protest against the BN government under Prime Minister **Abdullah Badawi** for neglecting the community's interests. This antipathy translated into a massive swing of ethnic Indian support away from the ruling coalition at the 2008 election, contributing to huge opposition gains. MIC's poor election performance saw longstanding party president, Samy Vellu, and two party vice-presidents lose their parliamentary seats. Vocal calls for party reform focused on Samy Vellu's leadership, and while he retained the party presidency for a record eleventh consecutive term in the party's 2009 internal elections, mounting pressure led to his resignation a year later. Still, the MIC failed to perform credibly at the 2013 elections, winning only four parliamentary seats and five state seats.

see also: Alliance Party; Badawi, Tun Abdullah; *Barisan Nasional*; Emergency 1948–60; Hindraf; Malaysian Chinese Association.

Malik, Adam (Indonesia)

Adam Malik served continuously with distinction as foreign minister of Indonesia from March 1966 to May 1977. He was appointed by General **Suharto**, who had assumed executive authority in the wake of an abortive coup (*see* ***Gestapu***) in October 1965 which politically discredited President **Sukarno**. Adam Malik played a key role in the regional and international rehabilitation of Indonesia after an assertive and exhibitionist phase of foreign policy. He was instrumental in promoting reconciliation with Malaysia and in helping to found **ASEAN** (Association of Southeast Asian Nations) as well as repairing economic relations with western states. Indonesia's reintegration into international society was registered by his election as president of the United Nations General Assembly in September 1971. Adam Malik was born on 22 July 1917 in Pematang Siantar in northern Sumatra. He combined an early interest in nationalism with that of journalism; at the age of twenty he founded the Antara press agency which after independence became the national news agency. At the end of the Pacific War, Adam Malik was a leading member of a group of young radical nationalists who wished to wrest independence from Japan rather than acquire it under their auspices. During the period of national revolution, he became involved in a plot against the socialist prime minister, Sutan Sjahrir, and was imprisoned until late 1948. His radical record prevented Adam Malik from playing a political role during the period of parliamentary democracy in the 1950s. Shortly after President Sukarno had instituted his system of **Guided Democracy** in July 1959, Adam Malik was sent as ambassador to the Soviet Union, which proved to be a disillusioning experience. In November 1963 he was appointed minister of trade but became progressively alienated from the Sukarno regime. He was an appropriate civilian choice for foreign minister in the military-dominated administration which replaced that of President Sukarno. Indeed, he ensured that Indonesia's conduct of foreign policy reflected an independent tradition and was not merely a crude expression of military priorities. After serving as foreign minister for eleven years, Adam Malik became briefly speaker of the country's **People's Consultative Assembly** and then in March 1978 was elected vice-president of the Republic. He retired from public life in March 1983 and died on 5 September 1984.

see also: ASEAN; *Gestapu;* Guided Democracy; People's Consultative Assembly; Sjahrir, Sutan; Suharto; Sukarno.

Maluku Violence 1999–2002
(Indonesia)

The Maluku Islands, also known as the Moluccas, are a group of islands located to the east of Sulawesi, Indonesia. They comprised a single province after Indonesian independence in 1945 but were subsequently split into two, North Maluku and Maluku, in 1999. North Maluku, whose capital is Ternate, has a predominantly Muslim population while Maluku, whose capital is Ambon, has a predominantly Christian population.

In January 1999, violence between Christian and Muslim communities broke out and lasted until the signing of the Malino II Accord on 13 February 2002 in Manilo, South Sulawesi. It was estimated that between 5,000 and 9,000 people died as a result of the violence, while another 300,000 to 700,000 were displaced. Approximately 29,000 houses and hundreds of mosques and churches were also destroyed. What triggered the catastrophe was a personal altercation between an Ambonese bus driver and a Bugis passenger in Ambon on 19 January 1999. From that incident, matters quickly escalated to altercations between Christian and Muslim gangs from neighbouring communities, eventually degenerating into widespread communal violence.

The unprecedented scale of violence in Maluku can be explained by multiple factors. While social and economic disparities had existed in Maluku society for decades, the fall of the **New Order** regime and the immediate turbulence of the *Reformasi* era amplified these uncertainties, allowing them to erupt into full-scale violence. Further intensifying the volatile atmosphere were demographic trends which saw immigration from South Sulawesi and transmigration from Java upsetting a hitherto Christian majority. Land and economic competition from these immigrants effectively displaced Christian Ambonese from many sectors of the economy, fuelling resentment towards Muslim immigrants who were perceived as receiving preferential treatment by the national government. This shifting ethno-religious balance further threatened traditional authority structures, such as the *pela* system which defined mutual obligations between villages. In addition, the sectarian violence was also linked to the newly disenfranchised members of the national elite who had a strategic interest in provoking violence to undermine the government of **Abdurrahman Wahid**. These elites were linked to the *preman* (street thugs) who were differentiated by ethnic and religious persuasions. Violence in Maluku worsened when ***Laskar Jihad*** recruited Muslims from across the archipelago to join Maluku Muslims to fight against Christians. Their arms, training and logistical superiority accelerated violence and worsened bloodshed across the region marked by savage mutilations, forced conversions and rampant destruction of property. The Indonesian military was also widely viewed to have been partisan, with some elements even arming Muslim factions and providing logistical support.

The spate of violence in Maluku ended with the government-sponsored Malino II Peace Accord in February 2002. In what was seen as decisive action by the coordinating minister for people's welfare, **Yusuf Kalla**, the peace accord established an eleven-point agreement to end conflict, restore the rule of law, protect the unitary state, establish freedom of movement, eliminate armed organizations, return displaced persons to their homes, rebuild infrastructure, maintain neutrality of security forces and reconstruct an integrated university.

see also: Kalla, Yusuf; *Laskar Jihad*; New Order; Wahid, Abdurrahman.

Manila Hostage Crisis 2010 (Philippines)

On 23 August 2010 a disgruntled policeman recently dismissed from the police force, Rolando Mendoza, took a tour bus and its passengers hostage in Manila in an attempt to get reinstated into the force. The bus was carrying twenty-five passengers at the time, most of whom were from Hong Kong. Negotiations with Mendoza, who was armed with a handgun and an M-16 assault rifle, were conducted by Philippine police superintendent Orlanddo Yebra, and chief inspector, Romeo Salvado. While the negotiation resulted in the release over several hours of nine hostages, uncertainty about the authorities' position in response to Mendoza's demands created confusion. Agitated by the live coverage and provoked by the presence of his brother, who apparently was introduced into the arena to assist with the hostage negotiations, Mendoza began shooting the hostages. Several attempts by the police at the scene to storm the bus failed, and the crisis only ended when Mendoza was eventually taken down by snipers. By then, Mendoza had killed eight hostages and injured several others.

The crisis was the first test for President **Benigno Aquino III**, who had been sworn into office barely three months earlier, and proved a major embarrassment for the Philippines government. The airing live across the world of the confusion surrounding attempts to address Mendoza's demands, and the failed attempts to storm the bus, revealed the incompetence of the police force during a hostage situation. The situation was compounded when investigations into the event, called for by President Aquino, revealed that several of the hostages may have in fact been killed by police fire. Criticism was particularly caustic from the authorities in China and Hong Kong who proceeded to place the Philippines on their travel alert list.

see also: Aquino III, Benigno Simeon Cojuangco.

Manila Pact 1954 (Cambodia/Laos/Philippines/Thailand/Vietnam)

The Southeast Asia Collective Defence Treaty, known as the Manila Pact, was concluded in Manila on 8 September 1954 between the governments of the United States, Britain, France, Australia, New Zealand, Pakistan, Thailand and the Philippines. The alliance was inspired by the United States, whose secretary of state, John Foster Dulles, had failed to mobilize united action in April 1954 to prevent the Vietnamese Communist victory at the Battle of **Dien Bien Phu**. As part of a global policy of containing international communism, the alliance was directed at the People's Republic of China and North Vietnam and designed to shore up the provisional territorial settlement reached in the **Geneva Agreements on Indochina** in July

1954. That settlement had divided Vietnam temporarily along the line of the seventeenth parallel of latitude and had recognized the independence of Laos and Cambodia. The obligation of the signatories of the Manila Pact to act under the central Article IV was extended through a separate protocol to 'the states of Cambodia and Laos and the free territory under the jurisdiction of the State of Vietnam'. The treaty took an institutionalized form from February 1955 when its council meeting in Bangkok approved the establishment of **SEATO** (Southeast Asia Treaty Organization) with headquarters in the Thai capital.

The alliance, which required unanimity for common action, was never effective because its members differed over security priorities from the outset. Only two of them were resident regional states. The Cambodian leader, Prince **Norodom Sihanouk**, repudiated the protection of the treaty in February 1956, while Laos was excluded from it in July 1962 under the terms of a neutralization agreement (*see* **Geneva Agreements on Laos**). South Vietnam never made an explicit appeal for assistance under the protocol. In March 1962 in a joint statement by Thai foreign minister, **Thanat Khoman**, and US secretary of state, Dean Rusk, the latter asserted that his country's obligation did not depend upon the prior agreement of all other parties to the treaty since that obligation was individual as well as collective. However, the most that the alliance ever managed was a limited show of force in Thailand in May 1962 by some of its members in response to a crisis in Laos. Pakistan had become alienated early on because of a failure to attract support against India. France openly opposed the United States' military intervention in Vietnam, while Britain withheld military cooperation, announcing disengagement from east of Suez in July 1967. Apart from the United States, of the original signatories only Australia, New Zealand, the Philippines and Thailand dispatched troops to Vietnam, but not collectively under the terms of the Manila Pact. The alliance lost its original *raison d'être* after US President Richard Nixon's historic visit to Beijing in February 1972, which confirmed Sino–US rapprochement.

A truncated Pakistan withdrew from the alliance in November 1972, following the secession of Bangladesh at the end of 1971. A Council meeting in September 1973, in the wake of the **Paris Peace Agreements** on Vietnam in January 1973, abolished the military structure of SEATO from February 1974. After Communist victories in Cambodia and South Vietnam in April 1975, Thailand's prime minister, **Kukrit Pramoj**, and the Philippine's president, **Ferdinand Marcos**, agreed informally to abolish SEATO during a meeting in Manila in July. That agreement was confirmed at a Council meeting in New York in September 1975 when it was decided that SEATO would be dissolved completely on 30 June 1977. The Collective Defence Treaty has never been revoked, however, primarily because it provides the only formal defence link between Thailand and the United States. In February 1979, following Vietnam's invasion of Cambodia, US President Jimmy Carter reaffirmed to Thailand's prime minister, **Kriangsak Chomanan**, the validity of the United States' commitment to his country under the Manila Pact. US defence cooperation with Thailand has been sustained but the Collective Defence Treaty survives only as a redundant vestige of the Cold War in Asia.

see also: Dien Bien Phu, Battle of, 1954; Geneva Agreements on Indochina 1954; Geneva Agreements on Laos 1962; Kriangsak Chomanan, General; Marcos, Ferdinand; Paris Peace Agreements 1973; SEATO; Sihanouk, King Norodom; Thanat Khoman.

Manila Summit (ASEAN) 1987

(Brunei/Indonesia/Malaysia/Philippines/Singapore/Thailand)

In December 1987 the six heads of government of **ASEAN** (Association of Southeast Asian Nations) met for two days in Manila. It was only the third such meeting in its history: the first was the **Bali Summit** in February 1976 and the second was the **Kuala Lumpur Summit** in August 1977. The Manila Summit was held amid tight security because of the series of abortive coups mounted against the administration of President **Corazón Aquino**, which had replaced that of **Ferdinand Marcos** in February 1986.

The meeting was not significant for any initiatives in political or economic cooperation. Nor did it lead to reconciliation between the Philippines and Malaysia over the **Philippines' Claim to Sabah**. The fleeting gathering was intended, above all, as a display of corporate solidarity for President Aquino's embattled administration on the understanding that failure to have so acted would have reflected adversely on the credibility of ASEAN.

see also: Aquino, Corazón; Bali Summit (ASEAN) 1976; Kuala Lumpur Summit (ASEAN) 1977; Philippines' Claim to Sabah.

Maphilindo (Indonesia/Malaya/Philippines)

Maphilindo is an acronym taken from the first parts of Malaya, the Philippines and Indonesia, which was coined by Indonesia's foreign minister, **Subandrio**, in June 1963. The term had its origins in regional contention (**Confrontation**) over the proposal for a Federation of Malaysia with Malaya as its political core. Both Indonesia and the Philippines objected, the latter because of its claim to part of northern Borneo included in the proposal (*see* **Philippines' Claim to Sabah**). As a blocking alternative, the Philippines' president, **Diosdado Macapagal**, advanced a plan for a confederation of nations of Malay origin predicated implicitly on a common anti-Chinese sentiment. At a meeting of senior ministers from the three states, which convened in Manila in June 1963, Subandrio supported the Maphilindo scheme as a flattering gesture to the Philippine president. Malaya's deputy prime minister, **Tun Abdul Razak**, endorsed the concept in an attempt to encourage Indonesia and the Philippines to accept Malaysia. A meeting of heads of government followed at the end of July which upheld the scheme but the apparent reconciliation did not last. Maphilindo foundered with the advent of Malaysia on 16 September 1963. Neither Indonesia nor the Philippines accorded recognition to the expanded state and diplomatic relations were broken off between the government in Kuala Lumpur and those in Jakarta and Manila. Despite attempts to revive the concept in 1964, Maphilindo never progressed beyond its declaratory establishment and failed to assume any institutional form.

see also: Confrontation; Macapagal, Diosdado; Philippines' Claim to Sabah; Razak, Tun Abdul; Subandrio.

Marcos, Ferdinand (Philippines)

Ferdinand Marcos was the most powerful political figure in the post-independence history of the Philippines. He held the office of president from January 1966 until February 1986. Ferdinand Edralin Marcos was born on 17 September 1917 in Ilocos Norte Province on the main island of Luzón. He came to national prominence when he was placed first in the bar finals after sitting the examinations in prison, prior to a successful appeal against a conviction for murdering a political rival of his father. After the Pacific War and national independence, his career was advanced by his claim to have been a distinguished guerrilla war commander. He entered politics in 1949, moving from the House of Representatives to the Senate in 1959. He was elected president in November 1965 and re-elected in November 1968.

In the face of rising political dissension and a constitutional impediment to a third term of office, Marcos declared martial law in September 1972. The break with constitutional legality was welcomed initially as a brave attempt to regenerate political and economic life. Within a decade, the promise of Marcos' New Society Movement had turned sour. Personal abuse of power undermined all independent institutions, while his family and business circle accumulated great wealth through corrupt practices. His wife **Imelda Marcos** attracted fierce animosity for her regal pretensions. Against a background of economic decline and burgeoning Communist insurgency, his personal authority crumbled visibly from August 1983 when his principal political rival, **Benigno Aquino**, was shot dead while in military custody at Manila airport on his return from exile in the United States. Unable to throw off the stigma of Aquino's assassination, stricken by illness, and unable to reverse economic failure, Marcos gambled on re-establishing his political authority through holding a snap election in February

1986. The opposition closed ranks around the popular widow of his assassinated rival, **Corazón Aquino**. Conspicuous electoral fraud, a military revolt led by the minister of defence, **Juan Ponce Enrile**, and the deputy chief of staff of the armed forces, **Fidel Ramos**, together with a massive display of popular support (**People Power**) for Corazón Aquino backed by Cardinal **Jaime Sin** and the Catholic Church, persuaded the US government to advise Marcos to leave the country. He was flown with his family via Guam to Hawaii where he remained in exile. After inspiring a number of feckless abortive attempts to promote a coup against the new government, recurrent ill health (and the warning of his host government) reduced him to a pathetic figure. He was refused permission to return to the Philippines and died in Hawaii on 28 September 1989. It was not until four years later that his family was granted permission by the government of President **Fidel Ramos** for his remains to be returned and entombed in a mausoleum in his hometown of Batac in the Ilocos region of Luzón. His persisting ill repute was demonstrated in June 1998, when president-elect Joseph Estrada revealed that he would permit Marcos' body to be buried in the country's Heroes Cemetery in Manila. The subsequent display of public outrage caused his widow, Imelda, to announce that the plan to bury her late husband would be postponed. It was only in February 1999, that the family of the late president agreed to pay substantial damages to victims of human rights abuses during his despotic and corrupt rule.

see also: Aquino, Benigno; Aquino, Corazón; Enrile, Juan Ponce; Estrada, Joseph; Marcos, Imelda; People Power; Ramos, Fidel; Sin, Jaime.

Marcos, Imelda (Philippines)

Imelda Marcos achieved political notoriety as the venal and controversial consort of President **Ferdinand Marcos** of the Philippines. She was born on 2 July 1929 to an impoverished branch of the wealthy Romuáldez family from Leyte in the central Visayan Islands. Much of her life was spent trying to overcome early social disability and material deprivation. She grew up to become a beautiful woman with a sweet soprano voice, subsequently put to her future husband's political service at election rallies. Ferdinand Marcos was attracted to her after Imelda had won the title Muse of Manila at the Philippines International Fair in 1953. In May 1954, after a whirlwind courtship, she married the up and coming congressman. Imelda proved to be a political asset to the future president but confined herself to only a ceremonial role during his first two terms of office.

After the introduction of martial law in September 1972, Imelda began to display personal political ambition and at one time came to be regarded as a likely successor to her ailing husband. Her formal political career began in 1975 when she was appointed governor of Metropolitan Manila. She entered the National Assembly in 1978, assuming the portfolio of human settlements later in the year. In 1982 she became a member of the Executive Council charged with responsibility for interim government in the event of the president's death or incapacity. In her political role, she exercised considerable patronage and acted as a plenipotentiary for her husband overseas. Imelda Marcos was an impulsive woman of boundless energy who was obsessed with grandiose schemes, material acquisition and cultivating a coterie of international celebrities. Her facility for political theatre served her and her husband well for a time. However, dynastic pretensions and insatiable greed had an alienating political effect nationally, especially after the blatant murder of opposition leader **Benigno Aquino**, which marked a political turning point. In February 1986, after military and popular reaction to fraudulently conducted elections had precipitated political change, she left for exile in Hawaii with her discredited husband. In exile, she continued to hold court among a small circle of émigrés and plotted Ferdinand Marcos' political return to the Philippines until thwarted by his death in September 1989. She was denied the right to bring her husband's body back in state to the Philippines. However, in November 1991 she returned to Manila with her son Bombong ostensibly to face civil and criminal charges relating to the expropriation of public funds. Her prime purpose was political vindication and ambition but she received only limited popular acclaim and did not pose a threat to the widow of the murdered Benigno Aquino, **Corazón Aquino**, who had succeeded Ferdinand Marcos as president. Imelda Marcos stood as a candidate in presidential elections in May 1992, but secured only just over ten per cent of the national vote, coming fifth behind **Fidel Ramos**, who as deputy chief of staff had led the military revolt which precipitated her husband's political downfall. In September 1993 she was sentenced in Manila to eighteen to twenty-four years in prison for criminal graft but was released on bail pending appeal. The same month, she was able to have Ferdinand Marcos' remains entombed in a mausoleum in his home town of Batac in what proved to be an abortive attempt to establish their son Bombong as his political successor. Further charges of embezzlement were brought against her in April 1994 and in September 1995. In May 1995, she secured election to the House of Representatives for a constituency in her home province of Leyte. In January 1998, the Supreme Court upheld the 1993 decision sentencing her to twelve years imprisonment but she was freed pending an appeal. Imelda Marcos then announced her candidacy for the presidential elections in May but withdrew at the end of April after opinion polls showed that she would secure only around two per cent of the vote. She subsequently supported the candidacy of the then vice-president, **Joseph Estrada**. In October 1998, the Supreme Court upheld her appeal overturning the only conviction, so far, on charges of graft relating to her late husband's despotic and corrupt rule. Corruption trials held in March 2008 acquitted Marcos of thirty-two cases against her. However, in September 2010, the Sandigabayan's Fifth Division ordered Marcos to return twelve million pesos of government funds withdrawn by her late husband from the National Food Authority in 1963.

Two of Imelda Marcos' children are involved in Philippine politics as well. Her daughter Maria Imelda Marcos has been Governor of Ilocos Norte since 2010, and her son Ferdinand Jr was elected to the Senate in the same year. In the 2010 election, Imelda Marcos ran once again for the House of Representatives for the second district of Ilocos Norte, which has long remained the main support base for the Marcos family. She achieved victory by a margin of sixty per cent from her nearest rival, Mariano Nalupta Jr. In October 2012, Marcos sought to renew her term as Ilocas Norte's second district representative by filing for candidacy. Notorious for her profligacy, Marcos remains a member of the House of Representatives at the age of eighty-three, despite persistent allegations of corruption hanging over her head.

see also: Aquino, Benigno; Aquino, Corazón; Estrada, Joseph; Marcos, Ferdinand; Ramos, Fidel.

Marshall, David (Singapore)

David Marshall was the first chief minister of Singapore, holding the office for fourteen months during 1955–6 in the initial phase of the island's decolonization. He was born in Singapore on 12 March 1908 to an Orthodox Jewish family from Iraq; his father was a successful trader. After failing to settle to a career in business, David Marshall trained in law as a barrister at the Middle Temple in London. His career as a criminal lawyer was interrupted by the Pacific War during which he was interned and then dispatched to Japan to work in coal mines. After the war, he established a reputation as an outstanding advocate. He also began to involve himself in Singapore's politics. In 1954 Marshall founded the Singapore Socialist Party, which he took into an alliance with the Labour Party as the Labour Front to make a strong showing in elections in 1955.

His period of office was turbulent, partly as a consequence of industrial unrest fomented by the Communist Party of Malaya and because of his own headstrong temperament. It was also shortlived, as he resigned when talks with the British government over self-government broke down; he was succeeded as chief minister by **Lim Yew Hock**. Marshall then resigned his parliamentary seat and went on to found the **Workers' Party**, which attracted Communist support, enabling him to win a by-election in 1962 which he then lost in general elections the following year. Marshall returned to legal practice but came into conflict with the government of **Lee Kuan Yew**, which was intolerant of dissent. In October 1972 he was suspended from legal practice for six months because he had breached an undertaking to the attorney general not to part with affidavits in *habeas corpus* proceedings, which were subsequently released at a conference of the International Press Institute. Reconciliation took place in 1978, however, when he was asked to become Singapore's ambassador to France, a post which he held continuously with distinction until his retirement in 1993. On his return to Singapore, he worked as a legal adviser, but became outspoken against the government. He died on 12 December 1995 aged eighty-seven.

see also: Lee Kuan Yew; Lim Yew Hock; Workers' Party.

Mas Selamat Kastari (Singapore)

Mas Selamat bin Kastari was the leader of ***Jemaah Islamiyah***'s (JI) Singapore branch and is currently held under Singapore's Internal Security Act that allows for detention without trial. Born on 23 January 1961 in Java, Indonesia, Mas Selamat Kastari migrated to Singapore with his family as a young boy. He joined ***Darul Islam***, the predecessor of JI, in the early 1990s and went to Afghanistan twice. It was in Afghanistan that he met **Hambali**, a leader of JI.

Mas Selamat is believed to be the mastermind behind JI plans to carry out attacks on western and local targets in Singapore, including the US Embassy and American Club, as well as the headquarters of various Singapore ministries. Investigations also suggested that he had made plans to crash a plane into Singapore's Changi Airport. In December 2001, Singapore's Internal Security Department (ISD) launched a crackdown on the JI cell in Singapore and Mas Selamat fled the country with his family. He was first arrested in the Indonesian island of Bintan in February 2003 by Indonesian authorities for carrying false identification papers. The absence of an extradition agreement between Singapore and Jakarta meant that he was released at the end of his detention. Mas Selamat was arrested again in January 2006 in Java on the same charges, and was later investigated for connections to the 2002 Bali bombings. He was subsequently deported to Singapore and held under the Internal Security Act.

Mas Selamat's escape from Singapore's Whitley Road Detention Centre on 27 February 2008 made headlines and placed Singapore under an uncomfortable spotlight. Investigations revealed that he had climbed out of the building through an unsecured bathroom window while he was in a cubicle, after requesting privacy from guards to change into civilian clothes for a scheduled family visit. A few days later, he reportedly swam more than one kilometre to the southern Malaysian state of Johor at night with the help of an improvized floatation device. A nationwide manhunt was conducted while an Interpol international red alert was also issued. It was later found that Mas Selamat received help from family members who had provided him with food, shelter, maps and some money before he escaped to Malaysia. Three of them were sentenced to time in prison. The Singapore government came under heavy criticism for failing to disseminate information on his escape to the public promptly. The mainstream media too, were criticized for failing to question how Mas Selamat was allowed to escape. Six officers from the ISD were subsequently charged, including the superintendent of the detention centre who was dismissed while his deputy and the guards in charge of Mas Selamat were demoted. A Commission of Inquiry uncovered numerous security lapses that led to the escape: the lack of grilles on the window in the toilet cubicle, the poor judgement of the guards and insufficient security around the Family Visitation Block from which Mas Selamat escaped.

On 1 April 2009, Mas Selamat was re-arrested by the Malaysian Special Branch in a small village in Johor in a joint operation involving intelligence agencies of both countries. His arrest was only made public in May as the Malaysian government had requested the news of his capture not to be released so as not to jeopardize ongoing security operations. He was subsequently returned to Singaporean custody on 24 September 2010 after being detained for eighteen months in Malaysia under its own Internal Security Act.

see also: Darul Islam; Hambali; *Jemaah Islamiyah.*

Masyumi (Indonesia)

Masyumi is an Indonesian acronym drawn from *Majelis Syuro Muslimin Indonesia*, which translates as Consultative Council of Indonesian

Muslims. It was established by the Japanese as an umbrella organization in October 1943. They conceived of the council as an instrument to serve their own wartime political purpose. After the proclamation of independence in August 1945, *Masyumi* became a part of the nationalist movement but with its own agenda of entrenching the values of Islam in the constitution of the Republic. Divisions between radical, traditional and modernist wings of the party led to successive defections. After the departure from party ranks of ***Nahdlatul Ulama*** in 1952, the modernist wing, drawn from the cultural and educational movement ***Muhammadiyah*** (Followers of the Prophet Muhammad), predominated but its political fortunes went into decline. *Masyumi* enjoyed representation in the early coalition cabinets which failed to address the country's economic problems. In the country's first general election in 1955, *Masyumi* secured just under twenty-one per cent of the vote, drawn primarily from the outer islands. That disappointing result undermined its claim to share office, from which it was excluded as parliamentary democracy gave way to **Guided Democracy** through the machinations of President **Sukarno**. Some of its leading members were implicated in abortive regional uprisings in 1958 which led to the party being banned in 1960. After President **Suharto** established his **New Order** from 1966, an attempt was made to reform the party in February 1968 through creating a legal successor as *Partai Muslimin Indonesia* (in acronym *Parmusi*). However, it was excluded from government. Following a weak showing in elections in 1971, it was merged with other Islamic parties into ***Partai Persatuan Pembangunan*** (United Development Party, PPP) in January 1973. In this form, it served to provide legitimacy for an electoral process whose main function was to lend legitimacy to President Suharto's authoritarian rule, which came to an end in May 1998.

see also: Guided Democracy; Islam; *Muhammadiyah*; *Nahdlatul Ulama*; New Order; *Partai Persatuan Pembangunan*; Suharto; Sukarno.

May 13 Racial Riots 1969 (Malaysia)

On 13 May 1969 communal violence erupted between Malays and non-Malays (mainly Chinese) in Kuala Lumpur, which took a toll of 196 lives, according to official figures. The violence occurred after a significant electoral reversal for the governing intercommunal **Alliance Party** coalition which had ruled Malaya and then Malaysia continuously from before independence in August 1957. The Alliance retained its parliamentary majority in the elections of 9 May but its Chinese component, the **Malaysian Chinese Association** (MCA) lost fourteen out of twenty-seven seats held previously, while **UMNO** (United Malays National Organization), the dominant party in the coalition, lost a high percentage of votes to its principal Malay opponent, ***Parti Islam Se-Malaysia*** (PAS), albeit not accurately reflected in seats retained.

Racial tension with a primary source in Malay political insecurity had been a striking feature of the election campaign. It had been heightened by the results for the federal Parliament and also by the uncertain outcome of the concurrent state elections in the case of Selangor, within which the national capital was situated. Selangor had long been assumed to be an exclusive Malay preserve, reflected in the constitutional provision that the chief minister had to be a Malay. The election produced a deadlocked state legislature and Malay anxieties were reinforced by the provocative nature of celebratory processions by supporters of successful non-Malay opposition parties in Kuala Lumpur. A counter-victory procession organized by Selangor UMNO for the evening of 13 May began with a huge gathering at the residence of the chief minister, Harun Idris. Communal violence at its fringes expanded in an orgy of killing by Malays, which was not fully contained for five days.

The riots proved to be the most significant event in the post-independence history of peninsular Malaysia. Parliamentary democracy was suspended until January 1971. The government was replaced temporarily by a National Operations Council headed by the deputy prime minister, **Tun Abdul Razak**. The format of politics in Malaysia was modified to ensure that the constitutional special position of the Malays was entrenched as one of dominance. A **New Economic Policy** foreshadowed on

1 July 1969 was later given content to shift the balance of material advantage more equitably in the Malay interest. The riots also demonstrated Malay loss of confidence in Prime Minister **Tunku Abdul Rahman**, who was obliged to resign in favour of his deputy Tun Razak in September 1970.

see also: Abdul Rahman, Tunku; Alliance Party; Malaysian Chinese Association; New Economic Policy; *Parti Islam Se-Malaysia*; Razak, Tun Abdul; UMNO.

Megawati Sukarnoputri (Indonesia)

Megawati Sukarnoputri was the first female president of Indonesia, holding high office from 2001 to 2004. Megawati was born on 23 January 1947 in Yogyakarta, then the revolutionary capital of the Republic of which her father was president. She was educated at Padjajaran University in Bandung but suffered personally from President **Sukarno**'s fall from political grace from the mid-1960s. Two broken marriages saw her in her forties entering politics in 1987 as a parliamentary representative of *Partai Demokrasi Indonesia* (PDI) but without displaying much interest in its proceedings. In July 1993, in reaction to an attempt by President **Suharto** to manipulate the choice of party leader, she was nominated as chairman, capitalizing on her parentage to secure election to that office in December that year. She was removed from office at a stage-managed party conference in Medan in June 1996, which was followed in July by the violent ejection of her supporters from the PDI headquarters in Jakarta by the police and army, which provoked rioting in the capital. Her faction had been excluded from participation in parliamentary elections in May 1997. Moreover, she was not in the forefront of agitation prior to the political downfall of President Suharto in May 1998. With the restoration of the democratic process, Megawati appeared as a symbol of political reform because of her persecution by the previous regime. Although she attracted substantial support as leader of the ***Partai Demokrasi Indonesia–Perjuangan*** (PDI–P) in parliamentary elections, a reformed PDI led by her *Perjuangan* (struggle) faction, she failed to impress as a potential leader with a concrete agenda for Indonesia's economic and political rehabilitation and also alienated the Islamic constituency because of the large number of Christians on her party list. She was elected vice-president of Indonesia by the **People's Consultative Assembly** (MPR) in October 1999 but, with her passive style, appeared a marginal figure beside an ailing president. Megawati failed to secure the presidency despite being the front-running candidate since the previous June because of her reluctance to engage in coalition building. Nevertheless, she emerged as an alternative when President **Abdurrahman Wahid**'s leadership style gradually alienated domestic and international support. On 23 July 2001, in the wake of strained relations between the president and military and with an economy still reeling from the **Asian Financial Crisis**, the MPR replaced Abdurrahman Wahid with Megawati.

Megawati's presidency proved largely tepid and uninspiring, albeit stabilizing. Due to the political circumstances that shaped her presidency, which saw her party win merely thirty-one per cent of the seats in the House of Representatives (DPR) and twenty-seven per cent in the MPR, she was forced to form weak alliances which effectively blocked successful policy implementation. Nevertheless, she did demonstrate a measure of resolve as she attempted to steer Indonesia through the early post-September 11 years of security challenges posed by terrorist groups. Megawati was the second head of state to visit Washington DC after September 11 and managed to secure the resumption of US military aid, hitherto frozen in reaction to alleged human rights abuses perpetrated by the Indonesian military in East Timor. She also presided over the introduction of an anti-terror mandate that allowed year-long detention of terrorist suspects without trial and the death sentence for convicted terrorists. This mandate was not well-received by a burgeoning civil society, or the DPR, which saw it as a return to the repression of the **New Order**. With her popularity diminished, Megawati's bid to be re-elected in 2004 failed when she lost to her former coordinating minister for political and security affairs, **Susilo Bambang**

Yudhoyono. Her disappointment at the loss was evident in her refusal to congratulate president-elect Yudhoyono on his victory.

Megawati attempted a comeback at the 2009 presidential elections. Yet, despite President Yudhoyono's dwindling popularity, she could not unseat him. Nevertheless, her strong performance indicated that she remains a political heavyweight and also revived her status within PDI–P, which became the only party not represented in President Yudhoyono's Cabinet. Megawati is also seen as the force behind the meteoric rise of popular Jakarta governor, **Joko Widodo**, who she eventually anointed in March 2014 to be the PDI–P's presidential candidate for the July 2014 presidential election, thereby quelling rumours that she planned to stand yet again.

see also: Asian Financial Crisis 1997–8; New Order; *Partai Demokrasi Indonesia–Perjuangan*; People's Consultative Assembly; Suharto; Sukarno; Wahid, Abdurrahman; Widodo, Joko; Yudhoyono, Susilo Bambang.

Mekong River Project (Cambodia/Laos/ Myanmar/Thailand/Vietnam)

The Mekong river rises in Tibet and flows south through southern China. It then continues in the same direction, serving as the boundary between Myanmar and Laos and most of that between Laos and Thailand, before passing through Cambodia and then southern Vietnam from where it empties into the **South China Sea** at the end of a course of some 2,600 miles. The lower Mekong River Basin, including Thailand, Laos, Cambodia and Vietnam, attracted the attention of the United Nations Economic Commission for the Far East (ECAFE) in the early 1950s as offering great potential for harnessing its resources for irrigation and energy purposes. The Committee for the Coordination of Investigations of the Lower Mekong Basin was set up in September 1957. Some progress was made during the 1960s, when a consortium of states began to collaborate in planning under United Nations aegis, with ECAFE subsequently becoming the Economic and Social Commission for Asia and the Pacific (ESCAP). The progress of the undertaking was obstructed by the **Indochina Wars**, with the government in Saigon presuming to speak for Vietnam. Cambodia withdrew from the undertaking when the **Khmer Rouge** seized power in 1975, while after its invasion by Vietnam in 1978, the government in Phnom Penh was excluded from the Mekong Committee.

The project was revived after the political settlement of the Cambodian conflict had been signed at the **International Conference on Cambodia in Paris** in October 1991. Acrimony then arose because of unilateral measures by Thailand to dam the river upstream but a joint communiqué was signed between the four riparian states on 5 February 1993. The terms of that communiqué committed the signatories to continued cooperation in the exploitation of the Mekong River and to the establishment of a Mekong Working Group with the task of drafting a framework agreement for future cooperation on the Mekong River based on an equitable and reasonable utilization of mainstream water. That agreement was concluded among the riparian states at a meeting in Thailand in April 1995 which set up a Mekong River Commission (MRC) with a regulatory mandate replacing an interim secretariat. The first official meeting of the Commission was convened in Phnom Penh in August 1995 to which Myanmar and China, as riparian states, were invited as dialogue partners. In 2001, the MRC passed new policies such as data sharing protocols. Subsequently, in 2002, China began to provide the MRC with daily water level data, and in 2003, agreed to scale back plans to blast rapids. However, China has not been cooperative in providing information concerning dam operations, and refused to attend emergency meetings that were held in 2004. In 2005, China finally agreed to hold technical discussions under the framework of cooperation with the MRC in Beijing, as a consequence of which China provided the MRC with data for flood forecasts in 2007, in exchange for monthly flow data. In April 2010, an MRC Summit was held in Thailand, with the attendance of all six riparian states. China remains the only country to have built hydropower dams on the main stream of the upper Mekong. In September 2012, the first power-generating unit was switched on at China's Nuozhadu hydroelectric dam, which will be the largest dam on the Mekong River upon completion in 2014. In contrast, in September 2011, the Myanmar government announced that it would suspend work on the US$3.6 million Myitsone dam project on the Irrawaddy River, partly in response to strong public opposition.

A key role in promoting the cooperative endeavour has been played by the United Nations Development Programme but, in June 1996, **ASEAN** (Association of Southeast Asian Nations) launched a complementary Mekong Basin Development Cooperation (AMBDC) programme with a second ministerial meeting convening in Hanoi in July 2000. Plans have been advanced for dams for hydro-electric power, irrigation and flood control. However, in some riparian states, especially in China and Laos, these dams have not always been established in consultation with downstream counterparts. In consequence, upstream reservoirs hold back vital waters in the dry season with serious environmental consequences such as silting up of Cambodia's Tonle Sap Lake and the intrusion of salt water into Vietnam's delta region. In late 2012, the government of Laos confirmed progress in constructing the US$5.2 billion **Xayaburi Dam**, which will be the first dam to be constructed on the lower Mekong River. The electricity generated from this dam is expected to be sold mainly to Thailand, thus generating critical income for Laos (estimated at more than US$2.5 billion a year). In doing so Laos has violated the 1995 Mekong Agreement (that all six riparian countries are signatories to) which requires consultation between these states prior to initiation of large projects on the Mekong river. Despite MRC requests for a delay to study the environmental impact of the Xayaburi Dam, and Laos' initial suspension of the project in compliance, Laos later moved ahead with project-related construction and signed a power purchasing agreement with Thailand, claiming that the decision was an internal affair. Environmentalists are concerned that the project could threaten the livelihoods of communities downstream, as key industries such as rice production and fishing could be affected, compounded by the resettlement of people living near the dam site. In response, the Laotian government has proposed several solutions such as a system that would flush sediment downstream, and a revised 'fish ladder' to help fish bypass the dam and reach spawning grounds.

see also: ASEAN; Indochina Wars; International Conference on Cambodia, Paris 1991; Khmer Rouge; South China Sea; Xayaburi Dam.

Melayu Islam Beraja (Brunei)

Melayu Islam Beraja (MIB) is a Brunei-Malay term which translates as Malay Islamic Monarchy. When Brunei resumed independence in January 1984 and joined the United Nations, Sultan **Hassanal Bolkiah** described his country in those terms in his address to the General Assembly. The concept of a Malay Islamic Monarchy was subsequently elevated into a national ideology by the sultan in July 1990 on his forty-fourth birthday. The ideology, which has been explained by the sultan as an attempt to return to national roots, has mixed functions. It serves to fend off any appeal from externally inspired Muslim fundamentalism. It also serves to legitimize the royal absolutism of Brunei by linking conservative values of Islam and traditional Malay culture with the unifying role of monarchy. MIB, which has become a compulsory subject in the university and schools, has been accompanied by a number of Islamic prohibitions within Brunei giving rise to social tensions.

see also: Bolkiah, Sultan Hassanal; Islam.

Memali Incident 1985 (Malaysia)

On 19 November 1985 members of the Malaysian Federal Reserve Unit (the elite anti-riot squad) and of the paramilitary Field Force became engaged in a violent confrontation with armed villagers while seeking to arrest an Islamic religious teacher and thirty-six other men in Kampung (village) Memali near Baling in the state of Kedah. Ibrahim Mahmud had been an official and a parliamentary candidate of the Malay opposition ***Parti Islam Se-Malaysia*** (PAS) and had refused to surrender to an arrest warrant issued in September 1984 under the Internal Security Act. He had studied for a time in Tripoli and was commonly known as Ibrahim Libya. During the exchange of fire, which lasted for five hours, eighteen people were killed, including Ibrahim Mahmud and four policemen. After the event, Prime Minister **Mahathir Mohamad** claimed that all thirty-seven wanted men had concentrated in Ibrahim Mahmud's house prior to the attempt by the security forces to arrest them. A curfew was imposed on the entire Baling area and the government took steps to control religious feelings from being further inflamed. However, the villagers of Kampung Memali insisted on burying the dead according to the rights due to those who had died as martyrs for the sake of **Islam**. In the event, the bloody incident proved to be an isolated one. At the time, there was deep concern that it might spark off further violent challenges to government by Islamic activists, especially in the rural areas where there were economic grievances.

see also: Islam; Mahathir Mohamad, Tun; *Parti Islam Se-Malaysia*.

Misuari, Nur (Philippines)

Nur Misuari was the founding leader of the **Moro National Liberation Front** (MNLF) ever since it took up arms against the government of President **Ferdinand Marcos** in 1972. He spent decades in exile, primarily in Libya where he enjoyed the patronage of Colonel Gaddafi. Although his movement made a military impact in the mid-1970s, they failed to sustain their initial success because of tribal differences and the ability of the Philippines government to exploit them and to neutralize external Islamic support. Nur Misuari was born in 1940 in the southern island of Sulu. He won a scholarship to the University of the Philippines and after graduating in arts worked as an instructor in Asian philosophies in the Institute of Asian Studies. At the University of the Philippines, he was drawn towards both Islamic and left-wing causes and in the late 1960s secured funding from traditional leaders on Sulu to enable him and other like-minded young Muslims to travel abroad for military training. He was party to an abortive agreement on Muslim autonomy negotiated by **Imelda Marcos** on behalf of the government in Manila. This **Tripoli Agreement** was concluded in December 1976. Nur Misuari has always maintained that President Marcos and his successors never kept to their side of the bargain. After the political downfall of Marcos, he resumed negotiations with representatives of President **Corazón Aquino** and signed a new accord in Jeddah in January 1987 but it failed to hold. From October 1993, he began negotiations with the government of **Fidel Ramos**, which were facilitated by Indonesian mediation. A political breakthrough was achieved in June 1996 leading to an agreement signed by Nur Misuari for the MNLF on 2 September in Manila, which established the Southern Philippines Council for Peace and Development (SPCPD) to supervise the peace process in those provinces with significant Muslim populations to be established as a Special Zone for Peace and Development to be funded from presidential funds. It also confirmed the retention of a controversial four-province Autonomous Region of Muslim Mindanao (ARMM), previously opposed by Misuari. On 9 September, he stood unopposed for the office of Governor of the Autonomous Region and was sworn in at the end of the month. In October 1996, Misuari was appointed chairman of the SPCPD. In July 1997, he assumed a mediatory role leading to a temporary ceasefire in government talks with the rival **Moro Islamic Liberation Front** (MILF), which had not endorsed the peace agreement of September 1996. He was also involved in negotiations following the abduction of foreign tourists from a Malaysian-held resort by members of the **Abu Sayyaf Group**.

In November 2001, Misuari broke the peace pact with the government, when he declared war on the government of **Gloria Macapagal-Arroyo**. Misuari was removed from office as governor by the president, being charged with leading attacks in 2001 that killed more than 100 people in Sulu and Zamboanga City. Subsequently, Misuari escaped to Malaysia, where he was arrested by Malaysian authorities. He was then deported to the Philippines in January 2002 and was detained until April 2008. In December 2007, Misuari's petition for bail was denied and he remained under house arrest in Manila. In April 2008, Misuari was replaced by Muslimim Sema as the leader of the MNLF. In December 2009, a Makati court found Misuari not guilty of rebellion charges, and in the same month Misuari was allowed to post bail. In October

2012, Misuari publicly criticized the **Framework Agreement on the Bangsamoro** between the Philippines government and the MILF, which he claimed was a conspiracy between the two sides. Misuari rejected an invitation to join a Transition Commission that would draft a new law to implement the peace agreement between the Philippines government and the MILF. The focus of the peace agreement was primarily on the creation of Bangsamoro, which would replace the Autonomous Region in Muslim Mindanao (ARMM). Misuari claimed such a move was an affront to the 1996 Agreement with the MNLF that created the ARMM. In September 2013, militants loyal to Misuari raided Muslim villages in the southern province of Zamboanga in a last-ditch attempt to derail the peace process. The rebels' action proved immensely unpopular with the local communities, and signalled the demise of Misuari's standing in the south. In truth, Misuari's standing had already diminished considerably by the 1990s, when he was unable to stop the fragmentation of the MNLF.

see also: Abu Sayyaf Group; Aquino, Corazón; Framework Agreement on the Bangsamoro; Macapagal-Arroyo, Gloria; Marcos, Ferdinand; Marcos, Imelda; Moro Islamic Liberation Front; Moro National Liberation Front; Ramos, Fidel; Tripoli Agreement 1976.

Mok, Ta (Cambodia) *see* **Ta Mok**.

Moro Islamic Liberation Front (Philippines)

The Moro Islamic Liberation Front (MILF) is a Muslim insurgency with religious-separatist goals based in the centre of the southern island of Mindanao. It established a distinct political identity in 1980 as a result of a split in 1978 within the **Moro National Liberation Front** (MNLF).

The MNLF had drawn its initial support from two main tribal constituencies among the Islamic community – the Tausugs from the Sulu islands and the Maguindanaos from central Mindanao. The MNLF leader was **Nur Misuari**, a Tausug. He was challenged by his deputy, Salamat Hashim, who was not only a Maguindanao but also an Islamic scholar who had been trained at Al-Azhar University in Cairo. Nur Misuari had a secular background and also links with the Communist movement which counted against him in the struggle to keep the MNLF intact; this was decided primarily on tribal-territorial grounds with support being attracted to the MILF from the other major Islamic tribal group on Mindanao, the Maranao.

The agreement in September 1996 on limited political autonomy between the Philippines government and the MNLF was opposed by the MILF, which continued to demand an independent Islamic state. By that juncture, it had established a territorial redoubt with a military headquarters in central Mindanao. Moreover, a *modus vivendi* had been worked out with elected provincial and municipal authorities. The military wing of the MILF has assumed a warlord role providing 'protection' in return for contributions from foreign companies and has engaged in kidnapping to ensure compliance. Recruitment to its ranks has been facilitated by local unemployment. The MILF combines a political with a religious agenda and has been able to attract external assistance in the form of funds and manpower. In January 1997, however, the MILF entered into peace talks with the government and signed a ceasefire. Those talks and the ceasefire were interrupted by recurrent hostilities, partly as a result of the MILF attempting to expand its territorial base and the determination of the security forces to reduce its operational zone. In clashes in the late 1990s, the MILF suffered heavy casualties, which may have provoked its announcement that its insurgents would come to the aid of the Communist **New People's Army** should it be hard pressed by army attacks. It has disavowed any connection, however, with the fundamentalist-Muslim **Abu Sayyaf Group** (ASG) responsible for murderous raids against civilian settlements and hostage taking in the southern Philippines. Formal peace talks were resumed in October 1999 but were interrupted by ceasefire violations. In March 2000, the MILF launched a major offensive against six military bases in Lanao del Norte Province in Mindanao, which was countered by a ground and air assault by government forces in April. The intensity of the fighting produced over 100,000 refugees, while the MILF demonstrated its ability to set off bombs, grenades and rockets in several towns in Mindanao. In July 2000, government forces overran the MILF headquarters, Camp Abubakar.

In June 2001, the MILF signed a peace agreement with the government of President **Gloria Macapagal-Arroyo**. Subsequently, relations between the MILF and the Philippines government improved progressively, and in December 2004, the two groups announced that they had formed a joint organization to clear the southern Philippines of two terrorist groups – the ASG and the ***Jemaah Islamiyah*** (JI). Despite the peace agreement, terrorist attacks alleged to have been instigated by the MILF continued periodically. In July 2003, the MILF leader Salamat Hashim passed away due to a heart attack and was succeeded by military chief and vice-chair for military affairs, Murad Ebrahim. In July 2008, representatives from the Philippines government and the MILF proposed the Memorandum of Agreement on Ancestral Domain (MOA-AD), which aimed to bring fighting to an end and begin formal talks that would lead to the drafting and signing of a Final Comprehensive Compact between the two groups. In the event, the agreement met strong public opposition, and in October 2008 the Philippine Supreme Court voted eight-to-seven to declare the MOA-AD unconstitutional and illegal. The Court's decision triggered attacks by MILF rebels on Christian communities in Mindanao and the violence displaced 750,000 people and left nearly 400 dead. These attacks were instigated by breakaway elements of the MILF, indicating the emergence of a split within the movement over Murad Ebrahim's willingness to strike a compromise with Manila. In March 2010, Commander Kato was ousted from the MILF for disobeying orders, and he went on to establish the Bangsamoro Islamic Freedom Fighters (BIFF), later renamed as the Bangsamoro Islamic Freedom Movement (BIFM) with Commander Bravo among those that pledged loyalty to him. In August 2011, negotiations were held between President **Benigno Aquino III** and Murad Ebrahim in Japan, leading to the signing of the **Framework Agreement on the Bangsamoro** in October 2012. Finally in March 2014, the MILF managed to conclude the **Comprehensive Agreement on the Bangsamoro** with the Manila government, ending almost three decades of its armed struggle.

see also: Abu Sayyaf Group; Aquino III, Benigno Simeon Cojuangco; Comprehensive Agreement on the Bangsamoro; Framework Agreement on the Bangsamoro; *Jemaah Islamiyah*; Macapagal-Arroyo, Gloria; Misuari, Nur; Moro National Liberation Front; New People's Army.

Moro National Liberation Front (Philippines)

The Moro National Liberation Front (MNLF) was set up in 1969 with the object of securing a separate state for Muslims concentrated in the southern islands of the Philippines. It has its own army known as the Bangsamoro Army, which is organized as a conventional army. At its height in the early 1990s, the Bangsamoro Army was believed to have around 17,000 fighters.

Longstanding Muslim alienation in Catholic-majority Philippines was acutely reinforced in the late 1960s after the **Corregidor Affair**, an alleged massacre of recruits in training for armed infiltration into Malaysia's state of Sabah, became public knowledge. Additional causes of grievance were acts of violence by Christian gangs acting on behalf of landed interests which culminated in bloodletting in a mosque in 1971 in Cotabato. The Moro National Liberation Movement was founded by a group of young secular Muslims who had become disillusioned with a traditional elite who had set up a Mindanao Independence Movement in 1968 without notable effect. They received some military training in Malaysia, whose government was determined to retaliate against the seeming bad faith of President **Ferdinand Marcos**. Their leader was **Nur Misuari**, who had been an instructor in Asian philosophies at the University of the Philippines and a one-time member of the radical Marxist *Kabataan Makabangan* (Patriotic Youth). The pejorative term Moro was included in the name of the separatist movement as a deliberate gesture of defiance. A central committee was established in Libya and produced a manifesto in April 1974 calling for political independence for the southern islands of Mindanao, Sulu, Palawan, Basilan and Tawi Tawi. Formal recognition from the Organization of the Islamic Conference was accorded in July 1975.

The MNLF began armed rebellion in October 1972 with an attack on the headquarters of the Philippine Constabulary in Marawi City in the wake of President Marcos' proclamation of martial law the month before. That proclamation had required all unregistered firearms to be handed in to the authorities and was construed in the south of the Philippines as a deliberate attempt to place the Muslims in a defenceless position against armed gangs of Christian settlers. Within twenty-four hours, the insurrection had spread with extensive violence and considerable loss of life, especially on the island of Sulu, where a major confrontation took place with security forces.

Negotiations in Tripoli took place under Libyan auspices in 1976 between Nur Misuari and **Imelda Marcos**, representing her husband. A compromise **Tripoli Agreement** was reached on Muslim political autonomy in thirteen provinces and nine cities but was never implemented because of charges of bad faith in the way a facilitating plebiscite had been conducted. The insurrection revived in 1977 but by that juncture, its momentum had passed its peak and President Marcos was able to play on tribal and regional divisions among the Muslim community to contain their challenge. He was able also to attract international Islamic diplomatic and financial support for alternative ways of providing for Muslim needs. It became evident that the MNLF was a loosely knit entity with the emergence of contending alternative leaderships. Indeed, in 1978 Nur Misuari's main rival Salamat Hashim set up the **Moro Islamic Liberation Front**. Muslim insurrection rumbled on without any attempt at resolution until **Corazón Aquino** succeeded Ferdinand Marcos in 1986. Nur Misuari returned to the Philippines in September 1986 to begin negotiations on Muslim autonomy. In January 1987 an agreement was signed in Jeddah between President Aquino's brother-in-law, Agapito Aquino, and Nur Misuari but once again implementation with the cooperation of both parties was frustrated. President Aquino insisted that political autonomy be made conditional on a plebiscite involving all inhabitants of the thirteen provinces, irrespective of religion. In addition, the cleavages within the Muslim community served to undermine Nur Misuari's claim to speak on behalf of all Filipino Muslims.

The Philippines government went ahead with the plan for political autonomy through a plebiscite in November 1989 in the thirteen provinces identified in the Tripoli Agreement in 1976. The outcome was the establishment in 1990 of an Autonomous Region of Muslim Mindanao in four provinces only – Maguindanao, Lanao del Sur (on the island of Mindanao), Sulu and Tawi Tawi. Elections were held in that region in February 1990 and a governor appointed to whom limited executive powers were accorded. The MNLF continued to oppose the new constitutional arrangement but with minimal effect. At the end of 1993, Indonesian good offices were employed for direct negotiations, which were transferred to the southern Philippines in early 1994. At the end of January 1994, the Philippines government and the MNLF signed a ceasefire agreement as a basis for proceeding with an accord on political autonomy in the southern islands. In September 1996, a compromise agreement was reached whereby the MNLF came to terms with the Autonomous Region of Muslim Mindanao (ARMM) with Nur Misuari as its governor and also endorsed the establishment of a Southern Philippines Council for Peace and Development (SPCPD) with Misuari as its chairman. As a result, hundreds of MNLF guerrillas were incorporated into the Philippines National Police and into its armed forces, which marked the transformation of the Front into a legitimate political entity. In the event, however, the agreement failed to live up to expectations. Economic crisis held up promised development assistance, while rampant corruption under Misuari's leadership prevailed. Meanwhile, Misuari's leadership of the MNLF was coming under heavy criticism for its authoritarian disposition. Matters came to a head in 2001 when MNLF split into four factions: the Misuari group, the Alvarej Isnaji group (which nevertheless remained supportive of Misuari), and two groups that were anti-Misuari, the Executive Council of 15 (EC-15) group and the Islamic Command Council. In the event, the EC-15, led by MNLF secretary-general Muslimin Sema, was recognized by the Philippines government as the official leadership of the MNLF.

An uprising orchestrated by Misuari in November 2001 failed and resulted in him being jailed until his acquittal in December 2009. In January 2002, the four factions signed a declaration of unity and conferred on Misuari the otiose title of chairman emeritus. The MNLF continued periodic attacks on Philippine security forces, notably in 2001, 2005 and 2007, even as it also clashed with other southern Philippines-based Muslim separatist groups such as MILF and the **Abu Sayyaf Group**, but it was becoming increasingly clear that it no longer had the capacity to pose the threat it did in the 1970s. Chronic factionalism compounded by ethnic and tribal faultlines and battlefield fatigue has seen the MNLF eclipsed by the MILF as the largest and most organized Moro armed resistance movement. In 2012, the MNLF found itself left out in the cold as the Philippines government concluded a landmark peace agreement with the MILF that would, among other things, conceive a new political entity to replace the ARMM, hitherto the symbolic pinnacle of the MNLF's struggle. In September 2013, almost 200 disgruntled fighters aligned with Nur Misuari raided five coastal villages in Zamboanga. The outbreak of violence displaced more than 30,000 residents while the Philippine military claimed to have killed more than thirty rebels. The raids proved unpopular and signalled the MNLF's demise as an actor of consequence in southern Philippine affairs.

see also: Abu Sayyaf Group; Aquino, Corazón; Corregidor Affair 1968; Islam; Marcos, Ferdinand; Marcos, Imelda; Misuari, Nur; Moro Islamic Liberation Front; Tripoli Agreement 1976.

Muhammadiyah (Indonesia)

Muhammadiyah (Followers of the Prophet Muhammad) is an urban-based religious organization which was set up in the Javanese city of Yogyakarta in 1912 by a mosque official. He was inspired by the ideas of the Egyptian theologist Mohammed Abduh, who had urged a cleansing of Islamic thought through a return to original texts. This enterprise in renewal was an attempt through education and social welfare to reconcile Islam with the modern world. *Muhammadiyah* was not engaged in politics under the Dutch, but with the proclamation of independence in 1945, it became a constituent part of ***Masyumi*** and aspired to create an Islamic state. *Masyumi* was banned in 1960 because of its implication in the regional revolts of the late 1950s. *Muhammadiyah* had continued in existence in pursuit of its original purposes, with an overlapping connection with the ***Partai Persatuan Pembangunan*** founded in 1973 by merging all Islamic parties. During the **Suharto** era, *Muhammadiyah* was obliged to dilute its Islamic identity by adhering to the state philosophy of ***Pancasila*** as its sole philosophy. In the wake of Suharto's political downfall, its leader, Amien Rais, established the ***Partai Amanat Nasional*** (PAN) with a reformist agenda directed beyond a narrow Islamic constituency, which secured some seven per cent of the vote and thirty-five out of 462 elective seats in parliamentary elections in June 1999. Through forging a coalition of Islamic-based parties, Amien Rais was elected speaker of the **People's Consultative Assembly** (MPR) in the following October. PAN never progressed beyond a marginal role in Indonesian politics, and its electoral support base has declined gradually. The lacklustre performance compelled a section of younger *Muhammadiyah* members to establish a new party, *Partai Matahari Bangsa* (the National Sun Party). In the event, the National Sun Party fared worse than its parent party, securing less than one per cent of the vote in the 2009 legislative elections, thereby failing to secure representation in the DPR. Though *Muhammadiyah*'s experience with electoral politics has not been particularly successful, it remains an important provider of social services in the form of educational institutions and medical facilities. It also plays an important role as a bulwark against the encroachment of religious conservatism and intolerance into Indonesia's pluralist society since the end of the **New Order**.

see also: Islam; *Masyumi*; New Order; *Pancasila*; *Partai Amanat Nasional*; *Partai Persatuan Pembangunan*; People's Consultative Assembly; Suharto.

Muhyiddin Yassin, Tan Sri (Malaysia)

Leadership transition in Malaysia after the 2008 election saw Prime Minister **Abdullah Badawi** step down from high office to make way for his deputy, **Najib Tun Razak**. With Najib as the newly appointed prime minister, the position of deputy prime minister was to be determined by a three-way fight at the **UMNO** (United Malays National Organization) 2009 party assembly in April among the party's three vice-presidents. The contest was won comfortably by Muhyiddin Yassin, an incumbent vice-president, after he defeated Muhammad Muhammad Taib, former chief minister of Selangor, and Malacca's former chief minister Ali Rustam, who was disqualified for suspected corruption involving his assistants.

As deputy prime minister and a close associate of Prime Minister **Mahathir Mohamad**, Muhyiddin is widely seen to favour conservative Malay nationalists within UMNO and Malay right-wing groups even though he was known to have worked well with ethnic Chinese businesses when he served as chief minister of Johor earlier in his career. Muhyiddin is arguably best known today for his controversial proclamation to be 'Malay first' rather than 'Malaysian first' when questioned by media after a parliamentary session. These public remarks sparked an outcry among non-Malays and appeared to contravene Prime Minister Najib's **One Malaysia** policy of multiculturalism. As education minister, he courted further controversy when he overturned an earlier policy on the study of science and mathematics in national schools in the English language and returned these subjects to the previous Malay curriculum. It is unclear though, whether his appeal as a conservative Malay nationalist is a deliberate and strategic attempt to balance Najib's more pluralist inclinations, or if it is calculated to undermine the prime minister.

Prior to becoming deputy prime minister, Muhyiddin held various positions in the federal government, such as the parliamentary secretary of the Ministry of Foreign Affairs, before rising up to hold ministerial positions in trade, youth and sports, domestic trade and consumer affairs, and agriculture. Within UMNO, Muhyiddin is a Supreme Council member and former vice-president (which he lost and won several times) before becoming deputy president. He was chief minister of his home state of Johor from 1986 to 1995.

see also: Badawi, Tun Abdullah; Mahathir Mohamad, Tun; Najib Tun Razak, Datuk Seri Mohamad; One Malaysia; UMNO.

Muoi, Do (Vietnam) *see* Do Muoi.

Murdani, General L. B. (Indonesia)

General Benny Murdani was commander of Indonesia's armed forces between March 1983 and February 1988 and minister of defence between March 1988 and March 1993. Leonardus Benjamin Murdani was born on 2 October 1932 in Cepu, central Java, to Catholic parents. He was literally a boy soldier during the national revolution, beginning his professional military training as a student reserve officer only after independence. As a young infantry officer with paracommando training, he distinguished himself in operations against regional rebels in Menado in northern Sulawesi and then survived a parachute drop into the jungles of Dutch-held West New Guinea (now **Irian Jaya**) which brought him to the attention of the regional commander and future president, General **Suharto**. He then began a career in military intelligence working directly for Colonel (later Lieutenant General) **Ali Murtopo** in clandestine negotiations to bring an end to Indonesia's ill-fated **Confrontation** of Malaysia. Diplomatic postings in Kuala Lumpur and Seoul were followed in 1974 by a series of senior military intelligence positions in Jakarta in which he served directly as security adviser to President Suharto, whose confidence he enjoyed for his personal loyalty and his dynamic style of leadership. As commander of the armed forces, he was responsible for revising their military doctrine and enhancing their professionalism. However, his relationship with President Suharto became subject to strain, in part because of attempts to restrict the business activities of the president's children, which were causing political alienation, together with his support for ***Partai Demokrasi Indonesia***. General Murdani was removed from military office in February 1988 shortly after his period of active service had been renewed in a calculated act of public humiliation by the president. He was subsequently appointed minister of defence in March 1988 without any powers of command in an evident attempt by Suharto to control any maverick political ambitions. With his removal from high office, his influence within the armed forces was undermined deliberately by Suharto through loyalist senior military appointments. However, with Suharto's fall from political grace, Murdani re-established close links with the former president. He passed away on 29 August 2004, aged seventy-two.

see also: Confrontation; Irian Jaya; Murtopo, General Ali; *Partai Demokrasi Indonesia*; Suharto.

Murtopo, General Ali (Indonesia)

General Ali Murtopo played a key role as an adviser to President **Suharto** in helping him to consolidate his power in the **New Order** of the late 1960s and early 1970s. He was responsible for the manipulation of the political system and also for the management of the so-called 'act of free choice' in **Irian Jaya**, which confirmed Indonesia's entitlement to the former Dutch possession. Ali Murtopo was born on 23 September 1923 in Blora, central Java. He was a student member of the revolutionary army from August 1945 and after independence continued as a professional soldier. He was educated in part at the Army Command and Staff School in Bandung, rising to battalion commander by the end of the 1950s. His career became entwined with that of the future president when General Suharto was in command of the central Javanese Diponegoro Division. Ali Murtopo was active as an intelligence officer in the operations to recover Irian Jaya and more significantly played a key clandestine role in negotiating an end to Indonesia's **Confrontation** of Malaysia in the mid-1960s. He was appointed minister of information in March 1978 but three months later suffered a heart attack during a visit to Malaysia. He never fully recovered and in March 1983 was relieved of his portfolio and made a member of the ceremonial Supreme Advisory Council. He died after a further heart attack on 18 May 1984.

see also: Confrontation; Irian Jaya; New Order; Suharto.

Musa Hitam, Tun (Malaysia)

Musa Hitam was deputy prime minister and minister of home affairs of Malaysia between July 1981 and February 1986, when he resigned after a personal conflict with Prime Minister **Mahathir Mohamad**. He then became engaged in an abortive challenge to Mahathir's leadership with a former political rival, **Tengku Razaleigh Hamzah**. Musa Hitam was born on 18 April 1934 in Johor. He was educated at the University of Malaya in Singapore and came into politics through involvement in international student affairs. After a short period in the civil service, he became executive secretary of **UMNO** (United Malays National Organization), entering Parliament in May 1969. Together with Mahathir, he was publicly identified with criticism of Prime Minister **Tunku Abdul Rahman** in the wake of intercommunal violence (**May 13 Racial Riots**) which followed the 1969 election. He then spent a year in virtual exile at the University of Sussex in England, but was able to return to political life and achieve ministerial office when **Tun Abdul Razak** became prime minister. After the failure to unseat Mahathir in 1987, Musa resigned his parliamentary seat in October 1988. He rejoined UMNO in January 1989 when Mahathir underwent a heart bypass operation. After he had made a complete recovery, a reconciliation of a kind took place with the prime minister, which led to Musa's appointment as Malaysia's Special Representative to the United Nations with ministerial rank and then as representative to the UN Human Rights Commission. In April 2000 he was appointed chairman of Malaysia's newly formed Human

Rights Commission. He also chaired the Eminent Persons Group that drafted the **ASEAN Charter**, and currently chairs the World Islamic Economic Forum.

see also: Abdul Rahman, Tunku; ASEAN Charter; Mahathir Mohamad, Tun; May 13 Racial Riots 1969; Razak, Tun Abdul; Razaleigh Hamzah, Tengku; UMNO.

Muslim Unity Front (Malaysia) *see Angkatan Perpaduan Ummah.*

Mustapha bin Datuk Harun, Tun (Malaysia)

Tun Mustapha was chief minister of Sabah between May 1967 and April 1976, during which he governed in the style of a Suluk chieftain and entertained ideas about taking Sabah out of Malaysia. Mustapha was born on 31 August 1918 in Kudat, where he succeeded his father as a native chief. He was the founding president of the **United Sabah National Organization** (USNO). He was appointed head of state on Sabah's entry into Malaysia in September 1963, holding the office for two years before becoming minister for Sabah affairs in the federal government. In April 1967 he secured election to the Sabah legislature and became chief minister in May. As chief minister, he encouraged mass conversion to Islam and also promoted Muslim insurgency in the south of the Philippines.

In the face of political challenges inspired from Kuala Lumpur which led to defections from the ruling party, Mustapha resigned as chief minister but remained head of USNO. He retained his parliamentary seat in elections in April 1976 won by dissidents from USNO grouped in *Berjaya* (Sabah People's Union) but remained in the political wilderness. In April 1985 he mounted an abortive constitutional coup which delayed the appointment as chief minister of Joseph Pairin Kitingan, whose *Parti Bersatu Sabah* (**Sabah United Party**, PBS) had won a clear majority of elective seats. After Kitingan's party defected from the federal ***Barisan Nasional*** (National Front) just before the general elections in October 1990, Mustapha became reconciled with the government in Kuala Lumpur. In May 1991 he stood as a successful candidate in a by-election for the Sabah legislature on behalf of **UMNO** within which USNO had been subsumed. The federal constitution was then amended specifically so that he could resume the office of minister for Sabah affairs. However, in January 1994 in a shock decision, he resigned his portfolio and also his party membership in a personal reaction to the failure of Ghafar Baba to retain his position as deputy president of UMNO and as deputy prime minister. In late February 1994 he joined PBS, which had just won a narrow victory in state elections but was then overturned by defections from among its ranks. He died on 2 January 1995 aged seventy-six.

see also: Barisan Nasional; Sabah United Party; UMNO; United Sabah National Organization.

N

Nacionalista Party (Philippines)

The Nacionalista Party was the first political organization advocating independence which was permitted after the imposition of US colonial rule in 1898. It represented a vehicle for the prosecution of elite family interests and as such was vulnerable to fragmentation. The party was formed in March 1907. From elections in June that year, it came to dominate Philippine political life up to the advent of the Pacific War in 1941 under the leadership of Manuel Quezón and Sergio Osmena. These two political rivals split the party over the struggle for the presidency in the early 1930s. The two factions healed the breach in June 1935 shortly before the establishment of the self-governing Commonwealth in November with Quezón as president. After the war, the Nacionalista Party split again as a result of personal rivalry and its so-called 'Liberal Wing' assumed power as the **Liberal Party**. The Nacionalista Party continued as a mirror-image elite network and a vehicle for personal political ambitions and patronage. Both **Ramón Magsaysay** and **Ferdinand Marcos** became presidents under its banner in 1953 and 1965 respectively after defecting from the rival Liberal Party. Marcos was re-elected in 1969 as the Nacionalista Party candidate but after the introduction of martial law in 1972, it became defunct. Later in the decade, Marcos established his own alternative New Society Movement to manipulate the electoral process until his downfall in 1986.

The Nacionalista Party was revived in 1989 to serve as the electoral vehicle for Salvador Laurel who, as **Corazón Aquino**'s running mate, had been elected as vice-president in 1986. In the presidential elections in May 1992, he secured a mere 3.4 per cent of the vote, which left the party politically moribund. Laurel was succeeded as party leader by Senator Manuel Villar Jr in 2003. In the 2005 general election the party secured five out of 235 seats. The Nacionalista Party was a member of the K-4 coalition in the 2004 presidential election and supported the candidacy of **Gloria Macapagal-Arroyo** for presidency and Noli de Castro for vice-presidency, both of whom emerged victorious. In the May 2007 election, the party won six seats. In April 2010, the Nacionalista Party and the Nationalist People's Coalition (NPC) formed an alliance for the upcoming elections that year. The Nacionalista Party put forward as its candidate Manuel Villar for presidency and supported the NPC vice-presidential candidate, Loren Legarda, but both campaigns ended in defeat. In May 2010 the Supreme Court declared the Nacionalista–NPC null and void on grounds that the parties' respective national conventions failed to approve the coalition.

see also: Aquino, Corazón; Liberal Party; Macapagal-Arroyo, Gloria; Magsaysay, Ramón; Marcos, Ferdinand.

Nahdlatul Ulama (Indonesia)

Nahdlatul Ulama (NU), which translates as Religious Scholars, is a traditional Islamic organization which was founded in east Java in 1926 in reaction to the modernism represented by ***Muhammadiyah*** (Followers of the Prophet Muhammad). It commands the support of some thirty million Indonesian Muslims mainly in Java and was also lead by **Abdurrahman Wahid** from 1984 to 1999 until he assumed the post of president in 1999. President Wahid's grandfather, Hashim Ashiri, founded the movement in 1926. Active in education and welfare, it became part of the wider ***Masyumi***, set up first under Japanese auspices in 1943 and then reconstituted as a political party after the proclamation of independence in 1945. The NU split from *Masyumi* in 1952 and contested the first national elections in 1955 in its own right, securing third place with 18.4 per cent of the vote. Religious prerogative was its priority and its leadership supported President **Sukarno**'s attack on parliamentary democracy, thus securing preferment under his political system of **Guided Democracy**. Alienation set in with the growing influence of the Communist Party of Indonesia and after an abortive coup (*see* ***Gestapu***) in October 1965, NU members joined with the military in exacting a bloody retribution.

The NU held its 1955 level of support in parliamentary elections in 1971. In 1973 it was forcibly merged with three other Islamic parties into the ***Partai Persatuan Pembangunan*** (United Development Party, PPP), which had been permitted only a perfunctory political role at elections every five years. In 1984 the NU withdrew from the PPP to devote itself to its educational and welfare roles when the government's policy obliging all organizations to accept the state philosophy of ***Pancasila*** as their sole principle appeared to threaten its identity. Nonetheless, in the following year, when the law making *Pancasila* the sole philosophical principle was passed, the NU endorsed it. When, in December 1990, President Suharto sought to counter military resistance to his continuation in office by mobilizing Islamic support through ICMI (Association of Indonesian Muslim Intellectuals), the NU was not a party to this initiative. In mid-1991 Abdurrahman Wahid set up an alternative *Forum Demokrasi* (Democracy Forum) as a counter to the attempt to mobilize the Islamic community on confessional grounds for President Suharto's political purpose. He also visibly displeased the president by refusing to have the NU nominate him for a further five-year term of office from March 1993. Under the leadership of Abdurrahman Wahid, the NU has been guided in the direction of religious tolerance and away from an Islamic political exclusivism. In the wake of Suharto's political downfall, Abdurrahman Wahid founded the ***Partai Kebangkitan Bangsa*** (National Awakening Party, PKB), which drew on his NU constituency. In parliamentary elections in June 1999, the PKB secured some seventeen per cent and fifty-one out of 462 elective seats. In the following October, Abdurrahman Wahid attracted support from a coalition of Islamic-based parties to secure presidential office. A paramilitary youth wing of the NU was deployed to intimidate critics of President Wahid in the media.

The NU continues to be one of the two largest socio-religious organizations in Indonesia that administer thousands of medical facilities, non-governmental organizations (NGOs) and educational institutions. It also has members who function as key agents of mainstream Javanese religious culture, such as mediators, healers, spiritual guides and martial arts exponents. Thus far the NU has shaped Indonesia's socio-political and religious landscape by being the dominant voice for Islam in the **New Order** and post-New Order period while working within the parameters of the state ideology of *Pancasila* and upholding the principles of pluralism and democracy. It has however experienced an erosion of its hitherto considerable influence in the face of a recent proliferation of more fundamentalist Islamic organizations. Unlike at the 2004 and 2009 elections when relations between the two were frosty, stout support from the NU accounted for the strong electoral showing by PKB at the 2014 elections.

see also: Gestapu; Guided Democracy; Islam; *Masyumi*; *Muhammadiyah*; New Order; *Pancasila*; *Partai Kebangkitan Bangsa*; *Partai Persatuan Pembangunan*; Suharto; Sukarno; Wahid, Abdurrahman.

Najib Tun Razak, Datuk Seri Mohamad (Malaysia)

Najib Tun Razak assumed high office in Malaysia on 3 April 2009 when his predecessor **Abdullah Ahmad Badawi** was pressured to step down after being held responsible for the ruling ***Barisan Nasional*** (National Front, BN) coalition's poor showing at the general election the year before.

Najib was born on 23 July 1954 in Kuala Lipis in the state of Pahang. His father, **Tun Abdul Razak**, became prime minister of Malaysia in 1970 but died prematurely in 1976. Najib was educated at the University of Nottingham in England and on his return to Malaysia began his career with the national oil company Petronas. He entered Parliament at the tender age of twenty-three years after winning his late father's Pekan (Pahang) parliamentary seat unopposed and has held the seat since. He subsequently held a series of junior ministerial appointments, including education and finance. In 1982 he stood successfully for the Pahang state legislature and was then appointed chief minister.

He returned to national politics in the elections of 1986 and held the portfolio of youth and sports and subsequently that of defence. During the intense struggle within **UMNO** (United Malays National Organization) in 1986–7, which led to an unsuccessful challenge to the position of Prime Minister **Mahathir Mohamad** by **Tengku Razaleigh Hamzah**, Najib's position was somewhat equivocal. He avoided committing himself irrevocably to either figure but after Mahathir's victory, he was able to use his Pahang state base to revive his political career. He was appointed minister of defence and oversaw the modernization of the Malaysian Armed Forces, and was later switched to the important post of minister of education. In 1999 he suffered a major setback at the federal elections when he barely scraped through in his parliamentary seat with a 241-vote majority. Nevertheless, his standing within UMNO, where he held one of the three vice-presidential posts, remained strong.

In January 2004, Najib was appointed deputy prime minister of Malaysia, and was elected deputy president of UMNO in July. In April 2008, Prime Minister Abdullah Badawi identified Najib as his probable successor. Meanwhile, Najib remained loyal to Badawi despite attempts by Mahathir to cast aspersions at the prime minister and precipitate a challenge to his leadership in UMNO. From September 2008, Najib carried the concurrent responsibility of minister of finance and navigated the Malaysian economy through the global financial crisis with several stimulus packages. Najib's prospects for high office were however tainted by revelations that a close advisor was embroiled in an extra-marital affair with undertones of corruption, and which ended with the murder of a Mongolian model and translator, Altanthuya Shaariibuu, in October 2006 allegedly by two members of Najib's security team. While both were eventually convicted, their conviction was overturned in August 2013.

In March 2009, Najib won the position of UMNO president unopposed and became Malaysia's sixth prime minister a month later. Najib moved swiftly to take on the role of reformist. He announced the implementation of the **New Economic Model** in March 2010, which was an economic plan to accelerate Malaysia's transition to a high-income country. In September 2010, Najib rolled out the **One Malaysia** campaign for ethnic harmony, national unity and efficient governance. Despite these attempts to placate grassroots discontent, the Najib-led BN managed only to secure forty-seven per cent of the popular vote and 133 parliamentary seats at the elections in May 2013. The opposition ***Pakatan Rakyat*** coalition secured fifty-one per cent of the popular vote and eighty-nine parliamentary seats. Not surprisingly, the loss of the popular vote piled pressure on Najib, as did the loss of considerable Chinese support.

see also: Badawi, Tun Abdullah; *Barisan Nasional*; Mahathir Mohamad, Tun; New Economic Model; One Malaysia; *Pakatan Rakyat*; Razak, Tun Abdul; Razaleigh Hamzah, Tengku; UMNO.

Nasakom (Indonesia)

Nasakom is an acronym and slogan conceived by President **Sukarno** to indicate the trinity of socio-political elements which were legitimately part of the political system of **Guided Democracy** that he inaugurated in July 1959. The acronym was drawn from the Indonesian *nasionalisme*, *agama* and *kommunisme*, meaning nationalism, religion and communism, represented as the three dominant strains in society. It reflected the syncretic disposition of Sukarno, who had published an essay entitled *Nationalism, Islam and Marxism* as early as 1926. The prime function of the slogan was to justify the political participation of the Communist Party of Indonesia, which served as a mobilizing vehicle for Sukarno against the armed forces. In the wake of an abortive coup (*see* ***Gestapu***) in October 1965 in which the Communists were implicated and which discredited Sukarno politically and also led to the dismantling of Guided Democracy, *Nasakom* soon disappeared from Indonesia's political lexicon.

see also: *Gestapu*; Guided Democracy; Sukarno.

Nasution, General Abdul Haris (Indonesia)

General Nasution was a distinguished military leader during and after the period of national revolution in Indonesia who conceived of the 'middle way' doctrine (*see* ***Dwi Fungsi***) justifying the prerogative political role of the armed forces. Abdul Haris Nasution was born in 1918 in Sumatra and trained before the Pacific War as an officer in the colonial army. During the Japanese occupation, he was involved with militant youth organizations in Bandung and then in the period of national revolution distinguished himself as a young commander of the west Java Siliwangi division. After independence, as head of the army, he was responsible for a display of force before the non-elected parliament but backed away from a coup. He resigned office at the end of 1952 but was reinstated in 1955. He played a critical role in crushing regional uprisings in the late 1950s and encouraged President **Sukarno** to introduce his authoritarian **Guided Democracy** in July 1959 but was then manoeuvred away from the centre of power. In October 1965 General Nasution narrowly avoided assassination during an abortive coup (*see* ***Gestapu***), which claimed the life of his young daughter. He threw his weight behind General **Suharto**, who took the lead in restoring order, but he did not play a central role in shaping the new political system based on military power. He served for a time as speaker of the **People's Consultative Assembly** but went into early retirement in the 1970s, becoming an open critic of Suharto's **New Order**. He signed the Petition of Fifty to Parliament in 1980 complaining of the perversion of the constitution, which angered the president into denying him foreign travel, among other restrictions. In mid-1993, however, in the wake of his further re-election in March, President Suharto received General Nasution, his former commander, in an act of reconciliation. He was then allowed to travel abroad for medical treatment. General Nasution died on 6 September 2000. He leaves behind a mixed reputation as a military commander and thinker and also as someone who was always out of his depth in politics, in which he was incapable of decisive action.

see also: Dwi Fungsi; Gestapu; Guided Democracy; New Order; People's Consultative Assembly; Suharto; Sukarno.

Natalegawa, Raden Mohammad Marty Muliana (Indonesia)

A highly competent diplomat, Marty Natalegawa was appointed foreign minister of Indonesia in October 2009 after a long and distinguished career in the foreign service. Born in Bandung, West Java, Natalegawa received his tertiary education at the London School of Economics and Corpus Christi College, University of Cambridge. He eventually obtained a doctoral degree from the Australian National University in 1993. Natalegawa was an activist during his student years, when he was a member of various anti-apartheid and nuclear disarmament movements. He joined the Indonesian foreign service in 1986 after obtaining his master's degree from the University of Cambridge and has held a number of senior positions, including as Indonesia's permanent representative to the United Nations in New York and ambassador to the United Kingdom. In Jakarta, he served as chief of staff of the Office of the Minister of Foreign Affairs, and as director-general for ASEAN Cooperation between 2002 and 2005, during which Indonesia chaired **ASEAN** (Association of Southeast Asian Nations). As Indonesian foreign minister, Natalegawa played an instrumental role in shuttle diplomacy during the **South China Sea** crisis in July 2012 which had led to ASEAN's failure to agree on a joint communiqué for the first time in the organization's history. In the wake of the crisis in Phnom Penh, Natalegawa shuttled between the capitals of the region to push for an ASEAN consensus on the issue. His efforts resulted in ASEAN's cobbling together a face-saving collective position on the importance of a code of conduct in governing differences over South China Sea claims.

see also: ASEAN; East Asia Summit; South China Sea.

National Congress for Timorese Reconstruction (Timor-Leste)

The National Congress for Timorese Reconstruction (*Conselho Nacional de Reconstrucao de Timor* (CNRT)) is a political party in Timor-Leste that champions the ideologies of anti-communism and social democracy. It was founded in March 2007 by former president, **José 'Xanana' Gusmão**. In the June 2007 general election, the CNRT captured twenty-four per cent of the vote and eighteen parliamentary seats, coming in second to ***Fretilin*** which won twenty-nine per cent of the vote and twenty-one seats. Given that no party commanded an absolute majority, the CNRT moved to form a governing coalition with the next two largest political parties – the Social Democratic Party–Timorese Social Democratic Association (PSD–ASDT) and the Democratic Party (PD) in July 2007. The resulting coalition mustered a combined majority of thirty-six seats and fifty-one per cent of the vote. Later that month it was announced that negotiations between the CNRT-led coalition and *Fretilin* had begun with the purpose of forming a national unity government. However, talks were unsuccessful given the lack of consensus over who should lead the government. In August 2007, the CNRT-led coalition announced that it would form the government, and that its leader, 'Xanana' Gusmão, would become prime minister. Though the move was declared unconstitutional by *Fretilin*, Gusmão was sworn in as the new prime minister in August 2007, while the president of the Democratic Party became the president of the National Parliament. The move prompted violent protests by *Fretilin* supporters and led to the destruction of property and other acts of violence in the following weeks. In February 2008, rebel East Timor soldiers attacked Prime Minister Gusmão and shot and seriously wounded President **José Ramos-Horta**. Subsequently, Gusmão declared a forty-eight hour state of emergency (later extended to two months) and described the events as an attempted coup. However, strong disagreements regarding the attacks emerged, and former prime minister **Mari Alkatiri** was among those who expressed doubts about the government's narrative of events surrounding the attacks.

During the CNRT-led coalition rule, Prime Minister Gusmão proposed a Strategic Development Plan to address issues of poverty and inequality. This policy generated considerable controversy both within Parliament and during public consultations due to the lack of an environmental impact assessment or any publicly released assessment of its financial viability. In the July 2012 general elections, the CNRT won 36.6 per cent of the vote, improving its share of parliamentary seats to thirty. This victory was achieved despite accusations that the CNRT-led coalition government was in a state of disarray, and engaged in systemic corruption and mismanagement. However, it still fell short of a majority, and had to once again form a coalition government with the Democratic Party which came in third with 10.3 per cent of the vote and eight seats.

see also: Alkatiri, Mari; *Fretilin*; Gusmão, José 'Xanana'; Ramos-Horta, José.

National Democratic Front (Philippines)

The National Democratic Front (NDF) was established by the Communist Party of the Philippines on 24 April 1973 in an attempt to capitalize on opposition to President **Ferdinand Marcos**' declaration of martial law in September 1972. The object was to create a political wing under which diverse opposition groupings could be mobilized in the party's interest. A manifesto was proclaimed in April 1973 which called for the unity of all anti-imperialist and democratic forces in order to establish a coalition government that would be truly democratic. The NDF attracted interest from left-wing clergy, intellectuals, students and labour groups and became especially active after general elections in 1978. It made a major strategic blunder in early 1986 in failing to appreciate the measure of popular support which had brought **Corazón Aquino** to high office in succession to President Marcos. In negotiations with her government, unrealistic demands were made for inclusion in a national coalition as the price for a political settlement. The NDF remained outside of the national political consensus; parties attracting its support failed abysmally to make any impact in the referendum in February 1987 on a new constitution and also in elections in May for a new Congress. The main threat to Corazón Aquino came from the right and not from the left; after her succession by **Fidel Ramos**, he was confident enough to permit the legalization of the Communist Party in September 1992. That party and the NDF suffered an evident marginalization reinforced by internal divisions.

Since the late 1980s the NDF has enjoyed more of a presence in the Netherlands than in the Philippines; it has maintained an office in Utrecht for fundraising and international public relations. The intellectual head of the party, **José María Sisón**, has lived in the Netherlands in exile for a number of years, ever since he was released from prison by Corazón Aquino under an amnesty. Negotiations between the NDF and the government in Manila were initiated in the early 1990s through the good offices of Vietnam in an attempt to find a place for the Communist front in national political life. However, intra-party squabbles have been an important factor in preventing those negotiations from bearing political fruit. The NDF took part in peace talks with the Philippines government in Utrecht in October 1994, which broke down. They were resumed in Brussels in June 1995 but lasted only one day ostensibly because Manila refused to release Sotero Llama, a Communist military commander arrested the previous May, who had been named subsequently as a member of the NDF negotiating panel. Talks were resumed in the Netherlands in June 1996 after Llama was released but then broke down after the **New People's Army** (NPA), the military wing of the NDF, seized hostages. They resumed again in early 1998. In February, representatives of the NDF and the government in Manila met in The Hague where an agreement on human rights was signed. The following month, they signed a second agreement on social and economic reforms. Despite this progress, the NDF was unwilling to continue negotiations in the Philippines, citing security reasons. Moreover, in May 1999, they called off further talks because the government had entered into a new visiting forces agreement with the United States. Mutual mistrust peaked in May 2013 when the NDF accused the government of reneging on the 1995 Joint Agreement on Safety and Immunity Guarantees that granted immunity to rebel negotiators, and which required written notice prior to termination by any party. NDF Chair Luis Jalandoni accused the government of unilaterally terminating the peace talks without informing the Norwegian mediators who played the role of third-party facilitator. Peace talks with the government stalled due to inability to arrive at a common understanding over pending criminal cases involving some nominated rebel negotiators. The NDF was dealt a major blow in March 2014 when two of its leaders, Benito Tiamzon and his wife, Wilma Austria, were captured in Cebu.

see also: Aquino, Corazón; Marcos, Ferdinand; New People's Army; Ramos, Fidel; Sisón, José María.

National League for Democracy (Myanmar)

The National League for Democracy (NLD) is the main opposition party in Myanmar. It was formed on 27 September 1988 as a political challenge to the **State Law and Order Restoration Council** (SLORC), which had assumed power on behalf of the military establishment six days before. That seizure of power followed a bloody confrontation on the streets of Yangon and other major towns in which the armed forces had opened fire on unarmed demonstrators.

The NLD was set up by **Aung San Suu Kyi**, the daughter of the nationalist leader and martyr, **Aung San**, and by Aung Gyi and Tin U, former senior officers who had become opponents of **Ne Win**'s regime. Aung Gyi left the party in December 1988, while Aung San Suu Kyi was arrested in July 1989. Yet when the NLD participated in general elections in May 1990, it won 392 out of 485 seats for the newly created People's Assembly, with some sixty per cent of the popular vote. In contrast, SLORC's **National Unity Party** (NUP) won only ten seats. The military establishment refused to convene the legislature until a new constitution had been drafted. SLORC also began to take repressive measures against members of the NLD, many of whom were deprived of their parliamentary status on spurious grounds. A National Convention to draft a new constitution began work in January 1993 with the armed forces intending to provide for themselves a prerogative political role. Selected members of the NLD were allowed to attend but the military establishment remained unwilling to recognize the outcome of the elections of May 1990. When Aung San Suu Kyi was released from detention in July 1995, the party had been reduced to a shadow of its former self through repression by SLORC. The NLD was subject to recurrent harassment and enforced resignations, although it was permitted to hold a congress in May 1998 to commemorate its electoral victory in May 1990. NLD headquarters were sealed off by security forces in September 2000 after Aung San Suu Kyi had been forcibly returned to her residence after trying to leave the capital. In 2001, some NLD branch offices were allowed to reopen and in May 2002, Aung San Suu Kyi was released from house arrest. Following several trips up-country, which were greeted with strong demonstrations of support, her motorcade was set upon by a mob allegedly organized by the junta, during which dozens of NLD members were killed and wounded. Aung San Suu Kyi and Tin Oo were arrested. Tin Oo was later released in February 2010, but Aung San Suu Kyi was not released until November 2010.

On 29 March 2010, the party decided not to register for elections to be held in November 2010 in protest at election rules which reserved a dominant role for the military in Parliament. The party was subsequently dissolved by the government on 6 May 2010, but the NLD ignored the order and continued to engage in social work. A breakaway faction calling itself the National Democratic Force (NDF) did contest the elections but received only three per cent of the vote. The majority of the party, however, boycotted the 2010 elections. In November 2011, political reforms initiated by the government seemed to offer a better chance for collaboration, including talks between Aung San Suu Kyi and **Thein Sein**. The NLD proceeded to announce its intention to register as a political party in order to contest future elections. Its application was approved by the Union Election Commission on 13 December 2011. During the 1 April 2012 by-election, the party won forty-three of forty-four seats it contested, out of a total forty-five seats available. The party is currently the largest opposition party in Parliament, albeit with less than seven per cent of the 644 seats. It operates on a platform of support for human rights, rule of law, national reconciliation, independence of the judiciary, media freedom and increasing social benefits. A chief aim of the party is amendment of the Constitution to reduce the military's continued dominant role in politics. The NLD is expected to pose a major challenge to the **Union Solidarity and Development Party** (USDP) in the next general elections, scheduled for 2015.

see also: Aung San; Aung San Suu Kyi; National Unity Party; Ne Win, General; State Law and Order Restoration Council; Thein Sein; Union Solidarity and Development Party.

National Liberation Front of South Vietnam (Vietnam)

The National Liberation Front of South Vietnam (NLF) was set up on 20 December 1960 through the initiative of the Communist Party to mobilize popular support south of the seventeenth parallel of latitude against the government of President **Ngo Dinh Diem** in Saigon. In its composition and declared political aspirations, which avoided Communist associations and reference to early unification, it replicated the **Viet Minh** (standing for the League for the Independence of Vietnam), which had served as a corresponding vehicle for the party from 1941. The NLF was established in a jungle area close to the Cambodian border under the figurehead chairmanship of Nguyen Huu Tho, a French-educated lawyer of liberal persuasion. It functioned through a myriad of functional groupings headed also by prominent personalities whose nationalist credentials were not touched by Communist affiliations. In effect, the NLF's activities were soon directly controlled by the People's Revolutionary Party, which was established in 1962 as a southern branch of the national party. In June 1969 the NLF, which had attracted a membership of several million, became a constituent part of the **Provisional Revolutionary Government of the Republic of South Vietnam**. This attempt to demonstrate a fuller international identity arose from the NLF's participation in quadripartite peace negotiations in Paris from January 1969. After the military collapse of the Saigon government in April 1975, the NLF had served its useful political purpose and, much to the chagrin of many of its leading non-Communist members, was merged into a northern counterpart, the Fatherland Front.

see also: Diem, Ngo Dinh; Paris Peace Agreements 1973; Provisional Revolutionary Government of the Republic of South Vietnam PRG 1969–76; Viet Minh; Vietnam War.

National Mandate Party (Indonesia) *see* ***Partai Amanat Nasional.***

National Unity Party (Myanmar)

The National Unity Party (NUP) was set up on 26 September 1988 as the successor to the **Burma Socialist Programme Party** (BSPP) through the intervention of the **State Law and Order Restoration Council** (SLORC). SLORC had seized power eight days previously in an attempt to reinforce the control of the military establishment in the wake of a bloody confrontation between security forces and unarmed civilian demonstrators. The NUP was intended to serve as the electoral vehicle for SLORC in polls held in May 1990. In the event, the NUP captured only ten seats in a People's Assembly of 485 seats, although it secured some twenty-five per cent of the popular vote. The opposition **National League for Democracy** won 392 seats but SLORC refused to permit the legislature to convene. Instead, a constitutional convention was held from January 1993 in which the NUP participated but only as the unpopular instrument of a resented military establishment.

Because of its close association with former strongman **Ne Win,** the NUP only played a marginal role in national politics throughout the 2000s, as their patron was gradually sidelined by General **Than Shwe**. At the 2010 elections, the NUP sought to distance itself from the ruling **Union Solidarity and Development Party** (USDP) despite its own ties to the junta, and contested as the second largest party in Myanmar with a surfeit of 999 parliamentary candidates nationwide. This led to speculation that the NUP could mount a formidable challenge to the ruling USDP. In the event, the party was soundly defeated by the USDP, securing only sixty-three seats compared to 883 for the USDP. During the campaign, the NUP attempted to display democratic credentials with gestures such as a promise to free the press, long muzzled by the ruling junta. The octogenarian former deputy commander of the armed forces, Tun Yi, currently leads the NUP.

see also: Burma Socialist Programme Party; National League for Democracy; Ne Win, General; State Law and Order Restoration Council; Than Shwe, Senior General.

Natuna Islands (Indonesia)

The Natuna Islands are a group of 272 islands located 400 miles northeast of Sumatra in the **South China Sea**. It is one of the largest natural gas fields in the world and is believed to contain over 210 trillion cubic feet of natural gas with an estimated forty-six trillion cubic feet of recoverable natural gas.

Indonesian sovereignty over the islands was unchallenged until 1993, when the People's Republic of China published a map containing a broken line in the South China Sea covering a gas field northeast of the islands. This line, which has entered the lexicon of regional affairs as Beijing's infamous 'nine-dotted line', delineates a Chinese claim over an area close to the Natuna Islands that breaches Indonesia's Exclusive Economic Zone (EEZ). In response, Jakarta dismissed these claims as baseless under international law and continued to assert Indonesia's sovereignty through exploration projects undertaken by the state-owned oil and natural gas corporation, Pertamina. Further demonstrating their strategic concerns about Chinese intentions, Jakarta signed a bilateral security treaty with Australia in 1995 (the treaty was later abrogated over East Timor). Concern about the escalation of tensions gave greater impetus to the Workshop Process on Managing Potential Conflicts in the South China Sea, which was initiated by Indonesia in 1990 as a confidence building measure with the purpose of providing an informal platform for South China Sea claimant states to discuss and better understand their respective claims. The efforts of the workshops however, proved fruitless even though tensions eased between the two governments.

In 2009, the appearance of Chinese fishing vessels off the islands provoked Indonesian navy

patrol boats to detain them. In a verbal note to the United Nations in 2009, China asserted its indisputable sovereignty over the islands in the South China Sea and the adjacent waters, laying claim over land territory and maritime areas to the north of the Natuna Islands. In 2010, Chinese fishermen guarded by Chinese fishery administration vessels threatened to fire on Indonesian naval patrols as they attempted to intercept Chinese fishing trawlers in the area. These events prompted Indonesia to send a diplomatic note to the United Nations challenging the Chinese claim as without a legal basis and tantamount to contravention of the United Nations Convention on the Law of the Sea (UNCLOS) treaty.
see also: South China Sea.

Naypyidaw (Myanmar)

Naypyidaw officially became the new administrative capital of Myanmar on 6 November 2005. The city was cut out of the jungle and shrubland near the town of Pyinmana in central Myanmar and has grown to become Myanmar's third largest city. Construction of the city began in 2002 and the government began moving ministries to the city in November 2005. The move was so hasty that government officials were told to relocate their offices within twenty-four hours, while their families were initially prohibited from relocating with them due to the lack of schools and other infrastructure and basic amenities. The first public event at Naypyidaw was a massive military parade to celebrate Armed Forces Day, held on 27 March 2006 when 12,000 troops marched in a review for Senior General **Than Shwe**. The rationale behind the move was debated for some time in Myanmar. The stated official explanation was that Yangon had grown too congested and there was little room for expansion of government offices, although it is also known that Than Shwe had taken an eccentric personal interest in the project. The new site is more central and strategically located than Yangon, also giving credence to the perception that the generals were concerned about foreign intervention. Most embassies have chosen to remain in Yangon. The city of Naypyidaw and the eight townships around it were collectively established as the Naypyidaw Union Territory under the **2008 Constitution**. It is under the direct administration of the president through a Naypyidaw Council which handles most of the day-to-day administration.
see also: Constitution 2008; Than Shwe, Senior General.

Ne Win, General (Myanmar)

General Ne Win was head of a military junta that ruled Burma/Myanmar autocratically and brutally in various guises for more than a quarter of a century. He was primarily responsible for inaugurating a pseudo-socialist order that impoverished the country, provoking popular revolt put down in 1988 with great loss of life. Ne Win was born on 14 May 1911 or 10 July 1910 in Paungdle in Prome District in lower Burma to a Sino-Burmese family, who gave him the name Shu Maung. He was educated at the University of Rangoon and, although a member of the nationalist movement, was not politically prominent. He left without a degree in 1932 to begin his working life as a postal clerk. He joined the *Dobama Asiayone* (Our Burma Association), a militant nationalist movement, and through it became associated with its leader **Aung San**, who recruited him as a member of a group of thirty comrades who were exfiltrated to Japan in 1940 to undergo military training. Ne Win, who acquired his *nom de guerre* (meaning Bright Son) in this period, returned with the Japanese army when they invaded Burma in December 1941.

Ne Win became a commander in the Japanese-sponsored Burma National Army, which in March 1945 switched to the side of the Allies as Japan's defeat seemed only a matter of time. The nationalist leader, Aung San, won the respect of Admiral Lord Mountbatten, the Supreme Allied Commander, who supported Burma's independence. Despite factional and ideological conflict within the nationalist movement, independence was set for January 1948, but in July 1947 Aung San and several cabinet ministers were assassinated. At the time, Ne Win was deputy to the commander-in-chief, Lieutenant General Smith-Dun, who was from the Karen minority which soon after rose in revolt. Smith-Dun was retired in early 1949 and Lieutenant General Ne Win took over as supreme commander of all armed forces and in April became deputy prime minister in charge of defence and home affairs until the following year, when the insurgent challenge to the Union of Burma was crushed. He returned to government temporarily as prime minister from 1958 to 1960 when civilian government was suspended for two years.

On 2 March 1962, as commander-in-chief, he led a successful coup which established a continuous period of military rule. He set up a ruling revolutionary council and also established the **Burma Socialist Programme Party** (BSPP) under whose exclusive aegis a Burmese Way to Socialism was promulgated. This ideology became the blueprint for a rigid system of central planning and bureaucratic control which brought the country to the point of economic collapse, so that it had to apply to the United Nations for 'least-developed status'. He became president of Burma on its establishment as a socialist republic in 1974, giving up that office in 1981 but remaining as president of the BSPP; he resigned in July 1988 in a context of political decay and chaos. Although government was placed in the charge of the **State Law and Order Restoration Council** (SLORC) in September 1988, Ne Win was believed to exercise a continuing influence over the military establishment and matters of political management. After not being seen in public since 1989, he was photographed in Jakarta in September 1997 looking pale and frail having travelled to Indonesia at the invitation of President **Suharto** for a short stay. He then flew on to Singapore, which he had visited for a medical check-up in 1993. In September 1998, he returned to Singapore for treatment for a clot on the brain. Ne Win's influence on the junta began to wane after 1998 and on 4 March 2002, he was placed under house arrest after an alleged plot to overthrow the government by Ne Win's son-in-law, Aye Zaw Win, was exposed. His favourite daughter and Aye Zaw Win's wife, Sandar Win was also placed under house arrest. Aye Zaw Win and his three sons were found guilty of treason and sentenced to death, but are thought to remain in custody in Insein Prison in Yangon. Ne Win died while under house arrest on 5 December 2002 at his lakeside house in Yangon. His death went unremarked by the junta or state media, nor was he given a state funeral.

see also: Aung San; Burmese Socialist Programme Party; State Law and Order Restoration Council; Suharto.

Neo Lao Hak Sat (Laos)

Neo Lao Hak Sat (Lao Patriotic Front) was established in January 1956 by the Lao People's Party, in effect the Communist Party, as a national front acting on behalf of the ***Pathet Lao*** (Lao Nation or State) movement. Headed by Prince **Souphanouvong**, the *Neo Lao Hak Sat* was constituted formally on a functional basis with representation, for example, from trade unions and women's and farmers' groups. It served also as a political party in the late 1950s enjoying significant success in supplementary national elections, whose outcome had a polarizing effect between right and left in Lao politics instead of promoting national reconciliation as intended by the terms of the **Geneva Agreements on Indochina of 1954**. Throughout its existence, until superseded by a corresponding Lao Front for National Construction in 1979, the *Neo Lao Hak Sat* was controlled by the Communist Party of Laos, initially as the Lao People's Party and then from 1972 in the name of the **Lao People's Revolutionary Party**, which has ruled the country since the end of 1975.

see also: Geneva Agreements on Indochina 1954; Geneva Agreements on Laos 1962; Lao People's Revolutionary Party; *Pathet Lao*; Souphanouvong, Prince.

New Aspiration Party (Thailand)

The New Aspiration Party (*Kwam Wang Mai*) was formed in October 1990 as the personal political vehicle of former army commander General **Chavalit Yongchaiyuth** who had been disappointed in a brief spell as deputy prime minister in the government of Prime Minister **Chatichai Choonhavan**. The New Aspiration Party secured fifty-one seats in elections conducted in September 1992. It then joined the coalition government headed by Prime Minister **Chuan Leekpai**, with General Chavalit assuming the office of minister of interior. Although not closely identified with the military which had employed violence against civilian demonstrators in May 1992, his party lost electoral support in September that year and also suffered factional tensions based on regional affiliations. In July 1994, its deputy leader defected to form a new party. General Chavalit was briefly deputy prime minister from October before withdrawing from the government coalition in December 1994 in an abortive bid to topple it. In elections in July 1995, the New Aspiration Party won fifty-seven seats and was invited to join the government headed by **Banharn Silpa-archa**, with General Chavalit given the positions of deputy prime minister and defence minister. It improved its position considerably in elections in November 1996 securing 125 seats, which made it the largest parliamentary party. General Chavalit went on to form a coalition government but was obliged to step down as prime minister in November 1997 in the wake of the **Asian Financial Crisis** for which his administration was held responsible. The New Aspiration Party was excluded from the new coalition government headed by the **Democrat Party**, and has remained in opposition. In June 2000, ninety-six of its members resigned from Parliament in an abortive attempt to force a snap election. In the run-up to the 2001 elections Chavalit formed a coalition with the ***Thai Rak Thai*** **Party** (TRT). Following TRT's strong win, the majority of New Aspiration Party members merged with TRT, and Chavalit became deputy prime minister in the government of **Thaksin Shinawatra**.

see also: Asian Financial Crisis 1997–8; Banharn Silpa-archa; Chatichai Choonhavan, General; Chavalit Yongchaiyuth, General; Chuan Leekpai; Democrat Party; *Thai Rak Thai* Party; Thaksin Shinawatra.

New Economic Mechanism (Laos)

The New Economic Mechanism (NEM) was a policy introduced by Prime Minister **Kaysone Phomvihan** in 1985 and announced at the 1986 party congress in response to the disappointing results of the **Lao People's Revolutionary Party**'s (LPRP) first decade in power. The new policy was couched in the appropriate socialist phraseology, but in effect amounted to an abandonment of state ownership and centralized control over the economy. Under the NEM, the inflated state bureaucracy was reduced, as was its role in economic management, and state subsidies to industries were abolished. Instead, managers were told to make their enterprises profitable and retail prices were deregulated. The policy was aimed at generating long-term benefits for the economy, but in the short-term resulted in inflation and unemployment, especially among workers in loss-making state sectors. This in turn gave rise to increased resentment and insecurity especially among the urban population. The standing of the ruling party was hurt by the reforms, especially due to the ideological compromise the NEM entailed. However, opposition forces within the country were too weak and disorganized to take advantage of the situation. While the collapse of communism in Eastern Europe came as a shock to the government, it also vindicated somewhat the wisdom behind the push for economic reforms in Laos. Still, the collapse of the Soviet Union meant the end of a major source of aid, forcing Laos to look to other sources; initially France and Japan, and later the World Bank and the Asian Development Bank. This move required further economic reforms. At the same time, the state of affairs also necessitated that Laos mend fences with its neighbours, particularly Thailand. Since then, Laos' Communist leaders have maintained a monopoly on political control, but have by and large allowed market forces to dictate the trajectory of the economy.

see also: Kaysone Phomvihan; Lao People's Revolutionary Party.

New Economic Model (Malaysia)

The New Economic Model (NEM) constitutes one of the four pillars of the National Transformation Programme that aims to transform Malaysia into a high-income nation with inclusive and sustainable economic growth to achieve the goals envisaged in Vision 2020. It is anchored on an Economic Transformation Programme (ETP) which will be driven by eight Strategic Reform Initiatives (SRIs) that provide the foundation for government policies. The rationale for the NEM stems from recognition that deep-seated structural reforms are necessary in order to stimulate sustainable economic growth. After several decades of rapid development, economic growth has stagnated since the **Asian Financial Crisis**. The Malaysian economy is now caught in a middle-income trap where it remains heavily dependent on trade and commodities, and as such is vulnerable to global imbalances and fluctuating commodity prices. Furthermore, the wealth gap in the country continues to widen, with political implications for the ruling ***Barisan Nasional*** coalition. Since the Asian Financial Crisis, the share of private investment in the economy has declined. Complex bureaucratic red-tape has raised the cost of investing and the competitiveness of the Malaysian economy has therefore declined. The goal of inclusive growth enshrined in the NEM has generated considerable controversy, in particular the notion that the NEM should work to benefit all Malaysians, regardless of race. Under the NEM, economic policies are to be refined in such a way as to encourage equitable growth, but Malay conservatives have expressed concern that this could encroach upon Malaysia's affirmative action policy.

see also: Asian Financial Crisis 1997–8; *Barisan Nasional*.

New Economic Policy (Malaysia)

In the wake of an electoral reverse in May 1969 followed by intercommunal violence, the **May 13 Racial Riots**, the Malay-dominated government of Malaysia introduced a New Economic Policy (NEP) in 1971. The policy, set out within the Second Malaysia Plan, comprised two related themes. These were 'to reduce and eventually eradicate poverty, by raising income levels and increasing employment opportunities for all Malaysians, irrespective of race' and also to accelerate 'the process of restructuring Malaysian society to correct economic imbalance, so as to reduce and eventually eliminate the identification of race with economic function'. To those ends, the target was set of raising holdings of corporate assets by the Malays from some two per cent to thirty per cent by 1990. The NEP was driven by political considerations. **UMNO** (United Malays National Organization) had experienced an electoral seepage from its natural constituency because of Malay apprehension that Chinese economic dominance might be translated into political expression. UMNO acted to protect the political birthright of the Malays and its prerogative guardian role of their interests through economic initiative. Sustained affirmative action to the advantage of the Malay community as well as ensuring that key economic portfolios in government were held by Malay ministers had the desired political effect to UMNO's advantage. It also led to the emergence of a Malay business elite associated with UMNO who enriched themselves to form a virtual new class. In June 1991 the prime minister, **Mahathir Mohamad**, announced details of his government's New Development Policy to replace the NEP which had applied between 1971 and 1990. The new policy was distinguished by an intention to moderate affirmative action in favour of the Malays and to lay greater stress on improved education and training. The target of thirty per cent of corporate assets to be held by the Malays was retained but without a set date for realization.

see also: Mahathir Mohamad, Tun; May 13 Racial Riots 1969; UMNO.

New Order (Indonesia)

The term New Order was employed to dignify and validate the regime established in Indonesia by General **Suharto** with the support of the armed forces in the wake of an abortive coup (*see* ***Gestapu***) in October 1965. The term was intended also to differentiate that regime based on the values of the 1945 Constitution and the state philosophy ***Pancasila*** from the alleged political deviations of President **Sukarno**. In July 1966, while Sukarno still occupied presidential office, the provisional **People's Consultative Assembly** endorsed Suharto's seizure of power in March, which was represented as an '*ordre baru*' or New Order. The unfortunate identification with the language of European fascism of the 1930s was seized on by critics of the regime. In time, the term New Order came to be superseded by that of *Pancasila* democracy as the legitimizing trope. President Suharto's so-called New Order was effectively terminated with his resignation on 21 May 1998.

see also: Gestapu; *Pancasila*; People's Consultative Assembly; Suharto; Sukarno.

New People's Army (Philippines)
The New People's Army (NPA) is the military arm of the Communist Party of the Philippines which was reconstituted on Maoist lines at a conference held between 26 December 1968 and 7 January 1969 in southern Tarlac Province on the island of Luzón. The New People's Army was established on 29 March 1969 in the same vicinity and drew support not only from a younger generation of political activists but from members of the longstanding Communist ***Hukbalahap*** Movement insurgency which had degenerated into banditry. Bernabe Buscayno (also known as Commander Dante) became the military leader in October 1970 after the capture of Faustino del Mundo (Commander Sumulong), who had switched political allegiance. The NPA adopted a strategy of military decentralization, exploiting the archipelagic condition of the Philippines to avoid a vulnerable concentration of forces. This strategy proved to be increasingly successful with the evident failure of the martial law regime of President **Ferdinand Marcos**, inaugurated in September 1972. The deteriorating economic condition of the country and feckless brutality of a rapidly expanded armed forces attracted recruits to the Communist cause. That cause was served further by the assassination of opposition leader **Benigno Aquino** in August 1983. By the mid-1980s, the NPA had an estimated strength of some 15,000 effectives and had established fighting presences in sixty-three of the country's seventy-three provinces where they engaged in ambush and selective assassination. Moreover, it demonstrated an organizational resilience, despite the capture of some of its senior figures.

The momentum of its military challenge was arrested, however, after the fall of President Marcos and the assumption of office by **Corazón Aquino** in February 1986. A miscalculation of political mood, expressed in a rejection of the constitutional process, led to a drain in popular support. Moreover, the Communist movement became subject to internal divisions as a consequence of the change in political system. Under new leadership, the security forces improved their performance and by the time that Corazón Aquino was succeeded as president by former army chief of staff, **Fidel Ramos**, in elections in May 1992, the NPA had declined as a fighting force. President Ramos was helped by the closure of all US military bases, such as the **Clark Air Base** and the **Subic Bay Naval Base**, which had long been a central nationalist demand by the Communist movement and in September 1992 he was sufficiently self-confident to persuade the Congress to legalize the Communist Party. The government has been engaged in intermittent negotiations with the **National Democratic Front**, which represents its interests but without being able to bring the limited insurgency to an end. The NPA has shown an ability to attack police stations and to kidnap senior military personnel.

The NPA was designated a terrorist group under the European Union Common Foreign and Security Policy, and a Foreign Terrorist Organization by the United States State Department in 2002. However, in 2011 the Philippines government delisted the NPA as a terrorist organization. In September 2005, President **Gloria Macapagal-Arroyo** signed the Amnesty Proclamation 1377 for the Communist Party of the Philippines and the NPA, among other Communist rebel groups. Nevertheless, the NPA has continued engaging in political violence. NPA membership has declined considerably from the heights of the mid-1980s. Numbers dwindled to 4,000 in 2013 as a consequence of factionalism, defections and surrenders. Even so, there is no indication that the NPA intends to disband, and it remains engaged in guerrilla activities in rural areas where poverty is rampant.

see also: Aquino, Benigno; Aquino, Corazón; Clark Air Base; *Hukbalahap* Movement; Macapagal-Arroyo, Gloria; Marcos, Ferdinand; National Democratic Front; Ramos, Fidel; Sisón, José María; Subic Bay Naval Base.

Ngo Dinh Diem (Vietnam) *see* **Diem, Ngo Dinh**.

Nguyen Ai Quoc (Vietnam) *see* **Ho Chi Minh**.

Nguyen Co Thach (Vietnam) *see* **Thach, Nguyen Co**.

Nguyen Manh Cam (Vietnam)

Nguyen Manh Cam was appointed Vietnam's foreign minister in August 1991 in succession to **Nguyen Co Thach**, who had become an obstacle to rapprochement with the People's Republic of China. He was a longstanding career diplomat chosen for his professional skills rather than for his political standing. Nguyen Manh Cam was born in 1929 in central Nghe Tinh Province and joined the Communist Party at the age of seventeen. He is believed to have received a university education and showed an early aptitude for diplomacy. He served extensively in Europe, including two periods as ambassador in Moscow, where he was in post at the time of his appointment as foreign minister. Possibly because he had not been directly involved in difficult negotiations with Chinese counterparts, Nguyen Manh Cam was regarded as a suitable plenipotentiary for repairing Sino-Vietnamese relations. He has also been active in developing relations with **ASEAN** (Association of Southeast Asian Nations), which Vietnam joined in July 1995. Nguyen Manh Cam became a member of the party's Politburo at its mid-term conference held in January 1994. In September 1997, he was appointed additionally to the office of deputy prime minister, which he retained on being succeeded as foreign minister by Nguyen Dy Nien in January 2000. He remained a member of the Politburo and a member of the Central Committee of the Communist Party of Vietnam until 2001. In 2005, he joined the Eminent Persons Group that outlined the **ASEAN Charter**.

see also: ASEAN; ASEAN Charter; Thach, Nguyen Co.

Nguyen Minh Triet (Vietnam)

Nguyen Minh Triet served as president of Vietnam from 2006 to 2011, making him the third in command after the general secretary and the prime minister. A southerner, Triet was born to a farming family in Ben Cat in October 1942, and joined the Communist Party of Vietnam in 1965 after studying mathematics and political science at Saigon University, where he was active in the leftist student movement. As a member of the Communist Party's youth movement, Triet saw military action in My Tho province during the early years of the **Vietnam War**.

Triet was appointed party chief for Song Be province in 1992, a post he held until 1997 when he moved to Binh Duong province. In 2000, he became party chief of Ho Chi Minh City, where he developed a reputation as a crusader against corruption. During his time as president, he was seen to be a strong advocate of market reforms and foreign investments. His political views, however, are more conservative. As president, Triet staunchly defended the government's crackdown on human rights lawyers, the Roman Catholic clergy and members of an outlawed trade union in 2007.

see also: Vietnam War.

Nguyen Phu Trong (Vietnam)

Nguyen Phu Trong was elected general secretary of the Central Committee of the Communist Party of Vietnam at the party's eleventh National Congress in January 2011. As general secretary, he is one part of the Troika that governs Vietnam. Nguyen Phu Trong was born in Hanoi in 1944 and graduated from the linguistics faculty of Hanoi General University in 1967. He joined the party in the same year. An intellectual heavyweight, Nguyen Phu Trong began his career in the *Tap chi Cong San* (*Communist Review*) in 1967, and was its editor-in-chief between 1991 and 1996. He completed his postgraduate studies at the High-Level Nguyen Ai Quoc Party School and his doctorate in Party Building from the Academy of the Social Sciences of the Soviet Union. He has been a member of the Politburo since 1997 and was elected chairman of the National Assembly in 2006. Nguyen Phu Trong is widely seen as a conservative with a reputation for consensus building. The latter quality has allowed him to play the role of mediator between the ultra-conservative president, **Truong Tan Sang**, and Prime Minister **Nguyen Tan Dung**, the two other parts of the ruling Troika. Developments during the seventh Plenum of the Communist Party of Vietnam in May 2013 indicated that Nguyen Phu Trong's influence has deteriorated considerably when the Central Committee produced its own list of candidates for election to the Politburo instead

of rubber-stamping the general secretary's list as was the previous practice. Moreover, several candidates endorsed by Nguyen Phu Trong failed in their quest for election onto the Politburo.
see also: Nguyen Tan Dung; Truong Tan Sang.

Nguyen Tan Dung (Vietnam)

Nguyen Tan Dung was appointed prime minister in 2006, replacing **Phan Van Khai** as part of a Cabinet reshuffle with the objective of revitalizing the country's leadership. He assumed office at the age of fifty-seven, making him the youngest prime minister since Vietnamese unification in 1975. Nguyen Tan Dung was born in 1949 and holds a Bachelor of Law degree in High-Level Political Theory. He joined the Vietnamese army in 1961 at the age of twelve during the country's struggle for reunification, and served in the military for two decades. He started off as a medic and was slowly promoted up the ranks to become a major and head of the Personnel Board of the Military Command in Kien Giang Province. During his time in the army, he was involved in the Third **Indochina War**. After the war, he climbed quickly up the party ranks to become a member of its Politburo in 1996. Prior to his appointment as prime minister, he became first deputy prime minister in 1997 and served as governor of the State Bank of Vietnam from 1998 to 1999.

Coming from the more commercial South, Nguyen Tan Dung has been a strong advocate of Vietnam's liberal economic reforms. Nevertheless, he was heavily criticized at the January 2011 National Congress by a conservative faction led by the newly appointed president, **Truong Tan Sang**, which drew attention to huge losses incurred by State Owned Enterprises (*see* **State Owned Enterprise Reform**) under the supervision of the prime minister. Further attacks were launched against him at the fourth Plenum (December 2011) and the sixth Plenum (October 2012). In the latter instance, he came close to removal when the Politburo of the Communist Party of Vietnam voted to discipline him for economic mismanagement. In the event, he managed to evade disciplinary action, which would have led to his removal, following a reversal by the Central Committee. Though these attempts to unseat him ultimately failed, they did diminish his influence. As a result of these pressures, Nguyen Tan Dung was compelled to publicly accept personal responsibility for the failure of several SOEs.
see also: Indochina Wars; Phan Van Khai; State Owned Enterprise Reform; Truong Tan Sang.

Nguyen Tat Thanh (Vietnam) *see* Ho Chi Minh.

Nguyen Van Linh (Vietnam) *see* Linh, Nguyen Van.

Nguyen Van Thieu (Vietnam) *see* Thieu, Nguyen Van.

Nik Abdul Aziz Nik Mat (Malaysia)

Nik Aziz was appointed chief minister of the northern Malay state of Kelantan in October 1990 and held that position until he stepped down, purportedly under pressure, in May 2013. He is also the spiritual leader of ***Parti Islam Se-Malaysia*** (PAS), and has come to personify austerity in contrast to the lavish and venal lifestyles of some senior **UMNO** (United Malays National Organization) politicians. Known endearingly in PAS by the sobriquets '*tok guru*' (teacher) and '*panglima perang*' (war admiral), he is one of Malaysia's most revered Islamic teachers and commands a strong following from both sides of the political divide. Nik Aziz was born in 1931 in Pulau Melaka, Kelantan, and received his education in Malaysia before attending Darul Uloom Deoband in India and Al-Azhar in Egypt, where he graduated with a master's degree in Islamic jurisprudence. He joined PAS in 1967 and quickly became a member of parliament for the seat of Pengkalan Chepa until 1986. In 1990, he helped PAS regain the state government of Kelantan, which was lost to UMNO in 1978, and became chief minister.

Nik Aziz's political career has been marked by frequent exchanges with UMNO leaders over religious credentials and the role of Islam in governing Malaysia. His attacks on UMNO, including during his sermons, have been especially visceral, where he has prayed for their downfall and called them heretics and infidels. His exchanges with the former prime minister, **Mahathir Mohamad**, in particular, have become Malaysian folklore. Nik Aziz has been a strong supporter of the close cooperation between PAS and other opposition parties in the ***Pakatan Rakyat***, including the **Democratic Action Party**. Nik Aziz is also popular among the non-Muslim community especially in his home state of Kelantan, and has been seen as a crucial factor in drawing greater support for PAS from the Chinese community. He has however also periodically expressed views that go against the grain of his presumed moderate, pluralist persona. For instance, he is a vocal proponent of stricter application of *shari'a* law to govern Muslims, and has also publicly criticized women who adorn themselves, suggesting that this was the cause of sexual crimes. In 2001, Nik Aziz's eldest son, Nik Adli Nik Aziz, was apprehended in a raid on the militant group ***Kumpulan Militan Malaysia***, and was detained without trial under the internal security act for five years. Nik Aziz survived a major heart attack in 2004. With his retirement as Kelantan chief minister, progressive elements in the Islamist opposition party have lost their most eminent and ardent champion.

see also: Democratic Action Party; *Kumpulan Militan Malaysia*; *Pakatan Rakyat*; *Parti Islam Se-Malaysia*; Mahathir Mohamad, Tun.

Nixon Doctrine 1969 (Vietnam)

On 25 July 1969 at a press briefing at a United States military base on the island of Guam shortly before embarking on a tour of southern Asian countries, President Richard Nixon set out revised criteria for his government's policy in the region. It was made explicit that the object of that revision was to avoid direct United States involvement in any future **Vietnam War**-type conflicts. In a speech in November and then in a report to Congress in February 1970, the president spelled out the terms of what had come to be known as the Nixon Doctrine. These terms were that:

> The United States will keep all its treaty commitments; we shall provide a shield if a nuclear power threatens the freedom of a nation allied with us, or of a nation whose survival we consider vital to our security and the security of the region as a whole. In cases involving other types of aggression, we shall furnish military and economic assistance when requested and as appropriate. But we shall look to the nation directly threatened to assume the primary responsibility of providing the manpower for its defence.

Nixon's remarks on Guam indicated the future direction of US policy in Southeast Asia leading to military disengagement from Vietnam and the rest of Indochina before the end of 1973 as provided for initially in the **Paris Peace Agreements.**

see also: Paris Peace Agreements 1973; Vietnam War.

Nol, Lon (Cambodia)

Marshal Lon Nol achieved notoriety as the leader of the coup which overthrew Prince **Norodom Sihanouk** on 18 March 1970. He ended the monarchy in Cambodia and in October 1970 established the shortlived **Khmer Republic**, which was superseded when the **Khmer Rouge** seized power in April 1975. Lon Nol was born on 13 November 1913 in Prey Veng province. He was educated at the Lycée Sisowath from which he joined the French colonial administration, rising rapidly to become a provincial governor at the age of thirty-two. At the end of the Pacific War, Lon Nol became chief of the Cambodian police and then transferred to military command, displaying loyalty to Norodom Sihanouk, who was then king. Lon Nol was appointed governor of the important border province of Battambang in 1954 and then chief of staff of the army in 1955. By the end of the decade, he had become both commander-in-chief and minister of defence. He was prime minister from 1966–7. In September 1969 he returned to the office of prime minister as Prince Sihanouk's political grip on Cambodia began to weaken.

After the removal of Prince Sihanouk, Lon Nol, who was a practising mystic, showed himself to be an incompetent military leader in the face of a Vietnamese-led insurgent challenge. In February 1971 he suffered a stroke from which he never fully recovered, yet still held on to power with US backing. His rule was both repressive and corrupt, contributing to the ultimate victory of the Khmer Rouge. He was persuaded to go into exile on 1 April 1975 but only in return for US$1 million being deposited in his name in a US bank. He settled in Hawaii until 1979 when he moved to California, where he died on 17 November 1985.

see also: Khmer Republic; Khmer Rouge; Sihanouk, King Norodom.

Nong Duc Manh (Vietnam)

Nong Duc Manh was elected general secretary of the Communist Party of Vietnam in 2001 at the ninth Party Congress and remained in office until January 2011 when he was succeeded by **Nguyen Phu Trong**. According to official Vietnamese records, he was born into an ethnic Tay family in 1940 but there has been speculation about his parentage. Nong's meteoric rise since becoming a member of the national party's Central Committee in 1989 raised many questions as to how a minority Tay orphan could have risen so far so fast. Rumours abound that he was one of many illegitimate children of **Ho Chi Minh**, Vietnam's revolutionary leader. Moreover when Nong succeeded **Le Kha Phieu** in 2001 as general secretary, he was the first from an ethnic minority background, the first to possess a university degree (he studied forestry in Leningrad from 1966 to 1971), and the first to have no military experience. He joined the Politburo in 1991.

Nong Duc Manh is perhaps best known for his nine-year tenure as the chairman of Vietnam's National Assembly from 1992 to 2001. He was credited with elevating the importance of the National Assembly in Vietnam's politics, which hitherto had been seen as little more than a rubber-stamping body. Widely considered a moderate reformist, his election as general secretary helped to strengthen the consensus behind further economic liberalization. Anti-corruption and rule of law were key themes of his leadership. He was a strong advocate of tough anti-corruption legislation and the need for greater accountability of party officials. He was also known for his political reform programme which improved the efficiency of state institutions. In recognition of his ability to unite the many factions within the party, he was re-elected by the party's newly expanded Central Committee in April 2006.

see also: Ho Chi Minh; Le Kha Phieu, General; Nguyen Phu Trong.

Norodom Ranariddh (Cambodia) *see* Ranariddh, Prince Norodom.

Norodom Sihanouk (Cambodia) *see* Sihanouk, King Norodom.

Nouhak Phoumsavan (Laos)

Nouhak Phoumsavan was elected president of the Lao People's Democratic Republic on 25 November 1992 by the Supreme People's Assembly on the death of **Kaysone Phomvihan**. Nouhak and Kaysone were close colleagues and veterans of the Laotian revolutionary movement. Nouhak was born in the southern town of Savannakhet either in 1910 or 1916, and is known to have run a transport business between Laos and Vietnam in the early 1940s, so coming into contact with Vietnamese Communists who recruited him to their cause. He was in Hanoi at the end of the Pacific War as representative of the Laotian revolutionaries. After the outbreak of hostilities with the French in the **Indochina Wars**, he directed guerrilla operations across the Lao–Vietnamese border. He was a ***Pathet Lao*** delegate to the conference that resulted in the **Geneva Agreements on Indochina in 1954**, after which he played a prominent role in the **Lao People's Revolutionary Party** following its formation in 1955. Although he engaged in negotiations with successive governments in Vientiane before 1975, his main contribution was as Kaysone's deputy and second-ranking member of the party's Politburo. After the establishment of the Communist government in 1975, Nouhak became minister of finance and then in 1982 one of four deputy prime ministers. As president, Nouhak was not believed to occupy as powerful a position as the prime minister, **Khamtay Siphandon**, who replaced Kaysone as head of the ruling party in November 1992. In March 1996, he was removed from the party's Politburo and, in February 1998, he was replaced as president by **Khamtay Siphandon**, after which he was given the role of advisor to the Executive Committee of the party's Central Committee. Nouhak died on 9 September 2008.

see also: Geneva Agreements on Indochina 1954; Indochina Wars; Kaysone Phomvihan; Khamtay Siphandon; Lao People's Revolutionary Party; *Pathet Lao*.

Nu, U (Burma/Myanmar)

U Nu was the first prime minister of Burma after independence from Britain in January 1948. He came to high office in tragic circumstances following the assassination of the nationalist leader, **Aung San**, and other cabinet colleagues in July 1947. He held office until 1958 with an interruption during 1956–7 and then again from 1960 to 1962 when military intervention marked an end to civilian politics. U Nu was born on 25 May 1907 in Wakema and was educated at Rangoon University where he became president of the Students' Union in the mid-1930s. After graduation, he became a schoolteacher and was active in the nationalist organization *Dobama Asiayone* (Our Burma Association). He was interned by the colonial authorities at the outbreak of the Second World War and then released after the Japanese occupied the country. He served as foreign minister in the wartime government headed by Ba Maw and then became deputy to Aung San in the **Anti-Fascist People's Freedom League** (AFPFL) which spearheaded the drive for independence after the defeat of the Japanese. As prime minister, he was faced with constant turbulence arising from having to cope with Communist and ethnic minority insurrection as well as factional infighting which proved to be beyond his capacity to control. U Nu was imprisoned between 1962 and 1966. He was allowed to leave Burma in April 1969 ostensibly for Buddhist pilgrimage but sought to organize resistance from Thailand against the rule of General **Ne Win** until 1973, when he left to spend a year in the United States before passing the rest of the decade in India. He returned to Burma to retire in 1980 after an amnesty but made an ineffectual attempt to return to active politics in August 1988 in the wake of the bloody confrontation between the armed forces and civilians demonstrating for greater democracy. He set up a League for Democracy and Peace and then proclaimed a 'parallel' government in September, which proved to be empty gestures incapable of significant impact. He was placed under house arrest in December 1989 and then released in April 1992. As a politician, U Nu has always been a respected figure of integrity but regarded as unworldly and not really suited to the turbulence of public life. He died in Yangon on 14 February 1995 aged eighty-seven.

see also: Anti-Fascist People's Freedom League; Aung San; Ne Win, General.

O

One Malaysia (1Malaysia) (Malaysia)

One Malaysia constitutes a key pillar of the National Transformation Programme that frames Malaysia's aspirations to attain high-income nation status as envisaged in the goals of Vision 2020. The concept was introduced by Prime Minister **Najib Razak**, and is aimed at fostering a greater sense of national unity amongst Malaysians of all races with the recognition that the country's further economic development would depend on its ability to unite its multi-ethnic, multi-religious population towards that end. It has never been clear, however, what concrete forms the concept has been expressed through. In part because of this, reactions to the articulation of this concept were mixed. Many were sceptical whether the concept represented anything more than a hollow political campaign slogan manufactured to win back the support of disenchanted ethnic Chinese and Indian voters to the ***Barisan Nasional*** (BN) coalition. This comes after the unprecedented losses in the 2008 general election. On the other hand, the reference to inclusive goals contained in the One Malaysia concept has also prompted Malay conservatives in the country and also within **UMNO** (United Malays National Organization) to demand clarification on what the introduction of One Malaysia would mean for the special position and privileges of Malays and other ***Bumiputra***. The flames of controversy surrounding One Malaysia were fanned further by opposition leader **Anwar Ibrahim**, who alleged that its campaign slogan, 'People First', was borrowed from the One Israel campaign of the Ehud Barak government, which utilized a similar slogan. According to Anwar, the similarity was contrived by APCO Worldwide, which consulted for both the Malaysian and Israeli governments.

see also: Anwar Ibrahim; *Barisan Nasional*; *Bumiputra*; Najib Tun Razak, Datuk Seri Mohamad.

Ong Boon Hua (Malaya/Malaysia)

see **Chin Peng**.

Ong Teng Cheong (Singapore)

Ong Teng Cheong was the first elected president of the Republic of Singapore and served from 1993 to 1999. Born in Singapore on 22 January 1936, Ong graduated with a degree in architecture from the University of Adelaide in Australia and began his career as an architect there. He later obtained a scholarship to pursue a Master of Civic Design at the University of Liverpool in the United Kingdom. Upon graduating in 1967, he joined the planning department of the Ministry of National Development as an architect and town planner. Four years later, he resigned from the civil service after repeated appeals to the Public Service Commission to adjust his salary in line with his qualifications failed. Thereafter, he established his own practice, Ong & Ong Architects and Town Planner, together with his wife, who later ran the firm after Ong entered politics.

Ong's political activities began with grassroots movements in the late 1960s. He was appointed chairman of the Resident's Association in Seletar Hills, and subsequently entered politics as a **People's Action Party** (PAP) member of parliament for Kim Keat in 1972. He remained in Parliament for the same ward for four more terms before leading a team to win the Toa Payoh Group Representation Constituency in 1991. Ong also rose to become a senior member of Cabinet, serving in the communications, culture and labour portfolios, and also as deputy prime minister. In addition, he held the posts of chairman of the PAP and secretary-general of the government-sanctioned labour union, the National Trade Union Congress (NTUC). Ong was also one of the four senior leaders who were considered potential successors to **Lee Kuan Yew**. Educated in Chinese and well-versed in Chinese poetics and culture, he enjoyed strong support from the Chinese majority. He resigned from Parliament in 1993 to run for president as a PAP-backed candidate. After a somewhat pedestrian campaign against a relatively unknown candidate, Ong won sixty per cent of the vote and became the country's fifth president. Ong was a vocal leader who spoke his mind. As a result, despite being a key member of the establishment his outspokenness has occasionally placed him at odds with the government. As secretary-general of the NTUC, he sanctioned a two-day strike for workers in the shipping industry in 1986 without prior Cabinet approval, irking some of his fellow ministers in the process. Two years after this incident, he led a public demonstration against what was then perceived as American interference in Singapore's internal affairs.

Despite enjoying the support of the PAP in his presidential campaign, he spent most of his years in presidential office locked in an antagonistic relationship with former cabinet colleagues over presidential responsibility in the matter of the safeguarding of Singapore's reserves, which was a key responsibility for the otherwise ceremonial position. In essence, Ong wanted greater access to information about the reserves than he claimed he was afforded. Ong also argued that the government's decision to sell the Post Office Savings Bank to the Development Bank of Singapore in 1998 without first informing him was inappropriate since, constitutionally, the bank's status as a government statutory board meant that decisions involving its reserves fell within the remit of the elected presidency. At the end of his six years in office, Ong declined invitations to stand for re-election on the grounds of poor health as well as difficulties he had faced in dealing with the government. The Cabinet had also, by then, decided to support S. R. Nathan, a former senior civil servant, as the government's favoured candidate. The latter subsequently succeeded Ong as president in 1999. After stepping down as president, Ong returned to his firm as an advisor until his death in 2002.

see also: Lee Kuan Yew; People's Action Party.

***Organisasi Papua Merdeka* (OPM)** (Indonesia) *see* **Free Papua Movement**.

P

Pakatan Rakyat (Malaysia)

Pakatan Rakyat (PR) is a political coalition that was formed on 1 April 2008 in the wake of Malaysia's twelfth general election. The coalition brings together ***Parti Keadilan Rakyat*** (PKR), the **Democratic Action Party** (DAP) and ***Parti Islam Se-Malaysia*** (PAS). The Sarawak National Party joined the coalition in April 2010 but quit a year later. While Malaysian parties have entered into various forms of political alliances and cooperative arrangements such as *Gagasan Rakyat* and ***Barisan Alternatif***, the creation of PR marked a new and deeper level of cooperation with, among other things, the formation of a leadership council, a common policy framework and an annual coalition convention.

A key to the early success of PR was its ability to harness a growing popular movement that was mobilizing against the government of Prime Minister **Abdullah Badawi**. With the help of former deputy prime minister and one time heir apparent to **Mahathir Mohamad**, Anwar Ibrahim, the various opposition political parties managed to set aside ideological differences to form the *Barisan Rakyat* (People's Front) in early 2008. At the time of its formation, the *Barisan Rakyat* included the three largest opposition political parties – DAP, PKR and PAS – as well as *Parti Sosialis Malaysia* (Socialist Party of Malaysia or PSM) and the United Pasok Nunukragang National Organization (PASAOK). The agreement among these parties to avoid three-cornered fights and to dispense with individual party manifestos and divisive policies laid the groundwork for political collaboration that resulted in the denial of a two-thirds parliamentary majority to the incumbent, the loss of five state legislatures and, eventually, the formation of PR. In December 2009, the first convention of PR was held to formally launch the coalition. PR's political platform and policies are outlined in the *Buku Jingga* (Orange Book). Published in December 2010, the book expands on the coalition's policy initiatives and ideas that touch on issues such as income distribution, administrative transparency, anti-corruption, improved education, and economic and political parity for the eastern Malaysian states of Sabah and Sarawak. While PR has provided a stronger, more formalized platform for oppositional coalition politics, it remains the case that its constituent parties still harbour different, and in some instances fundamentally contradictory, aspirations. In that respect, while all constituent parties champion clean governance, justice and welfare, the common issue that ultimately gels PR together remains their shared opposition to the incumbent ***Barisan Nasional*** (National Front, BN) and its ambitions to seize federal power. Nevertheless, ideological differences, while managed and contained, have not been eradicated. Indeed, these differences have surfaced frequently since the coalition's formation, such as differences between DAP and PAS over the question of *hudud* (the Islamic penal code) implementation and the Islamic state. This has forced PR leaders to regularly reiterate their respective party's commitment to the coalition. Another concern is the question of party discipline or lack thereof, which became evident when the PR coalition state government in Perak lost power in the **Perak Legislature Takeover** after several of their state representatives left the party to become 'BN-friendly' independents. A third issue that has strained the PR is power-sharing between the constituent members, particularly in states where they won control of the legislature. Nevertheless, PR still managed to secure the majority of the vote at the 2013 federal election, but failed in their ultimate objective of unseating the BN.

see also: Badawi, Tun Abdullah Ahmad; *Barisan Alternatif*; *Barisan Nasional*; Democratic Action Party; Mahathir Mohamad, Tun; *Parti Islam Se-Malaysia*; *Parti Keadilan Rakyat*; Perak Legislature Takeover 2009.

Pancasila (Indonesia)

Pancasila is a term of Sanskrit derivation for the five principles that comprise Indonesia's state philosophy. Those principles (a belief in one supreme god, humanism, nationalism, popular sovereignty and social justice) were enunciated by nationalist leader and future president **Sukarno** on 1 June 1945 in a speech before the Investigating Committee for the Preparation of Independence set up under Japanese auspices. The most important of the five principles is the belief in one supreme deity, qualified by the right of every Indonesian to believe in his or her own particular god. The prescription was employed originally by Sukarno to counter demands by devout Muslims that Indonesia should become an Islamic state and as a way of entrenching religious pluralism and tolerance in a culturally diverse and fissiparous archipelago. Controversial as a threat to Islamic prerogative, *Pancasila* was entrenched as the state philosophy by President **Suharto**, under whose administration the five principles were made the subject of compulsory courses of instruction for civil servants. In 1978 *Pancasila* was incorporated into the republic's constitution, which on promulgation on 18 August 1945 had included its principles only in general terms in the preamble. In 1985 all political parties and organizations became obliged under law to adopt *Pancasila* as their sole ideological basis, described in Indonesian as *asas tunggal*. President Suharto described Indonesia's political system as *Pancasila* Democracy, which was represented as an authentic Indonesian alternative to alien western values. Throughout the **New Order** period, *Pancasila* served as a vague but exclusive ideology which was useful as a demobilizing device against independent political elements seeking to appeal to a national audience. The charge of acting against *Pancasila* had sufficient of a treasonable implication to intimidate political dissidents. In practice, President Suharto reserved the monopoly right to determine what constituted an acceptable expression of the state philosophy. *Pancasila* became politically controversial to the extent that it came to be seen as the instrument of Suharto's purpose and not as a unifying neutral symbol. By May 1998, with the political downfall of Suharto, *Pancasila* had become discredited because of the way in which it had been abused. It then lost its political centrality but remained, in principle, Indonesia's state philosophy. The diminution of *Pancasila* was codified in the first sitting of the **People's Consultative Assembly** following the fall of Suharto, where it was decided that concepts such as *asas tunggal* would be abolished, and state indoctrination based on *Pancasila* ideology and institutionalization of the philosophy banned. Nevertheless, *Pancasila* has enjoyed something of a revival as a national philosophy of late in debates taking place in public and intellectual circles, where the concept has been suggested as a panacea for the centrifugal pull of rising ethnic and religious fundamentalisms unleashed by the demise of the strong New Order state.

see also: New Order; People's Consultative Assembly; Suharto; Sukarno.

Panglong Agreement (Burma/ Myanmar)

Held in February 1947, in the lead up to Burma's independence, the second Panglong Conference essentially established the basis for the formation of the Union of Burma. During the meeting **Aung San** did much to allay lingering fears among ethnic leaders about the possible unequal treatment of minorities in a future Union. Representatives of the Shan States, the Kachin hills and the Chin hills signalled their willingness to cooperate with the interim Burmese government by signing the final Panglong Agreement on 12 February 1947 and to join a future Union of Burma. The agreement accepted in principle 'full autonomy' in internal administration for the Frontier Areas, the colonial term for most of the areas where the country's ethnic minorities lived. The agreement provided for a representative of the Supreme Council of the United Hill Peoples, an ethnic minority organization representing several groups, to be appointed to the Governor's Executive Council and for the Frontier Areas to be brought within the purview of the Executive Council. The agreement meant that ethnicity had become part of the independence process as the Union of Burma came into being in January 1948. The successful outcome of the meeting convinced the British that Aung San and the **Anti-Fascist People's Freedom League** government would be able to mediate with the ethnic minorities' leaders in the Frontier Areas. The agreement would have far-reaching consequences for ethnic aspirations for self-rule. Clause Five guaranteed: 'Full autonomy in internal administration for the Frontier Areas is accepted in principle'. This formed the basis of the 'Spirit of Panglong' or the idea that the ethnic minorities were entitled to a form of self-rule, even if it was not expressly put into law. The constitution of 1947, devised later, would contain a clause that the Shan and Kayah States could opt to leave the Union after ten years through plebiscite.

The anniversary of the Panglong Agreement is still celebrated as a national holiday, Union Day, in Myanmar. Importantly, the **Karen** and Karenni had not participated in the conference, nor did representatives from other ethnic groups in Frontier Areas, or the Mon and Arakanese from Ministerial Burma. For many ethnic groups, however, the spirit of Panglong largely dissipated when General **Ne Win** took over power in 1962 and dispensed with the 1947 constitution. The coup was justified by the military as a response to ethnic agitation over issues of minority.

The 'Spirit of Panglong' has become almost more important than the agreement itself. Reforms since the 2010 elections have again prompted calls by ethnic minority leaders for another Panglong-style conference, but this time to include all ethnic minorities, to decide the status of ethnic minorities in Myanmar. While the government has shown some acceptance of a new conference, a substantial change in ethnic relations would necessitate amendment of the current **2008 Constitution**.

see also: Anti-Fascist People's Freedom League; Aung San; Constitution 2008; Karen; Ne Win, General.

Papua Freedom Movement (Indonesia) *see* Free Papua Movement.

Paris Peace Agreements 1973 (Vietnam)

On 27 January 1973 a set of agreements to end the war in Vietnam was concluded in Paris between representatives of the United States, the Democratic Republic of (North) Vietnam, the **Provisional Revolutionary Government of the Republic of South Vietnam** (PRG) – set up by the insurgent **National Liberation Front of South Vietnam** (NLF) in 1969 – and the Republic of (South) Vietnam. Formal talks to find a political settlement to the **Vietnam War** had begun in Paris in May 1968 between the United States and the Democratic Republic of Vietnam as a direct consequence of the impact in the United States of the dramatic **Tet Offensive** launched by the NLF in January 1968. Those talks were joined subsequently by representatives of the southern government and their revolutionary challengers who were part of a united Vietnamese Communist movement. The talks were deadlocked for some time because of the insistence of the Communist side that the United States should remove the incumbent government in Saigon as part of a political settlement. The Vietnamese Communists changed their priorities from July 1972 in the wake of their spring military offensive, which had been blunted by US aerial firepower. Their pressing concern then became to end direct US military involvement in Vietnam. That objective served as the centre-point of the agreements reached in Paris in January 1973 after an impasse from mid-December 1972 during which the intensive US 'Christmas Bombing' of North Vietnam was authorized in order to overcome opposition from South Vietnam's president, **Nguyen Van Thieu**. The agreements provided for US recognition of the territorial unity of Vietnam and a ceasefire, after which its forces would stop all military activities throughout the country, as well as a total military withdrawal within sixty days of signature. In return, the Communist side agreed to return all US prisoners of war, especially air force personnel. Provision was made for a political settlement among contending Vietnamese parties through the establishment of a National Council of National Reconciliation and Concord, which was charged with organizing free and democratic elections. Provision was made also for peaceful reunification between North and South through negotiations. The last US combat soldier left Vietnam by the end of March 1973.

A political settlement did not follow, however, despite the role of an international commission of control and supervision. The Paris Agreements did not make any provision for the withdrawal of northern troops from the southern half of the country. When the contending Vietnamese parties failed to set up the National Council of National Reconciliation and Concord because of irreconcilable political differences, the matter was finally resolved through superior force. The Ban Me Thuot Offensive launched by Communist forces in the mountains of South Vietnam in March 1975 led to the rout of Saigon's army and the fall of the capital on 30 April 1975.

The Paris Agreements also made provision for reconciliation between the United States and the Democratic Republic of Vietnam, with the former committing itself 'to healing the wounds of war and to post-war reconstruction of the Democratic Republic of Vietnam and throughout Indochina'. Normalization of relations was long delayed, however, by American bitterness at their evident defeat and humiliation, the manner of unification and by international reaction to Vietnam's invasion of Cambodia in December 1978. In addition, the issue of Vietnam providing a full accounting for US soldiers classified as Missing In Action served to delay normalization of relations. It was only in February 1994 that President Bill Clinton announced an end to the longstanding US trade and investment embargo against Vietnam but without authorizing diplomatic relations with the government in Hanoi beyond liaison offices in respective capital cities in the following May. Diplomatic relations were established in August 1995, partly in response to Vietnam's active cooperation in searching for those Missing In Action.

see also: National Liberation Front of South Vietnam; Provisional Revolutionary Government of the Republic of South Vietnam PRG 1969–76; Tet Offensive; Thieu, Nguyen Van; Vietnam War.

Partai Amanat Nasional (Indonesia)

Partai Amanat Nasional (PAN or the National Mandate Party) is an Indonesian political party founded on 23 August 1998. It is ideologically positioned as a moderate reformist Islamist party which bases itself on principles of religious morality and humanity. PAN was born out of the *Majelis Amanat Rakyat* (MARA or the People's Mandate Council), an organization which was founded on 14 May 1998 and included over fifty prominent intellectuals including Amien Rais, chairman of the ***Muhammadiyah*** organization. Upon the fall of the **New Order**, Rais announced the formation of PAN and served as its founding chairman. PAN participated in its first legislative election in 1999 and won seven per cent of the vote along with thirty-five seats in the People's Representative Council (DPR). Through the forging of a coalition of Islamic-based parties, Rais was elected speaker of the **People's Consultative Assembly** (MPR). In the 2004 legislative election, it won six per cent of the votes and fifty-two seats. Amien Rais was put forward as PAN's candidate for the presidential elections, but only managed to secure fifteen per cent of the vote along with vice-presidential candidate Siswono Yudo Husodo. At the 2009 legislative election, PAN managed to win six per cent of the votes and forty-three seats on the DPR. Its performance at the 2014 polls improved marginally to 7.5 per cent on the back of strong campaigning and visibility, especially in its traditional strongholds of East and Central Java. Initially put forward by his party to be a presidential candidate, PAN's longstanding chairman, Hatta Rajasa, was subsequently nominated by presidential election hopeful Prabowo Subianto to be his vice-presidential running mate. Hatta has been a member of Cabinet serving in the portfolios of research and technology as well as transport, and was most recently coordinating minister for economic affairs in the government of President **Susilo Bambang Yudhoyono**.

see also: Muhammadiyah; New Order; People's Consultative Assembly; Yudhoyono, Susilo Bambang.

Partai Bulan Bintang (Indonesia)

Partai Bulan Bintang (Crescent Star Party, PBB) was founded on 17 July 1998 as an Indonesian Islamist party which drew its legacy from the ***Masyumi*** party which was banned by former president Sukarno in 1960 following the alleged involvement of several party members in the PRRI rebellion (*Pemerintah Revolusioner Republik Indonesia* or the **Revolutionary Government of the Republic of Indonesia**). Following the fall of President **Suharto,** *Masyumi* was reformulated and renamed as PBB under the leadership of Yusril Ihza Mahendra.

Since its formation, PBB has been a marginal player in Indonesian politics. In the 1999 elections, PBB won barely two per cent of the vote and attained thirteen seats in the People's Representative Council. Nevertheless, Yusril was appointed minister of laws and legislation in the National Unity Cabinet under President **Abdurrahman Wahid**. PBB could not improve on this performance in subsequent elections. In 2004, it won 2.6 per cent of the popular vote and attained eleven seats in the Council, while in 2009 it only secured 1.8 per cent of the vote and failed to retain any of its seats. It could not fare better in 2014, winning only 1.5 per cent of the vote thereby failing to clear the parliamentary threshold. Drawing on its Masyumi Islamist legacy, PBB has championed the implementation of *shari'a* law in Indonesia as well as greater attention to Islamic education.

see also: Masyumi; Revolutionary Government of the Republic of Indonesia 1958–61; Suharto; Sukarno. Wahid, Abdurrahman.

Partai Demokrasi Indonesia (Indonesia) see *Partai Demokrasi Indonesia–Perjuangan*.

Partai Demokrasi Indonesia–Perjuangan (Indonesia)

Partai Demokrasi Indonesia (PDI), the Indonesian Democratic Party, was established in January 1973 as part of an attempt by the government of President **Suharto** to remould the political format of the republic. The political parties of the **Sukarno** era were regarded as fractious and nationally divisive. As an alternative vehicle for mobilizing support for President Suharto's **New Order**, a so-called association of Functional Groups, known in acronym as ***Golkar***, was rehabilitated for an electoral role. In order to lend legitimacy to elections as well as to control political activity, all legal parties were merged into two groupings. The PDI was formed primarily from the Indonesian National Party (*Partai Nasional Indonesia* – PNI), closely associated with Sukarno, and two Christian parties, while all Muslim parties were merged into the ***Partai Persatuan Pembangunan*** (PPP).

With civil servants virtually obliged to support *Golkar*, the PDI performed poorly in parliamentary elections in 1977 and in 1982. In consequence, it seemed likely to disappear and to undermine the legitimacy of the electoral process which had been devised to demonstrate the continuing legitimacy of the Suharto government. The PDI was revived to an extent in elections in 1987, in part through support from dissident elements in the armed forces and also because of growing urban discontent with the Suharto regime. Its rallies in the capital Jakarta were the most well-attended and it attracted support through its identification with President Sukarno. In parliamentary elections in June 1992, the PDI made an impact by its criticism of nepotism, which was construed as an attack on the rapacious business activities of President Suharto's family, as well as calling for the tenure of office of the president to be limited to two terms only. The PDI improved further on its electoral position but still managed to secure only some fifteen per cent of the total vote. In December 1993 **Megawati Sukarnoputri**, daughter of the late president, Sukarno, was elected to lead the party despite the known preference of the government for an alternative candidate. In June 1996, President Suharto contrived to remove Megawati from the party leadership at a conference in Medan. She and her supporters were excluded from the PDI list for parliamentary elections in May 1997 in which the party's vote was reduced to three per cent. After the political downfall of Suharto in May 1998, her *Perjuangan* (struggle) faction of the PDI, known as *Partai Demokrasi Indonesia–Perjuangan* (PDI–P), assumed the ascendency and in parliamentary elections in June 1999, it won 37.4 per cent of the vote and 154 of 462 elective seats, making it the largest party in the legislature. Meanwhile, the main PDI managed to secure only 0.62 per cent of the vote, relegating it to the periphery of Indonesian politics where it has languished. Having taken over the mantle, the PDI–P's electoral success gave rise to expectations that Megawati would become president, but, in the event, her path was blocked by a coalition of Islamic parties and she had to settle for the vice-presidency in October 1999. She did eventually become president in July 2001 after the removal of **Abdurrahman Wahid** from office.

After an unimpressive tenure in office, Megawati failed in her bid to retain the presidency at the 2004 election, and was forced to make way for **Susilo Bambang Yudhoyono**. Likewise, her presidential bid in 2009 also faltered. Since the heights of 1999, PDI–P's share of the popular vote fell to 18.5 per cent and fourteen per cent in 2004 and 2009 respectively. This has happened despite the party's attempt to position itself as the defender of small-scale farmers, petty traders and fishermen. The party however experienced something of a rejuvenation during the buildup to the 2014 election. This was in no small measure attributable to Megawati's eventual anointing of the hugely popular governor of Jakarta, **Joko Widodo** or 'Jokowi', as the party's presidential candidate. Following the announcement, the party's popularity skyrocketed according to a number of pre-election polls, particularly outside its traditional support bases in Java and Bali among younger voters. At the 2014 parliamentary poll itself, PDI–P emerged clear winners, although the margin of their victory in the popular vote fell short of the twenty-five per cent target which would have allowed them to nominate 'Jokowi' for the presidency without having to forge a political coalition. This was in part a result of the party's delayed formal nomination of 'Jokowi' as its presidential candidate, and accompanying failure to leverage his personal appeal until fairly late in the campaign. Subsequent rumours of a falling out between 'Jokowi' and Puan Maharani, daughter of Megawati and at one point a possible PDI–P presidential candidate as well, after the April election cast further doubt over the party's presidential aspirations.

see also: Golkar; Megawati Sukarnoputri; New Order; *Partai Persatuan Pembangunan*; Suharto; Sukarno; Wahid, Abdurrahman; Widodo, Joko; Yudhoyono, Susilo Bambang.

Partai Demokrat (Indonesia)

Partai Demokrat (Democratic Party, PD) is an Indonesian political party founded on 9 September 2001. PD served as the vehicle for **Susilo Bambang Yudhoyono**'s vice-presidential bid in 2001, which he eventually lost to **Hamzah Haz**.

During the 2004 legislative elections, PD won 7.5 per cent of the votes on the way to winning fifty-seven out of 560 seats. At the presidential polls, Yudhoyono stood with Yusuf Kalla as his vice-presidential running mate, and won 33.6 per cent of the vote. In a subsequent run-off election against the incumbent **Megawati Sukarnoputri**, Yudhoyono secured sixty per cent of the vote to win the presidency. During Yudhoyono's first term, the visibility of PD increased across the archipelago as it established itself as a formidable party with a national presence. This increased visibility paid dividends at the 2009 legislative elections when PD's performance improved significantly and it won 20.9 per cent of the vote, gaining 148 seats in the legislature. The party's popularity was further underscored by Yudhoyono's re-election with 60.8 per cent of the vote. PD's source of strength has been its broad appeal, anchored on the national ideology of ***Pancasila***. This has allowed PD to enter easily into political coalitions with other parties of different ideological stripes. At the same time, it is this character of PD that has led many to see it as merely a personal vehicle for President Yudhoyono's political aspirations since the 2004 elections rather than a party with any substantive ideology. To that end, it should be noted that there has been disquiet within the party itself over the centralization of power under Yudhoyono. Anas Urbaningrum's victory over Yudhoyono's preferred candidates, Andi Mallarangeng and Marzuki Alie, in the contest for party chairmanship in 2010 was seen as a reaction within segments of the party against the president's growing influence.

PD's prospects for the 2014 election were considerably diminished by a raft of corruption scandals that have rocked the party. Party treasurer Muhammad Nazaruddin was dismissed by Anas in April 2012 for his role in a graft case involving the provision of logistic support for the Southeast Asian Games in South Sumatra. Sports minister Andi Mallarangeng was forced to resign in December 2012 after allegations surfaced of corruption and mismanagement of a multi-million dollar sports complex project in Bogor, West Java. Anas himself was forced to resign in March 2013 after being named as a graft suspect. Given how Andi Mallarangeng and Anas Urbaningrum stood out as prominent reformists behind PD's rise to power, their misconduct has left the image of the party severely tarnished. Cognizant of the fact that the party's popularity had always relied on his own personality and popularity, Yudhoyono introduced a party convention through which to identify new candidates who could lead PD's defence of their presidency. This move however, failed to stem the haemorrhaging of support, and PD only managed to secure around eight per cent of the popular vote, a far cry from its performance in 2009.

see also: Haz, Hamzah; Megawati Sukarnoputri; *Pancasila*; Yudhoyono, Susilo Bambang.

Partai Keadilan Sejahtera (Indonesia)

Partai Keadilan Sejahtera (Prosperous Justice Party, PKS) is the third largest member of **Susilo Bambang Yudhoyono**'s governing coalition between 2009 and 2014, with fifty-seven members of parliament and three ministers. PKS was first formed as *Partai Keadilan* (Justice Party or PK) on 28 July 1998. Made up mostly of activists from the ***Tarbiyah*** movement, the Justice Party contested the 1999 elections and won a modest 1.44 per cent of the total vote. Even so, the party managed to secure a cabinet position when its president, Nur Machmudi Ismail, was appointed minister of agriculture and forestry.

Because electoral laws implemented in 1999 stipulated a two per cent threshold for political parties to be eligible for electoral contests, PK would have been barred from the 2004 contests. In order to continue their participation in party politics, members of the *Tarbiyah* movement led by Al-Muzammil Yusuf formed the PKS on 20 April 2003. PK subsequently merged with the PKS in July 2003.

Under the leadership of Hidayat Nurwahid, the PKS performed admirably in the 2004 election to win 7.34 per cent of the total vote and secure forty-five out of 550 seats to become the seventh largest party in Parliament. Hidayat himself was elected as chairman of the Assembly from 2004 to 2009. For the 2009 election, PKS joined a coalition led by President Yudhoyono's ***Partai Demokrat*** and won 7.88 per cent of the votes along with fifty-seven seats, becoming the fourth largest party in Parliament. Hidayat was succeeded by Tifatul Sembiring in May 2005, who served as party president for five years before passing the baton to Luthfi Hasan Ishaaq in June 2010. Meanwhile, prominent cleric Hilmi Aminuddin was appointed chair of the party's religious council in 2005, and continues in that position.

PKS's Islamist credentials rest on its mantra of 'Islam is the solution'. Party leaders have frequently articulated that the party's ideology rests on the inseparability of religion, politics and morality. The PKS objective of the Islamization of Indonesian society was pursued through proselytization and a strict cadre system. PKS's agenda of anti-corruption and social justice gradually gained currency especially among the urban electorate in Java. Much of the party's appeal rested on the fact that its representatives were seen to be 'clean', as opposed to the rampant corruption entrenched in Indonesian politics. At the same time, PKS has also taken conservative positions on social issues such as public morality, when it pushed a controversial anti-pornography law in 2008. Of note is the fact that while brandishing Islamist credentials, PKS also embraces religious pluralism. This is elaborated in its 1998 manifesto, which endorses the equality of all Indonesians and protects the human rights and dignity of all, regardless of religion, ethnicity or cultural background. PKS are also advocates of gender equality. However, their championing of gender equality has been questioned in recent times after the party's religious council issued a *fatwa* on women's participation in legislative elections, claiming that women should prioritize family over politics.

The image of PKS as a clean party free of corruption has in recent years been undermined by several controversies. This included the imprisonment of PKS lawmaker Muhammad Misbakhun for fraud, and resignation of another PKS lawmaker, Arifinto, for watching pornography during a parliamentary sitting. In addition to these internal crises, PKS's position in the coalition was struck a blow in 2011 when President Yudhoyono replaced the party's research and technology minister, Suharno Surapranata, with environment minister Gusti Muhammad Hatta, in a cabinet reshuffle, purportedly in reaction to several occasions when the Islamist party departed from coalition positions on policy issues. In February 2013, party president Luthfi Hasan Ishaaq was detained on corruption charges, and in early 2014 was sentenced to sixteen years imprisonment. Consequently, popular support for the party dipped at the 2014 polls, when it secured less than seven per cent of the vote. Nevertheless, the magnitude of the dip – barely one per cent between 2009 and 2014 – was remarkable given the severity of the corruption cases and their fallout. This was in part a result of the depth of the party's cadre system, effective strategic campaigning (including whistle-blowing on other graft cases), and the efforts of a dynamic new president, Anis Matta.

see also: Partai Demokrat; *Tarbiyah*; Yudhoyono, Susilo Bambang.

Partai Kebangkitan Bangsa (Indonesia)

Partai Kebangkitan Bangsa (National Awakening Party, PKB) was established specifically to contest parliamentary elections in June 1999 in the wake of the political downfall of former president **Suharto** in May 1998, and counts East Java as its stronghold. It was set up as the political arm of the ***Nahdlatul Ulama*** (NU), a rural-based Islamic organization of thirty million adherents with a liberal pluralist agenda, which had withdrawn from active politics in 1984. Chaired by Matori Abdul Djalil, its effective leader was **Abdurrahman Wahid**, who headed the NU. In the election of June 1999, it secured third place behind ***Partai Demokrasi Indonesia–Perjuangan*** and ***Golkar*** with 17.4 per cent of the vote and fifty-one out of 462 elective seats. Following the election, Abdurrahman Wahid was elected to the presidency by the **People's Consultative Assembly** after **Megawati Sukarnoputri**'s aspirations to high office were blocked in October 1999. The PKB has, however, been unable to sustain its momentum, managing to secure only 10.5 per cent of the votes in 2004 and five per cent in 2009 on the way to fifty-two seats and twenty-eight seats respectively. The poor performances can be attributed to internal conflicts and intra-family disputes arising from Abdurrahman Wahid's decision to sack a string of party chairmen, including his own nephew. The party however experienced a change in fortunes when Rusdi Kirana, a successful non-Muslim businessman and owner of Indonesia's largest airline, Lion Air, joined the party and became deputy chairman, and when the chairman of the NU, Said Agil Siraj, openly endorsed the party in its 2014 campaign. This resulted in a creditable increase in popular support to nine per cent at the 2014 polls.

see also: Golkar; Indonesian Democratic Party; Megawati Sukarnoputri; *Nahdlatul Ulama*; *Partai Demokrasi Indonesia–Perjuangan*; People's Consultative Assembly; Suharto; Wahid, Abdurrahman.

Partai Persatuan Pembangunan (Indonesia)

Partai Persatuan Pembangunan (United Development Party, PPP) was established in January 1973 through an enforced merger of four Muslim parties which had participated in national elections in 1971. The object of the merger was to make all political parties subordinate to the priorities of the **New Order** whereby they accorded it constitutional legitimacy without posing any effective electoral challenge. Over the years, the PPP has had its composite Islamic identity diluted as it has become obliged to give up using the *Ka'abah* (the sacred rock in Mecca) as its electoral symbol and to accept ***Pancasila*** as its sole ideology. It diminished as a political organization from 1984 when the ***Nahdlatul Ulama*** (NU) withdrew from formal politics to concentrate on social and educational activities. The effect was demonstrated in parliamentary elections in 1987 in which the PPP won only sixty-one seats compared to ninety-four seats in 1982. A marginal improvement in its electoral performance of sixty-two in 1992 had no impact on the overall political situation whereby parties were permitted to play a limited role only every five years, with the underlying purpose of endorsing the authority of the regime tied to the person of President **Suharto**. After his political downfall in May 1998, the PPP found itself in electoral competition with a number of newly formed Islamic parties. In parliamentary elections in June 1999, it secured 10.7 per cent of the vote and fifty-eight seats. Nonetheless, it was influential as a member of an Islamic-based coalition in opposing the bid for the presidency **Megawati Sukarnoputri**, who was accused of pro-Christian bias. In the event, the PPP helped to secure the election of President **Abdurrahman Wahid** in October 1999. Its leader, **Hamzah Haz**, was appointed coordinating minister for people's welfare, but resigned office in November that year, ostensibly to concentrate on leading his party, against a background of allegations of his involvement in corruption. However, the party was not particularly successful in the 2004 legislative elections, managing to gain only 8.2 per cent of the votes compared to 10.7 per cent in 1999.

The PPP's fortunes have not recovered since. A move to back Megawati in the 2004 presidential election misfired when party president Hamzah Haz was passed over by Megawati as her vice-presidential running mate. Soon, there was another setback when Megawati, whom the party continued to support after Hamzah Haz's disastrous attempt to put himself forward as an alternative presidential candidate, was defeated by **Susilo Bambang Yudhoyono** in a presidential run-off. At the 2009 legislative elections, the PPP secured only 5.33 per cent of the vote, although their new leader, Suryadharma Ali, managed to secure a cabinet position as minister of cooperatives and state and medium enterprises, and later as minister of religious affairs. This improved marginally to 6.5 per cent in 2014 mostly on the back of patronage on the part of Suryadharma Ali, who increased funding for Islamic education thereby securing the support of local Islamic scholars and teachers.

see also: Haz, Hamzah; Megawati Sukarnoputri; *Nahdlatul Ulama*; New Order; *Pancasila*; Suharto; Wahid, Abdurrahman; Yudhoyono, Susilo Bambang.

Partai Rakyat Brunei (Brunei) *see* People's Party.

Parti Bangsa Dayak Sarawak (Malaysia)

Parti Bangsa Dayak Sarawak (PBDS) may be translated as the Dayak Race Party of Sarawak. It is a communal-based political organization which seeks to advance the interests of the Dayak peoples of the north Bornean state of Sarawak in Malaysia. The various Dayak peoples constitute the largest indigenous grouping but politics has been dominated by a Malay-Melanau Muslim leadership since the mid-1960s with support from the Malaysian federal government in Kuala Lumpur. The Dayak party was formed in 1983 as a breakaway group from the mainly Dayak Sarawak National Party through the initiative of Leo Moggie, who then held the federal office of minister for energy. It won seven seats in elections to the state legislature in the year of its formation and in 1984 it became a member of the federal ruling coalition, ***Barisan Nasional*** (National Front, BN). It went on to secure fifteen seats in 1987 as part of a major challenge to the leadership of the chief minister, **Abdul Taib Mahmud**, and ***Parti Pesaka Bumiputera Bersatu*** but then failed to hold on to its political gains in 1991, when its representation fell back to seven. Although Dayak political alienation persists in Sarawak, PBDS has not been successful in mobilizing and focusing it beyond a limited constituency. In May 1994 it was admitted into the state ruling coalition. PBDS was deregistered in 2004 following a leadership crisis that brought about a split in the party between factions led by Datuk Daniel Tajem and James Jemust Masing. In the aftermath of the split, *Parti Rakyat Sarawak* was formed by Daniel Tajem and Datuk Sng Chee Hua. The party secured six seats at each of the 2008 and 2013 general elections, helping the BN retain its grip on Sarawak.

see also: Barisan Nasional; Parti Pesaka Bumiputera Bersatu; Sarawak National Party; Taib Mahmud, Datuk Patinggi Abdul.

Parti Bersatu Sabah (Malaysia) *see* Sabah United Party.

Parti Islam Se-Malaysia (Malaysia)

Parti Islam Se-Malaysia (PAS) translates from Malay as the Islamic Party of Malaysia. The party has long sought to entrench the religious values of Islam in the country's constitution and in November 1993 secured passage of a law in the Kelantan legislature which provided for an Islamic penal system. The party's origins, with support among a constituency of rural schoolteachers of leftist and pan-Malay disposition, go back to the radical Malay National Party which was founded at the end of the Pacific War. In 1951 it was reformed initially as the Pan Malayan Islamic Party which, with its fundamentalist message, posed the main Malay-Islamic challenge to **UMNO** (United Malays National Organization). The main political impact of PAS has been in the northeast of the Malay peninsula, where it won control of the Kelantan state legislature on two occasions before becoming a member of the ruling intercommunal *Barisan Nasional* (National Front, BN) in January 1973. That association was shortlived, with PAS being expelled in December 1977 after a revolt within the Kelantan state legislature against a chief minister appointed from Kuala Lumpur. That upheaval culminated in Mohamad Asri Muda's resignation as leader and paved the way for a younger generation more closely attuned to the Islamic resurgence, which had become a global phenomenon, to take over the helm of the party. Following this, the party became more vocal in its agitation for the transformation of Malaysia to an Islamic state. As part of ***Angkatan Perpaduan Ummah*** (Muslim Unity Front), PAS scored a notable success in winning all seats at the federal and state levels in Kelantan at the October 1990 election but was unable to prevent the BN from being returned to office with a two-thirds majority. In elections in April 1995, PAS held onto its seven seats in the federal Parliament and was also returned to office in the state of Kelantan. Despite this modest electoral performance, it continued to pose a threat to UMNO not only because of its Islamic credentials but also because of the probity of its leadership. PAS became the main political beneficiary of the outrage among the Malay community at the dismissal, arrest, detention, trial and imprisonment of former deputy prime minister, **Anwar Ibrahim**. In elections in November 1999, its federal parliamentary strength was increased to twenty-seven seats, and it gained control of the state legislature and government in Terengganu, while holding on to Kelantan. Its president, Fadzil Noor, became leader of the federal parliamentary opposition, while PAS assumed the dominant position within the ***Barisan Alternatif*** (Alternative Front), an inter-racial coalition of opposition parties, which had begun as an electoral pact. For its part, PAS sought to reconcile its religious priorities with a pragmatic approach to business, which drew a positive response from the non-Malay communities.

After the death of Fadzil Noor in 2002, **Abdul Hadi Awang** took over as president of the party. In the 2004 general elections, the party's decision to promote its Islamic State agenda prior to the elections proved to have a deleterious effect. This, in addition to positive popular sentiment towards the new prime minister, **Abdullah Badawi**, resulted in PAS losing Terengganu, narrowly defending Kelantan and retaining only seven parliamentary seats. PAS improved its showing at the 2008 general election when it formed an alliance with the Democratic Action Party (DAP) and *Parti Keadilan Rakyat* (PKR). During that campaign PAS significantly toned down its Islamic state agenda, campaigning instead for *Negara Berkebajikan* (welfare state), which saw it winning twenty-three parliamentary seats. In addition to Kelantan, PAS also wrestled control of the state of Selangor as part of the opposition coalition, which won a total of five states in 2008 (later reduced to four due to defections in Perak: *see* **Perak Legislature Takeover 2009**). Although the relationship between PAS and DAP remained rocky due to their ideological differences, the respective leaderships managed to contain differences in order to keep the coalition intact for the 2013 general election.

Paradoxically, PAS's recent electoral successes have come on the back of increased non-Muslim support for the party. This marks a crossroads for the Islamic opposition party which has had to grapple with internal discord between a pro-coalition faction harbouring transformative aspirations and conservatives who were wary of compromising PAS's core Islamic agenda for reasons of political expediency. The consequences of this discord were profoundly demonstrated at the 2013 election, where PAS struggled to win in Malay-Muslim majority seats on its way to securing twenty-one parliamentary seats, the lowest in the ***Pakatan Rakyat*** coalition. At the same time, conservatives in the party remain sceptical of the choice of Anwar Ibrahim as the favoured candidate for prime minister should the opposition coalition come to power.

see also: Alliance Party; *Angkatan Perpaduan Ummah*; Anwar Ibrahim; Badawi, Tun Abdullah Ahmad; *Barisan Alternatif*; *Barisan Nasional*; Islam; Mahathir Mohamad, Tun; *Pakatan Rakyat*; Perak Legislature Takeover 2009; UMNO.

Parti Keadilan Rakyat (Malaysia)

Parti Keadilan Rakyat (PKR), or the People's Justice Party, has its origins in the civil society reform movement precipitated by the **Asian Financial Crisis of 1997–8** in Malaysia. At the time, policy differences between the prime minister, **Mahathir Mohamad**, and his deputy, **Anwar Ibrahim**, led to the latter's dismissal from office. Anwar's dismissal, incarceration (during which time he sustained his infamous 'black eye' after being hit by the inspector-general of police), trial and subsequent conviction for corruption was met by a groundswell of popular discontent. In the wake of this political ferment, Anwar's wife, Wan Azizah Ismail, formed *Adil* (the Movement for Social Justice), an umbrella civil society organization that brought together activists from different class, ethnic and religious backgrounds. In April 1999, *Adil* morphed into a political party, *Parti Keadilan Nasional* (also known as *Keadilan*) or the National Justice Party, and in 2003, it merged with *Parti Rakyat Malaysia*, the Malaysian People's Party, to form PKR.

Since its early years as a civil society organization, PKR has sought to position itself at the centre of Malaysia's political spectrum. While its membership consisted of a large number of **UMNO** defectors who owed their allegiance to Anwar, it also drew support from non-Malays and non-Muslims, making it a rarity in Malaysian politics: a multi-ethnic party, albeit one that retains a strong Malay flavour as evidenced in the composition of its current leadership.

With its strength in urban constituencies across the Malaysian peninsula, PKR has since the 2004 general election worked in a political alliance with the ***Parti Islam Se-Malaysia***, which was carried over from the 1999 election when its precursor, *Keadilan*, was a member of the opposition ***Barisan Alternatif***. Nevertheless, in 2004 it could not build on the electoral success of 1999, when *Keadilan* won a commendable five seats in its maiden election contest. In fact, the party managed only a solitary seat in 2004, when Wan Azizah barely scraped through in Anwar's old constituency. Unsurprisingly, the poor performance led to predictions of its demise. In hindsight, those predictions proved premature. The party received a huge boost when Anwar was released from imprisonment in September 2004, and immediately positioned himself as the unofficial leader of the opposition, even though he did not officially join PKR until 2006 as the party's advisor, a position he retains until today. In 2008, PKR contributed thirty-one seats to the opposition's electoral windfall which denied the ruling coalition a two-thirds parliamentary majority. In 2013, the party managed to win thirty seats as part of the ***Pakatan Rakyat*** opposition coalition.

Despite its strong record in recent polls, PKR has also had its fair share of internal disputes. Notably, the party has lost a number of prominent members over the years who have either defected to UMNO or chosen to remain independents after leaving the party. The resignation of two of its members from the Perak legislature paved the way for the 2009 takeover of the Perak state government by the ***Barisan Nasional***.

Moreover, notwithstanding its commitment to an agenda of social justice and anti-corruption, since its formation PKR has been seen as a vehicle for Anwar Ibrahim to realize his political ambitions of becoming Malaysian prime minister. Anwar's influence in the party is very palpable: the party continues to be led by his wife, while a staunch ally, Azmin Ali, and his daughter, Nurul Izzah Anwar, occupy the deputy presidency and one of the vice-presidencies respectively. Discontent about Anwar's iron grip over the party has surfaced periodically, particularly in response to his unwavering endorsement of Azmin.

see also: Anwar Ibrahim; Asian Financial Crisis 1997–8; *Barisan Nasional*; *Pakatan Rakyat*; Mahathir Mohamad, Tun; *Parti Islam Se-Malaysia*; Perak Legislature Takeover 2009.

Parti Pesaka Bumiputera Bersatu (Malaysia)

Parti Pesaka Bumiputera Bersatu (PBB) which translates as the United Indigenous People's Inheritance Party, is the dominant political grouping in the north Bornean state of Sarawak in Malaysia. PBB was formed in 1973 as the result of a merger between the Iban-Dayak *Parti Pesaka* headed by their traditional leader, the Temenggong Jugah, and the Malay-Melanau *Parti Bumiputera* under the leadership of the chief minister, **Abdul Rahman Yakub**, and became a member of the newly established ruling federal ***Barisan Nasional*** (National Front) coalition. It has been controlled continuously by its Muslim component, led by current governor of Sarawak and former chief minister, Datuk Patinggi **Abdul Taib Mahmud**, which was a factor in Iban alienation leading to the splinter ***Parti Bangsa Dayak Sarawak*** being set up in 1983. PBB has ruled Sarawak in a coalition known as *Barisan Tiga* (Front of Three) with the **Sarawak United People's Party** (SUPP) and the **Sarawak National Party** (SNAP). In the state elections in September 1991, it won twenty-seven seats and its coalition partners twenty-two more, to command an overwhelming majority in the fifty-six seat legislature. It retained its dominant position in state elections in September 1996. In federal elections in April 1995, all of its eleven candidates won their seats. That number was reduced to ten in federal elections in November 1999. The party's dominance in Sarawak continued at the turn of the millennium. At the state elections, the party won all thirty seats it contested in 2001, later increasing its share to thirty-five seats in the subsequent 2006 and 2011 elections. In the federal elections, it won eleven seats in 2004, and fourteen seats in 2008 and 2013. Despite persistent allegations of corruption against Taib Mahmud, PBB's well-oiled grassroots machinery is still unmatched in rural Sarawak. PBB enjoys a sizeable representation of seven ministers and deputy ministers in the current Cabinet.

see also: Abdul Rahman Yakub, Tun; *Barisan Nasional*; *Parti Bangsa Dayak Sarawak*; Sarawak National Party; Sarawak United People's Party; Taib Mahmud, Datuk Patinggi Abdul.

Partido Liberal ng Pilipinas (Philippines)

The Liberal Party of the Philippines (*Partido Liberal ng Pilipinas*) was established in 1945 by Senate president, **Manuel Roxas**, Senator Elpidio Quirino and Senator Jose Avelino. At the point of its formation, it was considered a breakaway group from the dominant **Nacionalista Party**. It is the current majority and ruling party in the Philippines following the installation of President **Benigno Aquino III**. This party also enjoys majority control of the House of Representatives. It is considered the second oldest political party in the Philippines, and its membership has included notable politicians including **Benigno Aquino**, father of the current president, and Manuel Roxas, the first president of the Third Philippines Republic. Two other presidents were elected under this party banner as well – Elpidio Quirino and **Diosdado Macapagal**. The Liberal Party was an active critic of President **Ferdinand Marcos**' rule, and its outspokenness made it a target for political persecution. In recent years, the party has been instrumental in pushing controversial political decisions such as the rejection of the renewal of a new treaty on US bases in the country. It also expressed its endorsement of **EDSA II** and was active in support of Aquino's presidential campaign. The Liberal

Party consolidated power at the 2013 mid-term elections by winning 111 out of 234 seats in the House of Representatives. While the party only contested three of the twelve Senate seats that were vacant, it anchored Benigno Aquino III's 'Team PNoy' coalition that won a total of nine seats.

see also: Aquino, Benigno; Aquino III, Benigno Simeon Cojuangco; EDSA II; Macapagal, Diosdado; Marcos, Ferdinand; Nacionalista Party; Roxas, Manuel A.

Patani United Liberation Organization (Thailand)

The Patani United Liberation Organization (PULO) is a militant Muslim separatist group in southern Thailand. PULO was established in 1968 and drew support from a generation of frustrated young ethnic Malays living in Thailand's southern border provinces (*see* **Islam**), especially a small but significant number who had been educated abroad. It was founded in India by Kabir Abdul Rahman, who had studied at Aligarh Muslim University and who called himself Tengku Bira Kotanila when he went to Mecca to establish a base for overseas recruitment. PULO became an active insurgency with the politicization of Thai students in the early 1970s and mounted a number of military actions during the decade. In the repressive climate after the restoration of military rule in October 1976, Malay-Muslim students and intellectuals were attracted to the idea of autonomy and even independence for the southern provinces of Thailand. Organized attacks on government establishments in the south of the country as well as sporadic bombings in Bangkok continued after young activists had undergone military training in Libya and Syria in camps of the Palestine Liberation Organization. PULO membership reached its height in the 1980s, when it claimed to have several thousand fighters. While it claimed responsibility for sporadic attacks in the 1990s, including the bombing of a railway station in the southern town of Hatyai in 1992, a string of arson attacks on schools in the south in 1993 and the bombing of a bridge between Hatyai and Chana railway stations in 1994, the government's amnesty policy significantly eroded its support base during this period. The emergence of opportunities for Muslim political representation in the form of the *Santiparb* (Peace) Party and the Wadah faction of the ***Thai Rak Thai*** **Party** further undermined the appeal of PULO. In the event, PULO leaders retreated to live in exile in Malaysia, Indonesia and Europe. The organization also split in 1995 with the formation of New PULO.

International support for PULO has taken the form of Syrian and Libyan pleas before the United Nations as well as informal representation before the Organization of the Islamic Conference. Although a measure of support has come from coreligionists in the Malaysian state of Kelantan, especially from the Malay opposition ***Parti Islam Se-Malaysia*** (PAS), Muslim partners of Thailand within **ASEAN** (Association of Southeast Asian Nations) have never provided encouragement for its separatist goal. Attempts to win support from the Organization of Islamic Conference (OIC) initially faltered when Thailand was granted observer status in 1997, although OIC sympathy for PULO's cause increased after the resurgence of political violence in 2004. In April 1998, three alleged leaders of a new faction of PULO were extradited to Bangkok after having been arrested in Malaysia. In March 2000, Indonesian sources alleged that arms for rebels in **Aceh** were being shipped across the Malacca Strait by members of PULO.

With the resumption of political violence at the turn of the century, PULO has attempted to reassert its presence as commissars of the insurgency. An attempt to reunite the various factions of PULO towards that end in 2006 proved shortlived however, as leaders with different interests continued to clash. While much of the violence is believed to be perpetrated by a new generation of fighters purportedly under the loose leadership of the ***Barisan Revolusi Nasional-Coordinate***, PULO continues to claim to represent the interests of the insurgents at various peace talks.

see also: Aceh; ASEAN; *Barisan Revolusi Nasional-Coordinate*; Islam; *Parti Islam Se-Malaysia*; *Thai Rak Thai* Party.

Pathet Lao (Laos)

Pathet Lao, which translates as Lao Nation or State, is the name ascribed to the Laotian revolutionary movement aligned with the Communist-led **Viet Minh** during the first phase of the **Indochina Wars**. Its origins may be traced to the association established with Vietnam's Communists from October 1945 by the radical Lao nationalist Prince **Souphanouvong**. With Viet Minh military support, he organized resistance to the restoration of French colonial rule with conservative nationalists, including his half-brother Prince **Souvanna Phouma**. Driven into exile in Thailand, Prince Souphanouvong returned to Vietnam in November 1949 after an accommodation had been reached between the main body of Lao nationalists and the French. In August 1950, under Viet Minh patronage, he convened a so-called resistance congress close to the Vietnamese border. That congress set up a National Resistance government which adopted a twelve-point manifesto, at the bottom of which were the words *Pathet Lao*.

Pathet Lao soon became the generally accepted term for describing the Laotian revolutionary movement. The National Resistance government, however, was denied representation at the conference that led to the **Geneva Agreements on Indochina** in 1954. The ceasefire agreement for Laos concluded in July was signed between only French and Vietnamese military representatives, but the latter signed on behalf of the fighting units of *Pathet Lao*. Post-Geneva, the Laotian revolutionaries set up the ***Neo Lao Hak Sat*** (Lao Patriotic Front) which served as a front for the guiding **Lao People's Revolutionary Party** believed to have been established in 1951. Nonetheless, the term *Pathet Lao* remained in common usage to describe the revolutionary movement which assumed total power in December 1975.

see also: Geneva Agreements on Indochina 1954; Geneva Agreements on Laos 1962; Indochina Wars; Lao People's Revolutionary Party; *Neo Lao Hak Sat*; Souphanouvong, Prince; Souvanna Phouma, Prince; Viet Minh.

Paukphaw Relationship (Burma/Myanmar)

The *Paukphaw* relationship refers to a special association between Myanmar and the People's Republic of China begun in the 1950s. China is the only country for which this Burmese term, which translates as 'sibling,' is used. Chinese leaders, including Chou En-lai, cemented the relationship through a series of high-level visits. Since its inception the *Paukphaw* relationship has often followed a dual track allowing both countries to pursue state-to-state relations separate from party-to-party relations, a state of affairs that allowed China and Myanmar to maintain official relations while the Chinese Communist Party provided support for the Burmese Communist Party (BCP) in its struggle against Yangon. Throughout this period China provided various types of economic assistance, although until the 1990s trade with China was limited and the border trade was confined to a few crossings. Myanmar, as the younger brother in the relationship, was primarily concerned with regime preservation, and has skilfully played its China card in a way that allows it considerable space in international forums, while constantly repositioning itself towards China in an attempt to accommodate China's regional interests though resisting Chinese influence and interference in Myanmar's internal affairs.

Since the collapse of the BCP in 1989, relations between China and Myanmar have become closer. Chinese investments and trade have increased considerably, and Beijing has acted to block criticism and proposed Western sanctions in international forums, especially the United Nations Security Council. However, China still maintains relations with several armed ethnic insurgent groups on the Myanmar–China border, particularly the United Wa State Army (UWSA), the largest such organization in Myanmar. In recent years however, this relationship has cooled somewhat due to Myanmar's concern about China's growing influence. This became apparent in 2011 when the government suspended a large dam project financed and under construction by a Chinese state-owned company. The move was officially in response to public discontent with the project, but behind the scenes disquiet among the ranks of the military over what some perceived as too close a relationship to Beijing was also in play. The move also revealed a growing anti-Chinese sentiment among the Myanmar population.

Pedra Branca (Malaysia/Singapore) *see* **Horsburgh Lighthouse**.

Pembela (Malaysia)

The Organizations for the Defence of Islam (*Pertubuhan-Pertubuhan Pembela Islam*), known by the acronym *Pembela*, is a collection of more than seventy Muslim non-governmental organizations established in 2006 following controversial court cases which involved the conversion of Muslims to other religions. During the height of the **Lina Joy Issue**, *Pembela* was at the forefront of opposition to groups such as the **Article 11 Coalition** which were supporting Joy's freedom to renounce Islam. In that regard, *Pembela* represents the conservative Malay voices in Malaysia who fear the dilution of Islamic identity in the country, especially through Muslims leaving Islam through legal channels. Since its formation, *Pembela* has been a regular and vocal participant on the Malaysian civil society landscape. They are also non-partisan, in that they have criticized members of both the ruling ***Barisan Nasional*** (National Front) as well as the ***Pakatan Rakyat*** (People's Alliance) for taking liberal positions on conversion away from Islam.

see also: Article 11 Coalition; *Barisan Nasional*; Lina Joy Issue; *Pakatan Rakyat*.

***Pemerintah Revolusioner Republik Indonesia* (PRRI)** (Indonesia) *see* **Revolutionary Government of the Republic of Indonesia 1958–61**.

People Power (Philippines)

'People Power' is the term employed to describe the huge non-violent popular demonstration that took place from 22 February 1986 for four days in Epifanio de los Santos Avenue (EDSA) in Manila, close to the military camps Aguinaldo and Crame. That sustained demonstration in the wake of conspicuously fraudulent elections played a decisive part in persuading President **Ferdinand Marcos** to leave for exile in the United States and in bringing **Corazón Aquino** to office. The demonstration was precipitated by a revolt against President Marcos led by the minister of defence, **Juan Ponce Enrile**, and the deputy chief of staff of the armed forces, **Fidel Ramos**. With only some 200 supporters initially, they barricaded themselves into Camp Crame in anticipation of an armed attack. At that juncture, the Archbishop of Manila, Cardinal **Jaime Sin**, broadcast a call for people to pray and keep vigil outside the camp. The popular response was dramatic. A huge crowd established a human wall which interposed between the rebels and troops dispatched to crush them by the chief of staff of the armed forces, **Fabian Ver**. The security forces were reluctant to use force, while President Marcos prevaricated over giving an order to fire because he understood that in the event of bloodshed he would not be able to find refuge in the United States. The more he prevaricated, the more the armed forces began to side with the rebels' demand that Aquino be regarded as the rightful winner of the presidential elections. In the event, Marcos accepted the advice of Senator Paul Laxalt, speaking for President Ronald Reagan, that he 'should cut and cut cleanly', which he did in the evening of 25 February. Without the interposing display of People Power, the revolt against Marcos might well have been expeditiously crushed and the course of Philippine history would have been different.

see also: Aquino, Corazón; EDSA; Enrile, Juan Ponce; Marcos, Ferdinand; Ramos, Fidel; Sin, Cardinal Jaime; Ver, General Fabian.

People's Action Party (Singapore)

The ruling People's Action Party (PAP) has been continuously in power since the elections in May 1959 that immediately preceded Singapore's acquisition of self-governing status. The party was founded in November 1954 by English-educated professionals who sought the support of the island's Chinese-educated majority through aligning with radical trade unionists linked to the illegal Communist Party of Malaya. Their platform called for a democratic socialist non-Communist united Malaya, to include Singapore. When in 1961 a merger between peninsular Malaya and Singapore (together with British territories in northern Borneo) was sanctioned, tension arose between moderate and radical wings of the party leading to the defection of the latter, who formed the ***Barisan Sosialis*** (Socialist Front). The rump of the PAP governed with support in Parliament from right-wing parties. Merger into the Federation of Malaysia took place in September 1963 and in its immediate wake the PAP re-established an electoral majority in its own right.

In May 1964 the PAP made a provocative and unsuccessful electoral foray into peninsular Malaysian elections, which generated racial tensions. The outcome was Singapore's expulsion from Malaysia in August 1965, which had the effect of reinforcing popular support for the party. From elections in April 1968 until a by-election in October 1981, the PAP held every seat in the Legislative Assembly. In general elections in December 1984, two opposition candidates were successful, with the remaining seventy-seven seats going to the PAP. The opposition complement increased to four seats in the following elections in August 1991, including three won by the Singapore Democratic Party, in an enlarged legislature of eighty-one, with the PAP holding seventy-seven seats. By then, the reins of leadership had been passed from **Lee Kuan Yew**, who had served as prime minister for thirty-one consecutive years, to **Goh Chok Tong**. In elections in January 1997, the PAP won eighty-one seats in a legislature enlarged to eighty-three seats and raised its vote from sixty-one per cent to sixty-five per cent. This improved to 75.3 per cent in 2001, when the party won eighty-two out of eighty-four seats, including fifty-five uncontested seats. The magnitude of victory in 2001 was all the more remarkable given that Singapore was at the time in the throes of a major economic recession.

In August 2004, the PAP went through another leadership transition when **Lee Hsien Loong**, elder son of Lee Kuan Yew, succeeded Goh Chok Tong. The younger Lee sought to tone down the interventionist nature of the PAP-run state and also embarked on electoral reforms such as the reduction of the number of group representation constituencies. He also oversaw the increase in the number of non-constituency members of parliament (NCMPs), positions granted to losing opposition candidates who garnered the highest percentage of votes, and nominated members of parliament (NMPs), comprising prominent public figures who are not elected and do not have any party affiliation, to nine. In 2006, the PAP obtained 66.6 per cent of the vote, while continuing to hold eighty-two out of eighty-four parliamentary seats. The party is avowedly elitist, drawing parliamentary candidates from the ranks of successful bureaucrats, military officers and business people. Because of the longstanding absence of credible opposition, the PAP and the government of Singapore have become virtually indistinguishable. An initial commitment to democratic socialism has given way to an authoritarian pragmatism, justified with reference to outstanding economic achievement, which has been internationally acknowledged. This abiding nature of the party came under considerable strain at the 2011 general election, however, when the PAP saw its share of the popular vote drop markedly in 2011, dipping to 60.4 per cent. Even more significant was the party's loss of the **Aljunied Group Representation Constituency** to the **Workers' Party**, the first time that the PAP had lost a GRC. The erosion of support for the PAP was foremost due to growing resentment towards an economic policy that encouraged the influx of migrant labour, a liberal approach to granting of permanent residency and an alarming increase in the cost of living. Equally significant was the opposition's ability to recruit accomplished candidates of high calibre, something that had eluded them in previous elections. The PAP has lost both by-elections that have been conducted in the island-state since the 2011 general election.

see also: Aljunied Group Representation Constituency; *Barisan Sosialis*; Goh Chok Tong; Lee Hsien Loong; Lee Kuan Yew; Workers' Party.

People's Alliance for Democracy (Thailand)

The People's Alliance for Democracy (PAD), also known as the 'Yellow Shirts', was originally a coalition of protestors urging the removal of Prime Minister **Thaksin Shinawatra**. It later demonstrated for the ousting of the Thaksin-aligned **People's Power Party** (PPP)-led government. The movement also later played a prominent role in the border dispute between Thailand and Cambodia over the **Preah Vihear** temple.

The PAD arose out of the weekly public political talk shows of **Sondhi Limthongkul** which gradually turned into protest rallies against Thaksin. The PAD was eventually established on 8 February 2006 following the sale of Thaksin's family's shares in Shin Corp to Temasek Holdings of Singapore. It organized mass rallies against the Thaksin government, and dissolved itself two days after the military coup of 19 September 2006. The PAD was reconstituted on 28 March 2008 after the Thaksin-affiliated PPP won a majority in the December 2007 general election. Large street demonstrations began in May 2008 to pressure the government of **Samak Sundaravej** to resign, accusing the PPP of being a proxy party for Thaksin and his dissolved ***Thai Rak Thai* Party**. PAD protests escalated after Samak was disqualified for violating a law prohibiting government ministers from receiving salaries for other jobs. Violence during this period between PAD supporters, anti-PAD protesters and police left dozens injured and one PAD protestor dead. In August 2008, the PAD seized the grounds of Government House. It went on in November 2008 to seize Don Muang and Suvarnabhumi international airports in Bangkok as well as airports in Phuket, Krabi and Hat Yai. The PAD called off its protests on 3 December 2008 and relinquished control of the airports after the Constitutional Court dissolved the PPP and banned its leaders from politics. The PAD had stated during the height of the protests that the only prime minister they would accept was **Abhisit Vejjajiva** of the Democrat Party. PAD members would make recurring appearances in opposition to protests by the **United Front for Democracy Against Dictatorship** (UDD) during 2009, often resulting in violence. In April 2009, PAD leader Sondhi Limthongkul was wounded in an assassination attempt in Bangkok. Following their protest victory, PAD leaders claimed popular democracy had failed in Thailand and called for constitutional amendments that would make Parliament a largely royally appointed body. They have also suggested that the military and the traditional elite should have a greater role in politics. The issue had originally been used in 2008 as a *cause célèbre* by the PAD to attack the Samak government after it agreed to allow the Preah Vihear temple to be listed as a World Heritage Site. The PAD again came out in much smaller numbers in 2011 to protest the perceived soft stance of the Abhisit government over the ownership of Preah Vihear and several other temples along the Thai–Cambodian border. The PAD went so far as to call for Abhisit's resignation, using the issue to further its attempt to amend the constitution.

Prominent leaders of the PAD included media mogul Sondhi and former major general and Bangkok governor, **Chamlong Srimuang**. The PAD draws its core membership from upper and middle class Bangkokians with strong royalist feelings, as well as southerners. The group regularly invoked King **Bhumibol Adulyadej** in its protests, chose yellow as it is the king's colour and regularly denounced opponents as being disloyal to the monarchy. The PAD initially received support from factions within the military, and several Democrat Party leaders. PAD members also joined in the latest round of protests against the government of Yingluck Shinawatra that began in October 2013.

see also: Abhisit Vejjajiva; Bhumibol Adulyadej, King; Chamlong Srimuang, General; People's Power Party; Preah Vihear Temple Dispute; Samak Sundaravej; Sondhi Limthongkul; Thaksin Shinawatra; United Front for Democracy Against Dictatorship; Yingluck Shinawatra.

People's Constitution 1997 (Thailand)

Thailand's 1997 Constitution, popularly called the People's Constitution, was the first to be drafted by a popularly elected Constitutional Drafting Assembly. As such it was widely acclaimed as a landmark in Thai democratic reform. The constitution replaced the 1991 constitution put in place by a military junta following a coup that year. The timing of the constitution was also appropriate as it occurred at the height of the 1997 **Asian Financial Crisis** which prompted calls for reform. Among its more significant items, the People's Constitution provided for a bicameral legislature whose members would be directly elected. The document also contained provisions that addressed human rights concerns as well as measures designed to enhance the stability of elected governments. At the same time, the constitution also provoked strong criticism in reaction to clauses covering the creation of a constitutional court, the decentralization of government functions and requirements for members of parliament to possess higher education qualifications. While the People's Constitution was widely praised for how it went further than previous charters in granting greater power to ordinary citizens, it also facilitated the ascent of populist politicians and parties such as **Thaksin Shinawatra** and ***Thai Rak Thai* Party**. The 1997 constitution was abrogated by the military junta that took over the country after the September 2006 coup and later replaced by a new constitution.

see also: Asian Financial Crisis 1997–8; *Thai Rak Thai* Party; Thaksin Shinawatra.

People's Consultative Assembly (Indonesia)

The People's Consultative Assembly or MPR (*Majelis Permusyawaratan Rakyat*) was created to be the supreme constitutional authority to which the president of Indonesia is, in principle, accountable and to whom he or she reports. Provision for the MPR was made in the original independence constitution promulgated on 18 August 1945. That constitution lapsed with the attainment of independence in December 1949 but was reinstated by President **Sukarno** in July 1959 when he inaugurated the political system of **Guided Democracy**. That constitution was retained by President **Suharto**, who restored the People's Constitutional Assembly, which enjoyed only provisional status, on a partly elected and nominated basis in March 1973. During the **New Order** it comprised between 900 and 1,000 members, more than half of whom were nominated, with the rest drawn from a parliament elected every five years. That figure has been reduced to around 700 since the end of the New Order era. During Suharto's tenure, the MPR served as a rubber-stamping electoral college returning him to highest executive office recurrently until March 1998. With his resignation in May 1998, the MPR assumed a more active political role, especially after parliamentary elections in June 1999, which paved the way for radically new membership. In October 1999, faced with competition for highest office, it elected **Abdurrahman Wahid** as president. During the 2002 sitting of the MPR, additional constitutional amendments were introduced, including the establishment of a constitutional court and a direct presidential and vice-presidential election system. Once the supreme constitutional body, since 2003 the MPR's role in the Indonesian political system has been reduced considerably. Much of its previous remit has now been taken over by the House of Representatives (*Dewan Perwakilan Rakyat* or DPR), and it now enjoys authority only to amend the state constitution and swear in the president and vice-president. The current MPR speaker, Sidarto Danusubroto from the ***Partai Demokrasi Indonesia–Perjuangan***, is the thirteenth leader of the Assembly.

see also: Guided Democracy; New Order; *Partai Demokrasi Indonesia–Perjuangan*; Suharto; Sukarno; Wahid, Abdurrahman.

People's Party (Brunei)

The People's Party of Brunei (*Partai Rakyat Brunei*) was a radical Malay organization which mounted the abortive Brunei Revolt in the sultanate in December 1962. It was founded on 22 January 1956, initially as a branch of the left-wing People's Party of Malaya, but was not permitted to register until 15 August after expunging its foreign affiliation. Led by **A. M. Azahari**, the People's Party campaigned for independence within a unitary state of North Borneo under the constitutional auspices of the sultan, Sir Omar Ali Saifuddin. It opposed the agreement reached in September 1959 whereby the British protecting power granted the sultanate self-government and also the proposal in 1961 to incorporate Brunei within a Federation of Malaysia. The People's Party won all sixteen elective seats to the Legislative Council of thirty-three members in August 1962 and put down a motion opposing Malaysia for the meeting arranged for 5 December. It had planned to mount a revolt soon after, for which training had been under way for a year with Indonesian support. The sultan postponed the meeting of the **Legislative Council** but the revolt went ahead on 8 December, while Azahari was soliciting support in the Philippines. British troops from Singapore crushed the revolt at the request of the sultan, who banned the party on 10 December. It has remained proscribed within Brunei. In July 1973, however, a number of its leaders escaped from detention with Malaysian complicity. They reconstituted the People's Party in exile in May 1974, setting up an office in neighbouring Limbang in the Malaysian state of Sarawak (*see* **Limbang Claim**). After reconciliation between Brunei and Malaysia concurrent with the sultanate's independence and membership of **ASEAN** (Association of South-East Asian Nations) in January 1984, the external activities of the party effectively ceased.

see also: ASEAN; Azahari, A. M.; Brunei Revolt 1962; Confrontation; Legislative Council; Limbang Claim.

People's Power Party (Thailand)

The People's Power Party (PPP) was formed in 1998 but came into prominence following the September 2006 coup which ousted Prime Minister **Thaksin Shinawatra**. Comprising supporters of the former prime minister and members of the ***Thai Rak Thai* Party** that was dissolved following the coup, the PPP contested the 2007 elections, the first after the coup, on a populist platform. It managed to gain 233 out of 480 seats on its own, and with the contributions of five closely allied parties, who collectively won eighty-two seats, managed to form the government. Party leader and Thaksin ally **Samak Sundaravej** was appointed prime minister in December 2007 but was forced to resign in September the following year when, amidst mounting pressure from the **People's Alliance for Democracy**, he was disqualified by the Constitutional Court for receiving payment for his televised cooking shows. Besieged by growing street protests, Samak was replaced by **Somchai Wongsawat**, brother-in-law of Thaksin Shinawatra. In December 2008, the PPP was dissolved by the Constitutional Court along with allies, Matchima Party and ***Chart Thai* Party**, for electoral fraud. Somchai and other senior politicians from the party were sent into political exile and barred from politics for five years. After the party was dissolved, its members moved on to form the ***Pheu Thai* Party**.

see also: People's Alliance for Democracy; *Pheu Thai* Party; Samak Sundaravej; Somchai Wongsawat; *Thai Rak Thai* Party; Thaksin Shinawatra.

Perak Legislature Takeover 2009 (Malaysia)

The Perak state legislature takeover in 2009 was a controversial takeover of the opposition-controlled fifty-nine seat Perak legislature by the ruling ***Barisan Nasional*** (National Front, BN) coalition after the 2008 general election, which saw the state fall into opposition hands by a margin of three seats.

In February 2009 three ***Pakatan Rakyat*** members of the Perak state assembly resigned from their political parties, leaving both coalitions with twenty-eight seats each. While the three retained their seats as independents, they also declared their intention to align their votes with the BN. This effectively shifted the centre of gravity to the BN, which now claimed a *de facto* majority in the assembly. A request made by the sitting chief minister, Mohammad Nizar Jamaluddin, to dissolve the state parliament and call fresh elections was refused by the Perak sultan, Azlan Shah. Instead, the sultan handed the reins of the legislature to the BN and appointed Zambry Abdul Kadir as chief minister. On 7 May, the BN reconvened the state legislature amidst protests and arrests of several opposition state assemblymen. However, a few days later, on 11 May, the High Court in Kuala Lumpur ruled that Nizar's removal from his post was unconstitutional. According to the ruling, the sultan did not have the authority to dismiss the chief minister, and the removal of the latter from his position is legal only if he receives a vote of no-confidence by the legislature or

resigns. Upon appeal to the Court of Appeal, the BN managed to get the High Court's decision reviewed. In a unanimous decision on 9 February 2010, the constitutional crisis ended when the Federal Court, the apex judicial body in Malaysia, ruled that BN's Zambry Kadir was the lawful chief minister. It further ruled that a vote of no-confidence was not the only way of deciding if a chief minister still commanded the confidence of the legislature, thereby implicitly accepting the change of state government through defections.
see also: Barisan Nasional; Pakatan Rakyat.

Permesta (Indonesia)

Permesta is an acronym drawn from the Indonesian term *Piagam Perjuangan Semesta Alam,* meaning Universal Struggle Charter. The term was applied to the north Sulawesi (Celebes) dimension of abortive regional rebellions, which began formally in February 1958 and had fizzled out by the end of 1961. *Permesta* was the name adopted by a regionalist army council which seized power from civilian governors in eastern Indonesia in March 1957 in order to thwart attempts by the central government to prevent smuggling of copra and rubber. Corresponding army councils had been established in Sumatra from December 1956. When a **Revolutionary Government of the Republic of Indonesia** was proclaimed in west Sumatra in February 1958, open support was proffered from *Permesta.* The rebellion in Sulawesi, as well as the more significant one in Sumatra, originated in dissatisfaction with the central government in Jakarta over the maldistribution of political power and of economic returns from regional exports of raw materials, as well as in a resentment of its tolerance of the Communist Party of Indonesia. The rebellions were not secessionist but an attempt to remould the government of the republic by reducing the rising radical influence of President **Sukarno**. The seizure of power by army councils enabled Sukarno to declare martial law; the failure of the uprisings paved the way for him to introduce his political system of **Guided Democracy** in July 1959.
see also: Guided Democracy; Revolutionary Government of the Republic of Indonesia 1958–61; Sukarno.

Peta (Indonesia)

Peta is an Indonesian acronym drawn from *Pembela Tanah Air,* which translates as Defenders of the Fatherland. It was the term employed to describe the volunteer force of young Indonesians recruited by the Japanese in Java during the occupation of the Netherlands East Indies in order to supplement their military strength. Its inauguration was announced on 3 October 1943 by Lieutenant General Harada Kumakichi and attracted Indonesian nationalists who were provided with military training. A revolt by *Peta* forces against the Japanese in the east Javanese town of Blitar in February 1945 served as a prelude to national revolution. *Peta* was dissolved by the Japanese shortly after their surrender but it provided the nucleus of the army created after the proclamation of independence on 17 August 1945. Japanese training was limited but important in its emphasis on the role of *semangat* (spirit), which inspired the revolutionary army and which has become an integral part of Indonesian military tradition.

Pham Van Dong (Vietnam)

Pham Van Dong served continuously as prime minister of the Democratic Republic of Vietnam from 1955 and then of the reunited Socialist Republic of Vietnam until he retired from office in 1987. He was born on 18 March 1906 in Quang Nai Province into a mandarin family who served the court of Emperor Duy Tan. He was educated at the National Academy in Hue and then at the law faculty in Hanoi, where he came to prominence for organizing a strike in commemoration of the death of a nationalist leader. As a member of the Revolutionary Youth League, he fled to China where he joined in a close collaboration with **Ho Chi Minh**, who placed great trust in him. He was sent back to Vietnam in 1926 to organize Communist cells and was eventually arrested and imprisoned until 1936 when, after an amnesty, he returned to southern China to work again in partnership with Ho Chi Minh. Pham Van Dong demonstrated great talent as an administrator and also as a negotiator. He acted as finance minister from 1946 during the course of the first phase of the **Indochina Wars**. In 1954, as foreign minister, he headed the Vietnamese Communist delegation to the conference that resulted in **the Geneva Agreements on Indochina** and became prime minister in 1955. He was reputed to be a skilled conciliator between party factions and sought also to ensure that Vietnam did not align too closely with either China or the Soviet Union. After Ho Chi Minh's death in 1969, and more so after unification in 1975, his influence waned as **Le Duan** came to dominate party councils. Pham Van Dong announced his retirement from all governmental and party offices in December 1986 on grounds of advanced age and ill-health, giving up his posts in June 1987 to be succeeded by Pham Hung. He died in Hanoi on 29 April 2000.

see also: Geneva Agreements on Indochina 1954; Ho Chi Minh; Indochina Wars; Le Duan.

Phan Van Khai (Vietnam)

Phan Van Khai was elected Vietnam's prime minister in September 1997 and remained in office until 2006. A southerner, he was born in 1933 in Ho Chi Minh City. Phan Van Khai was a protégé of his predecessor, **Vo Van Kiet**, moving up the party ranks in Ho Chi Minh City before being appointed to the State Planning Committee in Hanoi. Widely considered to be an economic liberal by Vietnamese standards, he was a deputy prime minister prior to his appointment as prime minister and was charged with the responsibility for handling economic affairs. As prime minister, he was well known for pushing hard for the market reforms that drove Vietnam's economy in the 1990s despite resistance from conservative factions within the party, not least General Secretary **Le Kha Phieu**. Phan Van Khai made a landmark trip to the United States in 2005, the first visit by a sitting Vietnamese prime minister since the end of the **Vietnam War** thirty years earlier. His visit marked the tenth anniversary of normalized diplomatic relations and the fifth anniversary of the US–Vietnam Bilateral Trade Agreement, at the same time facilitating Vietnam's entry into the World Trade Organization and strengthening trade and investment ties with the United States.

As prime minister, Phan Van Khai was leader of the Cabinet and formed part of the troika that made up the Vietnamese top leadership. His term in office coincided with **Tran Duc Luong**'s as president, and Le Kha Phieu and subsequently **Nong Duc Manh** as general secretary of the party. Phan Van Khai, together with Tran Duc Luong, resigned from the Politburo in 2006 during the tenth Congress of the party as part of a strategy of leadership rejuvenation. He was succeeded by his nominee, Deputy Prime Minister **Nguyen Tan Dung**, who like him, is a southerner and dedicated economic reformer.

see also: Le Kha Phieu, General; Nguyen Tan Dung; Nong Duc Manh; Tran Duc Luong; Vietnam War; Vo Van Kiet.

Pheu Thai Party (Thailand)

The *Pheu Thai* Party was formed on 20 September 2008 in anticipation of the dissolution of the **People's Power Party** (PPP) through a constitutional court ruling implicating several of its party members in electoral fraud. It was the second attempt, after the shortlived PPP experiment, to reform the ***Thai Rak Thai* Party** after its leader, Prime Minister **Thaksin Shinawatra**, was ousted in a coup in September 2006 and the party was dissolved by the constitutional court in May 2007. Although party executives were banned from politics for five years, the majority of members of Parliament were unaffected and moved first to the PPP and later the *Pheu Thai* Party in the wake of the former's dissolution on 2 December 2008.

Yongyuth Wichaidit was elected the party's first leader the day after the dissolution of the PPP. The *Pheu Thai* Party lost the endorsement of the PPP's former allies who joined the **Democrat Party** under **Abhisit Vejjajiva** to form a new government, thereby leaving them in opposition. The party called for a national unity government to solve the nation's political problems, but this was rejected by the democrats and their allies. The party remained in opposition throughout the 2009–10 political turmoil. When the party contested its first elections in July it won an absolute majority in Parliament, paving the way for **Yingluck Shinawatra**, sister of Thaksin, to become prime minister. The highly populist formula used by the party in its election bid has since been criticized for allegedly reneging on promises. National reconciliation after years of political strife was a key component of the party's policies, but it has been accused of using the policy as a way to bring Thaksin back into the country under an amnesty. The party's credibility was further damaged by its seeming inability to effectively deal with massive floods that hit central Thailand later in the year. The party is closely aligned with the **United Front for Democracy against Dictatorship** (UDD) and several cadre are members of both. Although the party has been criticized for its shortcomings it remains widely popular, partly through its connection to the UDD. Under pressure from opposition rallies since October 2013, Prime Minister Yingluck was forced to dissolve Parliament and call fresh elections on 2 February 2014, which the *Pheu Thai* Party was believed to have won. In the event, the results were nullified by the Constitutional Court, which ruled that they had to be voided because voting failed to take place in all constituencies, and only forty-seven per cent of forty-three million voters cast their votes. The same court later found Prime Minister Yingluck guilty of abuse of power and forced her resignation on 7 May. The entire elected *Pheu Thai* government was removed on 22 May, when the military launched a coup against it.

see also: Abhisit Vejjajiva; Democrat Party; People's Power Party; Thaksin Shinawatra; United Front for Democracy against Dictatorship; Yingluck Shinawatra.

Phibul Songkram, Field Marshal (Thailand)

As a junior officer, Phibul Songkram was a leading military figure in the coup that overthrew Thailand's absolute monarchy in June 1932. He became virtual military dictator during the Pacific War, and again for a decade from 1948, until he was himself removed by a military coup. Phibul Songkram was born in 1897 of Sino-Thai origins and became a professional soldier after graduating from the Chulachomklao Royal Military Academy in Bangkok in 1915. He studied at the French artillery school in Fontainebleau during 1920–7; he became involved in a Thai political circle alienated by the privilege of the monarchy. After the successful coup in 1932, he held a series of command and cabinet positions. Phibul was responsible for stimulating Thai nationalism, in part at the expense of the resident Chinese community. He took Thailand close to an assertive Japan and used its support to secure territorial redress from France in Indochina. Japan invaded Thailand concurrently with its attack on the United States in December 1941. After offering a token resistance, Thailand joined Japan's side under Phibul's direction as supreme commander of the armed forces. He was eased from power in August 1944, however, when it had become apparent that Japan's defeat was only a matter of time. After the Pacific War, he was detained as a war criminal for several months but was then rehabilitated and even restored as army commander. His political fortunes revived considerably because of the Cold War and the United States' interest in an anti-Communist government. Following a military coup against the elected civilian government in November 1947, he became prime minister in April 1948, a post which he held until November 1957, when he was deposed. In 1955 Phibul returned from a tour of the United States and Britain apparently enamoured of democracy, especially the practice of free speech which he had observed in Hyde Park in London. The political turbulence that followed provided the context for his deposition by army commander Sarit Thanarat. Field Marshal Phibul was then exiled to Japan, where he died in 1964.

see also: Sarit Thanarat, Field Marshal.

Phieu, General Le Kha (Vietnam) *see* Le Kha Phieu, General.

Philippines–US Security Treaty 1951 (Philippines)

On 30 August 1951, the governments of the Philippines and the United States concluded a mutual security treaty, which was inspired by the advent of the Korean War and China's involvement and also by the need to pre-empt resistance to the Japanese Peace Treaty. Both parties agreed to act against any armed attack on the other in the Pacific with such action to be taken in accordance with each country's constitutional processes. Although the treaty has never been invoked, its terms of reference were criticized by nationalist opponents on the grounds that it did not provide the same automatic guarantee as the North Atlantic Treaty.

In April 1992, after the United States had given notice of its intention to vacate all of its military bases in the Philippines, foreign minister Raul Manglapus argued that the United States was obliged to come to the defence of the Philippines under the 1951 Treaty in the event of an attack on any of its vessels or possessions in the **South China Sea**. The American ambassador, Frank Wisner, countered by maintaining that his government's security obligations did not extend to islands in the South China Sea, which were disputed territories.

In the wake of the threat of **Terrorism in Southeast Asia** after September 11, the US–Philippine strategic partnership was revitalized with the aim of assisting the Philippines government with its counterterrorism and counter-insurgency efforts in the southern islands. Additionally, in the face of Chinese assertiveness in the South China Sea, the US further strengthened its defence assistance to and security presence in the Philippines. The signal move by US Secretary of State Hillary Clinton to refer to the disputed waters around the Spratly Islands as the West Philippine Sea in November 2011 emboldened Manila to take a stronger stand against China. American misgivings about Chinese assertiveness in the South China Sea were further reinforced by President Barack Obama during meetings with Chinese officials in Washington in July 2013. In November 2011, the sixtieth anniversary of the Security Treaty was celebrated as the foundation of the US–Philippine bilateral relationship. Further bilateral discussions in the wake of Chinese activities in the South China Sea triggered negotiations to strengthen the defence pact. In April 2014, negotiation on the terms of the strengthened pact were completed, which catered for US access to and use of Philippine military facilities at Manila's invitation.

see also: South China Sea; Terrorism in Southeast Asia.

Philippines' Claim to Sabah

(Malaysia/Philippines)

On 22 June 1962 the government of the Philippines, in response to a diplomatic note presented to its ambassador in London on 24 May, pointed out 'there is a dispute between the Sultanate of Sulu and the Philippines government on the one side and Her Majesty's Government on the other side regarding the ownership and sovereignty over North Borneo'. When on 16 September 1963 the British Crown transferred sovereignty over the colony of North Borneo (from then on known as Sabah) to the new Federation of Malaysia with its seat of government in Kuala Lumpur, that dispute became a matter of contention between the Philippines and Malaysia. It has remained unresolved ever since. Direct negotiations have proven fruitless, so far, in completely erasing the claim. At issue, in part, has been the question of succession to territorial domain in Southeast Asia, with the Philippines reluctant to make a unilateral concession. In addition, the claim has become enmeshed in the domestic politics of the republic.

The origins of the dispute are to be found in an agreement of January 1878 between the sultan of Sulu, the putative sovereign in the greater part of North Borneo, and representatives of a British commercial syndicate. The territory in question was either leased or ceded (depending on the translation used) in perpetuity in return for an annual payment of 5,000 Malayan dollars. In 1881 the British North Borneo Company took over the concession and began to administer the territory as well as to assume responsibility for the annual payments to the sultan of Sulu and his heirs. These administrative arrangements were not interrupted by Britain establishing a protectorate over North Borneo in 1888. The territory was occupied by the Japanese during the Pacific War and suffered much damage. In 1946 the British North Borneo Company relinquished all of its responsibilities to the British Crown; the territory became a colony until the transfer of sovereignty to Malaysia in 1963. The prospect of a claim emerged shortly after the independence of the Philippines in 1946, especially when its government successfully negotiated the transfer of the Turtle and Mangsee islands located in the Sulu Sea, which had been subject to British administration. The primary interest at the time was private, in particular on the part of the heirs of the Sulu sultanate, which had been extinguished in sovereign status during the period of US colonial rule. An attempt to pursue a financial settlement in the form of a lump sum was undertaken by a son of a former president without success. However, the coincidental incumbency of President **Diosdado Macapagal** with the proposal to establish Malaysia by Malaya's prime minister, **Tunku Abdul Rahman**, brought matters to a head. Macapagal had been in charge of the Philippines Foreign Affairs Department in 1946, responsible for his country's side in the negotiations which had led to the transfer of the Turtle and Mangsee islands. An effective press campaign inspired by private interests attracted the attention of the president, who was also doubtful about the credentials of the proposed new Federation of Malaysia, which had been represented as a vehicle for serving British interests. The claim, which he was responsible for presenting, has not been formally withdrawn and has continued to cause tension between the Philippines and Malaysia.

A major rupture occurred in 1968 following a state visit to Kuala Lumpur by President **Ferdinand Marcos**, which was construed as an act of reconciliation as well as a recognition of Malaysia's sovereignty. Reports of the **Corregidor Affair**, an alleged massacre of Filipino Muslim recruits being trained for armed infiltration into Sabah, provoked a temporary suspension of diplomatic relations. Relations between the two countries improved visibly with the visit by **Fidel Ramos** to Malaysia in January 1993, which was the first by a president of the Philippines since 1968, other than for an ASEAN occasion. Prime Minister **Mahathir Mohamad** paid a reciprocal visit in February 1994.

In February 2001, the Philippines filed for Application to Gain Access to the Pleadings at the International Court of Justice hearing on the **Sipadan–Ligitan** islands dispute between Malaysia and Indonesia with an eye to safeguarding its historical and legal rights arising from its claim to territorial sovereignty over the territory of North Borneo, and a month later petitioned the Court to intervene in their dispute with Malaysia. However, the Court denied the Philippine application in an October 2001 decision. The Philippines' claim to Sabah has been further complicated by disputes over legitimate leadership of the Sulu sultanate. In September 2005, the 'Royal Sultanate of Sulu Archipelago's Supreme Council' issued warnings to the Malaysian government to ignore claims by Sultan Rodinood Kiram regarding the North Borneo territorial dispute. In June 2006, Mohammad Fuad Kiram was installed as the thirty-fifth Sultan of Sulu and Sabah. In August 2008, President **Gloria Macapagal-Arroyo** issued a Memorandum Circular which stated that there would be no recognition of a foreign state's sovereignty over North Borneo. She later removed the mention of Sabah or North Borneo in the Archipelagic Baselines of the Philippine law in March 2009. Manila's claim over Sabah was further endorsed by the Supreme Court in July 2011. In February 2013, Jamalul Kiram III, a claimant to the throne of the Sulu sultanate dispatched a group of armed supporters from the 'Royal Security Forces of the Sultanate of Sulu and North Borneo' to occupy a village in the East Coast state of Sabah during the **Lahad Datu Crisis**. This prompted a response by the Malaysian security forces which escalated into an armed conflict in March 2013.

see also: Abdul Rahman, Tunku; Corregidor Affair; Lahad Datu Crisis 2013; Macapagal, Diosdado; Macapagal-Arroyo, Gloria; Mahathir Mohamad, Tun; Marcos, Ferdinand; Ramos, Fidel; Sipadan–Ligitan.

Phnom Penh Summit (ASEAN) 2002
(Brunei/Cambodia/Indonesia/Laos/Malaysia/Myanmar/Philippines/Singapore/Thailand/Vietnam)

The eighth meeting of the heads of government of **ASEAN** (Association of Southeast Asian Nations) convened in the Cambodian capital on 4–5 November 2002. It marked the first time that Cambodia hosted and chaired an ASEAN summit since it joined the organization in 1999. The Summit took place amidst tight security in the wake of the terrorist bombings in Bali a month earlier, which brought home the reality of **Terrorism in Southeast Asia**.

One of the key objectives of the Summit was to showcase ASEAN solidarity against terrorism as well as encourage cooperation in counter-terrorism efforts in the region to promote security. To that end, ASEAN members adopted the

Declaration on Terrorism that condemned the terrorist attacks and declared support for the United Nations in dealing with the issue of weapons of mass destruction in Iraq. The Phnom Penh Summit was also notable for the signing of the **Declaration on the Conduct of Parties in the South China Sea** (DOC) by ASEAN member states and China, where they reaffirmed their commitment to resolve their territorial and jurisdictional disputes by peaceful means. While a significant step forward for ASEAN–China relations, the DOC was nevertheless merely a non-binding interim political agreement falling short of the Code of Conduct ASEAN had sought for years. ASEAN and Chinese leaders also signed the Framework Agreement on ASEAN–China Economic Cooperation that set a timeline for the completion of the ASEAN–China Free Trade Area (ACFTA) by 2010 for the original six ASEAN countries and by 2015 for the less-developed ASEAN economies.

see also: ASEAN; Declaration on the Conduct of Parties in the South China Sea (ASEAN) 2002; Terrorism in Southeast Asia.

Phnom Penh Summit (ASEAN) April 2012 (Brunei/Cambodia/Indonesia/Laos/Malaysia/Myanmar/Philippines/Singapore/Thailand/Vietnam)

The twentieth meeting of the heads of government of **ASEAN** (Association of Southeast Asian Nations) convened in the capital of Cambodia on 3–4 April 2012 on the occasion of the organization's forty-fifth anniversary. At the top of the meeting agenda was a review of progress towards the ASEAN Economic Community as well as the Association's collective call for the lifting of sanctions against Myanmar after the successful conduct of elections in 2011. However, deliberations on economic integration were overshadowed by disagreements within ASEAN over the **South China Sea** territorial disputes. Tensions had been high in the buildup to the meeting over competing territorial and maritime claims that in fact led to naval clashes between claimant states even as ASEAN laboured on a Code of Conduct, a binding document that would codify the **Declaration on the Conduct of Parties in the South China Sea** (DOC). Specifically, members differed over whether China should be included in the drafting process of the code from the outset, or whether ASEAN should first formulate a common position on the proposed Code before entering into discussions with China. There were underlying tensions between the hosts on one side, and Vietnam and the Philippines on the other, over the extent to which the South China Sea claims should be allowed to dominate proceedings. This prompted concerns that Phnom Penh had gravitated into the Chinese orbit on the back of close economic and political ties. Despite denials by Cambodia's prime minister, **Hun Sen**, circumspection towards Cambodia was reinforced by the fact that Chinese president Hu Jintao had made a surprise official visit to the Cambodian capital a week prior to the Summit. The scarcely veiled tension over the South China Sea presaged developments at the ASEAN Ministerial Meeting in July in Phnom Penh, when differences between the Cambodian and Philippine foreign ministers culminated in ASEAN's inability to release a joint communiqué for the first time in its forty-five year history.

see also: ASEAN; Declaration on the Conduct of Parties in the South China Sea (ASEAN) 2002; Hun Sen; South China Sea.

Phnom Penh Summit (ASEAN) November 2012 (Brunei/Cambodia/Indonesia/Laos/Malaysia/Myanmar/Philippines/Singapore/Thailand/Vietnam)

The twenty-first meeting of heads of government of ASEAN (Association of Southeast Asian Nations) convened in the capital of Cambodia on 18–20 November 2012. The Summit was significant for the fact that it took place in the wake of a disastrous ASEAN Ministerial Meeting in July, when the organization failed for the first time in its forty-five year history to agree on a joint communiqué because of disagreements between Cambodia on the one hand and Vietnam and the Philippines on the other over how developments in the **South China Sea** should be reflected in the document. Despite attempts by China to divert attention from the South China Sea dispute, the conflicting territorial claims predictably became a central issue during the Summit. A replay of the July 2012 ASEAN Ministerial Meeting was averted at the last minute when Cambodia agreed to leave out mention of the non-internationalization of the South China Sea dispute from its final draft of the closing statement. At issue was Cambodian prime minister **Hun Sen**'s claim at the close of the ASEAN–Japan summit meeting that ASEAN had reached a consensus not to internationalize the South China Sea issue, which was immediately contradicted by the Philippines president, **Benigno Aquino III**. Cambodia had also attempted to include in its first draft of the post-summit Chairman's Statement mention of the non-internationalization of the South China Sea dispute, but this was later removed after objection from the Philippines and Vietnam. Predictably, the South China Sea issue overshadowed other notable developments during the Summit, including the adoption of an ASEAN human rights declaration, the launch of an ASEAN Institute of Peace and Reconciliation, and the initiation of talks towards the formation of a **Regional Comprehensive Economic Partnership**, the largest free trade agreement involving ASEAN and China, Japan, South Korea, India, Australia and New Zealand.

see also: Aquino III, Benigno Simeon Cojuangco; ASEAN; Hun Sen; Regional Comprehensive Economic Partnership; South China Sea.

Pol Pot (Cambodia)

Pol Pot was the notorious leader of the Communist Party of Cambodia, who presided over a reign of terror within the country between April 1975 and December 1978, when a Vietnamese invasion drove out his government. At least one million Cambodians died from execution, hunger and disease under his draconian regime, which was designed to restore the glory of a national past within a Marxist model of society. Pol Pot was a *nom de guerre* made public only in April 1976 when the State of **Democratic Kampuchea** was proclaimed. Pol Pot was born Saloth Sar on 19 May 1928 in a village in northerly Kompong Thom Province, the youngest of seven children in a moderately prosperous farming family. His early education was in Phnom Penh and Kompong Cham. Possibly because of his family's royal connections through concubinage, Saloth Sar was awarded a scholarship to study electrical engineering in France from 1949. He returned to Cambodia in January 1953 after failing to complete his studies. Saloth Sar's time in France was taken up in political study within a Marxist circle heavily influenced by the Stalinist persuasion of the Communist Party of France. This period is believed to have been formative in establishing a personal bond between him and a small group of politicized fellow Khmers and in developing a sense of mission. After initial involvement in anti-monarchist politics in 1953, Saloth Sar joined a Vietnamese-led insurgency in eastern Cambodia in August. He remained in Cambodia after the 1954 **Geneva Agreements on Indochina**, which recognized the country's independence, and from 1955 to 1963 worked as a schoolteacher in Phnom Penh. When the Communist Party of Cambodia was reconstituted in secret in 1960, he became a member of its central committee. When its general secretary disappeared, probably murdered, in 1962, Saloth Sar took his place.

In 1963 Saloth Sar fled the capital in fear of Prince **Norodom Sihanouk**'s police. He found refuge in a Vietnamese Communist sanctuary in the east and then moved north to spend time with tribal minorities. Their style of life without property, money and markets provided example and inspiration for his salvationist creed. Indeed, he and party colleagues recruited guerrilla fighters from among the deprived ranks of the tribal minorities who had a longstanding animus against urban dwellers. Armed struggle against the rule of Prince Sihanouk began in 1968 but assumed major proportions only after the coup in March 1970 which brought **Lon Nol** to power with United States support. The Vietnamese army decimated their Cambodian counterparts, so providing a shield behind which a **Khmer Rouge** fighting force could be protected while in recruitment and training. That force seized power in April 1975 and under the leadership of the pseudonymous Pol Pot emptied the cities and then began a horrific social experiment. He was revealed as prime minister in April 1976, holding that office with an interruption for a short period later that year that was probably the result of an intra-party power struggle.

Pol Pot escaped to the Thai border after Vietnam's invasion in December 1978, holding the position of the military commander of Democratic Kampuchea until his retirement was announced in September 1985. He was then described as director of a Higher Institute for National Defence, which he gave up in June 1989. In effect, he continued to exercise leadership over the Khmer Rouge insurgents from a base close to Trat on the Thai–Cambodian border. A photograph of him with other Khmer Rouge leaders dating from 1986 was discovered in March 1994 following Cambodian government military operations in the west of the country in March 1994. He is believed to have retained ultimate authority over the Khmer Rouge in its acceptance of the political settlement reached at the **International Conference on Cambodia** in Paris in October 1991. His influence is believed to have been decisive also in the subsequent boycott by the Khmer Rouge of the peace process and the elections conducted under United Nations auspices in May 1993 (*see* **UNTAC**). The failure of the Khmer Rouge to make significant military headway against the coalition government in Phnom Penh generated factional divisions within and defections from the Khmer Rouge with Pol Pot opposed to any accommodation. In June 1997, he ordered the murder of senior colleague **Son Sen**, his wife and sixteen members of his family. After fleeing with supporters into the jungle, Pol Pot was seized by **Ta Mok**, another senior figure also targeted for assassination, and put on trial in July 1997, which was observed by Nate Thayer, an American journalist. It was the first time that he had been seen by an independent observer since December 1979. After this show trial, he was sentenced to life imprisonment in the Khmer Rouge base at Anlong Veng close to the Thai border. In an interview with Thayer in October 1997, Pol Pot was quite unrepentant about his murderous record and claimed that although several thousand may have died in Cambodia, his conscience was clear. He died on 15 April 1998, reportedly of a heart attack, although his body was cremated before conclusive evidence of the cause of death could be established. Pol Pot left a bitter legacy, which affected virtually every Cambodian family. Those who met him have testified to his personal charm and qualities of leadership but there have been few more reviled men in the history of the twentieth century.

see also: Democratic Kampuchea; Geneva Agreements on Indochina 1954; International Conference on Cambodia, Paris 1991; Khmer Rouge; Nol, Lon; Sihanouk, King Norodom; Son Sen; Ta Mok; United Nations: Cambodia 1991–3; UNTAC.

Port Klang Free Zone Controversy (Malaysia)

The Port Klang Free Zone (PKFZ) controversy is a multi-billion dollar financial scandal in Malaysia that has implicated key officials in the ruling ***Barisan Nasional*** (National Front) coalition, and in particular the top leadership of the **Malaysian Chinese Association** (MCA). The 400-hectare PKFZ was originally conceived as a US$577 million development project that would create an industrial park with extensive and effective distribution and manufacturing facilities, as well as attractive tax exemptions and other investment initiatives. Initiated during the tenure of **Mahathir Mohamad**, the MCA was informally given the task of overseeing the PKFZ's development.

Since the project's inception, the PKFZ has been dogged by allegations of corruption and conflict of interests, not to mention problems of poor management and corporate governance. Early requests for a probe into these allegations were ignored by the Malaysian Anti-Corruption Commission, but they subsequently relented after glaring details of cost overruns emerged in 2009 following a PricewaterhouseCoopers audit which reported that the project costs had run up to RM4.6 billion from the initial estimate of RM1.845 billion. Following the probe, six people have been charged in court over the PKFZ scandal, including two former MCA ministers and the former head of the port authority. The six have been charged with criminal breach of trust, and are alleged to have issued letters of undertaking and support without the prior approval of the finance ministry, but which the

Cabinet had later authorized and ratified. The cost overruns have therefore been attributed to the implicit government guarantee attached to these massive loans. Both former MCA ministers were later acquitted.

see also: Barisan Nasional; Mahathir Mohamad, Tun; Malaysian Chinese Association.

Prabowo Subianto (Indonesia)

Prabowo Subianto is currently the leader of the nationalist party, ***Gerindra*** (*Gerakan Indonesia Raya*), and a strong contender for the presidency of Indonesia in the election scheduled for July 2014. Prabowo was born on 17 October 1951 in Jakarta. He is the son of Sumitro Djojohadikusumo, a prominent economist who served under President **Suharto**, and grandson of the prominent anti-colonialist, Margono. Prabowo was also once married to Titik Suharto, daughter of the late president.

A businessman with a military background, Prabowo manoeuvred to be a close confidante of the former president, Suharto, towards the end of the latter's thirty-two year rule. He graduated from the military academy in Malengeng in 1974, the same year as **Susilo Bambang Yudhoyono**, and served in both East Timor and **Irian Jaya**. He rose to the rank of lieutenant-general and during the final turbulent years of the Suharto administration commanded Kostrad, the army's Strategic Reserve Command which was first led by Suharto himself in 1961. A clash with then army general Wiranto over the top military position led to Prabowo being discharged from the military in August 1998 on grounds of having kidnapped anti-Suharto activists, and then being sidelined from national affairs. With assistance from his wealthy brother, Prabowo entered the commercial world and gradually built up a business empire with interests in oil, natural gas, oil palm plantations and fisheries. He resurfaced in the 2009 presidential race when he ran as vice-presidential candidate to **Megawati Sukarnoputri**, evidently on the understanding that Megawati would support a future presidential bid, which he publicly announced in 2011. In the event, this arrangement, known as the 'Batu Tulis Pact', was jettisoned by Megawati when she threw her support behind **Joko Widodo**. A fiery orator who campaigns for the presidency on a platform of firm leadership exemplified by his stated desire to take Indonesia back to the authoritarian 1945 Constitution, Prabowo is widely regarded as the second most popular candidate for the 2014 presidency after Joko Widodo. Nevertheless, controversies surround Prabowo's military past that might pose considerable obstacles to his political ambitions. While recognized as an effective military commander, Prabowo has been accused of human rights abuse during his service in East Timor, as well as against democracy activists during the height of popular protest against President Suharto.

see also: *Gerindra*; Irian Jaya; Megawati Sukarnoputri; Suharto; Widodo, Joko; Yudhoyono, Susilo Bambang.

Praphas Charusathien, Field Marshal (Thailand)

Field Marshal Praphas Charusathien was deputy prime minister of Thailand in October 1973 when student protest at the lack of constitutional progress erupted into a violent confrontation with the security forces. The civilian bloodshed prompted the intervention of King **Bhumibol Adulyadej**, which led to Praphas and the prime minister, Field Marshal **Thanom Kittikachorn**, going into exile as an act of contrition. Praphas Charusathien was born on 25 November 1912 in Udorn Province. He began his professional military training in 1933 at the Chulachomklao Royal Military Academy in Bangkok after the end of the absolute monarchy. As an infantry officer, he rose in rank as a protégé of Field Marshal **Sarit Thanarat** and served as minister of the interior under his aegis from 1957 and retained the position beyond Sarit Thanarat's death in 1963. Praphas held that post until 1973, with a brief interruption in 1971–2 when the nomenclature of his office was changed following an incumbency coup. He was also commander-in-chief of the Thai army between 1963 and 1973; his replacement by General Krit Sivara signalled a loss of political power. Praphas overshadowed Thanom and was, in effect, the strong man of Thai politics for a decade, acquiring a sinister reputation for financial manipulation and political intrigue. He was able to return to Thailand from exile in January 1977 after a coup in October 1976 (on the same day as the Thammasat University Massacre) had re-established military-based rule but he ceased to play any part in public life. He died in Bangkok on 18 August 1997.

see also: Bhumibol Adulyadej; Sarit Thanarat, Field Marshal; Thammasat University Massacre 1976; Thanom Kittikachorn, Field Marshal.

Prayuth Chan-ocha, General (Thailand)

General Prayuth Chan-ocha is the commander-in-chief of the Royal Thai Army. He oversaw the crackdown on so-called 'red shirt' demonstrators of the **United Front for Democracy Against Dictatorship** (UDD) in Bangkok's central business district in 2010 and later attempted to improve the military's public profile while still retaining its political influence. He is best known, however, for leading the military coup against the government of the ***Pheu Thai* Party** on 22 May 2014.

Prayuth graduated from the Armed Forces Academies Preparatory School with Class 12 and went on to receive his bachelor's degree from the Chulachomklao Royal Military Academy. His professional schooling included attending the National Defence College and the Command and General Staff College. Moving up through the ranks, he became deputy commander of the Second Infantry Division from 2002 to 2003, becoming its commander until 2005. He was promoted to deputy commanding general of the First Army Area providing security for Bangkok in 2005 and then its commanding general from 2006 to 2008. His Bangkok-based troops were key to the success of the 2006 putsch that ousted the **Thaksin Shinawatra** government. Prayuth was appointed army chief of staff in 2008, and General **Anupong Paochinda** as commander-in-chief of the Royal Thai Army in October 2010 after a year as his deputy. As the Army's deputy commander, Prayuth played a role in the negotiations that formed the Democrat-led coalition government in December 2008 as well as the crackdown on red shirt demonstrators in April 2009. He also played an important role in suppressing UDD-led anti-government protests in April and May 2010. As commander-in-chief he largely kept the army out of direct politics, although he made it clear that the army could play a role should there be further political instability. Prayuth is a member of the Queen's Guard, a faction within the military close to the palace and associated elites. With the election of the *Pheu Thai* Party-led government, he maintained a delicate political relationship with Prime Minister **Yingluck Shinawatra**. Though a staunch loyalist with close ties to the plotters of the 2006 coup, Prayuth attempted reconciliatory overtures towards the UDD while at the same time taking steps to improve the army's reputation, especially through its efficient handling of disaster relief during severe flooding in 2011. Despite pressure from both sides to intervene in the political crisis that began in October 2013 and the declaration of a state of emergency by the caretaker government of Yingluck Shinawatra, Prayuth repeatedly stated that the military would remain on the sidelines. Nevertheless things took an ominous turn predawn on 20 May 2014 when Prayuth announced that the army was declaring martial law in the country to address the worsening security situation. Initial denials that he had in effect launched a coup were dispelled two days later when, flanked by military leaders, he declared a *coup d'état* and assumed the position of prime minister.

see also: Anupong Paochinda, General; *Pheu Thai* Party; Thaksin Shinawatra; United Front for Democracy Against Dictatorship; Yingluck Shinawatra.

Preah Vihear Temple Dispute (Cambodia/Thailand)

A dispute over possession of the ruins of the ancient Khmer temple of Preah Vihear became a matter of tension between Cambodia and Thailand from the former's independence in November 1953, continuing even after legal resolution by the International Court of Justice in June 1962. The temple ruins are located to the north of Cambodia along the border with Thailand, on the edge of the Dang Raek escarpment which overlooks the Cambodian plain. This part of the boundary between Thailand and Cambodia (then a French protectorate) was delimited by a joint Franco-Siamese (Thai) border commission between 1905 and 1907. The commission should have based its delimitation on a boundary convention of February 1904, which stipulated that the line of demarcation follow the watershed of the Dang Raek range: this would have placed the temple in Thai territory. In the event, a French officer on the joint commission produced a map covering the area of the temple that showed its location on the Cambodian side of the boundary, which was not disputed at the time. That map was incorporated in an annexe to a subsequent boundary convention of March 1907.

Access to the ruins is exceedingly difficult from the Cambodian side, by contrast with its relative ease of access from the Thai side. Thailand occupied the temple site from time to time and continuously from 1949, but without objecting to the failure of the French-drawn map to reflect the terms of reference of the 1904 convention. The issue of Thailand's occupation of the temple site was raised after the end of the Pacific War, first by France and then by an independent Cambodia. A conference between the two governments in 1958 failed to resolve the issue, which was taken by Cambodia to the International Court of Justice in The Hague in the following year. The court decided in Cambodia's favour in June 1962, despite the terms of the 1904 convention, on the grounds that Thailand had never raised any objections to the authoritative map locating the temple site.

The dispute resurfaced in January 2008 when the Cambodian government announced its intention to apply for UNESCO's designation of Preah Vihear as a World Heritage Site. Thailand opposed this move on the grounds that the application should be a joint effort, and that such an application deemed the land surrounding the temple (which remained un-demarcated) Cambodian territory. A subsequent attempt at a joint communiqué failed as the Thai Constitutional Court declared it unconstitutional. Thailand's lack of enthusiasm, however, could not prevent the World Heritage Committee from listing the Preah Vihear temple as a World Heritage Site on 7 July 2008. On 15 July, Thai troops were dispatched as a signal of intent to the temple. This was met by a reciprocal mobilization of Cambodian forces, despite talks having been scheduled between senior officials from both countries. Matters came to a head in October when both militaries clashed at the border. Since then, attempts at a ceasefire have failed, and sporadic skirmishes have erupted, resulting in deaths and injuries on both sides as well as damage to the temple complex, even though a full-blown armed conflict has not materialized. Likewise, attempts by ASEAN to mediate, including the attempted posting of Indonesian observers to the border, have also floundered in the wake of national sovereignty claims, particularly by Thailand. In April 2013, the International Court of Justice (ICJ) began hearings on the ownership of the disputed 4.6 kilometres of land adjacent to the temple. On 11 November, the ICJ ruled in favour of Cambodian claims to sovereignty over the entire territory.

The dispute over Preah Vihear reflected mutual suspicions between two states which had been historical adversaries before the advent of colonialism and which adopted different positions in the Cold War. For Cambodia under the leadership of Prince **Norodom Sihanouk**, the temple represented a symbol of a newly won independence and provided an opportunity to challenge a perceived Thai reassertion of historical hegemony. To that end, it also provided a convenient domestic focus for nation-building. From the Thai perspective, the dispute reflected a traditional condescension towards Cambodia which turned into animosity when its foreign policy of neutrality, involving diplomatic relations with the People's Republic of China, was viewed as appeasement to communism in Southeast Asia. A lull in the years immediately after the end of the Cold War was broken for purposes of domestic political validation as politicians from first Cambodia and then Thailand mobilized their respective claims and stoked the flames of nationalism in the lead up to national elections.
see also: Sihanouk, King Norodom.

Prem Tinsulanonda, General
(Thailand)

Prem Tinsulanonda served as unelected prime minister of Thailand between 1980 and 1988.

He was born on 26 August 1920 and began his career as an army officer, training for the cavalry at the Chulachomklao Royal Military Academy. By 1977 he had risen to become assistant commander-in-chief of the army and served in the military government headed by General **Kriangsak Chomanan**. The **Young Turks** faction of officers, who had supported General Kriangsak, became alienated from him and engineered General Prem's succession. As prime minister, he successfully combined an activist policy towards Vietnam over Cambodia with a sober management of the economy, which flourished during his tenure. He survived two abortive coup attempts by disaffected officers and earned the respect of King **Bhumibol Adulyadej**, who sought his counsel during the street violence in May 1992 in protest at retired General **Suchinda Kraprayoon** becoming unelected prime minister. One reason Prem gave for his resignation in 1988 was that he believed that it was time the country had an elected prime minister; he had no inclination to participate in electoral politics. Since September 1988 Prem has held the position of president of the powerful Privy Council. From that vantage point he has continued to exercise considerable influence over Thai politics which is further amplified through his close personal relationship with King Bhumibol. Prem was a critic of Prime Minister **Thaksin Shinawatra**, and has been accused by the former prime minister of masterminding the September 2006 coup that removed him from office, as well as the events that followed, including the establishment of the unelected governments of **Surayud Chulanont** and **Abhisit Vejjajiva**. Prem has been an ardent supporter of the monarchy, and champions its role in defending the public interest and as the ultimate authority for the armed forces.

see also: Abhisit Vejjajiva; Bhumibol Adulyadej; Kriangsak Chomanan, General; Suchinda Kraprayoon, General; Surayud Chulanont, General; Thaksin Shinawatra; Young Turks.

Pribumi (Indonesia)

Pribumi is the Indonesian term used to identify indigenous citizens in contradistinction to those of ethnic Chinese origin. The term has an undoubted political significance because it is invariably applied to members of the business community and to the need to enable them to compete with Chinese entrepreneurs who came to dominate Indonesia's economy during the rule of President Suharto. The more well-known and corresponding term in Malaysia is *Bumiputra*.

see also: Bumiputra; Suharto.

Pridi Phanomyong (Thailand)

Pridi Phanomyong was the most influential civilian figure in the coup group that removed the absolute monarchy in Thailand in 1932. After the Pacific War, he served briefly as prime minister. He fled into exile in November 1947 following a military coup whose instigators accused him of responsibility for the death of King **Ananda Mahidol** in 1946. Pridi Phanomyong was born in 1901 into an ethnic Chinese family. He studied law in Bangkok and then spent seven years at university in Paris, where he was at the centre of radical thinking about Thai constitutional and economic development. On his return to Thailand, he served as an official at the Ministry of Justice before becoming a direct party to the end of the absolute monarchy. As a cabinet minister, he was a member of the constitutional drafting committee and also responsible for a controversial economic plan which led to charges of Communist inclination and his temporary banishment to France. On his return, Pridi was restored to cabinet office, including that of foreign minister. At the outbreak of the Pacific War in December 1941, he was appointed to the Regency Council in the absence of the young King Ananda, then living in Switzerland. During Thailand's alliance with Japan, he was the clandestine leader of the Free Thai Movement and was instrumental in having Parliament remove Field Marshal **Phibul Songkram** from the post of prime minister towards the end of hostilities. Pridi played a major part in securing Thailand's postwar international rehabilitation and took on the office of prime minister in March 1946 in difficult economic circumstances, but felt obliged to resign within two months of the violent death of King Ananda in June. He fled the country after the military coup in November 1947 and in February 1949 was implicated in an abortive attempt by the marines to restore him to power. Pridi then went to live in China, where he remained after the Communist Revolution for over twenty years. In 1970 he returned to Paris to spend the remainder of his life and died on 2 May 1983.

see also: Ananda Mahidol, King; Phibul Songkram, Field Marshal.

Provisional Revolutionary Government of the Republic of South Vietnam (PRG) 1969–76 (Vietnam)

On 8 June 1969 the Provisional Revolutionary Government of the Republic of South Vietnam (PRG) was established in 'a liberated zone' of South Vietnam by a self-proclaimed Congress of People's Representatives. The initiative for establishing the government was taken ostensibly by the insurgent **National Liberation Front of South Vietnam** (NLF) in company with a Vietnam Alliance of National Democratic and Peace Forces. In effect, the initiative was taken by the ***Lao Dong*** (Workers Party), which was the name used by Vietnam's Communist Party. The object was to challenge the legitimacy of the government in Saigon by creating an alternative internationally recognized locus of authority which would be a negotiating equal in talks in Paris. A collateral purpose was to demonstrate that the insurgency in the south of Vietnam was autonomous in origin and control and that reunification between the northern and southern halves of the country would be negotiated and take place on a step-by-step basis. In the event, reunification came on northern terms in July 1976 following the military overthrow of the government in Saigon in April 1975. Moreover, members of the Provisional Revolutionary Government, which was dissolved on reunification, were not accorded any tangible role in the Socialist Republic of Vietnam by the Communist Party, whose seat was in Hanoi.

see also: Lao Dong; National Liberation Front of South Vietnam.

Pulau Batu Puteh (Malaysia/Singapore)

see **Horsburgh Lighthouse**.

R

Rajaratnam, Sinnathamby (Singapore)

Sinnathamby Rajaratnam was the first foreign minister of an independent Singapore after it was separated from the Federation of Malaysia in August 1965. In that office, he participated actively in the formative stages of regional cooperation in Southeast Asia and was a strident early voice in challenging Vietnam's occupation of Cambodia in the third phase of the **Indochina Wars**. He played an important part in giving Singapore a regional influence out of proportion to the island-state's geopolitical significance, employing a colourful idiom and prose to that end. Sinnathamby Rajaratnam was born in Ceylon (Sri Lanka) on 23 February 1915 and was brought to Malaya by his parents as an infant. He was educated at Raffles Institution in Singapore and then at King's College in London, where he became politically active in close company with **Lee Kuan Yew**. He worked as a journalist in Singapore during the 1950s and became a founder member of the **People's Action Party** (PAP). He was initially appointed minister of culture and after 1965 held the office of foreign minister continuously until 1980. In June 1980 he became second deputy prime minister with an evident elder statesman role. In January 1985 he was made senior minister within the prime minister's office until retiring from public life shortly before the general elections in September 1988. He passed away on 22 February 2006 of heart failure at the age of ninety.

see also: Indochina Wars; Lee Kuan Yew; People's Action Party.

Ramos, Fidel (Philippines)

Fidel Ramos was president of the Philippines between July 1992 and June 1998. His election in May 1992 marked the first peaceful transfer of office in over a quarter of a century. Fidel Ramos has been credited with improving the governance of his country but was prohibited under the terms of the constitution from standing for a second term. He was born on 18 March 1928 in Lingayen, Pangasinan Province, and spent the greater part of his life in military service. Ramos was educated at the United States Military Academy at West Point, from which he graduated in 1950. He received further military training in the United States and saw service with Philippines forces in Vietnam. Ramos rose to become head of the paramilitary Philippine National Constabulary; when President **Ferdinand Marcos** declared martial law in 1972, Fidel Ramos served as a loyal lieutenant, rising to the position of deputy chief of staff of the armed forces. He was trusted by the president, partly because he was a cousin. He achieved fame and popular regard in February 1986 when with the defence minister, **Juan Ponce Enrile**, he led a successful military revolt against Marcos, who had tampered with the results of a snap presidential election. After **Corazón Aquino** had been confirmed as president, Ramos served her loyally, first as chief of staff and then as minister of defence. In the latter capacity, he was primarily responsible for defending constitutional government against a series of military coup attempts. President Aquino's gratitude became evident after the ruling party had rejected Fidel Ramos as their candidate for the presidential election in May 1992. He then formed his own political movement, ***Lakas*–NUCD**, and, with Aquino's support, won a closely fought contest against five other candidates with around only a quarter of the vote. Fidel Ramos became the first Protestant to occupy presidential office in the Philippines.

In his first state of the nation address in July 1992, he called on the Congress to legalize the Communist Party of the Philippines in an attempt to end more than two decades of insurgency. He was a resolute chief executive but met with congressional obstacles to his programme of macro-economic reform, especially over taxation policy. He was successful, however, in overcoming military dissidence, which had posed a threat to political stability during his predecessor's tenure. Towards the end of his term, he made a controversial and abortive attempt to revise the terms of the Constitution to permit him to stand for a second term. In retirement, Ramos has played the role of king-maker. He lent his support to calls for the resignation of President **Joseph Estrada** in 2000 due to allegations of corruption. President Estrada was eventually ousted by the **EDSA II** popular revolution in 2001. In 2005, Ramos defended President **Gloria Macapagal-Arroyo** against allegations of election rigging in what has come to be known as the Hello Garci scandal. In a *volte-face,* he later called for President Arroyo's resignation in a move that split the ***Lakas*–CMD** party into two factions in 2006: one supported Ramos while the other supported President Arroyo. In August 2009, Ramos (with former house speaker, Jose de Venecia Jr) led fifty *Lakas*–CMD members in opposition to the merger of the *Lakas*–CMD party with *Kabalikat ng Malayang Pilipino* (KAMPI) party which had taken place in June 2008 at the instruction of Arroyo, refusing the title of 'chairman emeritus' of the merged party which was contrived to marginalize him. Meanwhile, de Venecia filed a resolution at the Commission of Elections for the *Lakas*–KAMPI merger to be nullified. In the event, the Supreme Court denied the appeal, and upheld the legality of the resolution. In 2012, the *Lakas*–KAMPI merger was dissolved, and Ramos was approached to lead the reformed *Lakas*–CMD party, which by then had also distanced itself from Gloria Macapagal-Arroyo who was under hospital detention at the time. While Ramos publicly expressed his desire for *Lakas*–CMD to be granted legal accreditation by the Commission of Elections, he has yet to accept the position of leadership in the revamped party.

see also: Aquino, Corazón; EDSA II; Enrile, Juan Ponce; Estrada, Joseph; *Lakas*–CMD; *Lakas*–NUCD; Macapagal-Arroyo, Gloria; Marcos, Ferdinand.

Ramos-Horta, José (Timor-Leste)

José Ramos-Horta was the external representative of East Timorese resistance during the period of Indonesian occupation between 1975 and 1999. He was in Australia at the time of the invasion of East Timor and took ***Fretilin***'s case to the United Nations acting as a vigorous and persistent advocate of its cause as well as lobbying intensively around the world in order to keep it alive. In recognition of his activities, he shared the Nobel Peace Prize with Bishop Carlos Belo in November 1996. José Ramos-Horta was born in Dili in December 1949 of mixed Portuguese and Timorese parentage. He was involved from the outset with the Timorese Social Democratic Association, the forerunner of *Fretilin*. During his long period of exile, he spent much time in Australia where he found political and financial support. He also developed notable diplomatic skills which proved to be integral to his negotiations for an independent East Timor.

Ramos-Horta returned to Dili in December 1999 and thereafter was integral in laying the foundations for an independent East Timor. He worked closely with the United Nations Transitional Administration in East Timor (UNTAET) after his return to Dili, and through his negotiations the various domestic and international stakeholders agreed upon a blueprint for independence. On 27 September 2002, East Timor was admitted into the United Nations and Ramos-Horta was appointed as the country's first foreign minister. On 3 June 2006, Ramos-Horta also took on the added responsibility of being the interim minister of defence .He served in these two capacities until June 2006. With the resignation of Prime Minister **Mari Alkatiri**, President **José 'Xanana' Gusmão** appointed Ramos-Horta acting prime minister. He was subsequently confirmed as the country's second prime minister on 10 July 2006. On 25 February 2007, Ramos-Horta announced his candidacy for the April presidential elections and was eventually sworn into office as the second president of an independent East Timor having won sixty-nine per cent of the vote. It was during his term as president that an assassination attempt by rebels attempting a *coup d'état* in February 2008 severely wounded him and he had to be flown to Australia for emergency medical treatment. Ramos-Horta was in critical condition and was placed in an induced coma. He only regained consciousness ten days later and returned to Dili on 17 April 2008, after recuperating in Australia. Ramos-Horta's presidential term came to an end on 17 March 2012 when he was defeated in the 2012 presidential election, managing to gain only about nineteen per cent of the vote. He is currently the special representative of the secretary-general of the United Nations to Guinea-Bissau and head of the United Nations Integrated Peacebuilding Office in Guinea-Bissau (UNIOGBIS).

see also: Alkatiri, Mari; *Fretilin*; Gusmão, José 'Xanana'; United Nations: East Timor, 1999–2002.

Ranariddh, Prince Norodom (Cambodia)

Prince Norodom Ranariddh, eldest son of King **Norodom Sihanouk** by a minor wife, was born in Phnom Penh in 1944. He showed intellectual promise as a young man and studied law at the University of Aix-en-Provence, where he obtained a doctorate in Public International Law. He joined the faculty there in 1976 but in 1983 was drawn into Cambodian exile politics when his father appointed him as his personal representative based in Bangkok. He played a prominent representative role in the protracted negotiations over a political settlement from the late 1980s until the Paris Accords at the **International Conference on Cambodia** in October 1991. When Norodom Sihanouk became chairman of the four-party **Supreme National Council** in mid-1991, Prince Ranariddh succeeded his father as head of the **FUNCINPEC** party (National United Front for an Independent, Neutral, Peaceful and Cooperative Cambodia). In that role, he demonstrated qualities of leadership and statesmanship that were not sustained after assuming office in Cambodia, however. Indeed, he gave the impression of being more interested in its pomp and circumstance than the details of administration. He was Cambodia's first prime minister from October 1993 until ousted in July 1997. He assumed office in the wake of elections in May 1993 in which his party, FUNCINPEC, secured a plurality of votes. He shared power in a coalition with the **Cambodian People's Party** (CPP), with the former prime minister and his political adversary **Hun Sen** in the office of second prime minister. That coalition proved to be a fragile arrangement in which power was never truly shared by the CPP, while Prince Ranariddh was outmanoeuvred politically by Hun Sen and also lost the confidence of Western governments because of his *dilettante* conduct. Prince Ranariddh became chairman of Cambodia's National Assembly in November 1998 with the formation of a coalition government following general elections in the previous July. Their results, which Prince Ranariddh had initially declared to be fraudulent, confirmed the political dominance of Hun Sen as sole prime minister, which had been established through a violent coup in July 1997. As a result of that coup, Prince Ranariddh was removed as first prime minister, stripped of his parliamentary immunity, and then tried, found guilty and sentenced to thirty-five years imprisonment on charges of illegally importing arms and conducting clandestine negotiations with the Khmer Rouge. He had been out of the country at the time of the coup and only returned to participate in national politics after his father, King Norodom Sihanouk, had granted him an amnesty. His diminished role stood in contrast to his prominence in Cambodian politics earlier in the 1990s. His office of chairman of the National Assembly carried with it the right to serve as acting head of state in the absence or incapacity of an ailing King Sihanouk.

Despite an uneasy relationship with his temperamental and vain father, Prince Ranariddh was considered a favourite to succeed him when King Norodom Sihanouk abdicated in October 2004. However, he denied harbouring pretensions to the throne, and later that month was part of a nine-member council which chose **Norodom Sihamoni** to be the next king. In October 2006, Prince Ranariddh was removed from the position as chairman of FUNCINPEC by a party vote, a move initiated by his closest advisor, General Nek Bunchhay. Following this, he established the Norodom Ranariddh Party (NRP), which is currently the third largest political party in Cambodia. The NRP won two national assembly seats in the 2008 national elections. In March 2007, Prince Ranariddh was sentenced *in absentia* to eighteen months in prison for an illegal property sale of the FUNCINPEC party headquarters for 3.6 million dollars and for using the sales proceeds to purchase private property. However, in 2008, King Norodom Sihamoni granted his half-brother a royal pardon at the request of Prime Minister Hun Sen following the latter's re-election in the 2008 elections. Subsequently, Prince Ranariddh returned to Cambodia from Malaysia and retired from politics. In December 2008, King Norodom Sihamoni appointed Prince Ranariddh as the chief advisor of the Privy Council.

see also: Cambodian People's Party; FUNCINPEC; Hun Sen; International Conference on Cambodia, Paris 1991; Khmer Rouge; Sihamoni, Norodom; Sihanouk, King Norodom; Supreme National Council.

Razak, Tun Abdul (Malaysia)

Tun Abdul Razak was Malaysia's second prime minister, assuming office in September 1970 in succession to **Tunku Abdul Rahman**, who had lost the confidence of the politically dominant UMNO (United Malays National Organization). Tun Razak was born in Pahang in 1922 and was not able to receive a higher education in Britain until after the Pacific War. He completed his legal studies in 1950 and on returning to Malaya joined the civil service but soon left to enter politics. In Britain he had played a key role in the anti-colonial Malayan Forum and also acted as a mentor to the future prime minister, Tunku Abdul Rahman, whose deputy he became, holding portfolios for defence and rural development but acting also as *de facto* foreign minister. In that latter role, he led negotiations to ward off Indonesia's **Confrontation** and to form **ASEAN** (Association of Southeast Asian Nations). As prime minister, he was responsible for inaugurating the **New Economic Policy** designed to redress the balance of economic advantage from non-Malays to Malays, in part to entrench the political position of UMNO. He was responsible also for taking Malaysia into the Non-Aligned Movement in 1970 and for establishing diplomatic relations with the People's Republic of China in 1974. He died prematurely of leukaemia on 14 January 1976.

see also: Abdul Rahman, Tunku; ASEAN; Confrontation; New Economic Policy; UMNO.

Razaleigh Hamzah, Tengku (Malaysia)

Tengku Razaleigh Hamzah, also popularly known by the *nom de guerre* 'Ku Li', narrowly lost a leadership challenge to Prime Minister **Mahathir Mohamad** for the office of president of **UMNO** (United Malays National Organization) in April 1987. The following year, he established an alternative Malay party, ***Semangat '46*** (Spirit of 1946), which failed to make a significant impact. The party was dissolved in October 1996 when Tengku Razaleigh and his supporters resumed membership of UMNO.

Tengku Razaleigh was born in April 1937 in Kota Bharu to a former chief minister and member of the royal family of the east coast state of Kelantan. He was educated at Queen's University, Belfast, and completed legal studies at Lincoln's Inn, London. He became active in UMNO politics in Kelantan on his return, serving for some years in the state legislature before entering the federal parliament. He achieved national prominence from 1971 as executive director of PERNAS, the organization established to promote the economic interests of the Malays. He secured the most votes in elections for the three posts of vice-president of UMNO in 1975, but was passed over for the office of deputy prime minister in favour of Mahathir Mohamad in 1976. He was appointed finance minister but in 1984 was demoted to the portfolio of trade and industry after an unsuccessful challenge to deputy prime minister **Musa Hitam** for the office of UMNO deputy president. He resigned from cabinet office in 1986 and in his abortive bid for the UMNO presidency ironically had Musa Hitam as his running mate. After his return to UMNO, he was not identified with the political dissidence precipitated by the dismissal, arrest, trial and imprisonment of the deputy prime minister, **Anwar Ibrahim**. In the elections in November 1999 Tengku Razaleigh won a federal seat in Gua Musang, Kelantan, but was not offered a portfolio in the new cabinet. He made an abortive attempt to stand for deputy president and one of the posts of vice-president of UMNO at its General Assembly in May 2000 but failed to secure sufficient nominations. Tengku Razaleigh again expressed interest in contesting for the UMNO presidency in 2004 but was unable to obtain enough nominations to do so. He did however successfully defend his Gua Musang federal seat at the 2004, 2008 and 2013 elections. After the 2008 elections in which the ruling coalition performed poorly, Tengku Razaleigh led calls for the reform of UMNO, specifically, the party's internal election mechanism which concentrated party electoral power and influence in the hands of a few, thereby entrenching corruption.

see also: Anwar Ibrahim; Mahathir Mohamad, Tun; Musa Hitam, Tun; Razak, Tun Abdul; *Semangat '46*; UMNO.

Reform the Armed Forces Movement (RAM) (Philippines)

The Reform the Armed Forces Movement (RAM) played a key role in the mutiny that led to the overthrow of President **Ferdinand Marcos** in 1986. During the rule of his successor, **Corazón Aquino**, it served as a focus for military discontent and was responsible for mounting abortive coups and creating a climate of political instability. Its significance declined with the election to presidential office in May 1992 of the former chief of staff of the armed forces, **Fidel Ramos**.

The movement developed out of a personal rivalry between Marcos' minister of defence, **Juan Ponce Enrile**, and the then chief of staff of the armed forces, **Fabian Ver**. Partly as a vehicle for self-protection, Enrile set out to recruit a private army within the armed forces and attracted a group of discontented young officers to his cause. The RAM was set up in March 1985. A plot to seize the presidential palace against the background of a snap election called for February 1986 was discovered by Marcos. Fearing arrest, Enrile retreated with his supporters to Camp Aguinaldo, the site of the Defence Ministry. He was joined there by the deputy chief of staff of the armed forces, General **Fidel Ramos**, and the two of them shifted their base to the more defensible Camp Crame nearby (*see* **EDSA**) which became the focus of the '**People Power**' revolt that led to Marcos giving up office and going into exile.

After Corazón Aquino became president, Enrile was reinstated as minister of defence. But they were soon alienated from one another as Enrile and his youthful military supporters resented her exercise of power, which they regarded as rightfully theirs. Enrile was replaced as defence minister in November 1986 and the first of a number of abortive coups took place in January 1987, with Fidel Ramos appointed initially as chief of staff staying loyal to the president. Perhaps the most serious of the coups took place in August 1987 and was led by Colonel Grigorio Honasan, who had been a close aide to Enrile in February 1986. Honasan evaded capture for several months and subsequently escaped from detention in 1988 to launch another abortive coup in December 1989. Honasan and other dissident officers signed an accord with the government of Fidel Ramos in December 1992, which marked the effective end of challenge by the RAM.

see also: Aquino, Corazón; EDSA; Enrile, Juan Ponce; People Power; Ramos, Fidel; Ver, General Fabian.

Regional Comprehensive Economic Partnership (Brunei/Cambodia/Indonesia/Laos/Malaysia/Myanmar/Philippines/Singapore/Thailand/Vietnam)

Proposed at the **Bali Summit of ASEAN in 2011**, the Regional Comprehensive Economic Partnership (RCEP) is an ASEAN-inspired regional economic integration initiative that brings together the economies of **ASEAN** (Association of Southeast Asian Nations) and six dialogue partners – China, Japan, South Korea, Australia, New Zealand and India. If successful, it would create the largest trading bloc in the world. At its inception during the November 2012 **East Asia Summit**, RCEP was envisaged to reconcile the East Asian Free Trade Agreement which brought together ASEAN, China, Japan, and South Korea on the one hand, and the Comprehensive Economic Partnership in East Asia which also included Australia, New Zealand, and India, on the other. The basic premise of RCEP is an open regionalism where its accession scheme allows other members to join as long as they agree to comply with the grouping's guidelines and rules. These guiding principles were endorsed by the ASEAN economic ministers at their meeting in Cambodia in August 2012. While some see RCEP as competition to the US-led **Trans-Pacific Partnership** (TPP), which is far more ambitious in how it is attempting to create norms in investments, intellectual property rights and trade, others have suggested that RCEP can function as a vehicle for states to gradually liberalize their domestic economies in preparation for applying for membership of the TPP.

see also: ASEAN; Bali Summit (ASEAN) 2011; East Asia Summit; Trans-Pacific Partnership.

Reproductive Health Bills

(Philippines)

The Reproductive Health Bills, also known as the RH Bill, is legislation arising from government efforts to establish wider access to contraception or birth control, as well as maternal care, for Filipino women. The Bill has been the subject of controversy and major debate in the Philippines, a predominantly Roman Catholic country. Orthodox Roman Catholic beliefs advocate natural methods of contraception, and many Roman Catholics in the country are of the view that birth control not only contravenes their core belief, but also encourages promiscuity. Nevertheless, because of the booming population of the country lawmakers are compelled by circumstance to deliberate passing this law as a means of population control, in addition to other equally pressing aims of easing poverty and unemployment. If passed, the Bill will likely see the implementation of methods of contraception including condoms, birth control pills and IUDs (intrauterine devices). As a major policy initiative of his administration, President **Benigno Aquino III** has defied pressure from the Church by pushing the Bill through to its signing in December 2012. In response, the Church has appealed to the Supreme Court, and has threatened supporters of the Bill, including the president, with excommunication.

see also: Aquino III, Benigno Simeon Cojuangco.

Revolutionary Government of the Republic of Indonesia 1958–61

(Indonesia)

On 15 February 1958, a group of ill-matched dissident officers and politicians, who had met initially in Sungai Dareh in west Sumatra, proclaimed over Radio Bukit Tinggi a *Pemerintah Revolusioner Republik Indonesia* (PRRI), which translates as Revolutionary Government of the Republic of Indonesia. This reformist rather than separatist rebellion, which sought to change the structure of government in Jakarta, was rooted in regional discontent in Sumatra and Sulawesi (Celebes) in particular. It registered resentment at the distribution of power and resources between Java and the outer islands of the archipelago. It also incorporated resentment on the part of regional military commanders at the centralizing policies of the national military establishment. A revolt by the west Sumatra military command, which took over civil administration in December 1956, had precipitated corresponding actions in Sulawesi and Kalimantan (Borneo). In Sulawesi, a military movement known as *Piagam Perjuangan Semesta Alam* (in acronym ***Permesta***) meaning Universal Struggle Charter, which had been declared in March 1957, allied with the Sumatran rebels on 17 February 1958. The rebellion was also a reaction to the growing assertiveness and pro-Communist radicalism of President **Sukarno**, who maintained that the source of Indonesia's political turbulence was liberal democracy imported from the west. He declared martial law in March 1957 and acted to intimidate the modernist-Muslim ***Masyumi*** and the Socialist Party. He encouraged the seizure of Dutch business enterprises at the end of November 1957 in response to a failure to secure support in the United Nations General Assembly for Indonesia's position on **Irian Jaya**. This action, by causing economic disruption including a crisis in inter-island shipping, provoked the regional rebellion into a formal declaration of an alternative government. A firm military response from the centre in March 1958, however, saw the rebellion crumble and effectively collapse by June, although final defeat was not conceded until 1961. Its failure, despite clandestine support

from the United States' CIA, proved to be a political turning-point. It had the effect of consolidating the power of both Sukarno and the central military establishment, who together were able to inaugurate the authoritarian political system of **Guided Democracy** in July 1959.
see also: Guided Democracy; Irian Jaya; *Masyumi*; *Permesta*; Sukarno.

Rizal, José (Philippines)

José Rizal is regarded as the spiritual father of Filipino nationalism and the supreme martyr of its cause. His famous satirical novels exposing the venality of Spanish colonial rule produced an evocative response among his fellow Filipinos. He was born on 19 June 1861 in Calamba, south of Manila, to a wealthy Chinese-mestizo family. He was exceptionally gifted and went on from the Jesuit elite Ateneo High School to the University of Santo Tomas, where he qualified in medicine. Before he left the Philippines to pursue postgraduate studies in Madrid, he had suffered personal humiliation at Spanish colonial hands. He pursued a reformist political cause in metropolitan Spain and expressed his desire for equal status in two famous novels which were banned in the Philippines. He specialized in ophthalmology and spent time in England and then in Hong Kong. In June 1892 he returned to Manila, where he founded the Philippine League to advance his reformist political aims. Rizal was soon after banished to the southern island of Mindanao on a charge of sedition. In 1896 he volunteered for service in Cuba in the Spanish interest but was arrested while en route and taken back to Manila. He was charged with responsibility for the nationalist uprising which had begun in the Philippines earlier in the year and sentenced to death. Rizal was executed by firing squad on 30 December 1896 at the age of thirty-five. His poetic last testament, *Ultimos Adios*, has served as a romantic basic text for Philippine nationalism.

Roadmap to Democracy (Myanmar)

First announced in August 2003 by General **Khin Nyunt**, the 'Roadmap to Democracy' is a seven-step blueprint for a transition from military rule to a form of democracy wherein the military retains a strong influence. The roadmap essentially set out the process to re-establish democracy through a new constitution, the conduct of elections and the inauguration of a new parliament. The first step was to reconvene the stalled National Convention to draft principles for a new constitution. The second step was the piecemeal implementation of the foundation for a democratic system following the completion of the National Convention. The third step was to draft a constitution in accordance with the basic and detailed principles drawn up by the National Convention. The fourth step was the adoption of a new constitution through a national referendum. This was to be followed by step five, the conduct of free and fair elections for legislative bodies as laid out in the constitution. The sixth step was the convening of the new parliament. The seventh was the building of a 'modern, developed, and democratic nation' by the leaders elected by parliament, the government and other central organs. The seventh step is ongoing, but the others have all been accomplished, albeit not without controversy due to the military's strong regulation of the process and obvious bias to maintain its power through a 'disciplined flourishing democracy' at the completion of the process. Although not expressly listed as one of the steps, it was widely felt that the handover of arms by ethnic insurgent groups and their inclusion in mainstream politics was a part of this process. Though Khin Nyunt was removed from power in 2004, his 'Roadmap' appears to have unfolded over several years leading up to the 2010 election.
see also: Khin Nyunt, General.

Rohingya (Myanmar)

Rohingya is the name of the minority Muslim community in the north of the Arakan region of Myanmar who are the descendants of Arab and Persian traders who settled and intermarried over a period of several hundred years from the ninth century. Under colonial rule they enjoyed the protection of the government in Rangoon; their loyalty to the British during the Japanese occupation led to friction with the majority Burman Buddhists and the first of a series of forced population movements into east Bengal. Muslims in Arakan rose in abortive revolt with other ethnic minorities with independence in 1948 because of the central government's refusal to countenance their political autonomy. A government campaign disguised as a search for illegal immigrants in the late 1970s produced a second major wave of refugees into newly independent Bangladesh. Recurrent harassment continued until early 1992 when a third major exodus of some 300,000 took place as a result of an evident policy of 'ethnic cleansing' by the military regime. This action exercised the **ASEAN** (Association of Southeast Asian Nations) governments with significant Muslim communities such as Malaysia, Indonesia and Brunei. The policy of the government has been attributed to its interest in playing on communal tensions in order to distract popular attention from its economic failings and political repression. A process of repatriation of Rohingya was begun in September 1992 and some 200,000 have been reported as having returned to Myanmar by mid-1995. In April 2000, according to the International Federation of Human Rights, tens of thousands of Rohingya were forced to flee the country into Bangladesh as a result of a deliberate policy of ethnic cleansing in Arakan province where some 1.5 million reside.

In 2001, communal riots erupted in Sittwe, the capital of Rakhine State, with over twenty mosques destroyed. Notwithstanding their persecution, the Rohingya participated in the 2008 national referendum regarding the new constitution. Later that year, in December, several boatloads of Rohingya being smuggled from Bangladesh to Malaysia were detained in Thailand. Following this, Thailand initiated its new policy of 'pushing back' Rohingya boat people to drift at sea. In July 2009, Bangladesh began a new crackdown on undocumented Rohingya in Bangladesh, and the Bangladesh Border Guards began to force thousands of Rohingya back to Myanmar. In May 2011, the Bangladesh government refused a grant offered by the European Commission to reduce poverty in areas in Bangladesh with a majority of undocumented Rohingya refugees on grounds that it would encourage a greater exodus of refugees into the country. In 2012, riots broke out in Rakhine state in May, June and October between ethnic Rakhine Buddhists and Rohingya Muslims. The trigger was the rape and murder of a Rakhine woman earlier that year in May by a group of men claimed by locals to have been Rohingya Muslims. In response, a mob of ethnic Rakhine attacked a bus, killing ten Muslims, triggering violence between the two communities. The government of Myanmar responded to the violence by deploying troops and imposing curfews. In June 2012, a state of emergency was declared in Rakhine state. The violence resulted in more than 100 deaths, the displacement of more than 200,000 people (mostly Rohingya residents), and the destruction of thousands of homes. March 2013 saw the re-ignition of riots and attacks by the Rakhine Buddhist majority on the Muslim minority in Meiktila. This triggered further sectarian violence in April, May, August and October that year. To a great extent, this violence has been stoked by influential monks that the government has been unable or unwilling to act against. In some cases, violence is also believed to have been abetted by the military, which has otherwise been accused of targeting Rohingya Muslims through mass arrests and arbitrary violence in the course of security operations. At the heart of the issue remains the Myanmar government's continuation of its policy to deny Rohingya Muslims citizenship status and accompanying rights. Instead, they are classified as illegal immigrants from Bangladesh, despite the fact that many have resided in Myanmar for generations.
see also: ASEAN.

Roxas, Manuel A. (Philippines)

Manuel Roxas was the first president of the Republic of the Philippines on its independence from the United States. He was elected in April 1946 as president of the Commonwealth and then took the oath of office again in July with the full transfer of sovereignty. Manuel Roxas was born on 1 January 1892 in Capiz on the island of Panay and was educated at the University of the Philippines, where he graduated in law. He was an active politician between the two world wars, becoming speaker of the House of Representatives. He was involved in negotiating the transitional arrangement to independence in 1935, after which he held the office of secretary of finance. During the Pacific War, he had remained in the Philippines as a member of the Japanese-sponsored administration headed by Jose Laurel. He was saved from the political wilderness and worse by the active intervention of General Douglas MacArthur, who had been a close friend before hostilities. MacArthur's patronage was a decisive factor in Roxas's political rehabilitation and success. Restored as Senate president, he challenged the incumbent Sergio Osmena for high office and defected from the **Nacionalista Party** through the vehicle of its 'Liberal Wing', which was reconstituted as the **Liberal Party** under his leadership. He won a narrow victory with US support in a free-spending election. As president, he was faced with major problems of economic rehabilitation and political challenge from the peasant-based ***Hukbalahap* Movement**. He has been identified with protecting the United States' economic and military interests in the Philippines in return for payments for war damages. The military bases agreement which gave the United States a ninety-nine year tenure over twenty-three sites, including **Subic Bay Naval Base** and **Clark Air Base**, was negotiated under his aegis. Ironically he died on 15 April 1948 at Clark Air Base after making a speech to US service personnel.

see also: Clark Air Base; *Hukbalahap* Movement; Liberal Party; Nacionalista Party; Subic Bay Naval Base.

Ruak, Taur Matan (Timor-Leste)

Taur Matan Ruak is the third president of Timor-Leste. On 20 May 2012, he succeeded Nobel Peace Prize laureate **José Ramos-Horta** in a largely ceremonial position that has little policy role but which nevertheless remains crucial for peace and stability in a country that has been troubled with violence and unrest for decades.

Born in 1956 in Portuguese Timor as Jose Maria Vasconcelos, part of his appeal as a presidential candidate came from his extensive and decorated military background and in particular, his role in the resistance against Indonesian occupation of East Timor from 1975 to 1999. Known by his *nom de guerre*, which translates as 'two sharp eyes' in local dialect, he rose quickly through the ranks of *Falintil*, East Timor's national liberation army, and became its last commander-in-chief prior to independence. Upon independence from Indonesia in 2002, he was appointed major general of Timor-Leste's fledgling armed forces, a position which he relinquished in October 2011. He won the presidential election in April 2012, which observers have described as being generally free and fair, defeating his opponent Franscisco Guterres with sixty-one per cent of the vote. His past is not, however, free of controversy. A United Nations inquiry following the political crisis and deadly unrest of 2006 found that Taur Matan Ruak had armed civilians during the unrest, and recommended his prosecution for complicity in the violence (*see* **Timor-Leste Crisis 2006**). Taur Matan Ruak defended himself by claiming that he was merely following directives issued by the defence minister. No charges were subsequently pressed against him.

see also: Ramos-Horta, José; Timor-Leste Crisis 2006.

Rukunegara 1970 (Malaysia)

Translated literally as Basic Principles of the State, *Rukunegara* was promulgated on 31 August 1970 by Malaysia's Department of National Unity. Drawing inspiration from Indonesian practice, the concept was intended to provide a set of guidelines for communal coexistence in the wake of extensive violence that erupted in Kuala Lumpur in the May 13 Racial Riots 1969. The declaration read:

> Our Nation Malaysia, being dedicated to achieving a greater unity of all peoples; to maintaining a democratic way of life; to creating a just society in which the wealth of the nation shall be equitably shared; to ensuring a liberal approach to her rich and diverse cultural traditions; to building a progressive society which shall be oriented to modern science and technology;
>
> We, her people, pledge our united efforts to attain those ends guided by these principles:
>
> Belief in God
> Loyalty to King and Country
> Upholding the Constitution
> Rule of Law
> Good Behaviour and Morality

Rukunegara has never assumed the standing of a national ideology and lapsed as a practical political device after Malaysia resumed parliamentary government during the 1970s. The ability of the government to proceed with its **New Economic Policy** of redistributing wealth to the particular advantage of the Malay community without unleashing communal tensions has made the stratagem underlying *Rukunegara* redundant. The concept remains available for employment against political dissent with a racial connotation although in practice, it increasingly rings hollow in the wake of escalating Malay conservative right-wing rhetoric.

see also: May 13 Racial Riots 1969; New Economic Policy.

S

Sabah United Party (Malaysia)

The Sabah United Party (*Parti Bersatu Sabah*, PBS) was the ruling party in the Malaysian state of Sabah in northern Borneo from April 1985 until March 1994. It was established in February 1985 as the result of defections from the ruling *Berjaya* (Sabah People's Union) because of resentment on the part of ethnic Kadazans and Chinese at the pro-Muslim policies of the chief minister, Datuk **Harris Mohamad Salleh**. In state assembly elections in April, it won twenty-five out of forty-eight seats and after overcoming an artificial constitutional impediment, its leader, Datuk Joseph Pairin Kitingan, was sworn in as chief minister. In time, it was accepted as a member of the ruling federal coalition, ***Barisan Nasional*** (National Front, BN), and in July 1990 was returned to office despite apparent federal support for the opposition United Sabah National Organization (USNO). In mid-October 1990, just five days before elections to the federal legislature, PBS defected from the BN to join the opposition coalition. The BN, which retained office, expelled the PBS and sought to undermine its position in Sabah by establishing a branch of the politically dominant **UMNO** (United Malays National Organization) in the state as well as bringing a charge of corruption against the chief minister. This initiative appeared to backfire in April 1993, when leading members of the opposition USNO defected to join the PBS. Kitingan called state elections for February 1994, shortly before being found guilty of awarding a shophouse project to a company in which his brothers-in-law had an interest. However, he received a fine below the amount that would have disqualified him from contesting the elections. In the event, PBS was returned to power with a narrow majority. It secured twenty-five seats in the state legislature of forty-eight, with the remaining places being held by UMNO and three linked minor parties. Its parliamentary position was then undermined by a series of defections, including that of the chief minister's brother, Jeffrey Kitingan, which led to a loss of its majority four weeks after the result of the elections. Joseph Kitingan then resigned as chief minister in favour of Sakaran Dandai, the head of the Sabah division of UMNO. The key to the failure of PBS was the refusal of the federal government to encourage the economic development of Sabah as long as it remained in office. With the resignation of Datuk Kitingan, his party began to splinter into three factions which made their own accommodations with the BN government in the interest of sharing power and its spoils. It demonstrated its resilience in federal elections in April 1995 by holding eight seats compared to fourteen in 1990. In elections in November 1999, its federal strength was reduced to three seats, while in state elections won by the BN in the previous March, it secured seventeen out of forty-eight seats. In April 2000, however, six of its members in the state legislature defected to the ruling coalition. In January 2002, PBS rejoined the BN coalition and went on to contribute thirteen state seats and four parliamentary seats to the ruling coalition's landslide victory in March 2004. As an acknowledgement of PBS's contribution, Joseph Kitingan was made deputy chief minister and minister of rural development. While PBS has remained a member of the BN since, it has also laboured to regain a measure of local political autonomy and influence lost to UMNO when the latter entered the political fray in Sabah in 1990.

see also: Barisan Nasional; Harris Mohamad Salleh, Datuk; UMNO; United Sabah National Organization.

Saffron Revolution 2007 (Myanmar)

The 2007 protests, popularly known as the 'Saffron Revolution', took place in August and September 2007. Initially the result of dissatisfaction with the government's economic mismanagement, the demonstrations quickly took on political and anti-government overtones.

By 2007, Myanmar's civilian population was already increasingly restive over the slow pace of political reconciliation and a worsening economy. Economic mismanagement combined with Western sanctions had pushed many deeper into poverty while families of the military elite and their business partners amassed considerable wealth. Prices for daily necessities had been soaring since 2006, but a general tolerance for hardship built up over years of military rule kept the lid on. This changed on 15 August 2007 when the government removed a fuel subsidy resulting in price increases of between 100 and 500 per cent overnight, far beyond what ordinary people could afford. This sparked protests on 19 August that carried on into September despite government efforts to disperse the demonstrations with arrests. The protests took on a new form in mid-September as Buddhist monks took over the leadership of the movement, beginning in the northwest. Protests soon spread throughout the country, including Yangon, following the beating of protesting monks in Pakokku on 5 September. A boycott of donations from military families was called by monasteries in Mandalay, a powerful move that effectively denied them the Buddhist merit earned through donations.

While Buddhist monastic code forbids involvement in mundane politics, Myanmar's monks have been at the forefront of politics at numerous historic junctures, including anti-colonial activities and the 1988 demonstrations. The military was initially hesitant to stop the protests due to the reverence of monks by the largely Buddhist population and the enormous bad merit incurred by harming a monk. This changed on 26 September when the government ordered a general crackdown on the protests. Shots were fired into the crowds, monks and protesters were arrested, beaten, interrogated and many imprisoned. Monks were also defrocked. The crackdown horrified the international community, earning the regime strong criticism not only from western governments but also, surprisingly, China. Mass arrests and repressive measures over the following months eventually suppressed the protest movement and reaffirmed military rule. Notably, although there was early involvement by former 1988 student activists, the participation of the **National League for Democracy** was minimal.

see also: National League for Democracy.

Saloth Sar (Cambodia) *see* **Pol Pot**.

Sam Rainsy (Cambodia)

Sam Rainsy is the leader of the **Sam Rainsy Party** (SRP), a key opposition party in Cambodia. An outspoken critic of the Cambodian government's economic policies and prevalent corruption, he has a long-running feud with the ruling **Cambodian People's Party** (CPP) led by Prime Minister **Hun Sen** and has often been on the receiving end of government intimidation.

Born in Phnom Penh in 1949, Sam Rainsy moved to France in 1965 and started his career there in the finance sector. He joined Prince **Norodom Ranariddh**'s **FUNCINPEC** party and subsequently returned to Cambodia in 1992. After FUNCINPEC won the 1993 elections and formed a coalition government with the CPP, Sam Rainsy was appointed finance minister. In 1994, however, he was abruptly removed from his post and expelled from the party after a vote of no-confidence against him. A month later, he was also forced out of the National Assembly. In early November 1995, Sam Rainsy established the Khmer Nation Party (KNP) which eventually changed its name to the Sam Rainsy Party (SRP) prior to the 1998 elections. In February 2005, Rainsy was forced to flee the country after he and two other parliamentarians from his SRP were stripped of their parliamentary immunity and charged with defamation when he claimed that Hun Sen was involved in a grenade attack at a rally in 1997 which resulted in seventeen fatalities. He also faced defamation lawsuits from Norodom Ranariddh, whom he has accused of taking bribes from the ruling party. Rainsy was sentenced *in absentia* to eighteen months' imprisonment but was later pardoned by King **Norodom Sihamoni** just a few months after the sentence, at the request of the prime minister. The royal pardon allowed Rainsy to return to Cambodia and continue his political activities. Still smarting from that encounter, he was once again stripped of his parliamentary immunity in

2010 after allegedly falsifying information over the Vietnam–Cambodia border dispute as well as inciting protests and violence by villagers near the border. He was living in exile in Paris when he was sentenced *in absentia* to ten years' imprisonment. Sam Rainsy insisted that the charges against him were politically motivated and reflected broader attempts by the CPP to suppress opposition and criticism. Sam Rainsy received a royal pardon again from King Norodom Sihamoni in July 2013 at the behest of Prime Minister Hun Sen. He returned to invigorate the 2013 elections and led the **Cambodia National Rescue Party**, which included his SRP, to make significant inroads into the CPP's grip on power. Alleging widespread election fraud, Sam Rainsy has led an opposition boycott of parliament, calling for an independent investigation into election irregularities and a re-election. A meeting between Sam Rainsy and Hun Sen in October 2013 failed to resolve differences.

see also: Cambodia National Rescue Party; Cambodian People's Party; FUNCINPEC; Hun Sen; Ranariddh, Prince Norodom; Sam Rainsy Party; Sihamoni, King Norodom.

Sam Rainsy Party (Cambodia)

The liberal Sam Rainsy Party (SRP) came into being in March 1998 when it changed its name from Khmer Nation Party (KNP) and is a constituent of the **Cambodia National Rescue Party** (CNRP) in opposition to the ruling **Cambodian People's Party** (CPP). Formed in November 1995 by **Sam Rainsy** after he was expelled from **FUNCINPEC**, the KNP changed its name three years later as a result of internal party disputes that saw the emergence of a faction that had gravitated towards the ruling party.

The SRP won fifteen out of 122 seats in the Cambodian legislature in the 1998 elections, despite widespread allegations that the CPP had manipulated electoral process. In the 2003 elections, the SRP increased its share of seats to twenty-four, coming in second behind Prime Minister **Hun Sen**'s CPP. After eleven months of negotiations yielded no consensus between the three main parties, the SRP was eventually excluded from the coalition when FUNCINPEC agreed to join the CPP in forming the new government. SRP parliamentarians accused the new government of being unconstitutional and boycotted the new National Assembly. As an opposition party, SRP has borne the brunt of political repression and intimidation by the ruling CCP. In September 2012, the SRP formally combined with the Human Rights Party to form the CNRP to contest the 2013 elections in which they collectively won fifty-five seats to the CPP's sixty-eight seats.

see also: Cambodia National Rescue Party; Cambodian People's Party; FUNCINPEC; Hun Sen; Sam Rainsy.

Samak Sundaravej (Thailand)

Samak Sundaravej had a long political career which culminated as prime minister of Thailand in 2008 as well as leader of the **People's Power Party** (PPP). Samak was born in Bangkok on 13 June 1935 to a Chinese family. He earned a bachelor's degree from Thammasat University in Bangkok.

Samak joined the **Democrat Party** in 1968 and through his strong ties to the military became leader of its right-wing faction. After defeating veteran politician **Kukrit Pramoj** in the 1976 elections, Samak became deputy interior minister in the **Seni Pramoj** government. Samak was sent by Seni to Singapore in August 1976 to persuade former dictator Field Marshal **Thanom Kittikachorn** not to return to Thailand. Instead, Samak may have in fact encouraged the return by informing the general that he had the support of the monarchy, resulting in his removal from his cabinet position in October 1976. Samak responded by organizing an anti-government demonstration and attacked several ministers for allegedly being Communists. He played a prominent role in the events leading to the 6 October 1976 massacre of students at Thammasat University by inciting right-wing mobs to attack students, whom he labelled as Communists, protesting the return of Thanom. Samak became minister of interior in the government of **Thanin Kraivichian** which followed the coup of 6 October 1976 and initiated a campaign of arrests of alleged leftist students, writers and intellectuals. In 1979, Samak founded the *Prachakorn Thai* Party, which went on to defeat the incumbent Democrat Party in the 1979 elections. He was made minister of transport from 1983 to 1986 and again in 1990–1 under the governments of **Prem Tinsulanonda** and **Chatichai Choonhavan** respectively. In 1992, he was deputy prime minister in the military-appointed government of General **Suchinda Kraprayoon**, and defended the military's brutal suppression of pro-democracy protestors in May that year. Samak remained leader of his *Prachakorn Thai* Party until 2000 when he was elected governor of Bangkok. A popular governor, he served until 2003, when he concentrated on his popular cooking show. He would re-enter politics in 2006 as a senator following the coup of the same year.

Samak was the leader of the PPP and became prime minister when the party won general elections in December 2007. The **People's Alliance for Democracy** accused the PPP and Samak of being proxies for the exiled prime minister, **Thaksin Shinawatra**, and the disbanded ***Thai Rak Thai*** **Party**, and organized massive street protests to call for their removal. Samak refused to resign in the face of increasingly militant protests, but on 9 September 2008, he found himself disqualified by the Constitutional Court for receiving payment for his televised cooking shows while serving as prime minister, a violation of the constitution that bans ministers from accepting external paid positions. Samak with his loyalists tried to keep himself in position but gave up on 12 September when he resigned as leader of the PPP. Samak was later convicted on an old libel charge and sentenced to two years imprisonment. He jumped bail and left for the United States for cancer treatment. Returning to Thailand, Samak was hospitalized and died in Bangkok on 24 November 2009.

see also: Chatichai Choonhavan, General; Democrat Party; Kukrit Pramoj; People's Alliance for Democracy; People's Power Party; Prem Tinsulanonda, General; Seni Pramoj; Suchinda Kraprayoon, General; *Thai Rak Thai* Party; Thaksin Shinawatra; Thanin Kraivichian; Thanom Kittikachorn, Field Marshal.

Samphan, Khieu (Cambodia) *see* Khieu Samphan.

Samrin, Heng (Cambodia) *see* Heng Samrin.

San Yu, General (Myanmar)

General San Yu served as the faithful acolyte of **Ne Win** for over forty years. After Ne Win stood down as president of Burma in 1981, San Yu assumed the office until retiring from political life in 1988, when political turbulence caused the ruling military establishment to set up a new form of government. San Yu was born in Prome in 1919 and was studying medicine in Rangoon at the outbreak of the Pacific War. He became an officer in the Japanese-sponsored Burma Defence Army and continued with a military career after the end of hostilities, with some training in the United States. He rose rapidly in the military hierarchy and was a member of the Revolutionary Council under Ne Win which seized power in 1962; San Yu became general secretary of the Central Organizing Committee of the ruling **Burma Socialist Programme Party** (BSPP) in 1964. He subsequently held the positions of deputy prime minister and also of minister of defence and was at the time seen as a likely replacement for Ne Win, but his political role was that of loyal servant without great personal ambition. He died on 28 January 1996 aged seventy-six.

see also: Burma Socialist Programme Party; Ne Win, General.

Sangkum Reastre Niyum (Cambodia)

Sangkum Reastre Niyum, which translates as Popular Socialist Community, was a mass political organization established by Prince **Norodom Sihanouk** in March 1955 on his abdication from the throne. Through this organization, Prince Sihanouk commanded the heights of Cambodian politics for fifteen years until he was deposed in March 1970. The *Sangkum* served as a means through which he could encompass and also domesticate all shades of political opinion. It was employed initially to contest the general election held in September 1955. An overwhelming victory was secured with eighty-three per cent of the vote, which delivered all the seats in the National Assembly. The *Sangkum* functioned very much as a political stage for

Prince Sihanouk, who called periodic national congresses held in the open at which he could humiliate his ministers and national assemblymen in front of an urban mass for whom the occasion provided considerable entertainment. The heyday of the *Sangkum* and its national congresses was in the late 1950s and early 1960s. However, as Prince Sihanouk's political grip became less sure, in part because of external factors, the spectacle of the national congress lost its initial attraction. By the time Prince Sihanouk was overthrown in 1970, the *Sangkum* had long ceased to serve its initial political function.
see also: Sihanouk, King Norodom.

Sann, Son (Cambodia) *see* **Son Sann**.

Sanoh Thienthong (Thailand)

Sanoh Theinthong is a Thai politician and power-broker who has engineered the premierships of several of Thailand's recent prime ministers, although he has never held the position himself. Sanoh was born on 1 April 1934. He graduated with a law degree from Sripatum University in Bangkok in the 1970s. Sanoh entered politics in 1975, joining the ***Chart Thai*** **Party**, and was subsequently elected to Parliament for Prachinburi province in 1976. He was deputy minister for agriculture from 1986 to 1988 and deputy minister of transport for a short period in 1992. In 1994, Sanoh was made general secretary of the *Chart Thai* Party after **Banharn Silpa-archa** became its leader. When the *Chart Thai* Party formed a coalition government the following year, Banharn appointed Sanoh as minister of public health. Sanoh resigned in 1996 to join the **New Aspiration Party** of **Chavalit Yongchaiyuth**, becoming its secretary-general. Following its election win in 1996, Sanoh became minister of interior. Sanoh changed parties again in 2001, joining the new ***Thai Rak Thai*** **Party** under **Thaksin Shinawatra** and becoming its chief advisor. Upon the party's election victory in 2001, Sanoh did not receive a ministerial position, but his wife was alternately appointed minister of culture and labour. Within the party, Sanoh formed a powerful faction known as *Wang Nam Yen*. He however fell out with Thaksin and left the party in February 2006, later speaking at several **People's Alliance for Democracy** rallies following Thaksin's dissolution of Parliament later that year. In February 2006, Sanoh formed the *Pracharaj* (Royal People Party) and was declared its leader. In May 2011, he abandoned his party to join the ***Pheu Thai*** **Party,** and was elected in the July 2011 election. Sanoh supported the candidature of **Yingluck Shinawatra** as prime minister.
see also: Banharn Silpa-archa; *Chart Thai* Party; Chavalit Yongchaiyuth, General; New Aspiration Party; People's Alliance for Democracy; *Pheu Thai* Party, *Thai Rak Thai* Party; Thaksin Shinawatra; Yingluck Shinawatra.

Santri (Indonesia)

Santri is an Indonesian term deriving from *pesantran*, which is the name for a village religious school. It has come to be employed, primarily in Java, to distinguish Indonesian Muslims of a strict orthodoxy from the ***Abangan*** whose Islam is a synthesis comprising in part animist and Hindu–Buddhist beliefs with a mystical content. Since independence, *Santri* have been identified with political parties such as ***Masyumi*** and ***Nahdlatul Ulama*** and since the merger of all Islamic parties in 1973 with ***Partai Persatuan Pembangunan***. The term is a convenient category for foreign scholars rather than a precise basis for common identity on the part of devout Muslims. It began to lose its discrete quality when former President **Suharto** sought to mobilize urban Islamic elements in his own political interest during the 1990s. With his downfall and a mushrooming of Islamic-based parties, Islamic identity has served as more of a vehicle for ***Pribumi*** interests than as an indication of intra-religious divisions. Because of this, the boundaries between *Abangan* and *Santri* have become blurred owing to the complications of overlap between Islamic identity and political allegiance.
see also: Abangan; Islam; *Masyumi*; *Nahdlatul Ulama*; *Partai Persatuan Pembangunan*; *Pribumi*; Suharto.

Sarawak National Party (Malaysia)

The Sarawak National Party (SNAP) is a junior member of the federal ruling coalition, the ***Barisan Nasional*** (National Front). The party was established in March 1961 during a period of political ferment when the proposal to incorporate the British colony of Sarawak into a Federation of Malaysia was a matter of some controversy. It drew its support primarily from the Iban-Dayak community and was led by Stephen Ningkan, a former hospital assistant with Shell in Brunei, who became the first chief minister after entry into Malaysia in September 1963. His espousal of state rights and resistance to the model of Malay-Muslim dominance established in peninsular Malaysia led to his removal from office in 1966. SNAP moved into opposition but in time accommodated to the political supremacy of the minority Malay-Melanau Muslim communities. Iban-Dayak alienation at such accommodation led to defection and the breakaway ***Parti Bangsa Dayak Sarawak*** being established in 1983. The split within the Iban-Dayak community has ensured that SNAP remained a junior party in the coalition government, which was last returned to state office in September 1996. In federal elections in November 1999, SNAP held four seats, which was the same number as secured in April 1995.

In 2002, a leadership struggle split the SNAP party leadership into two factions, with one eventually forming the Sarawak Progressive Democratic Party. SNAP never recovered from this acrimonious split and its fortunes deteriorated significantly. In 2010, the party was expelled from the BN and joined the Pakatan Rakyat (PR). Disagreements with its PR partners led SNAP to exit the coalition in April 2012. SNAP failed to win any seats in the ensuing state election that month, and was deregistered in January 2013 when it failed to demonstrate that its leadership crisis had been resolved.

see also: Barisan Nasional; Pakatan Rakyat; Parti Bangsa Dayak Sarawak.

Sarawak United People's Party
(Malaysia)

The Sarawak United People's Party (SUPP) is a junior member of the ruling coalition government in the East Malaysian state of Sarawak. SUPP is also part of the federal ruling coalition, the ***Barisan Nasional*** (National Front, BN). SUPP was established in June 1959 in anticipation of municipal elections in Kuching and well before the proposal that the British colony be incorporated into a Federation of Malaysia had been mooted. Its founders were ethnic-Chinese businessmen who espoused a non-communal socialist agenda, but support for the party was along ethnic lines. Moreover, an active Communist component within the local Chinese community used SUPP as a vehicle for an abortive opposition to Sarawak's entry into Malaysia. During the 1960s, it formed part of the state opposition. But from the early 1970s, its leadership began practical collaboration with both state and federal governments, with SUPP becoming a founding member of the BN and then a member of the state ruling coalition. It still attracts Chinese support but on the basis of economic advantage through membership of the governing state coalition. Though SUPP remains a member of the BN, its performance has suffered from the swing of support away from the ruling coalition at the 2008 and 2013 federal elections. In the latter case, SUPP managed to win only one out of seven seats it contested. Similarly, at the 2011 Sarawak state elections, SUPP won only six out of the nineteen seats in which it featured.

see also: Barisan Nasional.

Sarit Thanarat, Field Marshal
(Thailand)

Sarit Thanarat was prime minister of Thailand from January 1959 until his death on 9 December 1963. He was a strong and forceful personality with an evident will to govern that commanded popular respect. During the period of political stability which he enforced as effective military dictator, the foundations were laid for Thailand's subsequent economic growth. In addition, the national standing of the monarchy was enhanced as a direct consequence of its employment by the regime to uphold its political legitimacy. Sarit Thanarat was born in the northeast of the country in 1908 and entered the Chulachomklao Royal Military Academy in Bangkok in the late 1920s. He was a junior officer at the time of the coup against the absolute monarchy in 1932. He rose steadily as an officer and was a colonel in command of an infantry battalion in Bangkok in

1947 at the time of the first coup after the Pacific War through which the military re-established its political dominance. By 1949 he had risen to the rank of lieutenant general with the key command of the First Army, charged with the defence of Bangkok, as part of an uneasy triumvirate with Field Marshal **Phibul Songkram** and the chief of police, General Phao Siyanond. Sarit and General Phao were direct rivals but when Sarit became commander-in-chief of the army in 1954, he was able to consolidate his power. He intervened to establish his dominance in September 1957 after a turbulent period of electoral politics fostered by the prime minister, Phibul. His deputy, General **Thanom Kittikachorn**, assumed the office of prime minister while Sarit went to the United States to receive medical treatment. Rumbling financial and political crises were not overcome until his return in October 1958 to launch a bloodless coup, after which he promulgated a new interim authoritarian constitution. Sarit assumed the office of prime minister in January 1959, drawing political inspiration from the recently established rule of Charles de Gaulle in France. In foreign policy, Thailand was sustained in its alliance relationship with the United States. After Sarit's death, a scandal arose over the number of wives he had taken as well as the considerable wealth that he had accumulated.

see also: Phibul Songkram, Field Marshal; Thanom Kittikachorn, Field Marshal.

Sary, Ieng (Cambodia) *see* Ieng Sary.

Scarborough Shoal Dispute (Philippines)

Consisting of a group of very small islands, rocks and reefs in the **South China Sea**, Scarborough Shoal, known to Chinese as Huangyan Island and Filipinos as Panatag Shoal, has been and continues to be the subject of a territorial dispute and source of deteriorating bilateral relations between the Philippines and China.

Both the People's Republic of China and the Republic of China (Taiwan) have claimed the islands on the historical basis that they have been their traditional fishing grounds for centuries. The shoal lies some 550 nautical miles from Hainan Island and 124 nautical miles off Zambales, which raises reasonable doubts over the logic of Chinese claim to the shoal, even though the shoal's location apparently falls within the area marked by the nine-dotted line which China has used to justify its claim to other disputed features of the South China Sea. The Philippines government has contested the legality of their claims and has publicly expressed its desire to resolve the dispute through peaceful negotiations and arbitration through the International Tribunal for the Law of the Sea. This has however been rejected by Beijing, which has insisted strongly on bilateral negotiations only.

In April 2012, tensions flared due to an attempt by the Philippines Navy to detain and arrest Chinese fishermen in the disputed waters, but they were blocked by two Chinese maritime surveillance ships that were patrolling in the vicinity. The military standoff between deployed gunboats in the area continued despite diplomatic assurances from both Beijing and Manila that all efforts were being made towards a peaceful resolution of the dispute. Relations between China and the Philippines continued to deteriorate as the latter accused the Chinese of imposing sanctions on tourism and fruit imports. While international law appears to be on the side of the Philippines, given that the UN Convention on the Law of the Sea (UNCLOS) provides for a 200 nautical mile Exclusive Economic Zone (EEZ) and continental shelf, Chinese officials have made no concessions, insisting that the issue would not be resolved until Chinese sovereignty over the shoal is recognized. In January 2013, Manila notified Beijing that it would seek international arbitration to decide on the legality of China's nine-dash line claim to the South China Sea. The dispute over the shoal became a matter of diplomatic contention between the Philippines and Cambodia at the **Phnom Penh Summit** of ASEAN (Association of Southeast Asian Nations) as well as its foreign ministers' meeting in 2012.

see also: ASEAN; Phnom Penh Summit (ASEAN), April 2012; South China Sea.

SEATO (Southeast Asia Treaty Organization) 1955–77 (Philippines/Thailand)

The Southeast Asia Treaty Organization (SEATO) was the institutional expression of the Southeast Asia Collective Defence Treaty concluded in the Manila Pact in September 1954. SEATO was established with its headquarters in Bangkok during a treaty council meeting held on 23–25 February 1955. As an organization, it initially comprised representatives of all council members, made up of all ambassadors of signatory states and a corresponding member of the Thai foreign service, a military advisers group as well as three committees concerned with economics, information and security. An international secretariat and a permanent working group of junior diplomats were set up at a council meeting in Karachi in March 1956. A meeting of military planners in Singapore in June 1956 recommended the establishment of a military planning office, which was endorsed at a council meeting in Canberra in March 1957 together with the office of secretary-general. After council meetings in Manila and Wellington in 1958 and 1959, some members declared specific military units for SEATO purposes.

Although SEATO arranged a series of military exercises, it never fulfilled an active military role, even during the **Vietnam War**. It found itself beset by internal tensions arising conspicuously from French dissidence but also from an underlying lack of common strategic interest. After the **Paris Peace Agreements** in January 1973, the organization began to be wound down because of its loss of any practical *raison d'être*. The military structure was abolished from 1 February 1974. At a council meeting held in New York on 24 September 1975, it was agreed to disband SEATO from 30 June 1977 but not to revoke the treaty on which it was based. Thailand, in particular, was keen to retain the vestigial security link with the United States.

see also: Manila Pact 1954; Paris Peace Agreements 1973.

Semangat '46 (Malaysia)

Semangat '46, which translates from Malay as the Spirit of 1946, was the name of a breakaway party from the politically dominant **UMNO** (United Malays National Organization). The schism arose from personal rivalry between the prime minister, **Mahathir Mohamad**, and the former minister of trade and industry, **Tengku Razaleigh Hamzah**, and the former deputy prime minister, **Musa Hitam**. The term Spirit of 1946 referred to the year in which UMNO was established in opposition to British constitutional revisionism and was intended to register that the breakaway group was the authentic legatee of UMNO's political values and traditions. *Semangat '46* was established in the wake of a decision by the federal High Court in February 1988 that UMNO was an unlawful society because thirty of its branches had not been properly registered when elections for highest party office were held at its General Assembly in April 1987. The party however, failed in its attempts at the 1990 and 1995 elections to unseat UMNO as the leading Malay-Muslim party in Malaysia. In October 1995, the party was formally dissolved and Tengku Razaleigh and his supporters were re-admitted to UMNO.

see also: Mahathir Mohamad, Tun; Musa Hitam, Tun; Razaleigh Hamzah, Tengku; UMNO.

Sen, Hun (Cambodia) *see* Hun Sen.

Seni Pramoj (Thailand)

Seni Pramoj enjoys the unique record of having been prime minister of Thailand in 1945 and then again for two short periods in 1975 and 1976. He was born on 26 May 1905 into a junior branch of the royal family; he is the older brother of **Kukrit Pramoj** (also prime minister 1975–6). Seni Pramoj received his main education in Britain, graduating in law from Worcester College, Oxford. He practised as a lawyer and entered the judiciary before heading Thailand's legation in Washington in 1940 as minister. In that capacity, he refused to communicate Thailand's declaration of war against the Allies made at Japan's insistence. In Washington he assumed the role of leader of the overseas Free Thai Movement; after the war he was briefly prime minister and foreign minister in interim governments before the restoration of a shortlived parliamentary democracy. He served as minister of justice in the **Democrat Party** cabinet led by Khuang Abhaiwongse during 1947–8 until it was overthrown by the military. Seni Pramoj returned to the practice of law but retained his association with the Democrat Party, becoming its leader after the death of Khuang in 1968. He re-entered Parliament in 1969, and during the democratic restoration from October 1973 until October 1976, he served for two periods as prime minister, leaving office first through electoral reverse and secondly through the military coup following the **Thammasat University Massacre**. He resigned as leader of the Democrat Party in 1979 and then retired from public life. He died on 28 July 1997 at the age of ninety-two.

see also: Democrat Party; Kukrit Pramoj; Thammasat University Massacre 1976.

Shan (Myanmar)

The Shan indigenous minority inhabit a hilly plateau of about 150,000 square kilometres or a quarter of the country in the eastern part of Myanmar which borders the People's Republic of China, Laos and Thailand. They share a cultural and linguistic affiliation with the people of Thailand and adhere to the Theravada branch of Buddhism. Under British administration, the traditional political system of rule by *Sawbwa* (hereditary princes) was made part of the colonial structure. The traditional leadership agreed to membership of a Shan state within the Union of Burma with the **Panglong Agreement** of 1947. The Shan did not join in the separatist challenge to the Union until 1959 after an attempt was made to remove the powers of their traditional leadership. A Shan States Army fought in an insurgency against the government in Rangoon until 1989, when a ceasefire agreement was reached with the ruling **State Law and Order Restoration Council** (SLORC). The Shan State Nationalities Liberation Organization formally abandoned its armed struggle against the Yangon government in October 1994. Insurgent activity continued under the leadership of the drug baron Khun Sa, but in June 1995 his Mong Tai Army split and a separate Shan State National Army resumed the insurgency. In December 2011, a ceasefire agreement was signed between the Shan State Army and the Myanmar government, but sporadic clashes have continued.

see also: Panglong Agreement; State Law and Order Restoration Council.

Shwe Mann (Myanmar)

Shwe Mann is the speaker of the Pyuthu Hluttaw, Myanmar's lower house of Parliament. A former general, Shwe Mann was born on 11 July 1947 at Kanyuntkwin in Bago Division. He attended the Defence Services Academy as part of Intake 11, graduating in 1969 as a second lieutenant. He rose steadily through the ranks, becoming a major in 1988 and later a battalion commander. He earned the honorific, 'Thura', in 1989 for bravery during operations against the Karen National Liberation Army. In 2000 he was promoted to major general. In November 2001 he became coordinator of Special Operations, a position that placed him in control of all military operations in Myanmar through the Bureau of Special Operations. In 2003 he was promoted to general. Shwe Mann rose to become a leading figure in the **State Peace and Development Council** and joint chief of staff of the Myanmar Armed Forces, eventually becoming the third-highest ranking member before resigning to contest elections as a civilian in 2010. He is widely respected in the military and among his soldiers for his service on the frontline. A protégé of **Than Shwe**, he was often seen as a likely successor to the position of commander of Myanmar's Armed Forces and leader of the military junta. He was made speaker of the Pyuthu Hluttaw on 31 January 2011 after winning his seat at the November 2010 election. In May 2011, he replaced **Thein Sein** as the leader of the **Union Solidarity and Development Party**.

Although a former high-ranking general and third-ranked member of the previous military regime who was close to Than Shwe, Shwe Mann has become a noted reformer who has developed good relations with **Aung San Suu Kyi**. On 7 February 2012, he acknowledged the issue of corruption at all levels of government during an address to the Pyuthu Hluttaw, a move seen as a significant step in the reform process underway in Myanmar politics. Shwe

Mann harbours political ambitions, and has expressed his intention to run for the presidency in 2015.

see also: Aung San Suu Kyi; State Peace and Development Council; Than Shwe, Senior General; Thein Sein; Union Solidarity and Development Party.

Sihamoni, King Norodom (Cambodia)

Norodom Sihamoni succeeded his father, King **Norodom Sihanouk**, as the King of Cambodia after the latter relinquished his title in 2004. Born in 1953, the year in which Cambodia gained independence, Norodom Sihamoni spent much of his formative and adult years abroad, first in Czechoslovakia where he completed high school and at the National Conservatory in Prague, where he pursued his passion for music and dance. He then moved to North Korea briefly to study filmmaking, an enthusiasm that his father, King Sihanouk also shared. He later returned to Cambodia when the **Khmer Rouge** regime came to power, and was placed under house arrest in the royal palace together with most of his family. When the Vietnamese invaded and toppled the Khmer Rouge regime in 1979, Sihamoni left for Paris where he taught classical dance and ballet for almost a decade. In 1993, he was selected as the Cambodian representative to UNESCO, a post he held until early 2004.

Shortly after Sihanouk's abdication, Sihamoni was elected by a nine-member Throne Council to the largely ceremonial role as King of Cambodia. A relatively unknown figure prior to his father's abdication, it has been suggested that his political neutrality and lack of controversy might have been the reason behind his selection as his father's successor, who during his reign had frequent confrontations with Prime Minister **Hun Sen** and his government. As King of Cambodia and with a flair for the performing arts, Sihamoni championed the revival of Cambodian cultural life after years of war and deprivation.

Recently, observers and close aides have suggested that, given Hun Sen's control over the royal family, Sihamoni has increasingly become a prisoner in his own palace. Sihamoni is constantly and closely surrounded by government officials both inside the palace and when he is out on rare visits to the countryside. Although the constitution bestows on him many rights and powers, Sihamoni has not exercised them in order to avoid antagonizing the government. The government has denied this, and maintains that the king continues to play an important role through providing recommendations on government policies and in particular on judicial, social and religious issues.

see also: Hun Sen; Khmer Rouge; Sihanouk, King Norodom.

Sihanouk, King Norodom (Cambodia)

Norodom Sihanouk was a dominating figure in the political life of Cambodia from the mid-1940s. As one of the great survivors of post-colonial politics in Southeast Asia, he drew his staying power from a tradition of divine monarchy, a unique flamboyant personality, and the failure of Cambodian regimes to transcend an endemic factionalism. He has to be regarded as a flawed personality, in part responsible for the tragedy that has befallen post-colonial Cambodia. His patriotism was always fused with an intense personal vanity which affected his judgement and prompted erratic behaviour.

Prince Sihanouk was born on 31 October 1922 to parents drawn from both the senior and junior wings of the royal family and received his secondary education at a French lycée in Saigon. In April 1941, after the death of King Sisowath Monivong, the colonial authorities decided to revert to the Norodom branch of the royal family because they judged that the young Sihanouk would make a malleable monarch. Initially he proved to be an accommodating figure in dealing in turn with representatives of Vichy France, Imperial Japan and Free France. That judgement was shown to be misplaced after the Pacific War, when King Sihanouk played the nationalist card to the political disadvantage not only of the French but of contending republican and social-revolutionary groupings. In June 1952 he assumed the office of prime minister, committing himself to achieving independence within three years. In February 1953 he embarked on a world tour in a successful attempt to embarrass the French into granting his political demands. He returned in triumph from a contrived internal exile in westerly Battambang Province to the capital, Phnom Penh, on 8 November 1953 to announce national independence. That independence was confirmed in 1954 by the **Geneva Agreements on Indochina**, which also imposed obligations on Cambodia to conduct internationally observed free elections. In March 1955, in order to escape the constraints of constitutional monarchy and to out-manoeuvre his political opponents, King Sihanouk abdicated his throne in favour of his father, Norodom Suramarit. He then set up a national front, ***Sangkum Reastre Niyum*** (Popular Socialist Community), which captured all seats in the National Assembly in elections in September 1955.

Prince Sihanouk then dominated Cambodian politics in a wilful and self-indulgent manner intolerant of any dissent until his overthrow in 1970. When his father died in 1960, Prince Sihanouk had himself created head of state in a monarchy without a monarch. He was overthrown in March 1970 by a coup which was justified by a failure to remove a Vietnamese Communist presence from the eastern parts of the country. Prince Sihanouk had been a pioneer of the foreign policy of non-alignment. He attended the **Asian–African Conference** at Bandung in Indonesia in April 1955 where his meeting with the People's Republic of China's prime minister, Zhou En-lai, served to convince him that non-alignment offered the best safeguard for Cambodia's security against neighbouring historical antagonists, both of whom were allied with the United States. Prince Sihanouk went on to reject the gratuitous protection of the **Manila Pact** of 1954 and committed his country to a foreign policy described as neutrality. Initially that policy coincided with conventional non-alignment but with the growing success of Communist insurgency in neighbouring South Vietnam, Prince Sihanouk revised the practice of neutrality to one of political accommodation to both North Vietnam and China. Toleration of Vietnamese Communist use of Cambodian territory as an active sanctuary from which to prosecute their revolutionary war against the Saigon regime provided an opportunity for his political opponents to move against him.

Prince Sihanouk was in Moscow on 18 March 1970 when he was deposed by the incumbent government in Phnom Penh headed by General **Lon Nol**. He continued a pre-arranged journey to Beijing where he joined the Vietnamese Communist prime minister, **Pham Van Dong**, to promote an opposition united front with a group of Cambodian insurgents whom Prince Sihanouk had dubbed the **Khmer Rouge**. In May 1970 he set up a government in exile with his new-found political partners and lent his name and authority to the cause of **Pol Pot**. With the victory of the Khmer Rouge in April 1975, he was reinstated as head of state but remained outside of Cambodia until the end of the year, except for a brief and disturbing visit in September. In Cambodia, Prince Sihanouk and his wife Monique lived under effective house arrest, while six of his fourteen children and a number of his grandchildren perished at Khmer Rouge hands. In April 1976, with the promulgation of the constitution for a republican **Democratic Kampuchea**, he resigned as head of state.

Coincident with Vietnam's invasion of Cambodia in December 1978, Prince Sihanouk was flown to Beijing on a Chinese aircraft and from there travelled to New York, where he denounced Vietnam's intervention before the General Assembly of the United Nations. He then went into exile in North Korea with whose late leader Kim Il Sung he had established a close rapport. A small resistance group loyal to him was set up among refugees along the border with Thailand and were organized into **FUNCINPEC** (the French acronym for the National United Front for an Independent, Neutral, Peaceful and Cooperative Cambodia). In June 1982 Prince Sihanouk was persuaded after much external pressure to become president of a so-called **Coalition Government of Democratic Kampuchea** (CGDK) comprising his Khmer Rouge tormentors and a non-Communist resistance movement of republican disposition. During the course of the 1980s he was able to transform his initial figurehead position into one of renewed political importance as the Vietnamese were obliged to withdraw effective support from the government which they had implanted in Phnom Penh. Towards the end of the decade, he resigned his office and began bilateral but abortive negotiations with its prime minister, **Hun Sen**. The failure of an **International Conference on Cambodia** in Paris in 1989 led to a major political initiative under the aegis of the permanent members of the United Nations Security Council, who concluded a framework agreement on a peace settlement in August 1990. Prince Sihanouk was seen as central to its successful application as the head of a symbolic repository of sovereignty, the **Supreme National Council**, which would delegate administrative responsibility to the United Nations in an interim period before elections were conducted to decide the political future of the country. That settlement was endorsed by a second stage of the **International Conference on Cambodia** in Paris in October 1991 and in the following month Prince Sihanouk returned to Cambodia after an absence of almost thirteen years to be reinstalled as head of state.

The Cambodian peace settlement was based on fragile political assumptions about the contending parties' commitment to national reconciliation. Although Prince Sihanouk was greeted on his return as a national saviour, all factions sought to exploit his personal standing. In failing health and lacking his former energy, he retreated to China and North Korea in periodic bouts of despair as Cambodia seemed to lapse into anarchy. Nevertheless, he was reinstated as King of Cambodia on 24 September 1993 at the age of seventy and in poor health, forty years after he abdicated the throne, by the coalition government of FUNCINPEC and the Cambodian People's Party. After his reinstatement as monarch, King Sihanouk returned to Beijing to receive treatment for prostate cancer. He reappeared in Phnom Penh in April 1994 and displayed some of his old political vigour in an attempt to effect an accommodation between the new coalition government and the Khmer Rouge, but to no avail. He went back to Beijing for more medical treatment in mid-May 1994 and also to demonstrate his continuing indispensability to stable government in Cambodia, pointing up the likely political vacuum that would be left with his departure from the scene. He returned to Cambodia at the beginning of 1995 without assuming an active political role. He stood above the growing rivalry between his son and Second Prime Minister Hun Sen and was publicly equivocal in response to the bloody coup in July 1997 which ousted Prince Ranariddh from senior political office. However, he did threaten to abdicate in an indication of the importance of his constitutional role to Hun Sen's consolidation of power. King Sihanouk went on to broker an agreement between Prince Ranariddh and Hun Sen initially by authorizing an amnesty for Prince Ranariddh who had been sentenced to thirty-five years' imprisonment for arms trafficking and negotiating clandestinely with the Khmer Rouge. When his son was relegated to the ceremonial role of chairman of the National Assembly after the July 1998 election, King Sihanouk readily accommodated himself to his son's political displacement, which indicated the nature of the filial relationship and also a characteristic disposition to defer to superior power. King Sihanouk died on 15 October 2012 in Beijing at the age of ninety.

see also: Asian–African Conference, Bandung 1955; Cambodian People's Party; Democratic Kampuchea; Democratic Kampuchea, Coalition Government of; FUNCINPEC; Geneva Agreements on Indochina 1954; Hun Sen; International Conference on Cambodia, Paris 1991; Khmer Rouge; Manila Pact 1954; Nol, Lon; Pham Van Dong; Pol Pot; Ranariddh, Prince Norodom; *Sangkum Reastre Niyum*; Supreme National Council; United Nations: Cambodia 1991–3; UNTAC.

Sin, Cardinal Jaime (Philippines)

Cardinal Jaime Sin, Archbishop of Manila, was head of the Roman Catholic Church in the Philippines from May 1976 to September 2003. He was born on 31 August 1928 in New Washington in Capiz Province on Panay Island in the central Philippines. Ordained in 1954, his early career was spent in the provincial ministry. He was surprised in January 1974 to be transferred from the archdiocese of Jaro to that of Manila. He achieved political prominence as an outspoken critic of the government of President **Ferdinand Marcos** and of the self-indulgence of his wife, **Imelda Marcos**. Long before the assassination of the opposition leader **Benigno Aquino** in August 1983, which marked a turning point in Filipino politics, Cardinal Sin had drawn public attention to growing poverty, corruption and the gross violation of human rights. After Aquino's death, he articulated the moral outrage of the Filipino people and encouraged public challenge to Marcos in the hope of promoting political reform.

Cardinal Sin was not a radical in politics and was never an enthusiast for liberation theology. His self-styled stance of 'critical collaboration' towards the Marcos administration indicated an evident ambivalence. That ambivalence arose from concern that exhortation to confrontation might unleash revolutionary forces to which the Church, as well as the state, might fall victim. He was influenced by the role which Buddhist monks had played in undermining the government of **Ngo Dinh Diem** in South Vietnam, so assisting the ultimate seizure of power by the Communists. Apprehension that the Communists might secure advantage from Marcos' decaying political system moved him to persuade **Corazón Aquino**, the widow of Benigno, to stand for president against Marcos in the snap election of February 1986. When conspicuous fraud resulted in military revolt led by **Juan Ponce Enrile** and **Fidel Ramos**, Cardinal Sin encouraged the mobilization and interposition of massive popular support, '**People Power**', which prevented Marcos from employing military force in order to cling on to power. He stood by Corazón Aquino on her elevation to high office but also made known his disappointment when her new government showed itself to be less than competent in addressing the fundamental economic and social ills of the Philippines. Cardinal Sin did not appear to welcome with enthusiasm the election of Fidel Ramos as the first Protestant president of the Philippines in May 1992 and opposed his efforts to promote birth control. In 2001, Cardinal Sin reprised his 1986 role and took an active part in the mobilization against President **Joseph Estrada** that culminated in the **EDSA II** revolt. It was later revealed that he had done this against the exhortations of the Vatican to remain non-partisan. Jaime Sin died on 21 June 2005 at the age of seventy-six.

see also: Aquino, Benigno; Aquino, Corazón; Diem, Ngo Dinh; EDSA II; Enrile, Juan Ponce; Estrada, Joseph; Marcos, Ferdinand; Marcos, Imelda; People Power; Ramos, Fidel.

Singapore Strait (Indonesia/Malaysia/Singapore)

The Singapore Strait is a constricted and congested waterway situated south of the island of Singapore and the southeastern tip of peninsular Malaysia and north of Indonesia's Riau Islands. Its length is approximately seventy miles. The narrowest land width is 3.2 miles; the narrowest breadth of navigable waters is 1.8 miles. At its most westerly point, the Singapore Strait merges with the Malacca Strait. At its corresponding easterly point, the strait merges with the **South China Sea**. Together with the linked **Malacca Strait**, the Singapore Strait was subject to a controversial joint statement on 16 November 1971 by Indonesia and Malaysia which challenged the customary legal regime in the context of making provision for safety of navigation. Singapore, which was a party to the provision, registered its reservations to that challenge. In the event, the three coastal states worked out a scheme for traffic separation in the linked straits on 24 February 1977 which was accepted by the maritime powers within the context of a new regime for straits used for international navigation. That regime was incorporated in the United Nations Convention on the Law of the Sea promulgated on 10 December 1982, which also recognized Indonesia's **Archipelago Declaration of 1957**.

The territorial sea boundary between Singapore and Indonesia was delimited in a treaty which was concluded on 25 May 1973. At its points of ingress and egress, the Singapore Strait is commanded by Indonesian and Malaysian territorial waters. A treaty concluded between Indonesia and Malaysia in July 1982 delimited the territorial sea boundary between the two countries, recognizing as a consequence the archipelagic status of the former. A dispute obtained between Malaysia and Singapore over the island of Pedra Branca (Singapore usage) or Pulau Batu Puteh (Malaysian usage) on which is situated the **Horsburgh Lighthouse**, which has been administered from Singapore since its construction in the mid-nineteenth century. The island is bounded by Malaysian and Indonesian waters but lies close to the middle of the navigable channel at the eastern egress of the Singapore Strait. The dispute was settled by the International Court of Justice in May 2008 which awarded the island (along with Horsburgh Lighthouse) to Singapore.

see also: Archipelago Declaration 1957; Horsburgh Lighthouse; Malacca Strait; South China Sea.

Singapore Summit (ASEAN) 1992

(Brunei/Indonesia/Malaysia/Philippines/Singapore/Thailand)

The fourth meeting of heads of government of **ASEAN** (Association of Southeast Asian Nations) convened in Singapore on 27 and 28 January 1992. The Summit took place in the wake of the **International Conference on Cambodia** in Paris in October 1991, which agreed a comprehensive political settlement of the Cambodian conflict. That conflict had engaged the corporate energies of ASEAN for more than a decade, enhancing the reputation of the Association as a diplomatic community. At issue at the Summit was the ability of ASEAN to demonstrate a renewal of its terms of cooperation, especially in economic matters. To that end, the six heads of government agreed to set up **AFTA** (ASEAN Free Trade Area) using their established Common Effective Preferential Scheme as the main mechanism within a timeframe of fifteen years beginning from 1 January 1993. A Malaysian initiative to establish an East Asian Economic Caucus exclusive of the United States and Australia failed to attract a consensus, with Indonesia opposed in particular. Adherence to ASEAN's Treaty of Amity and Cooperation by regional non-members was welcomed and a declaratory commitment to a regional **ZOPFAN** (Zone of Peace, Freedom and Neutrality) was reaffirmed, but security cooperation was not advanced in any substance. It was agreed, however, that external dialogues in political and security matters should be intensified by using the vehicle of the ASEAN post-ministerial conferences, which was undertaken from July 1992 in Manila. The heads of government agreed to meet formally every three years with informal meetings in between in a significant change from past practice. An important symbolic innovation was the decision to redesignate the secretary-general of the ASEAN Secretariat as the secretary-general of ASEAN with an enlarged mandate to initiate, advise, coordinate and implement ASEAN activities.

see also: AFTA; ASEAN; International Conference on Cambodia, Paris 1991; Treaty of Amity and Cooperation 1976; ZOPFAN.

Singapore Summit (ASEAN) 2007

(Brunei/Cambodia/Indonesia/Laos/Malaysia/Myanmar/Philippines/Singapore/Thailand/Vietnam)

The thirteenth meeting of heads of government of **ASEAN** (Association of Southeast Asian Nations) convened in Singapore from 18 to 22 November 2007 on the occasion of ASEAN's fortieth anniversary. Foremost of the achievements at the Summit was the signing of the **ASEAN Charter**, a historic agreement that would provide a legal and institutional framework for ASEAN as it committed itself to further strengthening community-building in the region. The Charter was drafted by a High Level Task Force (HLTF) consisting of senior government officials from each member state which had been established at the previous summit in Cebu. The Charter would be declared to have come into effect on the thirtieth day after it had been ratified in all member states and the tenth instrument of ratification deposited with the secretary-general of ASEAN. Under the Charter, ASEAN would acquire a legal personality distinct from that of its member states. Foreign ministers would form an ASEAN Coordinating Council (ACC) with the responsibility to prepare for meetings and implement decisions. The ASEAN Charter also provides for the convening of ASEAN summits twice a year instead of once a year. Provisions were also included for the establishment of an ASEAN human rights body.

Notwithstanding the monumental significance of the Charter's signing, the summit itself was overshadowed by Myanmar's bloody

suppression of demonstrations led by Buddhist monks during the **Saffron Revolution** just two months earlier. The decision to go ahead with the signing of the Charter led to criticisms, and questions were raised over the credibility of the document and, in particular, ASEAN's professed objectives to strengthen democratic accountability and the protection of human rights. While a collective decision was made to issue a strong statement condemning the violent clampdown in Myanmar, ASEAN was compelled to cancel a scheduled briefing by the UN envoy to Myanmar, Ibrahim Gambari, after Myanmar protested.
see also: ASEAN; ASEAN Charter; Saffron Revolution 2007.

Sipadan–Ligitan (Indonesia/Malaysia)

Sipadan is located in the Celebes Sea parallel to the eastern boundary between Malaysian Sabah and Indonesian Kalimantan. Together with the nearby reef of Ligitan, both islands were the subject of competing claims between Malaysia and Indonesia. Both based their respective claims on colonial agreements and documents, including an Anglo-Dutch boundary convention of 1891. The issue of jurisdiction arose when both states extended their territorial seas from three to twelve nautical miles. Malaysia's occupation dates from the formation of the Federation in 1963 when its troops were deployed to cope with Indonesia's **Confrontation**. In the early 1980s Indonesian patrol vessels were deployed to investigate reports of occupation by Malaysian troops, allegedly in violation of an understanding to avoid unilateral action in advance of negotiations. Indonesia has challenged Malaysia's occupation through recurrent acts of military display and in negotiations between heads of governments and officials. In September 1994, Indonesia rejected Malaysia's proposal that the dispute be referred to third-party arbitration but relented when their heads of government met again in October 1996. In May 1997, senior officials from both states concluded a draft agreement on submitting their contending claims to the International Court of Justice (ICJ) but Malaysia insisted on administering the islands until a judicial decision was forthcoming. At the end of April 2000, 21 people, including 10 foreign tourists, were abducted from Sipadan where Malaysia had built a diving resort, by armed Muslim insurgents from the Philippines. On 17 December 2002 the ICJ ruled by sixteen votes in favour of recognizing Malaysian sovereignty over Sipadan and Ligitan. While the ruling has periodically drawn a backlash from the Indonesian public, Jakarta has accepted the ICJ decision.
see also: Confrontation.

Sisón, José María (Philippines)

José María Sisón provided the intellectual vision in the reconstitution of the Communist Party of the Philippines which took place during a so-called 'Congress of Re-establishment' in Pangasinan Province between 26 December 1968 and 7 January 1969. He was responsible for drafting the new party's constitution which acknowledged the supreme guidance of Mao Tse Tung and also assumed the post of chairman. Sisón took the name Amado Guerrero (Beloved Warrior). In 1970, under that name, he wrote *Philippine Society and Revolution*, which served as the theoretical text for the party. Sisón was born on 8 February 1939 into a middle-income family in Ilocos Sur Province. He was educated at the University of the Philippines and became a leading activist in student politics as well as a member of the Communist Party. He began his career on the staff of the Manila Lyceum School of Journalism in 1954 where he helped to form the *Kabataan Makabayan* (KM: Patriotic Youth) which was a stridently anti-American nationalist movement. Sisón was expelled from the Communist Party in April 1967 because of his personal assertiveness and rejection of discipline. He then established an alternative politburo with inspiration from China's Cultural Revolution, which led on to his initiative for an alternative party. His small group of student radicals joined up with Bernabe Buscayno, who provided the leadership for the military wing of the party which was established on 29 March 1969 as the **New People's Army**. Sisón was captured by security forces in November 1977. He remained in prison until after the fall of President **Ferdinand Marcos**, when he was released in March 1986 by the new government of President **Corazón Aquino**. Sisón then established the People's Party to exploit so-called democratic space but with his colleagues misjudged the popular mood and failed to secure congressional representation in elections in May. He left the Philippines at the end of 1987 to take up residence in the Netherlands where he was granted political asylum and permitted to work for the National Democratic Front, which had long maintained its European office in Utrecht. Sisón continued to assert a leadership role in exile, pressing for a continuation of the initially successful strategy of peasant-based guerrilla war. In October 1988 a warrant was issued in the Philippines for Sisón's arrest after it had become known that he had resumed in exile the leadership of the Communist Party. He was involved in negotiations in Utrecht with representatives of the government in Manila in September 1992, but lost his role with a further split within the Communist Party which repudiated his leadership.

As a result of lobbying by the Philippines government, Sisón was blacklisted as a terrorist by the US and Netherlands governments, and then by the Council of Europe in 2002. Nevertheless, a decision to freeze his assets in Europe was reversed by the European Union General Court. In August 2007, Sisón was arrested by the International Crime Investigation Team of the Netherlands National Crime Investigation Department and detained for two weeks. He was charged along with other rebel leaders with three counts of murder in the Philippines – of Congressman Rodolfo in 2001 and two police officials following a rebel raid on a police station in 2002. Given that there was no extradition request, the trial was held in the Netherlands, where Sisón entered a plea of not guilty. The validity of the Netherlands' jurisdiction over the cases was questionable, given the fact that they had already been dismissed in July that year by the Philippine Supreme Court. On 13 September 2007 Sisón was released from jail for reasons of insufficient evidence. Several subsequent attempts by prosecutors to appeal the decision were denied. Sisón is currently the chief political consultant of the **National Democratic Front** (NDF).

see also: Aquino, Corazón; Marcos, Ferdinand; National Democratic Front; New People's Army.

Sjahrir, Sutan (Indonesia)

Sutan Sjahrir was the first prime minister of the revolutionary Republic of Indonesia, assuming office in November 1945. He was born in west Sumatra on 5 March 1909 and after showing great promise at secondary school went to the Netherlands to study law in Leiden. He returned to the Netherlands East Indies in 1931 at the suggestion of his more senior fellow-student **Mohammad Hatta** to help in organizing a new nationalist party, which he sought to infuse with socialist convictions. He was arrested in 1934 and sent into internal exile, first to New Guinea and then to Banda. During the Japanese occupation, he refused to collaborate and organized a small resistance movement whose members formed the core of the postwar Indonesian Socialist Party which he led. His anti-Japanese credentials were the key to his appointment as prime minister because of **Sukarno**'s taint of collaboration in the eyes of the Dutch and the western powers. Syahrir was an advocate of negotiations as the way to attain independence, which became a controversial strategy as the Dutch sought to re-establish their colonial dominion by force. He was displaced in June 1947 and then pleaded Indonesia's case before the United Nations but never again held public office. After independence, he became a marginal political figure despite a following of like-minded and gifted young people who came under the spell of his intelligence and personality. He led the Socialist Party but it went into decline after securing only two per cent of the vote in the first national elections in 1955. Syahrir was arrested in 1962 on suspicion of involvement in regional rebellion, but when his health deteriorated in 1965, he was permitted to leave the country for medical attention in Switzerland, where he died in April 1966. His political vision was set out in a pamphlet entitled 'Our Struggle' published in October 1945.

see also: Guided Democracy; Hatta, Mohammad; Sukarno.

Somchai Wongsawat (Thailand)

Born in Nakhon Si Thammarat in 1947, Somchai Wongsawat was prime minister of Thailand for the brief but turbulent period from September to December 2008. A distinguished civil servant, Somchai entered politics in 2007 when he joined the **People's Power Party** (PPP) as deputy leader during the height of popular protests by the **People's Alliance for Democracy** (PAD) against the party, which was seen as a vestige of the **Thaksin Shinawatra** government through which he continued to assert influence in national affairs. Somchai's short-lived government continued the populist policies that defined the terms of Thaksin and his immediate successor, **Samak Sundaravej**, whom Somchai replaced in September 2008 after a brief period as acting prime minister. In response, the PAD escalated their campaign against the PPP. In October 2008 the PAD blockaded parliament in an attempt to prevent Somchai from presenting the new government's policy statement. The ensuing crackdown by the police led to two deaths and numerous injuries. The PAD later also took over Bangkok's airports in an attempt to block Somchai's return from an overseas trip. In December that year, Somchai and his government were forced to step down after the PPP was found guilty of electoral fraud. Seen as a gentle and soft-spoken leader whose personal demeanour might have been able to heal the rift between the government he led and the PAD, Somchai Wongsawat was never able to shake off the baggage of his personal and political ties with Thaksin, his brother-in-law.

see also: People's Alliance for Democracy; People's Power Party; Samak Sundaravej; Thaksin Shinawatra.

Son Sann (Cambodia)

Son Sann was the leader of the republican-inclined **Khmer People's National Liberation Front** (KPNLF) which was established in October 1979 in opposition to the **Khmer Rouge** and the incumbent People's Republic of Kampuchea (PRK). He was born on 5 October 1911 in Phnom Penh to a family originating from southern Vietnam. Son Sann was educated in France, where he graduated in 1933 from the School for Advanced Commercial Studies. On his return to Cambodia, he served as deputy governor of the provinces of Battambang and Prey Veng in the French administration. After the Pacific War, Son Sann held a series of senior government offices beginning with finance minister; in 1954, as foreign minister, he represented Cambodia at the conference leading to the **Geneva Agreements on Indochina**. He became the first governor of Cambodia's National Bank in 1955, holding that position until 1968 and serving concurrently as prime minister during 1967–8. He was never in tune politically with Prince **Norodom Sihanouk** but after Sihanouk's overthrow in 1970, Son Sann left Cambodia to take up residence in Paris, where he was living when the Khmer Rouge seized power in 1975. As leader of the KPNLF, he took his movement in June 1982 into the **Coalition Government of Democratic Kampuchea** (CGDK), in which he held the office of prime minister. Poor military performance by the KPNLF led to dissension within its ranks but Son Sann, who attracted respect for his personal probity, held on to its political leadership. He took a hard line towards the incumbent government in Phnom Penh and was a party to the negotiations which culminated in a political settlement at the **International Conference on Cambodia** in Paris in October 1991. He returned to Cambodia in December 1991 and then transformed the KPNLF into the Buddhist Liberal Democratic Party for the elections in May 1993 under United Nations auspices. His party won only ten out of the 120 seats in the Constituent Assembly. Son Sann was elected its chairman and supervised its role in drafting a new constitution, which was promulgated in September. After the re-establishment of the constitutional monarchy, Son Sann retired from public life, giving up his chair of the National Assembly to Chea Sim. He lost his position as party president to the minister of information, Ieng Mouly, in July 1995. He subsequently set up his own Son Sann Party which contested elections in July 1998 without success. Following this, he took the Son Sann Party into alliance with **FUNCINPEC**. Son Sann died from heart failure in Paris in December 2000 at the age of eighty-nine.

see also: Democratic Kampuchea, Coalition Government of; FUNCINPEC; Geneva Agreements on Indochina 1954; International Conference on Cambodia, Paris 1991; Khmer People's National Liberation Front; Khmer Rouge; Sihanouk, King Norodom.

Son Sen (Cambodia)

Son Sen assumed the post of supreme commander of the insurgent national army of **Democratic Kampuchea** on the ostensible retirement of **Pol Pot** in August 1985. He was removed from that position some time after the Paris peace agreements following the **International Conference on Cambodia** in October 1991 because of contention among the **Khmer Rouge** leadership over complying with its provisions; but was reported as having been reinstated to senior command in April 1994. Son Sen was born in 1930 in southern Vietnam among the settled Cambodian minority. He was educated in Phnom Penh and then in the 1950s in Paris, where he became a member of a Marxist group of Cambodian students at whose centre was Saloth Sar (Pol Pot). On his return to Cambodia, he became director of studies at the National Teaching Institute as well as a leading member of the reconstituted Communist Party of Cambodia. He fled from the capital in 1963 to escape from Prince **Norodom Sihanouk**'s secret police and is believed to have spent time in Hanoi. By 1971 he had become chief of staff of the Cambodian People's National Liberation Armed Forces engaged in challenging the government in Phnom Penh headed by **Lon Nol**. After the Khmer Rouge seized power in April 1975, he became a deputy prime minister and minister of defence until the Vietnamese invasion at the end of 1978. He continued in that role in directing the military challenge of the ousted Khmer Rouge against the Vietnamese occupation and the government established in Phnom Penh. He was a party to the political machinery set up to implement the political settlement for Cambodia and was a Khmer Rouge member of the **Supreme National Council** in Phnom Penh until April 1993, when its delegation withdrew in protest at the forthcoming elections. At one time regarded as the fourth-ranking member of the Khmer Rouge hierarchy, he is believed to have engaged in factional rivalry with Pol Pot and to have been implicated in the murder of a British university teacher, Malcolm Caldwell, in Phnom Penh in December 1978. He was also in overall charge of the infamous **Tuol Sleng** interrogation centre. Son Sen was murdered on 10 June 1997, together with his wife and his nine children, on the instructions of Pol Pot after he had refused to attend a meeting at which the Khmer Rouge leader would have insisted on a continuation of armed struggle and on opposing a compromise deal with the government in Phnom Penh.

see also: Democratic Kampuchea; International Conference on Cambodia, Paris 1991; Khmer Rouge; Nol, Lon; Pol Pot; Sihanouk, King Norodom; Supreme National Council; Tuol Sleng.

Sondhi Limthongkul (Thailand)

Sondhi Limthongkul is a media mogul cum politician and leader of the **People's Alliance for Democracy** (PAD). Sondhi was born in Bangkok on 7 November 1947 to Chinese immigrant parents. He earned a bachelor's degree in history in 1969 from the University of California – Los Angeles, where he was also a reporter on the student newspaper, and completed an MA at Utah State University in 1972. He returned to Thailand and worked as a reporter and editor for several publications, setting up his own company in 1979. In 1982, Sondhi established *Phoojakarn* (*The Manager*), a business monthly that would eventually become a weekly, and later *Phoojakarn Rai Wan* (*Manager Daily*), a daily newspaper which would become his personal mouthpiece. Eventually, he set up the Manager Group, a publishing house and holding company for his numerous media outlets. Sondhi also branched into other markets including information technology and satellite television through a complex network of holding companies. His media outlets played a significant role in opposing military rule during the crackdown on pro-democracy protestors during May 1992.

The election of **Thaksin Shinawatra** in 2001 put several of Sondhi's associates in advantageous positions that allowed him to emerge from the brink of bankruptcy after his business empire unravelled during the 1997 **Asian Financial Crisis**, and Sondhi became a vocal supporter of Thaksin. This relationship soured in 2004 when, among other things, Sondhi's banker was forced out of a senior position at a major Thai bank in 2004 over problem loans, including Sondhi's. Sondhi began criticizing the Thaksin government through his media outlets in 2005. The government retaliated by cancelling Sondhi's weekly television show, but he switched to broadcasting over the internet and his popularity grew. Sondhi's criticism of Thaksin increasingly took on royalist overtones. A series of outdoor political talk shows hosted by Sondhi together with his broadcasts drew tens of thousands of protestors and became the focus for the formation of the new **People's Alliance for Democracy**, co-organized by Sondhi and aimed at removing the Thaksin government. A massive protest was called for 20 September 2006, but was called off due to the coup which ousted the Thaksin government and forced the prime minister into exile the day before. The PAD disbanded with Sondhi publicly supportive of the coup and continuing his criticism of Thaksin. When the **People's Power Party** (PPP) formed a government after a strong election win in December 2007, the PAD reformed in protest at what it considered a Thaksin proxy government. Sondhi was again at the forefront of the movement demanding the resignations of successive prime ministers, **Samak Sundaravej** and **Somchai Wongsawat**. He devoted much media time to the protests and was again a frequent speaker at demonstrations. In 2008, Sondhi together with other leaders led PAD supporters to occupy Government House for several months and later seize Suvarnabhumi International Airport. The protests ended with the Constitutional Court's dissolution of the PPP. On 17 April 2009, Sondhi narrowly avoided serious injury in an assassination attempt. It was never made public who carried out the attack. In June 2009, the New Politics Party was created as the political party of the PAD with Sondhi elected leader in October 2009. In 2011, infighting over the direction of the party resulted in Sondhi leaving the party and its effective dissolution.

see also: Asian Financial Crisis 1997–8; People's Alliance for Democracy; People's Power Party; Samak Sundaravej; Somchai Wongsawat; Thaksin Shinawatra.

Sonthi Boonyaratglin, General

(Thailand)

A former commander-in-chief of the Royal Thai Army, Sonthi Boonyaratglin was a major player behind the 2006 *coup d'état* and subsequently headed the ruling Council for National Security. Sonthi was born in the northeast Ubon Ratchathani province on 2 October 1946. He graduated from the Armed Forces Academies Preparatory School with Class 6 and went on to Chulachomklao Royal Military Academy, graduating in 1969 with Class 17. Sonthi served in the infantry and later the Special Forces, eventually commanding the Special Warfare Command. In August 2004, Sonthi was appointed deputy army commander, and was promoted to commander on October 2005. Sonthi's appointment made him the first Muslim army commander-in-chief. While the appointment was unexpected, he did have powerful backers in the Privy Council, including former general and privy councillor, **Surayud Chulanont**, and Privy Council president and former prime minister, **Prem Tinsulanonda**.

During his time as commander-in-chief, the army became increasingly involved in political disputes in Bangkok. At the time, Sonthi appeared to be attempting to keep the army above politics and repeatedly reassured the public that the army would not interfere in the crisis between Prime Minister Thaksin Shinawatra and the political opposition. However on 19 September 2006, Sonthi led other military leaders in carrying out a successful coup against Thaksin's government. After dissolving the Cabinet, Parliament and the Constitutional Court, he gave himself powers of prime minister, established the ruling Council for Democratic Reform, later changed to the Council for National Security, and declared that he would hand over power in two weeks. On the second day of the coup he received a formal mandate from King **Bhumibol Adulyadej**. Sonthi purged senior military ranks of Thaksin loyalists, oversaw the drafting of a new constitution and, together with the council, worked behind the scenes during the caretaker government of Surayud Chulanont. On 30 September 2007, Sonthi resigned his commission, handing over command of the army to General **Anupong Paochinda**. He also resigned as chairman of the Council for National Security on 1 October 2007, accepting a post as deputy prime minister for security in Surayud's government.

As army commander, Sonthi also presided over counterinsurgency operations in the south. His appointment came with the extension of an olive branch offer of dialogue with the insurgents, although it was never clear who were the leaders of the **southern provinces insurgency**. This attitude however hardened after the coup when Sonthi increased troop deployments to the south and ordered large cordon and search operations that had some impact on reducing the level of violence.

see also: Anupong Paochinda, General; Bhumibol Adulyadej, King; Insurgency, Southern Provinces; Prem Tinsulanonda, General; Surayud Chulanont, General.

Souphanouvong, Prince (Laos)

Prince Souphanouvong was instrumental in helping to found the revolutionary movement in Laos which achieved political victory under Vietnamese patronage. He was born on 13 July 1909, the youngest of the twenty sons of Prince Boun Khong. His best-known half-brother was Prince **Souvanna Phouma**. Prince Souphanouvong was educated at a school in Hanoi and went on to study engineering in France, where he became politically active during the period of the Popular Front. He returned to Indochina in 1937 and entered the colonial public works service. Posted to southern Vietnam, he married the daughter of a hotel owner. He drew on his Vietnamese connections in September 1945 when he travelled from Laos to the headquarters of **Ho Chi Minh** to seek an alliance against the French. Ho sent him back with a military escort with which Prince Souphanouvong launched an anti-French resistance movement. This movement was driven into exile in Thailand in 1946. When its more conservative members came to terms with France in 1949, Prince Souphanouvong joined the **Viet Minh** in the jungles of Vietnam, beginning a close association with the revolutionary leaders, **Kaysone Phomvihan** and **Nouhak Phoumsavan**. In August 1950 he was a party to establishing the ***Pathet Lao*** (Lao Nation) revolutionary movement. Although denied representation at the **Geneva Agreements on Indochina** in 1954, a Vietnamese vice-minister of defence signed the ceasefire agreement for Laos on their specific behalf with a French counterpart.

Prince Souphanouvong was a founding member of the **Lao People's Revolutionary Party** (LPRP) in 1955 and subsequently played an important negotiating role on behalf of the *Pathet Lao*, participating in a shortlived coalition government after a further conference resulting in the **Geneva Agreements on Laos** in 1961–2. That conference failed to end the civil war, which was eventually concluded to *Pathet Lao* advantage in 1975 after the end of the **Vietnam War**. Possibly because of his royal origins, Prince Souphanouvong was never a truly commanding figure in the ruling LPRP. He occupied senior positions, nonetheless, including membership of the Politburo. When the People's Democratic Republic of Laos was established in December 1975, he became its first president until obliged to give up on grounds of age and ill-health in 1986. He did not formally relinquish his office and Politburo position until the fifth national congress of the ruling party in March 1991. He died on 9 January 1995 aged eighty-six.

see also: Geneva Agreements on Indochina 1954; Geneva Agreements on Laos 1962; Ho Chi Minh; Kaysone Phomvihan; Lao People's Revolutionary Party; Nouhak Phoumsavan; *Pathet Lao*; Souvanna Phouma, Prince; Viet Minh; Vietnam War.

South China Sea (Brunei/Indonesia/Malaysia/Philippines/Vietnam)

The South China Sea has a semi-enclosed mediterranean quality. Its area of some 648,000 square miles is bounded by China, Vietnam, the Philippines, Indonesia, Malaysia and Brunei. The sea provides important maritime communication routes between the Indian and Pacific oceans, most notably for energy supply from the Gulf of Arabia to Japan's home islands. Within the South China Sea, there are four main island groups, none of which is the natural geographic extension of any coastal state's continental shelf. These groups, in different ways, are the object of serious contention between coastal states. The People's Republic of China is in control of the northerly Paracel Islands, which are contested by Vietnam and

Taiwan. At issue between China and Taiwan is the question of governmental legitimacy, not sovereignty over specific territories. Control of the northerly Pratas Islands by Taiwan is challenged only by China as part of its general challenge to the government in Taipei. The Macclesfield Bank is permanently submerged and the issue of control has not yet arisen. Greatest contention arises over the Spratly Islands comprising many reefs, shoals and sandbanks which spread out from the very centre of the sea. Jurisdiction is contested between China, Taiwan, Vietnam, Malaysia and the Philippines, with Brunei concerned only with maritime space arising from its continental shelf. The main attraction is the prospect of discovering and exploiting extensive reserves of oil and natural gas and fishing waters although strategic considerations may influence governments. In July 1992 the foreign ministers of **ASEAN** (Association of Southeast Asian Nations), at their annual meeting in Manila, issued a **Declaration on the South China Sea** which called on contending claimants to resolve issues of sovereignty without resort to force. The claim by China, exemplified in its nine-dash line map released in 2009, causes most concern within Southeast Asia because of the transformation of the strategic environment which would follow from the projection of its jurisdiction some 1,800 kilometres from its mainland into the maritime heart of the region. The nine-dash line map also includes Indonesia's **Natuna Islands** within its boundary. In 1995, Chinese forces occupied Mischief Reef, some 135 miles to the west of the Philippine island of Palawan. In 1990, Indonesia coordinated an informal Workshop on Managing Potential Conflicts in the South China Sea with financial support from Canada, but the results were negligible.

In November 2002, ASEAN and China made significant headway with the signing of the **Declaration on the Conduct of Parties in the South China Sea** (DOC). The DOC reaffirmed commitment to universally recognized principles of international law, freedom of navigation and overflight in the South China Sea, and peaceful settlement of jurisdictional disputes. It took another two years for agreement to be reached on the Terms of Reference for the ASEAN–China Joint Working Group tasked to implement the DOC, a task that remains elusive. In August 2005, a proposal that consultations on the DOC be undertaken among ASEAN states prior to discussions with China was rejected by Beijing on grounds that relevant parties should resolve their respective territorial disputes bilaterally, a position the Chinese had always insisted on. This resulted in a deadlock that lasted for six years until July 2011, when ASEAN agreed to drop its insistence on preliminary consultations and the Guidelines to implement the DOC were adopted. Discussions with Chinese senior officials on the implementation of the Guidelines commenced, and during a meeting held in Beijing in January 2012, agreement was reached to establish four expert committees on maritime scientific research, environmental protection, search and rescue, and transnational crime. The agreement on the Guidelines led to the revival of the longstanding proposal by the Philippines for a legally binding Code of Conduct (COC) that was included in the 2002 DOC.

Despite progress on the diplomatic front, China has continued to press its claims in the South China Sea assertively. In 2005, Chinese vessels opened fire on two Vietnamese fishing boats, killing nine people, and detained another ship with eight passengers on Hainan island. In 2009, Chinese fishing vessels harassed a US surveillance ship, purportedly for entering China's Exclusive Economic Zone. In February 2011, a Chinese vessel fired warning shots at Philippine fishing boats near Jackson Atoll, and in May that year three Chinese naval ships cut the cables of a Vietnamese oil and gas exploration vessel 120 km off the coast of Vietnam. In April 2012, an attempt by Philippine vessels to arrest Chinese fishermen near an outcrop of **Scarborough Shoal** for allegedly fishing government-protected marine species within the Philippines' 200 nautical miles limit was blocked by Chinese surveillance boats, leading to a tense standoff which lasted several months. By July 2012, China erected barriers to the entrance of Scarborough Shoal to ward off Filipino vessels. Meanwhile, national laws were passed in Vietnam and the Philippines that demarcated maritime borders. Tensions escalated further at the ASEAN Minister's Meeting in Cambodia in July 2012, when Chinese ally and ASEAN chair, Cambodia, blocked attempts to raise the issue of South China Sea tensions. The result was the embarrassment of ASEAN's inability to release a joint communiqué for the first time in its history. While China has since softened its position and indicated its readiness to continue discussions on the implementation of the DOC, four Chinese navy vessels sailed to James Shoal, a submerged reef in the South China Sea within fifty miles of the Malaysian coast, in May 2013. This is the farthest down the South China Sea that the Chinese navy has ventured and prompted expressions of concern from a Malaysian government that had hitherto been restrained in its responses to Chinese claims.

see also: ASEAN; Declaration on the Conduct of Parties in the South China Sea (ASEAN) 2002; Declaration on the South China Sea (ASEAN) 1992; Natuna Islands; Scarborough Shoal Dispute.

Southeast Asia Command 1943–6

The Southeast Asia Command was the title of the military authority responsible for dispossessing Japan of territorial gains acquired during the Pacific War. After the end of hostilities in 1945 that title was adopted into conventional usage to describe the region situated to the east of the Indian sub-continent and south of China. The decision to establish the Command was taken at a conference in Quebec City in August 1943, attended by the US president, Franklin Roosevelt, and the British prime minister, Winston Churchill, which appointed Vice-Admiral Lord Louis Mountbatten as Supreme Allied Commander. Based in Kandy in Ceylon (now Sri Lanka), its initial geographic responsibilities were limited to Burma, Thailand and Malaya, including Singapore and the island of Sumatra. In July 1945 at the Potsdam Conference in Germany attended by Marshal Stalin, President Truman, Prime Minister Churchill and his successor Clement Attlee, the decision was taken to transfer extensive geographic responsibilities from the South-West Pacific Command under General Douglas MacArthur so that it could devote itself to an assault on Japan's home islands. In consequence, the Southeast Asia Command was enlarged to include the whole of the Netherlands East Indies (except West Timor), northern Borneo and Indochina north of the sixteenth parallel of latitude. With the atomic bombing of Hiroshima and Nagasaki, its prime postwar tasks were to recover Allied prisoners of war and civilian internees and to take the surrender of Japanese forces. The Command's headquarters were transferred to Singapore in November 1945. British/Indian troops played a role in restoring French authority in southern Vietnam and came into armed conflict with Indonesian nationalists on the island of Java in the Battle of Surabaya. After a preliminary accord between Dutch and Indonesian representatives over the political future of the Indies in mid-November 1946, all British/Indian troops were withdrawn at the end of the month coincident with the Command being disbanded.

see also: Surabaya, Battle of.

Souvanna Phouma, Prince (Laos)

Prince Souvanna Phouma was prime minister of Laos on several occasions between 1950 and 1975 when the Communists assumed power. He was a man of liberal values who stood for a time as a symbol of national reconciliation among warring factions. His ability to fulfil that role depended in part on his personal relationship with his half-brother, Prince **Souphanouvong**, the nominal head of the pro-Communist ***Pathet Lao*** (Lao Nation) movement and for some years president of the People's Democratic Republic established in 1975. The obstacle which he could never overcome was that the main antagonists in Laos were never really interested in political compromise.

Souvanna Phouma was born on 7 October 1901 in Luang Prabang into the junior branch of the royal family. Trained in civil and electrical engineering in Vietnam and France, he became director of public works in French colonial Laos before the outbreak of the Pacific War. He became involved in politics at its close during the interregnum before the return of the French. With two brothers, he formed the Free Laos Movement in opposition to French rule and spent a short exile in Thailand, returning to Laos only after its independence was recognized in

1949. He first became prime minister in 1951 and negotiated the full transfer of sovereignty from France. After the **Geneva Agreements on Indochina** of 1954, which failed to resolve internal political divisions within Laos, he sought to engage the *Pathet Lao* in coalition government. Success in this enterprise prompted a right-wing military coup in July 1958 and Souvanna Phouma left office to serve as ambassador to France. He returned as prime minister after a neutralist coup in August 1960 but was forced into exile at the end of the year. He resumed high office after the **Geneva Agreements on Laos** in July 1962 as head of a government of national union. He was never able, however, to overcome deep internal divisions reinforced by external intervention. After the **Paris Peace Agreements** in January 1973, a corresponding accord for Laos, the **Vientiane Agreement on the Restoration of Peace and Reconciliation in Laos**, was concluded in the following month and Souvanna Phouma became the head of yet another coalition government. His role was little more than a caretaker one until his final resignation in December 1975. On giving up office, he was given a formal position as adviser to the new government but played no part in the political life of the People's Democratic Republic of Laos. Souvanna Phouma died in Vientiane on 10 January 1984 aged eighty-two.

see also: Geneva Agreements on Indochina 1954; Geneva Agreements on Laos 1962; Paris Peace Agreements 1973; *Pathet Lao*; Souphanouvong, Prince; Vientiane Agreement on the Restoration of Peace and Reconciliation in Laos 1973.

State Law and Order Restoration Council (Myanmar)

The State Law and Order Restoration Council (SLORC) was established on 18 September 1988 by the armed forces as the national instrument of government after a continuous period of public disturbance. Political disorder had been sparked off initially in September 1987 by a crude act of demonetization without government compensation, provoking student alienation which spread because of deep-seated economic discontent reaching a bloody culmination. SLORC was headed initially by the defence minister, General Saw Maung, who also assumed the post of prime minister. Martial law was introduced and all existing state organs abolished, including the ruling **Burma Socialist Programme Party** (BSPP), which re-emerged as the **National Unity Party** (NUP) a week later. Violent confrontation between student protestors and the armed forces intensified but was resolved with great loss of life through the indiscriminate use of firepower by the military.

Elections to the newly created People's Assembly were promised for May 1990 and were duly held to widespread surprise, but the overwhelming victory by the opposition **National League for Democracy** over the NUP and other minor groupings did not lead to political change because SLORC refused to allow the assembly to convene. By that juncture, opposition leader **Aung San Suu Kyi** had been under detention for nearly a year, while legal powers and violence were employed after the elections to crush all dissent. SLORC pressed ahead in an attempt to give its rule constitutional legitimacy. A National Convention was convened in January 1993; it concluded its work a year later by endorsing a prerogative political role for the armed forces in any new constitutional structure. In April 1992 General Saw Maung was replaced as head of SLORC and prime minister by his deputy, General **Than Shwe**, after reportedly suffering from mental disturbance. The real locus of power within SLORC at the time, however, was Brigadier General **Khin Nyunt**, the council's first secretary and head of military intelligence. In July 1995, SLORC felt able to release Aung San Suu Kyi from detention without serious fear of a challenge to its political position. On 15 November 1997, SLORC was dissolved and replaced by the **State Peace and Development Council** (SPDC). The firm grip on power by the military was not however lessened in any way by this change in nomenclature.

see also: Aung San Suu Kyi; Burma Socialist Programme Party; Khin Nyunt, General; National League for Democracy; National Unity Party; State Peace and Development Council; Than Shwe, Senior General.

State Owned Enterprise Reform (Vietnam)

State Owned Enterprise (SOE) reform in Vietnam, which began with ***Doi Moi*** (Renovation) in 1986, represents ongoing efforts by the Vietnamese government to restructure the SOE sector with the objective of making it more efficient and reducing the strain on the public budget and as a broader strategy for stimulating economic growth. However, after more than two decades, the reform process remains ambivalent, with large SOEs still underperforming, many with non-performing bank loans and some (e.g. Vinashin and Vinalines) defaulting on their debts.

In the early 1990s, SOEs found themselves unprepared to face the stiff competition in both the foreign and domestic markets. Many, if not most, of these SOEs were highly inefficient and running at a loss due to unclear objectives, poor management and soft budget constraints. Moreover, they also enjoyed the safety net of government bailouts in the event of failure. Still, unlike the economic restructuring of other formerly centrally planned economies, SOEs were envisaged by Vietnamese policymakers to play a lead role in the transformation to a market economy. It is in this respect that the reform of SOEs was vital. Equitization, in particular, was emphasized as a key strategy in reforming the SOE sector. In reality, the pace of equitization has been slow, and only small SOEs have been equitized. There was plenty of resistance to privatization from SOE managers who were concerned about the possible loss of privileges that came with running a SOE. Although a pilot privatization programme had been initiated as early as 1992, the pace of equitization did not pick up until much later. Out of the 2,600 firms equitized in the first thirteen years of the programme, approximately 2,000 took place between 2000 and 2005. The state continues to retain the controlling, albeit minority, share in most equitized firms; the varying degree of state engagement in these equitized firms depends on each's strategic importance. In addition to equitization, reduction of the number of SOEs also took place through the merging of SOEs that were too small to be competitive. Inspired by the Japan's Keiretsu and Korea's Chaebol models, the Vietnamese government established large-scale holding companies – General Corporations – with the aim of strengthening international competitiveness through concentration, internal linkages and economies of scale.

Despite the equitization programme, the state's share in the Vietnamese economy continues to hover at forty per cent over the reform period, suggesting that equitization was not so much an effort to reduce state involvement in the economy as a means of attracting capital to the equitized firms. Without transferring control of a firm to private capital, equitization cannot adequately tackle the efficiency issue. The remaining SOEs remain highly inefficient and unprofitable – eighty per cent of all SOE profits in 2011 can be accounted for by only four SOEs out of more than 1,300 – yet they continue to receive privileged access to capital and bank loans. The performance of SOEs became a major political issue at the eleventh National Congress held in January 2011, when it was believed that President **Truong Tan Sang** leaked information on huge losses incurred by the state conglomerate Vinashin in order to undermine the leadership of Prime Minister **Nguyen Tan Dung**, whose office had oversight of SOEs. This led to an intense struggle within the Communist Party which carried over into the fourth plenum of the Central Committee in December 2011 when the party launched its rectification campaign which had as its focus the matter of corruption among the top leadership.

see also: Doi Moi; Nguyen Tan Dung; Truong Tan Sang.

State Peace and Development Council (Myanmar)

On 15 November 1997, the **State Law and Order Restoration Council**, which had served as the vehicle for military rule in Myanmar since September 1988, was dissolved and replaced by the State Peace and Development Council (SPDC). The change of political label was purely cosmetic and was probably prompted by an attempt to improve the international image of the country following its controversial entry into ASEAN the previous July. Although the change of nomenclature suggested a revision of national priorities, the authoritarian nature of the government did not change. The commanders of Myanmar's various military regions were promoted and brought into the ruling council with the formation of the SPDC in a move that would be repeated several times to prevent the building of regional power centres. **Than Shwe** remained the chairman and together with army commander General Maung Aye continued to rule the country. Secretary-1 **Khin Nyunt** initially appeared to be ascendant in the SPDC, removing several of his rivals and promoting loyalists, but his influence was eliminated in 2004 when he was put under house arrest, his military intelligence apparatus largely dismantled, and many of his operatives imprisoned ostensibly on corruption charges. From this point until the handover of power in 2011, Than Shwe was the clear ruler.

Continued accusations of gross human rights abuses prompted the United States and several other Western nations to step up sanctions against the regime. Released from house arrest in 1995, **Aung San Suu Kyi** was again placed in detention by the regime in September 2000. The SPDC released her in May 2002, but detained her again in May 2003 after an attack on her motorcade in Depayin, Sagaing Division. Opposition politicians and rights advocates accused the military regime of masterminding the attack. The regime would go on to extend her detention three times. Aung San Suu Kyi would remain under house arrest until after national elections in November 2010. Several rounds of reconciliation talks were held between Aung San Suu Kyi and government interlocutors during the period, but all came to naught. In November 2005, the regime moved the capital from Yangon to **Naypyidaw**, a new capital city carved out of the jungle in central Myanmar. Unrest continued to simmer among the civilian population and, after the rescinding of fuel subsidies in August 2007, a series of protests erupted in several cities across the country (*see* **Saffron Revolution 2007**). Joined by monks from throughout Myanmar in September, the movement grew from dissatisfaction with the regime's economic mismanagement into nationwide anti-government protests. The government finally cracked down on 26 September, violently suppressing the protests and carrying out mass arrests of protestors, monks and organizers that would shock the international community and even bring reproach from China. The regime would come in for further criticism over its handling of the Cyclone Nargis disaster in May 2008 which killed over 130,000 in the southwest of the country. In the critical days following the disaster the regime threw up barriers to international relief efforts and only allowed in relief supplies and international experts after the successful intervention of the ASEAN secretary-general, **Surin Pitsuwan**, and the formation of the Tripartite Core Group consisting of the Myanmar government, **ASEAN** (Association of Southeast Asian Nations), and the United Nations and aid agencies to coordinate relief. The generals were further criticized for their refusal to postpone the constitutional referendum despite the huge loss of life.

Under SPDC rule ethnic insurgency continued to fester along Myanmar's borders, particularly in **Shan**, Karenni and **Karen** states. Many of the groups who had negotiated ceasefires in 1989–94 were growing restless and relations took a turn for the worse in 2009 when the SPDC pushed for these groups to hand over their weapons and join the military as a Border Guard Force while their political wings morphed into mainstream political parties. The arrest of Khin Nyunt, who had arranged most of the ceasefires, further eroded the regime's rapport with ethnic insurgents. In August 2003 the regime announced a seven-step '**Roadmap to Democracy**' intended to transform the country from military rule to a democracy under military guidance. One step was the reconvening of the National Convention in February 2005 in order to draft a new constitution. The military regime selected the participants from among small political and ethnic organizations, academics and other prominent figures. Major opposition parties, including the **National League for Democracy**, were banned from the convention. A constitution was eventually completed in September 2007 and a referendum held in 2008 which, although widely criticized, approved the draft (*see* **Constitution 2008**). On 13 August 2010, the SPDC announced national elections would be held on 7 November that year. A number of prominent members of the junta resigned from the military in the lead up to the polls in order to stand for election, including generals **Thein Sein** and **Shwe Mann**. In the campaigning that followed there were widespread allegations that the junta was directly assisting the **Union Solidarity and Development Party** (USDP) in its activities, prompting widespread doubt that the elections would be either free or fair. When the election results were announced on 17 November 2010, the USDP was the clear winner, and together with the 25 per cent of seats allocated to the military in parliament secured the military a key role in any future government. The SPDC acted as a caretaker government for the next four months before formally handing over power to the democratically elected government on 30 March 2011, after which generals Than Shwe and Maung Aye essentially faded from public view.

see also: ASEAN; Aung San Suu Kyi; Constitution 2008; Karen; Khin Nyunt, General; National League for Democracy; Naypyidaw; Roadmap to Democracy; Saffron Revolution 2007; Shan; Shwe Mann; State Law and Order Restoration Council; Surin Pitsuwan; Than Shwe, Senior General; Thein Sein; Union Solidarity and Development Party.

Subandrio (Indonesia)

Subandrio, who like many Javanese has only one name, was foreign minister of Indonesia between April 1957 and March 1966. He was the chosen political instrument of President **Sukarno**. As such, he directed and managed the radical leftist foreign policy of **Guided Democracy**, which was marked by **Confrontation** with Malaysia and a close alignment with the People's Republic of China. Subandrio was born on 15 September 1915 and trained as a medical practitioner in Jakarta under the Dutch. After the proclamation of independence, he was posted abroad by the embryonic Ministry of Information to engage in public relations and from 1947 was the republic's representative in London, becoming ambassador to Moscow between 1954 and 1956, returning to Jakarta in 1956 to become secretary-general of the Ministry of Foreign Affairs until being appointed foreign minister in 1957. In 1963 President Sukarno appointed him first deputy prime minister. In that position, he assumed control of the Central Intelligence Bureau and openly identified with the leftwards drift in politics to the extent that speculation arose over his possible succession to President Sukarno. After the abortive coup (*see* ***Gestapu***) in October 1965, Subandrio was subject to vociferous criticism from student and Muslim groups as well as from the armed forces. When General **Suharto** assumed executive authority in March 1966, Subandrio was arrested on charges of complicity in the alleged Communist-inspired coup attempt. After a trial before a military tribunal in October 1966, he was sentenced to death, which was commuted to life imprisonment in 1980. In August 1995, aged eighty-one, he was pardoned and released coincident with the fiftieth anniversary of the proclamation of Indonesia's independence. He died on 3 July 2004.

see also: Confrontation; *Gestapu;* Guided Democracy; Suharto; Sukarno.

Subic Bay Naval Base (Philippines)

Subic Bay Naval Base, situated some fifty miles west of Manila on the island of Luzón, was the most important US military installation in the Philippines. The base area comprised 62,000 acres and had been set aside for military use by US President Theodore Roosevelt in 1904. It was established as a major facility after the Philippines became independent in 1946, initially for ninety-nine years under a lease agreement concluded on 17 March 1947. It comprised a complex of facilities capable of supporting combat operations by several aircraft carrier groups throughout the Indian Ocean and the western Pacific Ocean. To serve that purpose, it became the largest US overseas supply depot. The term of the lease was reduced to twenty-five years in September 1965. The strategic significance of the base complex declined with the end of the Cold War. Nonetheless, the United States maintained an interest in retaining operational use of the facilities and engaged in

protracted negotiations with the government of the Philippines from the late 1980s over the financial terms for the renewal of the lease for an additional ten years. Although intergovernmental agreement on a new treaty was reached in August 1991, the Philippines Senate voted against ratification the following month with members motivated in part by the potential electoral benefits of demonstrating an assertive nationalism. The Philippines government then announced that negotiations with the United States designed to sanction withdrawal of its forces over a three-year period had collapsed. The United States was subsequently served with a one-year notice of termination, which required that Subic Bay Naval Base be returned to Philippine jurisdiction before the end of 1992. The United States began to comply without protest, immediately dismantling base installations and withdrawing floating docks. After the inauguration of President **Fidel Ramos** in July 1992, negotiations were resumed with the United States government on the continued servicing and repair of American vessels at Subic Bay. However, the naval base was formally transferred to Philippine control on 30 September 1992. The Cubi Point Naval Air Station on the western edge of the base complex was relinquished on 24 November that year when the last US service personnel left the Philippines.
see also: Ramos, Fidel.

Suchinda Kraprayoon, General
(Thailand)

General Suchinda Kraprayoon attained political notoriety in May 1992 when responsibility was attributed to him for ordering troops to fire on demonstrators in Bangkok protesting at his appointment as prime minister without prior election to Parliament. General Suchinda had become an army commander in March 1990 following the resignation of General **Chavalit Yongchaiyuth**, who had entered politics. In February 1991 General Suchinda led a bloodless coup which removed the government of the prime minister, **Chatichai Choonhavan**. After a period of interim government under a former diplomat and businessman, **Anand Panyarachun**, national elections were held in March 1992. The military-backed *Samakkhi Tham* Party (meaning Unity in Virtue) formed specifically for the elections, secured the largest number of seats and established a governing coalition with other pro-military parties. After their leader Narong Wongwan had been publicly discredited, General Suchinda resigned as army commander and accepted appointment as prime minister on 7 April, despite his commitment in November 1991 not to do so. Two weeks later demonstrations against his appointment were mounted in Bangkok, inspired by a fast by **Chamlong Srimuang**, the leader of the opposition *Palang Dharma* (Moral Force) Party. Demonstrations continued into May and after an initial use of armed force by the military, Chamlong was arrested, which inflamed political passions leading to an even bloodier confrontation with up to 200 deaths reported. On 20 May King **Bhumibol Adulyadej** summoned General Suchinda and Chamlong to his palace for a televised meeting which defused the crisis. General Suchinda resigned from office three days later and departed the country.

Suchinda Kraprayoon was born on 6 August 1933 in Phra Nakhon in northeast Thailand. He went straight from secondary school into the Chulachomklao Royal Military Academy in Bangkok, enrolling in its fifth class, whose cohort has dominated their military generation. He received advanced training in the United States at Fort Leavenworth Army Staff College and at Fort Seal Advanced Artillery College. His early career was spent as an artillery commander but he also spent three years in Washington in the early 1970s as deputy military attaché before transferring to army intelligence, whose head he became by 1982. On his way to the post of army commander-in-chief, he was army assistant chief of staff for operations in 1985 and army assistant commander-in-chief in 1987. General Suchinda represented a military tradition which assumed a prerogative role in public life and which had not been able to come to terms with the political consequences of economic and social change which had challenged that assumption.
see also: Anand Panyarachun; Bhumibol Adulyadej, King; Chamlong Srimuang, General; Chatichai Choonhavan, General; Chavalit Yongchaiyuth, General.

Suharto (Indonesia)

President Suharto dominated political life in Indonesia from 11 March 1966, when he seized power, until 21 May 1998 when he resigned from high office. In March 1966, he had used the threat of military force to assume executive authority from the incumbent President **Sukarno**. He concentrated and exercised power ruthlessly without significant challenge until Indonesia was beset by a devastating economic crisis from late 1997, unprecedented during his rule. He ruled Indonesia much like an erstwhile Javanese monarch employing a quiet but decisive authority. In so doing, he was moved by the conviction that he had been entrusted with a divinely inspired mission to guide the country along the path of political order and economic development. With evident success in this endeavour up to the late 1990s, he became the logical chairman of the Non-Aligned Movement whose heads of government met in Jakarta in September 1992. At the end of the month, he addressed the General Assembly of the United Nations as the movement's spokesman, so demonstrating the international standing of the republic and his own personal achievement. His personal credibility and that achievement were virtually dissipated overnight as he failed to comprehend, and to take appropriate action to cope with, the enormity of Indonesia's economic ills. On relinquishing office, he was succeeded initially by his vice-president, **B. J. Habibie**.

Suharto, like many Javanese, has only one name; he was born on 8 June 1921 in the village of Kemusu, near the town of Yogyakarta in central Java. He came from a peasant background and received only an elementary education but in June 1940 enlisted in the Royal Netherlands Indies Army, rising to the rank of sergeant before the Japanese occupation in 1942. In 1943 he joined the Japanese-sponsored ***Peta*** (*Pembela Tanah Air*, meaning Defenders of the Fatherland) within which he received officer training, rising to the rank of company commander. After the proclamation of Indonesia's independence in August 1945, Suharto joined the national army and distinguished himself as a brigade commander against the Dutch, rising to the rank of lieutenant colonel by the transfer of sovereignty in December 1949. He subsequently commanded the central Java Diponegoro Division and the forces deployed to liberate the western half of the island of New Guinea (**Irian Jaya**) from the Dutch. In May 1963, as a major general, he became commander of the army's Strategic Reserve (*Kostrad*) based in Jakarta, in the event a fateful posting.

In the early hours of 1 October 1965, dissident army units abducted and murdered six senior generals at the outset of an abortive coup (*see* ***Gestapu***). For reasons still not satisfactorily explained, Suharto's name was not on the list of generals abducted despite *Kostrad*'s assigned role in countering a coup attempt. Suharto seized the initiative and acted with skill and resolve to crush the revolt and then set about dismantling the political system of **Guided Democracy** established and dominated by President Sukarno. Responsibility for the abortive coup was attributed to the Communist Party of Indonesia, which had enjoyed the patronage of Sukarno. Suharto swept both away, leaving the armed forces under his command as the key national institution (*see* ***Supersemar***).

In March 1967 as a full general, Suharto was elected acting president by the provisional **People's Consultative Assembly** (MPR). In March 1968 that assembly confirmed him in office for a full term. He was re-elected unopposed by a formally constituted MPR in 1973 and then again in 1978, 1983, 1988 and 1993. From the outset, Suharto was instrumental in revising many of the republic's public priorities adopted by his predecessor. He set out to reverse the decline in Indonesia's economy by applying western orthodoxies, so attracting the support of the governments of the United States and Japan. To demonstrate a commitment to development and in repudiation of Sukarno's flamboyant adventurism, he brought the campaign of **Confrontation** against Malaysia to a speedy end. He also embarked on an unprecedented exercise in regional cooperation with the founding in August 1967 of **ASEAN** (Association of Southeast Asian Nations), which has remained at the centre of the republic's foreign policy. If seemingly attuned to western political sensibilities, Suharto has been no less a nationalist than his ill-fated predecessor. He was ruthless over the incorporation of Irian Jaya into the republic in 1969 and brutal in annexing East Timor from 1975 (*see* **Timor-Leste**).

Internally, Suharto imposed his so-called **New Order** through political demobilization. Political parties were obliged to amalgamate and subordinate their identities, while an existing organization of Functional Groups, ***Golkar*** (set up initially by the military to counter the Communists) became the electoral vehicle of a military establishment which he managed and manipulated. In addition, conscious of Indonesia's lack of a single cultural tradition, Suharto set out to impose nationally the syncretic formula ***Pancasila***, devised originally by Sukarno at the outset of independence in 1945 as a way of containing Islamic claims on the identity of the state. By the early 1990s, Suharto's political control had begun to slip a little as senior military officers became alienated by the extent to which his rule had become quasi-monarchical. Moreover, the rapacious business activities of his children and other relatives had generated a growing popular resentment and desire for political change. Suharto retained power, despite growing dissent, through manipulation and a masterly understanding of human weaknesses. The death of his wife, Ibu Tien, in April 1996, is believed to have affected his political judgement and also to have placed him under the malign influence of his greedy children. In March 1998, he was elected to a seventh consecutive term of office by the MPR indicating confidence that he could continue until 2003. The social and political consequences of economic crisis intervened to cut short his term. Social unrest was precipitated by sharp rises in fuel, transport and electricity prices, while basic staples were in short supply. A rising chorus of protest came to a head on 12 May 1998 when security forces in Jakarta opened fire on a student rally killing four young people. Urban violence assumed an anti-Chinese dimension with destruction and looting of property as well as the rape of Chinese women. In the middle of this mayhem, Suharto made a fundamental error of judgement in travelling to an international conference in Cairo in an attempt to demonstrate that his authority remained unimpaired. He was obliged to cut short his visit. He made an abortive attempt to form a so-called reform government but could not find candidates to fill its ranks. He left office as a reviled figure. In August 2000, he faced trial on a charge of siphoning off nearly US$600 million from charitable foundations but refused to appear in court on medical grounds.

With his authoritarian veil unceremoniously removed, Suharto's final years out of office were clouded by persistent allegations of corruption and abuse of power. Transparency International went on record in 2007 maintaining that Suharto was the world's most corrupt politician who allegedly amassed a fortune of between US$15 billion and US$35 billion. Meanwhile, members of his family and inner circle were also subject to accusations that they had abused their ties with Suharto to enrich themselves. In spite of these mounting allegations against him, in 2007 Suharto was successful in a lawsuit worth almost $106 million against *Time* magazine, which had accused him of siphoning off almost $15 billion to offshore bank accounts just before his forced resignation in 1998. Suharto passed away on 27 January 2008, closing one of the most controversial chapters in Indonesia's history. Such was the influence he wielded in life, even his harshest critics were present to pay their last respects to the former strongman. In spite of his legacy, some opinion polls have suggested that nearly fifty-eight per cent of Indonesians felt more content during the New Order period than what followed after Suharto's fall, although this could have been prompted by a sense of sympathy and nostalgia.

see also: ABRI; ASEAN; Confrontation; *Gestapu*; *Golkar*; Guided Democracy; Habibie, B. J.; Irian Jaya; New Order; *Pancasila*; People's Consultative Assembly; *Peta*; Sukarno; *Supersemar*; Timor-Leste.

Sukarno (Indonesia)

Sukarno, who in the Javanese tradition had only one name, was the first president of Indonesia. He was the pre-eminent nationalist leader of his generation. He enjoyed remarkable oratorical skills and an extraordinary ability to communicate with and mobilize the mass of the Indonesian people. He became a controversial international figure from the late 1950s when he led Indonesia into Confrontation successively with the Netherlands and Malaysia. His political career ended in disgrace, however, in the wake of the abortive coup (*see Gestapu*) in October 1965 (attributed to Indonesia's Communist Party) in which he appeared to be implicated. His political successor, General (later President) **Suharto**, kept him under virtual house arrest from March 1966 until his death in June 1970.

Sukarno was born in Blitar in east Java on 6 June 1901, the son of a schoolteacher. He was brought up in a politicized environment in the home of one of the early nationalist leaders. He graduated as a civil engineer from the Advanced School for Technical Studies in Bandung in 1925. Architecture was part of the curriculum, which Sukarno practised for a while but without much success. An active induction into nationalist politics occurred during his higher education. In 1927, he played the leading role in founding the secular Indonesian Nationalist Party, which uncompromisingly demanded independence from the Dutch. He was arrested in December 1929 and tried the following year in Bandung during which he made a spirited public defence of the nationalist cause. He was sentenced to four years' imprisonment in December 1930 but released a year later. He was detained for a second time in August 1933 and in February 1934 was sent with his family into internal exile in Flores from which he was transferred to Bengkulu in Sumatra in February 1938. He was still in internal exile when the Japanese overran the Netherlands East Indies in early 1942.

Sukarno collaborated with the Japanese but undoubtedly used his position to promote the idea of an independent Indonesian archipelago among a culturally diverse but increasingly receptive people. On 17 August 1945, two days after the Japanese capitulated, he proclaimed Indonesia's independence together with **Mohammad Hatta**, who became vice-president. During the violent independence struggle against the Dutch, he played more of a symbolic than an active role, one that was confirmed after independence in December 1949 when he became a constitutional president. However, during the 1950s, Indonesia's experiment with western parliamentary democracy began to test the integrity of the culturally diverse archipelago state. In the face of regional rebellion and a breakdown of political order, Sukarno seized the opportunity to move to the centre of the political stage. He appealed for a return to the roots of the national revolution and for the introduction of a **Guided Democracy** in keeping with the country's traditions. After a short period of martial law from March 1957, and with the support of the armed forces, Sukarno inaugurated the political system of Guided Democracy in July 1959 by reinstating the authoritarian 1945 constitution with an executive presidency.

During Guided Democracy, Sukarno acted as the personal embodiment of the Indonesian state. He enjoyed a major triumph in employing coercive diplomacy to manipulate the Dutch into transferring **Irian Jaya**, the western half of the island of New Guinea, retained after 1949, to Indonesian jurisdiction. When Sukarno sought to use the same tactic against the Federation of Malaysia, he was not successful. In addition, his close internal alignment with the Communist Party of Indonesia and external ties with the People's Republic of China alarmed the conservative military establishment which seized power after the failed coup in 1965 and proceeded to cast Sukarno into political oblivion (*see* ***Supersemar***). In his period of executive power, Sukarno was literally the resounding voice of Indonesia but brought his country more notoriety than prestige. In one respect, however, he demonstrated remarkable prescience. At the first meeting of the Non-Aligned Movement in Belgrade in 1961, Sukarno argued that the main problem facing the world was not that of superpower antagonism but conflict between the rich and poor countries. His management of his own country's economy was incompetent, however: on his overthrow it was in an impoverished condition as a consequence of profligate expenditure and corruption. His military usurpers nonetheless felt it politic to resurrect his reputation posthumously and also upheld his state philosophy of ***Pancasila***, which was first enunciated in June 1945. He was undoubtedly a charismatic unifying figure at a time when the identity and integrity of the state seemed to be in jeopardy. He died on 21 June 1970 in Bogor.

see also: Confrontation; *Gestapu*; Guided Democracy; Hatta, Mohammad; Irian Jaya; *Pancasila*; Suharto; *Supersemar*.

Sukarnoputri, Megawati (Indonesia)

see **Megawati Sukarnoputri**.

Supersemar (Indonesia)

Supersemar is an acronym from the Indonesian term *Surat Perintah Sebelas Maret*, which was an order signed by President **Sukarno** on 11 March 1966 to Lieutenant General **Suharto**, recently appointed minister/commander-in-chief of the army, instructing him 'to take all necessary steps to guarantee security and calm and the stability of the Government and the course of the Revolution'. The effect of the order was to transfer executive authority: it marked a critical stage in the ultimate deposition of President Sukarno. The use of the acronym *Supersemar* was to provide a basis in legitimacy for the transfer through invoking the name of *Semar*, a clown-god of Hindu mythology with a reputation for invincible authority. The process of transfer was precipitated by an abortive coup (*see* ***Gestapu***) in October 1965, which had the effect of undermining Sukarno's authority and also encouraging the leadership of the armed forces to seize power. Matters came to a head during a cabinet meeting in the presidential palace in Jakarta on 11 March 1966 against a background of rising student protest. Troops without insignia surrounded the palace, and Sukarno and close political associates fled by helicopter to the nearby resort town of Bogor. Three senior generals then drove to Bogor, where they confronted Sukarno who agreed to transfer executive authority. Lieutenant General Suharto then ordered the Communist Party of Indonesia banned and reconstituted the government. The transfer order was confirmed by the provisional **People's Consultative Assembly** in March 1967, with Sukarno retaining only nominal title. General Suharto was confirmed as president in succession to Sukarno in March 1968.

see also: *Gestapu*; People's Consultative Assembly; Suharto; Sukarno.

Supreme National Council (Cambodia)

The Supreme National Council was described in the accords on Cambodia reached at the **International Conference on Cambodia** in Paris on 23 October 1991 as 'the unique legitimate body and source of authority in which, throughout the transitional period, the sovereignty, independence and unity of Cambodia are enshrined'. Central to the contention over resolving the protracted Cambodian conflict was the problem of power-sharing between the warring Khmer factions in the transitional period before elections to determine the political future of the country. This problem was responsible for the failure of an earlier International Conference on Cambodia, Paris 1989. In the event, an initiative for a United Nations role in resolving the conflict gave rise to the proposal for a symbolic device comprising representatives of all factions which would be formally vested with sovereignty. Once established, it was to assume the Cambodian seat in the United Nations General Assembly and also delegate executive powers to **UNTAC** (United Nations Transitional Authority in Cambodia), which would run key ministries, oversee the disarmament and demobilization of contending forces, and organize national elections in a neutral political environment. The Council took on a formal existence at a meeting in the Indonesian capital, Jakarta, on 10 September 1990 and assumed a practical role after Prince **Norodom Sihanouk** was elected chairman in Beijing on 17 July 1991. After the accords reached in Paris in October 1991, the Supreme National Council convened for the first time in Cambodia on 30 December 1991. That meeting had been delayed because of political disorder in the capital Phnom Penh over the participation of **Khmer Rouge** representatives. Once established, it coexisted uneasily with the incumbent administration established by Vietnamese force of arms. The Khmer Rouge justified its failure to assume the government of Cambodia as an excuse for leaving the Council and for boycotting elections held under United Nations auspices in May 1993. The Supreme National Council was replaced when a provisional coalition government was established in

Phnom Penh in July 1993 without Khmer Rouge membership.

see also: International Conferences on Cambodia, Paris 1989, 1991; Khmer Rouge; Sihanouk, King Norodom; UNTAC.

Surabaya, Battle of, 1945
(Indonesia)

Surabaya is the principal port of east Java which serves as a base for Indonesia's navy. In November 1945 it was the site of the biggest battle of Indonesia's national revolution, which took place between Republican and British forces, and not the Dutch. Japan had occupied Indonesia during the course of the Pacific War; after the Japanese surrender, British forces from the **Southeast Asia Command** assumed initial responsibility for administering the Netherlands East Indies. They landed in small numbers some six weeks after the proclamation of national independence and faced the obvious suspicion that they were intent on helping to restore Dutch colonial rule. In early November 1945 Indonesian irregulars objected to a demand from the local British commander for the surrender of their arms, viewing it as a preliminary to a landing by Dutch troops. A violent confrontation ensued in which an entire brigade, comprising mainly Indian soldiers under British command, came close to being overrun. The refusal of Indonesian irregulars to heed an ultimatum to withdraw after a British brigadier had been killed while attempting to uphold a truce provoked a military onslaught at divisional strength. From 10 November, there followed three weeks of courageous and fanatical resistance by the Indonesians, who were ultimately pacified by superior force. The Battle of Surabaya is celebrated every year in Indonesia as Heroes' Day. At the time, it marked a turning point both for the British military authorities and Indonesia's nationalist leadership. Both parties saw the virtue of a negotiated solution to the problem of Indonesian independence. The British were conscious of the political costs of continued confrontation. The nationalist leadership judged it practical to give up a policy of armed struggle in favour of negotiations with the Dutch, in part because of concern not to alienate the great power support seen to be required for achieving full independence. In addition, that leadership had been disturbed by the prospect of being displaced by a radical youth element which had been prominent at Surabaya and which would be politically advantaged through continuing violence.

see also: Southeast Asia Command.

Surayud Chulanont, General
(Thailand)

General Surayud Chulanont is a privy counsellor and a former prime minister and commander-in-chief of the Royal Thai Army. Surayud was born in Prachinburi on 28 August 1943. Surayud's father, Phayom Chulananot, was an army colonel who later left his family and joined the Communist Party of Thailand, becoming a central committee member and chief of staff of the People's Liberation Army of Thailand. Surayud completed his primary education in Bangkok, then joined the inaugural class of the Armed Forces Academies Preparatory Academy. He subsequently graduated with Class 12 from the Chulachomklao Royal Military Academy in 1965 and later attended a number of service schools in Thailand and in the United States.

As an officer, Surayud served in a light artillery unit in 1966 and in the Special Forces from 1970. He participated in operations against the Communist Party of Thailand during the 1960s and 1970s. From 1972 to 1978 he was an instructor at the Special Warfare School. In 1983 he was the commander of the 1st Special Forces Division and four years later the commander of the 1st Special Forces. Surayud also served as an aide to General **Prem Tinsulanonda** during his time as army commander and later, prime minister. In 1992, Surayud was appointed commander of the Special Warfare Centre. Surayud's troops participated in the crackdown on protestors in Bangkok in May 1992, but asserted he never gave orders to his men to shoot. In 1994 he was appointed commander of the 2nd Army Region in the northeast of the country. In late 1998, he was appointed commander-in-chief of the army by the prime minister, **Chuan Leekpai**. By that time, Surayud had built a reputation in the service as incorruptible, tactful and effective. He had expressed displeasure at the use of violence in the 1992 crackdown and attempted to steer the army away from politics by making it more accountable. Under his command, the army became involved for the first time in a UN peacekeeping mission in East Timor. His troops also took a more active role in anti-narcotics activities along Thailand's northern border with Myanmar that occasionally led to border skirmishes with the Myanmar army. In 2003, clashes with Prime Minister **Thaksin Shinawatra** over narcotics suppression and promotion issues led to his 'promotion' to Supreme Commander of Thailand's armed forces, a substantially less influential post. Surayud resigned from the army later in 2003 and was appointed by King **Bhumibol Adulyadej** to the Privy Council on 14 November 2003. After spending some time as a Buddhist monk, Surayud, together with Prem, played key roles in arranging the promotion of General **Sonthi Boonyaratglin** to army commander. Following the 2006 coup, Surayud resigned from the Privy Council to become prime minister in the interim government until national elections in December 2007. He was confirmed as prime minister by junta leader General Sonthi on 1 October 2006. Surayud oversaw the drafting of a new constitution, held a constitutional referendum on 19 August 2007, and promised elections at the end of the year. He also increased the budget for security operations for the **Southern Provinces Insurgency**, and apologized for the loss of life during the Krue Se Mosque and Tak Bai incidents in 2004. His government also purged the senior ranks of the military of supporters of exiled prime minister Thaksin. Surayud was reappointed to the Privy Council in January 2008 after completing his term as prime minister.

see also: Bhumibol Adulyadej, King; Chuan Leekpai; Insurgency, Southern Provinces; Prem Tinsulanonda, General; Sonthi Boonyaratglin, General; Thaksin Shinawatra.

Surin Pitsuwan (Thailand)

Surin Pitsuwan was the first secretary-general of ASEAN (Association of Southeast Asian Nations) who served in the newly empowered office under the **ASEAN Charter**. Introduced with the formation of the ASEAN Secretariat 1976, the role of the secretary-general had largely been one of managing, rather than making, ASEAN policy. Nevertheless, the office has morphed over the years. In 1992, the ASEAN Secretariat was restructured and its chief officer was given the title 'Secretary-General of ASEAN' and accorded ministerial status. The office was further strengthened, albeit modestly, with the passing of the Charter.

Surin Pitsuwan was born on 28 October 1949 to an impoverished southern Thai family. His father was a prominent Muslim teacher. He received his higher education in the United States, acquiring a doctorate in political science from Harvard University in 1982. He then pursued an academic career, holding a post at Thammasat University in the mid-1980s. He entered politics in 1986 and was elected to parliament for the **Democrat Party** for a southern constituency in Nakhon Sri Thammarat Province, attracting strong support from the Muslim community whose faith he shares. Surin rose to become deputy leader of the Democrat Party, speaker of Parliament, and foreign minister from 1997 to 2001. On the occasion of the ASEAN ministerial meeting in Manila in July 1998, Surin famously proposed that the Association adopt an approach to regional cooperation he termed 'flexible engagement', which allowed member states to openly discuss the domestic affairs of fellow members inasmuch as they impacted on regional security. The suggestion was made in the wake of the **Asian Financial Crisis** and the environmental crisis, or 'haze' crisis, wrought by slash-and-burn farming practices in Indonesia that had beset the region. The proposal was not adopted for fear of excessive intervention.

In January 2008, Surin became the first secretary-general from outside of the civil service of a home government, although he had held the post of foreign minister of Thailand from 1997 to 2001. He was also the first secretary-general to be picked through an open recruitment exercise conducted for the position in the national selection process. Surin had to hit the ground running in order to handle the humanitarian crisis spawned by Cyclone Nargis which struck Myanmar in May 2008. In the aftermath of the cyclone, Surin had to muster his entire array of diplomatic talent to persuade the paranoid Myanmar junta to allow foreign aid into the country.

see also: ASEAN; ASEAN Charter; Asian Financial Crisis 1997–8; Democrat Party.

T

Ta Mok (Cambodia)

Ta Mok is the *nom de guerre* of the most notorious military commander of the **Khmer Rouge**. His true name is Chhit Choeun and he held senior military positions in the early 1970s during the successful challenge to the government of **Lon Nol**. He was seriously wounded in the fighting, losing a leg which was replaced with a wooden limb. Little is known of his personal background. His notoriety arises from his role as party secretary in the southwest region in conducting murderous purges after the Khmer Rouge came to power in April 1975, which is when he took the name Ta Mok, meaning Old Man. After their ousting by the Vietnamese, Ta Mok became vice-chairman of the supreme commission of the national army of **Democratic Kampuchea** and established a military fiefdom along Cambodia's northern border with Thailand. That position began to be challenged by the government which came to office in Cambodia in October 1993 after general elections held under United Nations aegis (*see* **UNTAC**). In a military encounter in February 1994, the government forces temporarily seized Ta Mok's base camp of Anlong Veng, but he had been able to move his headquarters some weeks before. In June 1997, forces loyal to Ta Mok arrested **Pol Pot** who was the subject of a show trial. Ta Mok then seized control of the rump of Khmer Rouge forces but was driven from his last camp into jungle along the Thai border by government units in June 1998. He was captured along the border in March 1999 and in September was charged with genocide under a decree issued in 1979 by the **People's Republic of Kampuchea**. Ta Mok's detention was repeatedly extended owing to the difficulty of convening a credible international tribunal (*see* **Khmer Rouge Trials**). It was only in July 2001 that the National Assembly approved legislation to establish a special tribunal to prosecute Khmer Rouge leaders. Ta Mok died in July 2006 after a long struggle with high blood pressure and tuberculosis before he could be tried for his part in the Khmer Rouge genocide.

see also: Democratic Kampuchea; Kampuchea, People's Republic of; Khmer Rouge; Khmer Rouge Trials; Nol, Lon; Pol Pot; UNTAC.

Taib Mahmud, Datuk Patinggi Abdul (Malaysia)

Abdul Taib Mahmud is currently governor of Malaysia's north Bornean state of Sarawak. Prior to that, he served as the state's chief minister from March 1981 to February 2014, making him the longest-serving chief minister in the Malaysian federal system. He continues to lead the ***Parti Pesaka Bumiputera Bersatu*** (PBB), which is dominated by a Muslim Malay–Melanau constituency of which he and his uncle are members. Taib Mahmud was born on 21 May 1936 in Miri, Sarawak, and studied law at the University of Adelaide in South Australia. He began his career as a Crown Counsel but entered Sarawak state politics when the former British colony joined Malaysia. He assumed ministerial position from the outset, holding first the portfolio of communications and works and then at the end of the 1960s entering the federal Parliament to assume cabinet office. His tenure as chief minister was marred after a time by tension with his uncle **Abdul Rahman Yakub**, who had become Sarawak's governor in 1981 but stood down from office in 1985. In March 1987 financially induced defections from the governing state coalition designed to unseat Taib Mahmud led to early elections which returned his government to office, but with a reduced majority. In subsequent elections in September 1991, Taib restored his coalition's fortunes with a resounding victory and in April 1995 delivered twenty-six out of twenty-seven Sarawak constituencies in federal elections. Datuk Taib has cultivated good relations with the federal government and his ability to deliver Sarawak to the ruling ***Barisan Nasional*** (National Front, BN), including landslide state election victories in 1996 and 1999, has been a key factor in his long political tenure.

Perennially confronted with allegations of corruption because of the huge personal wealth he has amassed, it was rumoured after the 2008 federal elections, which saw the BN lose its two-thirds parliamentary majority, that Taib might be sidelined by Prime Minister **Najib Razak**. Taib himself went on record to suggest he might retire in 'two to three years' time'. Yet despite this, as well as a major exposé in March 2013 that uncovered his involvement in controversial land deals in Sarawak, Taib still led the BN to a critical victory in the state during federal elections in 2013. This all but entrenched Taib's position in Sarawak, leading detractors to claim that even the prime minister was powerless against his political influence in the state. Taib Mahmud stepped down from the office of chief minister after thirty-three years in February 2014 and handed the reins to his political ally and former brother-in-law, Adenan Satem. The day after his resignation, he was sworn in as governor of Sarawak.

see also: Abdul Rahman Yakub, Tun; *Barisan Nasional*; Najib Tun Razak, Datuk Seri Mohamad; *Parti Pesaka Bumiputera Bersatu*.

Tanjung Priok Riot 1984
(Indonesia)

A violent confrontation between Muslim protestors and security forces took place with great loss of life during the night of 12 September 1984 in the Tanjung Priok port area of Jakarta, the capital of Indonesia. The protest had been precipitated by the arrest of four members of a local prayer hall, who had attacked two army officers in the course of demanding an apology for their having allegedly violated its sanctity. The large crowd which sought the release of the detainees was met at the police station by a hail of bullets from members of an air defence regiment, resulting in up to 200 deaths. The bloody episode took place against the background of Muslim resistance to the government's attempt to require all organizations to accept ***Pancasila***, the state philosophy, as their sole principle. Agitation against government policy had become vociferous in and around the Tanjung Priok prayer hall, leading to a military investigation which had in turn given rise to the incident that led on to the violence. After the fatal clash, there followed a series of fires and explosions in Jakarta; in January 1985, several small bombs went off within the historic Borobudur Buddhist monument near Yogyakarta. Acts of Muslim-inspired violence petered out by the end of the 1980s as the result of action by intelligence and security forces. Nearly a year after Suharto's political downfall, public interest was expressed in a full accounting of the Tanjung Priok episode with the senior officers concerned being questioned by the Human Rights Commission. In 2003 the House of Representatives (*Dewan Perwakilan Rakyat*) sanctioned the re-opening of the case. However the conviction of several senior military officers was overturned by the Supreme Court a year later and to date the case remains inconclusive.

see also: Islam; *Pancasila*.

Tarbiyah (Indonesia)

Tarbiyah refers to an Islamic reform movement prevalent in the tertiary education campuses across Indonesia during the 1970s and 1980s. The agenda of *Tarbiyah* was the creation of an Islamic society from the bottom up, where individuals formed familial units for the purpose of propagating Islamic values, which in turn would give rise to an Islamic society. This Islamic society will then result in the eventual creation of an Islamic state.

The *Tarbiyah* movement was non-violent and non-confrontational, and most of its activities focused on ***Dakwah*** (proselytization among the Muslim community). Because of its non-confrontational stance, the *Tarbiyah* movement managed to flourish under the **Suharto** government, particularly when the former president started to build an alliance with the Muslim community. The founding of the Association of Indonesian Muslim Scholars (ICMI), with Suharto ally **B. J. Habibie** as chairman, marked a turning point for the *Tarbiyah* movement when it was allowed to publicize its activities. With this endorsement, the *Tarbiyah* established Islamic boarding schools and associations that provided educational assistance to high school students. In addition to that, they established organizations for purposes of religious propagation and created informal religious educational circles known as *halqah* through which religious activities were conducted. The *Tarbiyah* movement also started to flourish in university student organizations, and a Union for Indonesian Muslim Students (KAMMI) was formed in 1998. In addition, existing Muslim student associations such as *Himpunam Mahasiswa Islam* (HMI) and Indonesia Islamic Student Movement (PMII) came under the control of *Tarbiyah* student activists. With the resignation of Suharto and the transition to a more democratic Indonesia, *Tarbiyah* activists formed *Partai Keadilan* (Justice Party) on 28 July 1998 in order to translate their social activism into a political agenda that held closely to its ideals. *Partai Keadilan* eventually became ***Partai Keadilan Sejahtera***.

see also: Dakwah; Habibie, B. J.; *Partai Keadilan Sejahtera*; Suharto.

Terrorism in Southeast Asia (Indonesia/Malaysia/Philippines/ Singapore)

While terrorism in the region has historically been perpetrated by Communist and nationalist groups, Islamist terrorist groups have emerged as a pernicious challenge for governments in Southeast Asia after September 11. As early as December 2001, Singaporean authorities arrested members of ***Jemaah Islamiyah*** (JI), a radical Muslim group with roots in the Indonesia-based ***Darul Islam*** movement and which sought to overthrow the governments in Malaysia, Indonesia, Singapore, Brunei, the Philippines and Thailand so as to create a regional caliphate. JI was formally founded by two *Darul Islam* activists, Abdullah Sungkar and **Abu Bakar Ba'asyir**, while they were taking refuge in Malaysia from the Suharto government in 1993. Other prominent JI leaders include Riduan Isamuddin (better known as **Hambali**), an Indonesian, and two Malaysians, Nordin Mohamed Top and Azhari Hussein. Many JI members also come from the network of the Pondok Ngruki, an Islamic boarding school started by Ba'asyir and Sungkar in 1972. Some observers have argued that the school's curriculum promotes an extreme interpretation of Islam which encourages violence. The group's violent turn occurred in 1998 during the communal conflicts in Maluku and Poso, when JI leaders deemed it an obligation for Muslims to engage in *jihad* to defend Islam in Indonesia against the perceived threat of Christian proselytization.

Post-September 11 terrorism in Southeast Asia possesses a transnational dimension that previously was less evident among the activities of the region's armed resistance groups. This transnational character was perhaps most profoundly demonstrated in the relationship between JI and Al-Qaeda that took on ideological and operational forms. JI also forged relationships of varying degrees with other armed groups in Southeast Asia such as the **Moro Islamic Liberation Front** (MILF) and the **Abu Sayyaf Group** (ASG). Contacts between JI and these groups were established in Afghanistan where Southeast Asian Muslims arrived to participate in the *jihad* against Soviet occupation in the 1980s. Members of JI were also known to have trained in Camp Abu Bakar As-Shiddiq, headquarters of the MILF until it was overrun in 2000.

On Christmas Eve of 2000, coordinated bomb attacks were launched in Jakarta and eight other Indonesian cities causing eighteen deaths. The attack was the first Al-Qaeda-inspired JI terrorist attack in the country. A document detailing planned attacks in Singapore, Malaysia and Indonesia was later discovered in December 2001 by Indonesian police, sparking concerns over the transnational footprint of the terrorist threat emanating from Indonesia. It was however, the devastating attacks in the Indonesian resort island of Bali in October 2002 that brought home the severity of the terrorist threat to the region. The 2002 Bali bombings involved a car bomb, which was detonated outside the Sari Club in Kuta, and a backpack mounted device carried by a suicide bomber which was detonated in Paddy's Pub across the street. The attack was the deadliest act of terror in Indonesian history with a death toll of over 200. Following the attack, an audio recording, purportedly of Osama Bin Laden, surfaced on various Al-Qaeda-linked websites lauding the Bali bombings as retaliation for the US War on Terror and Australia's support for the secession of East Timor. The Bali bombings were significant on several fronts. First, they signalled the escalation of the terrorist threat in Southeast Asia. Second, they forced the Indonesian government to acknowledge the presence of homegrown terrorists, even though the Indonesian leadership at the time continued to deny the existence of a terrorist group called JI.

The 2002 Bali bombings were followed by a suicide bomb blast at the JW Marriott Hotel in the business district of Jakarta in August 2003, the bombing of the Australian Embassy in Indonesia in September 2004 and a further attack in Bali in October 2005. All these attacks in Indonesia were connected to JI, and Al-Qaeda was believed to have provided US$30,000 to fund the 2003 attack. These attacks presaged heavy criticism of the Indonesian government for its alleged state of denial and lacklustre approach to counterterrorism. Jakarta responded by intensifying the training and operational preparedness of its crack counterterrorism task force, *Densus 88*, which has since acquired a reputation for operational decisiveness. With help from a carefully assembled intelligence network, *Densus 88* has managed to eliminate key JI leaders such as Azhari Hussein, Nordin Top and Dulmatin. At the same time, it has also been criticized for allegedly using torture to extract information. Meanwhile, terrorist attacks, while considerably reduced, were not eliminated, and in 2009 a radical faction within JI perpetrated attacks at the JW Marriot Hotel and the adjacent Ritz Carton Hotel, while a militant training camp was discovered in Aceh in 2010. Aside from counterterrorism operations, the Indonesian government has also used legal instruments to deal with terrorism. These include a 2003 anti-terror law that authorized the death penalty and detention without trial for perpetrators of terrorist acts. This legal instrument was deployed in the trial of the Bali bombers: Amrozi, Imam Samudra and Mukhlas.

Terrorist activity has been equally rife in the Philippines, and while the **New People's Army** have long adopted terrorism as a weapon in its struggle, it has been Islamist-inspired terrorist acts that have predominated in recent years. The southern islands of the Philippine archipelago, poorly governed and home to armed groups such as the **Moro National Liberation Front** (MNLF), the MILF and the ASG, have also proven to be a safe haven for JI members escaping authorities in Singapore, Malaysia and Indonesia. Since 2000, the region has also witnessed an upsurge in terrorist attacks of varying scale, including grenade attacks in markets, bombing of public transport facilities, and the taking of hostages by ASG from the Malaysian resort island of Sipadan in 2000 and from Palawan in 2001. The bombing of *SuperFerry 14* in February 2004, leading to more than 100 deaths, was the most lethal. Facing the magnitude of the problem, the Philippines government sought out American military assistance without hesitation.

The existence of internal security legislation, which allows for extended periods of detention without trial, and efficient policing and intelligence networks have provided the governments of Singapore and Malaysia the wherewithal to effectively contain the terrorist threats that have emerged within their borders. In addition to this, multinational cooperation among the four states and their **ASEAN** (Association of Southeast Asian Nations) neighbours has allowed for extensive exchange of information and joint operations that has helped national security and law enforcement agencies to effectively disrupt terrorist activities in the region.

see also: Abu Sayyaf Group; ASEAN; Ba'asyir, Abu Bakar; *Darul Islam*; Hambali; *Jemaah Islamiyah*; Moro Islamic Liberation Front; Moro National Liberation Front; New People's Army.

Tet Offensive 1968 (Vietnam)

Tet is the name of the holiday celebrated on the Vietnamese lunar new year. On the night of 30 January 1968, during that holiday, forces of the **National Liberation Front of South Vietnam** (NLF) launched a series of coordinated surprise attacks throughout South Vietnam. Apart from the capital Saigon, where the presidential palace was penetrated, thirty-four out of forty-four provincial capitals were attacked and ten were held temporarily. The citadel of the ancient capital of Hue was not retaken by United States and South Vietnamese forces until the end of February. The declared purpose of the attacks was to generate a popular uprising against the government of President **Nguyen Van Thieu**. To that end, the offensive, which involved a costly expenditure of human resources by the NLF, was a military failure. Politically, however, it proved to be a remarkable success due to its visual impact on television within the United States, where the **Vietnam War** had become increasingly unpopular. The domestic impact of the Tet Offensive led to the announcement by President Lyndon Johnson on 31 March that he would not seek re-election in November 1968 and that the bombing of North Vietnam would be restricted in order to start negotiations to end the war with the Vietnamese Communists. The Tet Offensive proved to be a critical psychological turning point in the Vietnam War, following which American resolve to fight the war was never the same.

see also: National Liberation Front of South Vietnam; Thieu, Nguyen Van; Vietnam War.

Thach, Nguyen Co (Vietnam)

Nguyen Co Thach was Vietnam's foreign minister between February 1980 and June 1991. He had prime responsibility for managing the adverse diplomatic consequences of the invasion of Cambodia, defending his country's interests with skill and determination in negotiations with **ASEAN** (Association of Southeast Asian Nations) and the People's Republic of China. He was forced from office at the seventh national congress of the Communist Party as part of the price of Vietnam's rapprochement with China. Nguyen Co Thach was born on 15 May 1923 into a peasant family in northern Vietnam. He entered the revolutionary movement as a young man and was arrested by the French. He rose to become a staff officer in the **Viet Minh** army and took part in the **Battle of Dien Bien Phu** in 1954. He then entered the diplomatic service and spent four years in New Delhi as consul-general. On returning to Hanoi, he played an important role in a series of international negotiations beginning with the **Geneva Agreements on Laos** in 1961–2. By the end of the 1970s he had risen to become the most senior official in the Ministry of Foreign Affairs. He was made an alternate member of the party Politburo in 1982 and a full member in 1986, the first diplomat to attain such rank. In March 1987 he was appointed a deputy prime minister, holding that office until June 1991 when all of his party and state posts were relinquished simultaneously. He died on 10 April 1998 aged seventy-seven.

see also: ASEAN; Dien Bien Phu, Battle of, 1954; Geneva Agreements on Laos 1962; Viet Minh.

Thai–Lao Border War 1987–8 (Laos/Thailand)

The Thai–Lao Border War was a brief and often overlooked armed conflict between Thailand and Laos over border demarcation that lasted from December 1987 to February 1988. At issue was the unclear ownership of four villages based on a 1907 French map of the border between then Siam and French Indochina. This same map is also at the heart of the **Preah Vihear Temple Dispute**. Thailand claimed Ban Rom Klao as part of its Phitsanulok Province and the other three villages as part of Uttaradit Province. In December 1987 Thai troops occupied Ban Rom Klao and raised the Thai flag. Vientiane issued strong protests, claiming the village is part of its Saiyabuli Province. Laotian army units staged a night attack on the Thai garrison, forcing them out of the village. Heavy fighting continued for several weeks until a ceasefire was arranged on 19 February 1988. Vietnamese units were sent to assist the Laotian Army but only arrived after the ceasefire was agreed. There were about a 1,000 casualties in total on both sides, with the Thais suffering more. General **Chavalit Yongchaiyuth**, commander of the Thai Army at the time, was criticized for fighting against the advice of the foreign ministry. In 1996 a Thai–Lao Joint Boundary Commission was established to clarify the 1,810-kilometre border between the two countries and ownership of the villages. Border demarcation is still ongoing.

see also: Chavalit Yongchaiyuth, General; Preah Vihear Temple Dispute.

Thai Rak Thai Party (Thailand)

The *Thai Rak Thai* (Thais Love Thais, TRT) Party was established on 14 July 1998 by successful entrepreneur cum politician, **Thaksin Shinawatra**. TRT was the governing party in Thailand from 2001 to September 2006, winning three landslide elections. In forming TRT, Thaksin wooed a considerable number of politicians from other parties and in some cases won whole factions over to the TRT banner. The party's first electoral foray resulted in a loss when its candidate failed in a bid to become governor of Bangkok in July 2000. TRT rebounded with a victory in January 2001 parliamentary elections by a wide margin over the incumbent **Democrat Party**. The elections were the first under the **People's Constitution** promulgated in 1997. TRT, which won 248 seats out of 500, more than any other party in previous elections, formed a government coalition with the ***Chart Thai* Party** and the **New Aspiration Party**. With a total of 325 seats, the TRT-led coalition had secured the largest majority in Thai electoral history. The New Aspiration Party of former army commander and prime minister, **Chavalit Yongchaiyuth**, merged with TRT shortly after the elections, as did the much smaller *Seritham* Party. TRT won an even larger majority in the 2005 elections when its own representatives won 376 seats, allowing the party to form a single-party government for the first time in Thai politics. The fact that TRT essentially comprised factions of other parties, and even entire parties as in the case of New Aspiration and *Seritham*, meant that it remained factionalized throughout its existence. Many of its politicians continued to maintain allegiance to their factions rather than to the party as a whole. Most important of these factions were *Wang Bua Ban* led by Thaksin's sister, Yaowapa Wongsawat, and which formed much of Thaksin's inner circle, and *Nam Wong Yen* led by kingmaker **Sanoh Thienthong** and which comprised politicians from the northeast.

Thaksin founded the party ostensibly as a vehicle for political and economic reform drawing mainly on support from Chiang Mai and the rural north and northeast and also from disaffected white-collar **Democrat Party** voters. This was articulated through a platform of populist policies that appealed directly to voters, especially those in rural areas of the north and northeast, the most populous in the country, and urban voters with roots in those areas. These policies included a universal health care scheme and a microcredit development fund for rural districts. The party has no real political ideology, but was skilful at convincing voters that the party listened to and empathized with their grievances, a marked change from traditional top-down Thai politics. Some of TRT's policies were controversial. Most prominently, the 2003 'war on drugs' led to intense international criticism for its reliance on extrajudicial killings. It was, however, popular with many Thais and did reduce the high levels of narcotics trafficking and use in the country. TRT's hardline policies in the restive southern region on the other hand, alienated many among the Malay-Muslim population and exacerbated an already deteriorating situation.

While TRT's policies were generally well received, especially by its support base, Thaksin's manoeuvring for personal political and economic advantage would result in the party's downfall. Chief among these was his sale of his family company Shin Corporation to Temasek Holdings of Singapore and attempts to evade taxes on this sale as well as on real estate dealings. The situation was compounded by his increasingly hostile attitude towards criticism by the press culminating in the closure of a weekly current affairs programme of former influential ally **Sondhi Limthongkul**. Angry protests over Thaksin's financial dealings soon coalesced into the **People's Alliance for Democracy** led by Sondhi and other prominent figures. Under this political pressure, Thaksin dissolved Parliament and called for new elections in an attempt to stave off the looming crisis. The Democrat Party and its allies boycotted the elections in April 2006 in which TRT won 460 of 500 seats. A rare intercession by King **Bhumibol Adulyadej,** who publicly declared the elections undemocratic, resulted in the Constitutional Court declaring them invalid and new elections being ordered. TRT became a caretaker government until new elections could be held later in the year. On 19 September 2006, the army staged a successful coup in Bangkok while Thaksin and much of the TRT leadership were abroad. Members of the leadership remaining in the country were arrested and detained by the junta, largely decapitating the party and making its reaction to the coup disorganized. Now in exile, Thaksin resigned from the party on 2 October 2006, a move that largely ended TRT as a political force. The party remained in existence until 30 May 2007 when the Constitutional Court officially banned it due to violations of electoral laws during the 2006 elections. The decision also banned 111 TRT politicians from participating in politics for five years. Most of the remaining TRT politicians would go on to join the **People's Power Party** (PPP), which would be seen as a proxy for TRT and Thaksin. The PPP would win a resounding victory in elections in 2007, but would also be dissolved by the Constitutional Court in December 2008 for electoral fraud. Many of the former TRT/PPP politicians moved to join the ***Pheu Thai* Party**, which became the main opposition party to the Democrat Party-led government until it won the 2011 election and formed the government.

see also: Bhumibol Adulyadej, King; *Chart Thai* Party; Chavalit Yongchaiyuth, General; Democrat Party; New Aspiration Party; People's Alliance for Democracy; People's Constitution; People's Power Party; *Pheu Thai* Party; Sanoh Thienthong; Sondhi Limthongkul; Thaksin Shinawatra.

Thaksin Shinawatra (Thailand)

One of the most divisive figures of his time, Thaksin Shinawatra served as prime minister of Thailand from February 2001 to September 2006 when he was removed in a military coup.

Thaksin Shinawatra, who was born on 26 July 1949, is a one-time senior police officer and successful telecommunications entrepreneur cum politician who was leader of the *Palang Dharma* Party from May 1995. During the first administration of **Chuan Leekpai**, he was foreign minister for three months but then resigned because of controversy over his lack of a parliamentary seat. He was elected to parliament in July 1995 and took his party back into coalition government as deputy prime minister to **Banharn Silpa-archa** but gave up office in August 1996 when *Palang Dharma* left the ruling coalition. After its dismal performance in elections in November 1996, Thaksin resigned as party leader. He was briefly deputy prime minister in the coalition headed by **Chavalit Yongchaiyuth** but lost office with the latter's resignation in November 1997 in the wake of the **Asian Financial Crisis**. In July 1998, he founded the ***Thai Rak Thai* Party** (TRT). On the basis of claiming to be in favour of political and economic reform, he emerged as a strong opposition rival to the prime minister, Chuan Leekpai. Thaksin led TRT to victory in elections held in January 2001, the first under the new **People's Constitution** promulgated in 1997, on the back of populist promises. The People's Constitution was a landmark in Thai democratic reform, providing guarantees of civil rights, creation of independent institutions, and implementation of executive powers designed to break the chronic political deadlock born of weak coalitions and factionalism since the end of military rule in Thailand. It was against this backdrop that Thaksin Shinawatra was appointed prime minister in a coalition government which included the ***Chart Thai* Party** and the **New Aspiration Party**.

Upon assuming high office, Thaksin moved quickly to entrench his position. He pushed through populist electoral promises such as universal healthcare and village credit, which further enhanced his popularity among the rural electorate. These populist measures led him and his TRT to another sweeping victory at the 2005 elections, when it won an even larger mandate with 375 seats. Some of his other policies in contrast, particularly his 'war on drugs' policy which led to multiple cases of extrajudicial killings, his hardline policies in relation to the **Southern Provinces Insurgency**, and the controversial sale of his family company Shin Corporation to Temasek Holdings of Singapore, sowed the seeds of discontent which would eventually contribute to his downfall. Thaksin's fall from grace was catalysed by his closure of the weekly current affairs programme of influential former ally **Sondhi Limthongkul**, which led to mass protest. Thaksin sought to stave off a brewing crisis by calling for fresh elections in April 2006, but faced with a collective boycott from opposition parties could only claim a pyrrhic victory. In the event, an unprecedented intervention by

King **Bhumibol Adulyadej** who publicly declared the election undemocratic led to judicial annulment of the election result, which in turn set in motion forces that eventually led to his removal through a coup in September 2006 while he was abroad. TRT suffered a similar fate when it was dissolved in May 2007 for reasons of electoral fraud. Thaksin returned briefly to Thailand in 2008 when the **People's Power Party**, comprised of his allies and former TRT colleagues, came to power after post-coup elections. Confronted with corruption charges, he skipped bail and left the country again, ostensibly to attend the opening ceremony of the August 2008 Olympics in Beijing, and has not returned since. In the event, Thaksin was charged *in absentia* for conflict of interest over a land deal involving his wife, Pojaman Shinawatra, and sentenced to two years' imprisonment. For that, he gained notoriety as the first Thai prime minister charged and convicted for a corruption offence that took place during his term.

While abroad in self-imposed exile, Thaksin remained involved in Thai politics, most profoundly through the **United Front for Democracy Against Dictatorship** (UDD), whose leaders he kept in regular contact with, and more recently though his sister and prime minister, **Yingluck Shinawatra**. In point of fact, at the height of the UDD protests Thaksin was ever-present at their rallies through satellite and phone-in links, often provocatively praising their actions and even calling for revolution. In November 2009, Thaksin accepted an invitation from Prime Minister **Hun Sen** to serve as an economic advisor to Cambodia at the height of the **Preah Vihear Temple Dispute**. Exercised by the prospect of Thaksin's return to Thailand, opposition forces blocked attempts by the government of Yingluck Shinawatra to embark on constitutional revisions, which they interpreted foremost as a vehicle to facilitate this return. In the event, the 22 May 2014 military coup has made this highly unlikely at least in the short term.

see also: Asian Financial Crisis 1997–8; Banharn Silpa-archa; Bhumibol Adulyadej, King; *Chart Thai* Party; Chavalit Yongchaiyuth, General; Chuan Leekpai; Insurgency, Southern Provinces; People's Constitution; People's Power Party; Preah Vihear Temple Dispute; Sondhi Limthongkul; *Thai Rak Thai* Party; United Front for Democracy Against Dictatorship; Yingluck Shinawatra.

Thammasat University Massacre 1976 (Thailand)

On 6 October 1976 armed border patrol and other police units, together with right-wing vigilante groups, stormed the campus of Thammasat University in Bangkok. Students had assembled there in protest against the return to the country in September of the former prime minister, Field Marshal **Thanom Kittikachorn**, who had gone into exile in the wake of a violent confrontation between soldiers and students in October 1973, after which parliamentary democracy had been re-established. There is reason to believe that Thanom's return was a deliberate attempt to engineer a political crisis in the military interest. Student theatre, including a mock hanging to draw attention to the extra-legal execution of two of their number in September, was seized on as an act of *lèse majesté* because of the striking resemblance of one of the actors to Crown Prince **Maha Vajiralongkorn**. The police onslaught led to carnage, with students being burned alive and lynched from trees as well as being shot dead. The official death toll was put at forty-six but the fatalities were almost certainly much greater, while hundreds of students were wounded and many thousands arrested. The same evening, Admiral Sangad Chaloryu, minister of defence in the elected government of the prime minister, **Seni Pramoj**, announced that a National Administrative Reform Council had seized power in order to restore law and order. The coup re-established military rule in Thailand with the evident blessing of King **Bhumibol Adulyadej**, who on 9 October appointed a former Supreme Court judge, Thanin Kraivichian, as a nominally civilian prime minister. He was replaced in a bloodless coup in October 1977 by a pragmatic military clique led by the army commander, General **Kriangsak Chomanan**. In the wake of the bloodbath at Thammasat University, hundreds of students fled the capital to join the insurgent Communist Party of Thailand, giving that movement a new momentum and significance less than two years after the end of the Vietnam War.

see also: Bhumibol Adulyadej, King; Kriangsak Chomanan, General; Maha Vajiralongkorn, Prince; Seni Pramoj; Thanom Kittikachorn, Field Marshal.

Than Shwe, Senior General

(Myanmar)

General Than Shwe was appointed prime minister of Myanmar and chairman of the **State Law and Order Restoration Council** (SLORC) on 23 April 1992 in succession to General Saw Maung, who was relieved from office apparently suffering from a mental disorder. Than Shwe was born on 2 February 1993 in Kyaukse, Mandalay Division. He received a secondary education only, but failed to finish and began employment as a postal clerk. He later enlisted in the military joining the ninth intake of the Army Officer Training School and after graduating in 1953 became an infantry officer and rose steadily in rank. In 1958, Than Shwe was assigned to the Directorate of Education and Psychological Warfare and later to psychological warfare field units. Throughout the late 1960s and 1970s he served in various field commands as well as general and divisional staff positions. By 1971, he was a battalion commander acquiring the rank of lieutenant colonel during 1972. In 1980, he became commander of the 88th Light Infantry Division overseeing several major military operations. In 1981 he was appointed to the Central Executive Committee of the **Burmese Socialist Programme Party**. In 1983 he was appointed commander of the Southwest Military Region and subsequently chairman of the Irrawaddy Division Party Committee. He was promoted to brigadier general in 1984. In 1985 he was promoted to major general and appointed vice chief of staff (army), effectively head of the army. Than Shwe was promoted to lieutenant general in November 1987. He became the deputy minister of defence in July 1988. Following the **1988 Democracy Uprising** and the 18 September 1988 coup that installed the SLORC, Than Shwe became its vice chairman. On 18 March 1990, Than Shwe became a full general, vice-commander of the Myanmar Armed Forces (*Tatmadaw*) and commander-in-chief of the Myanmar Army. When Senior General Saw Maung unexpectedly resigned on 23 April 1992 for health reasons, Than Shwe replaced him as chairman of the SLORC and commander-in-chief of the Armed Forces, at the same time promoting himself to senior general. He eventually gave up his command of the army in March 1993. When the **State Peace and Development Council** (SPDC) was created in November 1997, Than Shwe assumed the office of chairman.

Under Than Shwe, economic control over the economy was relaxed and Myanmar joined ASEAN (Association of Southeast Asian Nations) while at the same time maintaining tight controls over the media and political dissent. He released **Aung San Suu Kyi** in the late 1990s but returned her to detention in 2003. Throughout his rule, his government, and particularly the military, were widely criticized internationally for extensive human rights abuses. The government received especially virulent criticism in 2007 following its violent crackdown on the Buddhist monk-led '**Saffron Revolution**' and the delayed response to the Cyclone Nargis disaster in 2008. Than Shwe was frequently rumoured to be at odds with army commander and SPDC vice chairman, Vice Senior General Maung Aye. His paranoia led him to place the regime's third in command, **Khin Nyunt**, under house arrest during an ostensible anti-corruption drive that resulted in the dismantling of the intelligence service and cemented Than Shwe's grip on power. Although believed to be opposed to democratization, Than Shwe oversaw the seven-step '**Roadmap to Democracy**' including the completion of the National Convention in 2007, the referendum that approved the **2008 Constitution**, and the machinations that led up to the 2010 democratic vote and transition to nominal civilian rule in March 2011. After **Thein Sein** assumed the office of president, Than Shwe stepped down and largely retreated from public view. In ill health, he is still believed to maintain influence over the government, especially through the military and the National

Defence and Security Council, an extralegal body with undefined powers.

see also: ASEAN; Aung San Suu Kyi; Burma Socialist Programme Party; Constitution 2008; Democracy Uprising 1988; Khin Nyunt, General; Roadmap to Democracy; Saffron Revolution 2007; State Law and Order Restoration Council; State Peace and Development Council; Thein Sein.

Thanat Khoman (Thailand)

Thanat Khoman served as Thailand's foreign minister between 1959 and 1971. His major contribution was in promoting regional reconciliation and cooperation. He played a key role in mediating between Indonesia and Malaysia in the mid-1960s; the choice of Bangkok as the venue for the founding meeting of **ASEAN** (Association of Southeast Asian Nations) in August 1967 was a testament to his active part in institution-building. Thanat Khoman was born in 1914 in Bangkok into a Sino-Thai family. He studied law in France and entered his country's diplomatic service in 1940. He served in Tokyo during part of the Pacific War but on his return to Bangkok associated himself with the resistance to Japan's dominion. In that company, he was a member of a clandestine mission to the headquarters of the Allied **Southeast Asia Command** in Ceylon (Sri Lanka) in February 1945. After the war he held several diplomatic posts, rising to the rank of ambassador to Washington in 1957. He was removed as foreign minister with the incumbency coup by the military in 1971, in part because of his declared interest in a rapprochement with the People's Republic of China. After stepping down as a technocratic foreign minister, he entered politics and became the leader of the **Democrat Party** between 1979 and 1982 and a deputy prime minister between 1980 and 1982, after which he retired from political life.

see also: ASEAN; Democrat Party; Southeast Asia Command.

Thanin Kraivichian (Thailand)

Thanin Kraivichian became a controversial prime minister of Thailand in October 1976 when the deaths of students in the **Thammasat University Massacre** provided the opportunity for a military coup. He was in office for only a year when he was deposed by another military coup, but without bloodshed. Thanin was born on 5 April 1927 in Bangkok. He was trained as a lawyer at Gray's Inn, London. After a period in legal practice, he embarked on a career as a jurist and by 1976 had attained the position of senior judge in the country's Supreme Court. Thanin did not enjoy a political base. The key to his appointment as prime minister was his close association with King **Bhumibol Adulyadej**, who was suspicious of military rule and wished the country to have a civilian conservative leader. Thanin fitted the bill as a compromise candidate acceptable to the so-called National Administrative Reform Council in whose name the military had seized power. In office, however, he showed himself to be ideologically so dogmatic and ill-attuned to political responsibility that his removal in October 1977 by General **Kriangsak Chomanan** was greeted with a sense of national relief.

see also: Bhumibol Adulyadej, King; Kriangsak Chomanan, General; Thammasat University Massacre 1976.

Thanom Kittikachorn, Field Marshal (Thailand)

Field Marshal Thanom Kittikachorn was prime minister of Thailand in October 1973 when brutal military reaction to student protest at the lack of constitutional progress prompted King **Bhumibol Adulyadej** to advise him to go into exile overseas. His return to Thailand in September 1976, ostensibly to enter a Buddhist monastery, provoked a recurrence of protests which culminated the following month in many student deaths in the **Thammasat University Massacre** in Bangkok, which provided the opportunity for a military coup. Thanom Kittikachorn was born on 11 August 1911 and began his professional military training at the Chulachomklao Royal Military Academy in Bangkok before the coup in 1932 that put an end to the absolute monarchy. After rising to the rank of lieutenant general in the mid-1950s, he entered politics as a close associate of Field Marshal **Sarit Thanarat**, who was effective military dictator from 1957 until his death in 1963. Thanom, who was then deputy prime minister, became prime minister continuously (with one interruption) until his deposition in 1973. In that period, he depended conspicuously on the support of his deputy, General **Praphas Charusathien**. After his controversial return from exile, he lived a private life in retirement. He died on 16 June 2004.

see also: Bhumibol Adulyadej, King; Praphas Charusathien, Field Marshal; Sarit Thanarat, Field Marshal; Thammasat University Massacre 1976.

Thein Sein (Myanmar)

Thein Sein became president of Myanmar after being elected in the country's first democratic elections in decades in November 2011, and has been credited as the person who set Myanmar on its current path of political reform and liberalization.

Thein Sein was born in Kyonku village in Irrawaddy Division on 20 April 1945. He joined the ninth intake of the Defence Services Academy, graduating in 1968. He held few combat roles, serving mostly in bureaucratic positions. In 1993 he attained the rank of brigadier general and became the first brigadier to hold the position of general staff officer in the War Office in Yangon, an office he assumed in 1991. In 1996 he was promoted to major general and assigned the command of the newly established Triangle Military Region Command in northeastern Shan State where he served from 1997 to 2001. As a regional commander, Thein Sein also became a member of the **State Peace and Development Council** and Secretary-3 of the ruling junta in 2003. He became adjutant general of the War Office in 2001 and was promoted to lieutenant general in 2002. With the detention of **Khin Nyunt** in late 2004, Thein Sein became Secretary-1. During this time he also chaired the National Convention Convening Commission that oversaw the drafting of what would become Myanmar's current constitution. In April 2007, Thein Sein was appointed interim prime minister to replace the ailing Soe Win. After Soe Win's death on 12 October 2007, Thein Sein formally became prime minister (on 24 October). He was promoted to general in 2007 and continued to hold the position of Secretary-1 in the military junta, making him the country's fourth highest-ranking general. As prime minister he oversaw improvements in bilateral relations with Vietnam, Laos, Cambodia and Bangladesh. In the wake of the Cyclone Nargis disaster in May 2008, Thein Sein led the National Disaster Preparedness Central Committee tasked with emergency preparedness.

Thein Sein retired from the military on 29 April 2010, along with twenty-two other high-ranking military officers, to lead the **Union Solidarity and Development Party** for the November 2010 election. The party went on to win an overwhelming majority of seats in a controversial election marred by widespread irregularities. Thein Sein ran as a representative for Zabuthiri township in the Naypyidaw Union Territory where he won a purported 91.2 per cent of the vote. On 4 February 2011, he was elected by the Pyidaungsu Hluttaw's Presidential Electoral College as the president of the Republic of the Union of Myanmar, making him the first non-interim civilian president in forty-nine years. He is also concurrently the head of the National Defence and Security Council, an extralegal body with ill-defined powers, but definite authority to reinstitute military rule in an emergency. As president, Thein Sein sought and won Myanmar's bid to chair **ASEAN** (Association of Southeast Asian Nations) in 2014. He has also pushed numerous reform initiatives including relaxation of controls on the media, the suspension of a controversial dam project led by China, engagement with **Aung San Suu Kyi** which paved the way for the **National League for Democracy**'s involvement in by-elections in April 2012, and support for a peace process with the country's numerous ethnic insurgent organizations. Widely considered a moderate reformist, Thein Sein became the first Myanmar leader to visit the United States in forty-six years in September 2012. He was also nominated for the 2012 Nobel Peace Prize.

see also: ASEAN; Aung San Suu Kyi; Khin Nyunt, General; National League for Democracy; State Peace and Development Council; Union Solidarity and Development Party.

Thieu, Nguyen Van (Vietnam)

Nguyen Van Thieu was president and head of the government of the Republic of (South) Vietnam from September 1967 until April 1975, leaving Saigon for exile overseas shortly before the Communists seized power. He was born on 5 April 1923 into a Catholic family. He entered the army under French rule and received his professional training at the National Military Academy in Hue. He continued as an officer under the regime of **Ngo Dinh Diem**, receiving rapid promotion. As armed forces chief of staff and a lieutenant general, he was a member of the coup group which overthrew Diem in November 1963. He was initially deputy prime minister and then constitutional president during 1965–7. In September 1967, however, he secured election as executive president and held on to power. In that office, he resisted negotiations with the Communist insurgents and sought to prevent a private deal between Washington and Hanoi being translated into the **Paris Peace Agreements** for Vietnam in January 1973. It was his decision to order the retreat of southern forces following the Communist Ban Me Thuot Offensive in the central highlands in March 1975 which led to a military rout and the speedy collapse of his regime.

see also: Diem, Ngo Dinh; Paris Peace Agreements 1973.

Thongloun Sisoulith (Laos)

Thongloun Sisoulith is a deputy prime minister and minister of foreign affairs of Laos. Thongloun is a northerner born in Hua Phan Province in November 1945. He studied at the Neo Lao Hak Sat Pedagogical College in Hua Pan from 1962 to 1969 and was later educated in the Soviet Union. Thongloun was deputy minister of foreign affairs from 1987 to 1992, minister of labour and social welfare from 1993 to 1997, and a member of the National Assembly from 1998 to 2000. In March 2001 he became deputy prime minister and president of the State Planning Committee. Passed over for the position of prime minister in 2006, Thongloun was appointed deputy prime minister and foreign minister in 2006, replacing Somsavat Lengsavad. He is currently ranked fourth in the **Lao People's Revolutionary Party** (LPRP) Politburo. There is speculation that he is likely to become prime minister at the next five-year congress. He has the backing of younger members of the party who are more known for their political and technocratic credentials than their achievements in the revolution. Thongloun was instrumental in formulating policies for the economic advances in Laos over the past ten years.

see also: Lao People's Revolutionary Party.

Thongsing Thammavong (Laos)

Thongsing Thammavong is the current prime minister of Laos. He assumed the position on 23 December 2010 after the surprise resignation of **Bouasone Bouphavanh**. His position was strengthened after the Ninth Congress of the **Lao People's Revolutionary Party** (LPRP) in 2011. Thongsing has been a member of the LPRP's Politburo since 1991. He was previously president of the National Assembly from 2006 to 2010. Thongsing was born on 12 April 1944 in the northeastern province of Huaphan. He joined the revolutionary movement in August 1959 and became a member of the LPRP in July 1967. Thongsing studied military medicine and served during the war on the Lao–Vietnam border from 1959 to 1960 before becoming involved in education in Huaphan province and later at the national level from 1976 to 1979. After studying politics and administration from 1980 to 1981 he became a standby member of the Party Central Committee. Thongsing was minister of information and culture from 1983 to 1988. From 1989 to 1991 he was party secretary and vice-president of the People's Supreme Assembly, then promoted to acting president, a position he held during 1991–2. He was elected as a standing Politburo member and head of the Party Central Committee Organization Board at the fifth Party Congress in 1991, and re-elected at the sixth Congress. He was elected mayor of Vientiane in 2002. In 2006 he was elected president of the National Assembly. Thongsing was close to the former president, **Nouhak Phoumsavan**. Following the 2011 Congress, Tongsing moved up into the number two position in the Politburo, second only to **Choummaly Sayasone**, president of Laos and general secretary of the LPRP. Thongsing's steady and uncontroversial climb up the party hierarchy has put him in place to succeed Choummaly at the next Congress.

see also: Bouasone Bouphavanh; Choummaly Sayasone; Lao People's Revolutionary Party; Nouhak Phoumsavan.

Timor Gap Cooperation Treaty (Indonesia/Timor-Leste)

The Timor Gap Cooperation Treaty concluded by the governments of Indonesia and Australia on 27 October 1989 provided for the delimitation of the continental shelf boundary between the south coast of the then Indonesian island of Timor and the northern coast of Australia. The treaty came into force on 9 February 1991. Delimitation took the form of three zones, two to be subject respectively to the control of Indonesia and Australia and the third to be subject to joint control and exploitation. The prospect of rich oil and natural gas reserves in the Timor Sea was a determining factor in protracted negotiations and their outcome.

Contention over the terms of delimitation arose because of variations in the depth of the continental shelf overall. A shallow and vast continental shelf lies adjacent to the Australian coast whereas a narrow and deep continental shelf lies adjacent to the Timor coast. In between the two shelf features is the area known as the Timor Gap with a maximum depth of 3,000 metres. This depression lies some 300 miles north of Australia but only sixty miles south of Timor. The Australian government argued that because of the nature of that depression there were, in fact, two continental shelves between the two countries, which were themselves divided by the Timor Gap, which should itself be delimited equitably. The Indonesian government countered by maintaining that there was only one continental shelf and that the Timor Gap should not be the basis for delimitation because it was only a depression in the single shelf. They insisted on the employment of a median line between the two coasts, with obvious advantages for the Indonesian side. In the event, compromise was reached through an Australian initiative in the form of a proposal for a zone of joint exploration and exploitation comprising approximately half of the delimited area. The conclusion of the treaty was important, not only because it resolved a longstanding problem of competitive access to natural resources but because it set the seal on reconciliation between Jakarta and Canberra, especially over the issue of East Timor, which was annexed by Indonesia in 1976 in a move that Australia remained highly critical of but recognized. That issue was revived as a bone of political contention after the massacre of Timorese demonstrators by Indonesian security forces in the capital, Dili, in November 1991. That bloody episode, which provoked public protest in Australia, was not allowed to stand in the way of the practical implementation of the Timor Gap Cooperation Treaty. In December 1991 Indonesia and Australia signed agreements with a number of international oil companies, permitting them to explore for oil and natural gas in the zone of joint administration in the Timor Sea. The discovery of oil in the joint seabed zone was announced in February 1994. Portugal, which had left its Timor colony in 1974, brought an action against Australia before the International Court of Justice (ICJ) on the grounds that its rights as administering power had been violated by the treaty. In July 1995, the ICJ ruled that it did not have jurisdiction in the matter; it could not rule on the annexation of East Timor by Indonesia, which had not recognized the compulsory jurisdiction of the court and was not a party to the action.

After the UN-supervised referendum in August 1999 in which the vast majority of registered voters opted for independence, which was ratified by Indonesia's **People's Consultative Assembly** (MPR) in the following October, the status of the treaty was clarified. Acting on behalf of East Timor, in February 2000, the United Nations signed a Timor Gap oil and gas exploration treaty with Australia, which had the effect of upholding the terms of the 1989 treaty in favour of East Timor (not Indonesia) and Australia. This treaty established cooperation zones that covered about 65,000 kilometres divided into three zones, with the revenue being split between Dili and Canberra in accordance to the zonal divisions. On 20 May 2002, the Timor

Sea Treaty replaced the Timor Gap Cooperation Treaty of 1989 after East Timor gained independence. The new treaty was signed between the newly independent Government of East Timor (Timor-Leste) and Australia, after the latter refused to take the matter of contested maritime boundaries to the International Court of Justice, with the aim of developing the petroleum resources in a section of the seabed between Australia and East Timor known as the Joint Petroleum Development Area. This treaty had only a single zone with ninety per cent of the revenue derived from this area of the seabed going to Timor-Leste. In 2007 Timor-Leste and Australia signed the Treaty on Certain Maritime Arrangements in the Timor Sea (CMATS), which will in expire in 2057, and this treaty replaced Article 22 of the Timor Sea Treaty bringing its validity in line with CMATS's. The CMATS provided for the equal distribution of revenue derived from the disputed Greater Sunrise oil and gas field between Australia and Timor-Leste. The field is located in the Timor Gap where Australia and Timor-Leste have overlapping claims over the continental shelf or seabed. The Timor Sea Treaty can be renewed at any point if both Dili and Canberra are in consensus.
see also: People's Consultative Assembly.

Timor-Leste Crisis 2006 (Timor-Leste)

In May 2006, the state capital of Timor-Leste, Dili, descended into violence between competing factions of security forces that lasted for several months. This resulted in the displacement of around 150,000 people who fled their homes in Dili to escape the violence, taking shelter at United Nations' internally displaced persons camps. At least thirty people were reported killed.

The crisis was triggered by the poor handling of the dismissal of the 591 soldiers who went on a strike complaining of poor working conditions and that, as 'Westerners', they were being passed over for promotion because most of the military leadership were 'Easterners', where the original nationalist resistance movement was based. This deepened tensions between security forces in the eastern and western regions of the country, with the latter often being accused of 'half-hearted resistance' during Indonesia's occupation of the territory. But the crisis was also a consequence of pent-up frustration over high unemployment rates in Dili, as well as a general disillusionment with the ***Fretilin*** government in power amidst allegations of corruption. Unable to arrest the violence, the Timorese government requested help from the international community. Led by Australia, about 2,700 troops comprising military personnel from Australia, Malaysia, New Zealand and Portugal arrived in Dili to disarm the factions and restore order on the streets.

The descent into violence also reflected deep divisions within the political elite, particularly between the unpopular prime minister, **Mari Alkatiri**, and President **José 'Xanana' Gusmão**, which cast a dark shadow. Alkatiri, who had overseen the decision to dismiss the soldiers, resigned on 27 June after coming under intense domestic pressure for his handling of the crisis, as well as accusations that he and interior minister Rogerio Lobato had armed fighters against his political opponents, a charge which he denied. He was replaced by **José Ramos-Horta**, the foreign and defence minister, who was sworn in on 10 July. In response to the crisis, the United Nations Integrated Mission in Timor-Leste (UNMIT) was created on 25 August with the mandate of restoring order and stability, rebuilding the armed forces and the police, as well as providing assistance to the Timor-Leste government in the presidential and parliamentary elections in 2007. Accordingly, 1,500 foreign police were deployed in Timor-Leste to boost the police presence and capability.

What happened in those few months in 2006 reflected a political crisis involving internal divisions and revealed the weakness of the *Fretilin* government. Moreover, the reintroduction of foreign troops barely a year after UN mission peacekeepers withdrew also raised serious questions at the time about the viability of the young nation.
see also: Alkatiri, Mari; *Fretilin*; Gusmão, José 'Xanana'; Ramos-Horta, José.

Timor Sea Treaty 2002 (Timor-Leste)

see **Timor Gap Cooperation Treaty**.

Tonkin Gulf Dispute (Vietnam)

The Tonkin Gulf dispute between the People's Republic of China and Vietnam is a dispute over maritime boundary delimitation and territorial jurisdiction in the **South China Sea**, in particular within that body of water that is surrounded on three sides by Vietnam's northern provinces, China's Guangxi province and Hainan Island. Disagreement over the delimitation of the Sino-Vietnamese boundary stems from the differing interpretations of the Sino-French Treaty of 1887; its obscure content and vague language does not offer a readily identifiable line or the supporting evidence for such a line to be drawn.

Negotiations on the delimitation of the maritime boundary in the Gulf of Tonkin began in 1974, but talks stalled as relations between Vietnam and China deteriorated after 1978. Talks did not resume until 1991 with the normalization of relations between Hanoi and Beijing, where they decided to settle all outstanding border and territorial issues, including those in the Gulf of Tonkin. The first significant milestone was a Memorandum of Understanding signed by both parties in October 1993 on the principles for handling the Gulf of Tonkin dispute, which involved the establishment of an expert working group. On 25 December 2000, Chinese president Jiang Zemin and his Vietnamese counterpart, **Tran Duc Luong**, signed the Agreement on the Demarcation of Waters, Exclusive Economic Zones and Continental Shelves in the Gulf of Tonkin. With this, Beijing and Hanoi found consensus on a delimitation line in the Gulf which comprises twenty-one points from the Bei Lun river in the north to the southern mouth of the Gulf, as well as delineation of a territorial boundary, exclusive economic zones and continental shelves. At the same time, the two countries also signed an agreement on fishing cooperation in the Gulf of Tonkin. However, a resolution to the dispute over the demarcation of maritime boundaries beyond the mouth of the Gulf of Tonkin remains elusive due to their longstanding territorial dispute over the Paracel Islands, which have been under China's physical control since 1974.

see also: Luong, Tran Duc; South China Sea.

Tonkin Gulf Incident 1964 (Vietnam)

An alleged attack on two United States destroyers on patrol in the Gulf of Tonkin by North Vietnamese torpedo boats on 4 August 1964 prompted a US congressional resolution on 7 August. That resolution endorsed US military reprisals against naval bases and oil storage facilities and sanctioned a subsequent sustained aerial bombardment. It was revealed later that for the previous six months the United States had been sponsoring clandestine armed raids against North Vietnam and had also prepared a draft resolution for Congress which, if and when passed, would serve as a declaration of war and permit overt military action north of the seventeenth parallel of latitude. The retaliatory air strikes, launched some twelve hours after reports of the alleged North Vietnamese attacks had reached Washington, were possible only because of prior target planning. The Gulf of Tonkin Resolution, which authorized the president to 'take all necessary measures to repel any armed attack against the forces of the United States', was approved with only two dissenting votes. In January 1971 in an expression of congressional disillusionment with the conduct of the Vietnam War, the Gulf of Tonkin Resolution was repealed.

Tran Duc Luong (Vietnam) *see* Luong, Tran Duc.

Trans-Pacific Partnership (Brunei/Malaysia/Singapore/Vietnam)

The Trans-Pacific Partnership (TPP) is an ambitious attempt at establishing a multilateral free trade agreement comprising the economies of the United States, Australia, New Zealand, Peru, Chile, Japan, Singapore, Malaysia, Brunei and Vietnam. The TPP builds on the Trans-Pacific Strategic Economic Partnership Agreement (TPSEP) of 2005 involving Brunei, Chile, Peru and Singapore. The US and Australia expressed interest in joining the TPSEP in 2008, and this subsequently led to the conceptualization of the TPP. Unlike existing bilateral FTAs or the **Regional Comprehensive Economic Partnership** (RCEP), the TPP has set higher hurdles for membership, and thence has come to be seen as a more exclusive regional trade institution. For example, unlike these other mechanisms which essentially focus on border measures, the TPP's more comprehensive coverage includes 'behind border' measures that cover environmental and labour issues, intellectual property rights and telecommunications. Moreover, aside from moving beyond the traditional focus on the removal of trade barriers, the TPP is also potentially punitive for regional countries, particularly those with developing economies, as it appears to privilege commercial interests over consumer interest. Since September 2013, nineteen rounds of TPP negotiations have already been conducted. The high membership hurdles have also led the TPP to be viewed as a US-led trade institution, as opposed to the RCEP, which is seen to be anchored by **ASEAN** (Association of Southeast Asian Nations) and China.

see also: ASEAN; Regional Comprehensive Economic Partnership.

Treaty of Amity and Cooperation (ASEAN) 1976 (Brunei/Cambodia/Indonesia/Laos/Malaysia/Myanmar/Philippines/Singapore/Thailand/Timor-Leste/Vietnam)

A Treaty of Amity and Cooperation in Southeast Asia was concluded by the heads of government of **ASEAN** (Association of Southeast Asian Nations) on the island of Bali on 24 February 1976. Based on respect for the sanctity of national sovereignty, the **Bali Summit** treaty set out a code of conduct for regional relations. It also made provision for the pacific settlement of disputes with a High Council to facilitate that end among signatories in the event of a failure to resolve matters through direct negotiations. The promulgation of the treaty was part of an attempt by ASEAN to display political solidarity and confidence in the wake of revolutionary Communist success in Indochina during 1975. It was also made open for accession by other regional states in an abortive effort at the time to build political bridges to Indochina. Brunei signed the treaty on joining ASEAN in January 1984 while Papua New Guinea acceded to the document in July 1989.

It was not until after the end of the Cold War that Vietnam and Laos formally sought to adhere to the treaty at the annual meeting of ASEAN foreign ministers in Manila in July 1992. Reference to the utility of employing the dispute settlement provisions of the treaty was incorporated into the **Declaration on the South China Sea** issued at the same meeting. Cambodia and Myanmar acceded to the treaty in 1995.

In December 1987 a protocol was inserted into the treaty, which permitted states outside Southeast Asia to accede to the treaty following the consent of all the Southeast Asian states that were already signatories. A second protocol was inserted into the treaty in July 1998 to include the consent of all regional member states (including the new ones) for such accession. A third protocol was inserted into the treaty in July 2010 so as to allow the accession of regional organizations to the treaty with the consent of all regional member states. In July 2001, the rules of procedure of the treaty High Council were adopted. As of 2013, twenty High Contracting Parties outside the Southeast Asian region have acceded to the treaty: India and China in 2003; Japan, Pakistan, Russia and South Korea in 2004; New Zealand, Australia and Mongolia in 2005; France, Timor-Leste, Bangladesh and Sri Lanka in 2007; North Korea in 2008; the United States in 2009; the European Union, the United Kingdom and Brazil in 2012; and Norway in 2013. Accession to the Treaty of Amity and Cooperation was made a membership requirement of the **East Asia Summit**. The Treaty of Amity and Cooperation was also referenced in the **Declaration on the Conduct of Parties in the South China Sea** signed in Phnom Penh in November 2002. The machinery for dispute settlement has never been invoked by any of the ASEAN states to resolve intra-mural differences.

see also: ASEAN; Bali Summit (ASEAN) 1976; Declaration on the Conduct of Parties in the South China Sea (ASEAN) 2002; Declaration on the South China Sea (ASEAN) 1992; East Asia Summit.

Treaty of Friendship and Cooperation 1977 (Laos/Vietnam)

A Treaty of Friendship and Cooperation between the Lao People's Democratic Republic and the Socialist Republic of Vietnam, valid for a period of twenty-five years, was concluded between the two governments in Vientiane on 15 July 1977. The treaty set out to affirm the special relationship between the two states in the context of strained ties with **ASEAN** (Association of Southeast Asian Nations) governments and the deteriorating association between Vietnam and the People's Republic of China. The preamble stated that the two governments 'endeavouring to protect and develop the special Vietnam–Laos relationship to make the two countries inherently united in the national liberation cause, remain united forever in national construction and defence'. The treaty made provision for defence cooperation but the actual terms were incorporated in a secret protocol, as was the basis for the demarcation of their common border. At the time, the treaty was believed to make legal provision for the deployment in Laos of Vietnamese troops which had been in the country from the early 1950s and which were not withdrawn until the late 1980s. In February 2000, general-secretary of Vietnam's Communist Party, **Le Kha Phieu**, while receiving a high-level military delegation from Laos, spoke of the 'special friendship' between the two countries and peoples.
see also: ASEAN; Le Kha Phieu, General.

Treaty of Friendship and Cooperation 1978 (Vietnam)

A Treaty of Friendship and Cooperation between the Soviet Union and the Socialist Republic of Vietnam, valid for a period of twenty-five years, was concluded between the two governments in Moscow on 3 November 1978. Such a treaty had been sought by the Soviet Union for some time but had been resisted by Vietnam until faced with the prospect of external threat from the People's Republic of China. On Vietnam's part, signature constituted an attempt to deter China from military retaliation in response to its planned invasion of Cambodia, which began on 25 December 1978. Article Six of the treaty stipulated that 'In case either party is attacked or threatened with attack, the two signatories to the Treaty shall immediately consult each other with a view to eliminating that threat, and shall take appropriate and effective measures to safeguard peace and security of the two countries'. In the event, the treaty failed to deter China, which launched a punitive attack on Vietnam in February 1979. The Soviet Union provided considerable economic and military assistance to Vietnam in support of its policy in Cambodia until the late 1980s, when relations with China began to be repaired. The Soviet Union also deployed aircraft and naval vessels in Vietnam but did not at any time intervene on behalf of its treaty partner.

The treaty lapsed with the break-up of the Soviet Union in December 1991 to be succeeded by a new accord with Russia in June 1994 which covered continued use of **Cam Ranh Bay** and outstanding debts by Vietnam.
see also: Cam Ranh Bay.

Treaty of Peace, Friendship and Cooperation 1979 (Cambodia/Vietnam)

A Treaty of Peace, Friendship and Cooperation between the Socialist Republic of Vietnam and the **People's Republic of Kampuchea** (Cambodia), valid for a period of twenty-five years, was concluded between the two governments in Phnom Penh on 18 February 1979. The incumbent Cambodian administration had been established through force of Vietnamese arms only the previous month. The treaty was intended to give legal force to a special relationship between Vietnam and Cambodia demanded from 1976 by the government in Hanoi of the **Khmer Rouge** regime, which it had overthrown. The preamble asserted that 'the independence, freedom, peace and security of the two countries are closely interrelated'. The treaty served in particular to provide a legal basis for the presence in Cambodia of Vietnamese troops, who had been represented as volunteers when they invaded in December 1978, acting on behalf of the so-called Kampuchean National United Front for National Salvation. In the event, the treaty failed in its political and military purposes.

Vietnam withdrew its main force units from Cambodia in September 1989 and, in the interest of rapprochement with the People's Republic of China, was obliged to leave the government that it had implanted in January 1979 to its own political devices to come to a settlement of the Cambodian conflict.

see also: Kampuchea, People's Republic of; Khmer Rouge.

Tripoli Agreement 1976 (Philippines)

In December 1976, at a meeting in the Libyan capital, Tripoli, a provisional agreement was reached on regional autonomy between the Philippines government and the insurgent **Moro National Liberation Front** (MNLF). The MNLF had launched a separatist rebellion in the Muslim-inhabited southern provinces of the Philippines in October 1972 in the wake of a declaration of martial law by President **Ferdinand Marcos** in the previous month. Negotiations had begun from the end of 1974 but soon ran into difficulty. They were resumed two years later after a visit to Tripoli in November 1976 by **Imelda Marcos**, who enlisted the good offices of President Gaddafi who had become the most prominent international backer of Muslim nationalism in the Philippines. The Tripoli Agreement provided for a ceasefire and terms for political autonomy in thirteen provinces in the islands of Mindanao, Sulu and Palawan. The agreement was never implemented with the full consent of both parties, however, and subsequent negotiations broke down. Of the thirteen provinces identified, only four had Muslim majorities because of the internal migration of Christians from the north. President Marcos went ahead unilaterally to proclaim an autonomous region in March 1977 and to hold a referendum on the terms of autonomy within the thirteen provinces in April. The outcome was a predictable vote in favour of a very limited form of autonomy and against the kind of devolution of power favoured by the MNLF. The precarious ceasefire broke down during the remainder of 1977. Negotiations did not resume until after President Marcos was succeeded in office by **Corazón Aquino**. On the basis of a plebiscite conducted in 1989, the Aquino government established the Autonomous Region for Muslim Mindanao in four provinces in 1990. This set the stage for the Final Peace Agreement brokered by Indonesia between Manila and the MNLF in 1996. However, disagreements within the MNLF over whether the Final Peace Agreement reflected the spirit of the Tripoli Agreement led to the fragmentation of the movement and a resurgence of violence, which in turn shifted the initiative to the **Moro Islamic Liberation Front**.

see also: Aquino, Corazón; Marcos, Ferdinand; Marcos, Imelda; Moro Islamic Liberation Front; Moro National Liberation Front.

Truong Chinh (Vietnam)

Truong Chinh, who was born Dang Xuan Khu, was an influential member of the hierarchy of the Communist Party of Vietnam who served as head of state between 1981 and 1987. His ideological outlook owed much to Chinese example and his *nom de guerre* was a Vietnamese translation of the term Long March. Truong Chinh was born in 1907 in Nam Dinh Province into a well-known family of scholars. He was educated in Hanoi and after acquiring his baccalaureate worked as a schoolteacher. He was attracted to **Ho Chi Minh**'s revolutionary movement as a teenager and became a member of the Communist Party of Indochina on its foundation. He spent six years in prison from 1930 and on release worked for the Communist Party as a journalist. Truong Chinh was one of Ho Chi Minh's most trusted colleagues and was elected general secretary of the Communist Party in 1941, holding that position until 1956 when he was relieved of office because of his close identification with a harsh programme of land reform. He remained a member of the Politburo during the course of the **Vietnam War**, sustaining a reputation as a party hardliner. When **Le Duan** died in July 1986, Truong Chinh replaced him as general secretary of the Communist Party until the end of the year, when a radical change of economic course was signalled at its sixth national congress. He died on 1 October 1988 from injuries sustained in a fall.

see also: Ho Chi Minh; Le Duan; Vietnam War.

Truong Tan Sang (Vietnam)

Truong Tan Sang was elected by the National Assembly to the largely ceremonial post of president in July 2011. Seen as a conservative, Truong has been an outspoken critic of Prime Minister **Nguyen Tan Dung**'s economic reforms.

Truong was born in the southern province of Long An in 1949 and holds a Bachelor of Law degree. His political career began in 1969 when he joined the Communist Party of Vietnam. In 1971 he was imprisoned in Phu Quoc by the South Vietnamese government, and was released under the **Paris Peace Agreements** of 1973. From 1983 to 1986 Truong headed Ho Chi Minh City's forestry department, as well as its new economic zone development department. In 1986, Truong was promoted to the standing board of the city's Party committee. In 1991, Truong Tan Sang became a member of the national Party's central committee, and in the following year he became the chairman of Ho Chi Minh City Peoples' Committee. In 1996, he became secretary of the Party's Ho Chi Minh branch. It was also in this year that he joined the Politburo as its fourteenth ranking member. Following several promotions, Truong rose to become the second highest ranking member in the Politburo after **Nguyen Phu Trong** in 2001. He became the executive secretary of the Party's secretariat in 2006. Upon taking office as president in July 2011, Truong declared the objectives of his presidency to be the modernization and industrialization of Vietnam by 2020 and the peaceful resolution of its territorial claims with China in the Spratly Islands. His tenure however has been marked foremost by his excoriation of Prime Minister Nguyen Tan Dung, whose economic policies have come under fire for fostering widespread corruption and mismanagement of the country's debt-laden **State Owned Enterprises**. The acrimony between Truong and Nguyen peaked most recently at the sixth plenary of the Communist Party in October 2012, when Nguyen barely survived an unprecedented attempt to remove him from power.

see also: Nguyen Phu Trong; Nguyen Tan Dung; Paris Peace Agreements 1973; State Owned Enterprise Reform.

Tsunami 2004 (Indonesia/Malaysia/Thailand)

On 26 December 2004 an earthquake of 9.0 magnitude with an epicentre under the Indian Ocean near the west coast of the Indonesian island of Sumatra was triggered. It unleashed a series of massive waves, which reached heights of over ten metres and took over 230,000 lives in fourteen countries, including Indonesia, Malaysia and Thailand. Also known as the 2004 Indian Ocean tsunami, Indonesian tsunami and Boxing Day tsunami, it was one of the deadliest natural disasters on record. Indonesia was worst hit; specifically the western coast of Aceh including Banda Aceh, Calang and Melauboh, where over 170,000 were reported killed and about 500,000 left homeless.

The natural disaster saw an outpouring of immediate aid as governments, international organizations, humanitarian organizations, private sector corporations, community groups and individuals around the world pledged financial, medical and technical support. The World Bank had estimated the amount of aid needed at about USD$5 billion and by 1 January 2005 over USD$1.8 billion had been pledged. On top of financial aid, governments also dispatched rescue teams to aid in search and rescue, restoration and repair efforts. The pledging of support was not without controversy. In fact, UN secretary-general Kofi Annan assiduously called for contributors to honour their pledges while citing previous cases where they were dishonoured. The United States government was harshly criticized for its original pledge of USD$15 million, a sum many deemed paltry. Subsequently the amount was increased to USD$35 million, and eventually tenfold to USD$350 million.

Claims of inefficiency and corruption dogged the Indonesian government as Supreme Audit Agency chief Anwar Nasution admitted that administration of the USD$600 million National Disaster Management and Refugee Coordination Board fund was plagued by irregularities. Jakarta was also accused of being slow to accept foreign aid in Aceh, the worst hit region but also at the time a special region of Indonesia where the **Aceh Independence Movement** (*Gerakan*

Aceh Merdeka, GAM) was waging a separatist insurgency. While Jakarta and GAM declared an unofficial truce immediately following the disaster, tensions remained high as sporadic clashes between both sides erupted. The Indonesian government was also accused of using the tsunami disaster to penetrate hitherto impenetrable GAM strongholds by insisting that military personnel escort foreign aid workers entering areas of known insurgent activity. This led the UN to express concerns that these demands could create bottlenecks in the distribution of aid, prompting further allegations that the government was attempting to conceal corruption and human rights abuses in Aceh. However, the massive devastation that followed the tsunami of 2004 eventually compelled Jakarta and GAM to resolve their longstanding dispute. A series of negotiations culminated in a memorandum of understanding between both parties that confirmed commitment to a 'peaceful, comprehensive, and sustainable solution' to the conflict in Aceh. Dubbed the Helsinki Peace Accord, the agreement included a call to establish an immediate ceasefire, disarm rebel fighters, provide amnesty to GAM members, reduce and restrict government troop movements in Aceh, allow Aceh-based parties to participate in politics, allow Aceh to use its own regional flag, crest and hymn, establish a human rights court to expose abuses committed during the conflict, and establish a truth and reconciliation commission in Aceh. The memorandum was signed in Helsinki, Finland on 15 August 2005, and paved the way for the first democratic elections in Aceh after thirty years of insurgency.

see also: Aceh Independence Movement.

Tudung Controversy 2002

(Singapore)

In what was described by the *New York Times* as 'the most potent act of civil disobedience this tightly controlled nation has seen in years', four schoolgirls in Singapore were suspended in February 2002 after repeatedly turning up in their public schools wearing the *tudung* (headscarves worn by Malay-Muslim women), thereby violating a strict uniform policy set by the Ministry of Education. The parents of the four girls protested their suspension, arguing that the policy was unconstitutional as it violated their right to religious freedom. They threatened legal action and hired Karpal Singh, a Malaysian legal counsel, to represent them in their attempt to take the government to court over the issue. Singh however, failed to obtain the necessary practising certificate from the Singapore Supreme Court.

The Singapore government's justification for the policy was twofold. First, they opined that schools constituted public space for social interaction and the promotion of integration of different races at a young age. To that end, the *tudung* accentuates differences rather than emphasizes similarities and is therefore detrimental to social cohesion. Second, the government was concerned that allowing Muslim girls to wear the *tudung* to school would set an unwelcome precedent for other requests in the name of religious freedom. Critics however, pointed to the inconsistency in this policy given the government's support for Special Assistance Plan schools that cater to the ethnic Chinese elite as well as the freedom that Sikh students, based on a decree inherited from the British colonial administration, enjoyed in wearing their turbans in school.

Underlying the controversy is the government's sensitivity to issues of race and religion. Chronic race riots in the 1950s and 1960s have been seared into national memory in the island-state, and its government has demonstrated no qualms about bringing to bear the weight of the state against attempts to undermine harmony and stability among Singapore's various ethnic and religious groups. The timing of the controversy though was inopportune, for it occurred just after the secular state had cracked down on the Singapore cell of ***Jemaah Islamiyah*** which led to the arrest of thirteen suspected militants. Nevertheless, the domestic political fallout from the issue was marginal. The opposition Singapore Malay National Organization (PKMS) tried to increase pressure over this issue, but other Muslim organizations such as the Islamic Religious Council of Singapore, the highest Islamic body in the country, were quick to denounce their comments and offer support to the government's position on the grounds of

traditional Islamic knowledge. However, in what was derided by the Singapore government as a departure from the **ASEAN** (Association of Southeast Asian Nations) norm of non-interference in the internal affairs of member states, politicians and government officials from Malaysia and Brunei were vocal in their criticisms of Singapore's handling of the issue.
see also: ASEAN; *Jemaah Islamiyah*.

Tuol Sleng (Cambodia)

Tuol Sleng is the name of the notorious interrogation centre used by the **Khmer Rouge** regime during its rule in Cambodia between April 1975 and December 1978. The centre takes its name from the suburb in which it is located, while the actual building had served as a high school. Some 20,000 prisoners were brutally interrogated and done to death in Tuol Sleng, but only after having provided detailed confessions of political delinquency. The bulk of the inmates were themselves Khmer Rouge, including cadres of high standing, who were charged with a range of so-called counterrevolutionary offences. Tuol Sleng represented a savage symbol of the paranoia that progressively gripped the Khmer Rouge regime under **Pol Pot**. After Vietnam's invasion of Cambodia in December 1978 and the establishment in January 1979 of the **People's Republic of Kampuchea**, the centre was converted into a genocide museum, in part to justify the legitimacy of the implanted regime. In May 1999, Kang Kek Ieu (better known by his revolutionary *nom de guerre* of Duch), the Khmer Rouge commandant of Tuol Sleng was discovered working with relief organizations in northwestern Cambodia. His whereabouts had been known to the authorities for the previous two years but he was only arrested, ostensibly into protective custody, in the same month as his location had become public knowledge. In September 1999, he was formally indicted on a charge of genocide together with Khmer Rouge military commander, **Ta Mok**. In July 2007, Duch was officially charged with war crimes and crimes against humanity by the United Nations backed Extraordinary Chambers in the Courts of Cambodia. Duch's lawyers appealed against these charges but they were unsuccessful. In July 2010, Duch was found guilty of crimes against humanity, torture and murder, and sentenced to thirty-five years' imprisonment. A subsequent appeal was rejected. Tuol Sleng was renamed as the 'Tuol Sleng Genocide Museum' and is open to the public. The site has four buildings, Buildings A, B, C and D. Building A consists of the cells in which the bodies of the last victims were discovered; building B holds galleries of photographs of the late prisoners; building C consists of the schoolrooms that served as prison cells; and building D holds other memorabilia such as instruments of torture.
see also: Kampuchea, People's Republic of; Khmer Rouge; Pol Pot; Ta Mok.

U

UMNO (United Malays National Organization) (Malaya/Malaysia)

The United Malays National Organization (UMNO) is the most important political party in Malaysia. It was established in May 1946 as a Malay united front with which to challenge the British **Malayan Union Proposal**. The terms of that constitutional proposal included the deposition of the Malay rulers or sultans of the states of the peninsula as well as liberal provision for citizenship for Chinese and Indians of migrant origin. The British proposal had been influenced by the perceived mixed conduct of the different communities during the wartime Japanese occupation, with the Malays regarded as collaborators. The movement's founder and first president was Dato Onn bin Jafar, then Chief Minister of the state of Johor. He mobilized Malays on the basis of their acute concern that they would lose their political birthright in the country of which they were the indigenous people. He also drew on the support of a powerful lobby in Britain of former members of the Malayan civil service who were committed to the Malay cause, as well as that of the Malay rulers, who constituted living symbols of Malay identity. UMNO's campaign was successful and Britain withdrew the Malayan Union Proposal in favour of one setting up a Federation of Malaya, in which the rights of the Malay rulers were restored and access to citizenship would be made more difficult.

UMNO was then institutionalized as the main political party, claiming a prerogative right to protect the interests of the Malays which it has sustained ever since. Because the British colonial authorities, facing a Communist insurrection, believed that independence could be conceded only when the racial communities had come to political terms, Dato Onn attempted to turn UMNO into a multiracial party. This initiative proved to be premature and in the face of rank-and-file resistance, he was obliged to resign in favour of **Tunku Abdul Rahman**, who led the successful campaign for independence. To that end, he was able to work out a viable accommodation at elite level with corresponding Chinese and Indian parties which, as the **Alliance Party**, enjoyed notable electoral success. Malaya became independent in August 1957, with UMNO as the dominant party and providing the prime minister, a situation which continued with the advent of the wider Federation of Malaysia in September 1963. In the wake of an electoral reverse and communal violence in the **May 13 Racial Riots** in 1969, UMNO expanded the ruling coalition to include its main Malay political rival within a ***Barisan Nasional*** (National Front, BN) which was registered as a party in 1974. However, the separate identity and political pre-eminence of UMNO was maintained and strengthened through its extensive network of business activities cultivated in the 1980s by the leadership of **Mahathir Mohamad** and **Daim Zainuddin**.

A major split in the party occurred during the late 1980s. At the UMNO General Assembly in April 1987, prime minister and party president Mahathir Mohamad only narrowly fended off a challenge to his leadership by the minister for trade and industry, **Tengku Razaleigh Hamzah**. In February 1988 the federal High Court ruled that UMNO was an unlawful society because thirty of its branches had not been properly registered when its General Assembly and triennial elections had been held in 1987. Mahathir then secured permission to register an alternative party called UMNO *Baru* (New UMNO) to which all members of the deregistered party would have to apply to join. In May 1989 Mahathir's opponents secured permission to register a Malay party called ***Semangat '46*** (Spirit of 1946) which was an attempt to attach legitimacy arising from the founding of UMNO to the new entity. UMNO's political dominance was restored, however, in general elections in October 1990, when having dropped the 'new' label and still leading the BN, it succeeded in maintaining a two-thirds parliamentary majority at the expense of *Semangat '46* and its Malay and Chinese partners. At the end of that month, Mahathir was returned unopposed at its General Assembly as president of a politically restored party. UMNO's pre-eminent position was reinforced through a resounding electoral victory in April 1995 in which it won eighty-eight seats out of 101 contested, not to mention Tengku Razaleigh's return to the UMNO fold following the ignominious dissolution of *Semangat '46* a year later.

UMNO had confined its activities exclusively to peninsular Malaysia until 1991, when it contested by-elections in Sabah in northern Borneo in an attempt to pose a more effective challenge to the ruling **Sabah United Party** than the **United Sabah National Organization** (USNO). It succeeded in this enterprise in March 1994, when defections from the former, which had been returned to power with a narrow majority the month before, led to a loss of its parliamentary position.

UMNO's leading position diminished significantly with the outcome of the next elections in November 1999, when its strength in the federal Parliament was reduced to seventy-four seats. It also lost control of the state of Terengganu to ***Parti Islam Se-Malaysia***, which was the main beneficiary of the Malay vote swing against UMNO. That swing had been precipitated by the dismissal, arrest, trial and conviction of former deputy prime minister, **Anwar Ibrahim**, which elicited extensive domestic and international criticism.

In a surprise move, Mahathir announced in the 2002 UMNO General Assembly that he would step down from his position as prime minister. Amidst dramatic scenes on stage at the assembly, Mahathir later acceded to requests from colleagues to continue for a stipulated period in order to oversee a smooth transition in leadership. In October 2003, Mahathir finally stepped down as UMNO president and Malaysian prime minister after twenty-two years at the helm, and handed power to his designated successor, **Abdullah Ahmad Badawi**. The post-Mahathir era for UMNO and Malaysia began with a resounding victory at the March 2004 elections, when UMNO won 109 seats, thirty-two more than in 1999, as it led the BN to a landslide victory which included regaining the state government of Terengganu. Nevertheless, a combination of failed promises, under-achievements, and exasperating societal polarization, not to mention his falling out with his predecessor, turned the tables on Abdullah Badawi and UMNO at the following election in March 2008. The BN performed poorly and lost its two-thirds parliamentary majority for the first time in its electoral history, while UMNO won only seventy-nine seats. The dismal performance led immediately to calls for Abdullah Badawi's resignation. In order to avoid an acrimonious party election and a likely leadership challenge, Abdullah Badawi resigned from all posts in June 2009, paving the way for **Najib Tun Razak**, son of Malaysia's second prime minister **Tun Abdul Razak**, to come into office. Leadership change carried hopes for the restoration of confidence in UMNO and the BN. Najib moved swiftly to initiate several reforms within UMNO through an amendment to its constitution so as to enhance the party's credibility and improve transparency in its election process, long disparaged as extremely corrupt. The new system extended voting rights to 150,000 party grassroots leaders, departing from the previous practice which limited voting to 2,600 delegates privileged to attend the party assembly (a system that encouraged chronic vote-buying). It also abolished the quota system for nomination of candidates vying for party posts. In September 2010, Najib launched his **One Malaysia** (1Malaysia) campaign, which stressed national unity, ethnic tolerance and efficient governance. The results of these reforms were mixed. At the general election in May 2013, UMNO improved its performance by winning eighty-eight parliamentary seats. However, not only did UMNO fail to lead the BN to regain the two-thirds majority, the coalition in fact lost the popular vote to the opposition ***Pakatan Rakyat***. Invariably, this has fed rumours of yet another impending leadership change with members of the UMNO old guard such as Mahathir and Daim suggesting that Najib had to be held responsible for the BN's inability to turn the tide.

Since the Mahathir era, two trends have become evident in UMNO. First, the relationship between the party and business interests have deepened considerably. Once a party which drew its bedrock support from teachers and civil servants, UMNO has increasingly relied on its ties to big business in order to entrench and retain its influence in the country. Second, communalism has become a signal feature of UMNO's rhetoric, as demonstrated in the aspersions frequently cast with impunity at minorities, particularly the ethnic Chinese, at its general assemblies and on other occasions by some of its leaders.

see also: Abdul Rahman, Tunku; Alliance Party; Anwar Ibrahim; Badawi, Tun Abdullah Ahmad; *Barisan Nasional*; Mahathir Mohamad, Tun; Malayan Union Proposal 1946; May 13 Racial Riots 1969; Najib Tun Razak, Datuk Seri Mohamad; One Malaysia; *Pakatan Rakyat*; *Parti Islam Se-Malaysia*; Razaleigh Hamzah, Tengku; Sabah United Party; *Semangat '46*; United Sabah National Organization.

Union Solidarity and Development Association (Myanmar) *see* Union Solidarity and Development Party.

Union Solidarity and Development Party (Myanmar)

The Union Solidarity and Development Party (USDP) is Myanmar's majority party in Parliament. The party was registered on 2 June 2010 by the Union Election Commission and is the successor to the mass organization of the **State Peace and Development Council** (SLORC), the Union Solidarity and Development Association (USDA). The party is headquartered in **Naypyidaw**.

The USDA was formed by the SLORC on 15 September 1993 to act as a form of mass organization. To a large degree it replaced the **National Unity Party** (NUP) as the regime's chosen political vehicle after the poor showing of the NUP in the **1990 Elections**. The association was organized nationwide with an infrastructure extending down to the township level. The USDA disbanded with the creation of the USDP on 29 March 2010. Its members were enrolled in the new party and assets transferred over. Although it was supposed to purge itself of government officials and civil servants in accordance with the **2008 Constitution**, members like Prime Minister **Thein Sein**, who is party chairman, and junta number three, **Shwe Mann**, remained in the party. Although the inclusion of government officials was in violation of the constitution, the party was approved by the election commission. In the lead up to the **2010 Elections** the party was criticized for unethical recruitment practices, including offering low-interest loans to farmers and national identity cards to unregistered party sympathizers, especially in central Myanmar and Rakhine State. In the event, the USDP won 883 seats out of a total 1,154 seats contested. On formation of the government, the majority of cabinet members were appointees from the USDP who, as per constitutional rules, resigned their parliamentary seats. During by-elections to elect members of Parliament to replace those appointed to the cabinet the USDP was soundly defeated by the **National League for Democracy** (NLD), winning only one seat as opposed to the NLD's forty-three seats out of the forty-five available.

The party was initially led by Thein Sein until May 2011, when Shwe Mann took over as chairman. On 16 October 2012, Thein Sein was again elected as chairman of the USDP at its first party Congress in Naypyidaw. Shwe Mann is currently one of three party vice-chairmen. The Congress was believed to be held in part to discuss the party's poor showing in the April by-elections and ways forward to improve its popularity and chances in the next general elections in 2015, where it is expected the party will face a serious challenge from the NLD.

see also: Constitution 2008; Elections 1990; Elections 2010; National League for Democracy; Naypyidaw; Shwe Mann; State Peace and Development Council; Thein Sein.

United Front for Democracy Against Dictatorship (Thailand)

The United Front for Democracy Against Dictatorship (UDD), also known as the 'Red Shirts' for their distinctive apparel, is a political pressure group formed to oppose the **People's Alliance for Democracy** (PAD), the 2006 coup, and those supporting the coup, including the **Democrat Party**-led government of **Abhisit Vejjajiva**. Prominent leaders of the UDD include **Jatuporn Prompan** and Nattawut Saikua. The UDD is allied with the ***Pheu Thai* Party**, with several party members currently or formerly members of the group.

The UDD was established in 2006 to oppose the military coup that ousted Prime Minister **Thaksin Shinawatra**. It organized demonstrations during the 2006–7 period of military rule and opposed the military's 2007 constitution. While it halted protests after the December 2007 electoral win by the pro-Thaksin **People's Power Party** (PPP), the seizure of Government House by the PAD prompted the UDD to re-form, and several violent confrontations ensued between the two groups. The dissolution of the PPP and the ascent of Abhisit Vejjajiva and his Democrat Party-led coalition met with studied hostility, and major street demonstrations against the new government were organized by the UDD. A major rally held in April 2009 in Bangkok calling for Abhisit's resignation resulted in clashes with the military that injured at least 120 people. On 14 March 2010 the UDD held the largest political demonstration in Thai history in Bangkok, bringing in people from the north and northeast as well as organizing thousands of Bangkok-based supporters. The protests centred on the symbolic Democracy Monument in central Bangkok and later spread to the important Rajaprasong commercial district. The Abhisit government responded by imposing a number of security measures, including use of the Internal Security Act. On 10 April, military units attempting to disperse protestors were repulsed in a violent confrontation that left twenty-five killed and over 800 injured. On 19 May the military again moved to disperse protestors after almost a week of violent confrontations. Although military measures resulted in the surrender of key leaders Nattawut and Jatuporn, a number of protestors and soldiers were killed and injured. After two months of protests, ninety-one people had been killed and some 2,100 injured, mostly protestors.

One of the chief grievances of the UDD was that the Abhisit government was illegitimate because it came to power with backing from the military and the judiciary, and not via popular elections. The UDD called for the dissolution of Parliament and new general elections. They have been vocal about the perceived interference of the military, judiciary and certain members of the Privy Council in politics. The UDD drew its support from the rural areas of the north and northeast and Bangkok urban dwellers originally from those areas. UDD followers have taken pride in their rural and often lower class origins, although there are numerous middle class supporters and intellectuals involved as well. Closely identified with Thaksin Shinawatra, the UDD has campaigned for his return to Thailand, although not all its members support the exiled former prime minister. In any event, this has made the UDD a natural ally of the *Pheu Thai* Party and several of its members including Jatuporn and Nattawut were elected during the July 2011 general elections. In the wake of the 22 May 2014 coup that removed the democratically elected *Pheu Thai* government, talk has been rife of the remobilization of the UDD, particularly in the pro-Thaksin stronghold in the northeastern region, to oppose the military administration.

see also: Abhisit Vejjajiva; Democrat Party; Jatuporn Prompan; People's Alliance for Democracy; People's Power Party; *Pheu Thai* Party; Thaksin Shinawatra.

United Nations: Cambodia 1991–3

(Cambodia)

The United Nations became actively involved in the conflict in Cambodia from December 1978, following the Vietnamese invasion of the country. Vietnam's military occupation and the legitimacy of the government that it installed in Phnom Penh from January 1979 were challenged during the 1980s through the annual passage of resolutions in the UN General Assembly and by upholding the representation of the ousted **Khmer Rouge** regime. An **International Conference on Cambodia**, New York 1981, which convened under the auspices of the UN secretary-general, failed to resolve the conflict. A second **International Conference on Cambodia**, Paris 1989 (July–August), held as the Cold War was coming to an end, also proved abortive.

The four contending Cambodian factions were unable to agree on terms for power-sharing during an interim period before elections under international supervision to determine the political format and future of the country. In the wake of that failure, Stephen Solarz, a US Congressman, advocated publicly that the United Nations should assume the interim administration of Cambodia as the means to promote a political settlement. This suggestion was taken up by the Australian government, which conducted a feasibility study whose results were published early in 1990. The Australian study attracted the serious attention of the five permanent members of the United Nations Security Council. Their officials proceeded to draft a framework document, which was eventually accepted on 28 August 1990 by the four Cambodian factions as the basis for settling the conflict.

Central to the United Nations plan was a provision for bypassing the problem of power-sharing, which had stood in the way of an accord. In place of an instrument for effective power-sharing, it was proposed to have a **Supreme National Council** (SNC), on which all Cambodian factions would be represented. The SNC was described as the unique legitimate body and source of authority in which, throughout the transitional period, the sovereignty, independence and unity of Cambodia would be enshrined. This body would delegate to the United Nations all powers necessary to implement a peace agreement. The SNC was set up among the Cambodian parties at a meeting in Jakarta on 10 September 1990; the framework document was then endorsed unanimously in turn by the Security Council and the General Assembly of the United Nations. Contention among the Cambodian parties delayed the election of Prince **Norodom Sihanouk** as chairman of the SNC until July 1991. His election cleared the way for the reconvening of the **International Conference on Cambodia**, Paris 1991, and for a comprehensive political settlement to be concluded on 23 October.

The terms of the Paris accord called on the United Nations Security Council to establish **UNTAC** (United Nations Transitional Authority in Cambodia) with civilian and military components under the direct responsibility of the UN secretary-general. UNTAC was accorded a mandate to conduct free and fair elections for a Constituent Assembly in a neutral political environment. The Constituent Assembly would approve a new constitution and then transform itself into a legislative assembly which would have responsibility for creating a new Cambodian government. To serve this end, UNTAC assumed responsibility for supervising, monitoring and verifying a ceasefire and the withdrawal of all foreign forces, as well as the regroupment, cantonment and ultimate disposition of all Cambodian forces and their weapons during the transitional period before general elections ultimately scheduled for May 1993. In addition, in order to ensure a neutral political environment conducive to free and fair elections, five key ministries of the government in Phnom Penh, which was not to be dismantled, were to be placed under UNTAC's direct administrative control.

UNTAC was established formally in March 1992 after the Security Council had sanctioned the dispatch of some 22,000 civilian and military personnel with an initial budget of US$1.9 million in the largest and most costly United Nations peacekeeping operation then ever mounted. Headed by Yasushi Akashi, an under-secretary-general for disarmament, UNTAC faced early difficulty in upholding the ceasefire as military clashes between Khmer Rouge and Phnom Penh government forces took place in battles for territorial and population control with the elections in mind. However, even more serious problems set in from June 1992, when the demobilization of the four factions was to have begun in a part of the plan intended to regroup about seventy per cent of all contending forces in UNTAC-controlled regroupment zones. The Khmer Rouge, deployed primarily in western Cambodia, refused to cooperate. Their representatives on the SNC complained that UNTAC had not verified the withdrawal of Vietnamese forces, large numbers of whom were alleged to be still in Cambodia in disguise. They also took exception to the limited role of the SNC and the extent to which the administration of most of the country had remained in the hands of the incumbent government in Phnom

Penh, which had been installed as a direct result of Vietnam's original invasion. Indeed, they asserted that UNTAC was in active collusion with that government in its exclusive political interest. Khmer Rouge obstruction took the form of active harassment of UN personnel, including their detention and appropriation of their equipment, especially vehicles. The Khmer Rouge went further in refusing to participate in the elections arranged for May 1993. In October 1992 the UN Security Council acted unanimously in setting a deadline of the following month for Khmer Rouge compliance. When this did not materialize, trade sanctions were imposed from January 1993 on Khmer Rouge-controlled zones but without real effect. Nonetheless, the Security Council reaffirmed its intention that UNTAC proceed with elections in May. By the end of January 1993, a total of twenty political parties had registered to take part in the elections. Apart from murderous intimidation by the Khmer Rouge, directed primarily at Vietnamese residents, strong evidence emerged of political violence employed by agents of the Phnom Penh government at the expense of their non-Communist electoral rivals. Despite the absence of an ideal neutral political environment, UNTAC conducted the elections in late May 1993 as planned with considerable success.

With a turnout of some ninety per cent, most of the seats for the 120-member Constituent Assembly were shared between two parties, with fifty-eight seats for **FUNCINPEC** (National United Front for an Independent, Neutral, Peaceful and Cooperative Cambodia), led by Prince **Norodom Ranariddh**, a son of Prince Sihanouk, and fifty-one seats for the **Cambodian People's Party** (CPP), led by **Hun Sen**. Prince Sihanouk intervened to forge an interim coalition between the two rivals after the CPP sought to challenge the electoral outcome through threat of territorial secession. The Constituent Assembly convened in June 1993 and by September had agreed the terms of a new constitution, based in part on the restoration of the monarchy, resumed by Norodom Sihanouk on 24 September 1993. A new coalition government was formed at the end of October with Prince Ranariddh and Hun Sen as first and second prime ministers respectively. The constitutional process was endorsed by the United Nations, whose mandate for Cambodia came to a substantive end on 26 September with the departure of Yasushi Akashi, the head of UNTAC, although not all of its peacekeeping forces were withdrawn until mid-November 1993. Many aspects of the UN operation were flawed, in particular its quasi-administrative role in supervising and controlling key ministries within the incumbent government in Phnom Penh. Moreover, it was constrained by a peacekeeping mandate that prevented military enforcement against violent recalcitrant factions. In the event, a calculated risk in holding elections paid off because of the courage of the Cambodian people in taking part and also because the Khmer Rouge had begun to lose their military momentum and to fragment.

see also: Cambodian People's Party; FUNCINPEC; Hun Sen; International Conferences on Cambodia, New York 1981, Paris 1989, 1991; Khmer Rouge; Ranariddh, Prince Norodom; Sihanouk, King Norodom; Supreme National Council; UNTAC.

United Nations: East Timor 1999–2002 (Indonesia/Timor-Leste)

The United Nations Transitional Administration in East Timor (UNTAET) was established on 25 October 1999 by the Security Council with overall responsibility for administration and was empowered to exercise all legislative and executive authority. The United Nations has been involved with the issue of East Timor from the time of Indonesia's invasion of the former Portuguese territory in December 1975. It had never acknowledged Indonesia's jurisdiction but failed to make any impact on the government in Jakarta during the rule of President **Suharto**. With his political downfall in May 1998, Indonesia under the interim administration of President **B. J. Habibie** appeared unwilling to concede more than a status of special autonomy for the territory. That situation changed unexpectedly in January 1999 when Habibie offered the inhabitants of East Timor the choice between autonomy and independence. In May 1999 an agreement was reached between the secretary-general of the United Nations and the foreign ministers of Indonesia and Portugal whereby Indonesia would assume responsibility for security during the referendum in August, which would be conducted by a United Nations Assessment Mission in East Timor (UNAMET). That referendum took place on 30 August against a background of rising violence mounted by pro-integrationist armed militia inspired by the local military determined to block independence. That violence became endemic with the announcement of the referendum result on 4 September; almost four-fifths of voters had supported independence. The scorched-earth policy of the armed militia precipitated the withdrawal of the UNAMET. On 15 September, the UN Security Council adopted a unanimous resolution authorizing a multinational force to use all necessary means to restore peace in East Timor. It had been understood that Australia would provide the largest contingent in the International Force East Timor (INTERFET) whose advance units flew into Dili from Darwin on 20 September under the command of an Australian major general. That force was effective in restoring law and order to the ravaged territory but the conspicuous role of Australia generated political tensions with Indonesia and some other members of **ASEAN** (Association of Southeast Asian Nations). It was against that background that the UN Security Council established UNTAET in October 1999 and made provision for the replacement of INTERFET by a UN force led by a Filipino general who arrived in Dili in January 2000. INTERFET's role came to a formal end on 23 February 2000 when Australia's Major General Peter Cosgrove handed over responsibility for security in East Timor to a United Nations peacekeeping force led by Lieutenant General Jaime de los Santos.

UNTAET oversaw the establishment and operation of a National Consultative Council, later National Council, which comprised Timorese political and community leaders assembled to deliberate the matter of independence, and a transitional Cabinet. Elections for a Constituent Assembly were held on 30 August 2001, which resulted in a major victory for ***Fretilin***. The mandate of UNTAET ended with the independence of East Timor on 20 May 2002. The UN presence in the newly independent country would nevertheless continue with the formation of the United Nations Mission of Support to East Timor, UNMISET, for a few more years.

see also: ASEAN; *Fretilin*; Habibie, B. J.; Suharto.

United Nations: Irian Jaya 1962–9
(Indonesia)

Irian Jaya is the Indonesian term for the western half of the island of New Guinea which had been an integral part of the Netherlands East Indies. Although the Dutch agreed to transfer sovereignty to an independent Indonesia in December 1949, they insisted on retaining administrative control of West New Guinea, with the future of the territory to be subject to further negotiations. Their refusal to relinquish control became a matter of great controversy during the 1950s, leading to a breach in diplomatic relations, **Confrontation**, and an international crisis involving US–Soviet competition. A United States initiative prompted renewed negotiations in 1962 with formal mediation by a US diplomat, Ellsworth Bunker, under the auspices of U Thant, then acting secretary-general of the United Nations. An accord was concluded on 15 August 1962 whereby the territory would be transferred first to United Nations and then to Indonesian administration. In addition, it was agreed that an 'act of free choice' with United Nations advice, assistance and participation would take place before the end of 1969 in order to determine whether or not the territory's inhabitants wished to remain subject to Indonesian jurisdiction.

The initial transfer to United Nations authority took effect from 1 October 1962 with administration placed under a UN Temporary Executive Authority (UNTEA). Indonesia replaced UNTEA as agreed from 1 May 1963, despite a campaign by Jakarta to advance the date of transfer to 1 January and to suggest that a determination of opinion would not be necessary. Indonesia's assumption of administration was not popular within Irian Jaya and armed resistance was mounted by a **Free Papua Movement**. In the event, an 'act of free choice' of a kind was conducted in the territory during July and August 1969. But the overseeing UN representatives were denied full opportunity to judge

the true merits of a plebiscitary exercise by village notables alone, who voted by 1,025 to nil in favour of continued union with Indonesia. The report of the visiting United Nations mission on the test of opinion confirmed the result but contained clear reservations. When the report came before the General Assembly, it was endorsed but not before attracting criticism from a number of African countries, in particular. President **Suharto** announced Irian Jaya's incorporation into the Republic of Indonesia as its twenty-sixth province on 17 September 1969.
see also: Confrontation; Free Papua Movement; Irian Jaya; Suharto.

United Nations: Northern Borneo 1963 (Indonesia/Malaysia/Philippines)

The controversy over the formation of the Federation of Malaysia, which was contested by Indonesia and the Philippines, led to the United Nations playing a role in assessing the political preferences of the inhabitants of the British colonies of North Borneo and Sarawak. A meeting at ministerial level in Manila in June 1963 between representatives of Indonesia, Malaya and the Philippines resulted in the Manila Agreements in July to welcome the formation of Malaysia, to include the Borneo territories, provided the support of their people was 'ascertained by an independent and impartial authority, the Secretary-General of the United Nations or his representative'. Secretary-General U Thant agreed to dispatch such a representative with a team to northern Borneo to examine the conduct and verify the outcome of recent elections in North Borneo and Sarawak and, above all, to ascertain whether or not Malaysia had been a major, if not the main, issue. Further controversy arose over the participation of Indonesian and Philippine observers and more importantly the announcement by Malaya on 29 August 1963 that Malaysia would be established on 16 September that year, even though the findings of the United Nations mission were not due to be made public until 14 September. The United Nations team of nine assessors led by Laurence Michelmore, one of its officials, did not begin its work until 26 August. Nonetheless, the secretary-general published his report on 13 September, finding that 'there is no doubt about the wishes of a sizeable majority of the peoples of these [Borneo] territories to join in the Federation of Malaysia'. He felt obliged, however, to reprimand the government of Malaya for fixing the date for the establishment of the new Federation before his conclusions had been reached and made known. The Federation of Malaysia succeeded Malaya without difficulty in membership of the United Nations but the pointed admonition by the secretary-general became the basis of Indonesia's refusal to recognize the new Federation and to reinstate its campaign of **Confrontation**.
see also: Confrontation.

United Sabah National Organization (USNO) (Malaysia)

The United Sabah National Organization (USNO) was one of the first political parties to be formed in northern Borneo in the expectation of the establishment of Malaysia. It was set up in 1961 by Tun **Mustapha Harun**, a traditional Suluk leader, whose constituency was among the Muslim community. USNO played a leading part in the coalition government of the state from 1963. Mustapha began his political career in the office of constitutional head of state but stepped down in 1965 to return to USNO, leading it to electoral victory in April 1967, after which he assumed the position of chief minister. USNO, with a Chinese partner within the Sabah Alliance, then dominated state politics until defeated in elections in 1976 following a split within its ranks and federal suspicion that Mustapha had secessionist ambitions. Although in opposition in Sabah, USNO entered the federal ***Barisan Nasional*** (National Front, BN) but was never fully a political partner, which became evident when it opposed the transfer of the island of Labuan to the authority of the central government. USNO was expelled from the BN in 1984. It contested the state elections of 1985 under the leadership of Mustapha, who failed in a constitutional coup to unseat the duly elected government of Joseph Pairin Kitingan's **Sabah United Party** (*Parti Bersatu Sabah*, PBS). USNO remained in the political wilderness until

PBS withdrew from the BN just before federal elections in October 1990. This act of political betrayal revived Mustapha's utility to the government in Kuala Lumpur, which with his cooperation set up a branch of the nationally dominant **UMNO** (United Malays National Organization) in Sabah. Sabah's chief minister responded by forging a state-level coalition with dissident USNO members in April 1993. The BN acted in turn to expel USNO again from membership, while Mustapha was appointed as federal minister for Sabah affairs, a post which he had first held in 1966. In August 1993 USNO was formally deregistered, ostensibly on the initiative of the Registrar of Societies. A number of its senior members joined the incumbent PBS, while Mustapha resigned from the federal cabinet and from UMNO after Ghafar Baba had been replaced as its deputy president by **Anwar Ibrahim**. Since then, several subsequent attempts to re-register the party have been rejected by the Registrar of Societies on ambiguous grounds. Meanwhile, up to ninety-five per cent of the USNO membership is believed to have joined UMNO Sabah. An attempt by remnant USNO members to contest the 2013 federal and state elections under the banner of the Sabah State Reform Party led to resounding defeat.

see also: Anwar Ibrahim; *Barisan Nasional;* Mustapha bin Datuk Harun, Tun; Sabah United Party; UMNO.

UNTAC (United Nations Transitional Authority in Cambodia) (Cambodia)

The United Nations Transitional Authority in Cambodia (UNTAC) was established as a direct result of the peace agreement concluded at the **International Conference on Cambodia** held in Paris in October 1991. To ensure its implementation, the UN Security Council was invited to establish a transitional authority with civilian and military powers under the direct responsibility of the UN secretary-general delegated to it by the **Supreme National Council**. Apart from peacekeeping duties, UNTAC was allocated direct responsibility for ensuring a neutral political environment conducive to free and fair elections intended to resolve political conflict. UNTAC was authorized by the Security Council on 28 February 1992 and was provided with 22,000 military and civilian personnel and a budget of around US$1.7 million. It was headed by Yasushi Akashi, an under-secretary-general.

UNTAC became operational on 15 March 1992. From the outset, UNTAC faced intractable problems in implementing its mandate. Its major difficulty arose from the refusal of the **Khmer Rouge** to cooperate in implementing the military provisions of the Paris agreement from the middle of 1992. It also failed to assume control of key ministries in Phnom Penh, which allowed the incumbent government imposed by Vietnam to intimidate political opponents. Despite serious shortcomings in its peacekeeping role, UNTAC was able to conduct relatively free and fair elections and overcome a boycott and violence by the Khmer Rouge. A remarkable success was the registration of more than ninety per cent (4.7 million) of eligible voters, while some 360,000 refugees from camps along the border with Thailand were resettled within a nine-month period. Elections held in May 1993 led on to the restoration of a constitutional monarchy, with **Norodom Sihanouk** reinstated as king, despite intervening political turbulence, and then a coalition government. When Yasushi Akashi left Cambodia on 26 September 1993 on the completion of his mission as head of UNTAC, he claimed that the United Nations had succeeded in its objective of laying a firm foundation for Cambodian democracy. That statement exaggerated the achievement of UNTAC but the outcome of its intervention far exceeded all initial expectations of its peacekeeping role.

see also: International Conference on Cambodia, Paris 1991; Khmer Rouge; Sihanouk, King Norodom; Supreme National Council; United Nations: Cambodia 1991–3.

V

Ver, General Fabian (Philippines)

General Fabian Ver was chief of staff of the armed forces of the Philippines from August 1981 until February 1986, when he resigned his post in the interest of a beleaguered President **Ferdinand Marcos**. During the final stage of the martial law regime, Fabian Ver combined the role of head of the armed forces with that of principal bodyguard to Marcos, to whom he was closely related. Ver was born in 1920 in Ilocos Norte, the birthplace of President Marcos. He was educated at the University of the Philippines, which provided an opportunity for entry into the Reserve Officer Training Corps and then into the paramilitary Philippine Constabulary. He took part in counterinsurgency operations against the ***Hukbalahap* Movement** guerrillas, specializing in military intelligence. Fabian Ver's career took off after Marcos became president in 1966. In 1971 he had become chief of the Presidential Security Command and director-general of the National Intelligence and Security Authority. His power was based on his close personal relationship with President Marcos and also with **Imelda Marcos**, which permitted him considerable scope for patronage through control of military promotions. He acquired a reputation as a heartless advocate of punitive measures against political opponents of the president and was widely suspected of direct involvement in the assassination of **Benigno Aquino** in August 1983. He was charged with being an accessory in his murder in January 1985 and was suspended from military office, but Marcos reinstated him as chief of staff on his acquittal in December. Fabian Ver resigned his post on 16 February 1986 as Marcos sought to shift responsibility for the fraudulent conduct of presidential elections in which he had been challenged by **Corazón Aquino**. It was allegedly fear of arrest by troops still loyal to General Ver that prompted an act of rebellion by the deputy chief of staff, **Fidel Ramos**, and the defence minister, **Juan Ponce Enrile**, on 22 February 1986 which led to Marcos' political downfall three days later. The president overruled General Ver's advice to use force against '**People Power**' – civilian demonstrators blocking the path of his marines to the camp where the rebels were concentrated. After arriving in the United States, Fabian Ver is believed to have attempted to organize a revolt in the Philippines on Marcos' behalf. He is reported to have sought to recruit to Brunei Filipino workers, who would be armed and trained for assassination during a visit to the sultanate by Corazón Aquino in 1986, intended to precipitate such a revolt. In the event, the visit was postponed and arrests took place at a very senior level within the Brunei court. General Ver accumulated vast wealth as a result of his close association with the Marcos family, which he enjoyed during twelve years of foreign exile. He died in Bangkok in November 1998 and, as a former chief of staff, was buried with full military honours in his home town of Sarrat.

see also: Aquino, Benigno; Aquino, Corazón; Enrile, Juan Ponce; *Hukbalahap* Movement; Marcos, Ferdinand; Marcos, Imelda; People Power; Ramos, Fidel.

Vientiane Action Plan (ASEAN) 2004 (Brunei/Cambodia/Indonesia/Laos/Malaysia/Myanmar/Philippines/Singapore/Thailand/Vietnam)

The **ASEAN** (Association of Southeast Asian Nations) Vientiane Action Plan (VAP) was formulated in response to the Bali Concord II in October 2003 and was signed at the **Vientiane Summit** of ASEAN in November 2004. The VAP was the second in a series of action plans – succeeding the Hanoi Plan of Action (HPA) to be implemented for the period 2004–10 – to realize the goals of establishing an ASEAN Community by 2020 as envisioned by the Declaration of ASEAN Concord II. The VAP was a vehicle to unify the strategies and goals of the three pillars of the **ASEAN Community**, especially focusing on two dimensions – deepening regional integration and narrowing the development gap between the ten member countries. In order to realize aspirations of deeper regional integration, the VAP outlined a set of implementation mechanisms such as proposals to intensify dialogue, make binding commitments, identify appropriate implementation timetables and mechanisms, extend national and regional capacities and competences, and develop institutional frameworks, responses and human resources in a range of areas, especially in the economic sphere. Notably, the VAP also committed ASEAN to the promotion and protection of human rights among member states. The VAP was later replaced by the Roadmap for an ASEAN Community, which would be implemented between 2009 and 2015.

see also: ASEAN; ASEAN Community; Vientiane Summit (ASEAN) 2004.

Vientiane Agreement on the Restoration of Peace and Reconciliation in Laos 1973

(Laos)

The **Paris Peace Agreements** for Vietnam were signed on 27 January 1973. On 21 February a corresponding agreement was signed for Laos in Vientiane between the Royal government and the ***Pathet Lao*** (Lao Nation) represented as the Patriotic Forces which had been at odds with each other for nearly two decades. Internal conflict in Laos had been tied inextricably to that in neighbouring Vietnam ever since the Communist-led **Viet Minh** movement had challenged French rule at the end of the Pacific War in the first phase of the **Indochina Wars**. The revolutionary *Pathet Lao* had functioned as virtually a subordinate branch of the Viet Minh. After the division of Vietnam by the **Geneva Agreements on Indochina** in July 1954, the eastern uplands of Laos became of critical importance to Vietnam's Communists seeking to overturn the government in Saigon as an access route for personnel and military supplies from north to south. Effective control of the territory through which the **Ho Chi Minh Trail** passed was sufficient for Vietnam's Communists and their Laotian counterparts until the closing stages of the **Vietnam War**, when the United States' military disengagement undermined any residual political resolve of the government in Vientiane. The agreement reached in Vientiane provided for a ceasefire, the termination of all foreign military intervention and the establishment within thirty days of a Provisional Government of National Union responsible for conducting national elections. A protocol providing for such a coalition government was not signed until 14 September with the date of formation set for 10 October 1973. That government with Prince **Souvanna Phouma** as prime minister was installed only on 5 April 1974. The coalition failed to function according to the Vientiane Agreement, however, as its demoralized royalist members were subject to increasing intimidation. General elections did not take place and *Pathet Lao* forces assumed progressive control concurrently with the military campaign which brought the Communists to power in South Vietnam. By the end of 1975 power had passed to the **Lao People's Revolutionary Party** (LPRP). On 3 December it was announced that King Savang Vatthana had abdicated and that the Lao People's Democratic Republic had been established with **Kaysone Phomvihan**, the general secretary of the LPRP, as prime minister. A **Treaty of Friendship and Cooperation** was entered into with Vietnam on 18 July 1977. The Vientiane Agreement failed in its declared purpose, serving instead as the means through which the Laotian revolutionary movement came to power.

see also: Geneva Agreements on Indochina 1954; Ho Chi Minh Trail; Indochina Wars; Kaysone Phomvihan; Lao People's Revolutionary Party; Paris Peace Agreements 1973; *Pathet Lao*; Souvanna Phouma, Prince; Treaty of Friendship and Cooperation 1977; Viet Minh; Vietnam War.

Vientiane Summit (ASEAN) 2004

(Brunei/Cambodia/Indonesia/Laos/Malaysia/Myanmar/Philippines/Singapore/Thailand/Vietnam)

The tenth meeting of heads of government of **ASEAN** (Association of Southeast Asian Nations) convened in Vientiane on 29 and 30 November 2004. This was the first Summit to be hosted in and chaired by Laos. The main agenda of the Summit was to work towards achieving the end goals of the **ASEAN Community** and ASEAN Vision. To that end, ASEAN leaders signed the **Vientiane Action Plan** (VAP), a six-year plan that would succeed the Hanoi Plan of Action, which would focus on deepening ASEAN integration and narrowing the development gap between ASEAN members. ASEAN leaders also adopted the ASEAN Security Community (ASC) Plan of Action which had been drafted by Indonesia. The Summit was also notable for a moribund attempt at the creation of an ASEAN peacekeeping force, proposed by Indonesia, which was rejected for fear of its implications for sovereignty and the principle of non-interference. The meeting also witnessed the accession of the Russian Federation and the Republic of Korea to the **Treaty of Amity and Cooperation.**

see also: ASEAN; ASEAN Community; Treaty of Amity and Cooperation; Vientiane Action Plan (ASEAN) 2004.

Viet Cong (Vietnam)

Viet Cong is an abbreviation for *Viet-Nam Cong-San* (translated as Vietnamese Communists) which came into common usage in the years following the partition of Vietnam by the **Geneva Agreements on Indochina** in 1954. It was employed initially as a pejorative term by the southern government headed by **Ngo Dinh Diem** but was taken up by western governments and writers as a label for the Communist insurgent movement in the south of Vietnam. It was never used by the Vietnamese Communists, who founded the **National Liberation Front of South Vietnam** in December 1960 as a political vehicle with which to challenge the government in Saigon.

see also: Diem, Ngo Dinh; Geneva Agreements on Indonesia 1954; National Liberation Front of South Vietnam.

Viet Minh (Vietnam)

Viet Minh is an abbreviation of *Viet Nam Doc-lap Dong-ming Hoi* (which translates as League for the Independence of Vietnam) which was established in May 1941 in the Chinese border town of Chingsi. The Viet Minh was conceived of initially by the Communist leader **Ho Chi Minh** as a national united front with which to solicit Allied support, first for defeating Japan and then for liberating Vietnam from French colonial rule. It was founded as the result of a decision taken by the Communist Party of Indochina at the eighth plenum of its central committee. A guerrilla base was set up in the mountains of northern Vietnam where contact was established with agents of the US Office of Strategic Service, the forerunner of the Central Intelligence Agency (CIA). Viet Minh forces entered Hanoi in the **August Revolution** in 1945 in an attempt to foment a general insurrection. The independence of the Democratic Republic of Vietnam was declared by Ho Chi Minh on 2 September 1945 but the *coup de force* did not survive the Chinese Nationalist occupation and then the restoration of French rule. Armed conflict with France began at the end of 1946. In the previous May, the Viet Minh had sponsored the *Lien Viet* (League for the National Union of Vietnam) as an even broader front organization. When the Communist Party of Indochina, ostensibly dissolved in 1945, adopted the name ***Lao Dong*** (Vietnam Workers Party) in March 1951, the Viet Minh was absorbed into the *Lien Viet* and the term ceased to be employed by the Communists. Nonetheless, it remained in general usage to describe the Communist-led nationalist movement which successfully challenged French rule in Indochina from the end of the Pacific War until their military success in the **Indochina Wars** at the **Battle of Dien Bien Phu** in May 1954.

see also: August Revolution 1945; Dien Bien Phu, Battle of, 1954; Ho Chi Minh; Indochina Wars; *Lao Dong*.

Vietnam–US Strategic Partnership (Vietnam)

Even though the **Vietnam War** ended in 1975, normalization of relations between the United States and Vietnam did not occur until 1995. Yet even after normalization, while trade and investment links grew extensively as Vietnam sought to liberalize its hitherto centrally planned economy, domestic opposition in both countries hampered progress on closer defence cooperation, which only gradually materialized much later. It was only after the turn of the millennium that defence relations were strengthened as both countries found it in their interest to develop closer ties in the face of a rising and more assertive China. Vietnam, with a long history of disputes with its larger neighbour, was keen to deepen American engagement in the region at a time when the United States was preoccupied with the Middle East and terrorism. The decision taken at a plenary meeting of the Communist Party of Vietnam in July 2003 to step up defence ties and cooperation with the United States was quickly followed by Vietnamese Defence Minister Phan Van Tra's visit to Washington in November 2003 and a port call at Saigon by a US navy vessel. Relations continued to improve with successive visits by both Vietnamese and American leaders.

Since 2008, there has also been a significant increase in military-to-military engagement such as joint naval activities in the **South China Sea** and the convening of an inaugural annual defence dialogue, signalling a convergence of the strategic interests of the two countries. While Vietnamese interest in strengthening defence relations with the United States coincided with increasing Chinese assertiveness in the South China Sea, a healthy long-term strategic partnership will have to rest on more than just pragmatic cooperation over a particular issue. Indeed, US–Vietnam relations are likely to be held back by differing political beliefs on governance, democracy and human rights.

see also: South China Sea; Vietnam War.

Vietnam War (Cambodia/Laos/Vietnam)

The Vietnam War is commonly understood to refer to the armed conflict between the forces of the United States and the Communist Party of Vietnam which took place primarily from March 1965 until January 1973, when the **Paris Peace Agreements** were signed. The nature of the conflict was more complex and its course more protracted, but it was informed by the common feature of a struggle over the political identity of Vietnam. The Vietnam War passed through two clearly defined historical stages involving differing forms of American intervention. Its origins are to be found in the determined attempt by the Vietnamese-dominated Communist Party of Indochina (founded in 1930) to thwart the re-establishment of French colonial power after the end of the Pacific War and to set up a Marxist state. In the wake of Japan's surrender in August 1945, the Communist front, known as the **Viet Minh** (League for the Independence of Vietnam) seized power in Hanoi in the **August Revolution**; on 2 September **Ho Chi Minh** proclaimed the formation of the Democratic Republic of Vietnam. The Viet Minh attracted popular support because of its nationalist credentials, while the French were faced with rising opposition at home.

Direct military confrontation between the Viet Minh and the French first took place at the end of 1946 ostensibly over control of customs but, in effect, over entry of arms in the northern port of Haiphong. The first of the **Indochina Wars** began as a guerrilla struggle on the Communist side but progressively became one between conventional formations, culminating in the historic **Battle of Dien Bien Phu** in the early months of 1954. From 1950 the Viet Minh had the advantage of military assistance from the newly established People's Republic of China, whose provision of US-manufactured artillery captured during the Korean War was decisive in the Battle of Dien Bien Phu. The French had attracted military assistance from the United States because of an ability to represent their colonial interest as part of a global struggle against international communism. It took the form of economic aid, military supplies and logistical support; by the time of the Battle of Dien Bien Phu, the United States was bearing almost eighty per cent of the total cost of France's prosecution of the war.

As the French military position became progressively more untenable with growing popular opposition to the war, an agreement was reached to convene an international conference in Geneva to discuss Korea and Indochina. The fortress of Dien Bien Phu fell to Viet Minh assault on 7 May 1954 in a great psychological victory only the day before the Indochina phase of the conference began. This dramatic triumph did not immediately decide the political future of Vietnam, in part because China and the Soviet

Union wished to avoid a confrontation with the United States. They persuaded their Vietnamese allies to compromise on territorial control and to agree to a provisional demarcation of the country along the line of the seventeenth parallel of latitude prior to national elections in 1956. The Democratic Republic of Vietnam succeeded to power north of that line. To its south, an anti-Communist nationalist government was established, led by former exile **Ngo Dinh Diem**, who established a Republic of Vietnam in 1955 with the support of the United States. That government, with US backing, refused to implement the electoral provisions of the **Geneva Agreements on Indochina** and took effective military action against the southern branch of the Communist movement.

The second phase of the Vietnam War may be said to have begun with the establishment in December 1960 of the **National Liberation Front of South Vietnam** (NLF). This equivalent to the Viet Minh was set up on the instruction of the ruling ***Lao Dong*** (Workers Party) in Hanoi, which had changed its name from the Communist Party of Indochina in 1951. The NLF began a series of armed actions against the Saigon government with signal success in the rural areas. The insurgency was reinforced from the north through infiltration of personnel and supplies through a series of routes passing through Laos and then Cambodia known collectively as the **Ho Chi Minh Trail**. The United States became drawn progressively into the war in support of the southern government. This support took the initial form of economic and military assistance, including the provision of some 700 military advisers. US military intervention was incremental but the first major decision was made by President John F. Kennedy in 1961, which resulted in some 16,000 US ground troops being deployed in Vietnam by the end of 1963. The Vietnam conflict was perceived as a test case in defeating Communist-inspired national liberation wars. Countervailing American resolve was required to prevent countries falling to communism, one after another like dominoes, to use the imagery employed by President Dwight D. Eisenhower in April 1954 (*see* **Domino Theory**).

The year 1963 was a turning point in the course of the war. The evident unpopularity of the government in Saigon in the face of Buddhist protest as well as its lamentable military performance led to a withdrawal of US support for President Ngo Dinh Diem. His assassination in November 1963 was followed by the assumption of power by a series of military juntas, none of which demonstrated any grasp of the requirements for victory. In consequence, the United States took on a growing responsibility for the conduct of the war on the mistaken assumption that it would be possible to buy time for a better motivated South Vietnamese Army to resume the burden of fighting. But every addition of US military resources was matched from the north, which was driven by a nationalist zeal and supported materially and diplomatically by Communist allies.

In March 1965 the United States changed the nature of the conflict by embarking on the continuous aerial bombardment of North Vietnam. The United States had first bombed the north in August 1964 as an act of retaliation for alleged torpedo attacks on patrolling US destroyers in the **Tonkin Gulf Incident**. When this attempt to interdict the flow of supplies southwards and to impose a penal cost on Hanoi for prosecuting the war failed, more US combat troops were introduced into the south. By the end of President Lyndon Johnson's term of office in January 1969, the number of those troops had reached more than half a million but without having been able to inflict a decisive defeat on the Communist forces. The turning point in the second phase of the war came at the beginning of 1968 during the Tet festival for the Vietnamese new year. A series of well-coordinated offensives against urban targets were launched by the NLF from the end of January, which included the penetration of the US embassy compound in Saigon. The **Tet Offensive** was a military failure conducted at great loss of life by the NLF, which gave up control of rural strongholds as a consequence. It was, however, a great psychological victory because of its political impact within the United States, where a popular tide was rising in opposition to a war conducted at great expense in blood and treasure and which did not seem related to American interests. A political turning point came in March in a primary election in New Hampshire, in which the setback suffered by President Johnson was such that he decided not to stand for re-election in November 1968 and to countenance negotiations with the Communist side, which began in Paris by the end of the year.

Johnson's successor, President Richard Nixon, realized that his political future depended on his ability to end the war but was concerned to do so in a way that did not seem to impair the global credibility of the United States. He began to reduce US force levels and advanced in July 1969 a new policy, the '**Nixon Doctrine**', which placed the primary responsibility for conducting the war on the South Vietnamese. This policy of so-called **Vietnamization** was underpinned with continued bombing of North Vietnam from Guam and Thailand, as well as from offshore aircraft carriers. The declared US war aim was to maintain the separate political integrity of Vietnam south of the seventeenth parallel. This end was sustained in negotiations in Paris, which reached a turning point at the end of 1972 following the failure of a conventional military offensive by the North Vietnamese across the seventeenth parallel in March 1972. The Vietnamese Communists revised their long-held view that the United States should remove the government in Saigon and were prepared to settle for the priority of securing an American military withdrawal. After a renewal of US aerial warfare, a final peace agreement was concluded in Paris in January 1973 whereby, in addition to a ceasefire with Vietnamese forces in place, it was agreed that all US forces would be removed from Vietnam in return for the release of US prisoners of war, primarily air force personnel. A power-sharing National Council of National Reconciliation and Concord, a structure for organizing elections, could not be established, however, and the ceasefire broke down. Monitoring of the implementation of the accord by an international commission followed US military withdrawal and release of prisoners but without effect. American support for the Saigon government began to falter as the Watergate scandal undermined Richard Nixon's authority and his threat to resume bombing, should the Communists violate the peace accords.

In early 1975 the war began to move on to a dramatic culmination after the Communist side undertook military probes, which enabled them to seize the provincial capital of Phuoc Long. In March, the Ban Me Thuot Offensive in the central highlands led South Vietnam's President **Nguyen Van Thieu** to order a retreat to the plains, which turned into a spectacular rout. The progressive collapse of his army followed; on 30 April Communist forces entered Saigon to receive the surrender from President Dong Van Minh, who had succeeded to office after President Thieu's flight from the country into exile. The NLF had maintained that they sought an independent neutral southern state, but in July 1976 the two halves of the country were reunited formally into the Socialist Republic of Vietnam.

The Vietnam War was very costly in loss of life and casualties: 47,365 US personnel were killed in action and nearly 11,000 lost their lives through other causes, including accidents. The war memorial in Washington contains the names of 58,196 men and women who died in Vietnam. South Vietnamese military deaths amounted to 254,257. In May 1995, the government in Hanoi released approximate casualty figures of more than one million fatalities from North Vietnam and National Liberation Front of South Vietnam. Civilian casualties were very heavy both north and south, with more than two million deaths and injuries. The Vietnamese received engineering support from Chinese troops as well as material support from China, the Soviet Union and its bloc allies. The United States carried the main burden of prosecuting the war in support of the South Vietnamese, but was assisted by the limited military involvement of troops from Australia, New Zealand, South Korea, the Philippines and Thailand.

The Vietnam War had a wider Indochinese dimension. The Viet Minh had penetrated Laos and Cambodia in the early 1950s in order to pin down French forces and also to establish a fraternal political domain. Vietnamese troops remained in Laos after the Geneva accords in July 1954 to stiffen the counterpart ***Pathet Lao*** (Lao Nation) against the government in

Vientiane, in part to ensure control of military access routes from north to south Vietnam. The Vietnamese Communist military presence was extended to Cambodia during the 1960s for a corresponding purpose, which provided a pretext for the overthrow of Prince **Norodom Sihanouk** and the expansion of the war westwards. The destruction of the Cambodian army by the Vietnamese Communists during 1970–1 played an important part in helping the **Khmer Rouge** to seize power in April 1975 some two weeks before the fall of Saigon. In the case of Laos, the **Vientiane Agreement on the Restoration of Peace and Reconciliation in Laos** was signed in February 1973, following the Paris accords for Vietnam, but Laos did not fall under Communist rule until after the end of the Vietnam War in April 1975.

see also: August Revolution 1945; Diem, Ngo Dinh; Dien Bien Phu, Battle of, 1954; Domino Theory; Geneva Agreements on Indochina 1954; Ho Chi Minh; Ho Chi Minh Trail; Indochina Wars; Khmer Rouge; *Lao Dong*; National Liberation Front of South Vietnam; Nixon Doctrine 1969; Paris Peace Agreements 1973; *Pathet Lao*; Sihanouk, King Norodom; Tet Offensive 1968; Thieu, Nguyen Van; Tonkin Gulf Incident 1964; Vientiane Agreement on the Restoration of Peace and Reconciliation in Laos 1973; Viet Minh; Vietnamization.

Vietnamization (Vietnam)

Vietnamization was the term coined in the wake of President Nixon's historic press conference on the island of Guam in July 1969; the **Nixon Doctrine** presaged the United States' military disengagement from Vietnam. Vietnamization was meant to describe the assumption of principal responsibility for fighting the war by the army of the Republic of (South) Vietnam. Its first major test occurred in February 1971 with a military incursion (codenamed Lam Son 719) into Laos in an attempt to interdict the legendary Ho Chi Minh Trail. The action proved to be a military disaster. The failure of Vietnamization to substitute for US intervention was confirmed by the inability of the South Vietnamese Army to blunt the Communist offensive in March 1972 without the use of US air power. In the wake of the **Paris Peace Agreements** of January 1973, Vietnamization was exposed as no more than a slogan to extricate the United States from Vietnam when a rout of southern forces during the Ban Me Thuot Offensive in March 1975 led directly to decisive military defeat at the end of the following month.

see also: Nixon Doctrine 1969; Paris Peace Agreements 1973.

Vo Nguyen Giap, General (Vietnam) *see* Giap, General Vo Nguyen.

Vo Van Kiet (Vietnam)

Vo Van Kiet was appointed chairman of the Council of Ministers of Vietnam in August 1991, elevated from the position of deputy to **Do Muoi**, who had become secretary-general of the ruling Communist Party. His appointment indicated Vietnam's continuing commitment to market-based economic reforms with which Vo Van Kiet had been closely identified. He was born Phan Van Hoa in Can Tho in southern Vietnam in 1922 to a peasant family and became involved in the revolutionary movement in the early 1940s. He rose in the party hierarchy working in the south of the country and held the post of secretary of the Saigon Municipal Party Committee at the end of the **Vietnam War** in 1975. He continued to hold high party office in what became Ho Chi Minh City but demonstrated a signal interest in practical economic matters with growing impatience with sterile dogma. In 1982 he was elected a full member of the Politburo and also a vice-chairman of the Council of Ministers. He became identified with the programme of economic reform after the Communist Party's sixth National Congress in December 1986. He was appointed acting chairman of the Council of Ministers in March 1988 on the death of Pham Hung but failed to retain that position, which was filled in June by the more conservative Do Muoi. His succession to Do Muoi in 1991 was reconfirmed when the National Assembly elected him to the new office of prime minister in September 1992 in which he concentrated on economic matters and developing closer relationships with **ASEAN** (Association of Southeast Asian Nations). He continued in office until September 1997 when he was succeeded as prime minister by **Phan Van Khai**.

A pragmatic reformist and proponent of ***Doi Moi***, as prime minister Vo Van Kiet presided over a period of economic growth and development in Vietnam and sought to improve the country's relations with the international community. His efforts on the latter count led to the lifting of a trade embargo by the United States in 1994, membership in ASEAN in 1995, and the development of a personal rapport with several international statesmen, including **Lee Kuan Yew**. After leaving office in September 1997 and the Politburo of the Communist Party that December, Vo Van Kiet remained an outspoken supporter of reforms, calling for press freedom and dialogue with dissidents. He died on 11 June 2008.

see also: ASEAN; Do Muoi; *Doi Moi*; Lee Kuan Yew; Phan Van Khai; Vietnam War.

W

Wahid, Abdurrahman (Indonesia)

Abdurrahman Addakhil Wahid, often known by the sobriquet Gus Dur, was born on 7 September 1940 in Jombang, East Java. His paternal grandfather, Hasyim Asy'ari, was the founder of the ***Nahdlatul Ulama*** (NU), a highly influential traditionalist *Sunni* organization in Indonesia with over thirty million followers. His father, Abdul Wahid Hasyim, was Indonesia's first minister of religious affairs. Wahid's early education was in Jakarta where he subsequently assumed a position as a teacher at a *pesantren* (Islamic boarding school) in Jombang and later as a headmaster at a *madrasah* (Islamic school). In 1963, he received a scholarship from the Ministry of Religious Affairs to pursue further studies at the Al-Azhar University in Cairo, Egypt. In 1966, he enrolled at the University of Baghdad. Upon his return to Indonesia, Wahid worked as a journalist for major publications such as *Tempo* and *Kompas* and built a sound reputation as a social commentator. In 1977, he joined the Hasyim Asy'ari Islamic University as dean of the Faculty of Islamic Beliefs and Practices.

Though Wahid had twice previously declined membership in the NU's Religious Advisory Council, he was eventually persuaded to join by his maternal grandfather, Bisri Syansuri, a notable religious scholar and NU strongman. Wahid quickly positioned himself as a reformer in NU, which at this point was embroiled in controversy related to the massacre of Communist Party members after the fall of President **Sukarno**. As part of a seven-person internal reform committee, Wahid managed to distance NU from partisan politics by reorienting the party's attention to social engagement. In 1984, he was nominated as NU's new chairman at its National Congress, a move which was warmly received by the **New Order** regime. Under Wahid, NU supported President Suharto and his party, ***Golkar***, and endorsed the state ***Pancasila*** ideology. Other NU initiatives under Wahid's chairmanship included the reform of the *pesantren* education system and the creation of a new generation of NU Muslim intellectuals, known as NU *Muda* (Young NU Members), which promulgated alternative Islamic discourses widely described as progressive and secular. Because of his popularity and successful revitalization of NU, Wahid was re-elected for a second term in 1989.

With the advent of the political reform movement, NU came under mounting pressure to form its own party in order to challenge the scandal-stricken *Golkar*. In 1998, Wahid acceded and ***Partai Kebangkitan Bangsa*** (National Awakening Party, PKB) was formed. On 7 February, Wahid was announced as PKB's candidate for the presidential election. Following the withdrawal of incumbent president **B. J. Habibie**, Wahid secured the official nomination from the Central Axis, a political coalition put together by Amien Rais, chairman of the **People's Consultative Assembly** (MPR). On 20 October 1999, Wahid won the first ever democratic presidential election in Indonesia, winning with 373 votes to **Megawati Sukarnoputri**'s 313 votes, and became the country's fourth president.

Wahid's presidential administration focused heavily on political reform. Immediately after the election Wahid formed his first Cabinet, the National Unity Cabinet, and set about abolishing the ministries of Information and Welfare, both known to be among the most corrupt agencies under the New Order regime. In tandem with policies of decentralization, Wahid also moved to reform the armed forces by rolling back its ***Dwi Fungsi*** doctrine that mandated its involvement in national politics, and replacing generals who questioned his authority over the military. Not surprisingly, this move proved unpopular with certain segments in the military, and was initially met with resistance which placed the military's relationship with the president under considerable strain. This was manifested during the outbreak of violence between Christians and Muslims in Ambon, when Wahid's orders to the military not to permit ***Laskar Jihad*** to enter the fray went unheeded, leading the president to declare a state of emergency.

Aside from reforming the military, Wahid's presidency was known for its commitment to pluralism, religious tolerance and equality among races. Wahid set the stage for the transformation of difficult relations with the restive Aceh province, when he reopened negotiations with the **Aceh Independence Movement** and with the Chinese community, and when he ended decades of institutionalized discrimination by declaring Chinese New Year a holiday and lifting bans on Chinese script and the importing of Chinese publications. Wahid also adopted a more conciliatory approach towards the ***Ahmadiyah*** sect when he invited Mirza Tahir Ahmad, the fourth leader of the Ahmadi, to Jakarta as a goodwill gesture.

Notwithstanding its reformist credentials, the Wahid presidency was tainted by allegations of corruption involving the mismanagement of monies by the *Badan Urusan Logistic* (BULOG or State Logistics Agency) and misuse of donation funds from the Sultan of Brunei earmarked for humanitarian assistance to Aceh. Economic reforms also progressed at a glacial pace, leading to widespread impatience and dissatisfaction. The government struggled to attract foreign direct investment, and as a consequence the national debt ballooned. Matters came to a head in November 2000, when 151 members of the People's Representative Council signed a petition calling for Wahid's impeachment. On 23 July 2001, the MPR unanimously voted to impeach Wahid and replace him with Megawati Sukarnoputri. Wahid continued his involvement in national politics after his impeachment. He rallied to be considered a candidate for the 2004 elections but was disqualified on medical grounds. Abdurrahman Wahid died in Jakarta on 30 December 2009 as a result of multiple health problems and was buried in Jombang, East Java. A state funeral was held for him followed by a mourning period of seven days.

see also: Aceh Independence Movement; *Ahmadiyah*; *Dwi Fungsi*; *Golkar*; Habibie, B. J.; *Laskar Jihad*; Megawati Sukarnoputri; *Nahdlatul Ulama*; New Order; *Pancasila*; *Partai Kebangkitan Bangsa*; People's Consultative Assembly; Sukarno.

Widodo, Joko (Indonesia)

Joko Widodo, or 'Jokowi' as he is affectionately known, is currently governor of Jakarta, the most populous city in Southeast Asia. A relative political unknown only a few years ago, Jokowi was the favourite to win the Indonesian presidential election scheduled for July 2014 after his candidature was formally announced by **Megawati Sukarnoputri**, his mentor and leader of his party, ***Partai Demokrasi Indonesia–Perjuangan*** (PDI–P).

Jokowi's popularity rests on his humble demeanour, consultative style of administration and a natural connection with people. Also striking about his background is the fact that Jokowi does not hail from a political family, nor is he a business tycoon. On the contrary, the former furniture and flooring businessman is known for his frugal lifestyle, and for having refused a salary while he served as the elected mayor of Solo, a position he relinquished to become the governor of Jakarta on a PDI–P ticket in 2012. His popular appeal has also been enhanced by the policies he has introduced since winning the gubernatorial elections, such as a free healthcare scheme and the launch of a long awaited mass transit rail system in the sprawling city.

Jokowi was born on 21 June 1961, in the city of Solo (Surakarta) and possesses an engineering degree from Gadjah Mada University.

see also: Megawati Sukarnoputri; *Partai Demokrasi Indonesia–Perjuangan*.

Workers' Party (Singapore)

The Workers' Party (WP) has had a chequered record in Singapore politics for more than a quarter of a century, attaining only minimal parliamentary representation. It was founded in November 1957 by the former chief minister, **David Marshall**, and modelled on the British Labour Party. An immediate showing was made in city council elections with Communist support. Withdrawal of that support left it without any seats after general elections in 1959 brought the **People's Action Party** (PAP) to power. David Marshall then won a by-election in the Anson constituency in 1962 through a return of Communist backing after left-wing defection from the ruling PAP over the formation of Malaysia. After David Marshall resigned from the party in January 1963 in frustration at Communist control, the WP became moribund for nearly a decade. In 1971 Marshall's law partner, **J. B. Jeyaretnam**, revived the party, which became very much a personal political vehicle. Ten years later in October 1981, Jeyaretnam became the first opposition member of parliament for over a decade when he won a by-election, also in Anson. In Parliament, he distinguished himself with carping criticism of government and was returned by his constituency in general elections in December 1984. Jeyaretnam lost his seat and was disqualified from politics for five years in November 1986 after the High Court confirmed his conviction for making a false declaration of the WP accounts and being fined an amount which automatically carried that penalty.

The WP failed to secure any seats in elections in September 1988 but was successful in one constituency in August 1991, through **Low Thia Khiang**. In elections in January 1997, Low retained his seat, while J. B. Jeyaretnam entered Parliament as the sole non-constituency member, a position allocated to up to three losing opposition candidates. He was however removed from this position in 2001 after being declared bankrupt. A falling out between Jeyaretnam and Low in 2001 led to the former's departure from the party. Low took over as secretary-general, and after a period of rebuilding, the party experienced something of a revival under his leadership. In the April 2011 general election, Low led his team to a landmark victory at the **Aljunied Group Representation Constituency** (GRC) by wresting a GRC from the PAP for the first time since this electoral division was introduced in 1988. The fortunes of the WP improved further in the ensuing two years, when it won both by-elections it contested against the PAP in the single-seat wards of Hougang in May 2012 and Punggol East in January 2013.

see also: Aljunied Group Representation Constituency; Jeyaretnam, J. B.; Low Thia Khiang; Marshall, David; People's Action Party.

X

Xayaburi Dam (Cambodia/Laos/Thailand/Vietnam)

Situated on the lower stretches of the Mekong River in northern Laos, the Xayaburi Dam is a proposed US$3.5 billion, 1,285-megawatt hydropower project whose construction is spearheaded by Thailand's second largest construction company, C. H. Karnchang, and financed by Thai banks. Once completed, the Electricity Generating Authority of Thailand has also undertaken to purchase ninety-five per cent of the electricity generated by the dam.

While the success of the Xayaburi Dam project is critical to the Laotian economy, its construction has also proven to be controversial. Environmental activists have decried the construction of the dam, arguing that because it is located upstream its operation would impede the flow of sediment and the migration of fish downstream. Concomitantly, this would have negative consequences for the ecosystem as well as the livelihoods of more than sixty million people who reside in the Mekong Delta, many of whom rely heavily on fishing and agriculture. In addition to this, environmental activists have also expressed concern that the completion of the Xayaburi Dam might set a precedent for the building of other dams in the lower Mekong. In order to protect the ecosystem and ensure the environmental sustainability of the Mekong river, an inter-governmental body known as the Mekong River Commission (MRC) was established via the instrument of a treaty between Cambodia, Laos, Thailand and Vietnam in 1995. With the creation of this body, projects on the river envisaged by any one signatory state could only proceed after consultation with and agreement from other members of the MRC.

Because of environmental issues related to the construction of the dam, the government of Thailand has come under strong political pressure to enforce a moratorium on construction activities until environmental concerns have been addressed. Both Cambodia and Vietnam strongly oppose the Xayaburi Dam as their agriculture industries will be threatened by the hydropower project. Laos, however, is keen to proceed in earnest with construction, as electricity from the dam will generate much needed income for its economy.

Y

Yang di-Pertuan Agong (Malaysia)

Yang di-Pertuan Agong (Supreme Ruler) is the official title of Malaysia's reigning constitutional monarch. Monarchy in Malaysia has long enjoyed a special political standing, in part because of its symbolic role in the emergence of Malay nationalism during the **Malayan Union Proposal** crisis from 1946. Its prerogatives have been jealously guarded but have come under challenge as economic development has generated change within Malay society. The distinctive feature about monarchy in Malaysia is that the office is held for five years only on a rotational rather than on a hereditary basis. The constitutional predecessor of Malaysia, the Federation of Malaya, was created from a number of states in the Malay Peninsula which had been in formal treaty relations with the British Crown, making them sovereign entities in legal theory. On independence in 1957, the nine hereditary Malay rulers of Malaya agreed to occupy the office of Supreme Ruler in turn on an agreed notion of seniority. That arrangement has continued from the establishment of Malaysia in 1963.

In 1983 a political crisis occurred over the issue of the royal assent to Acts of Parliament which the government of **Mahathir Mohamad** had sought to remove by constitutional amendment. Another **Constitutional Crisis** arose early in 1993 over the same government's attempt to remove the right of the hereditary rulers to immunity from criminal prosecution after an alleged act of assault by a former king. In May 1994, Malaysia's Parliament passed an amendment to the constitution whereby any Bill which had been endorsed by both its houses would be deemed to have become law within thirty days, whether or not assented to by the king. On 13 December 2011, Abdul Halim Shah, the sultan of Kedah, was invested as the latest incumbent. He is the first monarch to hold the office twice, having first held the position from 1970 to 1975. He is also the oldest hereditary ruler to have ascended the throne.

see also: Constitutional Crises; Mahathir Mohamad, Tun; Malayan Union Proposal 1946.

Yeo, George Yong-Boon (Singapore)

George Yong-Boon Yeo is a former **People's Action Party** (PAP) Member of Parliament for **Aljunied Group Representation Constituency** (GRC) and former Minister for Foreign Affairs of the Republic of Singapore (2004–11). He retired from politics after losing his seat in Parliament in the 2011 general elections.

Born in 1954, Yeo studied for his bachelor's degree in engineering at Cambridge University on a prestigious President's and Singapore Armed Forces (SAF) scholarship before joining the SAF. In 1983, he graduated from Harvard Business School with an MBA with High Distinction. During his service in the SAF, he held the positions of Head of the Air Plans Department of the Republic of Singapore Air Force (RSAF), chief of staff of the Air Staff and Director of Joint Operations and Planning in the Ministry of Defence, before resigning from the SAF as a brigadier general to enter politics and contest the 1988 general election.

Yeo entered politics at the age of thirty-four and was one of the elected MPs for Aljunied GRC from 1988 to 2011. During his political career spanning twenty-three years, he served in the Cabinet as minister of information and the arts (1991–9), minister of health (1994–7) and minister for trade and industry before becoming the minister of foreign affairs. As foreign minister, he became known for his strong advocacy for a proactive and integrated **ASEAN**. He was a critic of the Myanmar junta during the **Saffron Revolution** in 2007, which took place just two months before the signing of the ASEAN Charter, arguing that ASEAN's credibility was at stake if the organization did not voice concern over developments in the country. In the realm of domestic politics he was widely seen as a progressive and liberal voice within the conservative PAP establishment.

Upon his defeat by the **Workers' Party** in Aljunied GRC, Yeo was succeeded as foreign minister by K. Shanmugam. In October 2011, he stepped down from the PAP's central executive committee. He is currently vice-chairman of the Hong Kong property developers, Kerry Group. He is a practising Roman Catholic who also has expressed appreciation for Taoist philosophy. In the wake of the 2011 electoral defeat, Yeo declared that he would not contest the next election.

see also: Aljunied Group Representation Constituency; ASEAN; People's Action Party; Saffron Revolution 2007; Workers' Party.

Yingluck Shinawatra (Thailand)

Yingluck Shinawatra was Thailand's first female prime minister. Yingluck was born in Chiang Mai on 21 June 1967. She earned a bachelor's degree from Chiang Mai University in 1988 and a master's in public administration in 1991 at Kentucky State University in the United States. She worked in her family's businesses, becoming an executive in several of her older brother's enterprises. Yingluck is the younger sister of exiled former prime minister, **Thaksin Shinawatra**, and the sister-in-law of another former prime minister, **Somchai Wongsawat**.

Yingluck's ascent to power was as dramatic as her downfall. Notwithstanding her relative inexperience and personal reluctance, Yingluck was named the ***Pheu Thai* Party**'s top candidate under the party-list system for the July 2011 elections despite being neither a party leader nor an executive committee member. With *Pheu Thai*'s absolute majority win, a coalition government was formed and Yingluck was appointed prime minister on 5 August. Against the backdrop of a deeply polarized political climate between pro- and anti-Thaksin forces, Yingluck's government faced constant criticism by detractors, including for its handling of the 2011 floods, and its apparent inability to fulfil promises made during the electoral campaign despite the fact that the Thai economy had stabilized during the early months of her tenure. As a *Pheu Thai* prime minister, she faced pressure in the form of demands from pro-Thaksin forces to craft an amnesty bill for those accused of politically motivated offences after the 2006 coup, ostensibly to secure his pardon.

Yingluck, who set political reconciliation as a major policy goal, laboured to establish a cordial relationship with the military. To defuse tensions, her government delayed proposed tabling of changes to the military-inspired constitution. Initially dismissed as merely a puppet of her brother, Yingluck did grow in confidence as prime minister during her term, demonstrating deft diplomatic skills while developing her own independent power base. In July 2013, Yingluck took on the important position of defence minister, purportedly with the support of army chief, General **Prayuth Chan-ocha**, making her the first female in a position traditionally the preserve of retired senior military officers.

She was however unable to mend fences with the traditional Bangkok elite and royalists who have been bent on removing all vestiges of her brother's rule. To that end, her political opponents brought charges of malfeasance and neglect against her for her government's controversial rice buy-back scheme, which they criticized was a populist ploy to secure the rural support base. At the same time, opposition forces also opposed her party's proposed amnesty bill, which they viewed as paving the way for Thaksin's return to Thailand. The traditional elite and royalists took to the streets in October 2013 and reignited mass protest, calling for Yingluck's dismissal. A gambit to dissolve Parliament and call elections, which were held on 2 February 2014 amidst protests and blockades at several voting stations, backfired on Yingluck when the Constitutional Court declared the election result null and void on the grounds that because voting could not be completed within the same day (because of the blockades), the process was unconstitutional. The same court found her guilty on charges of abusing her power by transferring a senior official out of the National Security Council and replacing him with a loyalist. In the event, Yingluck was forced to resign on 7 May 2014. She was detained and later released by the military after the coup of 22 May 2014.

see also: Pheu Thai Party; Prayuth Chan-ocha, General; Somchai Wongsawat; Thaksin Shinawatra.

Young Turks (Thailand)

Young Turks is the name given to a group of regimental and battalion commanders who became influential in Thai politics from the mid-1970s and who promoted an abortive coup in April 1981. The core of the group were graduates of class seven of the Chulachomklao Royal Military Academy. They had experienced advanced professional training as well as service in Vietnam and involvement in counter-insurgency in Thailand. The group coalesced in the wake of the collapse of military rule in October 1973 during a highly volatile democratic interlude brought to a close by a bloody coup in October 1976 following the **Thammasat University Massacre**. After an incumbency coup in October 1977 which made General **Kriangsak Chomanan** prime minister, the Young Turks, who took their name from the movement established at the heart of the Ottoman empire in 1908, played an arbiter role within a factionalized military. Their withdrawal of support from General Kriangsak prompted his resignation in February 1980 and the succession to office by General **Prem Tinsulanond**a. Charging weakness of political leadership, the Young Turks organized a coup attempt on 1 April 1981 but General Prem escaped from Bangkok to Korat in the northeast of the country with the royal family. The failure to attract support from King **Bhumibol Adulyadej**, who endorsed General Prem's action, led to the collapse of the coup attempt within days. Most of the Young Turks were dismissed or transferred within the army but some of their number were involved in a subsequent abortive coup in September 1985. They represented a complex mixture of self-seeking and professional interests concerned both to protect military privilege and to prevent a perceived degeneration of the political process allegedly influenced by civilian–business participation.

see also: Bhumibol Adulyadej, King; Kriangsak Chomanan, General; Prem Tinsulanonda, General; Thammasat University Massacre 1976.

Yudhoyono, Susilo Bambang (Indonesia)

Susilo Bambang Yudhoyono, also popularly known as 'SBY', was Indonesia's first directly elected president when he defeated **Megawati Sukarnoputri** in the October 2004 election. In July 2009, he secured a landslide victory with sixty-one per cent of the vote to become the first Indonesian president to be re-elected.

Susilo Bambang Yudhoyono was born in Pacitan in East Java on 9 September 1949 into a well-to-do family. After graduating from the Indonesian Military Academy and topping his class in 1973, he joined the army and undertook various tours of duty, steadily rising through the ranks. Yudhoyono also attended the Infantry Officer Advanced Course at Fort Benning in the United States in the 1980s as well as the US Army Command and General Staff College in Kansas in 1991, during which time he obtained a master's degree in business management from Webster University. Yudhoyono held territorial commands in Jakarta and South Sumatra, and served as chief of the armed forces social and political affairs staff. He received a doctorate in agricultural economics from Bogor Agricultural Institute in 2004. In 2005, he was awarded two honorary doctorates in law and political science, from Webster University and Thammasat University respectively. Yudhoyono retired from the military in January 2000 and began his political career in the government of **Abdurrahman Wahid**, where he served first as minister of mining and energy, and later, as coordinating minister for political, social and security affairs in August 2000. He was dismissed by President Wahid in 2011 when he disobeyed orders issued by the president, himself under siege and facing impeachment, to declare a state of emergency. This act of defiance earned him a reputation as a liberal and democrat. Yudhoyono returned to government as coordinating minister for political, social and security affairs in the '*Gotong Royong*' cabinet of Megawati Sukarnoputri, under instructions to improve counterterrorism efforts in the wake of the October 2002 terrorist bombings in Bali. However, he resigned in March 2004 after falling out with Megawati and announced his candidature for the upcoming presidential elections through the vehicle of ***Partai Demokrat***, with **Yusuf Kalla** as his running mate. Together, they managed to secure a sixty per cent majority mandate at the second round of the 2004 presidential election that allowed him to form the 'United Indonesia' Cabinet in October. In 2009, he secured a convincing first round victory for a second term, winning a 60.8 per cent majority, and proceeded to form a coalition government with ***Partai Keadilan Sejahtera***, ***Partai Amanat Nasional***, ***Partai Persatuan Pembangunan*** and ***Partai Kebangkitan Bangsa***.

While his supporters celebrate him as a democrat and a 'thinking general', his career has not been without controversy. As a soldier, Yudhoyono served as chief of staff when mobs linked to the military attacked Megawati Sukarnoputri's ***Partai Demokrasi Indonesia*** party headquarters in 1996. His complicity in those events was never conclusively proven. During East Timor's transition to independence in 1999, he was appointed chief of territorial affairs and reported directly to then-commander of the armed forces, General Wiranto. Though Wiranto was later indicted for war crimes by the East Timor tribunal, no charges were brought against Yudhoyono on the grounds that he was not part of the inner circle of military commanders accused of turning a blind eye to violence in East Timor. Nor has Yudhoyono been immune to controversy as a politician and as president. The Indonesian government's approval of a RP6.7 trillion bank bailout for Bank Century in 2008 was heavily criticized, and Yudhoyono was derided after auditors found evidence of violations by the bank. He has also been criticized for his reluctance to take action against the police chief and attorney general after evidence surfaced that they were complicit in attempts to frame officials from the Corruption Eradication Commission. On other occasions, Yudhoyono has been derided for being weak on domestic issues, particularly in relation to the assertiveness of religious groups. His inability or reluctance to take action against perpetrators of anti-***Ahmadiyah*** attacks was instructive in that regard, as was his government's impotence to prevent radical Muslim groups from disrupting plans to hold the Miss World beauty pageant in Jakarta (the pageant had to be relocated to Bali). Towards the end of his tenure, Yudhoyono was exercised by a series of corruption scandals that plagued his party, and his inability to find within its top ranks a successor to mount a challenge for the Indonesian presidency.

see also: *Ahmadiyah*; Kalla, Yusuf; Megawati Sukarnoputri; *Partai Amanat Nasional*; *Partai Demokrasi Indonesia*; *Partai Demokrat*; *Partai Kebangkitan Bangsa*; *Partai Persatuan Pembangunan*; Wahid, Abdurrahman.

Yusuf, Irwandy (Indonesia)

Irwandy Yusuf is the former governor of the special Indonesian province of Aceh. He was born in Bireuen, Aceh on 2 August 1960. A veterinarian who graduated from the Syiah Kuala University in Banda Aceh, he pursued a master's degree in veterinary science at the Oregon State University in the United States in 1993.

Irwandy was elected with 39.3 per cent of the popular vote at the 2006 elections, a historic democratic process for the people of Aceh after thirty years of brutal confrontation between the Indonesian military forces and the Acehnese separatist movement, the **Aceh Independence Movement** (*Gerakan Aceh Merdeka*, GAM). Irwandy himself was an active member of GAM from 1990, where he served in multiple roles, most notably as intelligence operations chief. He was arrested in 2003 and sentenced to nine years' imprisonment in the Keudah Prison in Banda Aceh, and was interred there during the **2004 Tsunami**. He managed to escape from his cell by fleeing to the second floor of the building and punching his way through the asbestos ceiling where he held on to the roof for two hours before the waves subsided. Following the tsunami, the Indonesian Government and GAM settled on a peace agreement which paved the way for an end to the insurgency and the advent of democratic elections in Aceh. The elections saw two factions emerge from within GAM to vie for the governorship of Aceh – one led by Irwandy who was in favour of integration into the Indonesian polity, and another by Malik Mahmud, a popular GAM stalwart who was a key voice that articulated the aspirations of the separatist movement from exile but who nevertheless was standing as a candidate of ***Partai Persatuan Pembangunan***. The contest was won by Irwandy, who ran as an independent. During his leadership, Irwandy actively championed the conservation of Aceh's rainforest, to the extent of personally joining official raids on illegal logging. He eventually found himself embroiled in controversy however, when he issued a permit for a palm-oil company, PT Kallista Alam, to use 1,605 hectares of peat swamp for a plantation in the Tripa conservation zone, one of the last refuges of the endangered Sumatran orang-utan, in 2011. This provoked widespread anger among Acehnese who claimed that he had betrayed his homeland and his cause. In 2012, he lost his re-election bid to fellow former GAM member **Zaini Abdullah**, amidst claims of voter fraud and intimidation.

see also: Abdullah, Zaini; Aceh Independence Movement; *Partai Persatuan Pembangunan*; Tsunami 2004.

Z

ZOPFAN (Zone of Peace, Freedom and Neutrality) 1971 (Indonesia/Malaysia/Philippines/Singapore/Thailand)

A joint declaration of determination 'to exert initially necessary efforts to secure the recognition of, and respect for, Southeast Asia as a Zone of Peace, Freedom and Neutrality, free from any form or manner of interference by outside Powers' was signed on 27 November 1971 in Kuala Lumpur by the foreign ministers of Indonesia, Malaysia, the Philippines and Singapore, and a special envoy of the National Executive Council of Thailand. The five delegates had convened to discuss a Malaysian proposal that Southeast Asia as a region be neutralized through guarantees from the United States, the Soviet Union and the People's Republic of China. Indonesia's strong objection to virtual policing rights being accorded to outside powers was primarily responsible for collective endorsement of an alternative proposal allocating exclusive responsibility for managing regional order to regional states. The **Kuala Lumpur Declaration** of the ZOPFAN formula was adopted officially as corporate policy at the **Bali Summit**, the first meeting of heads of government of **ASEAN** (Association of Southeast Asian Nations) held in February 1976 when it was included within a **Declaration of ASEAN Concord**. That declaration called on member states, individually and collectively, to take active steps for the early establishment of the zone. Subsequently, there have been recurrent reaffirmations by ASEAN of ZOPFAN's desirability, but practical steps towards its realization have not been taken.

The concept of ZOPFAN has been supported most strongly by Indonesia, whose foreign policy it closely reflects. Malaysia has also been supportive because of its role in pressing for neutralization, which was acknowledged as a desirable objective in Kuala Lumpur in November 1971. Other regional states have been willing to provide only formal backing because of the practical difficulties of implementation. A major obstacle to implementation has been the absence of a shared strategic perspective among the ASEAN states, which is pointed up by the very concept of ZOPFAN. That concept reflects the view of those governments that wish to see regional order determined by the resident states of Southeast Asia. Not all regional governments share this view because of a concern that they would be at the mercy of the strongest regional powers. For that reason, they prefer to maintain defence cooperation with states beyond the region in order to have access to external sources of countervailing power. It is noteworthy that all member governments of ASEAN have defence cooperation agreements of one kind or another with extra-regional states, while even Indonesia has permitted limited access by US naval vessels to its east Java port of Surabaya. Vietnam, which joined ASEAN in July 1995, still permits a residual Russian naval presence to remain in **Cam Ranh Bay**. In December 1995, in an attempt to lend substance to ZOPFAN, ASEAN's heads of government concluded a treaty purporting to establish a nuclear weapon-free zone in Southeast Asia. However, by the end of the century at the meeting of ASEAN foreign ministers in Singapore in July 1999, only passing reference was made to ZOPFAN, in noting consultations with nuclear weapon states over their accession to the protocol to the Southeast Asia Nuclear Weapon-Free Zone Treaty (SEANWFZ).

see also: ASEAN; Bali Summit (ASEAN) 1976; Cam Ranh Bay; Declaration of ASEAN Concord 1976; Kuala Lumpur Declaration 1971.

Postscript

Since the submission of this manuscript to the publishers, a number of major events have unfolded in Southeast Asia that warrant mention.

On 20 October 2014, **Joko Widodo** will be sworn in as the seventh president of the Republic of Indonesia. Earlier in August, "Jokowi," as Joko is affectionately known, had prevailed over a robust challenge from **Prabowo Subianto** for the presidency during a closely fought presidential election. Though he has emerged victorious, Jokowi faces some immediate challenges, not least of which is the fact that he presides over a minority government in the Indonesian parliament and indications are that his challenger Prabowo, whose coalition at the time of writing continues to hold the parliamentary majority, refuses to accept defeat. No less daunting for the new president, who possesses barely a decade's worth of municipal political and administrative experience before he took high office, is the need to balance potentially competing interests within his coalition between key supporters such as the former president, **Megawati Sukarnoputri**, her daughter, Puan Maharani, and several former military generals who are throwbacks to the **New Order** government of the late former president, **Suharto**.

In Thailand, the military coup of May 2014, the twentieth in modern Thai history, was followed by wide-ranging censorship, a clampdown on protests, the assumption of high office by the coup leader, **Prayuth Chan-ocha**, the establishment of a National Council of Peace and Order (NCPO) by the junta, and the appointment of an unelected National Legislative Assembly by the NCPO – unelected on account of the junta's aversion to electoral processes that threw up the populist, **Thaksin Shinawatra**. Promises of impartiality in appointments to the NLA did not quite materialize, and the eventual assembly comprised a large number of military officers and personalities with close ties to key members of the junta and other pro-Monarchists. Notably, the National Assembly that was set up after the 2006 coup was far more diverse in terms of its representation.

Amidst the humanitarian tragedy wrought by a lost airliner, the Malaysian carrier's MH370, and another, MH17, that was shot down by pro-Russia insurgents in Ukraine, Malaysia witnessed several months of political tumult and intrigue in the opposition-held state of Selangor, the country's richest state. The controversy revolved around the position of the Chief Minister of Selangor, until recently held by Abdul Khalid Ibrahim of the ***Parti Keadilan Rakyat*** (PKR). Because of displeasure within PKR ranks with Khalid's leadership and management of the state's bountiful resources, an attempt was made in early 2014 by PKR advisor Anwar Ibrahim to render Khalid's leadership untenable. In the event, Anwar's effort to position himself to replace Khalid was blocked by the ***Barisan Nasional*** government, which immediately had the former deputy prime minister banned from politics (Anwar's gambit against Khalid involved winning a by-election for a seat on the state legislature, which was required so as to qualify him for the Chief Minister post) on yet another sodomy charge. Meanwhile, Khalid was sacked from PKR in August 2014, and Anwar's wife and PKR president, Wan Azizah Wan Ismail, was put forward by the party as his replacement at the helm of the Selangor state government. Her nomination however, was not unanimously accepted within the ***Pakatan Rakyat*** opposition coalition. Several senior leaders of ***Parti-Islam Se-Malaysia***, including the party president in particular, **Abdul Hadi Awang**, harboured reservations towards Wan Azizah's candidature – for reasons of her gender as well as her connection to Anwar, thereby testing the opposition coalition's unity.

In Myanmar, a seemingly routine exercise of a national census witnessed several controversial developments that cast doubt over the democratization process currently underway in the once reclusive country. The fact that it was the first country-wide census in thirty years was laudable. However, the census was also criticized internationally for the government's refusal to accord **Rohingya** Muslims recognition as citizens, this time, according to government officials, on account of a technicality (their household cards listed them as "Bengali" so they could not claim to be "Rohingya"). The census also could not access areas in the states of **Kachin** and Arakan which were some of the last bastions of ethnic, armed insurgent movements. In June 2014, a thirty-one member constitution review committee voted overwhelmingly to reinforce article 59(F) of the Myanmar constitution, which bars anyone who has been married to a foreigner from running for the presidency. This meant that **Aung San Suu Kyi**'s aspirations to hold high office would continue to be blocked. While the committee's recommendation is not binding, prospects of the **Union Solidarity and Development Party**-controlled parliament revising that constitutional clause are unlikely.

Meanwhile, regional tensions over China's placement of an oil rig in **South China Sea** waters, claimed by Vietnam to be within its 200-nautical mile Exclusive Economic Zone in May 2014, appeared to ease when the former removed the rig in August, purportedly because of the monsoon season. The unilateral move was met by calls for self-restraint on the part of pro-Chinese leaders in Vietnam, particularly the party secretary, **Nguyen Phu Trong**, and the president, **Truong Tan Sang**, signaling strong sentiments against antagonizing China, particularly at a time when the Philippines was seeking regional support for litigation of its own competing claims with China. Vietnam's position appears to have shifted somewhat from that which was articulated at the May 2014 **ASEAN** Summit held for the first time in Yangon, Myanmar, when, together with the Philippine president, **Benigno Aquino III**, Vietnam's prime minister, **Nguyen Tan Dung**, spoke out on the need for the regional organization to take a stronger stance in the face of Chinese assertiveness in the South China Sea. Needless to say, as in the case of recent ASEAN summits the topic of competing claims and escalation of tension in the South China Sea overshadowed all other issues on the summit agenda.

see also: Anwar Ibrahim; Aquino III, Benigno Simeon Cojuangco; ASEAN; Aung San Suu Kyi; *Barisan Nasional*; Hadi Awang, Abdul; Kachin; Megawati Sukarnoputri; New Order; Nguyen Phu Trong; Nguyen Tan Dung; *Pakatan Rakyat*; *Parti Islam Se-Malaysia*; *Parti Keadilan Rakyat*; Prabowo Subianto; Prayuth Chan-ocha; Rohingya; South China Sea; Suharto; Thaksin Shinawatra; Truong Tan Sang; Union Solidarity and Development Party; Widodo, Joko.

Further Reading

General

Acharya, Amitav (2000) *Constructing a Security Community. ASEAN and the Problem of Regional Order*, Routledge, London.

Alagappa, Muthiah (ed.) (1985) *Political Legitimacy in Southeast Asia*, Stanford University Press, Stanford.

Bloodworth, Dennis (1987) *The Eye of the Dragon: Southeast Asia Observed, 1954–1986*, Times Books, Singapore.

Brown, David (1994) *The State and Ethnic Politics in Southeast Asia*, Routledge, London.

Colbert, Evelyn (1977) *Southeast Asia in International Politics, 1941–1956*, Cornell University Press, Ithaca, NY.

Collins, Alan (2000) *Security Dilemmas of Southeast Asia*, Macmillan, Basingstoke.

—— (2003) *Security and Southeast Asia: Domestic, Regional, and Global Issues*, Institute of Southeast Asian Studies, Singapore.

Emmers, Ralf (2003) *Cooperative Security and the Balance of Power in ASEAN and the ARF*, Routledge, London.

—— (2008) *Security and International Politics in the South China Sea: Towards a Cooperative Management Regime*, Routledge, London.

Emmerson, Donald (ed.) (2008) *Hard Choices: Security, Democracy, and Regionalism in Southeast Asia*, Institute of Southeast Asian Studies, Singapore.

Fitzgerald, Stephen (1972) *China and the Overseas Chinese*, Cambridge University Press, Cambridge.

Funston, John (ed.) (2001) *Government and Politics in Southeast Asia*, Institute of Southeast Asian Studies, Singapore.

Jorgensen-Dahl, Arnfinn (1982) *Regional Organization and Order in Southeast Asia*, Macmillan, London.

Kershaw, Roger (2000) *Monarchy in South-East Asia. The Faces of Tradition in Transition*, Routledge, London.

Kroef, Justus M. van der (1981) *Communism in South-East Asia*, Macmillan, London.

Leifer, Michael (1990) *ASEAN and the Security of South-East Asia*, Routledge, London.

Lim Joo-Jock and Vani, S. (eds) (1984) *Armed Communist Movements in Southeast Asia*, Institute of Southeast Asian Studies, Singapore.

Liow, Joseph Chinyong and Emmers, Ralf (eds) (2006) *Order and Security in Southeast Asia: Essays in Memory of Michael Leifer*, Routledge, London.

Neher, Clark D. (1991) *Southeast Asia in the New International Era*, Westview Press, Boulder, CO.

Nishikawa, Yukiko (2010) *Human Security in Southeast Asia*, Routledge, Abingdon.

Osborne, Milton (1971) *Region of Revolt*, Penguin, Harmondsworth.

—— (1990) *Southeast Asia: An Illustrated Introductory History*, Allen & Unwin, Sydney.

Palmujoki, Eero (2001) *Regionalism and Globalism in Southeast Asia*, Palgrave MacMillan, Basingstoke.

Shaplen, Robert (1979) *A Turning Wheel*, Random House, New York.

Southeast Asian Affairs (annually from 1974) Institute of Southeast Asian Studies, Singapore.

Steinberg, D. J., *et al.* (eds) (1987) *In Search of Southeast Asia: A Modern History*, University of Hawaii Press, Honolulu.

Storey, Ian (2011) *Southeast Asia and the Rise of China: The Search for Security*, Routledge, London.

Suryadinata, Leo (1985) *China and the ASEAN States: The Ethnic Chinese Dimension*, Singapore University Press, Singapore.

Wang Gung-wu (1981) *Community and Nation: Essays on Southeast Asia and the Chinese*, Heinemann Educational, Singapore.

Wilson, Dick (1975) *The Neutralization of Southeast Asia*, Praeger, New York.

Brunei

Bartholomew, James (1990) *The Richest Man in the World*, Penguin, Harmondsworth.

Braighlinn, G. (1992) *Ideological Innovation under Monarchy: Aspects of Legitimation Activity in Contemporary Brunei*, VU University Press, Amsterdam.

Hussainmiya, B. A. (1995) *Sultan Omar Ali Saifuddin III and Britain*, Oxford University Press, Sham Alam, Selangor.

Leake, Jr, David (1989) *Brunei: The Modern Southeast Asian Islamic Sultanate*, Forum, Kuala Lumpur.

Ooi Keat Gin (2013) *Post-war Borneo, 1945–1950: Nationalism, Empire, and State-building*, Routledge, London.

Singh, D. S. Ranjit (1984) *Brunei 1839–1983: The Problems of Political Survival*, Oxford University Press, Singapore.

Cambodia

Becker, Elizabeth (1986) *When the War Was Over*, Simon & Schuster, New York.

Brinkley, Joel (2009) *Cambodia's Curse: The Troubled History of a Modern Land*, The Rosen Publishing Group, New York.

Chanda, Nayan (1986) *Brother Enemy: The War after the War*, Harcourt Brace Jovanovich, San Diego, CA.

Chandler, David P. (1991) *The Tragedy of Cambodian History: Politics, War and Revolution since 1945*, Yale University Press, New Haven, CT.

Etcheson, Craig (1984) *The Rise and Demise of Democratic Kampuchea*, Westview Press, Boulder, CO.

Fawthrop, Ken and Jarvis, Helen (2005) *Getting Away with Genocide? Elusive Justice and the Khmer Rouge Tribunal*, UNSW Press, Sydney.

Gottesman, Evan (2003) *Cambodia after the Khmer Rouge: Inside the Politics of Nation Building*, Yale University Press, New Haven, CT.

Jackson, Karl D. (ed.) (1989) *Cambodia 1975–1978: Rendezvous with Death*, Princeton University Press, Princeton, NJ.

Kamm, Henry (1998) *Cambodia. Report from a Stricken Land*, Arcade Publishing, NY.

Kao, Kim Hourn (2002) *Cambodia's Foreign Policy and ASEAN: From Nonalignment to Engagement*, Cambodian Institute for Cooperation and Peace, Phnom Penh.

Kiernan, Ben (2002) *The Pol Pot Regime: Race, Power, and Genocide in Cambodia under the Khmer Rouge, 1975–1979*, Yale University Press, New Haven, CT.

Leifer, Michael (1967) *Cambodia: The Search for Security*, Praeger, New York.

Ollier, Leakthina Chan-Pech and Winter, Tim (2006) *Expressions of Cambodia: The Politics of Tradition, Identity, and Change*, Routledge, London.

Osborne, Milton (1973) *Politics and Power in Cambodia*, Longman Australia, Camberwell.

—— (1994) *Sihanouk: Prince of Light, Prince of Darkness*, Allen & Unwin, Sydney.

Peou, Sorpong (2001) *Cambodia: Change and Continuity in Contemporary Politics*, Ashgate, Aldershot.

Shawcross, William (1979) *Sideshow: Kissinger, Nixon and the Destruction of Cambodia*, André Deutsch, London.

—— (1984) *The Quality of Mercy: Cambodia, Holocaust and Modern Conscience*, André Deutsch, London.

Thion, Serge (1993) *Watching Cambodia*, White Lotus, Bangkok.

Widyono, Benny (2008) *Dancing in Shadows: Sihanouk, the Khmer Rouge, and the United Nations in Cambodia*, Rowman and Littlefield, New York.

Indonesia

Anderson, Benedict (1972) *Java in a Time of Revolution*, Cornell University Press, Ithaca, NY.

Aspinall, Edward (2009) *Islam and Nation: Separatist Rebellion in Aceh, Indonesia*, Stanford University Press, Palo Alto, CA.

Bresnan, John (1993) *Managing Indonesia: The Modern Political Economy*, Columbia University Press, New York.

—— (ed.) (2005) *Indonesia: The Great Transition*, Rowman and Littlefield, New York.

Crouch, Harold (1993) *The Army and Politics in Indonesia*, Cornell University Press, Ithaca, NY.

—— (2010) *Political Reform in Indonesia after Soeharto*, Institute of Southeast Asian Studies, Singapore.

Fealy, Greg and White, Sally (eds) (2008) *Expressing Islam: Religious Life and Politics in*

Indonesia, Institute of Southeast Asian Studies, Singapore.

Feith, Herbert (1962) *The Decline of Constitutional Democracy in Indonesia*, Cornell University Press, Ithaca, NY.

Forrester, Geoff and May, R. J. (eds) (1998) *The Fall of Soeharto*, Crawford Publishing House, Bathurst, NSW.

Hefner, Robert (2000) *Civil Islam: Muslims and Democratization in Indonesia*, Princeton University Press, Princeton, NJ.

Hellwig, Tineke and Tagliacozzo, Eric (eds) (2009) *The Indonesia Reader: History, Culture, Politics*, Duke University Press, Durham, NC.

Honna, Jun (2003) *Military Politics and Democratization in Indonesia*, Routledge, London.

Jenkins, David (1984) *Suharto and His Generals: Indonesian Military Politics 1975–1983*, Cornell Modern Indonesia Project, Ithaca, NY.

Kahin, George McT. (1952) *Nationalism and Revolution in Indonesia*, Cornell University Press, Ithaca, NY.

Legge, J. D. (1973) *Sukarno: A Political Biography*, Penguin, Harmondsworth.

Leifer, Michael (1983) *Indonesia's Foreign Policy*, Allen & Unwin, London.

Liow, Joseph Chinyong (2005) *The Politics of Indonesia–Malaysia Relations: One Kin, Two Nations*, RoutledgeCurzon, London.

McDonald, Hamish (1980) *Suharto's Indonesia*, Fontana, London.

Mietzner, Marcus (2008) *Military Politics, Islam, and the State in Indonesia*, Institute of Southeast Asian Studies, Singapore.

Perwita, Anak Agung Banyu (2007) *Indonesia and the Muslim World: Islam and Secularism in the Foreign Policy of Soeharto and Beyond*, NIAS Press, Copenhagen.

Platzdasch, Bernhard (2009) *Islamism in Indonesia: Politics in the Emerging Democracy*, Institute of Southeast Asian Studies, Singapore.

Polomka, Peter (1971) *Indonesia since Sukarno*, Penguin, Harmondsworth.

Ramage, Douglas (1995) *Politics in Indonesia: Democracy, Islam and the Ideology of Tolerance*, Routledge, London.

Reid, Anthony J. S. (1974) *Indonesian National Revolution 1945–50*, Longman Australia, Hawthorn.

Schwarz, Adam (1999) *A Nation in Waiting: Indonesia in the 1990s*, Allen and Unwin, St Leonards, NSW.

Sebastian, Leonard C. (2005) *Realpolitik Ideology: Indonesia's Use of Military Force*, Institute of Southeast Asian Studies, Singapore.

Suryadinata, Leo (1999) *Interpreting Indonesian Politics*, Times Academic Press, Singapore.

Tyson, Adam D. (2010) *Decentralization and Adat Revivalism in Indonesia*, Routledge, Abingdon.

Vatikiotis, Michael (1998) *Indonesian Politics under Suharto*, Routledge, London.

Laos

Adams, Nina S. and McCoy, Alfred W. (eds) (1970) *Laos: War and Revolution*, Harper & Row, New York.

Brown, MacAlister and Zasloff, Joseph (1986) *Apprentice Revolutionaries: The Communist Movement in Laos, 1930–1985*, Hoover Institution Press, Stanford, CA.

Pholsena, Vatthana (2006) *Post-war Laos: The Politics of Culture, History, and Identity*, Cornell University Press, Ithaca, NY.

Quincy, Keith (2000) *Harvesting Pa Chay's Wheat: The Hmong and America's Secret War in Laos*, Eastern Washington University Press, Spokane, Washington.

Stevenson, Charles (1972) *The End of Nowhere: American Policy toward Laos since 1954*, Beacon Press, Boston, MA.

Stuart-Fox, Martin (1986) *Laos: Politics, Economics and Society*, F. Pinter, London.

Tarling, Nicholas (2011) *Britain and the Neutralisation of Laos*, National University of Singapore Press, Singapore.

Toye, H. C. M. (1968) *Laos: Buffer State or Battleground?*, Oxford University Press, London.

Zasloff, Joseph J. and Unger, Leonard (eds) (1991) *Laos: Beyond the Revolution*, Macmillan, London.

Malaysia

Chin Kin Wah (1983) *The Defence of Malaysia and Singapore*, Cambridge University Press, Cambridge.

Crouch, Harold (1996) *Government and Society in Malaysia*, Cornell University Press, Ithaca, NY.

Funston, John (1980) *Malay Politics in Malaysia*, Heinemann Educational Books (Asia), Kuala Lumpur.

Gomez, Edmund Terence and Jomo, K. S. (1997) *Malaysia's Political Economy: Politics, Patronage, and Profits*, Cambridge University Press, Cambridge.

Jeshurun, Chandran (2008) *Malaysia: Fifty Years of Diplomacy, 1957–2007*, Talisman Publishing, Kuala Lumpur.

Lee, H. P. (1995) *Constitutional Conflicts in Contemporary Malaysia*, Oxford University Press, Kuala Lumpur.

Lee, Hock Guan and Suryadinata, Leo (eds) (2012) *Malaysian Chinese: Recent Developments and Prospects*, Institute of Southeast Asian Studies, Singapore.

Liow, Joseph Chinyong (2009) *Piety and Politics: Islamism in Contemporary Malaysia*, Oxford University Press, New York.

Means, Gordon (1991) *Malaysian Politics: The Second Generation*, Oxford University Press, Singapore.

Milne, R. S. and Mauzy, Diane K. (1999) *Malaysian Politics under Mahathir*, Routledge, London.

Saravanamuttu, Johan (2010) *Malaysia's Foreign Policy, the First Fifty Years: Alignment, Neutralism, Islamism*, Institute of Southeast Asian Studies, Singapore.

Short, Anthony (1975) *The Communist Insurrection in Malaya 1948–60*, Frederick Muller, London.

Sopiee, Mohammad Noordin (1974) *From Malayan Union to Singapore Separation*, Penerbit Universiti Malaya, Kuala Lumpur.

Voon, Phin Keong (ed.) (2008) *Malaysian Chinese and Nation-Building: Before Merdeka and Fifty Years After*, Two Volumes, Centre for Malaysian Chinese Studies, Kuala Lumpur.

Zakaria Haji Ahmad (2007) *The Encyclopedia of Malaysia: Government and Politics, 1940–2006*, Editions Didier Millet, Kuala Lumpur.

Myanmar

Aung-Thwin, Michael and Aung-Thwin, Maitrii (2012) *A History of Myanmar since Ancient Times: Traditions and Transformations*, Reaktion Books, London.

Callahan, Mary P. (2003) *Making Enemies: War and State Building in Burma*, Cornell University Press, Ithaca, NY.

Dittmer, Lowell (2010) *Burma or Myanmar? The Struggle for National Identity*, World Scientific, Singapore.

Holliday, Ian (2011) *Burma Redux: Global Justice and the Quest for Political Reform in Myanmar*, Columbia University Press, Columbia, NY.

Lintner, Bertil (1989) *Outrage: Burma's Struggle for Democracy*, Review Publishing, Hong Kong.

Maung, Mya (1992) *Totalitarianism in Burma*, Paragon House, New York.

Silverstein, Josef (1977) *Burma: Military Rule and the Politics of Stagnation*, Cornell University Press, Ithaca, NY.

Smith, Martin (1991) *Burma: Insurgency and the Politics of Ethnicity*, Zed Press, London.

Steinberg, David I. (2001) *Burma: The State of Myanmar*, Georgetown University Press, Washington, DC.

Taylor, Robert H. (2009) *The State in Myanmar*, University of Hawaii Press, Honolulu, HI.

Than, Mya (2005) *Myanmar in ASEAN: Regional Cooperation Experience*, Institute of Southeast Asian Studies, Singapore.

Tin Maung Maung Than (1999) *The Political Economy of Burma's (Myanmar's) Development Failure 1948–1988*, Institute of Southeast Asian Studies, Singapore.

Philippines

Bonner, Raymond (1987) *Waltzing with a Dictator*, Times Books, New York.

Bresnan, John (ed.) (1986) *Crisis in the Philippines: The Marcos Era and Beyond*, Princeton University Press, Princeton, NJ.

Greene, Fred (ed.) (1988) *The Philippine Bases: Negotiating for the Future*, Council on Foreign Relations, New York.

Hedman, Eva-Lotta and Sidel, John (2000) *Philippine Politics in the Twentieth Century: Colonial Legacies, Post-Colonial Trajectories*, Routledge, London.

Hodder, Rupert (2002) *Between Two Worlds: Society, Politics, and Business in the Philippines*, Routledge, London.

Hutchcroft, Paul D. (1998) *Booty Capitalism: The Politics of Banking in the Philippines*, Cornell University Press, Ithaca, NY.

Karnow, Stanley (1989) *In Our Image: America's Empire in the Philippines*, Random House, New York.

Kasuya, Yuko and Quimpo, Nathan Gilbert (eds) (2010) *The Politics of Change in the Philippines*, Anvil Publishers, Manila.

Kerkvliet, Benedict J. (1977) *The Huk Rebellion*, University of California Press, Berkeley, CA.

Kessler, Richard J. (1989) *Rebellion and Repression in the Philippines*, Yale University Press, New Haven, CT.

Kirk, Donald (1998) *Looted: The Philippines after the Bases*, St Martin's Press, New York.

McFerson, Hazel M. (2002) *Mixed Blessing: The Impact of the American Colonial Experience on Politics and Society in the Philippines*, Greenwood Press, Westport, CT.

McKenna, Thomas M. (1998) *Muslim Rulers and Rebels: Everyday Politics and Armed Separatism in the Southern Philippines*, University of California Press, Berkeley.

Severino, Rudolfo C. (2007) *Whither the Philippines in the 21st Century?*, Institute of Southeast Asian Studies, Singapore.

Steinberg, David Joel (1982) *The Philippines: A Singular and Plural Place*, Westview Press, Boulder, CO.

Wurfel, David (1988) *Filipino Politics: Development and Decay*, Cornell University Press, Ithaca, NY.

Singapore

Ang Cheng Guan (2013) *Singapore, ASEAN, and the Cambodian Conflict, 1978–1991*, National University of Singapore Press, Singapore.

Barr, Michael D. (2008) *Paths not Taken: Political Pluralism in Post-war Singapore*, National University of Singapore Press, Singapore.

Bloodworth, Dennis (1986) *The Tiger and the Trojan Horse*, Times Books, Singapore.

Chan Heng Chee (1976) *The Dynamics of One Party Dominance*, Singapore University Press, Singapore.

Chua Beng Huat (1995) *Communitarian Ideology and Democracy in Singapore*, Routledge, London.

da Cunha, Derek (2012) *Breakthrough: Roadmap for Singapore's Political Future*, Straits Times Press, Singapore.

Gunn, Geoffrey (2008) *Singapore and the Asian Revolutions*, Macau Editora, Hong Kong.

Hack, Karl (2010) *Singapore from Temasek to the 21st Century: Reinventing the Global City*, National University of Singapore Press, Singapore.

Hill, Michael and Lian Kwen Fee (1995) *The Politics of Nation Building and Citizenship in Singapore*, Routledge, London.

Hong, Lysa (2008) *The Scripting of a National History: Singapore and Its Pasts*, Hong Kong University Press, Hong Kong.

Lee Kuan Yew (1998) *The Singapore Story: Memoirs of Lee Kuan Yew*, Times Academic Press, Singapore.

—— (2000) *From Third World to First*, Harper Collins Publishers, New York.

Leifer, Michael (2000) *Singapore's Foreign Policy. Coping with Vulnerability*, Routledge, London.

Milne, R. S. and Mauzy, Diane K. (1990) *Singapore: The Legacy of Lee Kuan Yew*, Westview Press, Boulder, CO.

Minchin, James (1986) *No Man Is an Island*, Allen & Unwin, Sydney.

Raja, Jothie (2012) *Authoritarian Rule of Law: Legislation, Discourse, and Legitimacy in Singapore*, Cambridge University Press, Cambridge.

Sandhu, K. S. and Wheatly, P. (eds) (1989) *Management of Success: The Moulding of Modern Singapore*, Institute of Southeast Asian Studies, Singapore.

Vasil, Raj (1992) *Governing Singapore*, Mandarin, Singapore.

Yap, Sonny (2009) *Men in White: The Untold Story of Singapore's Ruling Political Party*, Singapore Press Holdings, Singapore.

Thailand

Alagappa, Muthiah (1987) *The National Security of Developing States: Lessons from Thailand*, Auburn House, Dover, MA.

Chacavalpongpun, Pavin (2010) *Reinventing Thailand: Thaksin and His Foreign Policy*, Institute of Southeast Asian Studies, Singapore.

Girling, John L. S. (1981) *Thailand: Society and Politics*, Cornell University Press, Ithaca, NY.

Hewison, Kevin (ed.) (1997) *Political Change in Thailand*, Routledge, London.

Kulick, Elliot and Wilson, Dick (1992) *Thailand's Turn*, Macmillan, London.

Liow, Joseph Chinyong and Pathan, Don (2010) *Confronting Ghosts: Thailand's Shapeless Southern Insurgency*, Lowy Institute Papers, Sydney.

McCargo, Duncan (2008) *Tearing Apart the Land: Islam and Legitimacy in Southern Thailand*, Cornell University Press, Ithaca, NY.

—— (2012) *Politics and the Press in Thailand: Media Machinations*, Routledge, London.

—— and Pathmanand, Ukrist (2005) *Thaksinization of Thailand*, NIAS Press, Copenhagen.

Morell, David and Samudavanija, Chai-anan (1981) *Political Conflict in Thailand*, Oelgeschlager, Gunn and Hain, Cambridge, MA.

Phongpaichit, Pasuk and Baker, Chris (2004) *Thaksin: The Business of Politics in Thailand*, Silkworm Books, Bangkok.

Stowe, Judith A. (1991) *Siam Becomes Thailand*, Hurst, London.

Ungpakorn, Giles Ji (2007) *A Coup for the Rich: Thailand's Political Crisis*, Workers Democracy Publishers, Bangkok.

Yoshifumi, Tamada (2008) *Myths and Realities: The Democratization of Thai Politics*, Trans Pacific Press, Kyoto.

Timor-Leste

Ballard, John R. (2008) *Triumph of Self-determination: Operation Stabilise and United Nations Peacemaking in East Timor*, Praeger, Westport, Conn.

Cotton, James (2006) *East Timor, Australia, and Regional Order: Intervention and Its Aftermath in Southeast Asia*, Routledge, London.

Hainsworth, Paul and McCloskey, Stephen (2000) *The East Timor Question: The Struggle for Independence from Indonesia*, I.B. Tauris, London.

Jolliffe, Jill (1978) *East Timor: Nationalism and Colonialism*, University of Queensland Press, St Lucia, Queensland.

Kingsbury, Damien and Leach, Michael (2007) *East Timor: Beyond Independence*, Monash University Press, Clayton, Vic.

Molnar, Andrea K. (2010) *Timor Leste: Politics, History, and Culture*, Routledge, London.

Tanter, Richard, van Klinken, Geert Arend and Ball, Desmond (2006) *Masters of Terror: Indonesia's Military and Violence in East Timor*, Rowman and Littlefield, Lanham, MD.

Taylor, John G. (2009) *East Timor: The Price of Freedom*, Zed Books, London.

Vietnam

Balme, Stéphanie and Sidel, Mark (2007) *Vietnam's New Order: International Perspectives on the State and Reform in Vietnam*, Palgrave MacMillan, Basingstoke.

Brown, T. Louise (1991) *War and Aftermath in Vietnam*, Routledge, London.

Chapman, Jessica M. (2013) *Cauldron of Resistance: Ngo Dinh Diem, the United States, and 1950s South Vietnam*, Cornell University Press, Ithaca, NY.

Duncanson, Dennis J. (1968) *Government and Revolution in Vietnam*, Oxford University Press, London.

Evans, Grant and Rowley, Kelvin (1984) *Red Brotherhood at War*, Verso, London.

Gainsborough, Martin (2010) *Vietnam: Rethinking the State*, Zed Books, London.

Gilks, Anne (1992) *The Breakdown of the Sino-Vietnamese Alliance, 1970–1979*, Institute of East Asian Studies, University of California, Berkeley, CA.

Herring, George (1979) *America's Longest War*, Wiley, New York.

Hy, V. Luong (ed.) (2003) *Postwar Vietnam: Dynamics of a Transforming Society*, Rowman and Littlefield, Lanham, MD.

Jeffries, Ian (2006) *Vietnam: A Guide to Economic and Political Developments*. Routledge, London.

Kahin, George McT. (1986) *Intervention*, Alfred A. Knopf, New York.

Karnow, Stanley (1983) *Vietnam: A History*, Viking Press, New York.

Kattenburg, Paul (1980) *The Vietnam Trauma in American Foreign Policy, 1945–75*, Transaction Books, New Brunswick, NJ.

Kolko, Gabriel (1986) *Intervention: Anatomy of a War 1940–1975*, Allen & Unwin, London.

Lancaster, Donald (1961) *The Emancipation of French Indochina*, Oxford University Press, London.

Morley, James W. and Nishihara, Masashi (eds) (1997) *Vietnam Joins the World*, M. E. Sharpe, Armonk, NY.

Randle, Robert F. (1969) *Geneva 1954: The Settlement of the Indochina War*, Princeton University Press, Princeton, NJ.

Ross, Robert (1988) *The Indochina Tangle*, Columbia University Press, New York.

Smith, R. B. (1983–91) *An International History of the Vietnam War, Vols I–III*, Macmillan, London.

Thayer, Carl and Amer, Ramses (eds) (1999) *Vietnamese Foreign Policy in Transition*, Institute of Southeast Asian Studies, Singapore.

Truong Nhu Tang (1986) *Journal of a Vietcong*, Jonathan Cape, London.

Turley, William S. (1986) *The Second Indochina War*, Westview Press, Boulder, CO.

West, Richard (1995) *War and Peace in Vietnam*, Sinclair-Stevenson, London.

Williams, Michael (1992) *Vietnam at the Crossroads*, Pinter, London.

Index by Country

Brunei, Sultanate of

ADMM (ASEAN Defence Ministers' Meeting)
AFTA (Association of Southeast Asian Nations Free Trade Area) 1993–
APEC (Asia-Pacific Economic Cooperation) 1989–
ASEAN (Association of Southeast Asian Nations) 1967–
ASEAN Charter (Charter of the Association of Southeast Asian Nations)
ASEAN Community
ASEAN Regional Forum (ARF) 1994–
Asia–Europe Meeting (ASEM) 1996–
Azahari, A. M.
Bali Summit (ASEAN) 2003
Bali Summit (ASEAN) 2011
Bandar Seri Begawan Summit (ASEAN) April 2013
Bandar Seri Begawan Summit (ASEAN) October 2013
Bangkok Summit (ASEAN) 1995
Bolkiah, Sultan Hassanal
Brunei Revolt 1962
Cebu Summit (ASEAN) 2006
Chiang Mai Initiative
Declaration of ASEAN Concord II 2003
Declaration of ASEAN Concord III 2011
Declaration on the Conduct of Parties in the South China Sea (ASEAN) 2002
Declaration on the South China Sea (ASEAN) 1992
East Asia Summit 2005–
Exchange of Letters 2009
Hanoi Summit (ASEAN) 1998
Hanoi Summit (ASEAN) April 2010
Hanoi Summit (ASEAN) October 2010
Hua Hin Summit (ASEAN) February 2009
Hua Hin Summit (ASEAN) October 2009
Islam
Jakarta Summit (ASEAN) 2011
Kuala Lumpur Summit (ASEAN) 2005
Legislative Council
Limbang Claim
Manila Summit (ASEAN) 1987
Melayu Islam Beraja
People's Party
Phnom Penh Summit (ASEAN) 2002
Phnom Penh Summit (ASEAN) April 2012
Phnom Penh Summit (ASEAN) November 2012
Regional Comprehensive Economic Partnership
Singapore Summit (ASEAN) 1992
Singapore Summit (ASEAN) 2007
South China Sea
Trans-Pacific Partnership
Treaty of Amity and Cooperation (ASEAN) 1976
Vientiane Action Plan (ASEAN) 2004
Vientiane Summit (ASEAN) 2004

Cambodia, Kingdom of

ADMM (ASEAN Defence Ministers' Meeting)
AFTA (Association of Southeast Asian Nations Free Trade Area) 1993–
ASEAN (Association of Southeast Asian Nations) 1967–
ASEAN Charter (Charter of the Association of Southeast Asian Nations)
ASEAN Community
ASEAN Regional Forum (ARF) 1994–
Asia–Europe Meeting (ASEM) 1996–
Bali Summit (ASEAN) 2003
Bali Summit (ASEAN) 2011
Bandar Seri Begawan Summit (ASEAN) April 2013
Bandar Seri Begawan Summit (ASEAN) October 2013
Bangkok Summit (ASEAN) 1995
Brevié Line
Buddhism
Cambodia National Rescue Party
Cambodian People's Party
Cebu Summit (ASEAN) 2006
Cham
Chea Sim
Chiang Mai Initiative
Communism in Southeast Asia
Declaration of ASEAN Concord II 2003
Declaration of ASEAN Concord III 2011

Declaration on the Conduct of Parties in the South China Sea (ASEAN) 2002
Declaration on the South China Sea (ASEAN) 1992
Democratic Kampuchea
Democratic Kampuchea, Coalition Government of (CGDK) 1982–90
Domino Theory
East Asia Summit 2005–
FUNCINPEC
Geneva Agreements on Indochina 1954
Hanoi Summit (ASEAN) 1998
Hanoi Summit (ASEAN) April 2010
Hanoi Summit (ASEAN) October 2010
Heng Samrin
Hua Hin Summit (ASEAN) February 2009
Hua Hin Summit (ASEAN) October 2009
Hun Sen
Ieng Sary
Indochina Wars
International Conference on Cambodia, New York 1981
International Conference on Cambodia, Paris 1989
International Conference on Cambodia, Paris 1991
Islam
Jakarta Conference on Cambodia 1970
Jakarta Summit (ASEAN) 2011
Kampuchea, People's Republic of (PRK)
Kampuchean People's Revolutionary Party (KPRP)
Khieu Samphan
Khmer People's National Liberation Front (KPNLF)
Khmer Republic
Khmer Rouge
Khmer Rouge Trials
Kuala Lumpur Summit (ASEAN) 2005
Manila Pact 1954
Mekong River Project
Nol, Lon
Phnom Penh Summit (ASEAN) 2002
Phnom Penh Summit (ASEAN) April 2012
Phnom Penh Summit (ASEAN) November 2012
Pol Pot
Preah Vihear Temple Dispute
Ranariddh, Prince Norodom
Regional Comprehensive Economic Partnership
Sam Rainsy
Sam Rainsy Party
Sangkum Reastre Niyum
Sihamoni, King Norodom
Sihanouk, King Norodom
Singapore Summit (ASEAN) 2007
Son Sann
Son Sen
Supreme National Council
Ta Mok
Treaty of Amity and Cooperation (ASEAN) 1976
Treaty of Peace, Friendship, and Cooperation 1979
Tuol Sleng
United Nations: Cambodia 1991–3
UNTAC (United Nations Transitional Authority in Cambodia)
Vientiane Action Plan (ASEAN) 2004
Vientiane Summit (ASEAN) 2004
Vietnam War
Xayaburi Dam

Indonesia, Republic of

Abangan
Abdullah, Zaini
ABRI
Aceh Independence Movement
ADMM (ASEAN Defence Ministers' Meeting)
AFTA (Association of Southeast Asian Nations Free Trade Area) 1993–
Ahmadiyah
Ambalat
APEC (Asia-Pacific Economic Cooperation) 1989–
Archipelago Declaration 1957
ASEAN (Association of Southeast Asian Nations) 1967–
ASEAN Charter (Charter of the Association of Southeast Asian Nations)
ASEAN Community
ASEAN Regional Forum (ARF) 1994–
Asia–Europe Meeting (ASEM) 1996–
Asian–African Conference, Bandung 1955
Asian Financial Crisis 1997–8
Ba'asyir, Abu Bakar
Bali Summit (ASEAN) 1976
Bali Summit (ASEAN) 2003

Bali Summit (ASEAN) 2011
Bandar Seri Begawan Summit (ASEAN) April 2013
Bandar Seri Begawan Summit (ASEAN) October 2013
Bangkok Declaration (ASEAN) 1967
Bangkok Summit (ASEAN) 1995
Boediono
Cebu Summit (ASEAN) 2006
Chiang Mai Initiative
Cobra Gold Military Exercises
Communism in Southeast Asia
Confrontation
Darul Islam
Declaration of ASEAN Concord 1976
Declaration of ASEAN Concord II 2003
Declaration of ASEAN Concord III 2011
Declaration on the Conduct of Parties in the South China Sea (ASEAN) 2002
Declaration on the South China Sea (ASEAN) 1992
Dwi Fungsi
East Asia Summit 2005–
Free Papua Movement
Front Pembela Islam
Gerindra
Gestapu
Golkar
Guided Democracy
Habibie, B. J.
Hambali (Riduan Isamuddin)
Hanoi Summit (ASEAN) 1998
Hanoi Summit (ASEAN) April 2010
Hanoi Summit (ASEAN) October 2010
Hatta, Mohammad
Haz, Hamzah
Hizbut Tahrir Indonesia
Hua Hin Summit (ASEAN) February 2009
Hua Hin Summit (ASEAN) October 2009
Irian Jaya
Islam
Jakarta Conference on Cambodia 1970
Jakarta Summit (ASEAN) 2011
Jemaah Islamiyah
Kalla, Yusuf
Kuala Lumpur Declaration 1971
Kuala Lumpur Summit (ASEAN) 1977
Kuala Lumpur Summit (ASEAN) 2005
Laskar Jihad
Madiun Revolt 1948
Majelis Mujahidin Indonesia
Majelis Ulama Indonesia
Malacca Strait
Malacca Strait Patrol
Malik, Adam
Maluku Violence 1999–2002
Manila Summit (ASEAN) 1987
Maphilindo
Masyumi
Megawati Sukarnoputri
Muhammadiyah
Murdani, General L. B.
Murtopo, General Ali
Nahdlatul Ulama
Nasakom
Nasution, General Abdul Haris
Natalegawa, Raden Mohammad Marty Muliana
Natuna Islands
New Order
Pancasila
Partai Amanat Nasional
Partai Bulan Bintang
Partai Demokrasi Indonesia – Perjuangan
Partai Demokrat
Partai Keadilan Sejahtera
Partai Kebangkitan Bangsa
Partai Persatuan Pembangunan
People's Consultative Assembly
Permesta
Peta
Phnom Penh Summit (ASEAN) 2002
Phnom Penh Summit (ASEAN) April 2012
Phnom Penh Summit (ASEAN) November 2012
Prabowo Subianto
Pribumi
Regional Comprehensive Economic Partnership
Revolutionary Government of the Republic of Indonesia 1958–61
Santri
Singapore Strait
Singapore Summit (ASEAN) 1992
Singapore Summit (ASEAN) 2007
Sipadan–Ligitan
Sjahrir, Sutan
South China Sea
Subandrio
Suharto

Sukarno
Supersemar
Surabaya, Battle of, 1945
Tanjung Priok Riot 1984
Tarbiyah
Terrorism in Southeast Asia
Timor Gap Cooperation Treaty
Treaty of Amity and Cooperation (ASEAN) 1976
Tsunami 2004
United Nations: East Timor 1999–2002
United Nations: Irian Jaya 1962–9
United Nations: Northern Borneo 1963
Vientiane Action Plan (ASEAN) 2004
Vientiane Summit (ASEAN) 2004
Wahid, Abdurrahman
Widodo, Joko
Yudhoyono, Susilo Bambang
Yusuf, Irwandy
ZOPFAN (Zone of Peace, Freedom and Neutrality) 1971

Laos, People's Democratic Republic of

ADMM (ASEAN Defence Ministers' Meeting)
AFTA (Association of Southeast Asian Nations Free Trade Area) 1993–
ASEAN (Association of Southeast Asian Nations) 1967–
ASEAN Charter (Charter of the Association of Southeast Asian Nations)
ASEAN Community
ASEAN Regional Forum (ARF) 1994–
Asia–Europe Meeting (ASEM) 1996–
Bali Summit (ASEAN) 2003
Bali Summit (ASEAN) 2011
Bandar Seri Begawan Summit (ASEAN) April 2013
Bandar Seri Begawan Summit (ASEAN) October 2013
Bangkok Summit (ASEAN) 1995
Bouasone Bouphavanh
Buddhism
Cebu Summit (ASEAN) 2006
Chiang Mai Initiative
Choummaly Sayasone
Communism in Southeast Asia
Declaration of ASEAN Concord II 2003
Declaration of ASEAN Concord III 2011
Declaration on the Conduct of Parties in the South China Sea (ASEAN) 2002
Declaration on the South China Sea (ASEAN) 1992
Domino Theory
East Asia Summit 2005–
Friendship Bridge
Geneva Agreements on Indochina 1954
Geneva Agreements on Laos 1962
Hanoi Summit (ASEAN) 1998
Hanoi Summit (ASEAN) April 2010
Hanoi Summit (ASEAN) October 2010
Hmong
Hua Hin Summit (ASEAN) February 2009
Hua Hin Summit (ASEAN) October 2009
Indochina Wars
Jakarta Summit (ASEAN) 2011
Kaysone Phomvihan
Khamtay Siphandon
Kuala Lumpur Summit (ASEAN) 2005
Lao People's Revolutionary Party
Manila Pact 1954
Mekong River Project
Neo Lao Hak Sat
New Economic Mechanism
Nouhak Phoumsavan
Pathet Lao
Phnom Penh Summit (ASEAN) 2002
Phnom Penh Summit (ASEAN) April 2012
Phnom Penh Summit (ASEAN) November 2012
Regional Comprehensive Economic Partnership
Singapore Summit (ASEAN) 2007
Souphanouvong, Prince
Souvanna Phouma, Prince
Thai–Lao Border War 1987–8
Thongloun Sisoulith
Thongsing Thammavong
Treaty of Amity and Cooperation (ASEAN) 1976
Treaty of Friendship and Cooperation 1977
Vientiane Action Plan (ASEAN) 2004
Vientiane Agreement on the Restoration of Peace and Reconciliation in Laos 1973
Vientiane Summit (ASEAN) 2004
Vietnam War
Xayaburi Dam

Malaysia, Federation of

Abdul Rahman, Tunku
Abdul Rahman Yakub, Tun
ABIM
ADMM (ASEAN Defence Ministers' Meeting)
AFTA (Association of Southeast Asian Nations Free Trade Area) 1993–
Al-Ma'unah
Alliance Party
Ambalat
Angkatan Perpaduan Ummah
Anglo-Malayan/Anglo-Malaysian Defence Agreement 1957–71
Anwar Ibrahim
APEC (Asia-Pacific Economic Cooperation) 1989–
Article 11 Coalition
ASA (Association of Southeast Asia) 1961–7
ASEAN (Association of Southeast Asian Nations) 1967–
ASEAN Charter (Charter of the Association of Southeast Asian Nations)
ASEAN Community
ASEAN Regional Forum (ARF) 1994–
Asia–Europe Meeting (ASEM) 1996–
Asian Financial Crisis 1997–8
Badawi, Tun Abdullah Ahmad
Bali Summit (ASEAN) 1976
Bali Summit (ASEAN) 2003
Bali Summit (ASEAN) 2011
Baling Talks 1955
Bandar Seri Begawan Summit (ASEAN) April 2013
Bandar Seri Begawan Summit (ASEAN) October 2013
Bangkok Declaration (ASEAN) 1967
Bangkok Summit (ASEAN) 1995
Bank Bumiputera Crisis
Barisan Alternatif (BA)
Barisan Nasional (BN)
Bersih
Bumiputra
Buy British Last Policy
Cebu Summit (ASEAN) 2006
Chiang Mai Initiative
Chin Peng
Chinese Communities in Southeast Asia
Cobbold Commission 1962
Cobra Gold Military Exercises
Communism in Southeast Asia
Confrontation
Constitutional Crises
Corregidor Affair 1968
Daim Zainuddin, Tun
Dakwah
Declaration of ASEAN Concord 1976
Declaration of ASEAN Concord II 2003
Declaration of ASEAN Concord III 2011
Declaration on the Conduct of Parties in the South China Sea (ASEAN) 2002
Declaration on the South China Sea (ASEAN) 1992
Democratic Action Party (DAP)
East Asia Summit 2005–
Emergency 1948–60
Exchange of Letters 2009
Five Power Defence Arrangements (FPDA) 1971–
Fuad, Tun Muhammad (Donald Stephens)
Gerakan Rakyat Malaysia
Ghazalie Shafie, Tun Mohamad
Hadi Awang, Abdul
Hanoi Summit (ASEAN) 1998
Hanoi Summit (ASEAN) April 2010
Hanoi Summit (ASEAN) October 2010
Harris Mohamed Salleh, Datuk
Herzog Affair 1986
Hindraf
Horsburgh Lighthouse
Hua Hin Summit (ASEAN) February 2009
Hua Hin Summit (ASEAN) October 2009
Hussein Onn, Tun
Iskandar Development Region
Islam
Jakarta Summit (ASEAN) 2011
Jemaah Islamiyah
Johor, Strait of
Kuala Lumpur Declaration 1971
Kuala Lumpur Summit (ASEAN) 1977
Kuala Lumpur Summit (ASEAN) 2005
Kumpulan Militan Malaysia
Lahad Datu Crisis 2013
Lim Guan Eng
Lim Kit Siang
Lim Yew Hock
Limbang Claim
Lina Joy Issue
Loi Tack
Mahathir Mohamad, Tun
Malacca Strait

Malacca Strait Patrol
Malayan Union Proposal 1946
Malaysian Chinese Association
Malaysian Indian Congress (MIC)
Manila Summit (ASEAN) 1987
Maphilindo
May 13 Racial Riots 1969
Memali Incident 1985
Muhyiddin Yassin, Tan Sri
Musa Hitam, Tun
Mustapha bin Datuk Harun, Tun
Najib Tun Razak, Datuk Seri Mohamad
New Economic Model
New Economic Policy
Nik Abdul Aziz Nik Mat
One Malaysia (1Malaysia)
Pakatan Rakyat
Parti Bangsa Dayak Sarawak
Parti Islam Se-Malaysia
Parti Keadilan Rakyat
Parti Pesaka Bumiputera Bersatu
Pembela
Perak Legislature Takeover 2009
Philippines' Claim to Sabah
Phnom Penh Summit (ASEAN) 2002
Phnom Penh Summit (ASEAN) April 2012
Phnom Penh Summit (ASEAN) November 2012
Port Klang Free Zone Controversy
Razak, Tun Abdul
Razaleigh Hamzah, Tengku
Regional Comprehensive Economic Partnership
Rukunegara 1970
Sabah United Party
Sarawak National Party
Sarawak United People's Party
Semangat '46
Singapore Strait
Singapore Summit (ASEAN) 1992
Singapore Summit (ASEAN) 2007
Sipadan–Ligitan
South China Sea
Taib Mahmud, Datuk Patinggi Abdul
Terrorism in Southeast Asia
Trans-Pacific Partnership
Treaty of Amity and Cooperation (ASEAN) 1976
Tsunami 2004
UMNO (United Malays National Organization)
United Nations: Northern Borneo 1963
United Sabah National Organization
Vientiane Action Plan (ASEAN) 2004
Vientiane Summit (ASEAN) 2004
Yang di-Pertuan Agong
ZOPFAN (Zone of Peace, Freedom and Neutrality) 1971

Myanmar (Burma)

ADMM (ASEAN Defence Ministers' Meeting)
AFTA (Association of Southeast Asian Nations Free Trade Area) 1993–
Anti-Fascist People's Freedom League (AFPFL)
ASEAN (Association of Southeast Asian Nations) 1967-
ASEAN Charter (Charter of the Association of Southeast Asian Nations)
ASEAN Community
ASEAN Regional Forum (ARF) 1994–
Asia–Europe Meeting (ASEM) 1996–
Aung San
Aung San Suu Kyi
Bali Summit (ASEAN) 2003
Bali Summit (ASEAN) 2011
Bandar Seri Begawan Summit (ASEAN) April 2013
Bandar Seri Begawan Summit (ASEAN) October 2013
Bangkok Summit (ASEAN) 1995
Buddhism
Burma Socialist Programme Party (BPSPP)
Cebu Summit (ASEAN) 2006
Chiang Mai Initiative
Chin
Constitution 2008
Constructive Engagement
Declaration of ASEAN Concord II 2003
Declaration of ASEAN Concord III 2011
Declaration on the Conduct of Parties in the South China Sea (ASEAN) 2002
Declaration on the South China Sea (ASEAN) 1992
Democracy Uprising 1988
East Asia Summit 2005–
Elections 1990
Elections 2010
Hanoi Summit (ASEAN) 1998

Hanoi Summit (ASEAN) April 2010
Hanoi Summit (ASEAN) October 2010
Hua Hin Summit (ASEAN) February 2009
Hua Hin Summit (ASEAN) October 2009
Insurgencies, Myanmar
Islam
Jakarta Summit (ASEAN) 2011
Kachin
Karen
Khin Nyunt, General
Kuala Lumpur Summit (ASEAN) 2005
Mekong River Project
National League for Democracy
National Unity Party
Naypyidaw
Ne Win, General
Nu, U
Panglong Agreement
Paukphaw Relationship
Phnom Penh Summit (ASEAN) 2002
Phnom Penh Summit (ASEAN) April 2012
Phnom Penh Summit (ASEAN) November 2012
Regional Comprehensive Economic Partnership
Roadmap to Democracy
Rohingya
Saffron Revolution 2007
San Yu, General
Shan
Shwe Mann
Singapore Summit (ASEAN) 2007
State Law and Order Restoration Council
State Peace and Development Council
Than Shwe, Senior General
Thein Sein
Treaty of Amity and Cooperation (ASEAN) 1976
Union Solidarity and Development Party
Vientiane Action Plan (ASEAN) 2004
Vientiane Summit (ASEAN) 2004

Philippines, Republic of

Abu Sayyaf Group (ASG)
ADMM (ASEAN Defence Ministers' Meeting)
AFTA (Association of Southeast Asian Nations Free Trade Area) 1993–
APEC (Asia-Pacific Economic Cooperation) 1989–
Aquino, Benigno
Aquino III, Benigno Simeon Cojuangco
Aquino, Corazón
ASA (Association of Southeast Asia) 1961–7
ASEAN (Association of Southeast Asian Nations) 1967–
ASEAN Charter (Charter of the Association of Southeast Asian Nations)
ASEAN Community
ASEAN Regional Forum (ARF) 1994–
Asia–Europe Meeting (ASEM) 1996–
Bali Summit (ASEAN) 1976
Bali Summit (ASEAN) 2003
Bali Summit (ASEAN) 2011
Bandar Seri Begawan Summit (ASEAN) April 2013
Bandar Seri Begawan Summit (ASEAN) October 2013
Bangkok Declaration (ASEAN) 1967
Bangkok Summit (ASEAN) 1995
Cebu Summit (ASEAN) 2006
Chiang Mai Initiative
Clark Air Base
Cobra Gold Military Exercises
Communism in Southeast Asia
Comprehensive Agreement on the Bangsamoro (CAB) 2014
Contemplacion, Flor: Hanging 1995
Corregidor Affair 1968
Declaration of ASEAN Concord 1976
Declaration of ASEAN Concord II 2003
Declaration of ASEAN Concord III 2011
Declaration on the Conduct of Parties in the South China Sea (ASEAN) 2002
Declaration on the South China Sea (ASEAN) 1992
East Asia Summit 2005–
EDSA
EDSA II
Enrile, Juan Ponce
Estrada, Joseph
Framework Agreement on the Bangsamoro 2012
Hanoi Summit (ASEAN) 1998
Hanoi Summit (ASEAN) April 2010
Hanoi Summit (ASEAN) October 2010
Hua Hin Summit (ASEAN) February 2009
Hua Hin Summit (ASEAN) October 2009
Hukbalahap Movement
Islam
Jakarta Summit (ASEAN) 2011

Jemaah Islamiyah
Kuala Lumpur Declaration 1971
Kuala Lumpur Summit (ASEAN) 1977
Kuala Lumpur Summit (ASEAN) 2005
Laban ng Demokratikong Pilipino (LDP)
Lahad Datu Crisis 2013
Lakas–CMD
Macapagal, Diosdado
Macapagal-Arroyo, Gloria
Magsaysay, Ramón
Maguindanao Massacre 2009
Manila Hostage Crisis 2010
Manila Pact 1954
Manila Summit (ASEAN) 1987
Maphilindo
Marcos, Ferdinand
Marcos, Imelda
Misuari, Nur
Moro Islamic Liberation Front
Moro National Liberation Front
Nacionalista Party
National Democratic Front
New People's Army
Partido Liberal ng Pilipinas
People Power
Philippines–US Security Treaty 1951
Philippines' Claim to Sabah
Phnom Penh Summit (ASEAN) 2002
Phnom Penh Summit (ASEAN) April 2012
Phnom Penh Summit (ASEAN) November 2012
Ramos, Fidel
Reform the Armed Forces Movement (RAM)
Regional Comprehensive Economic Partnership
Reproductive Health Bills
Rizal, José
Roxas, Manuel A.
Scarborough Shoal Dispute
SEATO (Southeast Asia Treaty Organization) 1955–77
Sin, Cardinal Jaime
Singapore Summit (ASEAN) 1992
Singapore Summit (ASEAN) 2007
Sisón, José María
South China Sea
Subic Bay Naval Base
Terrorism in Southeast Asia
Treaty of Amity and Cooperation (ASEAN) 1976
Tripoli Agreement 1976
United Nations: Northern Borneo 1963
Ver, General Fabian
Vientiane Action Plan (ASEAN) 2004
Vientiane Summit (ASEAN) 2004
ZOPFAN (Zone of Peace, Freedom and Neutrality) 1971

Singapore, Republic of

ADMM (ASEAN Defence Ministers' Meeting)
AFTA (Association of Southeast Asian Nations Free Trade Area) 1993–
Aljunied Group Representation Constituency
Anglo-Malayan/Anglo-Malaysian Defence Agreement 1957–71
APEC (Asia-Pacific Economic Cooperation) 1989–
ASEAN (Association of Southeast Asian Nations) 1967–
ASEAN Charter (Charter of the Association of Southeast Asian Nations)
ASEAN Community
ASEAN Regional Forum (ARF) 1994–
Asia–Europe Meeting (ASEM) 1996–
Bali Summit (ASEAN) 1976
Bali Summit (ASEAN) 2003
Bali Summit (ASEAN) 2011
Bandar Seri Begawan Summit (ASEAN) April 2013
Bandar Seri Begawan Summit (ASEAN) October 2013
Bangkok Declaration (ASEAN) 1967
Bangkok Summit (ASEAN) 1995
Barisan Sosialis
Cebu Summit (ASEAN) 2006
Chiam See Tong
Chiang Mai Initiative
Chinese Communities in Southeast Asia
Cobra Gold Military Exercises
Contemplacion, Flor: Hanging 1995
Declaration of ASEAN Concord 1976
Declaration of ASEAN Concord II 2003
Declaration of ASEAN Concord III 2011
Declaration on the Conduct of Parties in the South China Sea (ASEAN) 2002
Declaration on the South China Sea (ASEAN) 1992
East Asia Summit 2005–
Five Power Defence Arrangements (FPDA) 1971–

Goh Chok Tong
Goh Keng Swee
Hanoi Summit (ASEAN) 1998
Hanoi Summit (ASEAN) April 2010
Hanoi Summit (ASEAN) October 2010
Hertogh, Maria: Riots, 1950
Herzog Affair 1986
Horsburgh Lighthouse
Hua Hin Summit (ASEAN) February 2009
Hua Hin Summit (ASEAN) October 2009
Iskandar Development Region
Islam
Jakarta Summit (ASEAN) 2011
Jemaah Islamiyah
Jeyaretnam, J. B.
Johor, Strait of
Kuala Lumpur Declaration 1971
Kuala Lumpur Summit (ASEAN) 1977
Kuala Lumpur Summit (ASEAN) 2005
Lee Hsien Loong
Lee Kuan Yew
Lim Yew Hock
Low Thia Khiang
Malacca Strait
Malacca Strait Patrol
Manila Summit (ASEAN) 1987
Marshall, David
Mas Selamat Kastari
Ong Teng Cheong
People's Action Party
Phnom Penh Summit (ASEAN) 2002
Phnom Penh Summit (ASEAN) April 2012
Phnom Penh Summit (ASEAN) November 2012
Rajaratnam, Sinnathamby
Regional Comprehensive Economic Partnership
Singapore Strait
Singapore Summit (ASEAN) 1992
Singapore Summit (ASEAN) 2007
Terrorism in Southeast Asia
Trans-Pacific Partnership
Treaty of Amity and Cooperation (ASEAN) 1976
Tudung Controversy 2002
Vientiane Action Plan (ASEAN) 2004
Vientiane Summit (ASEAN) 2004
Workers' Party
Yeo, George Yong-Boon
ZOPFAN (Zone of Peace, Freedom and Neutrality) 1971

Thailand, Kingdom of

Abhisit Vejjajiva
ADMM (ASEAN Defence Ministers' Meeting)
AFTA (Association of Southeast Asian Nations Free Trade Area) 1993–
Anand Panyarachun
Ananda Mahidol, King
Anupong Paochinda, General
APEC (Asia-Pacific Economic Cooperation) 1989–
ASA (Association of Southeast Asia) 1961–7
ASEAN (Association of Southeast Asian Nations) 1967–
ASEAN Charter (Charter of the Association of Southeast Asian Nations)
ASEAN Community
ASEAN Regional Forum (ARF) 1994–
Asia–Europe Meeting (ASEM) 1996–
Asian Financial Crisis 1997–8
Bali Summit (ASEAN) 1976
Bali Summit (ASEAN) 2003
Bali Summit (ASEAN) 2011
Bandar Seri Begawan Summit (ASEAN) April 2013
Bandar Seri Begawan Summit (ASEAN) October 2013
Bangkok Declaration (ASEAN) 1967
Bangkok Summit (ASEAN) 1995
Banharn Silpa-archa
Barisan Revolusi Nasional
Bhumibol Adulyadej, King
Buddhism
Cebu Summit (ASEAN) 2006
Chamlong Srimuang, General
Chart Pattana Party
Chart Thai Party
Chatichai Choonhavan, General
Chavalit Yongchaiyuth, General
Chiang Mai Initiative
Chinese Communities in Southeast Asia
Chuan Leekpai
Cobra Gold Military Exercises
Communism in Southeast Asia
Constructive Engagement
Declaration of ASEAN Concord 1976

Declaration of ASEAN Concord II 2003
Declaration of ASEAN Concord III 2011
Declaration on the Conduct of Parties in the South China Sea (ASEAN) 2002
Declaration on the South China Sea (ASEAN) 1992
Democrat Party
Democratic Soldiers
East Asia Summit 2005–
Friendship Bridge
Hanoi Summit (ASEAN) 1998
Hanoi Summit (ASEAN) April 2010
Hanoi Summit (ASEAN) October 2010
Hua Hin Summit (ASEAN) February 2009
Hua Hin Summit (ASEAN) October 2009
Insurgency, Southern Provinces
Islam
Jakarta Summit (ASEAN) 2011
Jatuporn Prompan
Kriangsak Chomanan, General
Kuala Lumpur Declaration 1971
Kuala Lumpur Summit (ASEAN) 1977
Kuala Lumpur Summit (ASEAN) 2005
Kukrit Pramoj
Maha Vajiralongkorn, Prince
Malacca Strait Patrol
Manila Pact 1954
Manila Summit (ASEAN) 1987
Mekong River Project
New Aspiration Party
Patani United Liberation Organization
People's Alliance for Democracy
People's Constitution 1997
People's Power Party
Pheu Thai Party
Phibul Songkram, Field Marshal
Phnom Penh Summit (ASEAN) 2002
Phnom Penh Summit (ASEAN) April 2012
Phnom Penh Summit (ASEAN) November 2012
Praphas Charusathien, Field Marshal
Prayuth Chan-ocha, General
Preah Vihear Temple Dispute
Prem Tinsulanonda, General
Pridi Phanomyong
Regional Comprehensive Economic Partnership
Samak Sundaravej
Sanoh Thienthong
Sarit Thanarat, Field Marshal
SEATO (Southeast Asia Treaty Organization) 1955–77
Seni Pramoj
Singapore Summit (ASEAN) 1992
Singapore Summit (ASEAN) 2007
Somchai Wongsawat
Sondhi Limthongkul
Sonthi Boonyaratglin, General
Suchinda Kraprayoon, General
Surayud Chulanont, General
Surin Pitsuwan
Thai–Lao Border War 1987–8
Thai Rak Thai Party
Thaksin Shinawatra
Thammasat University Massacre 1976
Thanat Khoman
Thanin Kraivichian
Thanom Kittikachorn, Field Marshal
Treaty of Amity and Cooperation (ASEAN) 1976
Tsunami 2004
United Front for Democracy Against Dictatorship
Vientiane Action Plan (ASEAN) 2004
Vientiane Summit (ASEAN) 2004
Xayaburi Dam
Yingluck Shinawatra
Young Turks
ZOPFAN (Zone of Peace, Freedom and Neutrality) 1971

Timor-Leste, Democratic Republic of

Alkatiri, Mari
ASEAN Regional Forum 1994–
Fretilin
Gusmão, José 'Xanana'
Habibie, B. J.
National Congress for Timorese Reconstruction
Ramos-Horta, José
Ruak, Taur Matan
Timor Gap Cooperation Treaty
Timor-Leste Crisis 2006
Timor Sea Treaty 2002
Treaty of Amity and Cooperation (ASEAN) 1976
United Nations: East Timor 1999–2002

Vietnam, Socialist Republic of

ADMM (ASEAN Defence Ministers' Meeting)
AFTA (Association of Southeast Asian Nations Free Trade Area) 1993–
APEC (Asia-Pacific Economic Cooperation) 1989–
ASEAN (Association of Southeast Asian Nations) 1967–
ASEAN Charter (Charter of the Association of Southeast Asian Nations)
ASEAN Community
ASEAN Regional Forum (ARF) 1994–
Asia–Europe Meeting (ASEM) 1996–
August Revolution 1945
Bali Summit (ASEAN) 2003
Bali Summit (ASEAN) 2011
Bandar Seri Begawan Summit (ASEAN) April 2013
Bandar Seri Begawan Summit (ASEAN) October 2013
Bangkok Summit (ASEAN) 1995
Bao Dai, Emperor
Boat People
Brevié Line
Buddhism
Cam Ranh Bay
Cebu Summit (ASEAN) 2006
Cham
Chiang Mai Initiative
Communism in Southeast Asia
Declaration of ASEAN Concord II 2003
Declaration of ASEAN Concord III 2011
Declaration on the Conduct of Parties in the South China Sea (ASEAN) 2002
Declaration on the South China Sea (ASEAN) 1992
Diem, Ngo Dinh
Dien Bien Phu, Battle of, 1954
Do Muoi
Doi Moi
Domino Theory
Dung, Nguyen Tan
East Asia Summit 2005–
Elysée Agreement 1949
Geneva Agreements on Indochina 1954
Giap, General Vo Nguyen
Hanoi Summit (ASEAN) 1998
Hanoi Summit (ASEAN) April 2010
Hanoi Summit (ASEAN) October 2010
Ho Chi Minh
Ho Chi Minh Trail
Hua Hin Summit (ASEAN) February 2009
Hua Hin Summit (ASEAN) October 2009
Indochina Wars
Jakarta Summit (ASEAN) 2011
Kuala Lumpur Summit (ASEAN) 2005
Lao Dong
Le Duan
Le Duc Anh, General
Le Duc Tho
Le Kha Phieu, General
Linh, Nguyen Van
Luong, Tran Duc
Manila Pact 1954
Mekong River Project
National Liberation Front of South Vietnam
Nguyen Manh Cam
Nguyen Minh Triet
Nguyen Phu Trong
Nguyen Tan Dung
Nixon Doctrine 1969
Nong Duc Manh
Paris Peace Agreements 1973
Pham Van Dong
Phan Van Khai
Phnom Penh Summit (ASEAN) 2002
Phnom Penh Summit (ASEAN) April 2012
Phnom Penh Summit (ASEAN) November 2012
Provisional Revolutionary Government of the Republic of South Vietnam (PRG) 1969–76
Regional Comprehensive Economic Partnership
Singapore Summit (ASEAN) 2007
South China Sea
State Owned Enterprise Reform
Tet Offensive 1968
Thach, Nguyen Co
Thieu, Nguyen Van
Tonkin Gulf Dispute
Tonkin Gulf Incident 1964
Trans-Pacific Partnership
Treaty of Amity and Cooperation (ASEAN) 1976
Treaty of Friendship and Cooperation 1977
Treaty of Friendship and Cooperation 1978

Treaty of Peace, Friendship, and Cooperation 1979
Truong Chinh
Truong Tan Sang
Vientiane Action Plan (ASEAN) 2004
Vientiane Summit (ASEAN) 2004
Viet Cong
Viet Minh
Vietnam–US Strategic Partnership
Vietnam War
Vietnamization
Vo Van Kiet (Vietnam)
Xayaburi Dam